CONSUMER'S HANDBOOK OF VIDEO SOFTWARE

CONSUMER'S HANDBOOK OF VIDEO SOFTWARE

compiled by
VIDEOLOGS INC.
With an overview of
home video hardware
by Charles Bensinger

VNR VAN NOSTRAND REINHOLD COMPANY
NEW YORK   CINCINNATI   TORONTO   LONDON   MELBOURNE

First published in 1981

Copyright © 1981 by Videologs, Inc.

Library of Congress Catalog Number 81-51415

ISBN 0-442-29007-1

Printed in the United States of America

Van Nostrand Reinhold Company
135 West 50th Street
New York, NY 10020

Van Nostrand Reinhold Ltd.
1410 Birchmount Road, Scarborough, Ontario M1P 2E7

Van Nostrand Reinhold Australia Pty. Ltd.
17 Queen Street, Mitchan, Victoria 3132

Van Nostrand Reinhold Company Ltd.
Molly Millars Lane, Wokingham, Berkshire, England RG11 2PY

16 15 14 13 12 11 10 9 8 7 6 5 4 3 2 1

Contents

2189620

Preface

There was a time when the only way to see your favorite movie at home was to wait for it to show up on one of the broadcast networks. If you were lucky enough to find the movie scheduled at a convenient hour, you then had to endure incessant commercial interruption. And of course the broadcast network, for one reason or another, would usually edit out portions or even entire scenes from the film.

In the past few years the situation has improved considerably for movie enthusiasts. New video technologies, specifically the videocassette recorder and the videodisc player, have made it possible for you to see premium films in your own livingroom at your own convenience. You can now watch such classics as "Casablanca," "M*A*S*H," "The Wizard of Oz," or "The Godfather" in their original form, uninterrupted and uncut.

The number and variety of films available in video formats has increased dramatically. Back in 1977 Twentieth Century-Fox leased its first 50 titles to Magnetic Video. Two years later Paramount began making its titles available on videocassette. But 1980 was the turning point. In that single year almost all the other major Hollywood studios began releasing films on videocassette.

The laser optical (LaserVision) disc debuted at the end of 1978. At first the number of movie discs was limited, but in a short time, as production techniques improved, the library of titles expanded. The laser optical disc was joined by RCA's capacitance electronic disc (CED) in March 1981. At present there is an excellent selection of top-notch films available in both disc formats.

But the movie enthusiast has a problem finding out which films are available, at what price, in which formats, from whom. There are literally thousands of films on video offered by a multitude of producers and distributors. *The Consumer's Handbook of Video Software* brings together all the information you need for locating the films of your choice and comparing prices or rental terms of each producer/distributor. If you have not yet decided on the type of viewing equipment you should purchase, you can use this guide to find out how many of your favorite films are offered in each format. (Also, see the article by Charles Bensinger on p. ix.)

If you are looking for a specific title, you can turn directly to "Motion Pictures by Title" beginning on page 1. Or, if you are interested in a particular genre (e.g., westerns, science-fiction, animation/cartoons), you might check "Motion Pictures by Subject" on page 183. The Producer/Distributor Index, page 201, lists the addresses, phone numbers, and contact persons for those wishing to place an order or make further inquiries about a film.

Besides listing the classics and recent blockbusters, the handbook includes many of the lesser-known quality films. There are compilations of old comedy shorts, serials from the 1940s, vintage cartoons, and silent film adventures that are hardly ever shown on broadcast TV. Pornographic titles are listed for the viewer's discretion; the editors have chosen not to annotate these films.

The *Consumer's Handbook for Video Software* has been drawn from the data base of *The Videologs,* the authoritative guides to professional, educational, and consumer videocassette programs since 1979. Movie stills reprinted in this book have been selected by Jerry Vermilye from his extensive personal collection.

Home Video Equipment—
Making The Personal Decision

Home video has evolved considerably since Sony introduced the first true home videorecorder—The Betamax—in 1975. It was a one-hour only Beta format recorder that lacked a camera connector and could only record programs from broadcast TV. At the time, a one-hour recording capability seemed perfeclty adequate. Now, however, such shortsightedness seems incredible when considering the vast array of movies, special features, and the extended recording capabilities of most present home VCRs. Four-, five-, or six-hour recording capability is now established as normal and required.

It's always easy to pass judgment in the light of hindsight. It's much more difficult to accurately foresee or predict future events, especially in a field that evolves so rapidly. New models of VCRs, videodisc players, and cameras seem to appear almost monthly.

Fortunately, software programming does not become obsolete rapidly or need to be modified constantly. But, in order to access the ever-growing body of programming, one must confront the bewildering array of video equipment, formats, special features, accessories, styles, etc. For the person who does not enjoy researching, analyzing, and comparing technical specifications, features and assorted doodads, the purchase of video equipment may appear to be somewhat intimidating.

It is not really as frightening as it seems since most video equipment is made by only four or five Japanese manufacturers, and each product line has many of the same features of its competitors in the same price range. There are, however, some initial decisions you must make. The first of these regards the choice of whether you want to record your own programs as well as play back other program materials. If you do wish to record movies from TV or buy a camera to tape birthday parties and little league games, you eliminate videodisc players. The videodisc player can only play back pre-recorded videodiscs. A VCR, on the other hand, can both play back pre-recorded tapes and make its own recordings. The best analogy is to think of videodisc players as record players and VCRs as tape recorders.

If you have for now decided you want recording capability, the next decision is whether portability is a prime consideration. If it is, there is a wide range of portable VCRs that can also be powered off household AC electricity as well as battery power. Of course, for home movies a camera must also be purchased.

Most people buy VCRs to record TV programs off the air and therefore find the automatic programming features of certain VCRs to be most desirable. Different models offer a range of programming features that vary from the ability to automatically record one program within 24 hours up to 14 programs or more over a two or three week period on different channels. Although portable VCRs generally sacrifice these sophisticated programmable abilities, optional accessory programmable tuner/timers can often be purchased. It should also be mentioned that all home VCRs, whether portable or non-portable, can be used with most black and white or color cameras with the proper adaptors. All VCRs also record sound as well as pictures.

Perhaps the basis on which the final VCR decision will be made is on the various features that you personally find most desirable for the price that you are willing to pay. Most VCRs now offer such features as stop action, freeze frame, slow motion, and fast motion. Deluxe models offer remote control, variable slow-to-high-speed playback in forward and reverse, program-search ability, and excellent editing and scene review when used with the appropriate camera. Newer cameras feature automatic fade controls and automatic focusing. A color camera, though, will double your investment in a video system, and audio and lighting accessories also suddenly seem to become necessary.

Another very important criterion is format choice, which poses the question of Beta versus VHS. Both formats offer excellent quality and a wide range of features, although VHS provides slightly longer recording time, affords a wider assortment of models, and is more common. VHS machines comprise about 65% of all home VCRs sold and Beta about 35%. Factors that will influence your choice will be price and local availability and servicing.

If you decide to go with a videodisc system, you have three choices of formats—the laser optical system, the CED or capacitance needle and groove system, and the hybrid VHD grooveless capacitance system. All three systems play 60 minutes on each side of a 10 or 12 inch plastic disc (depending on the system), provide a picture quality slightly superior to the best VCRs, and offer a range of special features such as slow and fast motion and freeze frame. VHD and laser optical systems also provide random access, remote control, two audio tracks for stereo sound or bilingual recording, and optional digital audio processors.

The advantages of the videodisc system over the VCR are better picture quality, more accurate program access, and lower price of machine and programming. CED and VHD players retail for around $500, and laser units for $750. VCRs range from $700 to $1,400. While pre-recorded videotapes cost $30 and up, videodisc costs are in the $10 to $30 range for a 2 hour program.

There is much, much more to be said on this subject,[1] but whatever your video equipment choices, you will find that video provides a great deal of opportunity for personal learning and enjoyment as well as access to an incredible wealth of information and home entertainment.

Charles Bensinger

---

[1]For those interested in an in-depth examination of home video equipment, Charles Bensinger has authored *The Home Video Handbook*. This guide provides detailed information on how to choose and properly make use of VCRs, cameras, and accessories. It can be purchased for $9.95 plus $1 shipping and handling from Video-Info Publications, P.O. Box 2685, Santa Fe, NM 87501.

How to Use This Book

The *Consumer's Handbook of Video Software* provides detailed information on over 2,000 feature films available in video formats. Film titles are listed alphabetically. The following sample illustrates the information provided in a typical entry.

SAMPLE ENTRY:

1
TOPPER
2   **3**   **4** **5** **6**   **7**
The Nostalgia Merchant; Order No. 4005; 1937 • b/w; 1 hr, 37 min; ½″ Beta II, ½″ VHS •
8
Sale: $54.95

9
Adapts a novel by Thorne Smith about a mild-mannered, henpecked husband who is aided—and manipulated—by a playful ghostly couple and their dog. Stars Cary Grant, Constance Bennett, Roland Young, and Billie Burke, under the direction of Norman Z. McLeod.

1. Film Title.

2. Producer/Distributor (P/D). The name of the company through which the cassette or disc is available. See the Producer/Distributor Index on page 201 for the address, telephone number, and contact person.

3. Order Number. The specific number (if any) to reference when ordering a cassette or disc.

4. Date. The year of the film's release.

5. Hue. Indicates whether the film is in black-and-white or color.

6. Length.

7. Video Formats Available. Includes ½" Beta, ½" VHS, CED (RCA disc), and LaserVision (MCA and Pioneer disc).

8. Pricing Information. Includes sale, rental, preview, and lease arrangements offered by each producer/distributor.

9. Summary. Provides a brief plot synopsis, names of the stars, and the director. Pornographic films are listed but not summarized.

When a film is offered by more than one distributor, the information for each is listed and separated by a dotted line.

SAMPLE ENTRY WITH MULTIPLE DISTRIBUTORS:

THE GODFATHER
Fotomat Corp; Order No. B0011 for ½" Beta II, V0011 for ½" VHS; 1972 • color; 2 hrs, 51 min; ½" Beta II, ½" VHS • Sale: $69.95; Rental: $13.95/up to 5 days, applicable to purchase

MCA DiscoVision; Order No. P12-518; 1972 • color; 2 hrs, 51 min; LaserVision • Sale: $24.95

Paramount Home Video; 1972 • color; 2 hrs, 51 min; ½" Beta II, ½" VHS • Sale $79.95

RCA SelectaVision Videodiscs; Order No. 00604; 1972 • color; 2 hrs, 51 min; CED • Sale: $27.98

Paints a chilling portrait of a Sicilian family's rise and near fall from power in America. Balances the story between family life and the ugly business of crime in a film based on Mario Puzo's novel. Stars Marlon Brando, Al Pacino, James Caan, Robert Duvall, Talia Shire, and Diane Keaton, under the direction of Francis Ford Coppola.

The above example reveals that "The Godfather" is carried by four different distributors. The film can be either purchased or rented and is available in ½" Beta and VHS from Fotomat Corp. and Paramount Home Video, LaserVision from MCA DiscoVision, and CED from RCA SelectaVision.

When you find a film that you would like to buy or rent, check first with your local video retail store. Video dealers usually have the most popular titles in stock and are pleased to order any other titles not on hand. If there are no convenient video stores in your area, you can usually order by mail, using the addresses provided in the Producer/Distributor Index.

CONSUMER'S HANDBOOK OF VIDEO SOFTWARE

A

A NOUS LA LIBERTE
Budget Video; 1931 • b/w; 1 hr, 27 min; 1/2" Beta II, 1/2" VHS • Sale: $44.95

Relates the story of a tramp who becomes rich and powerful, only to long for the simple joys of his earlier life, in a satire on modern technology by Rene Clair. Features Raymond Cordy, Henri Marchand, Rolla Rance, and Paul Olivier; in French with subtitles.

ABBOTT AND COSTELLO CARTOON HOUR
Video Communications Inc; Order No. 1158; Date not listed • color; 1 hr; 1/2" Beta II, 1/2" VHS • Sale: $54.95

Presents a series of cartoons featuring the characters created by the comedy team of Abbott and Costello.

ABBOTT AND COSTELLO MEET CAPTAIN KIDD
Fotomat Corp; Order No. B0149 for 1/2" Beta II, V0149 for 1/2" VHS; 1952 • color; 1 hr, 10 min; 1/2" Beta II, 1/2" VHS • Sale: $39.95; Rental: $7.95/up to 5 days, applicable to purchase
- -
Video Communications Inc; 1952 • color; 1 hr, 10 min; 1/2" Beta II, 1/2" VHS • Sale: $54.95

Features the comic duo sailing to the pirate Isle of Tortuga for a rendezvous with Charles Laughton.

ABBOTT AND COSTELLO MEET FRANKENSTEIN
MCA DiscoVision; Order No. 22-008; 1948 • b/w; 1 hr, 23 min LaserVision • Sale: $15.95

Offers the comic possibilities of Abbott and Costello plus Frankenstein, Dracula, the Wolfman, and the Invisible Man, as the Count tries to get Lou's brain for Frankenstein. Stars Bela Lugosi, Lon Chaney, Jr., and Bud Abbott and Lou Costello.

ABE LINCOLN IN ILLINOIS
The Nostalgia Merchant; Order No. 8019; 1939 • b/w; 1 hr, 50 min; 1/2" Beta II, 1/2" VHS • Sale: $54.95

Presents a film version of Robert Sherwood's Pulitzer Prize-winning play. Dramatizes Abe's early years as lawyer and suitor. Stars Raymond Massey, Gene Lockhart, and Ruth Gordon.

ABILENE TOWN
Thunderbird Films; 1946 • b/w; 1 hr, 30 min; 3/4" U-Matic, 1/2" Beta I, 1/2" Beta II, 1/2" VHS • Sale: $69.95 for 1/2" Beta I, 49.95 for 1/2" Beta II & VHS, $89.95 for 3/4"

Chronicles the trouble between townfolk, cattlemen, and homesteaders in Abilene. Features Randolph Scott, Ann Dvorak, Lloyd Bridges, Rhonda Fleming, and Edgar Buchanan.

ABRAHAM LINCOLN
Northeast Video and Sound, Inc; Order No. 1705; 1930 • b/w; 1 hr, 31 min; 3/4" U-Matic, 1/2" EIAJ, 1/2" Beta II, 1/2" VHS • Sale: $295; Rental: $75/wk

Offers D.W. Griffith's biography of Lincoln. Stars Walter Huston, Una Merkle, and Edger Dearing in one of Griffith's few attempts to direct a sound film.

THE ABSENT-MINDED PROFESSOR
Fotomat Corp; 1961 • b/w; 1 hr, 37 min; 1/2" Beta II, 1/2" VHS • Sale: $49.95; Rental: $9.95/up to 5 days, applicable to purchase
- -
RCA SelectaVision VideoDiscs; Order No. 00702; 1961 • b/w; 1 hr, 37 min; CED • Sale: $19.98
- -
Walt Disney Home Video; 1961 • b/w; 1 hr, 37 min; 1/2" Beta II, 1/2" VHS • Sale: $59.95

Presents a Walt Disney Studios comedy about a professor who discovers flying rubber he calls "flubber." Features special effects. Stars Fred MacMurray, Nancy Olson, Keenan Wynn, Tommy Kirk, Ed Wynn, and Leon Ames.

ACCIDENT
Fotomat Corp; Order No. B0247 for 1/2" Beta II, V0247 for 1/2" VHS; 1967 • color; 1 hr, 45 min; 1/2" Beta II, 1/2" VHS • Sale: $49.95; Rental: $9.95/up to 5 days, applicable to purchase

Tells in flashbacks the emotional events that lead to an automobile crash. Explores the thoughts and actions of a married college professor who falls in love with a female student, and the consequences. Stars Dick Bogarde, Stanley Baker, Delphine Seyrig, Vivian Merchant, and Michael York, under the direction of Joseph Losey. Features a script by Harold Pinter.

ADAM'S RIB
MGM/CBS Home Video; Order No. M50010; 1949 • b/w; 1 hr, 41 min; 1/2" Beta II, 1/2" VHS • Sale: $49.95

- -

Niles Cinema; Order No. GM-718; 1949 • b/w; 1 hr, 41 min; 1/2" Beta II, 1/2" VHS • Sale: $49.95

- -

RCA SelectaVision VideoDiscs; Order No. 00201; 1949 • b/w; 1 hr, 41 min; CED • Sale: $14.98

Presents a Spencer Tracy/Katherine Hepburn Comedy directed by George Cuckor. Concerns a husband and wife who are lawyers opposing one another on the same case. Stars Tracy, Hepburn, Judy Holliday, Tom Ewell, Jean Hagen, Polly Moran, and David Wayne, in a screenplay written by Ruth Gordon and Garson Kanin.

ADVENTURES OF CAPTAIN MARVEL
The Nostalgia Merchant; Order No. 0056; 1941 • b/w; 3 hrs; 1/2" Beta II, 1/2" VHS • Sale: $109.95

Presents, on two videocassettes, a Republic motion picture serial in 12 episodes. Follows the adventures of Captain Marvel as he attempts to thwart the nefarious criminal Scorpion, who is intent on acquiring a device that turns ordinary metal into gold. Stars Tom Tyler, Frank Coghlan, Jr., and Louise Currie.

ADVENTURES OF CHIP 'N' DALE
Fotomat Corp; Order No. B1025 for 1/2" Beta II, V0125 for 1/2" VHS; Date not listed • color; 47 min; 1/2" Beta II, 1/2" VHS • Sale: $44.95; Rental: $7.95/5 days

- -

MCA DiscoVision; Order No. D61-506; Date not listed; LaserVision • color; hr • Sale: $9.95

- -

Niles Cinema; Order No. WD-22; Date not listed • color; 47 min; 1/2" Beta II, 1/2" VHS • Sale: $44.95

- -

Walt Disney Home Video; Order No. 22BS for 1/2" Beta II, 22VS for 1/2" VHS; Date not listed • color; 47 min; 1/2" Beta II, 1/2" VHS • Sale: $44.95

Presents a Walt Disney cartoon show starring Chip and Dale. Features "Two Chips and A Miss," "Chicken in the Rough," "Chips Ahoy," and "The Lone Chipmunks."

ADVENTURES OF FRONTIER FREMONT
Video Communications Inc; Order No. 6001; 1975 • color; 1 hr, 35 min; 1/2" Beta II, 1/2" VHS • Sale: $54.95

Follows the trials of a man who was a farmer and tinsmith in St. Louis during the 1830's. Shows him striking out west to live in the wilderness, and to lead a simpler life, only to encounter bears, rattlesnakes, and big cats. Features Dan Haggerty and Denver Pyle.

THE ADVENTURES OF HUCKLEBERRY FINN
Vid America ; Order No. 909; Date not listed • color; 1 hr, 37 min; 1/2" Beta II, 1/2" VHS • Rental: $10.95/wk

Adapts Mark Twain's book about the journey of Huckleberry Finn and Tom Sawyer down the Mississippi to become pirates. Provides a dramatization with young actors.

ADVENTURES OF MIGHTY MOUSE (PART 1)
Magnetic Video Corporation; Order No. CL-2027; Date not listed • color; 30 min; 1/2" Beta II, 1/2" VHS • Sale: $34.95

Offers a compilation of Terrytoon animated cartoons featuring Mighty Mouse.

ADVENTURES OF MIGHTY MOUSE (PART 2)
Magnetic Video Corporation; Order No. CL-2028; Date not listed • color; 30 min; 1/2" Beta II, 1/2" VHS • Sale: $34.95

See Part 1 for description.

ADVENTURES OF MIGHTY MOUSE (PART 3)
Magnetic Video Corporation; Order No. CL-2029; Date not listed • color; 30 min; 1/2" Beta II, 1/2" VHS • Sale: $34.95

See Part 1 for description.

THE ADVENTURES OF PINOCCHIO
Time-Life Video Club Inc; 1978 • color; 1 hr, 30 min; 1/2" Beta II, 1/2" VHS • Sale: $34.95 to members

- -

Video Games; 1978 • color; 1 hr, 30 min 1/2" Beta II, 1/2" VHS • Sale: $53.95

Presents an animated version of Carlo Collodi's story of the wooden puppet who tries to become a real boy, and whose nose betrays him when he does not tell the truth.

THE ADVENTURES OF RED RYDER
The Nostalgia Merchant; Date not listed • b/w; 3 hrs; 1/2" Beta II, 1/2" VHS • Sale: $109.95

Offers, on two videocassettes, a motion picture serial in 12 episodes. Stars Don "Red" Barry as Red Ryder.

THE ADVENTURES OF SHERLOCK HOLMES' SMARTER BROTHER
Magnetic Video Corporation; Order No. CL-1063; 1975 • color; 1 hr, 31 min; 1/2" Beta II, 1/2" VHS • Sale: $54.95

Offers a spoof of Sherlock Holmes films as his younger brother, Sigerson Holmes, sets out to solve a mystery involving international spies, a secret document, a damsel in distress, and the evil Professor Moriarty. Stars Leo McKern, Madeline Kahn, Marty Feldman, Dom DeLuise, and Gene Wilder, who also wrote and directed this film.

THE ADVENTURES OF SUPERMAN
Reel Images Inc ; Order No. 82; 1942-43 • b/w; 55 min; 1/2" Beta II, 1/2" VHS • Sale: $39.95 for 1/2" Beta II, $42.95 for 1/2" VHS

Presents seven cartoons from the Max Fleischer Studio. Includes "Underground World," "Terror On The Midway," "Volcano," "Destruction, Inc.," "Secret Agent," "Billion Dollar Limited," and "Showdown."

THE ADVENTURES OF TARZAN
Reel Images Inc; Order No. 466; 1921 • b/w; 2 hrs, 33 min; 1/2" Beta II, 1/2" VHS • Sale: $69.95 for 1/2" Beta II, $72.95 for 1/2" VHS

Recounts an early Tarzan jungle adventure. Presents a silent film starring Elmo Lincoln.

ADVISE AND CONSENT
National Film and Video Center; 1962 • b/w; 2 hrs, 19 min; 3/4" U-Matic, 1/2" Beta II, 1/2" VHS • Rental: $49/1 showing

Deals with the backroom politics involved when an ailing President asks the U.S. Senate to consent to the

Humphrey Bogart and Katharine Hepburn in _The African Queen_.

appointment of a controversial figure to the position of Secretary of State. Stars Henry Fonda, Charles Laughton, Walter Pidgeon, Peter Lawford, Gene Tierney, and Inga Swenson, in an Otto Preminger film.

AFFAIR
FHV Entertainment, Inc; Date not listed • color; 1 hr, 21 min; 1/2" Beta II, 1/2" VHS • Sale: $49.95

Presents a pornographic film.

AFFAIRS OF ANNABEL
Blackhawk Films, Inc; Order No. 506-01-0778 for 1/2" Beta II, 525-01-0778 for 1/2" VHS; 1938 • b/w; 1 hr, 8 min; 3/4" U-Matic, 1/2" Beta I, 1/2" Beta II, 1/2" VHS • Sale: $89.95 for 1/2" Beta I, $49.95 for 1/2" Beta II & VHS, $99.95 for 3/4"

Presents the first of the Annabel films. Offers the story of an adolescent who is pushed to movie stardom by her press agent. Stars Lucille Ball and Jack Oakie.

AFRICA SCREAMS
Discount Video Tapes; 1949 • b/w; 1 hr, 19 min; 1/2" Beta II, 1/2" VHS • Sale: $44.95

Offers a comic search for buried treasure in "deepest, darkest" Africa. Stars Bud Abbott and Lou Costello, Max and Buddy Baer, Hillary Brooke, and Shemp Howard.

AFRICA TEXAS STYLE
Video Warehouse, Inc; Order No. 1067; 1967 • color; 1 hr, 49 min; 1/2" Beta II, 1/2" VHS • Sale: $39.95

Follows the adventures of two U.S. cowboys in Kenya as they herd wild animals and fight a sabotage attempt. Stars Hugh O'Brian, John Mills, and Nigel Green.

THE AFRICAN QUEEN
Magnetic Video Corporation; Order No. CL-2025; 1951 • color; 1 hr, 45 min; 1/2" Beta II, 1/2" VHS • Sale: $54.95

Follows the adventures of a puritanical missionary lady and a hard-drinking riverman aboard his steamer in the war-torn African jungle. Stars Katharine Hepburn and Humphrey Bogart, under the direction of John Huston.

AFRICAN SAFARI
Video Communications Inc; Order No. 1002; 1975 • color; 1 hr, 38 min; 1/2" Beta II, 1/2" VHS • Sale: $54.95

Presents a documentary by Ron Shanin, who spent

over five years in Eastern and Central Africa photographing and editing it.

AGAINST A CROOKED SKY
Vid America; Order No. 986; 1975 • color; 1 hr, 27 min; 1/2" Beta II, 1/2" VHS • Sale: $49.95; Rental: $11.95/wk, applicable to purchase

Follows a young boy who sets out to find his sister, who has been kidnapped by Indians. Stars Richard Boone and Stewart Peterson.

THE AGONY AND THE ECSTASY
Golden Tapes Video Tape Library; Order No. F-1007; 1965 • color; 2 hrs, 20 min; 1/2" Beta II, 1/2" VHS • Sale: $49.95 for 1/2" Beta II & VHS, $124.95 for 3/4"

Magnetic Video Corporation; Order No. CL-1007; 1965 • color; 2 hrs, 20 min; 1/2" Beta II, 1/2" VHS • Sale: $64.95

The Video Library; Order No. MV-1007; 1965 • color; 2 hrs, 20 min; 1/2" Beta II, 1/2" VHS • Sale: $74.95

Recounts Michelangelo's conflicts with Pope Julius II during the period when he painted the Sistine chapel. Follows sections of the Irving Stone novel. Stars Charlton Heston, Rex Harrison, Diane Cilento, and Harry Andrews, under the direction of Carol Reed.

AIDA
Time-Life Video Club Inc; 1955 • color; 1 hr, 36 min; 1/2" Beta II, 1/2" VHS • Sale: $44.95 to members

Presents an Italian film of the opera by Giuseppe Verdi. Features Sophia Loren in the title role, with the voice of Renata Tebaldi.

AIRPLANE!
Paramount Home Video; Order No. 1305; 1980 • color; 1 hr, 28 min; 1/2" Beta II, 1/2" VHS • Sale: $79.95

Offers a spoof of the "Airport" disaster films. Centers on an ex-fighter pilot and his stewardess-girlfriend who must co-pilot a jumbo jet after a massive attack of food poisoning disables the jet in mid-flight. Uses cliché after cliché to humorous purpose. Stars Robert Hays, Julie Hagerty, Kareem Abdul-Jabbar, Lloyd Bridges, Leslie Nielsen, Robert Stack, Peter Graves, and Ethel Merman.

AIRPORT '77
MCA DiscoVision; Order No. 10-010; 1977 • color; 1 hr, 54 min; LaserVision • Sale: $24.95

Presents the story of a 747 jet liner which emergency-lands underwater, and the struggles of its crew to keep everyone alive until a rescue can be launched. Includes many personal subplots in the "Grand Hotel" style, as well as the complication of a skyjacking. Stars Jack Lemmon, Lee Grant, Brenda Vaccaro, Joseph Cotten, Olivia de Havilland, Darrin McGavin, Christopher Lee, George Kennedy, and James Stewart.

ALEXANDER NEVSKY
Ivy Video; 1938 • b/w; 1 hr, 45 min; 3/4" U-Matic, 1/2" Beta II, 1/2" VHS • Sale: $59.95 for 1/2" Beta II & VHS, trade-in plan available, $225 for 3/4"

Presents Eisenstein's epic on the military exploits of Russia's great medieval hero, Czar Alexander Nevsky. Contains much anti-Teutonic propaganda which the film-maker intended as an inspiration to his people in the impending war against Nazi Germany.

ALGIERS
Video Communications Inc; 1939 • b/w; 1 hr, 36 min; 1/2" Beta II, 1/2" VHS • Sale: $54.95

Video T.E.N.; 1938 • b/w; 1 hr, 36 min; ½″ Beta II, ½″ VHS • Sale: $49.95 for ½″ Beta II, $54.95 for ½″ VHS

Portrays a wealthy girl dazzled by the Casbah and its most notorious citizen, Pepe Le Moko. Stars Charles Boyer and Hedy Lamarr.

ALICE ADAMS
Blackhawk Films, Inc; Order No. 506300776 for ½″ Beta II, 525300776 for ½″ VHS; 1935 • b/w; 1 hr, 39 min; ½″ Beta II, ½″ VHS • Sale: $49.95

Adapts for the screen Booth Tarkington's book about a young social-climbing girl who falls in love with an unpretentious wealthy man. Stars Katharine Hepburn, Fred MacMurray, and Fred Stone, under the direction of George Stevens.

ALICE GOODBODY
FHV Entertainment, Inc; Date not listed • color; 1 hr, 23 min; ½″ Beta II, ½″ VHS • Sale: $49.95

Presents a pornographic film.

ALICE IN WONDERLAND
Meda/Media Home Entertainment Inc; Order No. M501; 1976 • color; 1 hr, 14 min; ½″ Beta I, ½″ Beta II, ½″ VHS • Sale: $59.95 for ½″ Beta I, $54.95 for ½″ Beta II & VHS

- -
Vid America; Order No. 967; 1976 • color; 1 hr, 12 min; ½″ Beta II, ½″ VHS • Rental: $12.95/wk

Presents a pornographic film.

ALICE SWEET ALICE
Blackhawk Films, Inc; Order No. 502-86-0124 for ½″ Beta II, 515-86-0124 for ½″ VHS; 1977 • color; 1 hr, 52 min; ½″ Beta II, ½″ VHS • Sale: $79.95

Recounts a series of macabre murders in which a masked person butchers his/her victims. Features Brooke Shields and Linda Miller.

ALICE'S ADVENTURES IN WONDERLAND
Fotomat Corp; Order No. B0133 for ½″ Beta II, V0133 for ½″ VHS; 1972 • color; 1 hr, 45 min; ½″ Beta II, ½″ VHS • Sale: $49.95; Rental: $9.95/up to 5 days, applicable to purchase

Video Communications Inc; 1972 • color; 1 hr, 45 min; ½″ Beta II, ½″ VHS • Sale: $54.95

Presents a musical version of the Lewis Carroll fantasy. Features Peter Sellers, Fiona Fullerton, Michael Crawford, Sir Robert Helpmann, Dame Flora Robson, and Dudley Moore.

ALIEN
Magnetic Video Corporation; 1979 • color; 2 hr, 4 min; ½″ Beta II, ½″ VHS • Sale: $59.95

Depicts the crew of a cargo spaceship attempting to defeat an alien being that has come aboard with an appetite for earthlings. Uses suspense, special effects, and bizarre violence. Features Sigourney Weaver, Tom Skerritt, John Hurt, Ian Holm, Yaphet Kotto, and Harry Dean Stanton.

ALIENS FROM SPACESHIP EARTH
Video Gems; 1977 • color; 1 hr, 47 min; ½″ Beta II, ½″ VHS • Sale: $59.95

Presents an "investigation" into such phenomena as levitation, mind-reading, walking through walls, and bringing back the dead. Features music by Donovan.

ALL ABOUT EVE
Magnetic Video Corporation; Order No. CL-1076; 1950 • b/w; 2 hrs, 18 min; ½″ Beta II, ½″ VHS • Sale: $44.95yn

Reveals the underside of Hollywood stardom, in the story of an aspiring actress whose passion to perform and jealousy cause her to betray her colleagues. Stars Bette Davis, Anne Baxter, George Sanders, and Celeste Holm, under the direction of Joseph L. Mankiewicz.

ALL IN A NIGHT'S WORK
Magnetic Video Corporation; Order No. CL-2017; 1961 • color; 1 hr, 34 min; ½″ Beta II, ½″ VHS • Sale: $54.95

- -
Red Fox; Order No. CL-2017; 1961 • color; 1 hr, 34 min; ½″ Beta II, ½″ VHS • Sale: $54.95

Stars Dean Martin, Shirley MacLaine, and Cliff Robertson in a comedy concerning what happens after a business tycoon is found dead with a smile on his face.

Anne Baxter, Gary Merrill, Celeste Holm, Bette Davis, and Hugh Marlowe in *All About Eve.*

ALL MINE TO GIVE
Video Communications Inc; 1957 • color; 1 hr, 42
min; 1/2" Beta II, 1/2" VHS • Sale: $54.95
Dramatizes the true story of a young Scottish immigrant couple who settled in the wilds of Wisconsin over
a century ago. Recounts how they braved the rigors of
northern winters and a raging epidemic. Stars Glynis
Johns, Cameron Mitchell, Rex Thompson, and Patty
McCormack.

ALL SCREWED UP
Magnetic Video Corporation; 1973 • color; 1 hr, 45
min; 1/2" Beta II, 1/2" VHS • Sale: $44.95
Reveals the incongruities of urban technological ad-
vances at the expense of human values, in a film
whose title is an Italian version of "S.N.A.F.U." Tells of
the problems encountered by a group of rural immi-
grants living communally in Milan. Stars Luigi Diberti
and Lina Polito, under the direction of Lina Wertmuller.

ALL STAR JAZZ SHOW
Time-Life Video Club Inc; Date not listed • color; 1 hr,
58 min; 1/2" Beta II, 1/2" VHS • Sale: $34.95, to mem-
bers
Provides a history of American Jazz. Traces the roots
of jazz from the Blues, Ragtime, and Swing, to the cur-
rent fusion of today. Features Dionne Warwick as host.
Stars Joe Williams, Count Basie, Gerry Mulligan, Max
Roach, Lionel Hampton, Stan Getz, and Herbie Han-
cock. Includes vintage clips of Count Basie, Fats Wal-
ler, and Charlie Barnet.

ALL THAT JAZZ
Magnetic Video Corporation; 1979 • color; 2 hrs, 3
min; 1/2" Beta II, 1/2" VHS • Sale: $69.95
- -
Niles Cinema; Order No. CL-1095; 1979 • color; 2
hrs, 3 min; 1/2" Beta II, 1/2" VHS • Sale: $69.95
Presents choreographer-director Bob Fosse's autobiographical musical. Includes Roy Scheider, as a Fosse-
like character, popping pills, seducing girls,staging
dance numbers, and having open-heart surgery. Features Jessica Lange, Ann Reinking, Leland Palmer,
Cliff Gorman, Ben Vereen, and Erzsebet Foldi.

ALL THE KING'S MEN
National Film and Video Center; 1949 • b/w; 1 hr, 49
min; 3/4" U-Matic, 1/2" Beta II, 1/2" VHS • Rental: $49/1
showing
Portrays a man who uses backwoods politics and big-
city dirty tricks to be elected governor. Shows how he
inaugurates an administration of reckless corruption
which leads to his downfall. Stars Broderick Crawford,
Mercedes McCambridge, John Ireland, and Joanne
Dru.

ALL THE PRESIDENT'S MEN
WCI Home Video Inc; 1976 • color; 2 hrs, 18 min; 1/2"
Beta II, 1/2" VHS • Sale: $60
Tells the behind-the-scenes story of the Watergate
scandal. Traces the attempts of "Washington Post" re-
porters Bob Woodward and Carl Bernstein to get the
facts which led to the eventual resignation of the Presi-
dent of the United States. Stars Robert Redford, Dustin
Hoffman, Jason Robards, Jack Warden, Martin Bal-
sam, Hal Holbrook, and Jane Alexander, under Alan J.
Pakula's direction. Adapts the book by Woodward and
Bernstein.

ALL THE WAY BOYS
Magnetic Video Corporation; Order No. CL-4050;
1973 • color; 1 hr, 45 min; 1/2" Beta II, 1/2" VHS • Sale:
$54.95

Highlights the adventures of two guys who'll do any-
thing for a buck, especially if it's dangerous, as they fly
rickety aircraft over the perilous Amazon River jungles.
Features Terence Hill and Bud Spencer.

ALL THINGS BRIGHT AND BEAUTIFUL
Time-Life Video Club Inc; Date not listed • color; 1 hr,
37 min; 1/2" Beta II, 1/2" VHS • Sale: $37.50, to mem-
bers
Adapts the best-selling novel about a young veterinar-
ian in Yorkshire. Follows Dr. Herriott as he decides
whether to practice among the simple farmers of the
small towns for whom animal medicine is of crucial
importance, or return to the city to take a more lucra-
tive offer. Uses location filming to enhance the story.

ALLEGHENY UPRISING
Blackhawk Films, Inc; Order No. 506-75-0775 for 1/2"
Beta II, 525-75-0775 for 1/2" VHS; 1939 • b/w; 1 hr,
21 min; 1/2" Beta II, 1/2" VHS • Sale: $49.95
Focuses on the clash, in 1759 America, between the
inept British commander who governs by the book,
and colonists who understand the danger of allowing
corrupt traders to deal with the Indians. Features John
Wayne, Claire Trevor, George Sanders, Brian Donlevy,
and Chill Wills.

ALMOST ANGELS
MCA DiscoVision; Order No. D18-509; 1962 • color; 1
hr, 33 min; LaserVision • Sale: $24.95
Adapts R.A. Stemmle's story of the son of a train conductor who is admitted to the Vienna Boy's Choir as
long as he can maintain his grades and endure whatever mischief the boy he replaced can devise. Stars
Peter Weck, Sean Scully, and The Vienna Boy's Choir.
Features music of Schubert, Brahms, and Strauss, and
Austrian locations in this Walt Disney studio production.

ALOHA, BOBBY AND ROSE
National Film and Video Center; 1975 • color; 1 hr, 29
min; 3/4" U-Matic, 1/2" Beta II, 1/2" VHS • Rental: $89/1
showing
Offers the story of a young couple who become involved in a tragic death, flee to Mexico, then return to
attempt to straighten out the mess. Stars Paul Le Mat,
Dianne Hull, Tim McIntire, and Leigh French.

ALPHA BETA
Cinema Concepts, Inc.; 1973 • color; 1 hr, 10 min;
3/4" U-Matic, 1/2" Beta II, 1/2" VHS • Sale: $54.95 for
1/2" Beta II & VHS, 149.95 for 3/4"
- -
The Video Library; Order No. CC-1001; 1974 • color;
1 hr, 10 min; 1/2" Beta II, 1/2" VHS • Sale: $54.95
Adapts for the screen the play by E.A. Whitehead.
Chronicles the disintegration of a marriage over a ten-
year period. Stars Albert Finney and Rachel Roberts,
under the direction of Anthony Page.

THE ALTAR OF LUST
Monarch Releasing Corporation; Date not listed •
color; 1 hr, 18 min; 3/4" U-Matic • Sale: $300
Presents a pornographic film.

ALVAREZ KELLY
Columbia Pictures Home Entertainment; Order No.
BE51008 for 1/2" Beta II, VH10010 for 1/2" VHS; 1966 •
color; 1 hr, 56 min; 1/2" Beta II, 1/2" VHS • Sale: $59.95
Offers a western set during the Civil War. Depicts a
cattle driver who is pressed into service by a Confederate colonel who wants him to steal cattle for his troops.

Stars William Holden, Richard Widmark, Janice Rule, and Patrick O'Neal.

THE AMAZING WORLD OF PSYCHIC PHENOMENA
Vid America; Order No. 988; 1976 • color; 1 hr, 31 min; 1/2" Beta II, 1/2" VHS • Sale: $44.95; Rental: $10.95/wk, applicable to purchase

Explores the claims of psychics Uri Geller, Jean Dixon, and others. Features Raymond Burr as host.

AMERICA AT THE MOVIES
Time-Life Video Club Inc; Date not listed • b/w & color; 1 hr, 56 min; 1/2" Beta II, 1/2" VHS • Sale: $39.95 to members

Offers a compilation of clips from over eighty films from the last fifty years of American cinema. Shows how the movies have explored and reflected American values and history. Contains favorite moments from Hollywood's classic features.

AMERICA BETWEEN THE GREAT WARS
Blackhawk Films, Inc; Order No. 506-66-0849 for 1/2" Beta II, 525-66-0849 for 1/2" VHS; Date not listed • b/w; 1 hr; 3/4" U-Matic, 1/2" Beta I, 1/2" Beta II, 1/2" VHS • Sale: $59.95 for 1/2" Beta I, $39.95 for 1/2" Beta II & VHS, $69.95 for 3/4"

Presents a documentary look at the major events in the United States from the 20's to the late 30's. Includes the Century of Progress in Chicago of 1933, the Prohibition era, the Hindenburg disaster, off-screen activities of Charlie Chaplin and Will Rogers, and light-hearted newsreels of Lew Lehr. Provides narration.

AMERICAN GIGOLO
Niles Cinema; Order No. PP-8989; 1980 • color; 1 hr, 57 min; 1/2" Beta II, 1/2" VHS • Sale: $64.95
- -
Paramount Home Video; Order No. 8989; 1980 • color; 1 hr, 57 min; 1/2" Beta II, 1/2" VHS • Sale: $79.95

Explores the seamy side of American life. Depicts a young man who accepts payment to be a guide, translator, chauffeur, and/or a companion. Relates how he is implicated in a murder. Stars Richard Gere, Lauren Hutton, Hector Elizondo, and Nina Van Pallandt.

AMERICAN GRAFFITI
MCA DiscoVision; Order No. 16-001; 1973 • color; 1 hr, 50 min; LaserVision • Sale: $24.95
- -
MCA Videocassette, Inc; Order No. 66010; 1973 • color; 1 hr, 50 min; 1/2" Beta II, 1/2" VHS • Sale: $60

Relates the last evening a group of high school graduates spend together in 1962 before going off to college, going into the army, or staying in town and looking for a job. Includes deejay Wolfman Jack spinning the rock 'n' roll on the radio as the cars drift down the boulevard, in a film directed by George Lucas and produced by Francis Ford Coppola. Stars Richard Dreyfus, Ronny Howard, Cindy Williams, and Paul Le Mat.

AMERICAN HOT WAX
Fotomat Corp; Order No. B0017 for 1/2" Beta II, V0017 for 1/2" VHS; 1978 • color; 1 hr, 31 min; 1/2" Beta II, 1/2" VHS • Sale: $49.95; Rental: $9.95/up to 5 days, applicable to purchase

Tells a story of Alan Freed, the New York disc jockey, who is planning the First Anniversary Rock & Roll Show in 1959. Features Chuck Berry performing "Sweet Little Sixteen," Jerry Lee Lewis with "Great Balls of Fire," and musical numbers by Screamin' Jay Hawkins and the Chesterfields. Stars Tim McIntire, John Lehne, Laraine Newman, and Jay Leno.

Gene Kelly and Leslie Caron in An American In Paris.

AN AMERICAN IN PARIS
MGM/CBS Home Video; Order No. M60006; 1951 • color; 1 hr, 53 min; 1/2" Beta II, 1/2" VHS • Sale: $59.95
- -
Niles Cinema; Order No. GM-719; 1951 • color; 1 hr, 53 min; 1/2" Beta II, 1/2" VHS • Sale: $59.95

Offers director Vincente Minnelli's film built around George Gershwin's music. Concerns an ex-G.I. artist living in Paris, trying to decide between two loves. Features Gene Kelly's singing and dancing. Stars Kelly, Leslie Caron, Nina Foch, Oscar Levant, and Georges Guetary.

THE AMERICANO AND VARIETY
Blackhawk Films, Inc; Order No. 506-30-0832 for 1/2" Beta II, 525-30-0832 for 1/2" VHS; 1926 • b/w; 54 min; 3/4" U-Matic, 1/2" Beta I, 1/2" Beta II, 1/2" VHS • Sale: $59.95 for 1/2" Beta I, $39.95 for 1/2" Beta II & VHS, $69.95 for 3/4"

Presents abridged versions of two silent films starring Douglas Fairbanks. Offers "The Americano," in which he saves a Caribbean country from revolt, and "Variety," which tells of a scandalous love affair within a trapeze act. Includes a musical score with narration.

ANASTASIA
Golden Tapes Video Tape Library; Order No. F-1040; 1956 • color; 1 hr, 50 min; 1/2" Beta II, 1/2" VHS • Sale: $49.95 for 1/2" Beta II & VHS, 124.95 for 3/4"
- -
Magnetic Video Corporation; Order No. CL-1040; 1956 • color; 1 hr, 45 min; 1/2" Beta II, 1/2" VHS • Sale: $44.95

Reveals the attempt to establish an amnesia victim as the possible surviving daughter and only living member of the assassinated Romanoff family, the Royal House of Russia, and shows the furor aroused when distant relatives try to prove and disprove her identity. Stars Ingrid Bergman, Yul Brynner, Helen Hayes, and Akim Tamiroff.

ANATOMY OF A MURDER
National Film and Video Center; 1959 • b/w; 2 hrs, 41 min; 3/4" U-Matic, 1/2" Beta II, 1/2" VHS • Rental: $49/1 showing

Depicts a murder trial in a small town: an uphill struggle for the defense until the lawyer manages to establish a motive. Stars James Stewart, Lee Remick, Ben Gazzara, Eve Arden, George C. Scott, and Orson Bean.

AND SO THEY WERE MARRIED
Discount Video Tapes; 1944 • b/w; 1 hr, 17 min; ½″
Beta II, ½″ VHS • Sale: $59.95

Tells of a young lady's apartment and the screwball
antics that originate there. Stars Robert Mitchum, Simone Simon, and James Ellison, and was retitled
"Johnny Doesn't Live Here Anymore."

AND THEN THERE WERE NONE
Fotomat Corp; Order No. B0121 for ½″ Beta II, V0121
for ½″ VHS; 1945 • b/w; 1 hr, 37 min; ½″ Beta II, ½″
VHS • Sale: $39.95; Rental: $7.95/up to 5 days, applicable to purchase
- -
Video Communications Inc; 1945 • b/w; 1 hr, 37 min;
½″ Beta II, ½″ VHS • Sale: $54.95

Adapts Agatha Christie's novel for the screen. Recounts the story of ten people invited to an isolated
island where they are killed off one by one. Features
Barry Fitzgerald, Walter Huston, Judith Anderson, and
Louis Hayward, under the direction of Rene Clair.

AN ANDALUSIAN DOG
Northeast Video and Sound, Inc; Order No. 108S;
1928 • b/w; 20 min; ¾″ U-Matic, ½″ EIAJ, ½″ Beta II,
½″ VHS • Sale: $79; Rental: $35/wk

Presents Luis Bunuel's first film, made in collaboration
with Salvador Dali and considered to be the vanguard
of the surrealistic film movement. Juxtaposes bizarre
events, illogical actions, and familiar objects in strange
places in an attempt to make a film in the subjective
language of the unconscious.

THE ANDERSON TAPES
Columbia Pictures Home Entertainment; 1972 • color;
1 hr, 38 min; ½″ Beta II, ½″ VHS • Sale: $59.95
- -
Time-Life Video Club Inc; 1972 • color; 1 hr, 38 min;
½″ Beta II, ½″ VHS • Sale: $49.95, plus $15 annual
membership fee

Focuses on an ex-con whose moves have been electronically recorded since his release, as he attempts a
major robbery. Features Sean Connery, Dyan Cannon,
and Martin Balsam, under the direction of Sidney Lumet.

THE ANDROMEDA STRAIN
MCA DiscoVision; Order No. 13-001; 1971 • color; 2
hrs, 17 min; LaserVision • Sale: $24.95

Adapts for the screen the novel by Michael Crichton,
as it traces the attempts of scientists to stop a virus that
threatens to wipe out mankind after a spacecraft falls
to Earth in a remote New Mexico village. Uses authentic technical effects. Stars Arthur Hill, David Wayne,
and James Olson under the direction of Robert Wise.

ANDY WARHOL'S DRACULA
Video Gems; 1975 • color; 1 hr, 46 min; ½″ Beta II,
½″ VHS • Sale: $59.95

Presents an "X" rated version of Bram Stoker's tale.
Includes explicit sexual material and violence.

ANDY WARHOL'S FRANKENSTEIN
Video Gems; 1975 • color; 1 hr, 35 min; ½″ Beta II,
½″ VHS • Sale: $59.95

Presents an "X"-rated version of Mary Shelley's novel.
Uses violence and explicit sexual material. Features
Joe Dallesandro, Monique Van Vooren, and Udokier.

ANGEL AND THE BADMAN
Cinema Concepts, Inc.; 1947 • b/w; 1 hr, 40 min; ¾″
U-Matic, ½″ Beta II, ½″ VHS • Sale: $54.95 for ½″

Beta II & VHS, $149.95 for ¾″
- -
The Nostalgia Merchant; Order No. 0050; 1947 • b/w;
1 hr, 40 min; ½″ Beta II, ½″ VHS • Sale: $54.95
- -
The Video Library; Order No. AE-6022; 1947 • b/w; 1
hr, 40 min; ½″ Beta II, ½″ VHS • Sale: $54.95

Features John Wayne in a western about a gunslinger
who is reformed by the love of a Quaker girl.

ANGEL ON MY SHOULDER
Budget Video; 1946 • b/w; 1 hr, 40 min; ½″ Beta II,
½″ VHS • Sale: $44.95
- -
Ivy Video; 1946 • b/w; 1 hr, 39 min; ¾″ U-Matic, ½″
Beta II, ½″ VHS • Sale: $59.95 for ½″ Beta II & VHS,
trade-in plan available, $250 for ¾″
- -
Northeast Video and Sound, Inc; Order No. 155S;
1946 • b/w; ½″ Beta II, ½″ VHS • Sale: $150

Relates the fantasy tale of a revenge-seeking gangster
whose deal with the Devil backfires when he becomes
a force for good over evil. Stars Paul Muni, Claude
Rains, and Anne Baxter.

ANGELA—FIREWORKS WOMAN
Quality X Video Cassette Company; Date not listed •
color; 1 hr, 25 min; ½″ Beta I, ½″ Beta II, ½″ VHS •
Sale: $99.50

Presents a pornographic film.

ANGELIQUE
Monarch Releasing Corporation; Date not listed •
color; 1 hr, 5 min; ¾″ U-Matic • Sale: $350

Presents a pornographic film.

**Chico, Groucho, and Harpo Marx
with Margaret Dumont in
Animal Crackers.**

ANIMAL CRACKERS
MCA DiscoVision; Order No. 22-005; 1930 • b/w; 1
hr, 37 min; LaserVision • Sale: $15.95
- -
MCA Videocassette, Inc; Order No. 55000; 1930 •
b/w; 1 hr, 37 min; ½″ Beta II, ½″ VHS • Sale: $50

Adapts the musical play by George S. Kaufman, Morrie
Ryskind, Bert Kalmar, and Harry Ruby, into the second
feature film vehicle for the Marx Brothers. Includes
"Hooray for Captain Spaulding" and a little plotting
around a stolen painting. Features Lillian Roth and
Margaret Dumont.

ANIMAL FARM

Budget Video; 1955 • color; 1 hr, 15 min; 1/2″ Beta II, 1/2″ VHS • Sale: $44.95

- -

Video Tape Network; Order No. CD 611 for 1/2″ Beta II, CD 612 for 1/2″ VHS; 1955 • color; 1 hr, 15 min; 1/2″ Beta II, 1/2″ VHS • Sale: $59.95

Presents an animated version of George Orwell's tale of farm animals who overthrow the dictatorship of their human master only to create one of their own.

ANIMAL HOUSE

MCA DiscoVision; Order No. 16-007; 1978 • color; 1 hr, 49 min; LaserVision • Sale: $24.95

- -

MCA Videocassette, Inc; Order No. 66000; 1978 • color; 1 hr, 49 min; 1/2″ Beta II, 1/2″ VHS • Sale: $60

Presents "The National Lampoon's" motion picture debut: a satirical look at campus life in the early '60's. Shows the "war" between fraternities as one of straight, clean-cuts vs. raunchy rule-breakers, R.O.T. C. vs. the beer party. Stars John Belushi, John Vernon, and Donald Sutherland.

ANIMATION IN THE 1930'S

Reel Images Inc; Order No. 81; Date not listed • b/w; 40 min; 1/2″ Beta II, 1/2″ VHS • Sale: $39.95 for 1/2″ Beta II, $42.95 for 1/2″ VHS

Presents a series of seven animated films. Includes "Crosby, Columbo and Vallee," "Daffy and the Dinosaur," and "Three's a Crowd," produced by Warner Bros.; "Minnie Yoo Hoo" by Walt Disney; "Betty in Blunderland" and "Margie," produced by Max Fleischer.

ANNE OF THE THOUSAND DAYS

MCA DiscoVision; Order No. 15-002; 1969 • color; 2 hrs, 25 min; LaserVision • Sale: $24.95

Studies the relationship between Henry VIII and Anne Boleyn, and traces the ensuing political and religious implications when the King's conscience is tormented by his passion for a new wife, and he must change the laws to gain her. Stars Richard Burton, Genevieve Bujold, and Anthony Quayle in an adaptation of Maxwell Anderson's play.

ANNIE HALL

Vid America; 1977 • color; 1 hr, 34 min; 1/2″ Beta II, 1/2″ VHS • Rental: $13.95/wk

Highlights the wit and humor of Woody Allen and Diane Keaton in this portrait of the love affair between a comedian and an aspiring singer. Examines the on-again/off-again romance with lovers battling and reconciling in the company of numerous one-liners and sight gags. Co-stars Tony Roberts, Paul Simon, Shelly Duvall, Carol Kane, and Colleen Dewhurst, under Allen's direction of a screenplay co-authored with Marshall Brickman.

ANYONE BUT MY HUSBAND

Entertainment Video Releasing, Inc; Order No. 1058; Date not listed • color; 1 hr, 20 min; 1/2″ Beta II, 1/2″ VHS • Sale: $69.95 for 1/2″ Beta II, $74.95 for 1/2″ VHS

Presents a pornographic film.

THE APE MAN

Cinema Concepts, Inc.; 1943 • b/w; 1 hr, 10 min; 3/4″ U-Matic, 1/2″ Beta II, 1/2″ VHS • Sale: $54.95 for 1/2″ Beta II & VHS, 149.95 for 3/4″

- -

Video Tape Network; Order No. CD 623 for 1/2″ Beta II, CD 624 for 1/2″ VHS; 1943 • b/w; 1 hr, 4 min; 1/2″ Beta II, 1/2″ VHS

Tells what happens to a scientist who experiments with a serum that turns him into a murdering ape. Stars Bela Lugosi.

THE APPLE DUMPLING GANG

Fotomat Corp; Order No. B1039 for 1/2″ Beta II, V1039 for 1/2″ VHS; 1975 • color; 1 hr, 40 min; 1/2″ Beta II, 1/2″ VHS • Sale: $54.95 Rental: $7.95 5 days

- -

Niles Cinema; Order No. WD-18; 1975 • color; 1 hr, 40 min; 1/2″ Beta II, 1/2″ VHS • Sale: $59.95

- -

Walt Disney Home Video; Order No. 18BS for 1/2″ Beta II, 18VS for 1/2″ VHS; 1975 • color; 1 hr, 40 min; 1/2″ Beta II, 1/2″ VHS • Sale: $59.95

Presents a western-comedy from the Walt Disney Studios. Follows the adventures of three orphans and a gambler trying to outwit slapstick outlaws who learn they've struck gold. Stars Bill Bixby, Susan Clark, Don Knotts, Tim Conway, David Wayne, Slim Pickens, and Harry Morgan.

APPOINTMENT IN HONDURAS

FHV Entertainment, Inc; 1953 • color; 1 hr, 19 min; 1/2″ Beta II, 1/2″ VHS • Sale: $49.95

Offers a drama in which a man with a mission and his treacherous companions trek through a deadly jungle to reach a political rendezvous. Stars Glenn Ford and Ann Sheridan.

ARIZONA DAYS

Fotomat Corp; Order No. B0105 for 1/2″ Beta II, V0105 for 1/2″ VHS; 1936 • b/w; 52 min; 1/2″ Beta II, 1/2″ VHS • Sale: $39.95; Rental: $7.95/up to 5 days, applicable to purchase

- -

Reel Images Inc; Order No. 553; 1936 • b/w; 52 min; 1/2″ Beta II, 1/2″ VHS • Sale: $39.95 for 1/2″ Beta II, $42.95 for 1/2″ VHS

Presents a musical western starring Tex Ritter and Eleanor Stewart. Tells of cowboys joining a minstrel group and saving the show from bad guys.

Diane Keaton and Woody Allen in _Annie Hall._

THE ARIZONA RANGER; ROAD AGENT

The Nostalgia Merchant; 1948; 1952 • b/w; 2 hrs; ½" Beta II, ½" VHS • Sale: $59.95

Offers a Tim Holt western double feature. Opens with "Arizona Ranger," co-starring Jack Holt and Nan Leslie in a frontier town with outlaw problems. Follows with "Road Agent," the story of a scheme to regain money stolen from a bank; co-stars Noreen Nash.

THE ARK OF NOAH

Video Communications Inc; Date not listed • color; 1 hr, 35 min; ½" Beta II, ½" VHS • Sale: $54.95

Examines the legend of Noah's ark and reveals evidence that the ark may actually have existed.

AS YOU LIKE IT

Reel Images Inc; Order No. 447; 1936 • b/w; 47 min; ½" Beta II, ½" VHS • Sale: $39.95 for ½" Beta II, $42.95 for ½" VHS

Presents the Shakespeare comedy, starring Sir Laurence Olivier and Elizabeth Bergner under the direction of Dr. Paul Czinner.

ASSAULT ON PRECINCT 13

Meda/Media Home Entertainment Inc; Order No. M132; 1976 • color; 1 hr, 30 min; ½" Beta II, ½" VHS • Sale: $54.95

Shows hoodlums laying siege to a police station, and a policeman joined with convicts for survival. Features Austin Stoker.

THE ASTRO ZOMBIES

Video T.E.N.; 1969 • color; 1 hr, 28 min; ½" Beta II, ½" VHS • Sale: $49.95 for ½" Beta II, $54.95 for ½" VHS

Relates how a scientist creates a half-human, half-mechanized creature with a killer's brain. Stars John Carradine, Wendell Corey, Tom Pace, Tura Satanna, and Joan Patrick.

ASTRONUT

Magnetic Video Corporation; Order No. CL-2039; Date not listed • color; 30 min; ½" Beta II, ½" VHS • Sale: $34.95

Offers a compilation of Terrytoon animated cartoons featuring Astronut.

AT HOME WITH DONALD DUCK

MCA DiscoVision; Order No. D61-505; Date not listed; LaserVision • color; 1 hr • Sale: $9.95

Offers the adventures of many Walt Disney cartoon characters. Features Donald Duck catching his nephews, Huey, Dewey, and Louie, with a box of cigars and punishing them for it. Shows Donald throwing a party and showing movies with Mickey Mouse, Goofy, and Pluto, and Donald himself. Presents animation by Al Coe, Jerry Hathcock, Bob Carlson, George Kreisl, Bill Justice, Volus Jones, George Nicholas, and Dan MacManus under C. August Nichols' direction.

AT SWORD'S POINT

Niles Cinema; Order No. NM-8046; 1952 • color; 1 hr, 21 min; ½" Beta II, ½" VHS • Sale: $54.95

- -

The Nostalgia Merchant; Order No. 8046; 1952 • b/w; 1 hr, 21 min; ½" Beta II, ½" VHS • Sale: $54.95

- -

Red Fox, Inc; Order No. 8046; 1952 • b/w; 1 hr, 21 min; ½" Beta II, ½" VHS • Sale: $54.95

Presents an adaptation of "The Three Musketeers," with much court intrigue and swordplay. Features Cornel Wilde, Maureen O'Hara, and Robert Douglas.

AT WAR WITH THE ARMY

Cinema Resources; 1950 • b/w; 1 hr, 33 min; ½" Beta II, ½" VHS • Sale: $45

Showcases the comedy team of Dean Martin and Jerry Lewis as they have girl trouble while in the service. Features Polly Bergen. Offers the first film appearance of Martin and Lewis.

ATTACK OF THE CRAB MONSTERS

Blackhawk Films, Inc; Order No. 502-86-0068 for ½" Beta II, 515-86-0068 for ½" VHS; 1957 • b/w; 1 hr, 10 min; ½" Beta II, ½" VHS • Sale: $59.95

Details how small land crabs on an isolated Pacific island become 25-foot monsters following H-bomb fallout, and how once they have devoured humans they acquire the knowledge of their victims. Features Richard Garland and Pamela Duncan.

ATTACK OF THE KILLER TOMATOES

Meda/Media Home Entertainment Inc; Order No. M108; 1979 • color; 1 hr, 27 min; ½" Beta II, ½" VHS • Sale: $54.95

Presents a musical-comedy spoof of science-fiction movies. Features David Miller, George Wilson, Sharon Taylor, and Jack Riley.

AUDITIONS

Meda/Media Home Entertainment Inc; Order No. M504; 1978 • color; 1 hr, 25 min; ½" Beta I, ½" Beta II, ½" VHS • Sale: $54.95 for ½" Beta I, $54.95 for ½" Beta II & VHS

Presents a pornographic film.

AUTOBIOGRAPHY OF A FLEA

Mitchell Brothers' Film Group; Date not listed • color; 1 hr, 26 min; ½" Beta II, ½" VHS • Sale: $69

- -

Video Home Library; Order No. VX-117; Date not listed • color; 2 hrs; ½" Beta II, ½" VHS • Sale: $99.95

Presents a pornographic film.

AUTUMN LEAVES

National Film and Video Center; 1956 • b/w; 1 hr, 48 min; ¾" U-Matic, ½" Beta II, ½" VHS • Rental: $49/1 showing

Profiles the marriage of an older woman to a younger man with a hidden past who is rapidly losing his grip on reality. Stars Joan Crawford, Cliff Robertson, Vera Miles, Lorne Greene, and Ruth Donnelly.

AUTUMN SONATA

Magnetic Video Corporation; 1978 • color; 1 hr, 37 min; ½" Beta II, ½" VHS • Sale: $59.95

- -

Niles Cinema; Order No. CL-9021; 1978 • color; 1 hr, 37 min; ½" Beta II, ½" VHS • Sale: $59.95

Portrays the first encounter in seven years between a famous concert pianist and her estranged daughter. Stars Ingrid Bergman, Liv Ullmann, and Gunnar Bjornstrand under Ingmar Bergman's direction.

AVANT GARDE AND EXPERIMENTAL FILM PROGRAM NO. 1

Reel Images Inc; Order No. 83; Date not listed • b/w; 1 hr, 14 min; ½" Beta II, ½" VHS • Sale: $49.95 for ½" Beta II, $52.95 for ½" VHS

Presents "Un Chien Andalou," by Luis Bunuel and Salvador Dali; "Rain," by Joris Ivens and Mannus Franken; "Ballet Mecanique," directed by Fernand Leger and photographed by Dudley Murphy; "Hearts of Age,'' directed by and starring Orson Welles; concludes the program with ''Unberfall'' under the direction of Erno Marzner.

THE AVENGING CONSCIENCE
Reel Images Inc; Order No. 463; 1914 • b/w; 1 hr, 17 min; ½" Beta II, ½" VHS • Sale: $49.95 for ½" Beta II, $52.95 for ½" VHS

Offers an early D.W. Griffith silent horror film reminiscent of Edgar Allan Poe stories. Presents a psychological study of a man having visions of murdering the uncle who wants to prevent his marriage. Features special effects that were considered new and daring for the time. Stars Henry B. Walthall, Blanche Sweet, Spottiswoode Aiken, and Mae Marsh.

AVIATION (VOLUME 1)
Blackhawk Films, Inc; Order No. 506-70-0823 for ½" Beta II, 525-70-0823 for ½" VHS; Date not listed • b/w; 1 hr; ¾" U-Matic, ½" Beta I, ½" Beta II, ½" VHS • Sale: $59.95 for ½" Beta I, $39.95 for ½" Beta II & VHS, $69.95 for ¾"

Offers a documentary which highlights aviation history from the Wright Brothers through the evolution of the helicopter. Uses a newsreel format. Includes the crash of de Pinedo, the Graf Zeppelin, Lindbergh's trans-Atlantic flight, and the Pan American Clippers, the amphibious experimental planes that circled the globe.

THE AWFUL TRUTH
National Film and Video Center; 1937 • b/w; 1 hr, 32 min; ¾" U-Matic, ½" Beta II, ½" VHS • Rental: $49/1 showing

Recounts the events leading up to and following the separation of a young couple. Shows that, although the husband accuses his wife of unfaithfulness and becomes engaged to a young socialite, she is determined to win him back. Stars Irene Dunne, Cary Grant, Ralph Bellamy, Alexander D'Arcy, and Cecil Cunningham, under the direction of Leo McCarey.

THE BABY
Niles Cinema; Order No. BT-06 for ½" Beta II, VH-06 for ½" VHS; 1973 • color; 1 hr, 40 min; ½" Beta II, ½" VHS • Sale: $59.95

Presents the story of a social worker who tries to rescue an environmentally deprived man-child from the clutches of his savage mother and sisters, with Anjanette Comer, Ruth Roman, and Mariana Hill.

BABY BLUE MARINE
National Film and Video Center; 1976 • color; 1 hr, 30 min; ¾" U-Matic, ½" Beta II, ½" VHS • Rental: $59/1 showing

Relates the story of a young man who fails the Marines' basic training and is sent home in the baby blue uniform which marks him as a failure. Tells how a deserting Marine trades uniforms with him—and he discovers that wearing the uniform of a hero leads people to demand heroic action of him. Stars Jan-Michael Vincent, Glynnis O'Connor, and Katherine Helmond.

BACHELOR AND THE BOBBY SOXER
Blackhawk Films, Inc; Order No. 506-07-0786 for ½" Beta II, 525-07-0786 for ½" VHS; 1947 • b/w; 1 hr, 35 min ; ½" Beta II, ½" VHS • Sale: $49.95

Relates how a playboy, convicted of a traffic charge, is sentenced by a lady judge to wine and dine her teenage niece until the girl loses her infatuation for him. Features Cary Grant, Myrna Loy, Shirley Temple, and Rudy Vallee.

BACK FROM ETERNITY
Video Communications Inc; Order No. 1006; 1956 • b/w; 1 hr, 37 min; ½" Beta II, ½" VHS • Sale: $54.95

Shows how an ex-Air Force ace crash lands a commercial airliner in the South American hunting grounds of Jivaro headhunters. Relates how the eleven survivors contend with the elements and threatened dangers from outside, and examines the horror within the group when it becomes necessary to decide which five will make it back to civilization. Stars Rod Steiger, Robert Ryan, and Anita Ekberg.

BACK STREET
MCA DiscoVision; Order No. 21-016; 1932 • b/w; 1 hr, 32 min; LaserVision • Sale: $15.95

Offers the first film version of Fannie Hurst's story of a woman in love with a married man who must accept her place in the background. Stars Irene Dunne, John Boles, and Zasu Pitts.

BACK TO BATAAN
Blackhawk Films, Inc; Order No. 506-39-0769 for ½" Beta II, 525-39-0769 for ½" VHS; 1945 • b/w; 1 hr, 35 min; ½" Beta II, ½" VHS • Sale: $49.95

Dramatizes the efforts of American soldiers to organize the Filipino freedom fighters to resist the Japanese during World War II. Stars John Wayne and Anthony Quinn.

BAD MAN'S RIVER
Tape Club of America; Order No. 2601 B; 1972 • color; 1 hr, 29 min; ½" Beta II, ½" VHS • Sale: $54.95
- -
Discount Video Tapes; 1972 • color; 1 hr, 29 min; ½" Beta II, ½" VHS • Sale: $49.95

Describes the exploits of the notorious King Gang. Tells how a Mexican revolutionary leader offers the gang a reward if they will blow up an arsenal used by the Mexican army. Stars Lee Van Cleef, Gina Lollobrigida, and James Mason.

THE BAD NEWS BEARS
Fotomat Corp; Order No. B0021 for ½" Beta II, V0021 for ½" VHS ; 1976 • color; 1 hr, 42 min; ½" Beta II, ½" VHS • Sale: $49.95; Rental: $9.95/up to 5 days, applicable to purchase
- -
Paramount Home Video; Order No. 8863; 1976 • color; 1 hr, 42 min; ½" Beta II, ½" VHS • Sale: $62.95
- -
RCA SelectaVision VideoDiscs; Order No. 00609; 1976 • color; 1 hr, 42 min; CED • Sale: $19.98

Portrays a grumbling, beer-guzzling former minor-league pitcher who gets roped into coaching a bunch of half-pints misfits somewhat loosely called a team. Stars Walter Matthau, Tatum O'Neal, Vic Morrow, and Joyce Van Patten.

THE BAD NEWS BEARS GO TO JAPAN
Fotomat Corp; Order No. B0025 for ½" Beta II, V0025 for ½" VHS; 1978 • color; 1 hr, 42 min; ½" Beta II, ½" VHS • Sale: $49.95; Rental: $9.95/up to 5 days, applicable to purchase

Cary Grant and Shirley Temple in *The Bachelor and the Bobby Soxer.*

Follows the Bears as they are spirited off to Tokyo by a slick con artist who sees in the team a perfect peg for a get-rich-quick scheme. Shows the strikeout-prone Bears pitted against a skillful Japanese baseball team. Stars Tony Curtis and Jackie Earle Haley.

THE BAD NEWS BEARS IN BREAKING TRAINING
Fotomat Corp; Order No. B0023 for ½″ Beta II, V0023 for ½″ VHS; 1977 • color; 1 hr, 37 min; ½″ Beta II, ½″ VHS • Sale: $49.95; Rental: $9.95/up to 5 days, applicable to purchase

Follows the Bears as they get a chance to play the Houston Toros for a shot at the Japanese champs. Shows how they devise a way to get to Texas to play at the Astrodome. Stars William Devane and Clifton James.

BAD PENNY
Quality X Video Cassette Company; Date not listed • color; 1 hr, 23 min; ½″ Beta I, ½″ Beta II, ½″ VHS • Sale: $99.50

Presents a pornographic film.

BADMEN OF NEVADA
Video Communications Inc; Order No. 1126; 1940 • b/w; 1 hr, 5 min; ½″ Beta II, ½″ VHS • Sale: $54.95

Recounts a story of the early days of Nevada, before law and order took over and peace came. Stars Victor Jory and Russell Hayden.

BALLAD OF A SOLDIER
Cinema Resources; 1960 • b/w; 1 hr, 29 min; ½″ Beta II, ½″ VHS • Sale: $45

Follows the attempts of a young Russian soldier to get home during World War II to see his mother and shows his love affair with a simple country girl. Stars Vladimir Ivashov, Shanna Prokhorenko, Antonina Maximova, and Nikolai Kruchkov.

BALLOONATIK
Golden Tapes Video Tape Library; Order No. CC6;

Date not listed • b/w; 45 min; ½″ Beta II, ½″ VHS • Sale: $49.95 for ½″ Beta II & VHS, $79.95 for ¾″

Presents a Buster Keaton silent comedy short in which Buster is accidently carried away on a balloon and copes with the situation in his own eccentric way.

BANDITS OF DARK CANYON; HIDDEN VALLEY OUTLAWS
The Nostalgia Merchant; Order No. 5005; 1948, 1944 • b/w; 2 hrs; ½″ Beta II, ½″ VHS • Sale: $59.95

Presents a western double feature. Opens with Rocky Lane in a western ghost town trying to clear an innocent man in "Bandits of Dark Canyon." Follows with "Hidden Valley Outlaws," with Wild Bill Elliott trying to corral a killer and avert a land swindle.

THE BANDITS OF OROGOSOLO
Thunderbird Films; 1964 • b/w; 1 hr, 40 min; ¾″ U-Matic, ½″ Beta I, ½″ Beta II, ½″ VHS • Sale: $69.95 for ½″ Beta I, $49.95 for ½″ Beta II & VHS, $89.95 for ¾″

Chronicles the trials of a shepherd pursued by the police because his hut has been used as a hideout by bandits.

BANG BANG YOU GOT IT
Quality X Video Cassette Company; Date not listed • color; 1 hr, 20 min; ½″ Beta I, ½″ Beta II, ½″ VHS • Sale: $99.50

Presents a pornographic film.

BAR 20 JUSTICE
Videobrary Inc; Order No. 13; 1938 • b/w; 1 hr, 10 min; ½″ Beta II, ½″ VHS • Sale: $39.95

Presents a Hopalong Cassidy western. Shows Cassidy trying to outsmart a devious gold mine thief. Stars William Boyd, George "Gabby" Hayes, and Pat O'Brien.

BAR 20 RIDES AGAIN
Videobrary Inc; Order No. 3; 1935 • b/w; 1 hr, 2 min;

½" Beta II, ½" VHS • Sale: $39.95

Presents a Hopalong Cassidy western. Features Cassidy posing as a foppish gambler to outwit a gang of rustlers led by a man who fancies himself an imitator of Napoleon. Stars William Boyd, George "Gabby" Hayes, and Chill Wills.

BAR 20 RIDES AGAIN; RUSTLER'S VALLEY
Videobrary Inc; Order No. 3-20; 1935 & 1937 • b/w; 2 hrs, 2 min; ½" Beta II, ½" VHS • Sale: $69.95

Presents a Hopalong Cassidy western double feature. Offers "Bar 20 Rides Again" in which Cassidy poses as a fop to outwit an outlaw who fancies himself another Napoleon, and "Rustler's Valley" in which a jealous fiance may not be who he says he is. Stars William Boyd and George "Gabby" Hayes.

BARABBAS
National Film and Video Center; 1962 • color; 2 hrs, 24 min; ¾" U-Matic, ½" Beta II, ½" VHS • Rental: $69/1 showing

Profiles Barabbas, the thief who is pardoned and freed when Christ is crucified in his place. Shows how he returns to his life of crime, but when in Rome tries to help the Christians. Stars Anthony Quinn, Silvana Mangano, Arthur Kennedy, Jack Palance, Ernest Borgnine, and Katy Jurado.

BARBARA BROADCAST
Quality X Video Cassette Company; 1977 • color; 1 hr, 27 min; ½" Beta I, ½" Beta II, ½" VHS • Sale: $99.50
- -
TVX Distributors; Order No. R.T. 83; Date not listed • color; 2 hrs; ½" Beta II, ½" VHS • Sale: $79.50 for ½" Beta II, $89.50 for ½" VHS

Presents a pornographic film.

BARBARELLA
Fotomat Corp; Order No. B0055 for ½" Beta II, V0055 for ½" VHS; 1968 • color; 1 hr, 38 min; ½" Beta II, ½" VHS • Sale: $49.95; Rental: $9.95/up to 5 days, applicable to purchase
- -
Paramount Home Video; 1968 • color; 1 hr, 38 min; ½" Beta II, ½" VHS • Sale: $59.95

Presents a film version of the comic strip, set on the planet Lython in the year 40,000, when Barbarella makes a forced landing while travelling through space. Portrays the heroine vanquishing evil in the forms of robots and monsters, while also rewarding, in an uninhibited manner, the men who assist her in the adventure. Stars Jane Fonda, John Philip Law, David Hemmings, and Milo O'Shea, under the direction of Roger Vadim.

BARE KNUCKLES
FHV Entertainment, Inc; 1976 • color; 1 hr, 30 min; ½" Beta II, ½" VHS • Sale: $49.95

Chronicles the saga of Zack Kane, the hunter, as he tracks down the wanted for a price. Stars Robert Viharo, Sherry Jackson, and Gloria Henry.

BAREFOOT IN THE PARK
Paramount Home Video; Order No. 8027; 1967 • color; 1 hr, 46 min; ½" Beta II, ½" VHS • Sale: $62.95

Adapts for the screen Neil Simon's Broadway comedy about newlyweds starting out in New York City with several strikes against them; he's a conservative lawyer, she's a free spirit, and New York is full of unexpected happenings. Stars Robert Redford, Jane Fonda, Charles Boyer, and Mildred Natwick.

THE BATTLE OF EL ALAMEIN
Video Warehouse, Inc; Order No. 1069; 1971 • color; 1 hr, 32 min; ½" Beta II, ½" VHS • Sale: $39.95

Recounts the World War II desert battle between Montgomery's Iron Back 8th Army and Rommel's crack AF Corps. Stars Frederick Stafford, George Hilton, and Michael Rennie.

BATTLESTAR GALACTICA
MCA DiscoVision; Order No. 19-007; 1978 • color; 2 hrs, 3 min; LaserVision • Sale: $24.95
- -
MCA Videocassette, Inc; Order No. 66011; 1978 • color; 2 hrs, 3 min; ½" Beta II, ½" VHS • Sale: $60

Offers the pilot for the TV series. Concerns the search by the only human survivors of many wars for a planet many galaxies away where they can exist—if not first hunted down by the evil force which chases them. Features the special effects of John ("Star Wars") Dykstra. Stars Lorne Greene, Richard Hatch, Dirk Benedict, Maren Jensen, Ray Milland, Lew Ayres, and Wilfred Hyde-White.

BATTLING HOOFER
Reel Images Inc; Order No. 449; 1936 • b/w; 1 hr, 22 min; ½" Beta II, ½" VHS • Sale: $49.95 for ½" Beta II, 52.95 for ½" VHS

Offers a musical melodrama about a tough bandleader who heads for Hollywood and stardom. Features a dancing number by star James Cagney.

THE BEACHCOMBER
Video T.E.N.; 1938 • b/w; 1 hr, 20 min; ½" Beta II, ½" VHS • Sale: $49.95 for ½" Beta II, $54.95 for ½" VHS

Relates a story of a beachcomber and a missionary's sister who at first loathe each other but later learn to love. Features Charles Laughton, Elsa Lanchester, Tyrone Guthrie, Robert Newton, and Dolly Mollinger in this adaptation of Somerset Maugham's "Vessel of Wrath."

THE BEARS AND I
Fotomat Corp; 1974 • color; 1 hr, 29 min; ½" Beta II, ½" VHS • Sale: $49.95; Rental: $9.95/up to 5 days, applicable to purchase
- -
RCA SelectaVision VideoDiscs; Order No. 00704; 1974 • color; 1 hr, 29 min; CED • Sale: $19.98

Offers a tale of bigotry against Indians living in the North Woods and the Vietnam veteran who tries to help. Features Patrick Wayne, Chief Dan George, Andrew Duggan, and Michael Ansara. Presents a Walt Disney Studios production.

BEAT THE DEVIL
National Film and Video Center; 1954 • b/w; 1 hr, 29 min; ¾" U-Matic, ½" Beta II, ½" VHS • Rental: $69/1 showing

Brings together a bunch of swindlers, all planning to double-cross one another over uranium lands, and then strands them when a explosion wrecks their ship. Stars Humphrey Bogart, Gina Lollobrigida, Jennifer Jones, Peter Lorre, and Robert Morley, under John Huston's direction.

BEAUTY AND THE BANDIT
Video Communications Inc; Order No. 1127; 1946 • b/w; 1 hr, 17 min; ½" Beta II, ½" VHS • Sale: $54.95

Portrays Chico, who robs the rich and gives to the poor, but is reformed by a beautiful woman bandit. Stars Gilbert Roland and Ramsey Amer.

THE BEDFORD INCIDENT
Columbia Pictures Home Entertainment; Order No. BE51015 for ½″ Beta II, VH10013 for ½″ VHS; 1965 • b/w; 1 hr, 42 min; ½″ Beta II, ½″ VHS • Sale: $59.95
- -
National Film and Video Center; 1965 • color; 2 hrs, 55 min; ¾″ U-Matic, ½″ Beta II, ½″ VHS • Rental: $69/1 showing

Offers a suspense tale of the Cold War. Depicts the men of an American destroyer who track a Russian submarine near Greenland. Stars Richard Widmark, Sidney Poitier, Martin Balsam, James MacArthur, Wally Cox, Eric Portman, and Donald Sutherland.

John Phillip Law and Jane Fonda in *Barbarella*.

BEDKNOBS AND BROOMSTICKS
Fotomat Corp; Order No. B1027 for ½″ Beta II, V1027 for ½″ VHS; 1971 • color; 2 hrs, 27 min; ½″ Beta II, ½″ VHS • Sale: $54.95; Rental: $7.95/5 days
- -
Walt Disney Home Video; Order No. 16BS for ½″ Beta II, 16VS for ½″ VHS; 1971 • color; 1 hr, 57 min; ½″ Beta II, ½″ VHS • Sale: $59.95
- -
Niles Cinema; Order No. WD-16; 1971 • color; 1 hr, 57 min; ½″ Beta II, ½″ VHS

Prsents a musical-fantasy from the Walt Disney Studios about an amateur witch who tries tohelp England during World War II. Features live action combined with animation. Stars Angela Lansbury, Roddy McDowall, David Tomlinson, Sam Jaffe, and Roy Snart.

BEDLAM
Niles Cinema; Order No. NM-8020; 1945 • b/w; 1 hr, 19 min; ½″ Beta II, ½″ VHS • Sale: $54.95
- -
The Nostalgia Merchant; Order No. 8020; 1945 • b/w; 1 hr, 19 min; ½″ Beta II, ½″ VHS • Sale: $54.95
- -
Red Fox, Inc; Order No. 8020; 1945 • b/w; 1 hr,.19 min; ½″ Beta II, ½″ VHS • Sale: $54.95

Presents the story of an 18th century madhouse and its sadistic overseer. Features Boris Karloff, Anna Lee, and Richard Fraser.

BEGGAR'S OPERA
Video Warehouse, Inc; Order No. 1081; Date not listed • color; 2 hrs; ½″ Beta II, ½″ VHS • Sale: $59.95

Presents a musical satire of life in 16th century England, from an off-Broadway production.

BEHIND THE GREEN DOOR
Mitchell Brothers' Film Group; Date not listed • color; 1 hr, 12 min; ½″ Beta II, ½″ VHS • Sale: $69

Presents a pornographic film.

BEHIND THE SHUTTERS
Cinema Concepts, Inc.; 1972 • color; 1 hr, 27 min; ¾″ U-Matic, ½″ Beta II, ½″ VHS • Sale: $54.95 for ½″ Beta II & VHS, $149.95 for ¾″

Presents a thriller about a revenge-seeking woman, her psychotic step-daughter, and a young hustler who may be a mass murderer. Stars Jean Seberg.

BEING THERE
MGM/CBS Home Video; Order No. C60026; 1979 • color; 2 hrs, 4 min; ½″ Beta II, ½″ VHS • Sale: $69.95

Adapts for the screen Jerzy Kosinski's short novel about a mentally retarded man who has tended the garden of a wealthy man for many years and is suddenly thrust by accident into the glamourous world of politics and TV. Stars Peter Sellers, Melvyn Douglas, Shirley Maclaine, Jack Warden, Richard Dysart, and Richard Basehart.

BEL AMI
Quality X Video Cassette Company; Date not listed • color; 1 hr, 30 min; ½″ Beta I, ½″ Beta II, ½″ VHS • Sale: $99.50

Presents a pornographic film.

BELL, BOOK AND CANDLE
Time-Life Video Club Inc; 1958 • color; 1 hr, 43 min; ½″ Beta II, ½″ VHS • Sale: $49.95, to members

Adapts the John Van Druten play about a wealthy, about-to-be-married publisher who is charmed by a Greenwich Village witch. Follows the comic attempts of her family to keep her in the fold when they discover she wants to leave her bewitching ways. Stars James Stewart, Kim Novak, Jack Lemmon, Ernie Kovacs, and Hermione Gingold.

BELLS OF CORONADO; KING OF THE COWBOYS
The Nostalgia Merchant; Order No. 5010; 1950, 1943 • b/w & color; 2 hrs; ½″ Beta II, ½″ VHS • Sale: $59.95

Presents a Roy Rogers western double feature. Opens with a color film in which Roy is an insurance investigator who is sent in to solve a murder and ore theft. Concludes with "King of the Cowboys" as Roy investigates a band of saboteurs.

BELLS OF ROSARITA
Cable Films; 1945 • b/w; 55 min; ½″ Beta I, ½″ Beta II, ½″ VHS • Sale: $45 for ½″ Beta I, $49.50 for ½″ Beta II & VHS

Presents a western featuring a movie within a movie. Offers songs as well as western action. Stars Roy Rogers, Dale Evans, and Trigger.

BELLS OF ROSARITA; UNDER WESTERN STARS
The Nostalgia Merchant; 1945; 1938 • b/w; 2 hrs; ½″

Beta II, 1/2" VHS • Sale: $59.95

Presents a Roy Rogers double bill. Opens with "Bells of Rosarita," in which Roy attempts to prevent a woman from being swindled out of her inheritance. Follows with "Under Western Stars," Roy Rogers' first starring role, in which he and Trigger fight an outlaw gang.

BEN HUR
MGM/CBS Home Video; Order No. M9004; 1959 • color; 3 hrs, 32 min; 1/2" Beta II, 1/2" VHS • Sale: $89.95
- -
Niles Cinema; Order No. GM-720; 1959 • color; 3 hrs, 32 min; 1/2" Beta II, 1/2" VHS • Sale: $89.95

Presents, on two videocassettes, the William Wyler adaptation of Lew Wallace's novel set during the time of Christ. Concerns a Jewish nobleman trying to overcome the tyranny of the Romans. Includes famous chariot race to the death. Stars Charlton Heston, Stephen Boyd, Jack Hawkins, Hugh Griffith, Martha Scott, and Sam Jaffe.

BEN TURPIN RIDES AGAIN (CROSS-EYED!)
Reel Images Inc; Order No. 528; 1923-28 • b/w; 45 min; 1/2" Beta II, 1/2" VHS • Sale: $39.95 for 1/2" Beta II, $42.95 for 1/2" VHS

Offers three slapstick Mack Sennett shorts starring Ben Turpin. Shows cross-eyed Ben as a Hollywood stunt man in "The Daredevil," then as a sheriff tracking two villains through the frozen North in "Yukon Jake." Finishes with Ben as a henpecked husband in "The Eyes Have It."

BENEATH THE PLANET OF THE APES
Magnetic Video Corporation; Order No. CL-1013; 1970 • color; 1 hr, 45 min; 1/2" Beta II, 1/2" VHS • Sale: $44.95
- -
The Video Library; Order No. MV-1013; 1970 • color; 1 hr, 45 min; 1/2" Beta II, 1/2" VHS • Sale: $54.95

Presents a science-fiction adventure about a futuristic world of apes that develops after a massive nuclear attack on the United States. Highlights a power struggle between a subterranean race of mutants and swarms of ape-men.

BENEATH THE SHEETS
Tape Club of America; Order No. 2816 B; Date not listed • color; 1 hr, 30 min; 1/2" Beta II, 1/2" VHS • Sale: $54.95

Presents a pornographic film.

BENEATH THE WAR OF THE WORLDS
Video Tape Network; Order No. CY 207 for 1/2" Beta II, CY 208 for 1/2" VHS; Date not listed • color; 40 min; 1/2" Beta II, 1/2" VHS • Sale: $49.95

Presents a parody of the science fiction live film genre. Details the end of mankind on live TV as alien beings land, with surprising results.

BENJI
Fotomat Corp; Order No. B0401 for 1/2" Beta II, V0401 for 1/2" VHS; 1973 • color ; 1 hr, 27 min; 1/2" Beta II, 1/2" VHS • Sale: $54.95; Rental: $9.95/5 days

Features the dog who can foil kidnappers and win hearts. Stars Benji, Peter Brek, Christopher Connelly, Patsy Garrett, Tom Lester, Mark Slade, and Deborah Walley.

BERLIN EXPRESS
The Nostalgia Merchant; Order No. 8063; 1948 • b/w; 1 hr, 26 min; 1/2" Beta II, 1/2" VHS • Sale: $54.95

Red Fox, Inc; Order No. 806; 1948 • b/w; 1 hr, 26 min; 1/2" Beta II, 1/2" VHS • Sale: $54.95

Recounts a World War II thriller about the underground working to save an endangered German scientist. Stars Robert Ryan, Merle Oberon, and Paul Lukas.

THE BERMUDA TRIANGLE
Vid America; Order No. 906; Date not listed • color; 1 hr, 34 min; 1/2" Beta II, 1/2" VHS • Rental: $12.95/wk

Investigates the area of the Atlantic Ocean which Columbus referred to as "The Sea of Fear" and modern terminology calls "The Bermuda Triangle." Recreates verified incidents from official reports, ships' logs, and eyewitness accounts in which boats and planes have disappeared. Proposes several possible explanations.

BERSERK
National Film and Video Center; 1967 • color; 1 hr, 36 min; 3/4" U-Matic, 1/2" Beta II, 1/2" VHS • Rental: $49/1 showing

Examines a series of murders which plague a traveling circus. Unfolds the personal lives of the performers as tension grows. Stars Joan Crawford and Ty Hardin.

THE BEST OF HECKLE & JECKLE (PART 1)
Magnetic Video Corporation; Order No. CL-2030; Date not listed • color; 30 min; 1/2" Beta II, 1/2" VHS • Sale: $34.95

Presents a compilation of Terrytoon animated cartoons featuring Heckle and Jeckle.

THE BEST OF HECKLE & JECKLE (PART 2)
Magnetic Video Corporation; Order No. CL-2031; Date not listed • color; 30 min; 1/2" Beta II, 1/2" VHS • Sale: $34.95

See Part 1 for description.

THE BEST OF HECKLE & JECKLE (PART 3)
Magnetic Video Corporation; Order No. CL-2032; Date not listed • color; 30 min; 1/2" Beta II, 1/2" VHS • Sale: $34.95

See Part 1 for description.

THE BEST OF SUPERMAN CARTOONS
Northeast Video and Sound, Inc; Date not listed • color; 1 hr, 8 min; 3/4" U-Matic, 1/2" EIAJ, 1/2" Beta II, 1/2" VHS • Sale: $159; Rental: $65/wk

Presents a composite of Superman and the Mad Scientist, Mechanical Monsters, The Magnetic Telescope, Tapoteurs, The Mummy Strikes, Bulleteers, and Jungle Drums.

BEYOND A REASONABLE DOUBT
Video Communications Inc; Order No. 1009; 1956 • b/w; 1 hr, 20 min; 1/2" Beta II, 1/2" VHS • Sale: $54.95

Shows how a novelist prepares to embarrass the District Attorney and win support for his cause, abolition of capital punishment. Relates how only his publisher holds the key to his innocence and how everything goes according to plan until the publisher, ready to deliver the eleventh hour evidence that will exonerate the writer, is killed in an auto crash. Details how one suspenseful twist follows another before the wheels of justice take their final ironic turn. Stars Dana Andrews and Joan Fontaine.

BEYOND AND BACK
Video Communications Inc; Order No. 6002; Date not listed • color; 1 hr, 35 min; 1/2" Beta II, 1/2" VHS • Sale: $54.95

Examines the question of an afterlife. Presents interviews with people who were pronounced clinically dead. Includes other areas such as parapsychology, spiritualism, and reincarnation.

BEYOND BELIEF
Video Communications Inc; Date not listed • color; 1 hr, 32 min; 1/2" Beta II, 1/2" VHS • Sale: $54.95

Explores the truth in some of the mysteries of our time such as "healing by hands," ESP, and reincarnation.

BEYOND FEAR
Cinema Concepts, Inc.; 1975 • color; 1 hr, 32 min; 3/4" U-Matic, 1/2" Beta II, 1/2" VHS • Sale: $54.95 for 1/2" Beta II & VHS, 149.95 for 3/4"
- -
The Video Library; Order No. CC-0104; 1975 • color; 1 hr, 32 min; 1/2" Beta II, 1/2" VHS • Sale: $54.95

Explores the moral implications of a man forced to help a vicious gang in a robbery when they hold his wife and son captive. Stars Michel Bouquet.

THE BIBLE
Blackhawk Films, Inc; Order No. 502-49-0015 for 1/2" Beta II, 515-49-0002 for 1/2" VHS; 1966 listed • color; 2 hrs, 35 min; 1/2" Beta II, 1/2" VHS • Sale: $74.95
- -
Golden Tapes Video Tape Library; Order No. F-1020; 1966 • color; 2 hrs, 34 min; 1/2" Beta II, 1/2" VHS • Sale: $49.95 for 1/2" Beta II & VHS, $124.95 for 3/4"
- -
Magnetic Video Corporation; Order No. CL-1020; 1966 • color; 2 hrs, 35 min; 1/2" Beta II, 1/2" VHS • Sale: $74.95
- -
The Video Library; Order No. MV-1020; 1966 • color; 2 hrs, 35 min; 1/2" Beta II, 1/2" VHS • Sale: $74.95

Presents an elaborate dramatization of the first twenty-two chapters of the Bible. Retells the stories of Adam and Eve, Cain and Abel, and Noah and the Flood. Stars Michael Parks, Richard Harris, Stephen Boyd, George C. Scott, Ava Gardner, and Peter O'Toole, under the direction of John Huston.

THE BIG CAT
Thunderbird Films; 1949 • color; 1 hr, 20 min; 3/4" U-Matic, 1/2" Beta I, 1/2" Beta II, 1/2" VHS • Sale: $69.95 for 1/2" Beta I, 49.95 for 1/2" Beta II & VHS, $89.95 for 3/4"

Relates the adventures of two families who put aside their long-standing feud to fight a deadly mountain lion. Features Lon McCallister, Peggy Ann Garner, Preston Foster, and Forrest Tucker.

BIG FOOT—MAN OR BEAST?
Video Communications Inc; Date not listed • color; 1 hr, 32 min; 1/2" Beta II, 1/2" VHS • Sale: $54.95

Investigates the legend of a giant manlike creature that is supposed to inhabit the forests of the Pacific Northwest. Features film footage that claims to show the creature itself.

THE BIG HUNT
Video Communications Inc; Date not listed • color; 1 hr, 30 min; 1/2" Beta II, 1/2" VHS • Sale: $54.95

Offers a safari to India featuring the capture of wild elephants, a tiger hunt, and a rhinoceros capture.

THE BIG LAND
Fotomat Corp; Order No. B0109 for 1/2" Beta II, V0109 for 1/2" VHS; 1957 • color; 1 hr, 38 min; 1/2" Beta II, 1/2" VHS • Sale: $39.95; Rental: $7.95/up to 5 days, applicable to purchase

Video Communications Inc; 1957 • color; 1 hr, 33 min; 1/2" Beta II, 1/2" VHS • Sale: $54.95

Shows cattle owners and grain farmers joining together to bring a railroad link to Texas. Stars Alan Ladd, Virginia Mayo, and Edmond O'Brien.

THE BIG MOUTH
National Film and Video Center; 1967 • color; 1 hr, 47 min; 3/4" U-Matic, 1/2" Beta II, 1/2" VHS • Rental: $49/1 showing

Features Jerry Lewis as a man who has a look-alike involved in a plot to steal diamonds from gangsters. Co-stars Harold Stone, Susan Bay, and Buddy Lester, under Lewis' direction.

BILLBOARD GIRL
Northeast Video and Sound, Inc; 1934 • b/w; 20 min; 3/4" U-Matic, 1/2" EIAJ, 1/2" Beta II, 1/2" VHS • Sale: $79; Rental: $29/wk

Features Bing Crosby as a man who falls in love with a girl in a billboard ad, and then tracks her down to a small college town.

BILLY THE KID RETURNS
Cable Films; 1938 • b/w; 55 min; 1/2" Beta I, 1/2" Beta II, 1/2" VHS • Sale: $45 for 1/2" Beta I, $49.50 for 1/2" Beta II & VHS

Presents a western in which Roy Rogers is mistaken for the legendary Billy the Kid. Features Rogers in a dual role, with Smiley Burnette.

BING CROSBY FESTIVAL
Discount Video Tapes; 1930-39 • b/w; 1 hr; 1/2" Beta II, 1/2" VHS • Sale: $49.95

Features three of Bing's musical short subjects. Includes "Billboard Girl," "Blue of the Night," and "I Surrender Dear."

BINGO LONG TRAVELLING ALL-STARS AND MOTOR KINGS
MCA DiscoVision; Order No. 16-011; 1976 • color; 1 hr, 51 min • Sale: $24.95

Follows the adventures of an all-black baseball team in 1939, which decides to try its luck on the road after being frustrated by the owners of the old Negro National League, and being barred from the Major Leagues by their color. Stars Billy Dee Williams, James Earl Jones, and Richard Pryor in an adaptation of William Brasher's novel.

THE BIOGRAPH SHORTS: D.W. GRIFFITH
Northeast Video and Sound, Inc ; Order No. 139S; 1909-12 • b/w; 55 min; 3/4" U-Matic, 1/2" EIAJ, 1/2" Beta II, 1/2" VHS • Sale: $150; Rental: $55/wk

Presents composite of shorts Griffith directed between 1908 and 1912. Includes "The Battle of Elderbush Gulch" and "Female of the Species."

THE BIONIC WOMAN
MCA DiscoVision; Order No. 20-001; 1975 • color; 1 hr, 36 min; LaserVision • Sale: $9.95

Offers the pilot for the TV series. Shows the Six Million Dollar Man's fiancee critically injured skydiving, her subsequent six-million-dollar operation, and her adventures as an indestructible government agent. Features Lindsay Wagner, Lee Majors, Richard Anderson, and Alan Oppenheimer.

BIRD OF PARADISE
Video T.E.N.; 1932 • b/w; 1 hr, 20 min; 1/2" Beta II, 1/2" VHS • Sale: $49.95 for 1/2" Beta II, $54.95 for 1/2" VHS

Recounts a romantic tale of the forbidden love of a south seas girl for a white man, as directed by King Vidor and Busby Berkeley. Includes Delores Del Rio, Joel McCrea, John Halliday, and Skeets Gallagher.

Tippi Hedren and Rod Taylor in *The Birds*.

THE BIRDS
MCA DiscoVision; Order No. 11-007; 1963 • color; 1 hr, 59 min; LaserVision • Sale: $24.95

- -
MCA Videocassette, Inc; Order No. 55010; 1963 • color; 2 hrs; 1/2" Beta II, 1/2" VHS • Sale: $55

Adapts a short story by Daphne DuMaurier for the screen. Shows a small California community trying to survive a growing number of attacks by birds of every shape and size, culminating in an all-out war: birds vs. mankind. Stars Rod Taylor, Tippi Hedren, and Jessica Tandy, under the direction of Alfred Hitchcock.

BIRTH OF A NATION
Cinema Concepts, Inc.; 1915 • b/w; 2 hrs; 3/4" U-Matic, 1/2" Beta II, 1/2" VHS • Sale: $54.95 for 1/2" Beta II & VHS , $149.95 for 3/4"

- -
Northeast Video and Sound, Inc; 1915 • b/w; 2 hrs, 10 min; 3/4" U-Matic, 1/2" EIAJ, 1/2" Beta II, 1/2" VHS • Sale: $395; Rental: $125/wk

- -
VCX; Order No. FC106; 1915 • b/w; 2 hrs, 39 min; 1/2" Beta II, 1/2" VHS • Sale: $45.00

- -
The Video Library; Order No. CC-0105; 1915 • b/w; 2 hrs; 1/2" Beta II , 1/2" VHS • Sale: $54.95

Presents D.W. Griffith's production which dramatizes the events leading up to and following the American Civil War. Features Lillian Gish, Mae Marsh, and Henry B. Walthall.

THE BITE
VTS; Date not listed • color; 1 hr, 20 min; 1/2" Beta I, 1/2" Beta II, 1/2" VHS • Sale: $99

Presents a pornographic film.

BITE THE BULLET
National Film and Video Center; 1975 • color; 2 hrs, 11 min; 3/4" U-Matic, 1/2" Beta II, 1/2" VHS • Rental: $89/1 showing

Brings together a group of gamblers, gunslingers, and prostitutes to compete in the Endurance Horse Race. Stars Gene Hackman, Candice Bergen, James Co-

burn, Jan-Michael Vincent, Ian Bannen, and Ben Johnson.

BITTER SWEET
Video T.E.N.; 1933 • b/w; 1 hr, 20 min; 1/2" Beta II, 1/2" VHS • Sale: $49.95 for 1/2" Beta II, $54.95 for 1/2" VHS

Recounts a Noel Coward story of an ill-fated romance between a young lady and a musician, with several songs written by Coward. Stars Anna Neagle, Fernand Graavey, Esme Percy, and Clifford Heatherley.

BITTERSWEET LOVE
Magnetic Video Corporation; Order No. CL-4001; 1977 • color; 1 hr, 32 min; 1/2" Beta II, 1/2" VHS • Sale: $54.95

- -
Red Fox, Inc; Order No. CL-4001; 1977 • color; 1 hr, 32 min; 1/2" Beta II, 1/2" VHS • Sale: $54.95

- -
Discount Video Tapes; 1977 • color; 1 hr, 32 min; 1/2" Beta II, 1/2" VHS • Sale: $54.95

Explores the destructive effects of a lie on an innocent couple in love. Stars Lana Turner, Robert Lansing, Celeste Holm, Robert Alda, Scott Hylands, and Meredith Baxter Birney.

BLACK AND WHITE IN COLOR
Time-Life Video Club Inc; 1977 • color; 1 hr, 30 min; 1/2" Beta II, 1/2" VHS • Sale: $44.95 to members

Presents the English language version of the French-African film that won the Academy Award for Best Foreign Film. Concerns the inhabitants of a West African outpost who decide to attack a nearby German garrison when they learn that World War I has begun; directed by Stars Jean-Jacques Annaud.

THE BLACK HOLE
Fotomat Corp; Order No. B1029 for 1/2" Beta II, V1029 for 1/2" VHS; 1979 • color; 1 hr, 37 min; 1/2" Beta II, 1/2" VHS • Sale: $54.95; Rental: $9.95/5 days

- -
Niles Cinema; Order No. WD-11; 1979 • color; 1 hr, 37 min; 1/2" Beta II, 1/2" VHS • Sale: $59.95

- -
Time-Life Video Club Inc; 1979 • color; 1 hr, 37 min; 1/2" Beta II, 1/2" VHS • Sale: $49.95 to members

- -
Walt Disney Home Video; Order No. 11BS for 1/2" Beta II, 11VS for 1/2" VHS; 1979 • color; 1 hr, 37 min; 1/2" Beta II, 1/2" VHS • Sale: $59.95

Presents a science-fiction film created at the Walt Disney Studios. Follows the attempts of a tyrannical explorer to brave a wonder of the universe, despite warnings from U.S. scientists. Uses the Disney art department's special effects. Stars Maximilian Schell, Anthony Perkins, Robert Forster, Joseph Bottoms, Yvette Mimieux, and Ernest Borgnine.

BLACK LIKE ME
Video Communications Inc; Order No. 4001; 1964 • b/w; 1 hr, 50 min; 1/2" Beta II, 1/2" VHS • Sale: $54.95

Presents a film version of the book by the same name. Relates how a white writer chemically changes the color of his skin and travels through the South, experiencing the humiliation and terror of the black man. Stars Roscoe Lee Browne and James Whitmore.

THE BLACK MARBLE
Magnetic Video Corporation; Order No. 4068; 1979 • color; 1 hr, 50 min; 1/2" Beta II, 1/2" VHS • Sale: $59.95

Offers a comedy-drama about a weary, hard-drinking Los Angeles detective who is assigned to track down a larcenous dog breeder. Stars Robert Foxworth, Paula Prentiss, and Harry Dean Stanton, under the direction of Harold Becker.

THE BLACK PIRATE
Reel Images Inc; Order No. 780; 1926 • b/w; 2 hrs, 2 min; 1/2" Beta II, 1/2" VHS • Sale: $49.95 for 1/2" Beta II, $52.95 for 1/2" VHS

Offers a silent swashbuckler that became the prototype for numerous action films to follow. Recounts the adventures of a nobleman who becomes a pirate. Includes a musical score. Stars Douglas Fairbanks, Sr. and Donald Crisp.

Clarence Muse, Kelly Reno, and Mickey Rooney in *The Black Stallion.*

THE BLACK STALLION
RCA SelectaVision VideoDiscs; Order No. 01409; 1979 • color; 1 hr, 43 min; CED • Sale: $19.98

Follows the adventures of a young boy and a magnificent Arabian stallion from a shipwreck to a championship horserace. Uses grand-scale photography by cinematographer-director Carroll Ballard. Stars Kelly Reno, Mickey Rooney, Teri Garr, Clarence Muse, Hoyt Axton, and Michael Higgens.

BLACK SUNDAY
Fotomat Corp; Order No. B0089 for 1/2" Beta II, V0089 for 1/2" VHS; 1977 • color; 2 hrs, 23 min; 1/2" Beta II, 1/2" VHS • Sale: $69.95; Rental: $9.95/up to 5 days, applicable to purchase

Portrays an Israeli commando who discovers a plot by Black September terrorists to blow up a Goodyear blimp over the Super Bowl with 80,000 people, including the President, in attendance. Offers a chilling portrait of people obsessed with a cause for which, if necessary, they will die. Stars Robert Shaw, Bruce Dern, Marthe Keller, Fritz Weaver, and Steven Keats, under the direction of John Frankenheimer.

THE BLACK WIDOW
The Nostalgia Merchant; Order No. 0029; 1947 • b/w; 3 hrs, 15 min; 1/2" Beta II, 1/2" VHS • Sale: $109.95

Presents, on two videocassettes, a Republic motion picture serial in 13 episodes. Follows the attempts of fortune-hunter Sombra, heiress to an Asian dynasty, to steal scientific secrets and plunge the world into enslavement. Stars Bruce Edwards, Carol Forman, and Anthony Warde.

BLACKENSTEIN
Discount Video Tapes; 1972 • color; 1 hr, 27 min; 1/2" Beta II, 1/2" VHS • Sale: $54.95

Relates how a soldier who has had all four limbs blown off is repaired by a master surgeon, but then becomes a monster due to a mix-up of medications. Stars John Hart, Ivory Stone, and Andrea King.

BLACKMAIL
Video T.E.N.; 1929 • b/w; 1 hr, 26 min; 1/2" Beta II, 1/2" VHS • Sale: $49.95 for 1/2" Beta II, $54.95 for 1/2" VHS

Provides a look at Hitchcock's first sound film, the story of a detective's girlfriend who tries to cover up her killing of an attacker. Stars Anny Ondra, John Longdon, and Sarah Allgood.

BLAZING SADDLES
Fotomat Corp; Order No. B0297 for 1/2" Beta II, V0297 for 1/2" VHS; 1974 • color; 1 hr, 30 min; 1/2" Beta II, 1/2" VHS • Sale: $49.95

- -
WCI Home Video Inc; 1974 • color; 1 hr, 33 min; 1/2" Beta II, 1/2" VHS • Sale: $55

Offers Mel Brooks' irreverent western. Centers around a black man who becomes the sheriff of a small western town. Stars Cleavon Little, Gene Wilder, Slim Pickens, Harvey Korman, Madeline Kahn, Mel Brooks, Alex Karras, and Dom DeLuise.

BLESS THE BEASTS AND THE CHILDREN
National Film and Video Center; 1972 • color; 1 hr, 46 min; 3/4" U-Matic, 1/2" Beta II, 1/2" VHS • Rental: $69/1 showing

Recounts the efforts of a group of boys to free a herd of buffalo before they are slaughtered by hunters. Uses this effort as a symbol of the boys' need to free themselves from the stigma of being losers and outcasts.

BLIND HUSBANDS
Reel Images Inc; Order No. 467; 1919 • b/w; 1 hr, 38 min; 1/2" Beta II, 1/2" VHS • Sale: $49.95 for 1/2" Beta II, 52.95 for 1/2" VHS

Presents the story of a rakish Austrian officer attracted to the wife of a dull surgeon. Stars Erich von Stroheim in the first film directed by him.

BLOCKHEADS AND I'LL TAKE VANILLA
The Nostalgia Merchant; Order No. 4009; 1938 • b/w; 1 hr, 15 min; 1/2" Beta II, 1/2" VHS • Sale: $54.95

Presents Stan Laurel and Oliver Hardy in "Blockheads," telling of how Ollie brings his old army buddy, Stan, home to meet his wife. Includes a comedy short, "I'll Take Vanilla," starring Charley Chase.

BLOOD AND SAND
Blackhawk Films, Inc; Order No. 506-55-0893 for 1/2" Beta II, 525-55-0893 for 1/2" VHS; 1922 • color; 53 min; 1/2" Beta II, 1/2" VHS • Sale: $39.95

Profiles a young matador who marries his childhood sweetheart and achieves the status of Spain's "primo" matador, only to be ensnared by another woman bent on his destruction. Stars Rudolph Valentino, Lila Lee, and Nita Naldi in a silent feature.

BLOOD AND SAND
Magnetic Video Corporation; Order No. CL-1073; 1941 • b/w 2hrs, 3min; 1/2" Beta II, 1/2" VHS • Sale: $64.95

Nita Naldi, Rudolph Valentino, and Lila Lee in *Blood and Sand.*

Offers a remake of the silent film. Stars Tyrone Power, under Rouben Mamoulian's direction

BLOOD MANIA
Video Communications Inc; 1970 • color; 1 hr, 28 min; ½" Beta II, ½" VHS • Sale: $54.95

Reveals the story of a young medic whose career is threatened by blackmail. Stars Peter Carpenter and Robert O'Neill.

BLOOD OF A POET
Ivy Video; 1930 • b/w; 55 min; ¾" U-Matic, ½" Beta II, ½" VHS • Sale: $59.95 for ½" Beta II & VHS, trade-in plan available, $150 for ¾"

- -
Northeast Video and Sound, Inc; Order No. 152S; 1930 • b/w; 55 min; ¾" U-Matic, ½" EIAJ, ½" Beta II, ½" VHS • Sale: $150; Rental: $55/wk

Depicts the metaphorical adventures of a poet in this avant-garde film. Highlights the writing and directing talents of iconoclast Jean Cocteau.

BLOOD OF DRACULA'S CASTLE
Video Communications Inc; Order No. 1014; 1969 • color; 1 hr, 24 min; ½" Beta II, ½" VHS • Sale: $54.95

Presents a tale of vampirism starring John Carradine and Paula Raymond.

BLOOD OF THE VAMPIRE
Magnetic Video Corporation; Order No. CL-2022; 1958 • color; 1 hr, 25 min; ½" Beta II, ½" VHS • Sale: $54.95

Tells of a doctor, executed in 1880 as a vampire, who is restored to life by a hunchback and becomes governor of a Transylvanian prison for the criminally insane. Features Donald Wolfit, Barbara Shelley, and Vincent Ball.

BLOOD ON THE MOON
Niles Cinema; Order No. NM-8021; 1948 • b/w; 1 hr, 28 min; ½" Beta II, ½" VHS • Sale: $54.95

The Nostalgia Merchant; Order No. 8021; 1948 • b/w; 1 hr, 28 min; ½" Beta II, ½" VHS • Sale: $54.95

- -
Red Fox, Inc; Order No. 8021; 1948 • b/w; 1 hr, 28 min; ½" Beta II, ½" VHS • Sale: $54.95

Presents a western drama of ranchers and land schemes. Features Robert Mitchum, Barbara Bel Geddes, Robert Preston, and Walter Brennan.

BLOOD ON THE SUN
Budget Video; 1945 • b/w; 1 hr, 38 min; ½" Beta II, ½" VHS • Sale: $44.95

Relates the accidental capture by an American journalist of top secret Imperial Japanese documents and his efforts to keep them from the Japanese secret police. Stars James Cagney, Sylvia Sydney, Wallace Ford, and Robert Armstrong.

BLOODLINE
Fotomat Corp; B0285 for ½" VHS; 1979 • color; 1 hr, 56 min; ½" Beta II, ½" VHS • Sale: $59.95; Rental: $9.95/5 Paramount Home Video; 1979 • color; 1 hr, 56 min; ½" Beta II, ½" VHS • Sale: $59.95

Marks Audrey Hepburn's return to the screen in the role of an attractive and privileged woman who inherits the controlling interest of the family-owned pharmaceutical empire and finds her life in jeopardy. Includes James Mason, Ben Gazzara, Gert Frobe, Romy Schneider, Omar Sharif, Michelle Phillips, and Irene Papas.

BLOW-UP
MGM/CBS Home Video; Order No. M60015; 1966 • color; 1 hr, 48 min; ½" Beta II, ½" VHS • Sale: $59.95

- -
Niles Cinema; Order No. GM-721; 1966 • color; 1 hr, 48 min; ½" Beta II, ½" VHS • Sale: $59.95

Presents director Michelangelo Antonioni's film concerning a pop-world photographer who may or may not have discovered evidence of a murder. Stars Vanessa Redgrave, David Hemmings, Sarah Miles, Jill Kennington, and Verushka.

THE BLUE ANGEL
Cinema Concepts, Inc.; 1930 • b/w; 1 hr, 30 min; 3/4"
U-Matic, 1/2" Beta II, 1/2" VHS • Sale: $54.95 for 1/2"
Beta II & VHS, $149.95 for 3/4"

- -
Golden Tapes Video Tape Library; Order No. CD5;
1929 • b/w; 1 hr, 34 min; 1/2" Beta II, 1/2" VHS • Sale:
$49.95 for 1/2" Beta II & VHS, $124.95 for 3/4"

- -
Ivy Video; 1930 • b/w; 1 hr, 30 min; 3/4" U-Matic, 1/8"
Beta II, 1/2" VHS • Sale: $59.95 for 1/2" Beta II & VHS,
trade-in plan avalable, $195 for 3/4"

- -
Northeast Video and Sound, Inc; 1930 • b/w; 1 hr, 30
min; 3/4" U-Matic, 1/2" EIAJ, 1/2" Beta II, 1/2" VHS • Sale:
$225; Rental: $75/wk

- -
VCX; Order No. FC127; 1930 • b/w; 1 hr, 30 min; 1/2"
Beta II, 1/2" VHS • Sale: $35.00

- -
The Video Library; Order No. CC-0104; 1930 • b/w; 1
hr, 30 min; 1/2" Beta II, 1/2" VHS • Sale: $54.95

Portrays cabaret life in post World War I Germany, in
this feature directed by Josef Von Sternberg which introduced a new star, Marlene Dietrich. Utilizes also the
talent of Emil Jannings as a professor who throws
away his career and status for the love of a night-club
singer. Features the song ''Falling In Love Again.''

BLUE COLLAR
MCA DiscoVision; Order No. 10-017; 1978 • color; 1
hr, 54 min; LaserVision • Sale: $24.95

Offers a tale of assembly line workers who try to deal
with the boredom of factory work with humor, and then
decide to rob their union local's safe where they uncover a scandal. Stars Richard Pryor, Harvey Keitel,
and Yaphet Kotto.

BLUE HAWAII
Magnetic Video Corporation; Order No. CL-2001;
1961 • color; 1 hr, 41 min; 1/2" Beta II, 1/2" VHS • Sale:
$44.95

- -
The Video Library; Order No. MV-2001; 1961 • color;
1 hr, 41 min; 1/2" Beta II, 1/2" VHS • Sale: $44.95

Offers a musical about a soldier who returns to the
islands and begins working for a tourist agency. Stars
Elvis Presley, Angela Lansbury, and Joan Blackman.

THE BLUE MAX
Magnetic Video Corporation; Order No. CL-1062;
1966 • color; 2 hrs, 35 min; 1/2" Beta II, 1/2" VHS •
Sale: $64.95

Chronicles the efforts of an ambitious German combat
pilot in World War I to win his country's most coveted
medal—even if it means eliminating his colleagues and
seducing his commander's wife. Stars George Peppard, James Mason, and Ursula Andress.

BLUE STEEL
Cable Films; 1934 • b/w; 54 min; 1/2" Beta I, 1/2" Beta
II, 1/2" VHS • Sale: $45 for 1/2" Beta I, $49.50 for 1/2"
Beta II & VHS

Features John Wayne as an undercover U.S. Marshal.

BLUE SUMMER
Monarch Releasing Corporation; Date not listed •
color; 1 hr, 11 min; 3/4" U-Matic • Sale: $300

Presents a pornographic film.

BLUEBEARD
Ivy Video; 1943 • b/w; 1 hr, 13 min; 3/4" U-Matic, 1/2"

Beta II, 1/2" VHS • Sale: '59.95 for 1/2" Beta II & VHS,
trade-in plan available $159 for 3/4"

- -
Video T.E.N.; 1944 • b/w; 1 hr, 13 min; 1/2" Beta II,
1/2" VHS • Sale: $49.95 for 1/2" Beta II, $54.95 for 1/2"
VHS

Stars John Carradine as a puppeteer strangler in this
''B'' film directed by Edgar G. Ulmer, and also featuring Jean Parker as the damsel in distress.

THE BLUES BROTHERS
MCA Videocassette, Inc; Order No. 77000; 1980 •
color; 2 hrs, 13 min; 1/2" Beta II, 1/2" VHS • Sale: $89

- -
Niles Cinema; 1980 • color; 2 hrs, 13 min, 1/2" Beta II,
1/2" VHS • Sale: $89.95

Presents, on two videocassettes, Dan Ackroyd and
John Belushi as The Blues Brothers who are enlisted
on a mission for charity and end up nearly destroying
Chicago. Features Aretha Franklyn and other rhythm
and blues artists.

BOARDWALK
Time-Life Video Club Inc; 1979 • color; 1 hr, 43 min;
1/2" Beta II, 1/2" VHS • Sale: $49.95 to members.

Explores the world of a couple celebrating their 50th
wedding anniversary. Shows how they cope with
change and danger, with a disintegrating neighbor-
hood, their love for each other and their family. Stars
Ruth Gordon and Lee Strasberg.

BOB & CAROL & TED & ALICE
National Film and Video Center; 1969 • color; 1 hr, 44
min; 3/4" U-Matic, 1/2" Beta II, 1/2" VHS • Rental: $89/1
showing

Focuses on a couple experimenting with extramarital
sex to try to make their relationship more honest.
Shows how the experiment broadens to include another couple who are their close friends. Stars Natalie
Wood, Robert Culp, Elliot Gould, and Dyan Cannon.

BOCCACCIO '70
Magnetic Video Corporation; Order No. CL-4031;
1962 • color; 2 hrs, 25 min; 1/2" Beta II, 1/2" VHS •
Sale: $74.95

Presents three short films directed by Italy's premier
directors: Federico Fellini, Luchino Visconti and Vittorio De Sica. Stars Sophia Loren, Anita Ekberg, and
Romy Schneider.

THE BODY SNATCHER
Niles Cinema; Order No. NM-8039; 1945 • b/w; 1 hr,
17 min; 1/2" Beta II, 1/2" VHS • Sale: $54.95

- -
The Nostalgia Merchant; Order No. 8039; 1945 • b/w;
1 hr, 17 min; 1/2" Beta II, 1/2" VHS • Sale: $54.95

- -
Red Fox, Inc; Order No. 8039; 1945 • b/w; 1 hr, 17
min; 1/2" Beta II, 1/2" VHS • Sale: $54.95

Relates the story of grave robbery for medical dissec-
tion in 19th century Edinburgh. Features Boris Karloff,
Bela Lugosi, and Henry Daniell.

THE BODY SNATCHER AND CAT PEOPLE
Vid America; Order No. 202; 1945 & 1942 • color; 2
hrs, 30 min; 1/2" Beta II, 1/2" VHS • Rental: $13.95/wk

Presents a classic horror double-feature. See individ-
ual films for descriptions.

BON VOYAGE, CHARLIE BROWN

Niles Cinema; Order No. PP-1158; Date not listed • color; 1 hr, 16 min; 1/2" Beta II, 1/2" VHS • Sale: $59.95

- -

Paramount Home Video; Order No. 1158; Date not listed • color; 1 hr, 16 min;1/2" Beta II, 1/2" VHS • Sale: 72.95

Features the characters created by Charles Schulz. Presents Charlie Brown and friends as exchange students in Europe. Shows Snoopy playing tennis at Wimbledon and drinking root beers at a French bistro.

BONJOUR TRISTESSE

National Film and Video Center; 1958 • color; 1 hr, 34 min; 3/4" U-Matic, 1/2" Beta II, 1/2" VHS • Rental: $49/1 showing

Brings together a widower, his daughter, and her godmother for emotional complications in a villa on the French Riviera. Stars Deborah Kerr, David Niven, Jean Seberg, and Mylene Demongeot.

BONNIE AND CLYDE

MCA DiscoVision; Order No. W12-516; 1967 • color; 1 hr, 51 min; LaserVision • Sale: $24.95

- -

WCI Home Video Inc; 1967 • color; 1 hr, 51 min; 1/2" Beta II, 1/2" VHS • Sale: $55

Presents the much-imitated film about Depression-era bank robbers who become folk-heroes. Follows their odd love affair as well as probing the social issue of misfits become popular heroes due to publicity. Features the first use of slow-motion violence sequences to alter the audience's perspective. Stars Warren Beatty, Faye Dunaway, Michael J. Pollard, Gene Hackman, and Estelle Parsons, in her Oscar-winning performance, under Arthur Penn's direction.

BOOK OF NUMBERS

Magnetic Video Corporation; Order No. CL-5006; 1973 • color; 1 hr, 20 min; 1/2" Beta II, 1/2" VHS • Sale: $54.95

Explores the rivalry between two opposing numbers operations—one run by blacks, the other by whites— in a small Arkansas town. Stars Raymond St. Jacques, who also directed.

BOOTS AND SADDLES

Reel Images Inc; Order No. 420; 1937 • b/w; 54 min; 1/2" Beta II, 1/2" VHS • Sale: $39.95 for 1/2" Beta II, $42.95 for 1/2" VHS

Presents a story, with musical interludes, of a young English lord who has inherited Gene Autry's ranch. Depicts Autry's efforts to make a real Westerner out of him. Features Smiley Burnette, Judith Allen, and Ra Hould.

BORDERLAND

Videobrary Inc; Order No. 15; 1937 • b/w; 1 hr, 18 min; 1/2" Beta II, 1/2" VHS • Sale: $39.95

Presents a Hopalong Cassidy western. Shows Cassidy disgraced and turned bad in order to set a trap for his arch enemy, The Fox. Stars William Boyd, George "Gabby" Hayes, and Stephen Morris.

BORN FREE

Columbia Pictures Home Entertainment; 1966 • color; 1 hr, 36 min; 1/2" Beta II, 1/2" VHS • Sale: $59.95

- -

Time-Life Video Club Inc; 1966 • color; 1 hr, 36 min; 1/2" Beta II, 1/2" VHS • Sale: $44.95 to members

Adapts for the screen Joy Adamson's true story of two

Bill Travers and Virginia McKenna in *Born Free*.

game wardens in Africa who adopt and domesticate a female lion cub. Features Virginia McKenna, Bill Travers, Geoffrey Keen, Peter Lukoye, Omar Chambati, and Elsa the lioness.

BORN YESTERDAY

Columbia Pictures Home Entertainment; 1950 • b/w; 1 hr, 43 min; 1/2" Beta II, 1/2" VHS • Sale: $59.95

- -

Time-Life Video Club Inc; 1951 • b/w; 1 hr, 43 min; 1/2" Beta II, 1/2" VHS • Sale: $59.95, to members.

Offers a comedy about a nouveau riche businessman who hires a young professor to teach culture to his dumb girl friend, against a backdrop of Washington corruption. Stars Judy Holliday, Broderick Crawford, and William Holden, under the direction of George Cukor.

THE BOSTON STRANGLER

Golden Tapes Video Tape Library; Order No. F-1015; 1968 • color; 1 hr, 56 min; 1/2" Beta II, 1/2" VHS • Sale: $49.95 for 1/2" Beta II & VHS, $124.95 for 3/4"

- -

Magnetic Video Corporation; Order No. CL-1015; 1968 • color; 1 hr, 56 min; 1/2" Beta II, 1/2" VHS • Sale: $44.95

- -

The Video Library; Order No. MV-1015; 1968 • color; 1 hr, 56 min; 1/2" Beta II, 1/2" VHS • Sale: $44.95

Presents the true detective story of the hunt for the murderer of thirteen women. Stars Tony Curtis and Henry Fonda.

THE BOY AND HIS DOG

Meda/Media Home Entertainment Inc; Order No. M104; 1976 • color; 1 hr, 50 min; 1/2" Beta II, 1/2" VHS • Sale: $54.95

Adapts the Harlan Ellison science-fiction novella. Fantasizes a future in which the survivors of World War IV have created an underground authoritarian society.

Shows how a boy and his dog rescue a girl from this underworld. Features Don Johnson, Susanne Benton, Alvy Moore, Jason Robards, and Helen Winston, under the direction of L.Q. Jones.

BOY ON A DOLPHIN
Magnetic Video Corporation; Order No. CL-1041; 1957 • color; 1 hr, 50 min; ½" Beta II, ½" VHS • Sale: $44.95

Focuses on a sunken art treasure off the coast of Greece and a romance between an American skindiver and his peasant girl assistant. Stars Alan Ladd and Sophia Loren in her U.S. film debut.

THE BOYS FROM BRAZIL
Magnetic Video Corporation; 1978 • color; 2 hrs, 3 min; ½" Beta II, ½" VHS • Sale: $59.95

- -
RCA SelectaVision VideoDiscs; Order No. 00502; 1978 • color; 2 hrs, 3 min; CED • Sale: $19.98

Adapts for the screen Ira Levin's suspense novel about a former Nazi's plan to clone Adolph Hitler, and the aging Jewish Nazi-hunter who is on his trail. Stars Laurence Olivier, Gregory Peck, James Mason, Lilli Palmer, Uta Hagen, John Rubenstein, Denholm Elliott, and Rosemary Harris.

THE BOYS IN THE BAND
MGM/CBS Home Video; Order No. C60017; 1970 • color; 2 hrs; ½" Beta II, ½" VHS • Sale: $59.95

- -
Niles Cinema; Order No. GM-722; 1970 • color; 2 hrs; ½" Beta II, ½" VHS • Sale: $59.95

Presents William Friedkin's adaptation of Mart Crowley's play about homosexuals gathered for a birthday party and the unspoken thoughts suddenly spoken. Stars Cliff Gorman, Laurence Luckinbill, Kenneth Nelson, Leonard Frey, Frederick Combs, and Reuben Greene.

BREAD AND CHOCOLATE
Meda/Media Home Entertainment Inc; 1978 • color; 1 hr, 51 min; ½" Beta II, ½" VHS • Sale: $59.95

Examines the life of a Italian worker who has moved to Switzerland and hopes to earn enough money to send for his wife and children. Shows how he is rejected by the German-speaking Swiss but finally receives sympathy from a Greek woman. Stars Nino Manfredi, Anna Karina, Johnny Dorelli, and Paulo Turco, under the direction of Franco Brusati.

BREAK OF HEARTS
The Nostalgia Merchant; Order No. 8032; 1935 • b/w; 1 hr, 20 min; ½" Beta II, ½" VHS • Sale: $54.95

Relates a romantic tale of two concert musicians who find their careers conflict with their love. Features Katharine Hepburn and Charles Boyer.

BREAKER BEAUTIES
Video Home Library; Order No. VX-107; Date not listed • color; 2 hrs; ½" Beta II, ½" VHS • Sale: $99.95

Presents a pornographic film.

BREAKFAST AT TIFFANY'S
Fotomat Corp; Order No. B0065 for ½" Beta II, V0065 for ½" VHS; 1961 • color; 1 hr, 54 min; ½" Beta II, ½" VHS • Sale: $49.95; Rental: $9.95/up to 5 days, applicable to purchase

- -
Paramount Home Video; 1961 • color; 1 hr, 54 min; ½" Beta II, ½" VHS • Sale: $59.95

Portrays Holly Golightly, a delicious eccentric determined to marry a Brazilian millionaire. Presents a

screen version of the Truman Capote novella. Stars Audrey Hepburn, George Peppard, Patricia Neal, Martin Balsam, Buddy Ebsen, and Mickey Rooney, under the direction of Blake Edwards.

BREAKFAST IN HOLLYWOOD
Reel Images Inc; Order No. 10; 1946 • b/w; 1 hr, 31 min; ½" Beta II, ½" VHS • Sale: $49.95 for ½" Beta II, 52.95 for ½" VHS

Presents entertainment based on the popular radio program. Stars Billie Burke, Zasu Pitts, Hedda Hopper, Spike Jones and his Orchestra, the King Cole Trio, Andy Russell, and Beulah Bondi.

BREAKING AWAY
Magnetic Video Corporation; Order No. CL-1081; 1979 • color; 1 hr, 40 min; ½" Beta II, ½" VHS • Sale: $44.95

Presents a comedy about a young man addicted to bicycle racing and his reactions to a crucial race. Stars Dennis Christopher, Dennis Quaid, Daniel Stern, and Jackie Earle Haley, under the direction of Peter Yates.

BREAKING GLASS
Paramount Home Video; Order No. 1392; 1980 • color; 1 hr, 34 min; ½" Beta II, ½" VHS • Sale: $62.95

Studies the cost of fame as a "New Wave" rock band and its female lead singer achieve it after a ruthless promotion. Stars Hazel O'Connor, who wrote and performs the 13 new songs, and Phil Daniels.

BREAKING THE ICE
Reel Images Inc; Order No. 578; 1938 • b/w; 1 hr, 19 min; ½" Beta II, ½" VHS • Sale: $49.95 for ½" Beta II, 52.95 for ½" VHS

Focuses on the Mennonites and a big city ice skating show. Includes songs by Victor Young sung by young tenor Bobby Breen. Features Bobby Breen, Charles Ruggles, Dolores Costello, and Billy Gilbert.

BREAKING UP
Time-Life Video Club Inc; Date not listed • color; 1 hr, 38 min; ½" Beta II, ½" VHS • Sale: $34.95 to members

Reveals the attempts of a woman to rediscover her single identity when her husband leaves her. Tells of her frustrations as she tries to raise her two children, struggles for financial independence, learns to deal with old friends, and confronts the business world. Stars Lee Remick.

BREAKOUT
Columbia Pictures Home Entertainment; 1975 • color; 1 hr, 36 min; ½" Beta II, ½" VHS • Sale: $59.95

- -
Fotomat Corp; Order No. V0429 for ½" Beta II, V0429 for ½" VHS; 1976 • color; 1 hr, 37 min; ½" Beta II, ½" VHS • Sale: $54.95; Rental: $9.95/5 days

- -
Time-Life Video Club Inc; 1976 • color; 1 hr, 36 min; ½" Beta II, ½" VHS • Sale: $44.95 to members

Dramatizes a prison break carried out, against impossible odds, by an adventurous pilot and a man being framed for murder by Mexican police. Stars Charles Bronson, Robert Duvall, and Jill Ireland.

BRIAN'S SONG
Columbia Pictures Home Entertainment; Order No. BE51105 for ½" Beta II, VH10100 for ½" VHS; 1970 • color; 1 hr, 13 min; ½" Beta II, ½" VHS • Sale: $59.95

Presents the TV-movie that set a standard for excellence. Follows the anguish between Chicago Bears teammates Gale Sayers and Brian Piccolo when Piccolo develops fatal cancer. Dramatizes a true story. Stars James Caan, Billy Dee Williams, Jack Warden, Shelley Fabares, and Judy Pace. Includes a musical score by Michel Legrand.

THE BRIDE OF FRANKENSTEIN

MCA DiscoVision; Order No. 23-003; 1935 • b/w; 1 hr, 15 min; LaserVision • Sale: $15.95

Offers the first sequel to the original "Frankenstein" and enlists the original production's stars and values. Features the scenes in which the Monster visits a blind man's cottage, and the finale in which the Monster has a mate created in the laboratory for him. Includes Franz Waxman's score and direction by James Whale. Stars Boris Karloff, Colin Clive, Elsa Lanchester, and Valerie Hobson.

BRIDE OF THE MONSTER

Reel Images Inc; Order No. 787; 1956 • b/w; 1 hr, 10 min; 1/2" Beta II, 1/2" VHS • Sale: $49.95 for 1/2" Beta II, $52.95 for 1/2" VHS

Follows a girl reporter on the trail of a mad scientist who experiments in the field of genetic mutation. Features Bela Lugosi, Tor Johnson, and Loretta King.

THE BRIDGE ON THE RIVER KWAI

National Film and Video Center; 1957 • color; 2 hrs, 41 min; 3/4" U-Matic, 1/2" Beta II, 1/2" VHS • Rental: $79/1 showing

Pits the courage and pride of a captured British Army colonel who must command his fellow prisoners to build a strategic railroad bridge against the determination of his vicious Japanese captor. Stars William Holden, Alec Guinness, and Jack Hawkins, under the direction of David Lean.

BRIMSTONE

The Nostalgia Merchant; Order No. 0171; 1949 • b/w; 1 hr, 30 min; 1/2" Beta II, 1/2" VHS • Sale: $54.95
- -
Red Fox, Inc; Order No. 0171; 1949 • b/w; 1 hr, 30 min; 1/2" Beta II, 1/2" VHS • Sale: $54.95

Tells of a marshal who poses as an ordinary cowboy to stop an outlaw family's reign of terror. Features Rod Cameron, Adrian Booth, and Walter Brennan.

BROKEN STRINGS

Reel Images Inc; Order No. 11; 1940 • color; 1 hr; 1/2" Beta II, 1/2" VHS • Sale: $39.95 for 1/2" Beta II, $42.95 for 1/2" VHS

Presents an all-black feature originally intended for black audiences. Relates the story of a concert violinist whose successful career is cut short when an automobile accident injures his hand. Stars Clarence Muse.

BROTHER JOHN

National Film and Video Center ; 1972 • color; 1 hr, 34 min; 3/4" U-Matic, 1/2" Beta II, 1/2" VHS • Rental: $49/1 showing

Tells the story of a man who, while visiting his home town to be with his dying sister, becomes involved with an old sweetheart, is suspected of being a union organizer, and is thrown into jail. Stars Sidney Poitier, Will Geer, Beverly Todd, and Bradford Dillman.

BROTHER OF THE WIND

Video Communications Inc; Date not listed • color; 1 hr, 32 min; 1/2" Beta II, 1/2" VHS • Sale: $54.95

Relates in documentary form the story of four wolf pups and a lonely mountaineer who rescues the pups when their mother is killed and saves them from starvation.

BROTHERS O'TOOLE

Video Communications Inc; Order No. 1016; 1973 • color; 1 hr, 34 min; 1/2" Beta II, 1/2" VHS • Sale: $54.95

Relates a tale of Colorado's poorest mining boom town, the residents of which refer to their city by a number of slightly strange nicknames. Shows what happens when a pair of slick drifters ride into town with ambitions of milking it even drier. Stars Lee Meriwether, John Astin, and Pat Carroll.

BRUBAKER

Magnetic Video Corporation; Order No. 1098; 1980 • color; 2 hrs, 11 min; 1/2" Beta II, 1/2" VHS • Sale: $69.95

Probes prison conditions and the attempts of an unorthodox warden at reform when unmarked gravesites are discovered. Adapts a story based on true incidents. Stars Robert Redford, Jane Alexander, and Yaphet Kotto.

BRUCE LEE SUPERDRAGON

Blackhawk Films, Inc; Order No. 502-30-0094 for 1/2" Beta II, 515-30-0094 for 1/2" VHS; 1976 • color; 1 hr, 14 min; 1/2" Beta II, 1/2" VHS • Sale: $54.95

Showcases an all-star Kung Fu cast in a biographical odyssey of Bruce Lee, compiled four years after his death.

BRUCE LI IN NEW GUINEA

Video Gems; 1980 • color; 1 hr, 38 min; 1/2" Beta II, 1/2" VHS • Sale: $59.95

Offers a martial arts film with Bruce Li, Chen Sing, Ho Chung Dao, and Danna.

BUCK AND THE PREACHER

National Film and Video Center ; 1972 • color; 1 hr, 42 min; 3/4" U-Matic, 1/2" Beta II, 1/2" VHS • Rental: $59/1 showing

Tells the story of an ex-Union Army Cavalry sergeant who becomes the guide for a wagon train of newly-freed slaves heading west to homestead. Stars Sidney Poitier, Harry Belafonte, and Ruby Dee in a film directed by Poitier.

BUCK PRIVATES

MCA DiscoVision; Order No. 22-007; 1941 • b/w; 1 hr, 22 min; LaserVision • Sale: $15.95

Offers Bud Abbott and Lou Costello's first feature. Follows the antics of two fellas who try to elude the police and end up in the Army taking orders from the policeman they tried to escape. Features the Andrews Sisters doing "Boogie Woogie Bugle Boy," "Rhumboogie," and "Beat Me, Daddy, Eight to Bar."

BUCK ROGERS CONQUERS THE UNIVERSE

Magnetic Video Corporation; Order No. CL-2026; 1939 • b/w; 1 hr, 31 min; 1/2" Beta II, 1/2" VHS • Sale: $54.95

Offers an edited version of a Buck Rogers serial, in which Buck takes on a gang of criminals on a futuristic Earth. Stars Buster Crabbe, Constance Moore, and Jackie Moran.

BUCK ROGERS (PLANET OUTLAWS)

Reel Images Inc; Order No. 560; 1939 • b/w; 1 hr, 10 min; 1/2" Beta II, 1/2" VHS • Sale: $49.95 for 1/2" Beta II, $52.95 for 1/2" VHS

Presents a serial made into a feature by deleting cliffhangers and plot recapitulations and adding narration. Shows how, after 500 years in suspended animation, Buck and Buddy wake to find the world ruled by Killer Kane, and recounts their efforts to battle this evil character. Features Buster Crabbe, Constance Moore, and Jackie Moran.

BUGS AND FRIENDS
Video Tape Network; Order No. KI 409 for ½" Beta II, KI 410 for ½" VHS; Date not listed • color; 1 hr; ½" Beta II, ½" VHS • Sale: $49.95

Presents cartoons featuring Bugs Bunny, Daffy Duck, Porky Pig, and Elmer Fudd.

THE BUGS BUNNY/ROAD RUNNER MOVIE
Fotomat Corp; Order No. B0293 for ½" Beta II, V0293 for ½" VHS; 1979 • color; 1 hr, 30 min; ½" Beta II, ½" VHS • Sale: $44.95

- -

WCI Home Video Inc; 1979 • color; 1 hr, 30 min; ½" Beta II, ½" VHS • Sale: $50

Provides a collection of classic Warner Brothers' cartoons featuring Bugs Bunny, Wile E. Coyote, the Road Runner, Daffy Duck, Porky Pig, Elmer Fudd, and Pepe LePew. Includes "Duck Amuck," "What's Opera, Doc?," "Duck Dodgers In The 24½ Century," plus never-before-seen animation.

BULLDOG DRUMMOND'S PERIL
Video T.E.N.; 1938 • b/w; 1 hr, 6 min; ½" Beta II, ½" VHS • Sale: $49.95 for ½" Beta II, $54.95 for ½" VHS

Relates how Bulldog Drummond is dragged away from his wedding to safeguard a formula for synthetic diamonds. Stars John Barrymore, John Howard, Louise Campbell, and Halliwell Hobbes.

BULLITT
MCA DiscoVision; Order No. W12-515; 1968 • color; 1 hr, 54 min; LaserVision • Sale:$24.95

- -

WCI Home Video Inc; 1968 • color; 1 hr, 54 min; ½" Beta II, ½" VHS • Sale: $55

Adapts the novel "Mute Witness," by Robert L. Pike, in which a police detective decides to take definitive steps when he discovers he is being set up by a politician and the underworld. Shows his routine assignment to protect a witness become more and more complicated when the witness is killed quite easily. Features a car chase through San Francisco which set the pattern for '70's chase sequences. Stars Steve McQueen, Robert Vaughn, Jacqueline Bisset, Robert Duvall, Simon Oakland, and Norman Fell in a film directed by Peter Yates.

BULLWINKLE
Video Communications Inc; Date not listed • color; 1 hr, 30 min; ½" Beta II, ½" VHS • Sale: $54.95

Offers a series of cartoons featuring the humor of Rocky the flying squirrel and Bullwinkle the moose.

BUNDLE OF JOY
Video Communications Inc; 1956 • color; 1 hr, 38 min; ½" Beta II, ½" VHS • Sale: $54.95

Recounts the troubles created when a single salesgirl takes custody of a baby boy and everyone believes she is the mother. Stars Eddie Fisher, Debbie Reynolds, Adolphe Menjou, and Tommy Noonan.

BURLESQUE ON CARMEN
Time-Life Video Club Inc; 1915 • b/w; 1 hr, 15 min; ½" Beta II, ½" VHS • Sale: $39.95 to members

Offers Charles Chaplin's slapstick version of "Car-

men," the gypsy who drove men wild. Uses restored footage, color-tones, and a music and sound effects track. Stars Chaplin, Edna Purviance, and Ben Turpin. Includes three rare Chaplin "one-reelers" from the French film archives.

BUS STOP
Blackhawk Films, Inc; Order No. 502-49-0019 for ½" Beta II, 515-49-0006 for ½" VHS; Date not listed • ; 1 hr, 34 min; ½" Beta II, ½" VHS • Sale: $54.95

- -

Magnetic Video Corporation; Order No. CL-1031; 1956 • color; 1 hr, 34 min; ½" Beta II, ½" VHS • Sale: $44.95

- -

The Video Library; Order No. MV-1031; 1956 • color; 1 hr, 34 min; ½" Beta II, ½" VHS • Sale: $54.95

Depicts a totally innocent young rancher who goes to town for a rodeo and "abducts" an experienced but naive B-girl he has decided to marry. Stars Marilyn Monroe, Don Murray, Arthur O'Connell, Betty Field, and Eileen Heckart in an adaptation of William Inge's play, under the direction of Joshua Logan.

BUSTER KEATON
Ivy Video; 1920 • b/w; 55 min; ¾" U-Matic, ½" Beta II, ½" VHS • Sale: $59.95 for ½" Beta II & VHS, trade-in plan avalable, $150 for ¾"

- -

Northeast Video and Sound, Inc; Order No. 139S; 1920 • b/w; 55 min; ¾" U-Matic, ½" EIAJ, ½" Beta II, ½" VHS • Sale: $149; Rental: $55/wk

Samples the short subjects written, directed by and starring the "great stone-face", Buster Keaton. Includes many gags later used by Keaton in his features.

Robert Redford and Paul Newman in
Butch Cassidy and the Sundance Kid.

BUTCH CASSIDY AND THE SUNDANCE KID
Magnetic Video Corporation ; Order No. CL-1061; 1969 • color; 1 hr, 52 min; ½" Beta II, ½" VHS • Sale: $54.95

- -

RCA SelectaVision VideoDiscs; Order No. 00101; 1969 • color; 1 hr, 52 min; CED • Sale: $19.98

Presents a comedy-western in which two of the West's most notorious train and bank robbers find themselves being pursued by the craftiest posse ever. Features a wise-cracking script by William Goldman, beautiful photography, and a score by Burt Bacharach. Stars Paul Newman, Robert Redford, Katherine Ross, Strother Martin, Henry Jones, Jeff Corey, George Furth, and Cloris Leachman, under the direction of George Roy Hill.

BUTLEY
Magnetic Video Corporation; 1973 • color; 2 hrs,.7 min; ½" Beta II, ½" VHS • Sale: $80

Offers the American Film Theatre's presentation of Simon Gray's play. Studies a professor who dislikes everyone and everything he comes into contact with. Shows his shattering influence on his students, wife, and male lover. Stars Alan Bates, Jessica Tandy, Richard O'Callaghan, Susan Engel, and Georgina Hale. Features the directorial debut of Harold Pinter.

BUTTERFLIES ARE FREE
National Film and Video Center; 1972 • color; 1 hr, 49 min; ¾" U-Matic, ½" Beta II, ½" VHS • Rental: $89/1 showing

Relates the story of a young blind man striving for independence and a frivolous, fickle young "hippie" who becomes his lover. Shows how the girl, who cannot make an emotional commitment, has as great a handicap to overcome. Stars Goldie Hawn, Eileen Heckart, and Edward Albert, Jr.

BYE, BYE BIRDIE
Columbia Pictures Home Entertainment ; 1963 • color; 1 hr, 52 min; ½" Beta II, ½" VHS • Sale: $59.95
- -
Time-Life Video Club Inc; 1963 • color; 1 hr, 51 min; ½" Beta II, ½" VHS • Sale: $49.95 to members

Offers a screen version of the Broadway musical about a rock and roll star, about to be drafted, who gives a final performance for his fans. Stars Dick Van Dyke, Ann-Margret, Janet Leigh, Maureen Stapleton, Paul Lynde, and Ed Sullivan, under the direction of George Sidney.

CABINET OF DR. CALIGARI
Northeast Video and Sound, Inc; Order No. 175S; 1919 • b/w; 1 hr, 8 min; ¾" U-Matic, ½" EIAJ, ½" Beta II, ½" VHS • Sale: $75/wk

Presents the classic German Expressionist film concerning a mesmerist's evil use of his somnambulist victim. Includes bizarre sets and lighting which inspired many horror films that followed. Stars Werner Krauss, Conrad Veidt, and Lil Dagover under the direction of Robert Wiene.

CACTUS FLOWER
National Film and Video Center; 1969 • color; 1 hr, 42 min; ¾" U-Matic, ½" Beta II, ½" VHS • Rental: $79/1 showing

Offers the story of a bachelor who has told his mistress that he is married; when he decides that he wants to marry her, she refuses to break up his home until she talks to his wife. Stars Goldie Hawn, Ingrid Bergman, and Walter Matthau.

CACTUS IN THE SNOW
FHV Entertainment, Inc; 1972 • color; 1 hr, 30 min;

½" Beta II, ½" VHS • Sale: $49.95
Stars Richard Thomas as an 18-year-old private in the Army on a 72-hour pass, in search of his first love adventure.

THE CAINE MUTINY
National Film and Video Center; 1954 • color; 2 hrs, 5 min; ¾" U-Matic, ½" Beta II, ½" VHS • Rental: $59/1 showing

Recounts the incidents which demonstrate the inability of the captain of the U.S.S. Caine to command the destroyer-minesweeper. Deals with the implications of the executive officer's actions in taking over the vessel. Stars Humphrey Bogart, Jose Ferrer, and Van Johnson.

THE CALICO QUEEN
Monarch Releasing Corporation; Date not listed • color; 1 hr, 21 min; ¾" U-Matic • Sale: $300

Presents a pornographic film.

CALIFORNIA SPLIT
National Film and Video Center; 1974 • color; 1 hr, 47 min; ¾" U-Matic, ½" Beta II, ½" VHS • Rental: $159/1 showing

Depicts two compulsive gamblers during a winning streak in Reno as they risk everything on one game with world champion poker player Amarillo Slim. Satirizes the gambling mentality by contrasting one partner's formal, white collar personality (George Segal) with the other's smalltime cloddish style (Elliot Gould).

CALL IT MURDER
Thunderbird Films; 1934 • b/w; 1 hr, 20 min; ¾" U-Matic, ½" Beta I, ½" Beta II, ½" VHS • Sale: $69.95 for ½" Beta I, 49.95 for ½" Beta II & VHS, 89.95 for ¾"

Offers an early Humphrey Bogart feature concerning a jury foreman whose daughter is involved with a gangster vitally interested in the case before the court. Co-stars Sidney Fox, O.P. Heggie, and Richard Wharf.

CALL ME ANGEL, SIR
Video Home Library; Order No. VX-122; Date not listed • color; 2 hrs; ½" Beta II, ½" VHS • Sale: $99.95

Presents a pornographic film.

CALL OF THE PRAIRIE
Videobrary Inc; Order No. 7; 1936 • b/w; 1 hr, 5 min; ½" Beta II, ½" VHS • Sale: $39.95

Presents a Hopalong Cassidy western. Shows Hopalong rescuing Johnny Nelson from a bizarre death trap devised for him by the pals with whom he has been drinking and gambling. Stars William Boyd, George "Gabby" Hayes, and Jimmy Ellison.

CALL OF THE PRAIRIE; PRIDE OF THE WEST
Videobrary Inc; Order No. 7-11; 1936 & 1938 • b/w; 2 hrs, 1 min; ½" Beta II, ½" VHS • Sale: $69.95

Offers a Hopalong Cassidy western double feature. Presents "Call of the Prairie" in which Hoppy must rescue his friend from a bizarre death trap, and "Pride of the West" in which an outlaw named Nixon is involved in a land swindle.

THE CALL OF THE WILD
FHV Entertainment, Inc; 1972 • color; 1 hr, 42 min; ½" Beta II, ½" VHS • Sale: $49.95

Offers Charlton Heston fighting against the perils of the

frozen North in this sweeping adventure based on Jack London's novel.

CALLING WILD BILL ELLIOTT; SANTA FE SADDLE-MATES
The Nostalgia Merchant; Order No. 5001; 1943, 1945 • b/w; 2 hrs; 1/2" Beta II, 1/2" VHS • Sale: $59.95

Offers a western double feature which opens with "Wild Bill Elliott" coming to the aid of homesteaders. Concludes with Sunset Carson breaking up a diamond smuggling ring in "Santa Fe Saddlemates."

CAMILLE 2000
Vid America; Order No. 969; Date not listed • color; 1 hr, 57 min; 1/2" Beta II, 1/2" VHS • Rental: $12.95/wk

Presents a pornographic film.

CAMOUFLAGE
Reel Images Inc; Order No. 13; 1943 • color; 21 min; 1/2" Beta II, 1/2" VHS • Sale: $29.95 for 1/2" Beta II, $32.95 for 1/2" VHS

Presents a cartoon with a Disney-like character, Yehudi the Chameleon, a likeable lizard who shows a group of Air Corps fliers the do's and don'ts of camouflage.

CAMPUS GIRLS
Quality X Video Cassette Company; Date not listed • color; 1 hr, 10 min; 1/2" Beta I, 1/2" Beta II, 1/2" VHS • Sale: $99.50

Presents a pornographic film.

CAMPUS PUSSYCATS
Tape Club of America; Order No. 2837 B; Date not listed • color; 1 hr, 16 min; 1/2" Beta II, 1/2" VHS • Sale: $54.95
- -
Video Warehouse, Inc; Order No. 1021; Date not listed • color; 1 hr, 16 min; 1/2" Beta II, 1/2" VHS • Sale: $54.95

Presents a pornographic film.

CAMPUS SWINGERS
Tape Club of America; Order No. 2840 B; Date not listed • color; 1 hr, 23 min; 1/2" Beta II, 1/2" VHS • Sale: $54.95

Presents a pornographic film.

CAN CAN
Blackhawk Films, Inc; Order No. 520-49-0002 for 1/2" Beta II, 515-49-0013 for 1/2" VHS; 1960 • color; 2 hrs, 11 min; 1/2" Beta II, 1/2" VHS • Sale: $74.95
- -
Golden Tapes Video Tape Library; Order No. F-1016; 1960 • color; 2 hrs, 10 min; 1/2" Beta II, 1/2" VHS • Sale: $49.95 for 1/2" Beta II & VHS, 124.95 for 3/4"
- -
Magnetic Video Corporation; Order No. CL-1016; 1960 • color; 2 hrs, 11 min; 1/2" Beta II, 1/2" VHS • Sale: $64.95
- -
The Video Library; Order No. MV-1016; 1960 • color; 2 hrs, 11 min; 1/2" Beta II, 1/2" VHS • Sale: $74.95

Presents the Cole Porter musical of 1890's Paris in which a lawyer defends his client's right to perform a daring new dance known as the can-can. Features 'C'est Magnifique,' 'I Love Paris,' 'Let's Do It,' and 'Just One Of Those Things.' Stars Frank Sinatra, Shirley MacLaine, Maurice Chevalier, Louis Jourdan, and Juliet Prowse.

THE CANDIDATE
WCI Home Video Inc; 1972 • color; 1 hr, 50 min; 1/2" Beta II, 1/2" VHS • Sale: $55

Probes the American political system in this story of a young reformer who has been convinced to run for the Senate. Reveals the candidate's faltering idealism as his chances for victory increase. Stars Robert Redford, Peter Boyle, Don Porter, Allen Garfield, Karen Carlson, and Melvyn Douglas, under the direction of Michael Ritchie.

CANDLESHOE
RCA SelectaVision VideoDiscs; Order No. 00705; 1977 • color; 1 hr, 41 min; CED • Sale: $19.98

Presents a Walt Disney Studio film about a con man who tries to pawn a young girl off as an heiress in order to get his hands on the inheritance. Uses location filming in Britain. Stars David Niven, Jodie Foster, Helen Hayes, Leo McKern, and Vivian Pickles.

CANDY STRIPERS
Arrow Films & Video; Date not listed • color; 1 hr, 30 min; 1/2" Beta II, 1/2" VHS • Sale: $99.90

Presents a pornographic film.

CAPRICORN ONE
Magnetic Video Corporation; Order No. 9007; 1978 • color; 2 hrs, 4 min ; 1/2" Beta II, 1/2" VHS • Sale: $59.95

Explores the premise that the first manned space flight to Mars is a hoax filmed in a TV studio. Follows the three astronauts blackmailed into helping the hoax when they realize they won't be allowed to survive otherwise. Stars Elliot Gould, James Brolin, Sam Waterston, Telly Savalas, Hal Holbrook, Brenda Vaccaro, Karen Black, and O.J. Simpson.

CAPTAIN AMERICA
The Nostalgia Merchant; Order No. 0112; 1944 • b/w; 3 hrs, 45 min; 1/2" Beta II, 1/2" VHS • Sale: $109.95

Presents, on two videocassettes, a Republic motion picture serial in 15 episodes. Follows Captain America as he combats the evil Scarab, a mad scientist who is intent on reaping fortunes by using fantastic scientific weapons and "the Purple Death" as blackmail devices. Stars Dick Purcell, Adrian Booth, and Lionel Atwill.

CAPTAIN APACHE
Tape Club of America; Order No. 2604 B; 1971 • color; 1 hr, 34 min; 1/2" Beta II, 1/2" VHS • Sale: $54.95

Depicts the destinies of a full-blooded Apache on assignment for Union Intelligence, an adventuress whose lover is involved in a plot to assassinate President Grant, and a ruthless soldier of fortune whose services are available to the highest bidder. Stars Lee Van Cleef, Carroll Baker, and Stuart Whitman.

CAPTAIN KIDD
Budget Video; 1945 • b/w; 1 hr, 23 min; 1/2" Beta II, 1/2" VHS • Sale: $44.95

Depicts the sea battles and swordplay of one of history's most notorious pirates. Stars Charles Laughton, Randolph Scott, Barbara Britton, and John Carradine.

CAR WASH
MCA DiscoVision; Order No. 16-003; 1976 • color; 1 hr, 37 min; LaserVision • Sale: $24.95

Presents a comic look at a day in the life of a Los Angeles car wash, and the hopes and frustrations of the men who work there. Includes a soul music score. Stars Franklin Ajaye, George Carlin, Professor Irwin Corey, the Pointer Sisters, and Richard Pryor.

THE CARDINAL
National Film and Video Center; 1963 • color; 2 hrs, 55 min; 3/4" U-Matic, 1/2" Beta II, 1/2" VHS • Rental: $69/1 showing

Portrays the life of a young priest who deals with many personal conflicts during his rise to Cardinal. Stars Tom Tryon, Romy Schneider, Carol Lynley, and Burgess Meredith, under Otto Preminger's direction.

CAREFREE
Niles Cinema; Order No. NM-8022; 1938 • b/w; 1 hr, 23 min; 1/2" Beta II, 1/2" VHS • Sale: $54.95

- -
The Nostalgia Merchant; Order No. 8022; 1938 • b/w; 1 hr, 23 min; 1/2" Beta II, 1/2" VHS • Sale: $54.95

- -
Red Fox, Inc; Order No. 8022; 1938 • b/w; 1 hr, 23 min; 1/2" Beta II, 1/2" VHS • Sale: $54.95

Features Fred Astaire and Ginger Rogers in a screwball comedy with music, Fred playing a psychiatrist and Ginger his client. Includes the Irving Berlin songs "Change Partners" and "I Used to Be Color Blind." Co-stars Ralph Bellamy, Luella Gear, and Jack Carson.

CARMEN JONES
Golden Tapes Video Tape Library; Order No. F-1048; 1955 • color; 1 hr, 45 min; 1/2" Beta II, 1/2" VHS • Sale: $49.95 for 1/2" Beta II & VHS, 124.95 for 3/4"

- -
Magnetic Video Corporation; Order No. CL-1048; 1955 • color; 1 hr, 45 min; 1/2" Beta II, 1/2" VHS • Sale: $44.95

Presents a musical comedy version of the opera starring Harry Belafonte, Dorothy Dandridge, and Pearl Bailey.

CARNAL KNOWLEDGE
Magnetic Video Corporation; Order No. CL-4003; 1971 • color; 1 hr, 36 min; 1/2" Beta II, 1/2" VHS • Sale: $54.95

- -
Red Fox, Inc; Order No. CL-4003; 1971 • color; 1 hr, 36 min; 1/2" Beta II, 1/2" VHS • Sale: $54.95

- -
Vid America; Order No. 451; 1971 • color; 1 hr, 36 min; 1/2" Beta II, 1/2" VHS • Rental: $13.95/wk

Satirizes the sexual relationships of two men from the mid-1940's into the 70's. Features Jack Nicholson, Candice Bergen, Arthur Garfunkel, Ann-Margret, and Rita Moreno, under the direction of Mike Nichols.

CARNY
MGM/CBS Home Video; Order No. C60028; 1980 • color; 1 hr, 42 min; 1/2" Beta II, 1/2" VHS • Sale: $59.95

Offers an adaptation of the Jack Kerouac story. Investigates life in a traveling carnival as two men fall in love with a young girl who joins up. Stars Gary Busey, Jodi Foster, Meg Foster, and Robbie Robertson of the rock group called The Band.

CARRY ON NURSE
Fotomat Corp; Order No. B0245 for 1/2" Beta II, V0245 for 1/2" VHS; 1959 • b/w; 1 hr, 24 min; 1/2" Beta II, 1/2" VHS • Sale: $49.95; Rental: $9.95/up to 5 days, applicable to purchase

- -
Reel Images Inc; Order No. 412; 1958 • b/w; 1 hr, 26 min; 1/2" Beta II, 1/2" VHS • Sale: $49.95 for 1/2" Beta II, 52.95 for 1/2" VHS

Offers the "Carry On" team attacking the British hospitals and nurses in this English comedy. Features Shirley Eaton and Kenneth Connor.

CARTOON CARNIVAL #1
Cinema Concepts, Inc.; 1940-45 • color; 1 hr; 3/4" U-Matic, 1/2" Beta II, 1/2" VHS • Sale: $39.95 for 1/2" Beta II & VHS, $79.95 for 3/4"

Presents Bugs Bunny, Porky Pig, and Daffy Duck cartoons.

CARTOON CARNIVAL #2
Cinema Concepts, Inc.; 1940-1945 • color; 1 hr; 3/4" U-Matic, 1/2" Beta II, 1/2" VHS • Sale: $39.95 for 1/2" Beta II & VHS, $79.95 for 3/4"

Presents "Merrie Melodies" and children's fables.

CARTOON FEST
Video Action Library; Order No. BH06; 1931-36 • color; 57 min; 1/2" Beta I, 1/2" Beta II, 1/2" VHS • Rental: $10/1 wk, $5 ea add'l wk

Presents a compilation of seven color cartoons: "Happy Days" (1936); "The Little Red Hen" (1934); "Jack and the Beanstalk" (1933); "Summertime;" "The Headless Horseman" (1934); "Fiddlestick" (1931); and "The Brave Tin Soldier" (1934).

CARTOON JAMBOREE
Northeast Video and Sound, Inc; Date not listed • color; 50 min; 3/4" U-Matic, EIAJ, 1/2" Beta II, 1/2" VHS • Sale: $150; Rental: $55/wk

Presents collection of cartoons including Felix the Cat, Popeye and Superman.

CARTOON PARADE NO. 1
The Nostalgia Merchant; Order No. 6001; Date not listed • color; 1/2" Beta II, 1/2" VHS • Sale: $54.95

Presents two hours of animation on one videocassette. Includes "Corny Concerto" with Bugs Bunny and Porky Pig, "The Mad Scientist" with Superman, "Popeye Meets Sinbad," "Henpecked Duck" with Daffy Duck, and "All This and Rabbit Stew" with Bugs Bunny and many others.

Ingrid Bergman and Humphrey Bogart in *Casablanca*.

26

CARTOON PARADE NO. 2
The Nostalgia Merchant; Order No. 6002; Date not listed • color; 1 hr, 57 min; ½" Beta II, ½" VHS • Sale: $54.95

Presents a compilation of color cartoon classics. Includes Bugs Bunny in "Wabbit Who Came to Supper," Popeye in "Popeye Meets Ali Baba," Superman in "Terror on the Midway," Little Luly in "Bored of Education," and others.

CARTOON PARADE NO. 3
The Nostalgia Merchant; Order No. 6003; Date not listed • color; 1 hr, 50 min; ½" Beta II, ½" VHS • Sale: $54.95

Presents a compilation of color cartoon classics. Includes "Falling Hare" with Bugs Bunny, "Cheese Burglar" starring Herman & Katnip, "Somewhere in Dreamland," "Robin Hood Makes Good," and others.

CASABLANCA
RCA SelectaVision VideoDiscs; Order No. 01420; 1942 • b/w; 1 hr, 42 min; CED • Sale: $19.98
- -
Vid America; Order No. 423; 1943 • b/w; 1 hr, 42 min; ½" Beta II, ½" VHS • Rental: $10.95/wk

Presents a World War II story of intrigue and romance which centers around a Casablanca nightclub owner who attempts to help his old love and her husband, a resistance fighter. Stars Humphrey Bogart, Claude Rains, Ingrid Bergman, Paul Henreid, Peter Lorre, Sydney Greenstreet, Conrad Veidt, and Dooley Wilson who sings "As Time Goes By." Features direction by Michael Curtiz.

CASANOVA '70
Magnetic Video Corporation; Order No. CL-4036; 1970 • color; 1 hr, 53 min; ½" Beta II, ½" VHS • Sale: $54.95

Follows the escapades of a handsome man whose problems include an unending thirst for women and a desire for danger and challenge to accompany his amorous conquests. Stars Marcello Mastroianni and Virna Lisi.

CASINO ROYALE
National Film and Video Center; 1967 • color; 1 hr, 46 min; ¾" U-Matic, ½" Beta II, ½" VHS • Rental: $89/1 showing

Traces the extravagant adventures of Sir James Bond when the famous spy comes out of retirement to refurbish the British Secret Service and his own legend. Features Peter Sellers, Dahliah Lavi, Deborah Kerr, William Holden, Woody Allen, Joanna Pettet, Orson Welles, and David Niven in a film based on Ian Fleming's first novel.

THE CASSANDRA CROSSING
Magnetic Video Corporation; Order No. 9005; 1977 • color; 2 hrs, 7 min; ½" Beta II, ½" VHS • Sale: $59.95

Presents a disaster film centering on a train travelling at high speed through Europe, with the plague aboard. Stars Sophia Loren, Richard Harris, Ava Gardner, Burt Lancaster, Martin Sheen, and O.J. Simpson.

CASSIDY OF BAR 20
Videobrary Inc; Order No. 2; 1938 • b/w; 1 hr; ½" Beta II, ½" VHS • Sale: $39.95

Presents a Hopalong Cassidy western. Shows Hoppy, Lucky, and Pappy trying to rescue a woman rancher

from a man who will stop at nothing to "buy" her ranch. Stars William Boyd, Russell Hayden, and Frank Darien.

CASSIDY OF BAR 20; SUNSET TRAIL
Videobrary Inc; Order No. 2-23; 1938 & 1939 • b/w; 2 hrs; ½" Beta II, ½" VHS • Sale: $69.95

Offers a Hopalong Cassidy western double feature. Presents "Cassidy of Bar 20" in which Hopalong must protect a woman rancher whose property and life are being threatened, and "Sunset Trail" in which Hoppy poses as a tenderfoot at a dude ranch to trap a killer. Stars William Boyd.

CASTLE OF FU MANCHU
Cinema Concepts, Inc.; 1972 • color; 1 hr, 27 min; ¾" U-Matic, ½" Beta II, ½" VHS • Sale: $54.95 for ½" Beta II & VHS, $149.95 for ¾"
- -
The Video Library; 1972 • color; 1 hr, 27 min; ½" Beta II, ½" VHS • Sale: $54.95

Presents an adventure thriller about Fu Manchu who terrorizes the world by creating catastrophies through the use of a mysterious chemical crystal formula. Stars Christopher Lee, Maria Perschy, and Richard Greene.

CAT BALLOU
National Film and Video Center; 1965 • color; 1 hr, 36 min; ¾" U-Matic, ½" Beta II, ½" VHS • Rental: $78/1 showing

Stars Lee Marvin as a gunslinger hired by several of Wolf City's establishment figures to kill a rancher and also as the gunslinger's drunken twin brother, who helps the rancher's daughter (Jane Fonda) foil the plot. Features Dwayne Hickman, Nat King Cole, Stubby Kaye, and Michael Callan.

CAT PEOPLE
Niles Cinema; Order No. NM-8047; 1942 • b/w; 1 hr, 13 min; ½" Beta II, ½" VHS • Sale: $54.95
- -
The Nostalgia Merchant; Order No. 8027; 1942 • color; 1 hr, 13 min; ½" Beta II, ½" VHS • Sale: $54.95
- -
Red Fox, Inc; Order No. 8047; 1942 • b/w; 1 hr, 13 min; ½" Beta II, ½" VHS • Sale: $54.95

Tells of a young bride who believes she is cursed to turn into a panther. Features Simone Simon, Kent Smith, and Tom Conway.

CATCH-22
Paramount Home Video; 1970 • color; 2 hrs, 1 min; ½" Beta II, ½" VHS • Sale: $59.95

Presents a film adaptation of Joseph Heller's novel. Offers a black-comedy, anti-war satire about a group of fliers stationed in the Mediterranean in 1944. Uses surrealistic and violent sequences based on Buck Henry's screenplay. Stars Alan Arkin, Martin Balsam, Art Garfunkel, Richard Benjamin, Jon Voight, and Orson Welles, under the direction of Mike Nichols.

CATHERINE & CO.
Vid America; Order No. 974; Date not listed • color; 1 hr, 31 min; ½" Beta II, ½" VHS • Rental: $12.95/wk

Presents a pornographic film.

CATHERINE THE GREAT
Golden Tapes Video Tape Library; Order No. CD2; 1934 • b/w; 1 hr, 34 min; ½" Beta II, ½" VHS • Sale: $49.95 for ½" Beta II & VHS, $124.95 for ¾"

Tells of a Russian czarina whose life is spoiled by a

marriage she did not plan on. Stars Douglas Fairbanks, Jr. and Elisabeth Bergner.

CATTLE QUEEN OF MONTANA
FHV Entertainment, Inc; 1954 • color; 1 hr, 28 min; 1/2" Beta II, 1/2" VHS • Sale: $49.95

Recounts the story of a woman who fights to protect her land from hired killers and renegade Indians in the 1880's Montana Territory. Features Barbara Stanwyck and Ronald Reagan.

C.B. MAMAS
Mitchell Brothers' Film Group; Date not listed • color; 1 hr; 1/2" Beta II, 1/2" VHS • Sale: $69

Presents a pornographic film.

C.C. AND COMPANY
Magnetic Video Corporation; Order No. CL-4002; 1970 • color; 1 hr, 34 min; 1/2" Beta II, 1/2" VHS • Sale: $54.95

- -
Video Communications Inc; Order No. 459; 1970 • color; 1 hr, 28 min; 1/2" Beta II, 1/2" VHS • Rental: $12.95/wk

Relates a story of love and death in the world of motorcycles, as a new member of a gang challenges its leader's reputation as best rider. Stars Joe Namath and Ann-Margret.

CENTERFOLD
Vid America; Order No. 983; 1980 • color; 1 hr; 1/2" Beta II, 1/2" VHS • Sale: $54.95; Rental: $12.95/wk, applicable to purchase

Presents a pornographic film.

CESAR
Budget Video; 1936 • b/w; 1 hr, 57 min; 1/2" Beta II, 1/2" VHS • Sale: $44.95

Recounts the final portion of Marcel Pagnol's trilogy of films, in which we encounter the characters of the earlier films after twenty years have elapsed. Details how, after the death of Panisse, Fanny and Marius are reunited through the agency of their son Andre. Features Raimu, Pierre Fresnay, Charpin, and Orane Demazis, under Pagnol's direction; in French with subtitles.

CHAIN GANG WOMEN
Video Communications Inc; Order No. 1018; 1971 • color; 1 hr, 25 min; 1/2" Beta II, 1/2" VHS • Sale: $54.95

Relates the story of a young man serving a short sentence in a Georgia state prison for selling marijuana who is transferred to a chain gang. Features Michael Stearns and Barbara Mills.

CHANDU ON THE MAGIC ISLAND
Reel Images Inc; Order No. 563; 1940 • b/w; 1 hr, 7 min ; 1/2" Beta II, 1/2" VHS • Sale: $49.95 for 1/2" Beta II, $52.95 for 1/2" VHS

Offers the main character from the radio serial "Chandu the Magician" in a film in which Chandu visits the lost island of Lemuria to battle an evil cult. Features Bela Lugosi, Maria Alba, and Clara Kimball Young.

CHANDU THE MAGICIAN
Northeast Video and Sound, Inc; Order No. 146S; 1932 • b/w; 1 hr, 12 min; 3/4" U-Matic, 1/2" EIAJ, 1/2" Beta II, 1/2" VHS • Sale: $195; Rental: $65/wk

Concerns the battle between the spiritualist Chandu and a madman who threatens to destroy the world. Stars Bela Lugosi, Marcel Varnel, and Edmund Lowe.

Barbara Stanwyck in
Cattle Queen of Montana.

THE CHANGELING
Time-Life Video Club Inc; 1980 • color; 1 hr, 53 min; 1/2" Beta II, 1/2" VHS • Sale: $44.95 to members

Depicts a man who, saddened by the death of his wife and daughter, moves into an old house in search of peace and quiet. Relates his growing—and finally justified—suspicions that the house is haunted. Stars George C. Scott and Trish Van DeVere.

CHAPLIN MUTUALS (VOLUME 1)
Video Action Library; Order No. BH09; 1916-17 • color; 1 hr; 1/2" Beta I, 1/2" Beta II, 1/2" VHS • Rental: $12.50/1 wk, $6.25 ea add'l wk

Offers three Charlie Chaplin silent comedies: "The Immigrant" (1917); "The Count" (1916); and "Easy Street" (1917).

CHAPLIN MUTUALS (VOLUME 2)
Video Action Library; Order No. BH10; 1916-17 • color; 1 hr; 1/2" Beta I, 1/2" Beta II, 1/2" VHS • Rental: $12.50/1 wk, $6.25 ea add'l wk

Presents three more Chaplin silent comedies: "The Adventurer" (1917); "One A.M." (1916); and "The Pawnshop" (1916).

CHAPLIN MUTUALS (VOLUME 3)
Video Action Library; Order No. BH11; 1916-17 • color; 1 hr; 1/2" Beta I, 1/2" Beta II, 1/2" VHS • Rental: $12.50/1 wk, $6.25 ea add'l wk

Offers another three Chaplin silent comedies: "The Cure" (1917); "The Floorwalker" (1916); and "The Vagabond" (1916).

CHAPLIN MUTUALS (VOLUME 4)
Video Action Library; Order No. BH12; 1916 • color; 1 hr; 1/2" Beta I , 1/2" Beta II, 1/2" VHS • Rental: $12.50/1 wk, $6.25 ea add'l wk

Presents three more Chaplin silent comedies: "Behind the Screen" (1916); "The Fireman" (1916); and "The Rink" (1916).

THE CHAPLIN REVIEW
Magnetic Video Corporation; Order No. CL-3001; 1958 • b/w; 1 hr, 59 min; ½" Beta II, ½" VHS • Sale: $44.95

Consists of three of his best short films: "A Dog's Life" (1918), "Shoulder Arms" (1918), and "The Pilgrim" (1922).

CHAPTER TWO
Columbia Pictures Home Entertainment; Order No. BE51135 for ½" Beta II, VH10130 for ½" VHS; 1979 • color; 2 hrs, 4 min; ½" Beta II, ½" VHS • Sale: $59.95
- -
Fotomat Corp; Order No. B0417 for ½" Beta II, V0417 for ½" VHS; 1979 • color; 2 hrs, 4 min; ½" Beta II, ½" VHS • Sale: $54.95; Rental: $9.95/5 days
- -
Vid America; Order No. 985; 1979 • color; 2 hrs, 4 min; ½" Beta II, ½" VHS • Sale: $59.95; Rental: $13.95/wk, applicable to purchase

Adapts for the screen Neil Simon's bittersweet autobiographical play about a man who falls in love before he has overcome his grief over his first wife's death. Stars James Caan, Marsha Mason, Valerie Harper, and Joseph Bologna.

CHARIOTS OF THE GODS
Vid America; Order No. F-1017; 1977 • color; 1 hr, 40 min; ½" Beta II, ½" VHS • Rental: $10.95/wk

Explores the theory that astronauts from other worlds might have brought advanced knowledge to Earth in ages past.

A CHARLIE BROWN FESTIVAL
RCA SelectaVision VideoDiscs; Order No. 01301; Date not listed • color; 1 hr, 39 min; CED • Sale: $19.98

Presents four animated stories previously seen on network TV. Features Charlie Brown as he tries to cope with Peppermint Patty, his losing baseball team, the Junior Olympics, and his love for the little red-haired girl. Includes "You're In Love, Charlie Brown," "There's No Time For Love, Charlie Brown," "It's Your First Kiss, Charlie Brown," and "You're The Greatest, Charlie Brown."

CHARLIE CHAN IN MEETING AT MIDNIGHT (BLACK MAGIC)
Reel Images Inc; Order No. 489; 1944 • b/w; 1 hr, 5 min; ½" Beta II, ½" VHS • Sale: $49.95 for ½" Beta II, $52.95 for ½" VHS

Presents one of the Charlie Chan murder-mysteries from the series which featured the Oriental detective on the Honolulu police force, created by Earl Derr Biggers. Concerns a killing which took place at a seance with hands held, no shot, no gun—just a mysterious bullet hole. Stars Sidney Toler and Mantan Moreland.

CHARLIE CHAPLIN SHORTS
Ivy Video; 1916 • b/w; 58 min; ¾" U-Matic, ½" Beta II, ½" Beta II • Sale: $59.95 for ½" Beta II & VHS, trade-in plan available, $150 for ¾"
- -
Northeast Video and Sound, Inc; Order No. 104S; 1915-17 • b/w; 58 min; ¾" U-Matic, ½" EIAJ, ½" Beta II, ½" VHS • Sale: $149; Rental: $55/wk

Affords a look at Chaplin in three of his early characterizations of the "little tramp." Comprises the short subjects entitled "Easy Street", "One A.M.", and "The Pawnshop".

CHARLOTTE'S WEB
Fotomat Corp; Order No. B0047 for ½" Beta II, V0047 for ½" VHS; 1972 • color; 1 hr, 34 min; ½" Beta II, ½" VHS • Sale: $49.95; Rental: $9.95/up to 5 days, applicable to purchase
- -
Paramount Home Video; 1972 • color; 1 hr, 34 min; ½" Beta II, ½" VHS • Sale: $59.95
- -
RCA SelectaVision VideoDiscs; Order No. 00624; 1973 • color; 1 hr, 25 min; CED • Sale: $19.98

Presents an animated, musical version of E.B. White's best-selling novel. Features the voices of Debbie Reynolds as Charlotte, Paul Lynde as Templeton the Rat, Agnes Moorehead as the Stuttering Goose, and Henry Gibson as Wilbur the Pig.

Charlotte's Web.

THE CHASE
National Film and Video Center; 1966 • color; 1 hr, 12 min; ¾" U-Matic, ½" Beta II, ½" VHS • Rental: $59/1 showing

Focuses on the efforts of a town sheriff to maintain his integrity: cattlebaron Val Rogers would like him to kill an escaped convict when he captures him to cover up an affair Rogers' son is having with the convict's wife. Features Marlon Brando, Jane Fonda, E.G. Marshall, Angie Dickinson, and Robert Redford.

CHECK AND DOUBLE CHECK
Golden Tapes Video Tape Library; Order No. CC9; 1930 • b/w; 1 hr, 13 min; ½" Beta II, ½" VHS • Sale: $49.95 for ½" Beta II & VHS, $124.95 for ¾"
- -
Ivy Video; 1929 • b/w; 1 hr, 20 min; ¾" U-Matic, ½" Beta II, ½" VHS • Sale: $59.95 for ½" Beta II and VHS, trade-in plan avalable, $195 for ¾"
- -
Northeast Video and Sound, Inc; Order No. 167S; 1929 • b/w; 1 hr, 20 min; ¾" U-Matic, ½" EIAJ, ½" Beta II, ½" VHS • Sale: $225; Rental: $75/wk
- -
Reel Images Inc; Order No. 12; 1930 • b/w; 1 hr, 17 min; ½" Beta II, ½" VHS • Sale: $49.95 for ½" Beta II, $52.95 for ½" VHS

Provides a chance to see radio stars Amos and Andy in person, as portrayed in black-face by their creators, Charles Correll and Freeman Gosden, both white men. Features the music of Duke Ellington and his Orchestra.

CHEECH AND CHONG'S NEXT MOVIE
MCA Videocassette, Inc; Order No. 66016; 1980 • color; 1 hr, 35 min; ½" Beta II, ½" VHS • Sale: $65

Presents the second movie featuring Cheech Marin and Tommy Chong. Follows them through a movie studio, a welfare office, a massage parlor, a police raid, a wealthy family's living room, a nightclub, and outer space.

CHEERING SECTION
Video Communications Inc; 1977 • color; 1 hr, 24 min; ½" Beta II, ½" VHS • Sale: $54.95

Offers an "R" rated film. Follows the pranks of rival high school students before the big football game. Shows the truce called when both teams decide to swap their cheerleaders for the party after the game. Features Rhonda Foxx and Tom Leindecker.

THE CHEERLEADERS
Monarch Releasing Corporation; Date not listed • color; 1 hr, 16 min; ¾" U-Matic • Sale: $350

Presents a pornographic film.

CHEERS FOR MISS BISHOP
Video T.E.N.; 1941 • b/w; 1 hr, 35 min; ½" Beta II, ½" VHS • Sale: $49.95 for ½" Beta II, 54.95 for ½" VHS

Portrays a turn-of-the-century woman who sacrifices marriage for a career as a university professor. Stars Martha Scott, William Gargan, Marsha Hunt, and Edmund Gwenn.

CHERRY, HARRY AND RAQUEL
Vid America; Order No. 625; Date not listed • color; 1 hr, 10 min; ½" Beta II, ½" VHS • Rental: $12.95/wk

Presents a pornographic film.

CHEYENNE RIDES AGAIN
Reel Images Inc; Order No. 51; 1938 • b/w; 56 min; ½"·Beta II, ½" VHS • Sale: $39.95 for ½" Beta II, $42.95 for ½" VHS

Offers a western saga in which the hero masquerades as an outlaw to discover the whereabouts of a gang of rustlers. Stars Tom Tyler.

CHEYENNE TAKES OVER; TULSA KID
The Nostalgia Merchant; Order No. 5009; 1947, 1940 • b/w; 2 hrs; ½" Beta II, ½" VHS • Sale: $59.95

Offers a western double feature. Presents Lash LaRue trying to prevent renegades from terrorizing a western town in "Cheyenne Takes Over." Concludes with "Tulsa Kid" in which Red Barry must face the gunfighter who raised him in a final showdown.

THE CHICKEN CHRONICLES
Magnetic Video Corporation; Order No. CL-4018; 1977 • color; 1 hr, 34 min; ½" Beta II, ½" VHS • Sale: $54.95

Follows a high school senior as he faces issues such as drugs and Vietnam as graduation day approaches in the late sixties. Features Phil Silvers, Steven Guttenberg, Ed Lauter, and Lisa Reeves.

CHILDREN SHOULDN'T PLAY WITH DEAD THINGS
Video Communications Inc; 1972 • color; 1 hr, 25 min; ½" Beta II, ½" VHS • Sale: $54.95

Tells of how a group of young filmmakers unknowingly desecrate a cemetery and bring back to life the cadavers of the wicked. Features Alan Ormsby.

CHILDREN'S COLLECTION I
Fotomat Corp; Order No. B0705 for ½" Beta II, V0705 for ½" VHS; 1972 • color; 32 min; ½" Beta II, ½" VHS • Sale: $39.95; Rental: $5.95/5 days

Provides three animated films produced by Xerox, all on one videocassette. Includes "The Peasant's Pea Patch," which instructs children about life's problems; "The World's Greatest Freak Show," about the meaning of beauty; and "The Seventh Mandarin," which tackles social conscience and the courage needed to speak the truth.

CHILDREN'S COLLECTION II
Fotomat Corp; Order No. B0703 for ½" Beta II, V0703 for ½" VHS; 1972-73 • color; 30 min; ½" Beta II, ½" VHS • Sale: $39.95; Rental: $5.95/5 days

Provides three animated films produced for children by Xerox, all on one videocassette. Includes "A Firefly Named Torchy," about feelings of inferiority; "The Most Marvelous Cat," about courage and love; and "The Strange Story of the Frog Who Became a Prince," about being happy with your own identity.

CHINA CAT
Freeway Video Enterprises; Date not listed • color; 1 hr, 20 min; ½" Beta II, ½" VHS • Sale: $75 for ½" Beta II, $85 for ½" VHS

Presents a pornographic film.

THE CHINA SYNDROME
Columbia Pictures Home Entertainment; Order No. BE51140 for ½" Beta II, VH10140 for ½" VHS; 1979 • color; 2 hrs, 3 min; ½" Beta II, ½" VHS • Sale: $59.95

- -
Fotomat Corp; Order No. B0449 for ½" Beta II, V0449 for ½" VHS; 1978 • color; 2 hrs, 2 min; ½" Beta II, ½" VHS • Sale: $54.95; Rental: $9.95/5 days
- -
Vid America; Order No. 984; 1978 • color; 2 hrs, 3 min; ½" Beta II, ½" VHS • Sale: $59.95; Rental: $13.95/wk, applicable to purchase

Details an attempted cover-up of an accident at a nuclear power plant as well as probing TV news practices. Reveals the consequences when one man tries to speak out and admit there is a problem. Stars Jack Lemmon, Jane Fonda, and Michael Douglas.

CHINATOWN
Fotomat Corp; Order No. B0077 for ½" Beta II, V0077 for ½" VHS; 1974 • color; 2 hrs, 11 min; ½" Beta II, ½" VHS • Sale: $69.95; Rental: $9.95/up to 5 days, applicable to purchase
- -
Paramount Home Video; 1974 • color; 2 hrs, 11 min; ½" Beta II, ½" VHS • Sale: $79.95

Offers a disillusioned vision of seedy, pre-war California, where what begins as a routine matrimonial snoop job mushrooms into a murderous regional and personal scandal. Stars Jack Nicholson, Faye Dunaway, John Huston, Burt Young, Diane Ladd, John Hillerman, and Perry Lopez, under the direction of Roman Polanski.

THE CHINESE GODFATHER
Home Theatre Movies; 1974 • color; 1 hr, 30 min; ½" Beta II, ½" VHS • Sale: $54.96

Presents a kung fu film starring Wu Chin, with Ting Pie and Pink Wu. Includes as well "The Final Days of Bruce Lee"

CHINESE GODS
Video Gems; 1980 • color; 1 hr, 30 min; ½" Beta II, ½" VHS • Sale: $59.95

Presents an animated film loosely based on Chinese mythology featuring a character patterned after the martial arts film star, Bruce Lee.

CHINO
FHV Entertainment, Inc; 1976 • color; 1 hr, 38 min; 1/2" Beta II, 1/2" VHS • Sale: $49.95

Fotomat Corp; Order No. B0197 for 1/2" Beta II, V0197 for 1/2" VHS; Date not listed • color; 1 hr, 38 min; 1/2" Beta II, 1/2" VHS • Sale: $49.95; Rental: $9.95/up to 5 days, applicable to purchase

Showcases Charles Bronson fighting for his land, his horses, his woman, and his life. Co-stars Jill Ireland.

THE CHOIRBOYS
MCA DiscoVision; Order No. 12-011; 1977 • color; 1 hr, 59 min; LaserVision • Sale: $24.95

Adapts the Joseph Wambaugh novel which looks inside the lifestyle of the rank-and-file policeman. Shows the frustration, fear, temptation, and revulsion on-duty and the drunken brawls, known as choir practice, off-duty. Features Charles Durning, Lou Gossett, Jr., Perry King, and Don Stroud.

CHORUS CALL
TVX Distributors; Order No. R.T. 75; Date not listed • color; 2 hrs; 1/2" Beta II, 1/2" VHS • Sale: $79.50 for 1/2" Beta II, 89.50 for 1/2" VHSI

Presents a pornographic film.

A CHRISTMAS CAROL
Fotomat Corp; Order No. B0137 for 1/2" Beta II, V0137 for 1/2" VHS; 1951 • b/w; 1 hr, 26 min; 1/2" Beta II, 1/2" VHS • Sale: $39.95; Rental: $7.95/up to 5 days, applicable to purchase

Video Communications Inc; 1951 • b/w; 1 hr, 26 min; 1/2" Beta II, 1/2" VHS • Sale: $54.95

Presents a classic film adaptation of the popular Dickens tale. Features the famous visitation of Marley's ghost and Scrooge's ecstatic antics upon awakening next morning. Stars Alistair Sim, Kathleen Harrison, Clifford Mollison, Jack Warner, and Mervyn Johns.

THE CHRISTMAS TREE
Fotomat Corp; Order No. B0119 for 1/2" Beta II, V0119 for 1/2" VHS; 1969 • color; 1 hr, 50 min; 1/2" Beta II, 1/2" VHS • Sale: $39.95; Rental: $7.95/up to 5 days, applicable to purchase

Video Communications Inc; Order No. 4002; 1969 • color; 1 hr, 50 min; 1/2" Beta II, 1/2" VHS • Sale: $54.95

Dramatizes the tender relationship between a father and his dying son. Traces the growth of love and sympathy between them, as well as the trust that develops. Stars William Holden, Virna Lisi, and Brook Fuller.

CIRCLE OF IRON
Magnetic Video Corporation; Order No. CL-4062; 1978 • color; 1 hr, 42 min; 1/2" Beta II, 1/2" VHS • Sale: $44.95

Presents a martial arts combat film about man's eternal quest for truth. Stars David Carradine, Christopher Lee, and Jeff Cooper.

THE CIRCUS AND A DAY'S PLEASURE
Magnetic Video Corporation; Order No. CL-3005; 1928 • b/w; 1 hr, 32 min; 1/2" Beta II, 1/2" VHS • Sale: $44.95

Presents two Charlie Chaplin films, "The Circus" which is reminiscent of his earlier work, and "A Day's Pleasure," one of Chaplin's rarest short films, which shows what he can do with such props as a Model T Ford and a folding deck chair.

CIRCUS WORLD
Video Communications Inc; Order No. 5003; Date not listed • color; 2 hrs, 11 min; 1/2" Beta II, 1/2" VHS • Sale: $74.95

Offers a story of a sharp-shooting trick rider who blazes a trail across Europe when he takes his three-ring traveling wild west show on tour. Stars John Wayne, Claudia Cardinale, Rita Hayworth, and Richard Conte.

CITIZEN KANE
Niles Cinema; Order No. NM-8002; 1941 • b/w; 2 hrs; 1/2" Beta II, 1/2" VHS • Sale: $54.95

The Nostalgia Merchant; Order No. 8002; 1941 • b/w; 2 hrs; 1/2" Beta II, 1/2" VHS • Sale: $54.95

RCA SelectaVision VideoDiscs; Order No. 00401; 1941 • b/w; 1 hr, 59 min; CED • Sale: $19.98

Red Fox, Inc; Order No. 8002; 1941 • b/w; 2 hrs; 1/2" Beta II, 1/2" VHS • Sale: $54.95

Time-Life Video Club Inc; 1941 • b/w; 1 hr, 59 min; 1/2" Beta II, 1/2" VHS • Sale: $44.95 to members

Vid America; Order No. 903; 1941 • b/w; 1 hr, 59 min; 1/2" Beta II, 1/2" VHS • Rental: $10.95/wk

Recounts the life and death of a powerful newspaper tycoon in this innovative, ground-breaking film by Orson Welles. Stars Welles, Joseph Cotten, and Agnes Moorhead.

Orson Welles in *Citizen Kane.*

CITIZEN'S BAND

Fotomat Corp; Order No. B0031 for ½" Beta II, V0031 for ½" VHS; 1977 • color; 1 hr, 38 min; ½" Beta II, ½" VHS • Sale: $49.95; Rental: $9.95/up to 5 days, applicable to purchase

Deals with the CB radio craze and the lives attached to the voices on the airwaves. Shows that the CB radio is a life-saving tool, an advertising medium, a weapon, a sexual instrument, and a mouthpiece for everything from gossip to the gospel. Stars Paul Le Mat, Candy Clark, Ann Wedgeworth, Marcia Rodd, and Ed Begley Jr., under the direction of Jonathan Glemme.

CITY LIGHTS

Magnetic Video Corporation; Order No. CL-3006; 1931 • b/w; 1 hr, 21 min; ½" Beta II, ½" VHS • Sale: $44.95

Offer Charlie Chaplin's silent comedy feature, which concerns the "little tramp's" efforts to obtain the money for an operation to restore sight to a blind flower girl. Co-stars Virginia Cherrill and Florence Lee, in a film written and directed by Chaplin.

Charles Chaplin and Virginia Cherrill in *City Lights.*

THE CLAMDIGGER'S DAUGHTER

Monarch Releasing Corporation; Date not listed • color; 1 hr, 24 min; ¾" U-Matic • Sale: $350

Presents a pornographic film.

CLASH BY NIGHT

Video Communications Inc; 1952 • b/w; 1 hr, 45 min; ½" Beta II, ½" VHS • Sale: $54.95

Examines the lives of a fishing boat skipper, his tired, defeated wife, and cynical friend. Contrasts the rugged beauty and terrible drabness of their Pacific town as reflected in the characters themselves. Stars Barbara Stanwyck, Paul Douglas, Robert Ryan, and Marilyn Monroe, under the direction of Fritz Lang.

CLASSIC SUPERMAN CARTOONS

Reel Images Inc; Order No. 82; Date not listed • b/w; 54 min; ½" Beta II, ½" VHS • Sale: $39.95 for ½" Beta II, $42.95 for ½" VHS

Features the following Superman cartoons: "Underground World," "Terror on the Midway," "Volcano," "Destruction, Inc.," "Secret Agent," "Billion Dollar Limited," and "Showdown."

CLEOPATRA

Blackhawk Films, Inc; Order No. 502-49-0004 for ½" Beta II, 515-49-0017 for ½" VHS; 1963 • color; 3 hrs, 12 min; ½" Beta II, ½" VHS • Sale: $74.95

- -

Golden Tapes Video Tape Library; Order No. F-1008; 1963 • color; 3 hrs, 12 min; ½" Beta II, ½" VHS • Sale: $49.95 for ½" Beta II & VHS, $124.95 for ¾"

- -

Magnetic Video Corporation; Order No. CL-1008; 1963 • color; 3 hrs, 12 min; ½" Beta II, ½" VHS • Sale: $64.95

- -

The Video Library; Order No. MV-1008; 1963 • color; 3 hrs, 12 min; ½" Beta II, ½" VHS • Sale: $74.95

Offers a lavish production in the DeMille tradition. Revolves around the four figures who were of the greatest importance in the establishment of the Roman Empire. Stars Richard Burton, Elizabeth Taylor, and Rex Harrison, under the direction of Joseph Mankiewicz.

A CLOCKWORK ORANGE

WCI Home Video Inc; 1971 • color; 2 hrs, 17 min; ½" Beta II, ½" VHS • Sale: $75

Presents Stanley Kubrick's adaptation of Anthony Burgess' novel. Takes a satirical look at the future when crime is rampant and science attempts to control the criminal mind. Stars Malcolm McDowell, Patrick Magee, Adrienne Corri, Aubrey Morris, and James Marcus.

CLOSE ENCOUNTERS OF THE THIRD KIND

Columbia Pictures Home Entertainment; 1977 • color; 2 hrs, 15 min; ½" Beta II, ½" VHS • Sale: $69.96

Presents Steven Speilberg's science-fiction spectacle concerning alien contacts with the human race. Centers on a small group of people obsessed with getting to a rendezvous point, not knowing why they must go there. Features highly acclaimed special effects. Stars Richard Dreyfuss, Francois Truffaut, Teri Garr, Melinda Dillon, Cary Guffey, and Bob Balaban.

CLOSE ENCOUNTERS OF THE THIRD KIND, SPECIAL EDITION

Vid America; Order No. 980; 1980 • color; 2 hrs, 12 min; ½" Beta II, ½" VHS • Sale: $69.95; Rental: $13.95/wk, applicable to purchase

Presents the re-edited version of Steven Speilberg's film about UFO's. Eliminates some scenes and adds a few moments. Concerns people who witness UFO's and their inexplicable need to travel to a remote mountain top. Stars Richard Dreyfuss, Teri Garr, Melinda Dillon, Francois Truffaut, Cary Guffey, and Bob Balaban.

THE CLOWNS

Meda/Media Home Entertainment Inc; Order No. M109; 1971 • color; 1 hr, 30 min; ½" Beta I, ½" Beta II, ½" VHS • Sale: $54.95 ½" Beta II & VHS

Recreates some of the most famous clown acts in circus history in a playful documentary directed by Federico Fellini. Shows the two kinds of clowns that have dominated the circus: the eternal tramp Auguste and the indestructible snob Pierrot or "the white clown."

Tomy Lee Jones
and Sissy Spacek
in *Coal Miner's
Daughter.*

COAL MINER'S DAUGHTER

MCA DiscoVision; 1980 • color; 2 hrs, 5 min • Sale: $24.95

MCA Videocassette, Inc; Order No. 66015; 1980 • color; 2 hrs, 4 min; 1/2" Beta II, 1/2" VHS • Sale: $65

Presents Sissy Spacek in a film biography of country singer Loretta Lynn, telling how she overcame numerous hardhips on her way to becoming "queen of country music." Co-stars Tommy Lee Jones and Beverly D'Angelo, under the direction of Michael Apted.

COAST TO COAST

Paramount Home Video; Order No. 1342; 1980 • color; 1 hr, 35 min; 1/2" Beta II, 1/2" VHS • Sale: $66.95

Offers a comedy concerning a cross-country trucker who is coerced into helping rescue a woman being pursued by her psychiatrist husband, who had her committed to avoid a costly divorce. Features Robert Blake and Dyan Cannon.

COCAINE COWBOYS

Meda/Media Home Entertainment Inc; Order No. M133; 1979 • color; 1 hr, 24 min; 1/2" Beta II, 1/2" VHS • Sale: $49.95

Presents a thriller in which a rock band smuggles cocaine from Colombia and runs afoul of the Mob.

COCKEYED CAVALIERS

Blackhawk Films, Inc; Order No. 506010766 for 1/2" Beta II, 525010776 for 1/2" VHS; 1934 • b/w; 1 hr, 10 min; 1/2" Beta II, 1/2" VHS • Sale: $49.95

Presents a slapstick comedy featuring Wheeler and Woolsey.

THE COLLECTOR

National Film and Video Center; 1965 • color; 1 hr, 59 min; 3/4" U-Matic, 1/2" Beta II, 1/2" VHS • Rental: $89/1 showing

Time-Life Video Club Inc; 1965 • color; 1 hr, 59 min; 1/2" Beta II, 1/2" VHS • Sale: $44.95 to members

Stars Terence Stamp and Samantha Eggar in a film based on the novel by John Fowles. Tells of a quiet London bank clerk who wins a lottery and kidnaps a girl he has been admiring for years.

COLLEGE

Video T.E.N.; 1927 • b/w; 1 hr, 10 min; 1/2" Beta II, 1/2" VHS • Sale: $49.95 for 1/2" Beta II, $54.95 for 1/2" VHS

Spotlights Buster Keaton in a silent comedy, also starring Florence Turner. Follows the tribulations of a brainy college student who, to avoid losing his girl, makes disastrous efforts to become an athletic hero.

THE COLOR ADVENTURES OF SUPERMAN

Reel Images Inc; Order No. 537; 1941-43 • color; 52 min; 1/2" Beta II, 1/2" VHS • Sale: $39.95 for 1/2" Beta II, $42.95 for 1/2" VHS

Features Bud Collyer as Superman's voice in seven animated adventures, including "Superman," "The Mechanical Monsters," "The Magnetic Telescope," "The Japoteurs," "The Bulleteers," "Jungle Drums," and "The Mummy Strikes."

COLOR CARTOON PARADE

Ivy Video; 1930 • color; 45 min; 3/4" U-Matic, 1/2" Beta II, 1/2" VHS • Sale: $59.95 for 1/2" Beta II & VHS, trade-in plan available, $195 for 3/4"

Presents five cartoons from the pen of I. W. Uwerks, an early pioneer of animation who started with Disney and later produced on his own these Mother Goose Fairy Tales.

COMA

MGM/CBS Home Video; Order No. M60013; 1978 • color; 1 hr, 53 min; 1/2" Beta II, 1/2" VHS • Sale: $59.95

Niles Cinema; Order No. GM-724; 1978 • color; 1 hr, 53 min; 1/2" Beta II, 1/2" VHS • Sale: $59.95

Presents director Michael Crichton's adaptation of his own suspense novel about bodies mysteriously disappearing from a modern Boston hospital. Follows a young female doctor who stumbles on to the truth when her best friend is admitted for a minor operation and lapses into a permanent coma. Stars Genevieve Bujold, Michael Douglas, Richard Widmark, Rip Torn, and Elisabeth Ashley.

*COMEDY CAVALCADE

Videobrary Inc; Order No. 1 to 35-SC; Date not listed • b/w; 1/2" Beta II, 1/2" VHS • Sale: $2098.25 full series, $419.65 ea volume, $69.95 ea tape for 1/2" Beta II, $2273.25 full series, $454.65 ea volume, $74.95 ea tape for 1/2" VHS • 35 units: Comedy Cavalcade (Volume 1, Part 1); Comedy

Offers a compilation, in five volumes of seven tapes each, of comedy shorts from the 1930's and 1940's. Presents, on each tape, six 20-minute shorts featuring such stars as Buster Keaton, Andy Clyde, Edgar Kennedy, Leon Errol, Bing Crosby, Ernest Truex, and Harry Langdon, among others.

COMEDY CAVALCADE (VOLUME 1, PART 1)

Videobrary Inc; Order No. 1-SC; Date not listed • Series: Comedy Cavalcade • b/w; 2 hrs; 1/2" Beta II, 1/2" VHS • Sale: $69.95 for 1/2" Beta II, $74.95 for 1/2" VHS

Presents a collection of comedy shorts from the 1930's and 1940's. Includes Buster Keaton in "Blue Blazes" and "Hayseed Romance"; Andy Clyde in "Don't Bite Your Dentist" and "The Giddy Age"; "Nose for News" with Joe Cook; and Willie Howard in "The Miss They Missed."

COMEDY CAVALCADE (VOLUME 1, PART 2)

Videobrary Inc; Order No. 2-SC; Date not listed • Series: Comedy Cavalcade • b/w; 2 hrs; 1/2" Beta II, 1/2" VHS • Sale: $69.95 for 1/2" Beta II, $74.95 for 1/2" VHS

Presents a collection of comedy shorts from the 1930's and 1940's. Includes Leon Errol in "Seeing Nellie Home" and "Down the Ribber"; "Whose Baby Are You" with Bert Lahr; "Two Lame Ducks" featuring Billy Gilbert and Vince Barnett; Willie Howard in "The Smart Way"; and Edgar Kennedy in "Gasoloons."

COMEDY CAVALCADE (VOLUME 1, PART 3)

Videobrary Inc; Order No. 3-SC; Date not listed • Series: Comedy Cavalcade • b/w; 2 hrs; 1/2" Beta II, 1/2" VHS • Sale: $69.95 for 1/2" Beta II, $74.95 for 1/2" VHS

Offers a collection of comedy shorts from the 1930's and 1940's. Presents "The Big Courtship" with Irene Ryan; Andy Clyde in "Boy, Oh Boy"; "He's a Honey" featuring Edgar Kennedy; Lloyd Hamilton in "His Big Moment"; Buster Keaton in "Gold Ghost"; and Danny Kaye starring in "Cupid Takes a Holiday."

COMEDY CAVALCADE (VOLUME 1, PART 4)

Videobrary Inc; Order No. 4-SC; Date not listed • Series: Comedy Cavalcade • b/w; 2 hrs; 1/2" Beta II, 1/2" VHS • Sale: $69.95 for 1/2" Beta II, $74.95 for 1/2" VHS

Offers a collection of comedy shorts from the 1930's and 1940's. Includes Leon Errol in "Who's a Dummy" and "Bested by a Beard"; "Scotch" with Andy Clyde; "Girls Will Be Boys" with Charlotte Greenwood; Fern Emmett in "Mother's Holiday"; and "Morning Judge" featuring Edgar Kennedy.

COMEDY CAVALCADE (VOLUME 1, PART 5)

Videobrary Inc; Order No. 5-SC; Date not listed • Series: Comedy Cavalcade • b/w; 2 hrs; 1/2" Beta II, 1/2" VHS • Sale: $69.95 for 1/2" Beta II, $74.95 for 1/2" VHS

Presents a collection of comedy shorts from the 1930's and 1940's. Offers Andy Clyde in "Bulls and Bears"

and "An Old Gypsy Custom"; Milton Berle starring in "Poppin' the Cork"; "One Quiet Night" with Walter Catlett; Joe Cook in "White Hope"; and "Idle Roomers" with Frank Melino.

COMEDY CAVALCADE (VOLUME 1, PART 6)

Videobrary Inc; Order No. 6-SC; Date not listed • Series: Comedy Cavalcade • b/w; 2 hrs; 1/2" Beta II, 1/2" VHS • Sale: $69.95 for 1/2" Beta II, $74.95 for 1/2" VHS

Offers a collection of comedy shorts from the 1930's and 1940's. Features Leon Errol in "Berthquake" and "Scrappily Married"; "Clancy at the Bat" with Andy Clyde; Buster West and Tom Patricola in "Hy Ya' Doc"; "That's My Meat" with Al St. John; and Edgar Kennedy in "Hillbilly Goat."

COMEDY CAVALCADE (VOLUME 1, PART 7)

Videobrary Inc; Order No. 7-SC; Date not listed • Series: Comedy Cavalcade • b/w; 2 hrs; 1/2" Beta II, 1/2" VHS • Sale: $69.95 for 1/2" Beta II, $74.95 for 1/2" VHS

Offers a collection of comedy shorts from the 1930's and 1940's. Presents Buster Keaton in "Love Nest on Wheels"; Lloyd Hamilton in "Pop's Pal"; "Ladies Love Hats" with Ernest Truex; Bing Crosby starring in "One More Chance"; Franklin Panghorn and Ray Cook in "Torchy's Kitty Coup"; and Willie Howard in "Affairs of Pierre."

COMEDY CAVALCADE (VOLUME 2, PART 1)

Videobrary Inc; Order No. 8-SC; Date not listed • Series: Comedy Cavalcade • b/w; 2 hrs; 1/2" Beta II, 1/2" VHS • Sale: $69.95 for 1/2" Beta II, $74.95 for 1/2" VHS

Offers a collection of comedy shorts from the 1930's and 1940's. Includes Leon Errol in "Borrowed Blonde" and "Fired Man"; Andy Clyde in "Hello Television"; "Bridge Wives" featuring Al St. John; "Dog Gone Babies" with Ernest Truex; and Edgar Kennedy in "Blasted Evens."

COMEDY CAVALCADE (VOLUME 2, PART 2)

Videobrary Inc; Order No. 9-SC; Date not listed • Series: Comedy Cavalcade • b/w; 2 hrs; 1/2" Beta II, 1/2" VHS • Sale: $69.95 for 1/2" Beta II, $74.95 for 1/2" VHS

Presents a collection of comedy shorts from the 1930's and 1940's. Features Danny Kaye in "Getting an Eyeful"; the Mack Sennett stars in "Who's Who at the Zoo"; "The Great Pie Mystery" with Harry Gribbon; Buster Keaton in "Grand Slam Opera"; "Only the Brave" with Ernest Truex; and Harry Langdon in "Big Flash."

COMEDY CAVALCADE (VOLUME 2, PART 3)

Videobrary Inc; Order No. 10-SC; Date not listed • Series: Comedy Cavalcade • b/w; 2 hrs; 1/2" Beta II, 1/2" VHS • Sale: $69.95 for 1/2" Beta II, $74.95 for 1/2" VHS

Presents a collection of comedy shorts from the 1930's and 1940's. Offers Leon Errol in "Counselitis" and "Maid to Order"; Moran and Mack in "Farmer's Fatal Follies"; Tim and Irene (Ryan) in "Modern Home"; "Tired Feet" with Harry Langdon; and Edgar Kennedy in "In-Laws are Out."

COMEDY CAVALCADE (VOLUME 2, PART 4)

Videobrary Inc; Order No. 11-SC; Date not listed • Series: Comedy Cavalcade • b/w; 2 hrs; 1/2" Beta II, 1/2" VHS • Sale: $69.95 for 1/2" Beta II, $74.95 for 1/2" VHS

Offers a collection of comedy shorts from the 1930's and 1940's. Features Moran and Mack in "Freeze Out"; "Parked in Paree" with Buster West and Tom Patricola; Andy Clyde and Harry Gribbon in "Uppercut O'Brien"; Tim and Irene (Ryan) in "One Big Happy

Family"; "Ticklish Business" with Monte Collins; and Andy Clyde in "His Weak Moment."

COMEDY CAVALCADE (VOLUME 2, PART 5)
Videobrary Inc; Order No. 12-SC; Date not listed • Series: Comedy Cavalcade • b/w; 2 hrs; 1/2" Beta II, 1/2" VHS • Sale: $69.95 for 1/2" Beta II, $74.95 for 1/2" VHS
Presents a collection of comedy shorts from the 1930's and 1940's. Features Edgar Kennedy in "Love on a Ladder" and "Dumb's the Word"; "When Wife's Away" with Leon Errol; "Boudoir Butler" with Andy Clyde; George Shelton and Harry Gribbon in "Sleepless Hollow"; and "Stagehand" with Harry Langdon.

COMEDY CAVALCADE (VOLUME 2, PART 6)
Videobrary Inc; Order No. 13-SC; Date not listed • Series: Comedy Cavalcade • b/w; 2 hrs; 1/2" Beta II, 1/2" VHS • Sale: $69.95 for 1/2" Beta II, $74.95 for 1/2" VHS
Offers a collection of comedy shorts from the 1930's and 1940's. Features Andy Clyde in "Fainting Lover" and "Cannonball"; Yorke and King in "How Am I Doing"; "Pennywise" with Joe Cook; "Way Up Thar" with Joan Davis; and Lloyd Hamilton in "Trouble for Two."

COMEDY CAVALCADE (VOLUME 2, PART 7)
Videobrary Inc; Order No. 14-SC; Date not listed • Series: Comedy Cavalcade • b/w; 2 hrs; 1/2" Beta II, 1/2" VHS • Sale: $69.95 for 1/2" Beta II, $74.95 for 1/2" VHS
Offers a collection of comedy shorts from the 1930's and 1940's. Presents Leon Errol in "Wholesailing Along" and "Twin Husbands"; Andy Clyde in "Feeling Rosy"; Bert Lahr in "Off the Horses"; "Light Fantastic" with Ernest Truex; and Edgar Kennedy in "Sock Me to Sleep."

COMEDY CAVALCADE (VOLUME 3, PART 1)
Videobrary Inc; Order No. 15-SC; Date not listed • Series: Comedy Cavalcade • b/w; 2 hrs; 1/2" Beta II, 1/2" VHS • Sale: $69.95 for 1/2" Beta II, $74.95 for 1/2" VHS
Offers a collection of comedy shorts from the 1930's and 1940's. Features Tim and Irene (Ryan) in "Heir Today"; "How's the Time" with Edgar Kennedy and Harry Barris; "Don't Be Nervous" with Lloyd Hamilton; Buster West and Tom Patricola in "Going, Going, Gone"; Andy Clyde starring in "Lunkhead"; and "He's a Prince" featuring Tom Howard and George Shelton.

COMEDY CAVALCADE (VOLUME 3, PART 2)
Videobrary Inc; Order No. 16-SC; Date not listed • Series: Comedy Cavalcade • b/w; 2 hrs; 1/2" Beta II, 1/2" VHS • Sale: $69.95 for 1/2" Beta II, $74.95 for 1/2" VHS
Offers a collection of comedy shorts from the 1930's and 1940's. Presents Leon Errol in "Lord Epping Returns" and "Hired Husband"; "The Inventors" featuring Stoopnagle and Budd; Buster Keaton in "Three on a Limb"; "Purely Circumstantial" with Lupino Lane; and Edgar Kennedy starring in "Merchant of Menace."

COMEDY CAVALCADE (VOLUME 3, PART 3)
Videobrary Inc; Order No. 17-SC; Date not listed • Series: Comedy Cavalcade • b/w; 2 hrs; 1/2" Beta II, 1/2" VHS • Sale: $69.95 for 1/2" Beta II, $74.95 for 1/2" VHS
Presents a collection of comedy shorts from the 1930's and 1940's. Offers "Who's Who" with Neila Goodelle; Andy Clyde starring in "For the Love of Ludwig"; "Dream House" featuring Bing Crosby; "Hollywood Lights" with Rita Ryan; The Ritz Brothers in "Hotel Anchovy"; and "Prize Puppies" with Lloyd Hamilton.

COMEDY CAVALCADE (VOLUME 3, PART 4)
Videobrary Inc; Order No. 18-SC; Date not listed • Series: Comedy Cavalcade • b/w; 2 hrs; 1/2" Beta II, 1/2" VHS • Sale: $69.95 for 1/2" Beta II, $74.95 for 1/2" VHS
Presents a collection of comedy shorts from the 1930's and 1940's. Offers Leon Errol in "Back Stage Follies" and "Wrong Room"; "Don't Give Up" with Buster West; Monte Collins in "The Mad House"; "Tied for Life" starring Harry Langdon; and "Beaux and Errors" featuring Edgar Kennedy.

COMEDY CAVALCADE (VOLUME 3, PART 5)
Videobrary Inc; Order No. 19-SC; Date not listed • Series: Comedy Cavalcade • b/w; 2 hrs; 1/2" Beta II, 1/2" VHS • Sale: $69.95 for 1/2" Beta II, $74.95 for 1/2" VHS
Offers a collection of comedy shorts from the 1930's and 1940's. Presents Andy Clyde in "The Golfers" and "The Chumps"; Bert Lahr starring in "Gold Bricks"; "His Pest Girl" with Tim and Irene (Ryan); "Gentlemen of the Bar" with Ernest Truex; and Bob Hope in "Going Spanish."

COMEDY CAVALCADE (VOLUME 3, PART 6)
Videobrary Inc; Order No. 20-SC; Date not listed • Series: Comedy Cavalcade • b/w; 2 hrs; 1/2" Beta II, 1/2" VHS • Sale: $69.95 for 1/2" Beta II, $74.95 for 1/2" VHS
Offers a collection of comedy shorts from the 1930's and 1940's. Includes Leon Errol in "Panic in the Parlor" and "Tattle Television"; "Screen Test" with Buster West and Tom Patricola; Tom Howard and George Shelton in "Stylish Stouts"; "The Chemist" starring Buster Keaton; and Edgar Kennedy in "Bric-A-Brac."

COMEDY CAVALCADE (VOLUME 3, PART 7)
Videobrary Inc; Order No. 21-SC; Date not listed • Series: Comedy Cavalcade • b/w; 2 hrs; 1/2" Beta II, 1/2" VHS • Sale: $69.95 for 1/2" Beta II, $74.95 for 1/2" VHS
Presents a collection of comedy shorts from the 1930's and 1940's. Features Bing Crosby in "Billboard Girl"; Billy Gilbert and Vince Barnett together in "Brain Busters"; "Taxi Troubles" with Andy Clyde; "Ready to Serve" featuring Buster West and Tom Patricola; Harry Langdon starring in "Hooks and Jabs"; and "Honk Your Horn" with Lloyd Hamilton.

COMEDY CAVALCADE (VOLUME 4, PART 1)
Videobrary Inc; Order No. 22-SC; Date not listed • Series: Comedy Cavalcade • b/w; 2 hrs; 1/2" Beta II, 1/2" VHS • Sale: $69.95 for 1/2" Beta II, $74.95 for 1/2" VHS
Presents a collection of comedy shorts from the 1930's and 1940's. Features "Dumb Duck" with Easy Aces; "Super Stupid" with Billy Gilbert; Harry Langdon in "Knight Duty"; and Shirley Temple starring in "Pie Covered Wagon," "Pollytix in Washington," "Kid'n Hollywood," "Kid's Last Fight," "Glad Rags to Riches," and "War Babies."

COMEDY CAVALCADE (VOLUME 4, PART 2)
Videobrary Inc; Order No. 23-SC; Date not listed • Series: Comedy Cavalcade • b/w; 2 hrs; 1/2" Beta II, 1/2" VHS • Sale: $69.95 for 1/2" Beta II, $74.95 for 1/2" VHS
Offers a collection of comedy shorts from the 1930's and 1940's. Presents "It Happened All Right" with Tim and Irene (Ryan); "Don't Get Excited" with Harold Goodwin; "Playboy Number One" featuring Willie Howard; Imogene Coca starring in "The Bashful Ballerina"; "The Lion's Roar" with Daphne Pollard; and Monte Collins in "It's a Cinch."

COMEDY CAVALCADE (VOLUME 4, PART 3)
Videobrary Inc; Order No. 24-SC; Date not listed • Series: Comedy Cavalcade • b/w; 2 hrs; 1/2" Beta II, 1/2"

VHS • Sale: $69.95 for ½″ Beta II, $74.95 for ½″ VHS

Presents a collection of comedy shorts from the 1930's and 1940's. Features Leon Errol in "Cutie on Dutie" and "Poppa Knows Worst"; Edgar Kennedy starring in "Parlour, Bedroom and Wrath"; "Her Accidental Hero" with Harry Gribbon; "Million Dollar Melody" featuring Lillian Roth; and Tim and Irene (Ryan) in "Hamlet and Eggs."

COMEDY CAVALCADE (VOLUME 4, PART 4)
Videobrary Inc; Order No. 25-SC; Date not listed • Series: Comedy Cavalcade • b/w; 2 hrs; ½″ Beta II, ½″ VHS • Sale: $69.95 for ½″ Beta II, $74.95 for ½″ VHS

Presents a collection of comedy shorts from the 1930's and 1940's. Includes Andy Clyde in "No, No, Lady" and "Half Baked Relations"; Tom Howard and George Shelton in "Grooms in Gloom" and "Time Out"; "Hooray for Hooligan" with Buster West and Tom Patricola; and "Hitch Hiker" starring Harry Langdon.

COMEDY CAVALCADE (VOLUME 4, PART 5)
Videobrary Inc; Order No. 26-SC; Date not listed • Series: Comedy Cavalcade • b/w; 2 hrs; ½″ Beta II, ½″ VHS • Sale: $69.95 for ½″ Beta II, $74.95 for ½″ VHS

Presents a collection of comedy shorts from the 1930's and 1940's. Features Leon Errol in "Dear Deer" and "Stage Fright"; Charlotte Greenwood in "Love Your Neighbor"; "The Big Meow" with Tom Howard and George Shelton; Andy Clyde starring in "Just a Bear"; and "Quiet Please" featuring Edgar Kennedy.

COMEDY CAVALCADE (VOLUME 4, PART 6)
Videobrary Inc; Order No. 27-SC; Date not listed • Series: Comedy Cavalcade • b/w; 2 hrs; ½″ Beta II, ½″ VHS • Sale: $69.95 for ½″ Beta II, $74.95 for ½″ VHS

Offers a collection of comedy shorts from the 1930's and 1940's. Features June Allyson in "Pixilated"; Bing Crosby in "I Surrender Dear"; "Ditto" starring Buster Keaton; "Tamale Vendor" with Tom Patricola; Roondy and Timberg in "Freshies"; and Ernest Truex in "Mr. Adam."

COMEDY CAVALCADE (VOLUME 4, PART 7)
Videobrary Inc; Order No. 28-SC; Date not listed • Series: Comedy Cavalcade • b/w; 2 hrs; ½″ Beta II, ½″ VHS • Sale: $69.95 for ½″ Beta II, $74.95 for ½″ VHS

Offers a collection of comedy shorts from the 1930's and 1940's. Features Leon Errol in "Beware of Redheads" and "Framing Father"; Bert Lahr starring in "Montague the Magnificent"; "Blue Blackbirds" with Moran and Mack; Andy Clyde in "Artists and Muddles"; and "Good Housewrecking" with Edgar Kennedy.

COMEDY CAVALCADE (VOLUME 5, PART 1)
Videobrary Inc; Order No. 29-SC; Date not listed • Series: Comedy Cavalcade • b/w; 2 hrs; ½″ Beta II, ½″ VHS • Sale: $69.95 for ½″ Beta II, $74.95 for ½″ VHS

Presents a collection of comedy shorts from the 1930's and 1940's. Offers Buster Keaton in "Tars and Stripes" and "Allez Oop"; "Polished Ivory" with Lloyd Hamilton; "Kiss the Bride" featuring Buster West and Tom Patricola; Andy Clyde starring in "Dog Doctor"; and Pert Kelton in "Albany Branch."

COMEDY CAVALCADE (VOLUME 5, PART 2)
Videobrary Inc; Order No. 30-SC; Date not listed • Series: Comedy Cavalcade • b/w; 2 hrs; ½″ Beta II, ½″ VHS • Sale: $69.95 for ½″ Beta II, $74.95 for ½″ VHS

Presents a collection of comedy shorts from the 1930's and 1940's. Offers Leon Errol in "Follow That Blonde"

and "Too Many Wives"; "One Run Elmer" starring Buster Keaton; "Their Wive's Vacation" with Pert Kelton; Andy Clyde in "Frozen Assets"; and "South Seasickness" featuring Edgar Kennedy.

COMEDY CAVALCADE (VOLUME 5, PART 3)
Videobrary Inc; Order No. 31-SC; Date not listed • Series: Comedy Cavalcade • b/w; 2 hrs; ½″ Beta II, ½″ VHS • Sale: $69.95 for ½″ Beta II, $74.95 for ½″ VHS

Presents a collection of comedy shorts from the 1930's and 1940's. Offers Edgar Kennedy in "Spot on the Rug"; "North of Zero" with Tom Patricola; Imogene Coca and Danny Kaye starring in "Dime a Dance"; Moran and Mack in "Pair of Socks"; Buster Keaton as the "Timid Young Man"; and "Happy Heels" with Buster West and Tom Patricola.

COMEDY CAVALCADE (VOLUME 5, PART 4)
Videobrary Inc; Order No. 32-SC; Date not listed • Series: Comedy Cavalcade • b/w; 2 hrs; ½″ Beta II, ½″ VHS • Sale: $69.95 for ½″ Beta II, $74.95 for ½″ VHS

Presents a collection of comedy shorts from the 1930's and 1940's. Features Leon Errol in "Pretty Dolly" and "Oil's Well That Ends Well"; Edgar Kennedy starring in "Poisoned Ivory"; "Hold It" with Pat Rooney, Jr.; Billy Gilbert and Vince Barnett in "Nifty Nurses"; and "Palooka from Paducah" with Buster Keaton.

COMEDY CAVALCADE (VOLUME 5, PART 5)
Videobrary Inc; Order No. 33-SC; Date not listed • Series: Comedy Cavalcade • b/w; 2 hrs; ½″ Beta II, ½″ VHS • Sale: $69.95 for ½″ Beta II, $74.95 for ½″ VHS

Presents a collection of comedy shorts from the 1930's and 1940's. Stars Shirley Temple in "Managed Money," "Dora's Dunkin Doughnuts," and "Pardon My Pups." Includes also "Where Is Wall Street" with Howard and Shelton; "Mr. Widget" with Joe Cook; and Harry Gribbon in "Dance Hall Marge."

COMEDY CAVALCADE (VOLUME 5, PART 6)
Videobrary Inc; Order No. 34-SC; Date not listed • Series: Comedy Cavalcade • b/w; 2 hrs; ½″ Beta II, ½″ VHS • Sale: $69.95 for ½″ Beta II, $74.95 for ½″ VHS

Offers a collection of comedy shorts from the 1930's and 1940's. Features Leon Errol in "Moving Vanities" and "Home Boner"; Buster Keaton in "E-Flat Man"; Willie Mahoney in "She's My Lillie, I'm Her Willie"; "That Rascal" with Harry Barris; and Edgar Kennedy in "Tramp Trouble."

COMEDY CAVALCADE (VOLUME 5, PART 7)
Videobrary Inc; Order No. 35-SC; Date not listed • Series: Comedy Cavalcade • b/w; 2 hrs; ½″ Beta II, ½″ VHS • Sale: $69.95 for ½″ Beta II, $74.95 for ½″ VHS

Presents a collection of comedy shorts from the 1930's and 1940's. Offers Buster Keaton in "Jailbait"; "Who's Crazy" with Harry Gribbon; "Just the Type" featuring Pat Rooney, Jr.; Alberta Vaughn in "Love Bargain"; Arthur Stone in "Lady, Please"; and "Expectant Father" with Ernest Truex.

COMING ATTRACTIONS (PART 1)—THE SUPER STARS
Reel Images Inc; Order No. 554; 1930-75 • color; 31 min; ½″ Beta II, ½″ VHS • Sale: $29.95 for ½″ Beta II, $31.95 for ½″ VHS

Presents preview shorts for twelve movies. Includes "Presenting Lily Mars," with Judy Garland, Tommy Dorsey, Bob Crosby, and Van Heflin; "The Singing Kid," "Mammy," and "Go into Your Dance," three films starring Al Jolson; two Barbara Streisand films, "Funny Girl" and "Funny Lady"; "King Creole," with

Elvis Presley and Carolyn Jones; and two James Cagney films, "Yankee Doodle Dandy" and "Footlight Parade." Concludes with "The Maltese Falcon" and "The Treasure of the Sierra Madre," two films starring Humphrey Bogart.

COMING HOME
Vid America; Order No. 470; 1978 • color; 2 hrs; 1/2" Beta II, 1/2" VHS • Rental: $13.95/wk

Examines the relationship between the wife of a marine who has left for the Vietnam War and an embittered paraplegic who has returned. Shows the wife's changing attitudes, growing self-awareness, and awkward attempts to re-establish a lost marriage when her husband comes home. Stars Jane Fonda, Jon Voight, and Bruce Dern.

A COMING OF ANGELS
Entertainment Video Releasing, Inc; Order No. 1049; Date not listed • color; 1 hr, 20 min; 1/2" Beta II, 1/2" VHS • Sale: $69.95 for 1/2" Beta II, $74.95 for 1/2" VHS

Presents a pornographic film.

THE CONDOMINIUM
FHV Entertainment, Inc; Date not listed • color; 1 hr, 28 min; 1/2" Beta II, 1/2" VHS • Sale: $49.95

Presents a pornographic film.

CONGRESSIONAL PLAYGIRLS
Tape Club of America; Order No. 2833 B; Date not listed • color; 1 hr, 26 min; 1/2" Beta II, 1/2" VHS • Sale: $54.95

Presents a pornographic film.

CONVERSATION PIECE
Magnetic Video Corporation; Order No. CL-2048; 1977 • color; 2 hrs, 2 min; 1/2" Beta II, 1/2" VHS • Sale: $64.95

Analyzes an American professor living in Rome, devoted entirely to intellectual pursuits, who rents his house to a rich Marchesa and her German gigolo. Details his growing obsession with his decadent tenants and their affairs. Stars Burt Lancaster, Silvana Mangano, and Helmut Berger, under the direction of Luchino Visconti.

COPKILLERS
FHV Entertainment, Inc; Date not listed • color; 1 hr, 38 min; 1/2" Beta II, 1/2" VHS • Sale: $49.95

Chronicles the story of two young men whose plans for easy money backfire as they discover they have no choice but to flee from the law and to survive at any cost. Stars Jason Williams.

CORRIDORS OF BLOOD
Cinema Concepts, Inc.; 1962 • b/w; 1 hr, 25 min; 3/4" U-Matic, 1/2" Beta II, 1/2" VHS • Sale: $54.95 for 1/2" Beta II & VHS, 149.95 for 3/4"

- -
The Video Library; 1962 • b/w; 1 hr, 26 min; 1/2" Beta II, 1/2" VHS • Sale: $54.95

Dramatizes the tale of an English surgeon who performs many crude experiments until he develops anesthetics for his patients. Stars Boris Karloff and Betta St. John.

THE COUNT OF MONTE CRISTO
RCA SelectaVision VideoDiscs; Order No. 00519; 1975 • color; 1 hr, 40 min; CED • Sale: $19.98

Presents the TV-movie adaptation of Alexandre Dumas' tale of a man unjustly shut up in an island-prison because a rival covets his fiance. Shows his escape

and eventual attempt at revenge. Stars Richard Chamberlain, Tony Curtis, Trevor Howard, Louis Jourdan, Donald Pleasance, and Taryn Power.

COUNT THE WAYS
TVX Distributors; Order No. R.T. 84; Date not listed • color; 2 hrs; 1/2" Beta II, 1/2" VHS • Sale: $79.50 for 1/2" Beta II, $89.50 for 1/2" VHS

Presents a pornographic film.

COUNTDOWN TO WORLD WAR II
Blackhawk Films, Inc; Order No. 506-75-0885 for 1/2" Beta II, 525-75-0885 for 1/2" VHS; Date not listed • b/w; 59 min; 3/4" U-Matic, 1/2" Beta I, 1/2" Beta II, 1/2" VHS • Sale: $59.95 for 1/2" Beta I, $39.95 for 1/2" Beta II & VHS, $69.95 for 3/4"

Presents a collection of newsreels from the 1930's which record the events which led to the Second World War—the rise of Hitler, the achievements of Mussolini. Offers color-toned films with narration.

COUPLES
Video Home Library; Order No. VX-114; Date not listed • color; 2 hrs; 1/2" Beta II, 1/2" VHS • Sale: $99.95

Presents a pornographic film.

COURAGEOUS CAT
Video Tape Network; Order No. KI 413 for 1/2" Beta II, KI 414 for 1/2" VHS; Date not listed • color; 1 hr; 1/2" Beta II, 1/2" VHS • Sale: $49.95

Offers cartoon characters conceived and written by Bob Kane, creator of Batman and Robin. Features Courageous Cat and Minute Mouse who live in their cat cave headquarters and ride in their "catmobile" and help the local authorities to solve mysteries.

COUSIN, COUSINE
Meda/Media Home Entertainment Inc; 1976 • ; 1 hr, 35 min; 1/2" Beta II, 1/2" VHS • Sale: $59.95

Examines the relationship of two cousins by marriage who become acquainted when their respective spouses have an affair together. Shows how their friendship develops into love and how their relatives are forced to cope with romantic trysts at family gatherings. Stars Marie-Christine Barrault and Victor Lanoux.

COVER GIRL
National Film and Video Center; 1944 • color; 1 hr, 47 min; 3/4" U-Matic, 1/2" Beta II, 1/2" VHS • Rental: $79/1 showing

Stars Rita Hayworth as a chorus girl who is offered a job on Broadway and fired by her nightclub owner boyfriend who is afraid he will hinder her success. Ends with her returning to him. Features Gene Kelly, music by Jerome Kern, and lyrics by Ira Gershwin.

COWBOY COMMANDOS
Thunderbird Films; 1944 • b/w; 1 hr; 3/4" U-Matic, 1/2" Beta I, 1/2" Beta II, 1/2" VHS • Sale: $59.95 for 1/2" Beta I, $39.95 for 1/2" Beta II & VHS, $79.95 for 3/4"

Presents a comic western with cowboys attempting to overcome the plots of Nazi spies and saboteurs. Stars Ray Corrigan, Dennis Moore, and Max Terhune.

THE COYOTE'S LAMENT
MCA DiscoVision; Order No. D61-507; Date not listed; LaserVision • color; 1 hr • Sale: $9.95

Presents the misadventures of a coyote family as they attempt, again and again, to raid the sheep farm guarded by Pluto. Features the animation artistry of the Walt Disney Studios. Offers the work of John Lounsberry, Cliff Nordberg, Robert Youngquist, Bill Keil, Eric Larson, George Nicholas, George Kreisl, and Phil Duncan.

CRASH
Fotomat Corp; Order No. B0185 for ½" Beta II, V0185 for ½" VHS; 1976 • color; 1 hr, 25 min; ½" Beta II, ½" VHS • Sale: $39.95; Rental: $7.95/up to 5 days, applicable to purchase

Portrays a jealous invalid-husband determined to kill his supernaturally-influenced wife. Includes numerous car chases and scenes of the occult. Features Jose Ferrer, John Carradine, Sue Lyon, John Ericson, and Leslie Parrish.

Ben Chapman as the creature in *The Creature From The Black Lagoon.*

CREATURE FROM THE BLACK LAGOON
MCA Videocassette, Inc; Order No. 66018; 1954 • b/w; 1 hr, 19 min; ½" Beta II, ½" VHS • Sale: $65

Niles Cinema; Order No. MC-6018; 1954 • b/w; 1 hr, 19 min; ½" Beta II, ½" VHS • Sale: $64.95

Offers a science-fiction film shot in 3-D. Includes 4 pairs of 3-D glasses. Centers on a prehistoric gill-man with an eye for the ladies who resides in the Amazon River and is discovered by an expedition of scientists. Stars Richard Carlson, Julia Adams, Richard Denning, Antonio Moreno, and Nestor Paiva.

THE CREATURE'S REVENGE
Thunderbird Films; Date not listed • color; 1 hr, 30 min; ¾" U-Matic, ½" Beta I, ½" Beta II, ½" VHS • Sale: $69.95 for ½" Beta I, $49.95 for ½" Beta II & VHS, $89.95 for ¾"

Presents a chiller about a dying diplomat, a mad doctor, and a series of brain transplants. Features Grant Williams, Kent Taylor, Angelo Di Angelo, and Gus Peters.

THE CRICKET IN TIMES SQUARE
Fotomat Corp; Order No. B0707 for ½" Beta II, V0707 for ½" VHS; 1973 • color; 26 min; ½" Beta II, ½" VHS • Sale: $39.95; Rental: $5.95/5 days

Provides an animated film for children, produced by Xerox. Centers on the efforts of Tucker Mouse, Harry Cat, and Chester Cricket to aid some people who run a shabby newstand in noisy, bustling Times Square. Uses characters created by George Selden.

CRIME AND PUNISHMENT
National Film and Video Center; 1935 • b/w; 1 hr, 30 min; ¾" U-Matic, ½" Beta II, ½" VHS • Rental: $69/1 showing

Brings Dostoevsky's novel to the screen as Raskolnikov kills and robs an old pawnbroker and is then hounded to the edge of sanity by his feeling that his capture is imminent. Stars Peter Lorre, Marian Marsh, and Edward Arnold, under the direction of Josef von Sternberg.

THE CRIMSON GHOST
The Nostalgia Merchant; Order No. 0039; 1946 • b/w; 3 hrs; ½" Beta II, ½" VHS • Sale: $109.95

Presents, on two videocassettes, a Republic motion picture serial in 12 episodes. Traces the attempts of the hooded villain, the Crimson Ghost, to steal the atomic powered Cyclotrode, a futuristic weapon he would use to enslave the world. Stars Charles Quigley, Linda Stirling, and I. Stanford Jolley.

CROMWELL
National Film and Video Center; 1970 • color; 2 hrs, 19 min; ¾" U-Matic, ½" Beta II, ½" VHS • Rental: $79/1 showing

Profiles Cromwell, the commoner who connived his way to the title of Grand Protector of the British Isles as the leader of the revolution that toppled King Charles I from the throne. Stars Richard Harris and Alec Guinness.

CRUISERS
VTS; Date not listed • color; 1 hr, 27 min; ½" Beta I, ½" Beta II, ½" VHS • Sale: $99

Presents a pornographic film.

CRUISING
MGM/CBS Home Video; Order No. C60029; 1980 • color; 1 hr, 42 min; ½" Beta II, ½" VHS • Sale: $59.95

Offers the controversial film directed by William Friedkin. Follows an undercover policeman as he searches for the killer of homosexuals. Stars Paul Sorvino, Al Pacino, Karen Allen, Richard Cox, and Don Scardino.

CRY BLOOD APACHE
Niles Cinema; Order No. BT-03 for ½" Beta II, VH-03 for ½" VHS; 1970 • color; 1 hr, 15 min; ½" Beta II, ½" VHS • Sale: $49.95

Presents a Western saga of hidden gold, reckless prospectors, and an Indian girl and warrior, featuring Joel McCrea and Jody McCrea.

CRY FOR ME BILLY
Magnetic Video Corporation; Order No. CL-5013; 1977 • color; 1 hr, 33 min; ½" Beta II, ½" VHS • Sale: $54.95

Relates a tale of a white man who dares to love an Indian girl in a country where violence and massacre are the law. Stars Cliff Potts, Xochitl, and Harry Dean Stanton.

CRY UNCLE!
Entertainment Video Releasing, Inc; Date not listed • color; 1 hr, 20 min; ½" Beta II, ½" VHS • Sale: $79.95

Presents a pornographic film.

CURLY TOP

Magnetic Video Corporation; Order No. CL-1067; 1935 • b/w; 1 hr, 15 min; ½″ Beta II, ½″ VHS • Sale: $54.95

Presents a little girl playing cupid for her sister and a handsome young man. Stars Shirley Temple, John Boles, Rochelle Hudson, Jane Darwell, and Arthur Treacher. Features the song "Animal Crackers in My Soup."

THE CURSE OF THE CAT PEOPLE

The Nostalgia Merchant; Order No. 8048; 1944 • b/w; 1 hr, 10 min; ½″ Beta II, ½″ VHS • Sale: $54.95

Red Fox, Inc; Order No. 8048; 1944 • b/w; 1 hr, 10 min; ½″ Beta II, ½″ VHS • Sale: $54.95

Presents a fantasy of a sensitive child who is guided by the vision of her dead mother. Stars Simone Simon, Kent Smith, and Jane Randolph.

CURSE OF THE HEADLESS HORSEMAN

Monarch Releasing Corporation; Date not listed • color; 1 hr, 15 min; ¾″ U-Matic • Sale: $350

Presents a pornographic film.

CURSE OF THE VOODOO

Cinema Concepts, Inc.; 1965 • b/w; 1 hr, 17 min; ¾″ U-Matic, ½″ Beta II, ½″ VHS • Sale: $54.95 for ½″ Beta II & VHS, $149.95 for ¾″

The Video Library; Order No. CC-0109; 1965 • b/w; 1 hr, 17 min; ½″ Beta II, ½″ VHS • Sale: $54.95

Presents a story about hunter who, after killing a lion which is sacred to a village of Africans, is put under a spell by the village witchdoctor. Stars Bryant Halliday, Dennis Price, and Lisa Daniely.

CYBORG: THE SIX MILLION DOLLAR MAN

MCA DiscoVision; Order No. 19-003; 1973 • color; 1 hr, 15 min; LaserVision • Sale: $9.95

Adapts the novel by Martin Caiden and presents the pilot for the TV series as Steve Austin, astronaut, is severely injured and "repaired" to become a "bionic" man, stronger than any normal human, and now serving as a government operative. Features Lee Majors and Martin Balsam.

CYRANO DE BERGERAC

Cinema Resources; 1950 • b/w; 1 hr, 52 min; ½″ Beta II, ½″ VHS • Sale: $45

Presents the film version of Edmond Rostand's play of 17th century Paris. Follows the tragic, comic, and romantic adventures of the soldier of fortune with a nose larger than most. Stars Jose Ferrer, Mala Powers, William Prince, Morris Carnovsky, and Elena Verdugo.

DAKOTA

Niles Cinema; Order No. NM-0125; 1945 • b/w; 1 hr, 22 min; ½″ Beta II, ½″ VHS • Sale: $54.95

The Nostalgia Merchant; Order No. 0125; 1945 • b/w; 1 hr, 22 min; ½″ Beta II, ½″ VHS • Sale: $54.95

Red Fox, Inc; Order No. 0125; 1945 • b/w; 1 hr, 22 min; ½″ Beta II, ½″ VHS • Sale: $54.95

Relates a saga of greedy land grabbers in the Dakota Territory. Features John Wayne, Vera Ralston, and Walter Brennan.

DAMIEN, OMEN II

Magnetic Video Corporation; 1978 • color; 1 hr, 47 min; ½″ Beta II, ½″ VHS • Sale: $59.95

Offers the first sequel to "The Omen." Presents a horror-suspense film which shows the teenage antichrist child slowly coming to realize his identity. Uses explicit violence. Stars William Holden, Lee Grant, Robert Foxworth, Lew Ayres, Sylvia Sydney, and Jonathan Scott-Taylor.

THE DANCING PIRATE

Reel Images Inc; Order No. 14; 1936 • color; 1 hr, 24 min; ½″ Beta II, ½″ VHS • Sale: $49.95 for ½″ Beta II, $52.95 for ½″ VHS

Presents a musical romance set in southern California. Features music and lyrics by Richard Rodgers and Lorenz Hart. Stars Charles Collins, Frank Morgan, and Jack La Rue under the direction of Lloyd Corrigan.

DANGEROUS HOLIDAY

Reel Images Inc; Order No. 409; 1937 • b/w; 54 min; ½″ Beta II, ½″ VHS • Sale: $39.95 for ½″ Beta II, $42.95 for ½″ VHS

Presents a family film in which a young violin prodigy runs away from his greedy relatives to just be a kid with his new friends, a gang of kidnappers. Stars Hedda Hopper, Ra Hould, Guinn "Big Boy" Williams, Jack La Rue, and Franklin Pangborn.

DANIEL BOONE

Thunderbird Films; 1937 • b/w; 1 hr, 20 min ; ¾″ U-Matic, ½″ Beta I, ½″ Beta II, ½″ VHS • Sale: $69.95 for ½″ Beta I, 49.95 for ½″ Beta II & VHS, $89.95 for ¾″

Video T.E.N.; 1937 • b/w; 1 hr, 17 min; ½″ Beta II, ½″ VHS • Sale: $49.95 for ½″ Beta II, $54.95 for ½″ VHS

Tells of the founding and battle for Boonesboro. Stars George O'Brien as Daniel Boone, with Heather Angel and John Carradine.

DANISH PASTRIES

Quality X Video Cassette Company; Date not listed • color; 1 hr, 29 min; ½″ Beta I, ½″ Beta II, ½″ VHS • Sale: $99.50

Presents a pornographic film.

DANNY BOY

Reel Images Inc; Order No. 470; 1941 • b/w; 1 hr, 7 min; ½″ Beta II, ½″ VHS • Sale: $49.95 for ½″ Beta II, $52.95 for ½″ VHS

Depicts the difficulties of a returning war dog's adjustment to civilian life, despite the help of his young master. Shows the complications that arise when Danny Boy is accused of still being dangerous.

DAREDEVILS OF THE RED CIRCLE

The Nostalgia Merchant; Date not listed • b/w; 3 hrs; ½″ Beta II, ½″ VHS • Sale: $109.95

Presents, on two videocassettes, a motion picture serial in 12 episodes. Stars Charles Quigley, Herman Brix, and David Sharpe.

THE DARING ADVENTURER
Video Communications Inc; Order No. 1129; 1949 • b/w; 1 hr, 5 min; ½" Beta II, ½" VHS • Sale: $54.95

Presents a western in which Chico poses as a husband-father to stop a marriage, thereby exposing a conspiracy. Stars Duncan Renaldo and Leo Carrillo.

THE DARING ROGUE; THE DEVIL'S DEN
Video Communications Inc; Order No. 1124; 1946, 1948 • b/w; 2 hrs, 3 min; ½" Beta II, ½" VHS • Sale: $74.95

Offers a western double feature starring Duncan Renaldo and Leo Carrillo as Chico and Pablo. Presents "The Daring Rogue," in which the two are in trouble with the U.S. Cavalry but, with the aid of a senorita, emerge as heroes. Features "The Devil's Den," in which the duo clean up Silver City after narrowly escaping death.

THE DARK COMMAND
The Nostalgia Merchant; 1940 • b/w; 1 hr, 40 min; ½" Beta II, ½" VHS • Sale: $54.95
- -
Red Fox, Inc; 1940 • b/w; 1 hr, 40 min; ½" Beta II, ½" VHS • Sale: $54.95

Presents a Raoul Walsh saga of the Civil War, focusing on Quantrill and his raiders. Features John Wayne, Claire Trevor, Walter Pidgeon, and Roy Rogers.

DARK JOURNEY
Video T.E.N.; 1937 • b/w; 1 hr, 22 min; ½" Beta II, ½" VHS • Sale: $49.95 for ½" Beta II, $54.95 for ½" VHS

Portrays a fashion designer who is a double agent in World War I, and the German agent who is her lover and enemy. Stars Vivien Leigh, Conrad Veidt, Joan Gardner, and Anthony Bushell.

DARK MOUNTAIN
Thunderbird Films; 1944 • b/w; 1 hr; ¾" U-Matic, ½" Beta I, ½" Beta II, ½" VHS • Sale: $59.95 for ½" Beta I, $39.95 for ½" Betá II & VHS, $79.95 for ¾"

Tells of a young ranger who has lost his old girlfriend to a rich importer. Features a chase down Dark Mountain after it is discovered that the rich importer is a gangster. Stars Robert Lowry, Ellen Drew, and Regis Toomey.

DARK STAR
Video Communications Inc; 1974 • color; 1 hr, 28 min; ½" Beta II, ½" VHS • Sale: $54.95

Traces the twenty-year mission of the scoutship "Dark Star" to seek and destroy "unstable" planets proving to be hazardous to other ships. Features Dan O'Bannon.

DARLING
Magnetic Video Corporation; Order No. CL-4032; 1965 • b/w; 2 hrs, 2 min; ½" Beta II, ½" VHS • Sale: $54.95
- -
Vid America; Order No. 329; 1965 • b/w; 2 hrs; ½" Beta II, ½" VHS • Rental: $11.95/wk

Focuses on a young model desperately searching for love in a world of television, night clubs, and the jet set. Stars Julie Christie, Laurence Harvey, and Dirk Bogarde under the direction of John Schlesinger.

DAVID COPPERFIELD
Magnetic Video Corporation; Order No. CL-1078; 1970 • color; 1 hr, 57 min; ½" Beta II, ½" VHS • Sale: $54.95

Dramatizes Charles Dickens' story of a downtrodden orphan boy who in his growth to manhood acquires a set of extraordinary friends and equally extraordinary enemies. Stars Robin Phillips, Richard Attenborough, Cyril Cusack, Edith Evans, Pamela Franklin, and Susan Hampshire.

DAVY CROCKETT, KING OF THE WILD FRONTIER
Fotomat Corp; Order No. B1031 for ½" Beta II, V1031 for ½" VHS; 1955 • color; 1 hr, 33 min; ½" Beta II, ½" VHS • Sale: $54.95; Rental: $7.95/5 days
- -
Niles Cinema; Order No. WD-14; 1955 • color; 1 hr, 32 min; ½" Beta II, ½" VHS • Sale: $59.95
- -
Walt Disney Home Video; Order No. 14BS for ½" Beta II, 14VS for ½" VHS; 1955 • color; 1 hr, 32 min; ½" Beta II, ½" VHS • Sale: $59.95

Presents a feature film compiled from three segments of the Walt Disney TV series. Traces the famous Indian scout and his sidekick from the Indian Wars to the U.S. Congress to the Alamo. Stars Fess Parker, Buddy Ebsen, and Hans Conried.

DAWN ON THE GREAT DIVIDE
Cable Films; 1943 • b/w; 1 hr, 13 min; ½" Beta I, ½" Beta II, ½" VHS • Sale: $65 for ½" Beta I, $49.50 for ½" Beta II & VHS
- -
Video Communications Inc; Order No. 1130; 1942 • b/w; 57 min; ½" Beta II, ½" VHS • Sale: $44.95

Presents a saga of early American history with the railroads pushing west against the outlaws who preferred the wide-open frontiers. Stars Buck Jones in his last film.

THE DAY OF THE DOLPHIN
Magnetic Video Corporation; Order No. CL-4004; 1973 • color; 1 hr, 44 min; ½" Beta II, ½" VHS • Sale: $54.95
- -
Red Fox, Inc; Order No. CL-4004; 1973 • color; 1 hr, 44 min; ½" Beta II, ½" VHS • Sale: $54.95
- -
Vid America; Order No. 460; 1973 • color; 1 hr, 44 min; ½" Beta II, ½" VHS • Rental: $12.95/wk

Recounts the attempts of a scientist to communicate with dolphins and the political intrigue resulting from his success. Stars George C. Scott and Trish Van Devere, under the direction of Mike Nichols.

Michael Rennie and Patricia Neal in
The Day The Earth Stood Still..

40

THE DAY OF THE JACKAL
MCA DiscoVision; Order No. 11-004; 1973 • color; 2
hrs, 24 min; LaserVision • Sale:$24.95

Details the step-by-step attempt to assassinate General
Charles de Gaulle in 1963 by the man known only as
"the Jackal." Shows the police stalking him as he
hunts his prey from France to Austria, Italy, and back
again to France, in this adaptation of Frederick
Forsyth's novel. Stars Edward Fox, under the direction
of Fred Zinneman.

THE DAY OF THE TRIFFIDS
Niles Cinema; Order No. BT-26 for ½" Beta II, VH-26
for ½" VHS; 1963 • color; 1 hr, 34 min; ½" Beta II,
½" VHS • Sale: $59.95

Relates a science-fiction tale of showers of meteorites
that cause small plants to grow huge and destroy civilization. Stars Howard Keel and Nicole Maurey.

DAY OF WRATH
Cable Films; 1943 • b/w; 1 hr, 50 min; ½" Beta I, ½"
Beta II, ½" VHS • Sale: $65 for ½" Beta I, $49.50 for
½" Beta II & VHS

Relates a psychological horror story based on records
of witch trials of the early 1600's. Features the understated touch of director Carl Theodor Dreyer.

THE DAY THE EARTH STOOD STILL
Blackhawk Films, Inc; Order No. 502-49-0008 for ½"
Beta II, 515-49-0011 for ½" VHS; 1951 • b/w; 1 hr,
32 min; ½" Beta II, ½" VHS • Sale: $54.95
- -
Golden Tapes Video Tape Library; Order No. F-1011;
1951 • b/w; 1 hr, 32 min; ½" Beta II, ½" VHS • Sale:
$49.95 for ½" Beta II & VHS, $124.95 for ¾"
- -
Magnetic Video Corporation; Order No. CL-1011;
1951 • b/w; 1 hr, 32 min; ½" Beta II, ½" VHS • Sale:
$44.95
- -
The Video Library; Order No. MV-1011; 1951 • b/w; 1
hr, 32 min; ½" Beta II, ½" VHS • Sale: $54.95

Presents a science-fiction film about an exploratory
visit from an alien who wishes to help the human race
learn from its mistakes. Stars Michael Rennie, Patricia
Neal, Hugh Marlowe, and Sam Jaffe, under the direction of Robert Wise.

THE DAY TIME ENDED
Meda/Media Home Entertainment Inc; Order No.
M137; Date not listed • color; 1 hr, 20 min; ½" Beta II,
½" VHS • Sale: $49.95

Shows alien spaceships, an alien pyramid with flashing
lights, two huge lizard creatures, and a mechanical alien—all in a house that is slipping into different dimen-
sions. Features Chris Mitchum, Jim Davis, Dorothy
Malone, Marcy Lafferty, Scott Kolden, and Natasha
Ryan.

DAYS OF HEAVEN
Fotomat Corp; Order No. B001 for ½" Beta II, V001 for
½" VHS; 1978 • color; 1 hr, 34 min; ½" Beta II, ½"
VHS • Sale: $69.95; Rental: $13.95/up to 5 days, applicable to purchase
- -
Paramount Home Video; 1978 • color; 1 hr, 34 min;
½" Beta II, ½" VHS • Sale: $59.95

Follows a poor young man and woman from Chicago
to the Texas Panhandle in their search for an existence
in the period preceding World War I. Studies the influence on their lives of a young, wealthy, shy man who is
dying while falling in love with the young woman. Fea-

tures evocative cinematography. Stars Richard Gere,
Brooke Adams, and Sam Shepard, under the direction
of Terrence Malick, from his screenplay.

**Brooke Adams and Richard Gere
in *Days of Heaven*.**

THE DAYS OF THRILLS AND LAUGHTER
Magnetic Video Corporation; Order No. CL-2024;
1961 • b/w; 1 hr, 33 min; ½" Beta II, ½" VHS • Sale:
$54.95

Presents a compilation of the greatest of film comedy,
a non-stop avalanche of chase scenes, exploding
houses, monsters, slapstick, and sight gags.

DEADLY FATHOMS
Video Communications Inc; Date not listed • color; 1
hr, 33 min; ½" Beta II, ½" VHS • Sale: $54.95

Portrays an underwater adventure-documentary study
of the Bikini Atoll in the Marshall Islands in the Pacific.

DEADLY HERO
Magnetic Video Corporation; Order No. CL-4005;
1976 • color; 1 hr, 42 min; ½" Beta II, ½" VHS • Sale:
$54.95
- -
Red Fox, Inc; Order No. CL-4005; 1976 • color; 1 hr,
42 min; ½" Beta II, ½" VHS • Sale: $54.95

Presents a crime drama concerning the relationship of
a veteran New York cop and a young off-Broadway
orchestra conductor. Features Don Murray, Diahn Williams, and James Earl Jones.

DEAR DEAD DELILAH
Cinema Concepts, Inc.; 1975 • color; 1 hr, 27 min;
¾" U-Matic, ½" Beta II, ½" VHS • Sale: $54.95 for
½" Beta II & VHS, $149.95 for ¾"
- -
The Video Library; Order No. CC-0110; 1975 • color;
1 hr, 27 min; ½" Beta II, ½" VHS • Sale: $54.95

Features Agnes Moorehead, Will Geer, and Michael
Ansara in a mystery thriller about a Southern family
that is systematically being murdered.

THE DEATH KISS
Cable Films; 1932 • b/w; 1 hr, 14 min; ½" Beta I, ½"
Beta II, ½" VHS • Sale: $65 for ½" Beta I, $49.50 for
½" Beta II & VHS
- -
Video T.E.N.; 1933 • b/w; 1 hr, 15 min; ½" Beta II,
½" VHS • Sale: $49.95 for ½" Beta II, $54.95 for ½"
VHS

Features the cast of Dracula in a murder mystery that

takes place in a movie studio. Stars Bela Lugosi, Edward Van Sloan, and David Manners.

DEATH RIDES THE PLAINS
Reel Images Inc; Order No. 59; 1944 • b/w; 54 min; ½" Beta II, ½" VHS • Sale: $39.95 for ½" Beta II, $42.95 for ½" VHS

Recounts the story of a ranch owner who lures prospective buyers to his home through newspaper ads, then murders them and steals their money. Stars Bob Livingston, Al "Fuzzy" St. John, Nica Doret, and Ray Bennett.

DEATH WISH
Fotomat Corp; Order No. B0091 for ½" Beta II, V0091 for ½" VHS; 1974 • color; 1 hr, 33 min; ½" Beta II, ½" VHS • Sale: $49.95; Rental: $9.95/up to 5 days, applicable to purchase

- -
Paramount Home Video; 1974 • color; 1 hr, 33 min; ½" Beta II, ½" VHS • Sale: $59.95

Offers a violent, controversial film about a liberal who has a change of opinion after his wife and daughter are violently attacked. Follows him as he turns vigilante and stalks the streets of New York on the prowl for muggers, hoodlums, and the like. Stars Charles Bronson, Vincent Gardenia, William Redfield, and Hope Lange.

THE DEBAUCHERS
Quality X Video Cassette Company; Date not listed • color; 1 hr, 16 min; ½" Beta I, ½" Beta II, ½" VHS • Sale: $99.50; Lease: $19

Presents a pornographic film.

DEBBY DOES DALLAS
Direct Video; 1979 • color; 1 hr, 20 min; ½" Beta II, ½" VHS • Sale: $99.50

Presents a pornographic film.

THE DEEP
Columbia Pictures Home Entertainment; 1977 • color; 2 hrs, 3 min; ½" Beta II, ½" VHS • Sale: $59.95
- -
Fotomat Corp; Order No. B0421 for ½" Beta II, V0421 for ½" VHS; 1977 • color; 2 hrs, 5 min; ½" Beta II, ½" VHS • Sale: $54.95; Rental: $9.95/5 days
- -
Time-Life Video Club Inc; 1977 • color; 2 hrs, 3 min; ½" Beta II, ½" VHS • Sale: $59.95 to members

Offers underwater suspense in Peter Benchley's tale of a couple who innocently stumble on a cache of contraband off Bermuda. Features Jacqueline Bisset, Nick Nolte, and Robert Shaw, under the direction of Peter Yates.

THE DEEP SIX
Fotomat Corp; Order No. B0125 for ½" Beta II, V0125 for ½" VHS; 1958 • color; 1 hr, 50 min; ½" Beta II, ½" VHS • Sale: $39.95; Rental: $7.95/up to 5 days, applicable to purchase
- -
Video Communications Inc; 1958 • color; 1 hr, 48 min; ½" Beta II, ½" VHS • Sale: $54.95

Examines a Quaker naval officer during World War II who compensates for past inaction by heading a dangerous shore mission. Stars Alan Ladd, William Bendix, James Whitmore, Keenan Wynn, Efrem Zimbalist, Jr., and Joey Bishop.

THE DEER HUNTER
MCA Videocassette, Inc; Order No. 88000; 1978 •

color; 3 hrs, 3 min; ½" Beta II, ½" VHS • Sale: $82

Presents the saga of a group of blue collar friends from Pennsylvania who must deal directly and indirectly with the Vietnam War. Stars Robert DeNiro, Christopher Walken, John Savage, John Cazale, and Meryl Streep, under Michael Cimino's direction.

Robert De Niro in
The Deer Hunter.

A DELICATE BALANCE
Magnetic Video Corporation; 1974 • color; 2 hrs, 14 min; ½" Beta II, ½" VHS • Sale: $80
- -
MCA DiscoVision; Order No. 10-013; 1973 • color; 2 hrs, 14 min; LaserVision • Sale: $24.95

Offers the American Film Theatre adaptation of Edward Albee's play about a Connecticut family with hostile feelings towards one another. Stars Katharine Hepburn, Paul Scofield, Lee Remick, Kate Reid, Joseph Cotton, and Betsy Blair.

DELIGHTFULLY DANGEROUS
Video T.E.N.; 1945 • b/w; 1 hr, 33 min; ½" Beta II, ½" VHS • Sale: $49.95 for ½" Beta II, 54.95 for ½" VHS

Traces the efforts of two sisters, one a quiet girl, the other a stripper, to win the same man in this romantic comedy with music. Features Jane Powell, Constance Moore, Ralph Bellamy, Arthur Treacher, and the Morton Gould Orchestra.

DELIVERANCE
Fotomat Corp; Order No. B0309 for ½" Beta II, V0309 for ½" VHS; 1972 • color; 1 hr, 45 min; ½" Beta II, ½" VHS • Sale: $59.95
- -
MCA DiscoVision; Order No. W10-519; 1972 • color; 1 hr, 49 min; LaserVision • Sale: $24.95
- -
WCI Home Video Inc; 1972 • color; 1 hr, 49 min; ½" Beta II, ½" VHS • Sale: $55

Adapts for the screen James Dickey's novel concerning four Atlanta businessmen who decide to canoe down the Cahulawasee River. Follows their attempts to survive as they are pursued by Appalachian men for sport, sex, and cruelty. Stars Burt Reynolds, Jon Voight, Ned Beatty, Ronny Cox, and James Dickey, under the direction of John Boorman.

DEMENTIA 13
Budget Video; 1963 • b/w; 1 hr, 15 min; ½" Beta II, ½" VHS • Sale: $44.95

Presents a gory thriller as an axe-murderer terrorizes a lonely Scottish estate. Stars William Campbell and Luana Anders.

THE DEMI-PARADISE
Thunderbird Films; 1945 • b/w; 1 hr, 50 min; ¾" U-Matic, ½" Beta I, ½" Beta II, ½" VHS • Sale: $69.95 for ½" Beta I, $49.95 for ½" Beta II & VHS, $89.95 for ¾"

Recounts the problems of a Russian engineer (played by Laurence Olivier) when he tries to adjust to life in England. Shows his changing relationship with an English woman played by Margaret Rutherford.

THE DENTIST AND THE FATAL GLASS OF BEER
Golden Tapes Video Tape Library; Order No. CC1; Date not listed • b/w; 40 min; ½" Beta II, ½" VHS • Sale: $49.95 for ½" Beta II & VHS, $79.95 for ¾"

Presents two W.C. Fields comedy shorts.

DEPUTY DAWG
Magnetic Video Corporation; Order No. CL-2010; Date not listed • color; 30 min; ½" Beta II, ½" VHS • Sale: $44.95

Features Terrytoon cartoons, including "Space Varmint," "Mighty Mouse," "The Mysterious Package," "Heckle & Jeckle," "Moose on the Loose," "Little Roquefort," "The Haunted Cat," "Astronut," and "Space Cowboy."

THE DESERT FOX
Golden Tapes Video Tape Library; Order No. F-1014; 1951 • color; 1 hr, 27 min; ½" Beta II, ½" VHS • Sale: $49.95 for ½" Beta II & VHS, $124.95 for ¾"
- -
Magnetic Video Corporation; Order No. CL-1014; 1951 • b/w; 1 hr, 27 min; ½" Beta II, ½" VHS • Sale: $44.95
- -
The Video Library; Order No. MV-1014; 1951 • b/w; 1 hr, 27 min; ½" Beta II, ½" VHS • Sale: $54.95

Depicts the defeat of Field Marshal Rommel in World War II Africa and his disillusioned return to Germany. Stars James Mason, Cedric Hardwicke, Jessica Tandy, and Luther Adler, under the direction of Henry Hathaway.

DESERT TRAIL
Cable Films; 1933 • b/w; 54 min; ½" Beta I, ½" Beta II, ½" VHS • Sale: $45 for ½" Beta I, $49.50 for ½" Beta II & VHS

Presents a western in which a woman comes to John Wayne's aid in order to prove his innocence.

DESIRES WITHIN YOUNG GIRLS
Vid America; Order No. 966; Date not listed • color; 1 hr, 18 min; ½" Beta II, ½" VHS • Rental: $12.95/wk

Presents a pornographic film.

DESTINATION SATURN
Cable Films; 1939 • b/w; 1 hr, 30 min; ½" Beta I, ½"

Beta II, ½" VHS • Sale: $65 for ½" Beta I, $49.50 for ½" Beta II & VHS

Offers a version of the Buck Rogers adventures in which Buck travels to the 25th century. Stars Buster Crabbe and Constance Moore.

DESTRY RIDES AGAIN
MCA DiscoVision; Order No. 24-002; 1939 • b/w; 1 hr, 34 min; LaserVision • Sale: $15.95

Adapts the Max Brand story of a peaceful sheriff who comes to town to tame it, and the saloon gal who causes trouble but eventually falls in love with him. Stars James Stewart, Marlene Dietrich, who sings "See What the Boys in the Back Room Will Have," and features Brian Donleavy, Una Merkel, Billy Gilbert, Jack Carson, and Mischa Auer.

THE DETECTIVE
Blackhawk Films, Inc; Order No. 502-49-0038 for ½" Beta II, 515-49-0026 for ½" VHS; 1968 • color; 1 hr, 54 min; ½" Beta II, ½" VHS • Sale: $54.95
- - - - - - - - - - - - - - - - - - -•- - - - - - - - - -
Golden Tapes Video Tape Library; Order No. F-1018; 1968 • color; 1 hr, 56 min; ½" Beta II, ½" VHS • Sale: $49.95 for ½" Beta II & VHS, $124.95 for ¾"
- -
Magnetic Video Corporation; Order No. CL-1018; 1968 • color; 1 hr, 54 min; ½" Beta II, ½" VHS • Sale: $44.95
- -
The Video Library; Order No. MV-1018; 1968 • color; 1 hr, 54 min; ½" Beta II, ½" VHS • Sale: $54.95

Presents a behind-the-scenes look at a big city police department based on Roderick Thorpe's best-selling novel. Follows a detective's investigation into the murder of a young homosexual. Stars Frank Sinatra, Jack Klugman, and Jacqueline Bisset.

THE DEVIL AT 4 O'CLOCK
National Film and Video Center; 1961 • color; 2 hrs, 6 min; ¾" U-Matic, ½" Beta II, ½" VHS • Rental: $49/1 showing

Sets up a situation in which three criminals and a young priest parachute into the mountains of a small Pacific island to rescue the staff and patients of a remote hospital after an earthquake and volcanic eruption devastate the island. Stars Spencer Tracy and Frank Sinatra.

DEVIL DOLL
Cinema Concepts, Inc.; 1964 • b/w; 1 hr, 20 min; ¾" U-Matic, ½" Beta II, ½" VHS • Sale: $54.95 for ½" Beta II & VHS, $149.95 for ¾"
- -
The Video Library; Order No. CC-0111; 1964 • b/w; 1 hr, 20 min; ½" Beta II, ½" VHS • Sale: $54.95

Presents a film about a crazed hypnotist and a wooden dummy who is able to walk and talk without any visible control by its master. Stars Bryant Haliday, William Sylvester, and Yvonne Romain.

THE DEVIL'S DAUGHTER
Reel Images Inc; Order No. 15; 1939 • b/w; 52 min; ½" Beta II, ½" VHS • Sale: $39.95 for ½" Beta II, $42.95 for ½" VHS

Relates a tale of a sister's hatred set against the background of voodoo drums in the West Indies. Features comic relief provided by Hamtree Harrington. Stars Nina Mae McKinney.

THE DEVIL'S NIGHTMARE
Tape Club of America; Order No. 2704 B; 1972 • color; 1 hr, 30 min; ½" Beta II, ½" VHS • Sale: 54.95

Poses the question: "Can you be possessed by the devil?" Tells a tale of exorcism, the one last hope for the possessed, and shows how the devil wins this time. Stars Erika Blane, Jean Servais, Daniel Emilfork and Lucien Raimbourg.

THE DEVIL'S RAIN
Video Communications Inc; Order No. 1183; 1975 • color; 1 hr, 25 min; 1/2" Beta II, 1/2" VHS • Sale: $54.95

Offers a tale of devil worshippers. Features Ernest Borgnine, Eddie Albert, Ida Lupino, William Shatner, Keenan Wynn, and John Travolta. Includes elaborate special effects and makeup.

DIABOLIQUE
Cinema Concepts, Inc.; 1955 • b/w; 1 hr, 20 min; 3/4" U-Matic, 1/2" Beta II, 1/2" VHS • Sale: $54.95 for 1/2" Beta II & VHS, $149.95 for 3/4"
- -
VCX; Order No. FC113; 1955 • b/w; 1 hr, 47 min; 1/2" Beta II, 1/2" VHS • Sale: $35.00
- -
The Video Library; 1955 • b/w; 1 hr, 20 min; 1/2" Beta II, 1/2" VHS • Sale: $54.95 • Foreign languages: French

Presents a mystery concerning a complicated murder plot concocted by the mistress of a schoolmaster and her lover. Creates an atmosphere of ever-increasing suspense as the story proceeds to its twist ending. Stars Simone Signoret, Vera Clouzot, and Paul Meurisse, under the direction of Henri-Georges Clouzot.

DIAL-A-GIRL
Tape Club of America; Order No. 2815 B; Date not listed • color; 1 hr, 30 min; 1/2" Beta II, 1/2" VHS • Sale: $54.95

Presents a pornographic film.

DIAMONDS
Magnetic Video Corporation; Order No. CL-4019; 1975 • color; 1 hr, 48 min; 1/2" Beta II, 1/2" VHS • Sale: $54.95

Features the world's greatest safecracker pitted against the world's toughest vault, which houses a billion dollars in diamonds. Stars Robert Shaw and Richard Roundtree.

DIARY OF A MAD HOUSEWIFE
MCA DiscoVision; Order No. 10-006; 1970 • color; 1 hr, 40 min;LaserVision • Sale: $24.95

Shows the dilemma of a dissatisfied housewife living in a suburban townhouse and married to an egomaniacal social-climber, who demands she help his career at the expense of her own sanity and individuality. Stars Carrie Snodgrass, Richard Benjamin, and Frank Langella, in an adaptation of the Sue Kaufmann novel.

THE DIARY OF ANNE FRANK
Magnetic Video Corporation; Order No. CL-1074; 1959 • color; 2 hrs, 50 min; 1/2" Beta II, 1/2" VHS • Sale: $64.95

Dramatizes the diary of a young Jewish woman, describing her family's two years of hiding in an Amsterdam attic to escape being shipped to a concentration camp. Details her courage against the daily terror; continues until shortly before the Nazi police discover the group. Stars Millie Perkins, Joseph Schildkraut, Shelley Winters, Richard Beymer, and Ed Wynn.

DICK DEADEYE
FHV Entertainment, Inc; Date not listed • color; 1 hr, 27 min ; 1/2" Beta II, 1/2" VHS • Sale: $49.95

Offers a zany animated musical in which Dick Deadeye is the only man who can save the world from evil sorcerers, bloodthirsty pirates, and the clutches of boredom.

DICK TRACY
Reel Images Inc; Order No. 552; 1937 • b/w; 4 hrs, 50 min; 1/2" Beta II, 1/2" VHS • Sale: $129.95

Presents, on two videocassettes, a Republic motion picture serial with 15 episodes. Follows the adventures of Dick Tracy as he battles the Spider Gang, which has turned Tracy's brother into a mindless robot. Stars Ralph Byrd, Kay Hughes, Smiley Burnette, Lee Van Atta, Carleton Young, and Francis X. Bushman.

DICK TRACY DOUBLE FEATURE
Video Communications Inc; Order No. 1026; Date not listed • b/w; 2 hrs, 2 min; 1/2" Beta II, 1/2" VHS • Sale: $74.95

Offers two detective thrillers featuring Dick Tracy as portrayed by two different stars. Begins with Morgan Conway in "Dick Tracy—Detective" tracking down "Scarface," and concludes with "Dick Tracy's Dilemma," starring Ralph Byrd.

DICK TRACY MEETS GRUESOME
Northeast Video and Sound, Inc; 1947 • b/w; 1 hr, 10 min; 3/4" U-Matic, 1/2" EIAJ, 1/2" Beta II, 1/2" VHS • Sale: $179; Rental: $70/wk

Follows the detective as he tracks down a gang of bank robbers who are using a special nerve gas. Stars Ralph Byrd, Boris Karloff, Anne Gwynne, and Edward Ashley.

DICK TRACY'S DILEMMA
Reel Images Inc; Order No. 785; 1947 • b/w; 1 hr, 1 min; 1/2" Beta II, 1/2" VHS • Sale: $39.95 for 1/2" Beta II, $42.95 for 1/2" VHS

Presents Chester Gould's comic strip detective in pursuit of the Claw, who kills with his hook-hand. Features Ralph Byrd, Lyle Latell, Kay Christopher, and Jack Lambert.

A DIFFERENT STORY
Magnetic Video Corporation; Order No. CL-4051; 1978 • color; 1 hr, 47 min; 1/2" Beta II, 1/2" VHS • Sale: $54.95

Spotlights the contemporary love story of two of the most improbable lovers imaginable: a man and a woman, both of them gay. Stars Perry King, Meg Foster, and Valerie Curtin.

DINGAKA
Magnetic Video Corporation; Order No. CL-5004; 1965 • color; 1 hr, 32 min; 1/2" Beta II, 1/2" VHS • Sale: $54.95

Examines the concept of justice in contemporary Africa as a tribesman tries to kill the man who murders his daughter and is himself convicted of attempted murder by the white legal authorities. Stars Stanley Baker and Juliet Prowse.

DINKY DUCK
Magnetic Video Corporation; Order No. CL-2036; Date not listed • color; 30 min; 1/2" Beta II, 1/2" VHS • Sale: $34.95

Presents a compilation of Terrytoon animated cartoons featuring Dinky Duck.

DINNER AT THE RITZ
Reel Images Inc; Order No. 445; 1938 • b/w; 1 hr, 18

min; 1/2" Beta II, 1/2" VHS • Sale: $49.95 for 1/2" Beta II, 52.95 for 1/2" VHS

Presents a melodrama in which the daughter of a murdered Parisian banker sets out to find his murderer. Stars David Niven, Annabella, and Paul Lukas.

THE DIRTY DOZEN
MGM/CBS Home Video; Order No. M70008; 1967 • color; 2 hrs, 30 min; 1/2" Beta II, 1/2" VHS • Sale: $59.95

- -

Niles Cinema; Order No. GM-725; 1967 • color; 2 hrs, 30 min; 1/2" Beta II1/2" VHS • Sale: $59.95

- -

RCA SelectaVision VideoDiscs; Order No. 00203; 1967 • color; 2 hrs, 30 min; CED • Sale: $22.98

Follows the attempts of an Army major to train a group of criminal misfits into a fighting unit for a suicidal mission into Nazi territory. Stars Lee Marvin, Robert Ryan, Ernest Borgnine, Charles Bronson, Jim Brown, John Cassavetes, Richard Jaekel, George Kennedy, Trini Lopez, Telly Savalas, Ralph Meeker, Clint Walker, and Robert Webber.

DIRTY GERTIE FROM HARLEM USA
Reel Images Inc; Order No. 454; 1946 • b/w; 1 hr; 1/2" Beta II, 1/2" VHS • Sale: $39.95 for 1/2" Beta II, 42.95 for 1/2" VHS

Presents an all-black variation of Somerset Maugham's "Rain." Relates the story of Gertie, who goes to Trinidad to hide out from the boyfriend she has jilted. Features the direction of Spencer Williams.

DIRTY HARRY
Fotomat Corp ; Order No. B0305 for 1/2" Beta II, V0305 for 1/2" VHS; 1971 • color; 1 hr, 43 min; 1/2" Beta II, 1/2" VHS • Sale: $59.95

- -

MCA DiscoVision; Order No. W12-514; 1972 • color; 1 hr, 43 min; LaserVision • Sale: $24.95

- -

WCI Home Video Inc; 1971 • color; 1 hr, 42 min; 1/2" Beta II, 1/2" VHS • Sale: $55

Follows San Francisco Police Detective Harry Calahan as he takes on jobs considered too dirty for others. Portrays a lawman who prefers to rely more on his .44 Magnum than the law. Stars Clint Eastwood, Harry Guardino, Reni Santoni, Andy Robinson, and John Vernon, under the direction of Don Siegel.

DIRTY MARY, CRAZY LARRY
Magnetic Video Corporation; Order No. CL-1053; 1974 • color; 1 hr, 32 min; 1/2" Beta II, 1/2" VHS • Sale: $54.95

Offers a comedy in which a race car driver, an ace mechanic, and an excitement-seeking young lady steal$150.000 from a supermarket. Depicts an armada of police closing in on the escaping trio. Stars Peter Fonda, Susan George, Adam Roarke, and Vic Morrow.

DISCO 9000
Home Theatre Movies; 1977 • color; 1 hr, 41 min; 1/2" Beta II, 1/2" VHS • Sale: $54.96

Presents a movie about the action at a disco. Stars John Poole, Jeanie Bell, and Johnnie Taylor.

DISNEY CARTOON PARADE, VOLUME I
RCA SelectaVision VideoDiscs; Order No. 00709; Date not listed • color; 1 hr, 36 min; CED • Sale: $19.98

Presents two complete cartoon shows from the Walt Disney Studios. Includes "On Vacation with Mickey Mouse and Friends," with Mickey, Minnie, Pluto, and Goofy; and "The Adventures of Chip 'n' Dale," with Donald Duck and Peg-leg Pete, the bank robber.

DISORDER IN THE COURT
Northeast Video and Sound, Inc; Order No. 101S; 1936 • b/w; 20 min; 3/4" U-Matic, 1/2" EIAJ, 1/2" Beta II, 1/2" VHS • Sale: $79; Rental: $29/wk

Features the Three Stooges in a comedy short with crazy antics and even crazier predicaments.

D.O.A.
Video Communications Inc; Order No. 1027; 1950 • b/w; 1 hr, 23 min; 1/2" Beta II, 1/2" VHS • Sale: $54.95

Shows how a man is accidentally given a lethal, slow-acting poison and, as his time to live runs out, how he frantically seeks to learn the truth as to why he was poisoned. Relates how he eventually uncovers a grim maze of deceit and death. Stars Edmond O'Brien and Luther Adler.

DOCTOR DOLITTLE
Blackhawk Films, Inc; Order No. 502-49-0005 for 1/2" Beta II, 515-49-0014 for 1/2" VHS; 1967 • color; 2 hrs, 32 min; 1/2" Beta II, 1/2" VHS • Sale: $74.95

- -

Golden Tapes Video Tape Library; Order No. F-1025; 1968 • color; 2 hrs, 32 min; 1/2" Beta II, 1/2" VHS • Sale: $49.95 for 1/2" Beta II & VHS, $124.95 for 3/4"

- -

Magnetic Video Corporation; Order No. CL-1025; 1967 • color; 2 hrs, 32 min; 1/2" Beta II, 1/2" VHS • Sale: $64.95

- -

The Video Library; Order No. MV-1025; 1967 • color; 2 hrs, 32 min; 1/2" Beta II, 1/2" VHS • Sale: $74.95

Presents a musical fantasy based on the stories of Hugh Lofting. Concerns the adventures of a nineteenth-century English doctor who is able to communicate with his animal patients. Stars Rex Harrison and Samantha Eggar.

Julie Christie and Omar Sharif in *Doctor Zhivago*.

45

DOCTOR FAUSTUS
National Film and Video Center; 1968 • color; 1 hr, 33 min; ¾" U-Matic, ½" Beta II, ½" VHS • Rental: $89/1 showing

Dramatizes Christopher Marlowe's version of the Faust story: an aging scholar sells his soul to the devil in exchange for youth, knowledge, power, and a woman, and is distracted by Mephistopheles with visions and games so he cannot realize the consequences of his bargain—and repent. Stars Richard Burton and Elizabeth Taylor.

DOCTOR IN TROUBLE
Tape Club of America; Order No. 2212 B; 1970 • color; 1 hr, 30 min; ½" Beta II, ½" VHS • Sale: $54.95

Offers a comedy feature in which a daring "Doctor Team" is portrayed in all their adventures with the ladies surrounding them. Stars Leslie Phillips, Robert Morley, Harry Secombe, and James Robertson Justice.

DOCTOR ZHIVAGO
MGM/CBS Home Video; Order No. M90003; 1965 • color; 3 hrs, 17 min; ½" Beta II, ½" VHS • Sale: $89.95
- -
Niles Cinema; Order No. GM-726; 1965 • color; 3 hrs, 17 min; ½" Beta II, ½" VHS • Sale: $89.95

Presents, on two videocassettes, the David Lean film adaptation of Boris Pasternak's novel of life during the Russian Revolution. Stars Omar Sharif, Julie Christie, Alec Guinness, Geraldine Chaplin, Rod Steiger, Ralph Richardson, Tom Courtney, and Rita Tushingham.

DOG DAY AFTERNOON
WCI Home Video Inc; 1975 • color; 2 hrs, 10 min; ½" Beta II, ½" VHS • Sale: $60

Dramatizes the true story of a man who attempted to rob a Brooklyn bank in order to raise the money needed for his lover's sex-change operation. Stars Al Pacino, John Cazale, Charles Durning, and James Broderick, under the direction of Sidney Lumet.

DOLL FACE
National Film and Video Center; 1945 • b/w; 1 hr, 20 min; ¾" U-Matic, ½" Beta II, ½" VHS • Rental: $49/1 showing

Depicts the life of a woman who charms everyone around her—a life of love and confusion. Features Perry Como singing "Huba-Huba" and Carmen Miranda doing "Chico-Chico," with a cast that includes Dennis O'Keefe.

DOLLARS
National Film and Video Center; 1972 • color; 2 hrs; ¾" U-Matic, ½" Beta II, ½" VHS • Rental: $79/1 showing

Involves complicated bank heist, in which the bank's security expert fakes a bomb scare as an excuse to lock himself in the safety deposit vault, where he transfers the contents of the boxes belonging to three criminals into one held by his girlfriend, Dawn Devine. Stars Goldie Hawn, Warren Beatty, and Gert Frobe.

DON'T DRINK THE WATER
Magnetic Video Corporation; Order No. CL-4048; 1969 • color; 1 hr, 40 min; ½" Beta II, ½" VHS • Sale: $54.95

Concerns a family stranded behind the Iron Curtain after a hijacking who are suspected of being spies. Stars Jackie Gleason and Estelle Parsons in this comedy based on Woody Allen's play.

DON'T FENCE ME IN; SHERIFF OF WICHITA
The Nostalgia Merchant; Order No. 5004; 1945, 1948 • b/w; 2 hrs; ½" Beta II, ½" VHS • Sale: $59.95

Presents a western double feature. Opens with Roy Rogers protecting the legend of "Wildcat" Kelly from reporter Dale Evans, in "Don't Fence Me In." Follows with "Sheriff of Wichita" in which a frontier investigator goes to a deserted outpost to solve a crime; stars Allan "Rocky" Lane.

DON'T GIVE UP THE SHIP
Magnetic Video Corporation; Order No. CL-2021; 1959 • color; 1 hr, 29 min; ½" Beta II, ½" VHS • Sale: $54.95
- -
Red Fox, Inc; Order No. CL-2021; 1959 • b/w; 1 hr, 29 min; ½" Beta II, ½" VHS • Sale: $54.95

Spotlights the antics of Jerry Lewis in the story of a missing Navy destroyer after World War II. Co-stars Dina Merrill and Mickey Shaughnessy, under the direction of Norman Taurog.

DON'T LOOK IN THE BASEMENT
Video Communications Inc; 1972 • color; 1 hr, 35 min; ½" Beta II, ½" VHS • Sale: $54.95

Reveals the mayhem that results in an eerie insane asylum when the inmates stage a rebellion. Features William Bill McGhee, Anne Macadams, and Rosie Holotik.

DON'T LOOK NOW
Niles Cinema; Order No. PP-8704; 1973 • color; 1 hr, 50 min; ½" Beta II, ½" VHS • Sale: $59.95
- -
Paramount Home Video; Order No. 8704; 1973 • color; 1 hr, 50 min; ½" Beta II, ½" VHS • Sale: $66.95

Adapts for the screen Daphne DuMaurier's story of a young British couple whose daughter dies in a drowning accident but seems to reappear on a visit to Venice. Stars Donald Sutherland and Julie Christie, under Nicolas Roeg's direction.

DON'T RAISE THE BRIDGE, LOWER THE RIVER
Columbia Pictures Home Entertainment; 1968 • color; 1 hr, 39 min; ½" Beta II, ½" VHS • Sale: $59.95

Presents Jerry Lewis in a comedy about an American in England trying to strike it rich without wrecking his marriage. Co-stars Terry-Thomas, Jacqueline Pearce, Bernard Cribbins, and Patricia Routledge, under the direction of Jerry Paris.

DOOMED TO DIE
Cable Films ; 1940 • b/w; 1 hr, 8 min; ½" Beta I, ½" Beta II, ½" VHS • Sale: $65 for ½" Beta I, $49.50 for ½" Beta II & VHS

Presents Boris Karloff as the super sleuth, Mr. Wong, in a mystery thriller.

DOUBLE INDEMNITY
MCA DiscoVision; Order No. 21-004; 1944 • b/w; 1 hr, 47 min; LaserVision • Sale: $15.95

Offers a murder mystery set in sunny California where an insurance agent and a blonde plan to murder her husband for his insurance money. Features a screenplay by Billy Wilder and Raymond Chandler. Stars Barbara Stanwyck, Fred MacMurray, Edward G. Robinson, Porter Hall, and Tom Powers, under Billy Wilder's direction.

THE DOUBLE MCGUFFIN
Fotomat Corp; Order No. B0407 for ½" Beta II, V0407

Barbara Stanwyck and Fred MacMurray in *Double Indemnity.*

for ½″ VHS; 1979 • color; 1 hr, 40 min; ½″ Beta II, ½″ VHS • Sale: $49.95; Rental: $7.95/5 days

Presents a comedy-thriller from the creator of "Benji." Follows the attempts of six teenagers to alert the authorities to an assassination plot. Features Ernest Borgnine, George Kennedy, Elke Sommer, Ed "Too Tall" Jones, Lyle Alzado, and Rod Browning.

DOWN TO EARTH

National Film and Video Center; 1947 • color; 1 hr, 41 min; ¾″ U-Matic, ½″ Beta II, ½″ VHS • Rental: $69/1 showing

Stars Rita Hayworth as the muse of dance who comes down from Mount Parnassus to star in a jazz musical about the Nine Muses. Co-stars Larry Parks, Roland Culver, James Gleason, Edward Everett Horton, Adele Jergens, and William Frawley.

DOWNHILL RACER

Niles Cinema; Order No. PP-6910; 1969 • color; 1 hr, 42 min; ½″ Beta II, ½″ VHS • Sale: $59.95

- -

Paramount Home Video; Order No. 6910; 1969 • color; 1 hr, 42 min; ½″ Beta II, ½″ VHS • Sale: $62.95

Studies the world of athletic competition as an Olympic-hopeful must decide which means more to him: his new love or being "the best." Provides character study of the empty life-style of a man driven by his own ego. Includes actual sport footage and location photography. Stars Robert Redford, Gene Hackman, and Camilla Sparv, under the direction of Michael Ritchie.

DR. FEELGOOD

Monarch Releasing Corporation; Date not listed • color; 1 hr, 20 min; ¾″ U-Matic • Sale: $350

Presents a pornographic film.

DR. KILDARE'S STRANGE CASE

Video T.E.N. • b/w; ½″ Beta II, ½″ VHS • Sale: $49.95 for ½″ Beta II, $54.95 for ½″ VHS

Highlights Doctors Kildare and Gillespie trying to treat a man with a dangerous mental disorder, and the

young doctor's romance with a nurse. Stars Lew Ayres, Lionel Barrymore, Laraine Day, Shepperd Strudwick, and Samuel S. Hinds.

DR. SYN

Cable Films; 1937 • b/w; 1 hr, 20 min; ½″ Beta I, ½″ Beta II, ½″ VHS • Sale: $65 for ½″ Beta I, $49.50 for ½″ Beta II & VHS

Offers a film adaptation of Russell Thorndyke's novel about the smuggling vicar of Dymchurch. Stars George Arliss, Margaret Lockwood, and John Loder.

DRACULA

MCA DiscoVision; Order No. 23-001; 1931 • b/w; 1 hr, 15 min; LaserVision • Sale: $15.95

- -

MCA Videocassette, Inc; Order No. 55003; 1931 • b/w; 1 hr, 15 min; ½″ Beta II, ½″ VHS • Sale: $50

Presents the film version of the stage role that made Bela Lugosi famous. Offers the count from Transylvania who has been "undead" for 700 years challenging ladies from London. Adapts the novel and play by Bram Stoker. Stars Lugosi, David Manners, Helen Chandler, and Dwight Frye, under the direction of Tod Browning.

DRACULA

MCA Videocassette, Inc; Order No. 66004; 1979 • color; 2 hrs; ½″ Beta II, ½″ VHS • Sale: $60

Presents a new version of the Bram Stoker story based on the Broadway play. Stars Frank Langella, Kate Nelligan, and Donald Pleasance. Features on-location shots of Cornwall, England.

DRACULA SUCKS

Meda/Media Home Entertainment Inc; Date not listed • color; 1 hr, 31 min; ½″ Beta II, ½″ VHS • Sale: $54.95

Presents a pornographic film.

A DREAM OF PASSION

Magnetic Video Corporation; Order No. CL-4055;

1978 • color; 1 hr, 50 min; 1/2″ Beta II, 1/2″ VHS • Sale: $54.95

Offers a psychological study of the fascination of an actress portraying Medea with a real-life mother who has murdered her children to spite her unfaithful husband. Stars Melina Mercouri and Ellen Burstyn, under the direction of Jules Dassin.

DREAMER
Magnetic Video Corporation; Order No. 1096; 1979 • color; 1 hr, 26 min; 1/2″ Beta II, 1/2″ VHS • Sale: $59.95
- -
Niles Cinema; Order No. CL-1096; 1979 • color; 1 hr, 26 min; 1/2″ Beta II, 1/2″ VHS • Sale: $59.95

Offers a "Rocky"-type story set in the world of professional bowling. Stars Tim Matheson, Susan Blakely, Jack Warden, and Richard B. Schull.

DREAMING LIPS
Blackhawk Films, Inc; Order No. 506-30-0826 for 1/2″ Beta II, 525-30-0826 for 1/2″ VHS; Date not listed • b/w; 1 hr, 10 min; 1/2″ Beta II, 1/2″ VHS • Sale: $49.95

Depicts what happens when the wife of an orchestra conductor falls in love with a violinist friend of her husband's. Features Raymond Massey and Elizabeth Bergner.

DREAMING OUT LOUD
Video T.E.N.; 1940 • b/w; 1 hr, 5 min ; 1/2″ Beta II, 1/2″ VHS • Sale: $49.95 for 1/2″ Beta II, $54.95 for 1/2″ VHS

Showcases the radio team of Lum and Abner in a film about a small town trying to bring progress in the form of a mobile medical unit. Includes Frances Langford, Frank Craven, Robert Wilcox, and Phil Harris.

DRESSED TO KILL
Budget Video; 1946 • b/w; 1 hr, 12 min; 1/2″ Beta II, 1/2″ VHS • Sale: $44.95
- -
Reel Images Inc; Order No. 714; 1946 • b/w; 1 hr, 12 min; 1/2″ Beta II, 1/2″ VHS • Sale: $49.95 for 1/2″ Beta II, $52.95 for 1/2″ VHS

Shows Sherlock Holmes and Dr. Watson on the trail of a crime ring that has stolen a set of bank plates from the Bank of England. Presents Holmes faced with the puzzling clue of three identical music boxes. Stars Basil Rathbone and Nigel Bruce.

DRUM BEAT
Fotomat Corp; Order No. B0113 for 1/2″ Beta II, V0113 for 1/2″ VHS; 1954 • color; 1 hr, 51 min; 1/2″ Beta II, 1/2″ VHS • Sale; $39.95; Rental: $7.95/up to 5 days, applicable to purchase
- -
Video Communications Inc; 1954 • color; 1 hr, 47 min; 1/2″ Beta II, 1/2″ VHS • Sale: $54.95

Depicts an Indian fighter after the Civil War assigned to negotiate peacefully with a warring Indian group. Stars Alan Ladd and Charles Bronson.

THE DUCHESS AND THE DIRTWATER FOX
Magnetic Video Corporation; Order No. CL-1059; 1976 • color; 1 hr, 44 min; 1/2″ Beta II, 1/2″ VHS • Sale: $54.95

Presents a western which uses contemporary humor about a card sharp and a dance hall girl. Stars George Segal, Goldie Hawn, Conrad Janis, and Roy Jenson, under the direction of Melvin Frank.

DUCK SOUP
MCA Videocassette, Inc; Order No. 55012; 1933 • b/w; 1 hr, 10 min; 1/2″ Beta II, 1/2″ VHS • Sale: $55

Offers the Marx Brothers in a comedy about a mythical land called Freedonia with Groucho as Rufus T. Firefly, the King. Stars Groucho, Harpo, Chico, and Zeppo Marx, Margaret Dumont, Louis Calhern, and Edgar Kennedy, under the direction of Leo McCarey.

DUEL
MCA DiscoVision; Order No. 19-002; 1971 • color; 1 hr, 31 min; LaserVision • Sale: $15.95

Presents a TV movie directed by Steven ("Jaws," "Close Encounterof the Third Kind") Spielberg. Offers a tale of suspense by Richard Matheson, as a businessman finds himself having to drive extremely defensively when a diesel truck repeatedly tries to run him off the road—and he can't ever seem to see the driver's face. Stars Dennis Weaver.

THE DUELLISTS
Paramount Home Video; Date not listed • color; 1 hr, 41 min; 1/2″ Beta II, 1/2″ VHS • Sale: $59.95

Presents an adventure-drama based on a factual story by Joseph Conrad. Stars Keith Carradine and Harvey Keitel as two Hussar officers in Napoleon's army who confront each other in a series of violent duels.

DUMMY TROUBLE
Video T.E.N.; 1940 • b/w; 1 hr, 15 min; 1/2″ Beta II, 1/2″ VHS • Sale: $49.95 for 1/2″ Beta II, $54.95 for 1/2″ VHS

Focuses on the 20th anniversary of a department store owner, who due to a series of misunderstandings, almost loses his wife in this comedy-drama. Features Harry Langdon, Betty Blythe, and Ralph Byrd.

DUNDER KLUMPEN
Video Gems; 1979 • color; 1 hr, 25 min; 1/2″ Beta II, 1/2″ VHS • Sale: $53.95
- -
Video Warehouse, Inc; Order No. 4005; Date not listed • color; 1 hr, 25 min; 1/2″ Beta II, 1/2″ VHS • Sale: $4495

Presents a Swedish animated film that provides a magical trip to a fantasy land for children.

DUTCH TREAT
Video Home Library; Order No. VX-111; Date not listed • color; 2 hrs; 1/2″ Beta II, 1/2″ VHS • Sale: $99.95

Presents a pornographic film.

D.W. GRIFFITH
Ivy Video; 1912 • b/w; 55 min; 3/4″ U-Matic, 1/2″ Beta II, 1/2″ VHS • Sale: $59.95 for 1/2″ Beta II & VHS, trade-in plan available, $150 for 3/4″

Spotlights the talents of Griffith in his series of Biograph shorts directed between 1908 and 1912. Includes Lionel Barrymore, Mae Marsh and Lillian Gish in "The Battle of Elderbush Gulch", Mary Pickford and Lillian Gish in "Female of the Species", and two other films.

D.W. GRIFFITH: AN AMERICAN GENIUS
Blackhawk Films, Inc; Order No. 506-34-0682 for 1/2″ Beta II, 525-34-0682 for 1/2″ VHS; 1975 • color; 56 min; 3/4″ U-Matic, 1/2″ Beta I, 1/2″ Beta II, 1/2″ VHS • Sale: $59.95 for 1/2″ Beta I, $49.95 for 1/2″ Beta II & VHS, $69.95 for 3/4″

Presents a documentary look at the work of D.W. Griffith, narrated by film critic Richard Schickel. Includes excerpts from early Biographs, "Birth of a Nation," the ice floe rescue from "Way Down East," and "Intolerance." Reveals that Griffith was more concerned with ideas and stories of his own choosing, and using film as an expressive medium, than he was influenced by the box office.

DYNAMITE CHICKEN
Cinema Concepts, Inc.; 1972 • color; 1 hr, 16 min; 3/4" U-Matic, 1/2" Beta II, 1/2" VHS • Sale: $54.95 for 1/2" Beta II & VHS, 149.95 for 3/4"

- -
The Video Library; Order No. CC-0113; Date not listed • color; 1 hr, 16 min; 1/2" Beta II, 1/2" VHS • Sale: $54.95

Presents a documentary focusing on the attitudes of American youth in the 1970's. Includes performances by Joan Baez, Lenny Bruce, Jimi Hendrix, B.B. King, Richard Pryor, Sha-Na-Na, Nina Simone and others.

DYNAMITE RANCH; LOCAL BADMAN
Video Communications Inc; Order No. 1119; 1932 • b/w; 2 hrs; 1/2" Beta II, 1/2" VHS • Sale: $74.95

Offers a western double feature. Stars Ken Maynard in "Dynamite Ranch," a story of the struggle of ranchers to hold on to their property. Presents Hoot Gibson in "Local Badman," a comedy set in the Old West.

THE EAGLE
Golden Tapes Video Tape Library; Order No. CD10; 1925 • b/w; 1 hr, 17 min; 1/2" Beta II, 1/2" VHS • Sale: $49.95 for 1/2" Beta II & VHS, $124.95 for 3/4"

- -
Ivy Video; 1926 • b/w; 1 hr, 12 min; 3/4" U-Matic, 1/2" Beta II, 1/2" VHS • Sale: $59.95 for 1/2" Beta II & VHS, trade-in plan available, $195 for 3/4"

Recounts the story of a Russian Robin Hood, an evil land owner, and his beautiful daughter during the time of Catherine the Great. Stars Rudolf Valentino in this silent film.

THE EAGLE HAS LANDED
Magnetic Video Corporation; Order No. 9006; 1977 • color; 2 hrs, 3 min; 1/2" Beta II, 1/2" VHS • Sale: $59.95

Centers on a fanciful plot set during World War II as the Nazi High Command decides to kidnap Winston Churchill and use him as ransom. Stars Michael Caine, Donald Sutherland, Robert Duvall, Jenny Agutter, Donald Pleasance, and Anthony Quayle.

THE EAGLE'S BROOD
Videobrary Inc; Order No. 8; 1935 • b/w; 59 min; 1/2" Beta II, 1/2" VHS • Sale: $39.95

Presents a Hopalong Cassidy western. Offers Cassidy "undercover" trying to find a young boy who witnessed the murder of his parents, before the murdering gang can locate him. Stars William Boyd and George "Gabby" Hayes.

EARTH VS. THE FLYING SAUCERS
National Film and Video Center; 1956 • b/w; 1 hr, 23 min; 3/4" U-Matic, 1/2" Beta II, 1/2" VHS • Rental: $49/1 showing

Recounts how experimental satellites are mysteriously shot down as soon as they are launched and strange humanoids in flying saucers attack the air base from which the rockets were sent. Stars Hugh Marlowe, Joan Taylor, and Donald Curtis.

EARTHQUAKE
MCA DiscoVision; Order No. 10-002; 1974 • color; 2 hrs, 9 min; LaserVision • Sale: $24.95

Shows what happens to people in Los Angeles before, during, and after a monumental natural disaster, and tells many personal stories along the way. Uses Academy Award-winning special effects. Stars Charlton Heston, Ava GardGeorge Kennedy, Lorne Green, and Genevieve Bujold.

James Dean in *East of Eden*.

EAST OF EDEN
MCA DiscoVision; Order No. W21-515; 1955 • color; 1 hr, 55 min; LaserVision • Sale: $24.95

- -
WCI Home Video Inc; 1955 • color; 1 hr, 55 min; 1/2" Beta II, 1/2" VHS • Sale: $55

Adapts John Steinbeck's novel and introduces James Dean in a film which tells the story of two brothers' rivalry for the love of their stern father. Stars James Dean, Raymond Massey, Julie Harris, Jo Van Fleet, Burl Ives, and Albert Dekker, under the direction of Elia Kazan.

EAST SIDE KIDS
Video Tape Network; Order No. CD 627 for 1/2" Beta II, CD 628 for 1/2" VHS; 1940 • b/w; 1 hr; 1/2" Beta II, 1/2" VHS • Sale: $49.95

Offers the mad adventure of murder and mayhem that started the East Side Kids series. Stars Leo Gorcey, Huntz Hall, and Bobby Jordan.

THE EAST SIDE KIDS: LET'S GET TOUGH
Video Tape Network; Order No. CD 629 for 1/2" Beta II,

CD 630 for ½" VHS; 1942 • b/w; 1 hr; ½" Beta II, ½" VHS • Sale: $49.95

Presents the East Side Kids as they tackle a spy ring and capture the deadly saboteurs of the Black Dragon Society.

THE EAST SIDE KIDS: SMART ALECKS
Video Tape Network; Order No. CD 631 for ½" Beta II, CD 632 for ½" VHS; 1942 • b/w; 1 hr; ½" Beta II, ½" VHS • Sale: $49.95

Pits the East Side Kids against the police and gangsters as they hunt a convict to prevent the execution of an innocent man.

EASTER PARADE
RCA SelectaVision VideoDiscs; Order No. 00213; 1948 • color; 1 hr, 43 min; CED • Sale: $14.98

Presents an Irving Berlin musical about a dancer who takes on a new partner while trying to forget his former one. Stars Fred Astaire, Judy Garland, Peter Lawford, Ann Miller, and Jules Munshin.

Fred Astaire and Judy Garland in *Easter Parade.*

EASY ALICE
Quality X Video Cassette Company; Date not listed • color; 1 hr, 15 min; ¾" U-Matic, ½" Beta II, ½" VHS • Sale: $99.50

Presents a pornographic film.

EASY COME, EASY GO
Fotomat Corp; Order No. B0263 for ½" Beta II, V0263 for ½" VHS ; 1967 • color; 1 hr, 35 min; ½" Beta II, ½" VHS • Sale: $49.95; Rental: $9.95/up to 5 days, applicable to purchase
- -
Paramount Home Video; Order No. 6615; 1967 • color; 1 hr, 35 min; ½" Beta II, ½" VHS • Sale: $59.95

Offers a musical adventure about a Navy frogman who

discovers a treasure chest and tries to bring it to the surface, with the help of a beautiful girl—and in spite of two unscrupulous characters. Stars Elvis Presley, Dodie Marshall, Pat Priest, Pat Harrington, Frank McHugh, and Elsa Lanchester, under the direction of John ("All in the Family") Rich.

EASY WOMAN
Mitchell Brothers' Film Group; Date not listed • color; 1 hr, 36 min; ½" Beta II, ½" VHS • Sale: $69

Presents a pornographic film.

ECSTASY
Golden Tapes Video Tape Library; Order No. CD1; 1933 • b/w; 1 hr, 22 min; ½" Beta II, ½" VHS • Sale: $49.95 for ½" Beta II & VHS, $124.95 for ¾"

Portrays a young woman who, after marrying an older man, takes a lover her own age. Features explicit scenes that have been praised by critics for their beauty and sophistication. Introduces Hedy Lamarr to the screen in this Czech film under the direction of Gustav Machaty.

THE EIGER SANCTION
MCA DiscoVision; Order No. 12-002; 1975 • color; 2 hrs, 5 min; LaserVision • Sale: $24.95

Adapts the novel by Trevanian, in which a killer comes out of retirement for the asking price of a painting by Pissarro. Uses mountain climbing as a backdrop to create a suspenseful thriller..Stars Clint Eastwood, who also directed, and features George Kennedy and Jack Cassidy.

8½
Time-Life Video Club Inc; 1963 • b/w; 2 hrs, 18 min; ½" Beta II, ½" VHS • Sale: $59.95 to members

Presents Federico Fellini's portrait of a successful film director. Shows the director about to begin his next movie when he realizes his own artistic and emotional mid-life crisis. Follows him as he proceeds to "take the cure" at a resort; depicts his own imaginings, comic and serious. Stars Marcello Mastroianni, Anouk Aimee, and Claudia Cardinale. Offers the English language version.

EIGHTEEN CARAT VIRGIN
Monarch Releasing Corporation; Date not listed • color; 1 hr, 10 min; ¾" U-Matic • Sale: $300

Presents a pornographic film.

EISENSTEIN
Reel Images Inc; Order No. 408; 1958 • b/w; 48 min; ½" Beta II, ½" VHS • Sale: $39.95 for ½" Beta II, $42.95 for ½" VHS

Presents a Soviet-made biography of Sergei Eisenstein, the film director. Includes rare footage of his early life, first films, and famous classics. Provides evidence of Eisenstein's contributions to cinematic editing, montage, composition, and technique.

EL CID
Time-Life Video Club Inc; 1961 • color; 3 hrs, 4 min; ½" Beta II, ½" VHS • Sale: $69.95 to members
- -
Video Communications Inc; Order No. 5001; 1961 • color; 3 hrs, 4 min; ½" Beta II, ½" VHS • Sale: $74.95

Presents a film based on fact and legend, filmed on location in Spain. Details the struggle of this legendary figure to free his people and his country from Moslem occupation. Stars Charlton Heston, Sophia Loren,

Genevieve Page, and Raf Valone, under the direction of Anthony Mann.

EL DORADO
Fotomat Corp; Order No. B0217 for ½" Beta II, V0217 for ½" VHS; 1967 • color; 2 hrs, 6 min; ½" Beta II, ½" VHS • Sale: $69.95; Rental: $9.95/up to 5 days, applicable to purchase

Presents, on two cassettes, a retelling of "Rio Bravo," another Howard Hawks western starring John Wayne, in which an alcoholic sheriff teams up with an old buddy-turned-gunslinger to clean up his town and prevent a greedy cattleman from taking over. Uses humor blended with action. Stars John Wayne, Robert Mitchum, James Caan, Arthur Hunicutt, and Charlene Holt, under Hawks' direction.

ELEANOR AND FRANKLIN
Time-Life Video Club Inc; 1979 • color; 3 hrs, 25 min; ½" Beta II, ½" VHS • Sale: $79.95 to members

Presents a television movie concerning the courtship of Eleanor and President Frenklin D. Roosevelt. Tells the story of the sheltered Eleanor, her meeting with her cousin Franklin, and his mother's objection to their marriage. Shows the world of debutante balls that they both grew up in, the years of the Presidency, Franklin's infidelity and Eleanor's loyalty, Franklin's struggle with polio, and his death. Stars Jane Alexander and Edward Herrmann.

THE ELECTRIC HORSEMAN
MCA Videocassette, Inc; Order No. 66006; 1979 • color; 2 hrs, 1 min; ½" Beta II, ½" VHS • Sale: $60

Relates the tale of a former rodeo star who now makes his living selling cereal. Follows his attempts to return a valuable racehorse to the wilderness, while fending off a determined lady reporter. Features Robert Redford, Jane Fonda, and Willie Nelson, under the direction of Sydney Pollack.

EMANUELLE IN BANGKOK
Monarch Releasing Corporation; Date not listed • color; 1 hr, 36 min; ¾" U-Matic • Sale: $350
- -
Vid America; Order No. 970; Date not listed • color; 1 hr, 34 min; ½" Beta II, ½" VHS • Rental: $12.95/wk

Presents a pornographic film.

EMILIENNE
Vid America; Order No. 968; Date not listed • color; 1 hr, 34 min; ½" Beta II, ½" VHS • Sale: $59.95; Rental: $12.95/wk, applicable to purchase

Presents a pornographic film.

EMMANUELLE
Columbia Pictures Home Entertainment; Date not listed • color; ½" Beta II, ½" VHS • Sale: $59.95
- -
Paramount Home Video; Order No. 8890; 1974 • color; 1 hr, 32 min; ½" Beta II, ½" VHS • Sale: $66.95
- -
Vid America; Order No. 979; 1974 • color; 1 hr, 32 min; ½" Beta II, ½" VHS • Sale: $69.95; Rental: $13.95/wk, applicable to purchase

Presents a pornographic film.

EMPEROR JONES
Northeast Video and Sound, Inc; 1934 • b/w; 1 hr, 12 min; ¾" U-Matic, ½" EIAJ, ½" Beta II, ½" VHS • Sale: $195; Rental: $75/wk

Presents an adaptation of the Eugene O'Neill play con-

cerning Brutus Jones, a Pullman porter who becomes King of Haiti. Features Paul Robeson, Dudley Digges, Frank Wilson, and Fredi Washington.

ENCHANTED FOREST
Video Communications Inc; Order No. 1031; 1945 • color; 1 hr, 17 min; ½" Beta II, ½" VHS • Sale: $54.95

Tells the story of a boy, lost in a dense forest, who is found by an old man who teaches him the value of the life and enchantment of the forest. Features Edmund Lowe, Harry Davenport, and Brenda Joyce.

ENCHANTED ISLAND
Video Communications Inc; Order No. 1032; 1958 • color; 1 hr, 34 min; ½" Beta II, ½" VHS • Sale: $54.95

Recounts a story in which a boatload of hard-bitten whalers in search of provision wander into an enchanted Eden. Shows that what they find are the dreaded Typee warriors, cannibals as savage as their land is serene. Stars Dana Andrews and Jane Powell.

ENCOUNTER WITH THE UNKNOWN
Video Communications Inc; Date not listed • color; 1 hr, 30 min; ½" Beta II, ½" VHS • Sale: $54.95

Features Rod Serling telling the story of three fully documented super-normal events concerning a death prophecy, a mysterious "deep hole," and a chillingly beautiful ghost.

THE END
Vid America; Order No. 454, 1978 • color; 1 hr, 40 min; ½" Beta II, ½" VHS • Rental: $13.95/wk, applicable to purchase

Offers a black comedy about a man who learns he is terminally ill and decides to commit suicide. Stars Burt Reynolds, Sally Field, Don DeLuise, Joanne Woodward, Kresty McNichol, Robby Benson, David Steinberg, Norman Fell, Carl Reiner, Myrna Loy, and Pat O'Brien, under Burt Reynolds' direction.

END OF THE ROAD
Discount Video Tapes; 1970 • color; 1 hr, 50 min; ½" Beta II, ½" VHS • Sale: $59.95

Presents a film version of the John Barth novel. Concerns an unstable college instructor who becomes involved with the wife of a professor. Stars Stacy Keach, James Earl Jones, Harris Yulin, Dorothy Tristan, Grayson Hall, and James Coco.

END OF THE WORLD
Meda/Media Home Entertainment Inc; Order No. M136; 1976 • color; 1 hr, 28 min; ½" Beta II, ½" VHS • Sale: $49.95

Follows a priest as he attempts to escape an unknown terror. Presents a science-fiction thriller featuring Christopher Lee.

ENTER THE DRAGON
WCI Home Video Inc; 1973 • color; 1 hr, 37 min; ½" Beta II, ½" VHS • Sale: $50

Presents a martial arts action film which stars Bruce Lee in his last role, as he infiltrates a strange tournament on an island fortress. Features John Saxon and Jim Kelly.

EROTIC MEMOIRS OF A MALE CHAUVINIST PIG
Quality X Video Cassette Company; Date not listed • color; 1 hr, 10 min; ½" Beta I, ½" Beta II, ½" VHS • Sale: $99.50

Presents a pornographic film.

AN EROTIC MUSICAL VERSION OF CINDERELLA
Vid America; Order No. 971; Date not listed • color; 1 hr, 36 min; ½" Beta II, ½" VHS • Sale: $59.95; Rental: $12.95/wk, applicable to purchase

Presents a pornographic film.

ESCAPADE IN JAPAN
Video Communications Inc; 1957 • color; 1 hr, 33 min; ½" Beta II, ½" VHS • Sale: $54.95

Follows the adventures of a seven-year-old boy who is a victim of a plane wreck off the coast of Japan. Tells of his adoption by a Japanese fishing family and his attempt to reach Tokyo with a boy from the family. Stars Cameron Mitchell, Teresa Wright, and Jon Provost.

ESCAPE FROM ALCATRAZ
Fotomat Corp; Order No. B0375 for ½" Beta II, V0375 for ½" VHS; 1979 • color; 1 hr, 52 min; ½" Beta II, ½" VHS • Sale: $54.95; Rental: $11.95/5 days
- -
Paramount Home Video; Order No. 1256; 1979 • color; 1 hr, 52 min; ½" Beta II, ½" VHS • Sale: $66.95
- -
RCA SelectaVision VideoDiscs; Order No. 00635; 1979 • color; 1 hr, 52 min ; CED • Sale: $24.98

Tells the true story of three men who dared to try to escape from the infamous prison and were never found. Stars Clint Eastwood, Patrick McGoohan, Roberts Blossom, and Jack Thibeau, under the direction of Donald Siegel.

ESCAPE TO BURMA
FHV Entertainment, Inc; 1955 • color; 1 hr, 27 min; ½" Beta II, ½" VHS • Sale: $49.95

Combines romance, adventure, and action in the Burmese jungle, blending wild animal scenes and human drama. Stars Barbara Stanwyck and Robert Ryan.

ESCAPE TO WITCH MOUNTAIN
Fotomat Corp; 1975 • color; 1 hr, 37 min; ½" Beta II, ½" VHS • Sale: $49.95; Rental: $9.95/up to 5 days, applicable to purchase

Niles Cinema; Order No. WD-13; 1975 • color; 1 hr, 34 min; ½" Beta II, ½" VHS • Sale: $59.95
- -
Walt Disney Home Video; Order No. 13BS for ½" Beta II, 13VS for ½" VHS; 1975 • color; 1 hr, 37 min; ½" Beta II, ½" VHS • Sale: $59.95

Follows the adventures of two children with mysterious powers who try to learn their origins. Reveals the plot to capture them for their powers. Stars Eddie Albert, Ray Milland, Kim Richards, Ike Eisenmann, and Donald Pleasance. Presents a Walt Disney Studios production.

ETERNALLY YOURS
Discount Video Tapes; 1939 • b/w; 1 hr, 35 min; ½" Beta II, ½" VHS • Sale: $49.95

Presents a magician's wife who is jealous of her husband's preoccupation with his work. Stars David Niven, Loretta Young, Billie Burke, Hugh Herbert, Zasu Pitts, and Eve Arden.

THE EUROPEANS
Time-Life Video Club Inc; 1979 • color; 1 hr, 30 min; ½" Beta II, ½" VHS • Sale: $44.95 to members

Adapts for the screen Henry James' novel set in 19th Century New England. Traces the attempts of a fortune-seeking brother and sister from England to find new lives with their American relatives. Uses authentic locales and costumes to tell the story of three romances. Stars Lee Remick, Robin Ellis, Wesley Addy, Tim Choate, and Lisa Eichhorn.

EVERGREEN
Budget Video; 1935 • b/w; 1 hr, 30 min; ½" Beta II, ½" VHS • Sale: $44.95
- -
Reel Images Inc; Order No. 473; 1934 • b/w; 1 hr, 34 min; ½" Beta II, ½" VHS • Sale: $49.95 for ½" Beta II, $52.95 for ½" VHS

Presents a musical comedy in which the daughter of a British music hall star is mistaken for her mother and is advertised as an example of eternal youth. Features a Rodgers and Hart score and stars Jessie Matthews, Sonnie Hale, Betty Belfour, and Barry Mackay.

Robin Ellis and Lee Remick in *The Europeans.*

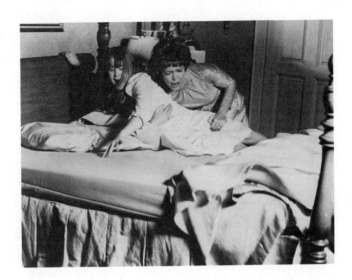

Linda Blair and Ellen Burstyn in _The Exorcist_.

EVERY INCH A LADY
Quality X Video Cassette Company; Date not listed •
color; 1 hr, 20 min; ½" Beta I, ½" Beta II, ½" VHS •
Sale: $99.50

Presents a pornographic film.

EVERY WHICH WAY BUT LOOSE
WCI Home Video Inc; 1978 • color; 1 hr, 59 min; ½"
Beta II, ½" VHS • Sale: $60

Presents Clint Eastwood's first departure from his
"Dirty Harry" character into a screwball comedy. Follows a romantic blue collar Californian while he chases
after a female country and western singer accompa-
nied by his best friend, an orangutan named Clyde.
Stars Eastwood, Sondra Locke, Geoffrey Lewis, Beverly D'Angelo, and Ruth Gordon.

**EVERYTHING YOU ALWAYS WANTED TO KNOW
ABOUT SEX, BUT WERE AFRAID TO ASK**
Vid America; 1972 • color; 1 hr, 27 min; ½" Beta II,
½" VHS • Rental: $13.95/wk

Presents a film conceived and directed by Woody Allen. Offers a series of sketches which satirize sexual
appetites and practices. Models each sketch as a parody of some well-known film genre, such as a science-
fiction thriller or an historical romance. Stars Woody
Allen, Anthony Quayle, Lynn Redgrave, John Carradine, Louise Lasser, Gene Wilder, and Burt Reynolds.

THE EVIL MIND
VCX; Order No. FC111; 1935 • b/w; 1 hr, 12 min; ½"
Beta II, ½" VHS • Sale: $35

- -
Video T.E.N.; 1935 • b/w; 1 hr, 12 min; ½" Beta II,
½" VHS • Sale: $49.95 for ½" Beta II, 54.95 for ½"
VHS

Features Claude Rains as a clairvoyant with fantastic
powers, in a film originally titled "Clairvoyant." Co-
stars Fay Wray.

EXECUTIVE ACTION
WCI Home Video Inc; 1973 • color; 1 hr, 30 min; ½"
Beta II, ½" VHS • Sale: $55

Offers a political thriller concerning the assassination
of John F. Kennedy. Stars Burt Lancaster, Robert
Ryan, Will Geer, and Gilbert Green.

EXIT THE DRAGON—ENTER THE TIGER
Video Communications Inc; Order No. 1188; Date not
listed • color; 1 hr, 24 min; ½" Beta II, ½" VHS • Sale:
$54.95

Presents a martial arts action film that explores the
causes of Bruce Lee's death. Features Bruce Li, the
successor to Lee.

THE EX-MRS. BRADFORD
The Nostalgia Merchant; Order No. 8060; 1936 • b/w;
1 hr, 20 min; ½" Beta II, ½" VHS • Sale: $54.95

Presents a comedy-mystery in which a divorced couple team up to solve a murder case. Stars William
Powell, Jean Arthur, and James Gleason.

THE EXORCIST
WCI Home Video Inc; 1973 • color; 2 hrs, 1 min; ½"
Beta II, ½" VHS • Sale: $60

Depicts a young girl of twelve years whose body is
possessed by a demon, and the attempts of Jesuit
priests to drive the demon out of the girl. Uses elaborate special effects. Stars Linda Blair, Ellen Burstyn,
Max von Sydow, Lee J. Cobb, Jason Miller, and Mercedes McCambridge's voice as the voice of the demon. Adapts William Peter Blatty's novel under the direction of William Friedkin.

EXORCIST II: THE HERETIC
WCI Home Video Inc; 1977 • color; 1 hr, 57 min; ½"
Beta II, ½" VHS • Sale: $55

Presents the sequel to the 1973 box office hit. Follows
the efforts of a priest (Richard Burton) to help the ever-

possessed young girl (Linda Blair). Co-stars Louise Fletcher, Kitty Winn, James Earl Jones, Ned Beatty, and Max von Sydow, under the direction of John Boorman.

EXPECTATIONS
TVX Distributors; Order No. R.T. 71; Date not listed • color; 2 hrs; 1/2" Beta II, 1/2" VHS • Sale: $79.50 for 1/2" Beta II, 89.50 for 1/2" VHS

Presents a pornographic film.

THE EYES OF LAURA MARS
Fotomat Corp; Order No. B0413 for 1/2" Beta II, V0413 for 1/2" VHS; 1978 • color; 1 hr, 43 min; 1/2" Beta II, 1/2" VHS • Sale: $54.95; Rental: $9.95/5 days
- -
Time-Life Video Club Inc; 1978 • color; 1 hr, 43 min; 1/2" Beta II, 1/2" VHS • Sale: $54.95 to members

Depicts a high fashion photographer who "sees" grisly murders as they are about to occur. Stars Faye Dunaway, Tommy Lee Jones, Brad Dourif, Rene Auberjonois, and Raul Julia.

EYES RIGHT
Reel Images Inc; Order No. 465; 1926 • b/w; 1 hr, 5 min; 1/2" Beta II, 1/2" VHS • Sale: $49.95 for 1/2" Beta II, $52.95 for 1/2" VHS

Portrays life in a military academy during the 1920's. Presents a silent film starring Francis X. Bushman.

THE FABULOUS DORSEYS
Video T.E.N.; 1947 • b/w; 1 hr, 31 min; 1/2" Beta II, 1/2" VHS • Sale: $49.95 for 1/2" Beta II, $54.95 for 1/2" VHS

Follows the careers of Tommy and Jimmy Dorsey in this biographical musical. Features the Dorsey brothers, Janet Blair, Paul Whiteman, William Lundigan, Arthur Shields, and many big band stars.

THE FABULOUS FIFTIES
Blackhawk Films, Inc; Order No. 506-66-0678 for 1/2" Beta II, 525-660678 for 1/2" VHS; Date not listed • ; 5 hrs; 3/4" U-Matic, 1/2" Beta I, 1/2" Beta II, 1/2" VHS • Sale: $249.95 for 1/2" Beta I, $199.95 for 1/2" Beta II & VHS, $349.95 for 3/4"

Presents, on three tapes, the decade of the 1950's in documentary form featuring the major news stories. Includes the Brinks robbery, MacArthur's "Old Soldiers" speech, Eisenhower, Nixon, Korea, Stalin's death, Mt. Everest conquered, the testing of the first H-bomb, Grace Kelly's marriage, The Cold War, and Castro's overthrow of Batista's Cuban government.

THE FABULOUS WORLD OF JULES VERNE
Video Communications Inc; 1958 • b/w; 1 hr, 27 min; 1/2" Beta II, 1/2" VHS • Sale: $54.95

Compiles various Jules Verne stories in a Czech film combining live action, puppets, and animation reminiscent of 19th century woodcuts. Stars Louis Tock, under the direction of Karel Zeman.

FAIL SAFE
National Film and Video Center; 1964 • color; 1 hr, 41 min; 3/4" U-Matic, 1/2" Beta II, 1/2" VHS • Rental: $49/1 showing

Depicts the results of the malfunction of a "fail-safe" computer which dispatches war planes containing nuclear weapons: a bomber on its way to destroy Moscow must be stopped. Stars Henry Fonda, Walter Matthau, Dan O'Herlihy, and Frank Overton.

FAIRYTALES
Meda/Media Home Entertainment Inc; Order No. M509; 1978 • color; 1 hr, 25 min; 1/2" Beta I, 1/2" Beta II, 1/2" VHS • Sale: $54.95 1/2" Beta II & VHS

Presents a pornographic film.

FALL OF THE HOUSE OF USHER
Golden Tapes Video Tape Library; Order No. CD6; 1958 • b/w; 55 min; 1/2" Beta II, 1/2" VHS • Sale: $49.95 for 1/2" Beta II & VHS, $79.95 for 3/4"

Dramatizes the Poe tale of an insane man who buries his sister alive and is then haunted by her. Stars Tom Tryon and Marshall Thompson.

THE FALL OF THE ROMAN EMPIRE
Video Communications Inc; Order No. 5004; 1964 • color; 2 hrs, 32 min; 1/2" Beta II, 1/2" VHS • Sale: $74.95

Traces the why and wherefores, both political and personal, that led to the demise of the Pax Romana and the culture of one of the world's greatest civilizations. Stars Anthony Quayle, Mel Ferrer, James Mason, Stephen Boyd, Sophia Loren, Alec Guinness, Christopher Plummer, Omar Shariff, and John Ireland, under the direction of Anthony Mann.

THE FALLEN IDOL
Budget Video; 1949 • b/w; 1 hr, 32 min; 1/2" Beta II, 1/2" VHS • Sale: $44.95
- -
Fotomat Corp; Order No. B0253 for 1/2" Beta II, V0253 for 1/2" VHS; 1948 • b/w; 1 hr, 34 min; 1/2" Beta II, 1/2" VHS • Sale: $49.95; Rental: $9.95/up to 5 days, applicable to purchase

Dramatizes the Graham Greene story of an ambassador's son who idolizes the embassy butler, only to become the latter's nemesis after the butler's wife is found murdered. Features Ralph Richardson, Michele Morgan, Jack Hawkins, and Bobby Henrey, under the direction of Carol Reed.

THE FALLEN SPARROW
Niles Cinema; Order No. NM-8038; 1943 • b/w; 1 hr, 34 min; 1/2" Beta II, 1/2" VHS • Sale: $54.95
- -
The Nostalgia Merchant; Order No. 8038; 1943 • b/w; 1 hr, 34 min; 1/2" Beta II, 1/2" VHS • Sale: $54.95
- -
Red Fox, Inc; Order No. 8038; 1943 • b/w; 1 hr, 34 min; 1/2" Beta II, 1/2" VHS • Sale: $54.95

Recounts the adventures of a Spanish Civil War returnee pursued by Nazis. Stars John Garfield, Maureen O'Hara, and Walter Slezak.

FAME
MGM/CBS Home Video; Order No. M70027; 1980 • color; 2 hrs, 13 min; 1/2" Beta II, 1/2" VHS • Sale: $69.95

Looks at the quest for excellence and the urge to become famous at the New York High School for the Performing Arts. Stars Irene Cara, Eddie Barth, Lee Curreri, Laura Dean, and Joanne Merlin.

THE FAMILY
Video Communications Inc; 1970 • color; 1 hr, 34 min; ½" Beta II, ½" VHS • Sale: $54.95

Chronicles the attempts of a professional hit-man to capture an underworld chief who has framed him. Stars Charles Bronson, Jill Ireland, and Telly Savalas.

FAMILY PLOT
MCA DiscoVision; Order No. 11-005; 1976 • color; 2 hrs; LaserVision • Sale: $24.95

Details a complex murder plot and a phony psychic who eventually becomes involved in it. Stars Bruce Dern, Karen Black, Barbara Harris, and William Devane, under Alfred Hitchcock's direction.

FANNY
Budget Video; 1932 • b/w; 2 hrs, 8 min; ½" Beta II, ½" VHS • Sale: $44.95

Portrays the second episode in Marcel Pagnol's film trilogy, in which Fanny finds she is pregnant and marries the rich Panisse. Tells how the sailor Marius returns home to claim Fanny as his bride, only to be confronted by his own father who has taken Fanny's side. Stars Raimu, Pierre Fresnay, Charpin, and Orane Demazis, under the direction of Marc Allegret; in French with subtitles.

FANTASTIC PLANET
Reel Images Inc; Order No. 722; 1973 • color; 1 hr, 8 min; ½" Beta II, ½" VHS • Sale: $49.95 for ½" Beta II, $52.95 for ½" VHS

Offers an animated science-fiction film from France and Czechoslovakia, directed by Rene Laloux. Tells of the revolt of the humanoid beings called Oms against their conquerors, the towering blue Draags.

THE FANTASTIC PLASTIC MACHINE
Video Communications Inc; Order No. 1037; 1969 • color; 1 hr, 33 min; ½" Beta II, ½" VHS • Sale: $54.95

Relates the story of a group of surfers from the Windansea Surf Club. Follows them on their journey across the South Pacific to compete with Australia's finest.

FANTASTIC VOYAGE
Blackhawk Films, Inc; Order No. 502-49-0032 for ½" Beta II, 515-49-0023 for ½" VHS; 1966 • color; 1 hr, 40 min; ½" Beta II, ½" VHS • Sale: $54.95
- -
Golden Tapes Video Tape Library; Order No. F-1002; 1966 • color; 1 hr, 45 min; ½" Beta II, ½" VHS • Sale: $49.95 for ½" Beta II & VHS, $124.95 for ¾"
- -
Magnetic Video Corporation; Order No. CL-1002; 1966 • color; 1 hr, 40 min; ½" Beta II, ½" VHS • Sale: $44.95
- -
The Video Library; Order No. MV-1002; 1966 • color; 1 hr, 40 min; ½" Beta II, ½" VHS • Sale: $54.95

Follows, through the use of special effects, a crew of scientists on a journey through the human body and into the brain. Stars Stephen Boyd, Raquel Welch, and Edmund O'Brien.

FANTASY IN BLUE
Meda/Media Home Entertainment Inc; Order No. M503; Date not listed • color; 1 hr, 25 min; ½" Beta I, ½" Beta II, ½" VHS • Sale: $54.95 for ½"

Presents a pornographic film.

A FAREWELL TO ARMS
Cinema Concepts, Inc.; 1932 • b/w; 1 hr, 18 min; ¾"

U-Matic, ½" Beta II, ½" VHS • Sale: $54.95 for ½" Beta II & VHS, $149.95 for ¾"
- -
Ivy Video; 1932 • b/w; 1 hr, 30 min; ¾" U-Matic, ½" Beta II, ½" VHS • Sale: $59.95 for ½" Beta II & VHS, trade-in plan available, $195 for ¾"
- -
Vid America; Order No. 919; 1932 • b/w; 1 hr, 18 min; ½" Beta II, ½" VHS • Rental: $10.95/wk
- -
The Video Library; Order No. CC-0014; 1932 • color; 1 hr, 18 min; ½" Beta II, ½" VHS • Sale: $54.95

Dramatizes Ernest Hemingway's novel concerning a wounded American soldier who falls in love with his British nurse during World War I in Italy. Stars Helen Hayes, Gary Cooper, Adolphe Menjou, Mary Philips, Jack LaRue, and Blanche Frederici, under the direction of Frank Borzage.

A FAREWELL TO ARMS
Golden Tapes Video Tape Library; Order No. F-1050; 1957 • color; 2 hrs, 32 min; ½" Beta II, ½" VHS • Sale: $49.95 for ½" Beta II & VHS, $124.95 for ¾"

Presents a remake of the 1932 film adaptation of Ernest Hemingway's novel. Stars Rock Hudson, Jennifer Jones, Vittorio De Sica, Alberto Sordi, Mercedes McCambridge, Elaine Stritch, and Oscar Homolka, under the direction of Charles Vidor.

Raquel Welch, Arthur Kennedy, William Redfield (above), Donald Pleasence, and Stephen Boyd in *Fantastic Voyage.*

FARMER'S DAUGHTERS
VTS; Date not listed • color; 1 hr, 14 min; ½" Beta I, ½" Beta II, ½" VHS • Sale: $99

Presents a pornographic film.

FAT CITY
National Film and Video Center; 1972 • color; 1 hr, 36 min; ¾" U-Matic, ½" Beta II, ½" VHS • Rental: $89/1 showing

Traces the career of an ex-prizefighter who decides to begin training again: he wins his first fight, but when he must pay his backer most of the prize money and he learns that his girlfriend is pregnant, he begins drinking again. Stars Stacy Keach as the boxer who finally returns to the ring as a winner; features Jeff Bridges and Susan Tyrrell.

FATE OF THE ANDREA DORIA
Video Communications Inc ; Order No. 1042; 1978 • color; 1 hr, 31 min; ½" Beta II, ½" VHS • Sale: $54.95

Follows divers as they explore the legendary "unsinkable" luxury liner—deserted except for sharks and other sea life for whom the ship is now a home.

FEARLESS FIGHTERS
Niles Cinema; Order No. BT-28 for ½" Beta II, VH-28 for ½" VHS; 1973 • color; 1 hr, 23 min; ½" Beta II, ½" VHS • Sale: $59.95

Presents an epic of oriental revenge and martial arts, using Kung-Fu, karate, judo, and Chinese shadowboxing, and the talents of Chang Ching, Yee Yuang, and Chen Lieh.

FELICIA
Quality X Video Cassette Company; Date not listed • color; 1 hr, 38 min; ½" Beta I, ½" Beta II, ½" VHS • Sale: $99.50

Presents a pornographic film.

FELLINI'S CASANOVA
MCA DiscoVision; Order No. 15-004; 1977 • color; 2 hrs, 35 min; LaserVision • Sale:$24.95

Presents Federico Fellini's first film in English, an unflattering depiction of the famous lover. Choreographs Casanova's lovemaking escapades to make them appear grotesque and humorous. Stars Donald Sutherland, Tina Aumont, Cicely Browne, and Dudley Sutton, under the direction of Fellini.

FIDDLER ON THE ROOF
RCA SelectaVision VideoDiscs; Order No. 01404; 1971 • color; 3 hrs, 1 min; CED • Sale: $27.98
- -
Vid America; Order No. 464; 1971 • color; 3 hrs, 4 min; ½" Beta II, ½" VHS • Rental: $13.95/wk, applicable to purchase

Adapts for the screen Joseph Stein's Broadway musical based on the stories of Sholem Aleichem. Concerns a Jewish milkman who clings to traditional values while living in Revolutionary Russia. Features Isaac Stern's violin and the Sheldon Harnick and Jerry Bock score. Stars Chaim Topol, Norma Crane, Leonard Frey, Molly Picon, Paul Mann, Rosalind Harris, Michele Marsh, Neva Small, and Candice Bonstein.

FIEND WITHOUT A FACE
Cinema Concepts, Inc.; 1958 • b/w; 1 hr, 14 min; ¾" U-Matic, ½" Beta II, ½" VHS • Sale: $54.95 for ½" Beta II & VHS, $149.95 for ¾"
- -
The Video Library; Order No. CC-0115; 1958 • b/w; 1 hr, 14 min; ½" Beta II, ½" VHS • Sale: $54.95

Presents a science-fiction-horror adventure of bloodsucking "mental vampires" that are invisible and cause ghastly death to all around them. Stars Marshall Thompson, Kim Parker, and Terence Kilburn.

THE 5TH DAY OF PEACE
Tape Club of America; Order No. 2302 B; 1972 • color; 1 hr, 35 min; ½" Beta II, ½" VHS • Sale: 54.95

Describes the brotherhood of military men in a movie which is based on a true World War II incident. Recounts the story of two Germans who are court-martialed for desertion and sentenced to death in a prisoner-of-war camp, commanded by a Canadian captain,

but run by a German colonel. Stars Franco Nero, Richard Johnson, Larry Aubrey, and Helmut Scheider.

55 DAYS AT PEKING
Time-Life Video Club Inc; 1963 • color; 2 hrs, 30 min; ½" Beta II, ½" VHS • Sale: $54.95 to members
- -
Video Communications Inc; Order No. 5002; 1963 • color; 2 hrs, 34 min; ½" Beta II, ½" VHS • Sale: $74.95

Depicts the siege of Peking during the Boxer Rebellion at the turn of the century. Reveals the plight of international representatives trapped inside Peking's foreign compound. Stars Charlton Heston, Ava Gardner, and David Niven, under the direction of Nicholas Ray.

FIGHTER PILOTS
FHV Entertainment, Inc; 1976 • color; 1 hr, 38 min; ½" Beta II, ½" VHS • Sale: $49.95

Probes the interactions of two enemies, thrown together by fate, who learn that the bond of friendship is more important than the meaningless agony of war. Stars Will Roberts and John Hardy.

FIGHTING CARAVANS
Reel Images Inc; Order No. 414; 1932 • b/w; 1 hr, 20 min; ½" Beta II, ½" VHS • Sale: $49.95 for ½" Beta II, $52.95 for ½" VHS

Offers an early Gary Cooper feature based on a story by Zane Grey. Follows the westward journey of a young caravan guide, his romance with a French girl, and his attempt to repel an Indian attack. Co-stars Lily Damita, Ernest Torrence, and Fred Kohler.

THE FIGHTING DEVIL DOGS
The Nostalgia Merchant; Date not listed • b/w; 3 hrs; ½" Beta II, ½" VHS • Sale: $109.95

Presents, on two videocassettes, a motion picture serial in 12 episodes. Stars Lee Powell and Herman Brix.

THE FIGHTING KENTUCKIAN
Niles Cinema; Order No. NM-0126; 1949 • b/w; 1 hr, 40 min; ½" Beta II, ½" VHS • Sale: $54.95
- -
The Nostalgia Merchant; Order No. 0126; 1949 • b/w; 1 hr, 40 min; ½" Beta II, ½" VHS • Sale: $54.95
- -
Red Fox, Inc; Order No. 0126; 1949 • b/w; 1 hr, 40 min; ½" Beta II, ½" VHS • Sale: $54.95

Recounts a story of romance and adventure on the frontierland of 1814. Features John Wayne, Vera Ralston, and Oliver Hardy.

FILLMORE
All Star Video Corp; 1972 • color; 1 hr, 45 min; ½" Beta II, ½" VHS • Sale: $79.95

Presents a rock documentary about the final days of the Fillmore West and its owner Bill Graham. Features The Grateful Dead, Santana, Jefferson Airplane, Quicksilver Messenger Service, and It's A Beautiful Day.

FILM FIRSTS
Blackhawk Films, Inc; Order No. 506-66-0882 for ½" Beta II, 525-66-0882 for ½" VHS; Date not listed • b/w; 51 min; ¾" U-Matic, ½" Beta I, ½" Beta II, ½" VHS • Sale: $59.95 for ½" Beta I, $39.95 for ½" Beta II & VHS, $69.95 for ¾"

Offers a color-toned, narrated segment from The History of the Motion Picture Series. Presents a documentary glimpse of many early film achievements. Includes the first science-fiction film, George Melies' "Trip to the

Moon," from 1902; the first cartoon, "Gertie the Dinosaur," from 1909; the first western, "The Great Train Robbery," Edwin S. Porter's film of 1903; and more.

FINGERS
Magnetic Video Corporation ; Order No. CL-5002; 1978 • color; 1 hr, 30 min; ½" Beta II, ½" VHS • Sale: $54.95

Focuses on the son of a gangster and a concert pianist, who is torn between the vicious world of his father and the gentle world of classical piano music. Stars Harvey Keitel, Tisa Farrow, Michael Gazzo, and Jim Brown.

FIONA ON FIRE
TVX Distributors; Date not listed • color; 2 hrs; ½" Beta II, ½" VHS • Sale: $79.50 for ½" Beta II, $89.50 for ½" VHS

Presents a pornographic film.

FIRE OVER ENGLAND
Video T.E.N.; 1937 • b/w; 1 hr, 21 min; ½" Beta II, ½" VHS • Sale: $49.95 for ½" Beta II, $54.95 for ½" VHS

Dramatizes the events leading up to the attempted invasion of England by the Spanish Armada. Includes Flora Robson, Raymond Massey, Laurence Olivier, Vivien Leigh, and Robert Newton.

Vivien Leigh and Laurence Olivier in Fire Over England.

FIRST LOVE
Fotomat Corp; Order No. B0061 for ½" Beta II, V0061 for ½" VHS; 1977 • color; 1 hr, 32 min; ½" Beta II, ½" VHS • Sale: $49.95; Rental: $9.95/up to 5 days, applicable to purchase

- -

Paramount Home Video; Date not listed • color; 1 hr, 32 min; ½" Beta II, ½" VHS • Sale: $59.95

Tells a story of Caroline and Elgin as they experience "first love." Stars William Katt, Susan Dey, John Heard, Beverly D'Angelo, and Robert Loggia, under the direction of Joan Darling.

FIRST MEN IN THE MOON
National Film and Video Center; 1964 • color; 1 hr, 43 min; ¾" U-Matic, ½" Beta II, ½" VHS • Rental: $49/1 showing

Tells how investigating U.N. Moon Project representatives find evidence of an earlier moon landing in the person of aging Arnold Bedford, who tells his story in a flashback that makes up most of the movie. Stars Edward Judd, Martha Hyer, and Lionel Jeffries.

THE FIRST NUDIE MUSICAL
Tape Club of America; Order No. 2842 B; 1976 • color; 1 hr, 30 min; ½" Beta II, ½" VHS • Sale: 54.95

Presents the first R-rated musical comedy. Stars Cindy Williams, Diana Canova, Stephen Nathan, and Bruce Kimmel. Includes the songs "Dancing Dildos," "Perversion," "Orgasm," and "I'll Kick You with Boots."

FIRST SPACESHIP ON VENUS
Video Communications Inc; 1960 • color; 1 hr, 20 min; ½" Beta II, ½" VHS • Sale: $54.95

Shows eight world-famous scientists setting out for Venus who, after great efforts, discover a civilization far more advanced than Earth's. Stars Yoko Tani.

THE FIRST TRAVELING SALESLADY
Video Communications Inc; Order No. 1039; 1956 • color; 1 hr, 32 min; ½" Beta II, ½" VHS • Sale: $54.95

Tells the story of a corset designer who heads west with her secretary in 1897 to sell barbed wire after a Broadway show is closed by police because of a number using her corsets. Features Ginger Rogers, Barry Nelson, Carol Channing, and James Arness.

FIST OF FURY II
Video Gems; 1980 • color; 1 hr, 30 min; ½" Beta II, ½" VHS • Sale: $59.95

Presents a martial arts film with Bruce Li.

THE 5,000 FINGERS OF DR. T.
National Film and Video Center; 1953 • color; 1 hr, 22 min; ¾" U-Matic, ½" Beta II, ½" VHS • Rental: $79/1 showing

Relates the fantasy of a young boy forced by his mother to practice the piano: the author of his exercise book—Dr. T—has imprisoned 500 boys at a giant keyboard on which they must practice 365 days a year. Stars Peter Lind Hayes, Mary Healy, Hans Conried, and Tommy Rettig.

FLAME OF BARBARY COAST
The Nostalgia Merchant; Order No. 0162; 1945 • b/w; 1 hr, 31 min; ½" Beta II, ½" VHS • Sale: $54.95

- -

Red Fox, Inc; Order No. 0162; 1945 • b/w; 1 hr, 31 min; ½" Beta II, ½" VHS • Sale: $54.95

Tells of a cowboy vying with a gambling czar for a dance hall queen and control of the Barbary Coast. Stars John Wayne, Ann Dvorak, and Joseph Schildkraut.

FLASH GORDON
MCA Videocassette, Inc; Order No. 66022; 1980 • color; 1 hr, 50 min; ½" Beta II , ½" VHS • Sale: $65

Follows the adventures of Flash Gordon, the quarterback for the New York Jets football team, as he is kidnapped to foil Ming the Merciless' plot to destroy the Earth. Stars Sam J. Jones, Max Von Sydow, Brian Blessed, Melody Anderson, Topol, Ornella Muti, Timothy Dalton, and Peter Wyngarde. Features music by "Queen."

Harry Shannon, Buster
Crabbe, and Jean Rogers
in *Mars Attacks The World.*

FLASH GORDON CONQUERS THE UNIVERSE

Cinema Concepts, Inc.; 1940 • b/w; 1 hr, 20 min; ¾″
U-Matic, ½″ Beta II, ½″ VHS • Sale: $54.95 for ½″
Beta II & VHS, $149.95 for ¾″

- -

Golden Tapes Video Tape Library; 1940 • b/w; 1 hr;
½″ Beta II, ½″ VHS • Sale: $49.95 for ½″ Beta II &
VHS, $79.95 for ¾″

- -

Northeast Video and Sound, Inc; Order No. 109S;
1940 • b/w; 4 hrs; ¾″ U-Matic, ½″ EIAJ, ½″ Beta II,
½″ VHS • Sale: $495; Rental: $175/wk

- -

The Video Library; Order No. VN-0407; 1940 • b/w; 1
hr, 20 min; ½″ Beta II, ½″ VHS • Sale: $49.95

Presents a re-edited version of the serial re-released as
"Purple Death from Outer Space." Recounts Flash's
attempt to thwart Ming the Merciless, who plans to gain
control of Earth. Features Buster Crabbe, Carol
Hughes, and Charles Middleton.

FLASH GORDON: MARS ATTACKS THE WORLD

Northeast Video and Sound, Inc; 1938 • b/w; 1 hr, 10
min; ¾″ U-Matic, ½″ EIAJ, ½″ Beta II, ½″ VHS • Sale:
$179; Rental: $70/wk

Features many special effects as Flash attempts to
save Earth from alien invasion. Stars Buster Crabbe,
Jean Rogers, Charles Middleton, and Frank Shannon.

FLASH GORDON:ROCKETSHIP

The Video Library; 1935 • b/w; 1 hr, 15 min; ½″ Beta
II, ½″ VHS • Sale: $54.95

Presents a compilation of films from the "Flash Gordon" serial, featuringBuster Crabbe.

A FLASK OF FIELDS

Reel Images Inc; Order No. 515; 1930-33 • b/w; 1 hr,
1 min; ½″ Beta II, ½″ VHS • Sale: $39.95 for ½″ Beta
II, $42.95 for ½″ VHS

Offers a compilation of three W.C. Fields comedy
shorts. Includes "The Golf Specialist," in which Fields
teaches a lady to golf; "The Fatal Glass of Beer," set in
the frozen North; and "The Dentist," featuring a very
ill-humored Dr. Fields and his hapless patients.

FLESH FACTORY

Mitchell Brothers' Film Group; Date not listed • color;
1 hr, 32 min; ½″ Beta II, ½″ VHS • Sale: $69

Presents a pornographic film.

THE FLIGHT OF THE COUGAR

The Nostalgia Merchant; Order No. 7010; 1967 •
color; 1 hr, 15 min; ½″ Beta II, ½″ VHS • Sale: $54.95

Shows Lassie saving a wounded cougar and taming a
wild stallion amid the splendor of the national parks.
Features Robert Bray and Merry Anders.

FLYING ACQUAINTANCES

Monarch Releasing Corporation; Date not listed •
color; 1 hr, 26 min; ¾″ U-Matic • Sale: $350

Presents a pornographic film.

THE FLYING DEUCES

Fotomat Corp; Order No. B0151 for ½″ Beta II, V0151
for ½″ VHS; 1939 • b/w; 1 hr, 7 min; ½″ Beta II, ½″
VHS • Sale: $39.95; Rental: $7.95/up to 5 days, applicable to purchase

- -

Golden Tapes Video Tape Library; Order No. CC4;
1939 • b/w; 1 hr, 10 min; ½″ Beta II, ½″ VHS • Sale:
$49.95 for ½″ Beta II & VHS, $124.95 for ¾″

- -

Northeast Video and Sound, Inc; Order No. 102S;
1939 • b/w; 1 hr, 10 min; ¾″ U-Matic, ½″ EIAJ, ½″
Beta II, ½″ VHS • Sale: $195; Rental: $70/wk

- -

Reel Images Inc; Order No. 501; 1939 • b/w; 1 hr, 9
min; ½″ Beta II, ½″ VHS • Sale: $49.95 for ½″ Beta II,
$52.95 for ½″ VHS

- -

Video Communications Inc; 1939 • b/w; 1 hr, 7 min;
½″ Beta II, ½″ VHS • Sale: $54.95

Shows Stan Laurel and Oliver Hardy joining the Foreign Legion so that Ollie can forget an unhappy romance.

FLYING DOWN TO RIO

Niles Cinema; Order No. NM-8003; 1933 • b/w; 1 hr,
29 min; ½″ Beta II, ½″ VHS • Sale: $54.95

The Nostalgia Merchant; Order No. 8003; 1933 • b/w; 1 hr, 29 min; 1/2" Beta II, 1/2" VHS • Sale: $54.95

Red Fox, Inc; Order No. 8003; 1933 • b/w; 1 hr, 29 min; 1/2" Beta II, 1/2" VHS • Sale: $54.95

Spotlights Fred Astaire and Ginger Rogers in the first musical they starred in together. Includes a dance on the wings of a flying plane. Co-stars Dolores Del Rio, Gene Raymond, and Raul Roulien.

FLYING LEATHERNECKS
Niles Cinema; Order No. NM-8004; 1951 • color; 1 hr, 42 min; 1/2" Beta II, 1/2" VHS • Sale: $54.95

The Nostalgia Merchant; Order No. 8004; 1951 • color; 1 hr, 42 min; 1/2" Beta II, 1/2" VHS • Sale: $54.95

Red Fox, Inc; Order No. 8004; 1951 • color; 1 hr, 42 min; 1/2" Beta II, 1/2" VHS • Sale: $54.95

Vid America; Order No. 934; 1951 • color; 1 hr, 42 min; 1/2" Beta II, 1/2" VHS • Rental: $10.95/wk

Presents John Wayne as a rugged Marine officer during World War II who is hated by his men, with Robert Ryan and Don Taylor.

FLYING TIGERS
Niles Cinema; Order No. NM-0003; 1942 • b/w; 1 hr, 40 min; 1/2" Beta II, 1/2" VHS • Sale: $54.95

The Nostalgia Merchant; Order No. 0003; 1942 • b/w; 1 hr, 40 min; 1/2" Beta II, 1/2" VHS • Sale: $54.95

Red Fox, Inc; Order No. 0003; 1942 • b/w; 1 hr, 40 min; 1/2" Beta II, 1/2" VHS • Sale: $54.95

Relates the story of World War II's Flying Tigers, outnumbered but never outfought. Features John Wayne, Anna Lee, and John Carroll.

FM
MCA DiscoVision; Order No. 16-012; 1978 • color; 1 hr, 50 min; LaserVision • Sale: $24.95

Offers a look at the workings of an all-music rock station. Shows the personal and professional goings-on, humorous and serious, and includes a continuous flow of music provided by Linda Ronstadt, Jimmy Buffett, Steely Dan, the Eagles, and Lynyrd Skynyrd. Stars Michael Brandon, Eileen Brennan, Alex Karras, Cleavon Little, and Martin Mull.

THE FOG
Magnetic Video Corporation; 1979 • color; 1 hr, 30 min; 1/2" Beta II, 1/2" VHS • Sale: $59.95

Niles Cinema; Order No. CL-4067; 1979 • color; 1 hr, 30 min; 1/2" Beta II, 1/2" VHS • Sale: $59.95

Offers a tale of a revived curse and murdering zombies. Stars Hal Holbrook and Adrienne Barbeau, under John Carpenter's direction.

FOLLOW THE FLEET
Niles Cinema; Order No. NM-8013; 1936 • b/w; 1 hr, 50 min; 1/2" Beta II, 1/2" VHS • Sale: $54.95

The Nostalgia Merchant; Order No. 8013; 1936 • b/w; 1 hr, 50 min; 1/2" Beta II, 1/2" VHS • Sale: $54.95

Red Fox, Inc; Order No. 8013; 1936 • b/w; 1 hr, 50 min; 1/2" Beta II, 1/2" VHS • Sale: $54.95

Stars Fred Astaire as a sailor and Ginger Rogers as a dance hall hostess, in a song and dance film scored by Irving Berlin. Includes "Let's Face the Music and Dance," "Let Yourself Go," and "We Saw the Sea."

Co-stars Randolph Scott, Harriet Hilliard, and Betty Grable.

FOLLOWING THE TUNDRA WOLF
Home Vision; Order No. 825-7001 for 1/2" Beta II, 825-9001 for 1/2" VHS; Date not listed • color; 44 min; 1/2" Beta II, 1/2" VHS • Sale: $49.95

Presents a wildlife film about the tundra wolf and the land he shares with the caribou, grizzly bear, musk-ox, wolverine, fox, and migratory birds. Features narration by Robert Redford.

FOOTBALL WIDOW
Scorpio, Etc; 1979 • color; 30 min; 1/2" Beta I, 1/2" Beta II, 1/2" VHS • Sale: $39.95

Presents a pornographic film.

FOR PETE'S SAKE
Columbia Pictures Home Entertainment; Order No. BE51475 for 1/2" Beta II, VH10470 for 1/2" VHS; 1974 • color; 1 hr, 30 min; 1/2" Beta II, 1/2" VHS • Sale: $59.95

Presents a comedy about a wife trying to raise money for her cab-driver husband's education. Stars Barbra Streisand, Michael Sarrazin, and Estelle Parsons.

FOR THE LOVE OF BENJI
Fotomat Corp; Order No. B0403 for 1/2" Beta II, V0403 for 1/2" VHS; 1977 • color; 1 hr, 25 min; 1/2" Beta II, 1/2" VHS • Sale: $54.95; Rental: $9.95/5 days

Presents the canine Benji on the trail of spies while vacationing in Greece with his humans. Stars Benji, Patsy Garrett, Cynthia Smith, Allen Fiuzat, and Ed Nelson.

FORBIDDEN TRAIL
Fotomat Corp; Order No. B0103 for 1/2" Beta II, V0103 for 1/2" VHS; 1942 • b/w; 1 hr; 1/2" Beta II, 1/2" VHS • Sale: $39.95; Rental: $7.95/up to 5 days, applicable to purchase

Offers a western featuring Buck Jones and Tim Mc-Coy.

FOREIGN CORRESPONDENT
Time-Life Video Club Inc; 1940 • b/w; 1 hr, 59 min; 1/2" Beta II, 1/2" VHS • Sale: $39.95 to members

Recounts the adventures of a naive young American reporter in Europe on the eve of World War II, who gets involved with a pacifist group and a spy ring. Stars Joel McCrea, Laraine Day, Herbert Marshall, George Sanders, and Robert Benchley, under the direction of Alfred Hitchcock.

A FORMAL FAUCETT
VTS; Date not listed • color; 1 hr, 10 min; 1/2" Beta I, 1/2" Beta II, 1/2" VHS • Sale: $99

Presents a pornographic film.

FORT APACHE
The Nostalgia Merchant; Order No. 8014; 1948 • b/w; 2 hrs, 5 min; 1/2" Beta II, 1/2" VHS • Sale: $54.95

Presents the first John Ford large-scale historical western. Stars John Wayne, Henry Fonda, Shirley Temple, and Ward Bond.

THE FORTUNE
National Film and Video Center; 1975 • color; 1 hr, 35 min; 3/4" U-Matic, 1/2" Beta II, 1/2" VHS • Rental: $89/1 showing

Presents a chaotic farce set in the Jazz Age: an heiress is kidnapped, a bank teller is blackmailed into marrying her, and her abductors fail in several inept attempts to murder her. Stars Warren Beatty, Jack Nicholson, and Stockard Channing.

FORTUNE'S FOOL
Reel Images Inc; Order No. 17; 1921 • b/w; 1 hr, 22 min; 1/2" Beta II, 1/2" VHS • Sale: $49.95 for 1/2" Beta II, 52.95 for 1/2" VHS

Depicts the life of a post-World War I beef king and profiteer in Germany. Examines his domestic situation as it brings out the absurdity of his life. Inclu des English text titles in a silent film starring Emil Jannings.

FORTY CARATS
National Film and Video Center; 1973 • color; 1 hr, 50 min; 3/4" U-Matic, 1/2" Beta II, 1/2" VHS • Rental: $59/1 showing

Probes the relationship between an older woman and the 22-year-old she meets while vacationing in Greece. Explores the social complications involved when they decide to marry. Stars Liv Ullmann, Gene Kelly, Edward Albert, and Binnie Barnes.

FORTY THIEVES
Videobrary Inc; Order No. 24; 1944 • b/w; 1 hr; 1/2" Beta II, 1/2" VHS • Sale: $39.95

Presents a Hopalong Cassidy western starring William Boyd and Andy Clyde.

FORTY THIEVES; SANTA FE MARSHALL
Videobrary Inc; Order No. 24-25; 1944 & 1940 • b/w; 2 hrs; 1/2" Beta II, 1/2" VHS • Sale: $69.95

Presents a Hopalong Cassidy western double feature. Stars William Boyd.

FOUL PLAY
Fotomat Corp; Order No. V0009 for 1/2" Beta II, V0009 for 1/2" VHS; 1978 • color; 1 hr, 58 min; 1/2" Beta II, 1/2" VHS • Sale: $54.95; Rental: $9.95/5 days
- -
Paramount Home Video; 1978 • color; 1 hr, 58 min; 1/2" Beta II, 1/2" VHS • Sale: $59.95
- -
RCA SelectaVision VideoDiscs; Order No. 00603; 1978 • color; 1 hr, 56 min; CED • Sale: $24.98

Tells of a young San Francisco librarian embroiled in a murder plot and her policeman protector. Stars Goldie Hawn, Chevy Chase, Burgess Meredith, Rachel Roberts, and Dudley Moore.

THE FOUNTAIN OF LOVE
Video Communications Inc; Order No. 1040; 1967 • color; 1 hr, 23 min; 1/2" Beta II, 1/2" VHS • Sale $54.95

Tells of a sleepy mountain town, seeking a subsidy from the Bureau of Tourism, that hires a press agent who heralds the village fountain "the Fountain of Youth." Stars Eddie Arent and Ann Smyrner.

THE FOUNTAINHEAD
Vid America; Order No. 326; 1949 • b/w; 1 hr, 54 min; 1/2" Beta II, 1/2" VHS • Rental: $10.95/wk

Adapts Ayn Rand's novel concerning an architect who defies the establishment with his unusual concept for a housing project, and then destroys the buildings when they do not measure up to his design. Stars Gary Cooper and Patricia Neal.

4D MAN
Video T.E.N.; 1959 • color; 1 hr, 25 min; 1/2" Beta II, 1/2" VHS • Sale: $49.95 for 1/2" Beta II, $54.95 for 1/2" VHS

Reveals how a scientist learns to project himself into

the fourth dimension and drain others' life energy. Stars Robert Lansing, Lee Meriwether, and Robert Strauss.

FRANCIS, THE TALKING MULE
MCA DiscoVision; Order No. 22-003; 1950 • b/w; 1 hr, 30 min; LaserVision • Sale: $15.95

Presents the first of seven films which feature a bumbling soldier who is lead in and out of trouble by a mule that speaks to him only. Shows Francis adopting the lost young man in the Burmese jungle during World War II, and making a hero out of him by whispering the enemy's whereabouts to him. Adapts the novel by David Stern and stars Donald O'Connor, Patricia Medina, Zasu Pitts, and Tony Curtis, as well as the voice of Chill Wills.

FRANKENSTEIN
MCA DiscoVision; Order No. 23-002; 1931 • b/w; 1 hr, 11 min; LaserVision • Sale:$15.95
- -
MCA Videocassette, Inc; Order No. 55004; 1931 • b/w; 1 hr, 11 min; 1/2" Beta II, 1/2" VHS • Sale: $50

Dramatizes the Mary Shelley novel in one of the first major horror films. Uses a gothic atmosphere to relate the tale of a driven scientist, who defies nature to produce the first man-made living being. Features special make-up and effects, and Boris Karloff's film debut. Stars Colin Clive, Mae Clarke, and John Boles, under James Whale's direction.

FRANKENSTEIN 1970
Blackhawk Films, Inc; Order No. 502-86-0071 for 1/2" Beta II, 515-86-0071 for 1/2" VHS ; 1958 • b/w; 1 hr, 23 min; 1/2" Beta II, 1/2" VHS • Sale: $59.95

Follows the adventures of a film company that has come to Baron Frankenstein's castle to make a horror movie, only to discover they are dealing with the real thing. Features Boris Karloff, Tom Duggan, and Jana Lund.

FRANKIE AND JOHNNY
Reel Images Inc; Order No. 483; 1935 • b/w; 1 hr, 7 min; 1/2" Beta II, 1/2" VHS • Sale: $49.95 for 1/2" Beta II, $52.95 for 1/2" VHS

Depicts the well-known relationship of the two lovers of the title. Features songs by blues singer Helen Morgan and stars Chester Morris.

FRANTIC
Reel Images Inc; Order No. 439; 1958 • b/w; 1 hr, 32 min; 1/2" Beta II, 1/2" VHS • Sale: $49.95 for 1/2" Beta II, $52.95 for 1/2" VHS

Dramatizes the story of a former commander, in love with the wife of his employer, who commits a murder and tries to make it look like suicide. Shows how fate steps in when he is trapped in an elevator, his escape car is stolen, and he is accused of murders he did not commit. Stars Maurice Ronet and Jeanne Moreau under the direction of Louis Malle, with music by Miles Davis.

FRATERNITY ROW
Fotomat Corp; Order No. B0081 for 1/2" Beta II, V0081 for 1/2" VHS; 1977 • color; 1 hr, 41 min; 1/2" Beta II, 1/2" VHS • Sale: $49.95; Rental: $9.95/up to 5 days, applicable to purchase

Recounts a story about pledging a fraternity in the early 1950's that follows the comical exploits of a dozen pledges to Gamma Nu Pi at a fictional Eastern college. Focuses on the pledge-master, who hopes for some mature change in the senseless ritual, but is opposed by older members, especially when it comes to hazing and the physical abuse of pledges. Stars Peter Fox, Gregory Harrison, Scott Newman, Nancy Morgan, and Wendy Phillips, under the direction of Thomas J. Tobin.

FRECKLES COMES HOME
Video T.E.N.; 1942 • b/w; 1 hr, 3 min; 1/2" Beta II, 1/2" VHS • Sale: $49.95 for 1/2" Beta II, 54.95 for 1/2" VHS

Dramatizes a nostalgic story of a former "bad boy" who returns from college to his home town to help a friend who has been swindled. Stars Johnny Downs, Gale Storm, Mantan Moreland, and Irving Bacon.

THE FRENCH CONNECTION
Blackhawk Films, Inc; Order No. 502-49-0012 for 1/2" Beta II, 515-49-0008 for 1/2" VHS; 1971 • color; 1 hr, 42 min; 1/2" Beta II, 1/2" VHS • Sale: $54.95

Golden Tapes Video Tape Library; Order No. F-1009; 1971 • color; 1 hr, 42 min; 1/2" Beta II, 1/2" VHS • Sale: $49.95 for 1/2" Beta II & VHS, $124.95 for 3/4"

Magnetic Video Corporation; Order No. CL-1009; 1971 • color; 1 hr, 42 min; 1/2" Beta II, 1/2" VHS • Sale: $44.95

RCA SelectaVision VideoDiscs; Order No. 00103 *; 1971 • color; 1 hr, 44 min; CED • Sale: $19.98

The Video Library; Order No. MV-1009; 1971 • color; 1 hr, 42 min; 1/2" Beta II, 1/2" VHS • Sale: $54.95

Presents a thriller about two real-life New York City narcotics detectives and their attempt to smash an international ring of heroin smugglers. Stars Gene Hackman, Fernando Rey, Roy Scheider, and Tony Lo Bianco.

FRENCH LINE
Blackhawk Films, Inc; Order No. 506-88-0749 for 1/2" Beta II, 525-88-0749 for 1/2" VHS; 1954 • color; 1 hr, 42 min; 1/2" Beta II, 1/2" VHS • Sale: $59.95

Relates the woes of a girl who is too rich, since all of the men she meets are out for her money, until she pretends to be poor and falls in love with a rich Parisian travelling incognito because he, too, is wary of fortune hunters. Stars Jane Russell and Gilbert Roland in this musical originally presented in 3-D.

FRENCH POSTCARDS
Fotomat Corp; Order No. B0387 for 1/2" Beta II, V0387 for 1/2" VHS; 1979 • color; 1 hr, 35 min; 1/2" Beta II, 1/2" VHS • Sale: $54.95; Rental: $9.95/5 days

Recounts the experiences of three American students who spend their junior year in Paris. Presents a comedy written by Gloria Katz and Willard Huyck, who previously wrote "American Graffiti." Features Miles Chapin, Blanche Baker, David Marshall Grant, and Mandy Patinkin.

FRENZY
MCA DiscoVision; Order No. 11-006; 1972 • color; 1 hr, 56 min; LaserVision • Sale: $24.95

MCA Videocassette, Inc; Order No. 55011; 1972 • color; 1 hr, 56 min;1/2" Beta II1/2" VHS • Sale: $55

Traces the story of the "Necktie Murderer" of London. Uses suspense and macabre humor in this adaptation of "Goodbye Picadilly, Farewell Leicester Square," Arthur La Bern's novel. Marks director Alfred Hitchcock's return to England, the first time in many years. Stars Jon Finch, Barry Foster, Anna Massey, and Alex McCowan.

FRIDAY THE 13TH
Paramount Home Video; Order No. 1395; 1980 • color; 1 hr, 35 min; 1/2" Beta II, 1/2" VHS • Sale: $79.95

Offers a horror tale which centers on a camp by a lake closed for twenty years due to unsolved murders. Follows the attempts of the new counselors to escape execution. Features Adrienne King and Betsy Palmer.

FROM BROADWAY TO HOLLYWOOD
Blackhawk Films, Inc; Order No. 506-66-0880 for 1/2" Beta II, 525-66-0880 for 1/2" VHS; Date not listed • b/w; 48 min; 3/4" U-Matic, 1/2" Beta I, 1/2" Beta II, 1/2" VHS • Sale: $59.95 for 1/2" Beta I, $39.95 for 1/2" Beta II & VHS, $69.95 for 3/4"

Presents a color-toned, narrated documentary of show business in the early 1930's. Includes Shirley Temple's "Biggest Little Star of the Thirties," Lew Lehr's "Cwazy Monkies," a thirties fashion show, a ride on a Mississippi riverboat, and Ed Sullivan's newspaper beat interviewing Eddie Cantor, Jack Dempsey, the Little Rascals, and others.

Don Dubbins, Montgomery Clift, and Frank Sinatra in *From Here to Eternity*.

FROM HERE TO ETERNITY
National Film and Video Center; 1953 • b/w; 1 hr, 58 min; 3/4" U-Matic, 1/2" Beta II, 1/2" VHS • Rental: $49/1 showing

Tells the story of a soldier who is befriended by only one man in his outfit—when that man is beaten to death after going AWOL, the soldier kills the man who beat him and deserts. Climaxes in the bombing of Pearl Harbor, when the soldier is killed while trying to rejoin his unit. Stars Montgomery Clift, Burt Lancaster, Deborah Kerr, Frank Sinatra, Donna Reed, and Ernest Borgnine.

FROM THE EARTH TO THE MOON
Fotomat Corp; Order No. B0165 for 1/2" Beta II, V0165 for 1/2" VHS; 1958 • color; 1 hr, 40 min; 1/2" Beta II, 1/2" VHS • Sale: $49.95; Rental: $9.95/up to 5 days, applicable to purchase

Video Communications Inc; 1958 • color; 1 hr, 40 min; 1/2" Beta II, 1/2" VHS • Sale: $54.95

Dramatizes the Jules Verne story of Victor Barbicane's attempt to launch to the moon. Features Joseph Cotten, George Sanders, and Debra Paget.

FROM THE TERRACE
Golden Tapes Video Tape Library; Order No. F-1036; 1960 • color; 2 hrs, 24 min; 1/2" Beta II, 1/2" VHS • Sale: $49.95 for 1/2" Beta II & VHS, $124.95 for 3/4"
- -
Magnetic Video Corporation; Order No. CL-1036; 1960 • color; 2 hrs, 24 min; 1/2" Beta II, 1/2" VHS • Sale: $64.95
- -
The Video Library; 1960 • color; 2 hrs, 24 min; 1/2" Beta II, 1/2" VHS • Sale: $74.95

Presents the dramatization of John O'Hara's novel of a man's search for wealth and power, starring Paul Newman and Joanne Woodward.

THE FRONT PAGE
Video T.E.N.; 1931 • b/w; 1 hr, 41 min; 1/2" Beta II, 1/2" VHS • Sale: $49.95 for 1/2" Beta II, $54.95 for 1/2" VHS

Offers one of the earliest sound films, directed by Lewis Milestone, and starring Adolph Menjou, Pat O'Brien, Mary Brian, Edward Everett Horton, and Mae Clark in a comedy of a newspaper office.

FRONTIER JUSTICE; BULLDOG COURAGE
Video Communications Inc; Order No. 1122; 1937 • b/w; 2 hrs, 3 min; 1/2" Beta II, 1/2" VHS • Sale: $74.95

Offers a western double feature. Features Hoot Gibson in "Frontier Justice," a story of how the law handles cattle rustlers. Presents Tim McCoy, in "Bulldog Courage," as a young man out to avenge his father's murder, thereby prompting speedy action from the law.

THE FRONTIERSMAN
Videobrary Inc; Order No. 1; 1938 • b/w; 1 hr, 14 min; 1/2" Beta II, 1/2" VHS • Sale: $39.95

Offers a Hopalong Cassidy western. Presents Cassidy trailing a cattle rustler, and trying to protect the new schoolmarm. Stars William Boyd, George "Gabby" Hayes, and Evelyn Venable.

FUN FACTORY AND CLOWN PRINCES OF HOLLYWOOD
Blackhawk Films, Inc; Order No. 506-01-0878 for 1/2" Beta II, 525-01-0878 for 1/2" VHS; Date not listed • b/w; 56 min; 3/4" U-Matic, 1/2" Beta I, 1/2" Beta II, 1/2" VHS • Sale: $59.95 for 1/2" Beta I, $39.95 for 1/2" Beta II & VHS, $69.95 for 3/4"

Presents two color-toned, narrated, compilations of silent film comic performances with musical accompaniment. Offers "Fun Factory" from the Mack Sennett Studios with the Keystone Kops, Fatty Arbuckle, Mabel Normand, Chaplin, Sennett, The Bathing Beauties, 16-year-old Gloria Swanson, and young Carole Lombard: and "Clown Princes of Hollywood" which features Ben Turpin, Charley Chase, Billy West, Oliver Hardy, Finlayson, Harold Lloyd, Buster Keaton, Harry Langdon, and Charlie Chaplin. Provides two segments from The History of the Motion Picture Series.

FUN IN ACAPULCO
Magnetic Video Corporation; Order No. CL-2002; 1963 • color; 1 hr, 37 min; 1/2" Beta II, 1/2" VHS • Sale: $44.95
- -
The Video Library; Order No. MV-2002; 1963 • color; 1 hr, 37 min; 1/2" Beta II, 1/2" VHS • Sale: $44.95

Presents an Elvis Presley musical in which Elvis works as a part-time lifeguard and nightclub entertainer while romancing two women. Co-stars Ursula Andress, Elsa Cardenas, and Paul Lukas.

FUN WITH DICK AND JANE
Columbia Pictures Home Entertainment; 1977 • color; 1 hr, 35 min ; 1/2" Beta II, 1/2" VHS • Sale: $59.95
- -
Fotomat Corp; Order No. B0423 for 1/2" Beta II, V0423 for 1/2" VHS; 1976 • color; 1 hr, 36 min; 1/2" Beta II, 1/2" VHS • Sale: $54.95; Rental: $9.95/5 days
- -
Time-Life Video Club Inc; 1977 • color; 1 hr, 35 min; 1/2" Beta II, 1/2" VHS • Sale: $59.95 to members

Tells a comic story of a man who loses his job and turns to burglary after a series of disappointments. Features George Segal, Jane Fonda, Ed McMahon, and Dick Gautier, under the direction of Ted Kotcheff.

FUNNY GUYS AND GALS OF THE TALKIES
Reel Images Inc; Order No. 78; 1930-43 • b/w; 1 hr, 2 min; 1/2" Beta II, 1/2" VHS • Sale: $39.95 for 1/2" Beta II, $42.95 for 1/2" VHS

Presents four comedy shorts from the 1930's and 1940's. Features "The Golf Specialist" with W.C. Fields; "Pardon My Pups" with Shirley Temple; "Girls Will Be Boys" with Charlotte Greenwood; and "Groucho Marx and Carole Landis" in footage taken during a live radio broadcast.

FUNSTUFF
Video Action Library; Order No. BH05; 1918-29 • color; 59 min; 1/2" Beta I, 1/2" Beta II, 1/2" VHS • Rental: $12.50/1 wk, $6.25 ea add'l wk

Includes five short comic films, beginning with "French Paint" (1920) starring Snub Pollard..Follows with Harold Lloyd and Bebe Daniels in "The Non Stop Kid" (1918). Continues with Shirley "Funny Face," a Betty Boop cartoon. Concludes with Andy Clyde in "The Brides' Relations" (1929), an early talkie by Mack Sennett.

THE FURY
Magnetic Video Corporation; Order No. 1097; 1978 • color; 1 hr, 58 min; 1/2" Beta II, 1/2" VHS • Sale: $59.95
- -
Niles Cinema; Order No. CL-1097; 1978 • color; 1 hr, 58 min; 1/2" Beta II, 1/2" VHS • Sale: $59.95

Follows the attempts of a father to rescue his son from an agency that wishes to exploit his psychokinetic powers. Stars Kirk Douglas, Carrie Snodgrass, John Cassavetes, Amy Irving, Andrew Stevens, Charles Durning, and Fiona Lewis under Brian De Palma's direction. Uses bizarre violence.

FUTURE WOMEN
Niles Cinema; Order No. BT-31 for 1/2" Beta II, VH-31 for 1/2" VHS; 1971 • color; 1 hr, 30 min; 1/2" Beta II, 1/2" VHS • Sale: $59.95

Tells the story of an army of women which kidnaps wealthy men and holds them for ransom, starring Shirley Eaton, Richard Wyler, and George Sanders.

GABRIELLE
Monarch Releasing Corporation; Date not listed • color; 1 hr, 5 min; 3/4" U-Matic • Sale: $300

Presents a pornographic film.

GANDY GOOSE
Magnetic Video Corporation; Order No. CL-2037; Date not listed • color; 30 min; 1/2" Beta II, 1/2" VHS • Sale: $34.95

Offers a compilation of Terrytoon animated cartoons featuring Gandy Goose.

GANGBUSTERS
Cable Films; 1942 • b/w; 4 hrs, 20 min; 1/2" Beta I, 1/2" Beta II, 1/2" VHS • Sale: $109.50

Reel Images Inc; Order No. 788; 1942 • b/w; 4 hrs, 13 min; 1/2" Beta II, 1/2" VHS • Sale: $129.95

Offers a thirteen-chapter serial from the 1930's based on the radio drama. Stars Kent Taylor, Irene Hervey, and Robert Armstrong.

GANGWAY
Budget Video; 1937 • b/w; 1 hr, 28 min; 1/2" Beta II, 1/2" VHS • Sale: $44.95

Reel Images Inc; Order No. 484; 1937 • b/w; 1 hr, 37 min; 1/2" Beta II, 1/2" VHS • Sale: $49.95 for 1/2" Beta II, $52.95 for 1/2" VHS

Tells of a female film critic who is mistaken for an international jewel thief in a musical spoof of gangster movies. Follows the heroine through a series of increasing complications from England to America. Stars Jessie Matthews, Nat Pendleton, Barry Mackay, Olive Blakeney, Noel Madison, and Alastair Sim.

THE GARDEN OF THE FINZI-CONTINIS
Time-Life Video Club Inc; 1971 • color; 1 hr, 35 min; 1/2" Beta II, 1/2" VHS • Sale: $49.95 to members

Enters the world of Ferrara, Italy in 1938 when the fascist government of Mussolini has begun to enforce racial laws against Jewish citizens. Unfolds from the perspective of people who live on a secluded estate, relating their gradual awareness of events that threaten their gentle way of life. Stars Dominique Sanda and Helmut Berger, under the direction of Vittorio De Sica.

THE GATLING GUN
Video Communications Inc; Order No. 1043; 1970 • color; 1 hr, 29 min; 1/2" Beta II, 1/2" VHS • Sale: $54.95

Presents an action-packed epic revolving around the newest destructive weapon of the period: a Gatling gun. Features Guy Stockwell, Robert Fuller, Barbara Luna, and Woody Strode.

THE GAY DIVORCEE
Niles Cinema; Order No. NM-8015; 1934 • b/w; 1 hr, 47 min; 1/2" Beta II, 1/2" VHS • Sale: $54.95

The Nostalgia Merchant; Order No. 8015; 1934 • b/w; 1 hr, 47 min; 1/2" Beta II, 1/2" VHS • Sale: $54.95

Red Fox, Inc; Order No. 8015; 1934 • b/w; 1 hr, 47 min; 1/2" Beta II, 1/2" VHS • Sale: $54.95

Time-Life Video Club Inc; 1934 • b/w; 1 hr, 47 min; 1/2" Beta II, 1/2" VHS • Sale: $54.95 to members

Presents a song and dance spectacular starring Fred Astaire and Ginger Rogers. Includes the Cole Porter songs "Night and Day" and "The Continental." Co-stars Alice Brady, Edward Everett Horton, Erwin Rhodes, and Betty Grable.

GAY RANCHERO
Cable Films; 1942 • b/w; 55 min; 1/2" Beta I, 1/2" Beta II, 1/2" VHS • Sale: $45 for 1/2" Beta I, $49.50 for 1/2" Beta II & VHS

Presents a western in which dishonest men are planning to take over a small airline that is in danger of going out of business. Stars Roy Rogers and Andy Devine.

A GEMINI AFFAIR
Tape Club of America; Order No. 2813 B; Date not listed • color; 1 hr, 33 min; 1/2" Beta II, 1/2" VHS • Sale: $54.95

Presents a pornographic film.

THE GENERAL
Ivy Video; 1927 • b/w; 1 hr, 14 min; 3/4" U-Matic, 1/2" Beta II, 1/2" VHS • Sale: $59.95 for 1/2" Beta II & VHS, trade-in plan available, $195 for 3/4"

Northeast Video and Sound, Inc; Order No. 103S; 1927 • b/w; 1 hr, 14 min; 3/4" U-Matic, 1/2" EIAJ, 1/2" Beta II, 1/2" VHS • Sale: $225; Rental: $75/wk

Reel Images Inc; Order No. 527; 1926 • b/w; 1 hr, 48 min; 1/2" Beta II, 1/2" VHS • Sale: $49.95 for 1/2" Beta II, $52.95 for 1/2" VHS

Features the acting and directing talents of Buster Keaton in this tale of a southerner who chases a stolen train, the "General" of the title, behind Union lines during the Civil War, with much mayhem, confusion, excitement and adventure in this silent comic version of a true historical story.

GENERATION
Magnetic Video Corporation; Order No. CL-4042; 1969 • color; 1 hr, 44 min; 1/2" Beta II, 1/2" VHS • Sale: $54.95

Examines the generation conflict between a young, anti-establishment, newly married couple who plan to deliver their baby in their own home, and the wife's dubious father. Stars David Janssen, Kim Darby, and Carl Reiner.

GENGHIS KHAN
National Film and Video Center; 1965 • color; 2 hrs, 4 min; 3/4" U-Matic, 1/2" Beta II, 1/2" VHS • Rental: $59/1 showing

Dramatizes, in epic fashion, the youth and rise to power of the Mongolian conqueror. Traces his conquest of Asia. Features Omar Sharif, Stephen Boyd, James Mason, Eli Wallach, and Francoise Dorleac.

Marilyn Monroe and Jane Russell in
Gentlemen Prefer Blondes.

GENTLEMAN'S AGREEMENT

Magnetic Video Corporation; Order No. CL-1077; 1947 • b/w; 1 hr, 58 min; ½" Beta II, ½" VHS • Sale: $44.95

Adapts Laura Z. Hobson's novel about a writer who assumes a Jewish identity in order to learn first-hand about anti-semitism. Explores his unexpected experiences with prejudice, as well as the indignities suffered by his family and fiancée. Stars Gregory Peck, Celeste Holm, Dorothy McGuire, John Garfield, June Havoc, Albert Dekker, Jane Wyatt, and Dean Stockwell, under the direction of Elia Kazan.

GENTLEMEN PREFER BLONDES

Blackhawk Films, Inc; Order No. 502-49-0010 for ½" Beta II, 520-49-0010; 1953 • color; 1 hr, 31 min; ½" Beta II, ½" VHS • Sale: $79.98

Golden Tapes Video Tape Library; Order No. F-1019; 1953 • color; 1 hr, 31 min; ½" Beta II, ½" VHS • Sale: $49.95 for ½" Beta II & VHS, $124.95 for ¾"

The Video Library; Order No. MV-1019; 1953 • color; 1 hr, 41 min; ½" Beta II, ½" VHS • Sale: $44.95

Presents a musical comedy based on Anita Loos' story about two American girls trying to make good in Paris. Stars Jane Russell, Marilyn Monroe, Charles Coburn, Tommy Noonan, and George Winslow, under the direction of Howard Hawks.

GEORGE

Tape Club of America; Order No. 2001 B; 1972 • color; 1 hr, 26 min; ½" Beta II, ½" VHS • Sale: $54.95

Recounts a tale of a swinging airline pilot in his quest to find love when he is saddled with a 250 lb. St. Bernard dog named George that's afraid of heights, fears cats, knocks down tables and sulks in the bathtub. Tells of his flighty sister who marries an Arabian maharajah and sends George to live with him. Stars Marshall Thompson, Jack Mullaney, Inge Schoner, and George.

GEORGE WHITE'S SCANDALS

Blackhawk Films, Inc; Order No. 506-88-0748 for ½" Beta II, 525-88-0748 for ½" VHS; 1945 • b/w; 1 hr, 35 min; ¾" U-Matic, ½" Beta I, ½" Beta II, ½" VHS • Sale: $89.95 for ½" Beta I, $49.95 for ½" Beta II & VHS, $99.95 for ¾"

Offers a musical-comedy look at the showbiz world. Highlights the antics of Joan Davis. Includes slapstick and jazz by the Gene Krupa Band. Features Jack Haley, Phillip Terry, Martha Holliday, and Jane Greer.

GEORGY GIRL

National Film and Video Center; 1966 • b/w; 1 hr, 40 min; ¾" U-Matic, ½" Beta II, ½" VHS • Rental: $49/1 showing

Portrays a gawky, badly-dressed, soft-hearted young woman who acts clownish to cover her inadequacies and envy of her roommate's casual love affairs. Stars Lynn Redgrave, James Mason, and Alan Bates.

GET HAPPY

Blackhawk Films, Inc; Order No. 506-01-0845 for ½" Beta II, 525-01-0845 for ½" VHS; Date not listed • b/w; 59 min; ¾" U-Matic, ½" Beta I, ½" Beta II, ½" VHS • Sale: $59.95 for ½" Beta I, $39.95 for ½" Beta II & VHS, $69.95 for ¾"

Presents a color-toned collection of comedy shorts. Includes Shirley Temple in "Glad Rags to Riches;" Weber and Fields in "Beer is Here;" Bessie Smith, the queen of the blues, in "St. Louis Blues;" and a Ub Iwerks cartoon featuring Flip the Frog.

GHIDRAH, THE THREE HEADED MONSTER

Discount Video Tape; 1965 • color; 1 hr, 25 min; ½" Beta II, ½" VHS • Sale: $49

VCX; Order No. FC122; 1965 • color; 1 hr, 25 min; ½" Beta II, ½" VHS • Sale: $35.00

Presents Japanese monsters Mothra, Rodan, and Godzilla joining forces to stop Ghidrah. Co-stars Yosuke Natsuki and Emi Ito.

GHOST TOWN LAW

Cable Films; 1942 • b/w; 1 hr, 5 min; ½" Beta I, ½" Beta II, ½" VHS • Sale: $65 for ½" Beta I, $49.50 for ½" Beta II & VHS

Follows the Rough Riders as they investigate bizarre events in a deserted ghost town. Stars Tim McCoy, Buck Jones, and Ray Hatton.

GHOST TOWN RENEGADES

Thunderbird Films; 1944 • b/w; 1 hr; ¾" U-Matic, ½" Beta I, ½" Beta II, ½" VHS • Sale: $59.95 for ½" Beta I, $39.95 for ½" Beta II & VHS, $79.95 for ¾"

Highlights Lash LaRue and Fuzzy Knight attempting to save prospective victims from a ruthless lawyer who plans to gain ownership of a gold mine by murder.

GHOST TOWN RENEGADES; SANTA FE UPRISING

The Nostalgia Merchant; 1947; 1946 • b/w; 2 hrs; ½" Beta II, ½" VHS • Sale: $59.95

Provides a western double feature. Probes the mystery of an old ghost town with Lash LaRue starring in "Ghost Town Renegades." Follows with "Santa Fe Uprising," in which Red Ryder protects a duchess from highwaymen who want to prevent her from taking over a toll road; stars Alan "Rocky" Lane and Bobby Blake.

GHOSTS ON THE LOOSE

Cable Films; 1943 • b/w; 1 hr, 4 min; ½" Beta I, ½" Beta II, ½" VHS • Sale: $65 for ½" Beta I, $49.50 for ½" Beta II & VHS

Offers a mystery-comedy complete with a haunted house, dim-witted cops, and an aura of supernatural events. Stars Bela Lugosi, Ava Gardner, the East Side Kids, Huntz Hall, and Leo Gorcey.

GHOSTS THAT STILL WALK

Video Communications Inc; Order No. 1044; 1978 • color; 1 hr, 32 min; ½" Beta II, ½" VHS • Sale: $54.95

Shows how a doctor's desperate attempt to unlock the secret of a possessed boy leads to a startling discovery—the evil power in control could be the work of ghosts haunting Death Valley.

G.I. BLUES

Magnetic Video Corporation; Order No. CL-2003; 1960 • color; 1 hr, 44 min;

RCA SelectaVision VideoDiscs; Order No. 01502; 1960 • color; 1 hr, 44 min; CED • Sale: $19.98

The Video Library; Order No. MV-2003; 1960 • color; 1 hr, 44 min; ½" Beta II, ½" VHS • Sale: $54.95

Presents a musical-romance set in peacetime Germany in which soldiers start a music group. Stars Elvis Presley, Juliet Prowse, Letitia Roman and Robert Ivers.

A GIFT FOR HEIDI

Fotomat Corp; Order No. B0135 for ½" Beta II, V0135 for ½" VHS; Date not listed • color; 1 hr, 11 min; ½"

Beta II, ½" VHS • Sale: $39.95; Rental: $7.95/up to 5 days, applicable to purchase

Video Communications Inc; 1962 • color; 1 hr, 11 min; ½" Beta II, ½" VHS • Sale: $54.95

Recounts the tale of a young girl and the lessons she learns while growing up in the Alp country.

Leslie Caron, Hermione Gingold, and Louis Jourdan in *Gigi*.

GIGI
RCA SelectaVision VideoDiscs; Order No. 00204; 1958 • color; 1 hr, 56 min; CED • Sale: $14.98

Presents Vincente Minnelli's musical film adaptation of Colette's story of a turn-of-the-century Parisian girl who becomes a lady. Features "I Remember It Well," "Thank Heaven For Little Girls" and "Gigi." Stars Leslie Caron, Maurice Chevalier, Louis Jourdan, Hermione Gingold, Jacques Bergerac, and Eva Gabor.

GILDA
Columbia Pictures Home Entertainment; 1946 • b/w; 1 hr, 50 min; ½" Beta II, ½" VHS • Sale: $59.95

Relates how a South American casino owner unknowingly hires his wife's former boy friend as his assistant, with tense emotional consequences. Stars Rita Hayworth, Glenn Ford, and George Macready, under the direction of Charles Vidor. Includes Hayworth singing "Put the Blame on Mame, Boys."

GIMME SHELTER
Columbia Pictures Home Entertainment; Order No. BCF7120 for ½" Beta II, VCF3075 for ½" VHS; 1970 • color; 1 hr, 31 min; ½" Beta II, ½" VHS • Sale: $59.95

RCA SelectaVision VideoDiscs; Order No. 01801; 1970 • color; 1 hr, 31 min; CED • Sale: $19.98

Time-Life Video Club Inc; 1970 • color; 1 hr, 31 min; ½" Beta II, ½" VHS • Sale: $44.95 to members

Presents a documentary of the Rolling Stones' Altamont Speedway concert that resulted in violence and murder. Shows performances by Ike and Tina Turner and The Jefferson Airplane.

GINGER IN THE MORNING
FHV Entertainment, Inc; 1973 • color; 1 hr, 32 min; ½" Beta II, ½" VHS • Sale: $49.95

Offers a story of a young hitchhiker and the man she befriends. Stars Sissy Spacek as "Ginger," with Monte Markham and Susan Oliver.

THE GIRL FROM STARSHIP VENUS
FHV Entertainment, Inc; Date not listed • color; 1 hr, 27 min; ½" Beta II, ½" VHS • Sale: $49.95

Presents a pornographic film.

GIRL MOST LIKELY
Video Communications Inc; 1957 • color; 1 hr, 38 min; ½" Beta II, ½" VHS • Sale: $54.95

Offers music, dancing, and comedy in the story of a girl who fakes a drowning to meet the owner of a yacht and is rescued by a mechanic instead. Stars Cliff Robertson, Jane Powell, and Kaye Ballard.

GIRLS, GIRLS, GIRLS
Magnetic Video Corporation; Order No. CL-2004; 1962 • color; 1 hr, 46 min; ½" Beta II, ½" VHS • Sale: $44.95

The Video Library; Order No. MV-2004; 1962 • color; 1 hr, 46 min; ½" Beta II, ½" VHS • Sale: $44.95

Features Elvis Presley in the story of a boy who refuses to accept a boat from the girl he loves until another boy begins to compete for her favor. Co-stars Stella Stevens, Laurel Goodwin, Jeremy Slate, Guy Lee, and Benson Fong.

GLEN OR GLENDA?
Video T.E.N.; 1953 • b/w; 1 hr, 10 min; ½" Beta II, ½" VHS • Sale: $49.95 for ½" Beta II, $54.95 for ½" VHS

Focuses on an early version of the sex change operation, to the befuddlement of a police inspector. Features Bela Lugosi, Lyle Talbot, Timothy Farrell, Dolores Fuller, and Daniel Davis.

GLORIFYING THE AMERICAN GIRL
Video T.E.N.; 1929 • b/w; 1 hr, 20 min; ½" Beta II, ½" VHS • Sale: $49.95 for ½" Beta II, $54.95 for ½" VHS

Recreates the world of Ziegfeld musicals in a story of a girl determined to make it as a dancer, and her egotistical partner. Features Mary Eaton, Dan Healey, Edward Crandall, Kaye Renard, Eddie Cantor, Helen Morgan, and Rudy Vallee.

GLORY
Video Communications Inc; Order No. 1049; 1956 • color; 1 hr, 40 min; ½" Beta II, ½" VHS • Sale: $54.95

Shows how a dewy-eyed teenager's faith prevents a filly from being sold or turned from the track. Relates how the filly is prepared for the Kentucky Derby despite opposition. Stars Margaret O'Brien and Walter Brennan.

GO DOWN DEATH
Northeast Video and Sound, Inc; Order No. 174S; Date not listed • b/w; 1 hr, 3 min; ¾" U-Matic, ½" EIAJ, ½" Beta II, ½" VHS • Sale: $195; Rental: $75/wk

Presents an all-black film, directed by Spencer Williams, which looks at religion, death and guilt in a small-town setting. Stars Myra Hemmings, Eddy Houston, and Samuel Jones.

GO TELL THE SPARTANS
Time-Life Video Club Inc; Date not listed • color; 1 hr, 54 min; ½" Beta II, ½" VHS • Sale: $39.95 to members

Portrays a group of American soldiers in Vietnam in 1964, when they were still called "advisers" and were unaware of the profundity of the conflict. Features Burt Lancaster.

THE GO-BETWEEN
National Film and Video Center; 1971 • color; 1 hr, 56 min; 3/4" U-Matic, 1/2" Beta II, 1/2" VHS • Rental: $89/1 showing

Recounts the secret love affair between an heiress and a poor tenant farmer who use a boy as their unwitting message-bearer. Climaxes with her mother's discovery of the affair. Stars Julie Christie and Alan Bates.

THE GODFATHER
Fotomat Corp; Order No. B0011 for 1/2" Beta II, V0011 for 1/2" VHS; 1972 • color; 2 hrs, 51 min; 1/2" Beta II, 1/2" VHS • Sale: $69.95; Rental: $13.95/up to 5 days, applicable to purchase

- -
MCA DiscoVision; Order No. P12-518; 1972 • color; 2 hrs, 51 min; LaserVision • Sale: $24.95
- -
Paramount Home Video; 1972 • color; 2 hrs, 51 min; 1/2" Beta II, 1/2" VHS • Sale: $79.95
- -
RCA SelectaVision VideoDiscs; Order No. 00604; 1972 • color; 2 hrs, 55 min; CED • Sale: $27.98

Paints a chilling portrait of a Sicilian family's rise and near fall from power in America, and the passage of rites from father to son. Balances the story between family life and the ugly business of crime in a film based on Mario Puzo's novel. Stars Marlon Brando, Al Pacino, James Caan, Robert Duvall, Talia Shire, and Diane Keaton, under the direction of Francis Ford Coppola.

THE GODFATHER, PART II
Fotomat Corp; Order No. B0013 for 1/2" Beta II, V0013 for 1/2" VHS; 1975 • color; 3 hrs, 20 min; 1/2" Beta II, 1/2" VHS • Sale: $69.95; Rental: $13.95/up to 5 days, applicable to purchase

- -
MCA DiscoVision; Order No. P12-519; 1975 • color; 3 hrs, 20 min; LaserVision • Sale: $24.95
- -
Paramount Home Video; 1975 • color; 3 hrs, 20 min; 1/2" Beta II, 1/2" VHS • Sale: $79.95

Continues the saga of two generations of power within the Corleone family. Tells two stories: the roots and rise of a young Don Vito, and the ascension of Michael as the new Don. Stars Al Pacino, Robert De Niro, Robert Duvall, Talia Shire, Diane Keaton, and Lee Strasberg, under the direction of Francis Ford Coppola.

GOD'S LITTLE ACRE
Niles Cinema; Order No. BT-10 for 1/2" Beta II, VH-10 for 1/2" VHS; 1958 • b/w; 1 hr, 58 min; 1/2" Beta II, 1/2" VHS • Sale: $59.95

Presents Erskine Caldwell's story of a Georgia farm family and the dreams of its members, with Robert Ryan, Tina Louise, Michael Landon, Buddy Hackett, and Aldo Ray.

THE GODSEND
Time-Life Video Club Inc; 1978 • color; 1 hr, 33 min; 1/2" Beta II, 1/2" VHS • Sale: $34.95 to members

Presents a horror film in the "Omen" mood. Follows a married couple who help a woman deliver her baby in a meadow while they are picnicing. Shows the terror they live after they adopt the child and their own children die, one by one.

GODZILLA VS. MEGALON AND GODZILLA VS. THE COSMIC MONSTER
Vid America; Order No. 927; 1976 • color; 2 hrs, 30 min; 1/2" Beta II, 1/2" VHS • Rental: $13.95/wk

Offers a double-feature starring Japan's favorite resur-

rected dinosaur. Opens with "Godzilla vs Megalon," in which he rescues Earth from a monstrous insect. Concludes with "Godzilla vs the Cosmic Monster," in which he has an encounter with an immense robot.

GOIN' COCONUTS
Time-Life Video Club Inc; Date not listed • color; 1 hr, 36 min; 1/2" Beta II, 1/2" VHS • Sale: $49.95 to members

Presents Donny and Marie Osmond in their first theatrical film, set in Hawaii. Offers a musical comedy as Donny and Marie pursue a gang of crooks.

GOIN' SOUTH
Fotomat Corp; Order No. B0043 for 1/2" Beta II, V0043 for 1/2" VHS; 1978 • color; 1 hr, 48 min; 1/2" Beta II, 1/2" VHS • Sale: $69.95; Rental: $13.95/up to 5 days, applicable to purchase

- -
Paramount Home Video; 1978 • color; 1 hr, 48 min; 1/2" Beta II, 1/2" VHS • Sale: $59.95

Offers a tongue-in-cheek western love story about an outlaw who is saved from the hangman's noose by a young woman, who agrees to marry him if he will work her gold mine before the railroad takes over her land. Stars Jack Nicholson and Mary Steenburgen, under Nicholson's direction.

GOING IN STYLE
WCI Home Video Inc; 1979 • color; 2 hrs; 1/2" Beta II, 1/2" VHS • Sale: $55

Follows the misadventures of three senior citizens who have grown tired of their mundane life style and decide to rob a bank. Stars George Burns, Art Carney, and Lee Strasberg, under the direction of Martin Brest.

GOING MY WAY
MCA DiscoVision; Order No. 21-017; 1944 • b/w; 2 hrs, 6 min; LaserVision • Sale: $15.95

Depicts the attempts of a young priest to save a mortgage-ridden parish and win over his gruff, conventional superior. Includes the songs "Going My Way," "Swinging on a Star," and "To-ra-loo-ra-loo-ra." Stars Bing Crosby, Barry Fitzgerald, Rise Stevens, Gene Lockhart, and Frank McHugh, in a film directed by Leo McCary which won seven Academy Awards, including "Best Picture."

THE GOLD BUG; RODEO RED AND THE RUNAWAY
RCA SelectaVision VideoDiscs; Order No. 02021; Date not listed • color; 1 hr, 32 min; CED • Sale: $14.98

Presents two complete dramas for children. Offers Edgar Allan Poe's "The Gold Bug," in which a teenager battles quicksand, a terrifying storm, and Captain Kidd's curse; and "Rodeo Red and the Runaway," in which a rugged farm woman teaches a young girl about facing life's problems by teaching her about horses.

THE GOLD RUSH
Cinema Concepts, Inc.; 1925 • b/w; 1 hr, 20 min; 3/4" U-Matic, 1/2" Beta II, 1/2" VHS • Sale: $54.95 for 1/2" Beta II & VHS, $149.95 for 3/4"

- -
Golden Tapes Video Tape Library; Order No. CC7; 1925 • b/w; 1 hr, 12 min; 1/2" Beta II, 1/2" VHS • Sale: $49.95 for 1/2" Beta II & VHS, $124.95 for 3/4"
- -
Ivy Video; 1925 • b/w; 1 hr, 12 min; 3/4" U-Matic, 1/2" Beta II, 1/2" VHS • Sale: $59.95 for 1/2" Beta II & VHS, trade-in plan available, $175 for 3/4"
- -
Northeast Video and Sound, Inc; Order No. 106S;

1925 • b/w; 1 hr, 12 min; ¾" U-Matic, ½" EIAJ, ½"
Beta II, ½" VHS • Sale: $195; Rental: $75/wk

Epitomizes the acting and directorial style of Charlie
Chaplin in this silent feature. Follows the misadventures of the Tramp as a hapless prospector in the frozen Yukon. Includes a scene of Charlie and Mack
Swain eating their boots for dinner in a cabin teetering
over the edge of a cliff.

THE GOLD RUSH AND PAY DAY
Magnetic Video Corporation; Order No. CL-3004;
1925 • b/w; 1 hr, 32 min; ½" Beta II, ½" VHS • Sale:
$44.95

Presents "The Gold Rush," the most ambitious of
Charlie Chaplin's early films which tells the story of
turn-of-the- century Klondike gold fever, and "Pay
Day," a rare short, starring Chaplin and his brother
Sydney, which focuses on a day in the life of a belea-
guered construction worker.

THE GOLDEN AGE OF COMEDY
Cinema Concepts, Inc.; 1957 • b/w; 1 hr, 18 min; ¾"
U-Matic, ½" Beta II, ½" VHS • Sale: $54.95 for ½"
Beta II & VHS, $149.95 for ¾"

- -
Vid America; Order No. 216; Date not listed • b/w; 1
hr, 28 min; ½" Beta II, ½" VHS • Rental: $7.95/wk
- -
The Video Library; Order No. CC-0118; 1957 • b/w; 1
hr, 16 min; ½" Beta II, ½" VHS • Sale: $54.95

Offers a compilation of scenes from old comedies, featuring performances by Laurel & Hardy, Ben Turpin,
Keystone Cops, Jean Harlow, Harry Langdon, and
others.

Charles Chaplin in *The Gold Rush*.

THE GOLDEN STALLION; THE CHEROKEE FLASH
The Nostalgia Merchant; 1949; 1945 • b/w; 2 hrs; ½"
Beta II, ½" VHS • Sale: $59.95

Presents a western double feature. Opens with "The
Golden Stallion," starring Roy Rogers, Dale Evans,
Estelita, and Pat Brady. Traces the life and numerous
good deeds of Trigger, the horse. Follows with "Cherokee Flash," in which Sunset Carson plays an ex-out-
law still haunted by association with his former gang.

THE GOLDEN VOYAGE OF SINBAD
National Film and Video Center; 1974 • color; 1 hr, 45
min; ¾" U-Matic, ½" Beta II, ½" VHS • Rental: $79/1
showing

Pits Sinbad, the Grand Vizier of Marabia, and the slave
girl Margiana against Prince Koura in a struggle for
control of the kingdom of Marabia that includes battle
with many strange and evil creatures. Stars John Phillip Law, Caroline Munro, Tom Baker, and Douglas Wil-
mer.

THE GOLF SPECIALIST AND THE PHARMACIST AND THE POOL SHARK
Golden Tapes Video Tape Library; Order No. CC2;
Date not listed • b/w; 54 min; ½" Beta II, ½" VHS •
Sale: $49.95 for ½" Beta II & VHS, $79.95 for ¾"

Stars W.C. Fields in three short comedies.

GOOD GUYS WEAR BLACK
Time-Life Video Club Inc; Date not listed • color; 1 hr,
40 min; ½" Beta II, ½" VHS • Sale: $44.95 to mem-
bers

Presents undefeated six-time world karate champ
Chuck Norris as John T. Booker, a mild-mannered professor and former Viet Nam commando leader, who
discovers he is marked for assassination by the C.I.A.
Includes a championship auto race, the ski slopes of
Squaw Valley, and Washington, D.C. locations, for this
martial arts action feature.

GOOD-BYE NANA
FHV Entertainment, Inc; Date not listed • color; 1 hr,
30 min; ½" Beta II, ½" VHS • Sale: $49.95

Offers an unconventional love story, set in a Swedish
summer landscape. Focuses on a warm and tender
relationship between a little boy and his nana. Stars
Mats Ahlfeldt and Anne Nord.

THE GORILLA
Budget Video; 1939 • b/w; 1 hr, 7 min; ½" Beta II, ½"
VHS • Sale: $44.95

- -
Reel Images Inc; Order No. 761; 1939 • b/w; 1 hr, 7
min; ½" Beta II, ½" VHS • Sale: $49.95 for ½" Beta II,
$52.95 for ½" VHS

Follows the adventures of three "detectives" in their
efforts to free the city of the fiendish terrors of the mad
criminal known only as The Gorilla. Stars the Ritz
Brothers, Anita Louise, Lionel Atwill, and Bela Lugosi.

THE GRADUATE
Blackhawk Films, Inc; Order No. 502-30-0120 for ½"
Beta II, 515-30-0120 for ½" VHS; 1967 • color; 1 hr,
46 min; ½" Beta II, ½" VHS • Sale: $54.95

- -
Magnetic Video Corporation; Order No. CL-4006;
1967 • color; 1 hr, 46 min; ½" Beta II, ½" VHS • Sale:
$54.95
- -
RCA SelectaVision VideoDiscs; Order No. 00801; 1967
• color; 1 hr, 45 min;CED • Sale: $19.98

Vid America; Order No. 471; 1967 • color; 1 hr, 45 min; ½" Beta II, ½" VHS • Rental: $13.95/wk

Recounts the experiences of a college graduate during the summer before he embarks upon his career. Focuses on his love affairs with a mother and her daughter, and the ensuing consequences. Stars Dustin Hoffman, Katherine Ross, and Anne Bancroft under the direction of Mike Nichols, with a soundtrack by Simon and Garfunkle.

THE GRAND ILLUSION

Cinema Concepts, Inc.; 1938 • b/w; 1 hr, 50 min; ¾" U-Matic, ½" Beta II, ½" VHS • Sale: $54.95 for ½" Beta II & VHS, $149.95 for ¾"

The Video Library ; Order No. CC-0119; 1938 • b/w; 1 hr, 50 min; ½" Beta II, ½" VHS • Sale: $49.95

Explores the human aspect of war in this Jean Renoir film about the relationships between French prisoners of war and their German commandant, and the conflicts between different classes of society among the prisoners. Stars Jean Gabin, Pierre Fresnay, and Erich von Stroheim.

THE GRAPES OF WRATH

Golden Tapes Video Tape Library; Order No. F-1024; 1940 • b/w; 2 hrs, 9 min; ½" Beta II, ½" VHS • Sale: $49.95 for ½" Beta II & VHS, $124.95 for ¾"

Magnetic Video Corporation; Order No. CL-1024; 1940 • b/w; 2 hrs, 9 min; ½" Beta II, ½" VHS • Sale: $64.95

Presents the drama of an Oklahoma dust bowl family which migrates to California, in this John Steinbeck classic starring Henry Fonda.

GRAY LADY DOWN

MCA DiscoVision; Order No. 12-005; 1978 • color; 1 hr, 51 min; LaserVision • Sale: $24.95

Shows the rescue operation launched to save 42 men trapped inside anuclear submarine that has been sunk 60 miles off the Eastern seaboard after a collision with a tramp steamer. Portrays the efforts of the U.S. Navy's Deep Submergence Rescue Unit to save the men, who have only 48 hours of oxygen. Stars Charlton Heston, David Carradine, and Stacy Keach, in an adaptation of the novel "Event 1000" by David Lavallee.

GREASE

Fotomat Corp; Order No. B0005 for ½" Beta II, V0005 for ½" VHS; 1978 • color; 1 hr, 50 min; ½" Beta II, ½" VHS • Sale: $69.95; Rental: $13.95/5 days

Paramount Home Video; 1978 • color; 1 hr, 50 min; ½" Beta II, ½" VHS • Sale: $59.95

RCA SelectaVision VideoDiscs; Order No. 00601; 1978 • color; 1 hr, 50 min; CED • Sale: $24.98

Adapts for the screen the Broadway musical about the 1950's, high school, and rock and roll. Includes "Grease," "You're the One That I Want," and "Hopelessly Devoted To You." Stars John Travolta, Oliva Newton-John, Stockard Channing, Eve Arden, Frankie Avalon, Joan Blondell, Edd Byrnes, Sid Caesar, and Sha-Na-Na.

THE GREAT DICTATOR

Magnetic Video Corporation; Order No. CL-3008; 1940 • b/w; 2 hrs, 8 min; ½" Beta II,½" VHS • Sale: $64.95

Offers Charlie Chaplin's first dialogue film in which he turned to political satire to express the deteriorating world conditions of the late 1930s. Plays on the simi-larities in appearance between Hitler and Chaplin's tramp character to create an indictment of the tyrannies of the dangerous world leader.

THE GREAT ESCAPE

Vid America; Order No. 461; 1963 • color; 2 hrs, 50 min; ½" Beta II, ½" VHS • Rental: $13.95/wk

Recounts a true story of how a group of Allied prisoners in a World War II German P.O.W. camp joined in a single mass breakout. Stars Steve McQueen, James Garner, Richard Attenborough, Charles Bronson, and James Coburn, under the direction of John Sturges.

THE GREAT GABBO

Reel Images Inc; Order No. 19; 1929 • b/w; 1 hr, 36 min; ½" Beta II, ½" VHS • Sale: $49.95 for ½" Beta II, $52.95 for ½" VHS

Video T.E.N.; 1929 • b/w; 1 hr, 22 min; ½" Beta II, ½" VHS • Sale: $49.95 for ½" Beta II, $54.95 for ½" VHS

Presents an early sound film in which an egotistical ventriloquist becomes controlled by his dummy. Stars Erich Von Stroheim.

THE GREAT GATSBY

Fotomat Corp; Order No. B0063 for ½" Beta II, V0063 for ½" VHS; 1974 • color; 2 hrs, 26 min; ½" Beta II ½" VHS • Sale: $69.95; Rental: $9.95/up to 5 days, applicable to purchase

Presents a screen version of the F. Scott Fitzgerald novel. Portrays Jay Gatsby, a dashing, enigmatic millionaire obsessed with the elusive and spoiled Daisy Buchanan. Stars Robert Redford, Mia Farrow, Bruce Dern, Karen Black, and Sam Waterston, under the direction of Jack Clayton, with screenplay by Francis Ford Coppola.

GREAT GUY

Cable Films; 1936 • b/w; 1 hr, 7 min; ½" Beta I, ½" Beta II, ½" VHS • Sale: $65 for ½" Beta I, $49.50 for ½" Beta II & VHS

Recounts the story of a hard-hitting investigator and his exposure of crooked politicians. Stars James Cagney and Mae Clarke.

GREAT LEADERS (GIDEON AND SAMSON)

Video Communications Inc; Order No. 1191; Date not listed • color; 2 hrs, 22 min; ½" Beta II, ½" VHS • Sale: $74.95

Stockard Channing and Jeff Conaway in Grease.

Tells the combined stories of Gideon and Samson from the Old Testament. Features Ivo Garrani, Fernando Rey, and Giogio Ceridni.

THE GREAT LOCOMOTIVE CHASE

Fotomat Corp; 1956 • color; 1 hr, 25 min; ½" Beta II, ½" VHS • Sale: $49.95; Rental: $9.95/up to 5 days, applicable to purchase

- -

RCA SelectaVision VideoDiscs; Order No. 00707; 1956 • color; 1 hr, 25 min; CED • Sale $19.98

Presents an updated version of Buster Keaton's "The General," which tells the true story of Andrews' Raiders. Follows a Union spy who captures a Confederate railroad train during the Civil War with the help of some colorful friends. Stars Fess Parker, Jeffrey Hunter, and Kenneth Tobey. Offers a film produced by Walt Disney Studios.

THE GREAT WALDO PEPPER

MCA DiscoVision; Order No. 10-004; 1975 • color; 1 hr, 47 min; LaserVision • Sale: $24.95

Recounts the days of "barnstormers"—the early aviators, the daredevils who enjoyed their freedom in the sky. Uses exciting aerial photography to illustrate the stunt flying of the 1920's. Stars Robert Redford, Bo Svenson, Bo Brundin, and Susan Sarandon.

GREEK STREET

Thunderbird Films; 1930 • b/w; 51 min; ¾" U-Matic, ½" Beta I, ½" Beta II, ½" VHS • Sale: $59.95 for ½" Beta I, $39.95 for ½" Beta II & VHS, $79.95 for ¾"

Presents an early musical about a girl's rise from singing in the street to performing as a night club star and the consequent changes in her personal life. Features Sari Maritzia, Arthur Hambling, and Martin Lewis.

THE GREEK TYCOON

MCA DiscoVision; Order No. 10-011; 1978 • color; 1 hr, 45 min; LaserVision • Sale: $24.95

Reveals the growing romance between one of the wealthiest and most powerful men in the world and the wife of a soon-to-be assassinated U.S. President. Shows the notoriety which surrounds this pair when her husband dies and the dormant relationship becomes front page news. Stars Anthony Quinn, Jacqueline Bisset, and James Franciscus.

THE GREEN ARCHER

Reel Images Inc; Order No. 710; 1940 • b/w; 4 hrs, 43 min; ½" Beta II, ½" VHS • Sale: $129.95

Offers a Columbia Studio serial in fifteen episodes, starring Victor Jory. Presents a tale of a jealous man who imprisons his brother in his castle until the Green Archer can find a way to help him.

THE GREEN BERETS

WCI Home Video Inc; 1968 • color; 2 hrs, 21 min; ½" Beta II, ½" VHS • Sale: $55

Depicts the Special Forces of the United States military and their involvement in the Vietnam War. Presents a film that has been criticized for its chauvinistic approach to the conflict in East Asia. Stars John Wayne, David Jansson, and Raymond St. Jacques, under the direction of John Wayne and Ray Kellogg.

GREYFRIARS BOBBY

MCA DiscoVision; Order No. D18-507; 1971 • color; 1 hr, 31 min; LaserVision • Sale:$24.95

Presents a Walt Disney Studio production. Tells of a terrier who stood guard over his master's grave in 19th century Scotland for fourteen years in spite of a law which forbade dogs to enter the cemetery reserved for heroes. Shows the ingenuity of "Bobby" to keep his vigil. Stars Donald Crisp and Laurence Naismith, in a story adapted from "Greyfriars Bobby" by Eleanor Atkinson.

THE GRIZZLY AND THE TREASURE

Video Communications Inc ; Order No. 1046; 1975 • color; 1 hr, 38 min; ½" Beta II, ½" VHS • Sale: $54.95

Presents a family adventure about a father's obsession to search for gold in the Alaskan Klondike territory with the aid of a nugget-finding raccoon.

GROOVE TUBE

Meda/Media Home Entertainment Inc; Order No. M101; 1972 • color; 1hr, 15 min; ½" Beta I, ½" Beta II, ½" VHS • Sale: $59.95

Offers a series of humerous and irreverent skits spoofing television. Stars Chevy Chase and Richard Belzer under the direction of Ken Shapiro.

GUADALCANAL ODYSSEY

Video Communications Inc; Date not listed • color; 1 hr, 36 min; ½" Beta II, ½" VHS • Sale: $54.95

Illustrates how nature works to heal the ravages wrought by man. Offers Leslie Nielsen narrating this underwater adventure interspersed with World War II film clips.

GUERRILLAS IN PINK LACE

Video Communications Inc; 1964 • color; 1 hr, 36 min; ½" Beta II, ½" VHS • Sale: $54.95

Follows the adventures of a man trying to escape in a cleric's disguise as the Japanese advance on Manila early in World War II. Relates how he finds himself the "chaperone" of a group of five showgirls. Stars George Montgomery and Joan Shawlee.

GUESS WHO'S COMING TO DINNER

National Film and Video Center; 1967 • color; 1 hr, 48 min; ¾" U-Matic, ½" Beta II, ½" VHS • Rental: $69/1 showing

Revolves around a white woman's engagement to a black doctor, her parents' reactions upon discovering that he is black, and his parents' dismay upon discovering that he intends to marry a white. Concludes, after some painful confrontations, with both sets of parents reconciled to their children's decisions. Stars Spencer Tracy, Katharine Hepburn, Sidney Poitier, and Katherine Houghton.

GULLIVER'S TRAVELS

Cinema Concepts, Inc.; 1939 • color; 1 hr, 15 min; ¾" U-Matic, ½" Beta II, ½" VHS • Sale: $54.95 for ½" Beta II & VHS, 149.95 for ¾"

- -

National Film and Video Center; 1939 • color; 1 hr, 17 min ; ¾" U-Matic, ½" Beta II, ½" VHS • Rental: $59/1 showing

- -

Reel Images Inc; Order No. 22; 1939 • color; 1 hr, 17 min; ½" Beta II, ½" VHS • Sale: $49.95 for ½" Beta II, $52.95 for ½" VHS

- -

VCX, Order No. FC-102; 1939 • color; 1 hr, 14 min; ½" Beta II, ½" VHS • Sale: $35.00

- -

Vid America; Order No. 701; 1939 • color; 1 hr, 10 min; ½" Beta II, ½" VHS • Rental: $10.95/wk

- -

The Video Library; Order No. ME-1048; 1939 • color; 1 hr, 15 min; ½" Beta II, ½" VHS • Sale: $54.95

Presents Max Fleischer's animated film based on the Jonathan Swift story.

THE GUN HAWK
Blackhawk Films, Inc; Order No. 502-57-0004 for 1/2" Beta II, 515-57-0004 for 1/2" VHS; 1963 • color; 1 hr, 32 min; 1/2" Beta II, 1/2" VHS • Sale: $59.95

Recounts how a "good" outlaw tries to keep a young man from becoming a gunslinger, only to be put into the position of a showdown with his best friend. Features Rory Calhoun, Ruta Lee, and Rod Cameron.

GUNFIGHT AT THE O.K. CORRAL
Fotomat Corp; Order No. B0039 for 1/2" Beta II, V0039 for 1/2" VHS; 1957 • color; 2 hrs; 1/2" Beta II, 1/2" VHS • Sale: $49.95; Rental: $9.95/up to 5 days, applicable to purchase
- -
Paramount Home Video; 1957 • color; 2 hrs; 1/2" Beta II, 1/2" VHS • Sale: $59.95

Tells a story of two of the west's most celebrated legends: Wyatt Earp, a U.S. Marshal, and Doc Holliday, a dentist-turned-gambler who knows how to handle a gun. Shows how the two foes become friends after Earp saves Holliday from mob violence, and how they then join forces to rid the West of the lawless Clanton gang, all leading up to the legendary gunfight. Stars Burt Lancaster, Kirk Douglas, Rhonda Fleming, Jo Van Fleet, and John Ireland, under the direction of John Sturges.

GUNG HO!
Video T.E.N.; 1943 • b/w; 1 hr, 28 min; 1/2" Beta II, 1/2" VHS • Sale: $49.95 for 1/2" Beta II, $54.95 for 1/2" VHS

Depicts the training and eventual battle success of a fighting unit in World War II. Features Randolph Scott, Grace McDonald, J. Carrol Naish, Robert Mitchum, Rod Cameron, and Milburn Stone.

GUNGA DIN
Niles Cinema; Order No. NM-8016; 1939 • b/w; 1 hr, 57 min; 1/2" Beta II, 1/2" VHS • Sale: $54.95
- -
The Nostalgia Merchant; Order No. 8016; 1939 • b/w; 1 hr, 57 min; 1/2" Beta II, 1/2" VHS • Sale: $54.95
- -
Red Fox, Inc; Order No. 8016; 1939 • b/w; 1 hr, 57 min; 1/2" Beta II, 1/2" VHS • Sale: $54.95
- -
Time-Life Video Club Inc; 1939 • b/w; 1 hr, 57 min; 1/2" Beta II, 1/2" VHS • Sale: $54.95 to members
- -
Vid America; Order No. 911; 1939 • b/w; 1 hr, 57 min; 1/2" Beta II, 1/2" VHS • Rental: $10.95/wk

Tells the story of three British soldiers and an Indian water-boy in the Punjab. Features Cary Grant, Douglas Fairbanks, Jr., and Victor McLaglen.

THE GUNMAN FROM BODIE
Fotomat Corp; Order No. B0101 for 1/2" Beta II, V0101 for 1/2" VHS; 1941 • b/w; 1 hr, 2 min; 1/2" Beta II, 1/2" VHS • Sale: $39.95; Rental: $7.95/up to 5 days, applicable to purchase

Presents a western featuring Buck Jones and Tim McCoy.

THE GUNS OF NAVARONE
National Film and Video Center; 1961 • color; 2 hrs, 39 min; 3/4" U-Matic, 1/2" Beta II, 1/2" VHS • Rental: $69/1 showing

Follows the actions of an Allied commando team assembled to sabotage the German-held guns of Navar-

one, which guard a vital sea channel. Stars Gregory Peck, David Niven, and Anthony Quinn.

GUNS OF THE TIMBERLAND
Fotomat Corp; Order No. B0111 for 1/2" Beta II, V0111 for 1/2" VHS; 1960 • color; 1 hr, 31 min; 1/2" Beta II, 1/2" VHS • Sale: $39.95; Rental: $7.95/up to 5 days, applicable to purchase
- -
Video Communications Inc; 1960 • color; 1 hr, 34 min; 1/2" Beta II, 1/2" VHS • Sale: $54.95 Discount Video Tapes; 1960 • color; 1 hr, 35 min; 1/2" Beta II, 1/2" VHS • Sale: $54.95

Depicts two partners in a logging operation being given a cold reception when they set up camp near a village where the citizens oppose the cutting down of their virgin forests. Stars Alan Ladd, Jeanne Crain, Gilbert Roland, and Frankie Avalon.

GUS
Fotomat Corp; 1976 • color; 1 hr, 36 min; 1/2" Beta II, 1/2" VHS • Sale: $49.95; Rental: $9.95/up to 5 days, applicable to purchase

Follows the comic adventures of a last-place football team that acquires a new kicker, a mule named Gus. Includes a plot to kidnap him and a slapstick chase. Features Edward Asner, Don Knotts, Gary Grimes, Tim Conway, and Dick Van Patton. Presents a Walt Disney Studios production.

HAIR
Vid America; 1979 • color; 1 hr, 58 min; 1/2" Beta II, 1/2" VHS • Rental: $13.95/wk

Presents an adaptation of the Broadway musical about the 1960's. Offers a rock-influenced score in the story of a naive young man who is side-tracked by love and the peace movement while on his way to be drafted. Includes the songs "Aquarius," "Easy to Be Hard," and "Hair." Stars Treat Williams and John Savage, under the direction of Milos Foreman.

The Central Park "be-in" from *Hair*.

HALLOWEEN

Meda/Media Home Entertainment Inc; Order No. M131; 1978 • color; 1 hr, 25 min; ½" Beta II, ½" VHS • Sale: $59.95

- -
Time-Life Video Club Inc; 1978 • color; 1 hr, 25 min; ½" Beta II, ½" VHS • Sale: $44.95 to members

Follows the murderous exploits of a deranged man who escapes from prison to terrorize his home town. Features Donald Pleasance, Jamie Lee Curtis, P. J. Soles, and Nancy Loomis, under the direction of John Carpenter.

HAMLET

RCA SelectaVision VideoDiscs; Order No. 01004; 1948 • b/w; 2 hrs, 33 min; CED • Sale: $22.98

Presents Laurence Olivier's interpretation of Shakespeare's tragedy. Uses location filming at Elsinore, Denmark, plus swirling wind and raging seas to suggest mood. Stars Laurence Olivier in the title role, Jean Simmons, Eileen Herlie, Basil Sydney, and Felix Aylmer, under Olivier's direction.

HANKY PANKY

Tape Club of America; Order No. 2835 B; Date not listed • color; 1 hr, 30 min; ½" Beta II, ½" VHS • Sale: $54.95 for ½" VHS

Presents a pornographic film.

HANSEL AND GRETEL

Fotomat Corp; Order No. B0177 for ½" Beta II, V0177 for ½" VHS; 1954 • color; 1 hr, 22 min; ½" Beta II, ½" VHS • Sale: $49.95; Rental: $9.95/up to 5 days, applicable to purchase

Presents the opera for children by Engelbert Humperdinck, which follows the adventures of a young boy and his sister who discover a house in the woods made of candy and owned by a witch. Features three-dimensional animation of the ''Kinemins,'' electronically operated, one-third life-size puppets. Includes the voices of Constance Brigham, Anna Russell, Mildred Dunnock, the Apollo Boys Choir, and a 100-piece orchestra.

HAPPY BIRTHDAY, WANDA JUNE

National Film and Video Center; 1971 • color; 1 hr, 45 min; ¾" U-Matic, ½", Beta II, ½" VHS • Rental: $79/1 showing

Relates the story of a young boy who has grown up worshipping his absent father's adventurous image. Shows his disillusionment when his father returns. Stars Rod Steiger and Susannah York in a film based on a novel by Kurt Vonnegut.

THE HAPPY HOOKER

Time-Life Video Club Inc; 1975 • color; 1 hr, 36 min; ½" Beta II, ½" VHS • Sale: $34.95 to members

Adapts the memoirs of Xaviera Hollander, who began as a secretary and ended up as America's most successful Madam. Features Lynn Redgrave and Jean Pierre Aumont, under the direction of Nicholas Sgarro.

THE HAPPY HOOKER GOES TO WASHINGTON

Time-Life Video Club Inc; 1977 • color; 1 hr, 26 min; ½" Beta II, ½" VHS • Sale: $39.95 to members

Offers the second film about Xaviera Hollander, the famous madam and columnist. Presents a spoof on hypocrisy, focusing on U.S. Senators. Features Joey Heatherton and George Hamilton.

Laurence Olivier and Jean Simmons in *Hamlet*.

THE HAPPY PRINCE AND THE LITTLE MERMAID

Vid America; Order No. 915; Date not listed • color; 51 min; ½" Beta II, ½" VHS • Rental: $9.95/wk

Presents animated versions of two fairy tales. Begins with ''The Happy Prince'' by Oscar Wilde, about the friendship between a statue and a swallow. Concludes with ''The Little Mermaid'' by Hans Christian Andersen, the bittersweet story of a mermaid's love for a young prince.

HARD SOAP HARD SOAP

Freeway Video Enterprises; Date not listed • color; 1 hr, 20 min; ½" Beta II, ½" VHS • Sale: $75 for ½" Beta II, 85 for ½" VHS

Presents a pornographic film.

THE HARDER THEY COME

RCA SelectaVision VideoDiscs; Order No. 00902; 1973 • color; 1 hr, 28 min; CED • Sale: $19.98

Studies a Jamaican pop singer who struggles to escape the ghetto through his reggae music. Stars Jimmy Cliff, Janet Barkley, Carl Bradshaw, Ras Daniel Hartman, and Bobby Charlton. Features a reggae musical soundtrack.

THE HARDER THEY FALL

Columbia Pictures Home Entertainment; 1956 • b/w; 1 hr, 49 min; ½" Beta II, ½" VHS • Sale: $59.95

- -
Time-Life Video Club Inc; 1956 • b/w; 1 hr, 49 min; ½" Beta II, ½" VHS • Sale: $44.95 to members

Offers a drama of corruption in the prize ring, scripted by Budd Schulberg, and featuring Humphrey Bogart in his last role, as a press agent coming to grips with the exploitation of fighters by managers. Co-stars Rod Steiger and Jan Sterling.

HARLAN COUNTY U.S.A.
Columbia Pictures Home Entertainment; Order No. BCF7160 for ½" Beta II, VCF3100 for ½" VHS; 1977 • color; 1 hr, 43 min; ½" Beta II, ½" VHS • Sale: $59.95

Documents the 13-month Kentucky coal-miners' strike that began in 1973 against the Eastover Mining Company. Features the direction of Barbara Kopple.

THE HARLEM GLOBETROTTERS
National Film and Video Center; 1951 • b/w; 1 hr, 20 min; ¾" U-Matic, ½" Beta II, ½" VHS • Rental: $49/1 showing

Spotlights the Globetrotters, the most famous professional basketball team in the U.S., in a story about a young college player who quits school to become a Globetrotters star. Features Thomas Gomez, Dorothy Dandridge, and Bill Walker.

HAROLD AND MAUDE
Fotomat Corp; Order No. B0075 for ½" Beta II, V0075 for ½" VHS; 1971 • color; 1 hr, 31 min; ½" Beta II, ½" VHS • Sale: $49.95; Rental: $9.95/up to 5 days, applicable to purchase
- -
Paramount Home Video; 1971 • color; 1 hr, 31 min; ½" Beta II, ½" VHS • Sale: $59.95

Follows the adventures of, and love affair between, a twenty-year-old boy who is intensely interested in death, and a 79-year-old swinger who revels in life's goodness. Offers a black comedy which includes a point of view considered objectionable to some. Stars Ruth Gordon, Bud Cort, Vivian Pickles, and Ellen Geer.

HAROLD LLOYD SHORTS
Northeast Video and Sound, Inc; 1920-30 listed • b/w; 50 min; ¾" U-Matic, ½" EIAJ, ½" Beta II, ½" VHS • Sale: $150; Rental: $55/wk

Features Lloyd's screen character—the typical all American man—full of ambition and ingenuity. Offers Lloyd performing all his own acrobatics and stunts.

THE HARRAD EXPERIMENT
Niles Cinema; Order No. BT-18 for ½" Beta II, VH-18 for ½" VH8; 1973 • color; 1 hr, 35 min; ½" Beta II, ½" VHS • Sale: $59.95

Details life at a coeducational college where honest sexual relations between students are an essential part of the curriculum. Features James Whitmore, Tippy Hedren, and the Ace Trucking Company.

HARRY AND WALTER GO TO NEW YORK
Columbia Pictures Home Entertainment; 1976 • color; 2 hrs, 3 min; ½" Beta II , ½" VHS • Sale: $59.95
- -
Fotomat Corp; Order No. B0433 for ½" Beta II, V0433 for ½" VHS; 1976 • color; 1 hr, 52 min; ½" Beta II, ½" VHS • Sale: $54.95; Rental: $9.95/5 days

Offers a comedy about two unsuccessful turn-of-the-century vaudevillians who take up safecracking. Features James Caan, Elliott Gould, Michael Caine, and Diane Keaton.

THE HAUNTED STRANGLER
Cinema Concepts, Inc.; 1958 • b/w; 1 hr, 18 min; ¾" U-Matic, ½" Beta II, ½" VHS • Sale: $54.95 for ½"Beta II & VHS, $149.95 for ¾"
- -
The Video Library; Order No. CC-0122; 1658 • b/w; 1 hr, 18 min; ½" Beta II, ½" VHS • Sale: $54.95

Features Boris Karloff in a play on the Dr. Jekyll-Mr. Hyde theme.

HAUNTS
FHV Entertainment, Inc; 1976 • color; 1 hr, 30 min; ½" Beta II, ½" VHS • Sale: $49.95

Examines a lonely woman, obsessed by her past and driven to madness in this psychosexual thriller, set in a peaceful coastal town. Stars May Britt, Cameron Mitchell, and Aldo Ray.

HAVE ROCKET, WILL TRAVEL
National Film and Video Center; 1959 • b/w; 1 hr, 16 min; ¾" U-Matic, ½" Beta II, ½" VHS • Rental: $49/1 showing

Features the Three Stooges en route to Venus, where they baffle the creatures there with their bungling.

HAWK OF THE WILDERNESS
The Nostalgia Merchant; Order No. 0082; 1938 • b/w; 3 hrs; ½" Beta II, ½" VHS • Sale: $109.95

Presents, on two videocassettes, a Republic motion picture serial in 12 episodes. Tells the story of a shipwrecked infant, reared by Indians on a remote island, who battles modern pirates and protects a scientific expedition in the wilderness. Stars Herman Brix, Mala, and William Royle.

HAWMPS!
Fotomat Corp; Order No. B0405 for ½" Beta II, V0405 for ½" VHS; 1976 • color; 1 hr, 38 min; ½" Beta II, ½" VHS • Sale: $49.95; Rental: $7.95/5 days

Presents a comedy based on a true story. Tells of U.S. Soldiers stationed in the western desert after the Civil War who must learn to ride camels. Features James Hampton, Christopher Connelly, Slim Pickens, Denver Pyle, and Jack Elam.

HAY COUNTRY SWINGERS
Tape Club of America; Order No. 2836 B; Date not listed • color; 1 hr, 10 min; ½" Beta II, ½" VHS • Sale: $54.95

Presents a pornographic film.

HE WALKED BY NIGHT
Thunderbird Films; 1949 • b/w; 1 hr, 20 min; ¾" U-Matic, ½" Beta I, ½" Beta II, ½" VHS • Sale: $69.95 for ½" Beta I, 49.95 for ½" Beta II & VHS, $89.95 for ¾"

Stars Richard Basehart, Scott Brady, and Jack Webb in his film debut. Concerns a criminal expert in electronics and police tactics who becomes the target of the largest manhunt in Los Angeles history.

THE HEADLESS HORSEMAN AND WILL ROGERS
Blackhawk Films, Inc; Order No. 506-66-0829 for ½" Beta II, 525-66-0829 for ½" VHS; Date not listed • b/w; 52 min; ¾" U-Matic, ½" Beta I, ½" Beta II, ½" VHS • Sale: $59.95 for ½" Beta I, $39.95 for ½" Beta II & VHS, $69.95 for ¾"

Presents two Will Rogers comedy shorts, with narration. Includes Will as Ichabod Crane in "The Legend of Sleepy Hollow," followed by a tribute to him which traces his career from Vaudeville to Ziegfeld and his Hal Roach features.

HEALTH SPA
TVX Distributors; Order No. R.T. 75; Date not listed • color; 2 hrs; ½" Beta II, ½" VHS • Sale: $79.50 for ½" Beta II, 89.50 for ½" VHS

Presents a pornographic film.

HEART OF ARIZONA
Videobrary Inc; Order No. 6; 1938 • b/w; 1 hr, 8 min;

½" Beta II, ½" VHS • Sale: $39.95

Offers a western featuring Hopalong Cassidy. Reveals Belle Starr's love for Cassidy and her sacrifice. Stars William Boyd, George "Gabby" Hayes, and Natalie Moorehead.

HEART OF THE WEST
Videobrary Inc; Order No. 16; 1936 • b/w; 1 hr; ½" Beta II, ½" VHS • Sale: $39.95

Presents a Hopalong Cassidy western. Tells a tale of a cattle rustler who wants Cassidy to work for him on his ranch. Stars William Boyd and George "Gabby" Hayes.

THE HEARTBREAK KID
Magnetic Video Corporation; Order No. CL-1083; 1972 • color; 1 hr, 44 min; ½" Beta II, ½" VHS • Sale: $44.95

Presents a comedy by Neil Simon concerning the embarrassment of a young bridegroom who falls for another woman on his honeymoon. Features Charles Grodin, Cybill Shepherd, and Jeannie Berlin, under the direction of Elaine May.

HEART'S DESIRE
Reel Images Inc; Order No. 482; 1937 • b/w; 1 hr, 19 min; ½" Beta II, ½" VHS • Sale: $49.95 for ½" Beta II, 52.95 for ½" VHS

Offers an English musical romance in which a Viennese tenor in London's Albert Hall makes the mistake of becoming involved with an English socialite. Stars Richard Tauber and Leonora Corbett.

HEARTS OF THE GOLDEN WEST
Northeast Video and Sound, Inc; Order No. 111S; 1942 • b/w; 60 min; ¾" U-Matic, ½" EIAJ, ½" Beta II, ½" VHS • Sale: $150; Rental: $60/wk

Features Roy Rogers in a confrontation involving a shipping company that has run afoul of the law.

HEAT
Meda/Media Home Entertainment Inc; Order No. M110; 1972 • color; 1 hr, 40 min; ½" Beta I, ½" Beta II, ½" VHS • Sale: $54.95

Offers an odyssey through the Andy Warhol/Paul Morrissey universe established in "Flesh" and "Trash"— this time in a dumpy Hollywood motel and a large old mansion. Examines the lives of bored, out-of-work movie actors. Stars Joe Dallassandro and Sylvia Miles.

HEAVEN CAN WAIT
Fotomat Corp; Order No. B0007 for ½" Beta II, V0007 for ½" VHS; 1978 • color; 2 hr, 40 min; ½" Beta II, ½" VHS • Sale: $69.95; Rental: $13.95/5 days
- -
MCA DiscoVision; Order No. 10-527; 1978 • color; 1 hr, 40 min • Sale: $24.95
- -
Paramount Home Video; 1978 • color; 1 hr, 40 min; ½" Beta II, ½" VHS • Sale: $59.95
- -
RCA SelectaVision VideoDiscs; Order No. 00605; 1978 • color; 1 hr, 40 min; CED • Sale: $24.98

Offers an updated version of the 1941 film "Here Comes Mr. Jordan." Concerns a Los Angeles Ram quarterback who is taken to heaven ahead of his time by mistake. Follows his adventures as he is provided with a new body and returned to earth. Stars Warren Beatty, Julie Christie, James Mason, Jack Warden, Dyan Cannon, Charles Grodin, and Buck Henry, under Beatty and Henry's co-direction of a screenplay written by Beatty and Elaine May.

HEAVENS ABOVE!
Fotomat Corp; Order No. B0233 for ½" Beta II, V0233 for ½" VHS; 1963 • b/w; 1 hr, 45 min; ½" Beta II, ½" VHS • Sale: $49.95; Rental: $9.95/up to 5 days, applicable to purchase
- -
Time-Life Video Club Inc; 1963 • b/w; 1 hr, 45 min; ½" Beta II, ½" VHS • Sale: $39.95 to members

Provides a satirical look at the British clergy as a well-meaning Reverend makes things difficult for his parishioners and ends up as the Bishop of Outer Space. Stars Peter Sellers, Cecil Parker, Isabel Jeans, Eric Sykes, and Ian Carmichael, under the direction of the Boulting Brothers.

HECKLE AND JECKLE
Magnetic Video Corporation; Order No. CL-2009; Date not listed • color; 30 min; ½" Beta II, ½" VHS • Sale: $44.95

Presents 5 Terrytoon cartoons featuring Heckle and Jeckle.

HECTOR HEATHCOTE
Magnetic Video Corporation; Order No. CL-2043; Date not listed • color; 30 min; ½" Beta II, ½" VHS • Sale: $34.95

Offers a compilation of Terrytoon animated cartoons featuring Hector Heathcote.

HEDDA
Magnetic Video Corporation; Order No. CL-5012; 1975 • color; 1 hr, 44 min; ½" Beta II, ½" VHS • Sale: $54.95

Presents the Royal Shakespeare Company production of Henrik Ibsen's "Hedda Gabler." Offers a tale of a strong-willed woman married to a weak husband in the 19th century who is nonetheless alluring to the men in her community in Norway. Includes many textual cuts. Stars Glenda Jackson, Timothy West, and Jennie Linden.

HEIDI
Magnetic Video Corporation; Order No. CL-1066; 1937 • b/w; 1 hr, 15 min; ½" Beta II, ½" VHS • Sale: $54.95

Adapts Johanna Spyri's classic children's story about a girl who lives in the Swiss mountains with her grandfather. Details the attempts to separate them against their will so that Heidi will provide companionship for a young girl who is confined to a wheelchair. Stars Shirley Temple, Jean Hersholt, and Helen Westley.

Jean Hersholt and Shirley Temple in *Heidi*.

HEIDI
RCA SelectaVision VideoDiscs; Order No. 01203; 1968 • color; 1 hr, 50 min; CED • Sale: $19.98

Presents the TV-movie adaptation of Johanna Spyri's children's tale of the young girl who leaves the Swiss Alps and her grandfather to discover the world below. Stars Maximilian Schell, Jean Simmons, Michael Redgrave, Walter Slezak, Jennifer Edwards, and Peter Van Eyck.

HELL ON FRISCO BAY
Fotomat Corp; Order No. B0127 for ½" Beta II, V0127 for ½" VHS; 1956 • color; 1 hr, 33 min; ½" Beta II, ½" VHS • Sale: $39.95; Rental: $7.95/up to 5 days, applicable to purchase
----
Video Communications Inc; 1955 • color; 1 hr, 38 min; ½" Beta II, ½" VHS • Sale: $54.95

Offers police action on the San Francisco waterfront as a wrongly-convicted ex-cop emerges from prison bent upon finding the man responsible for the crime and his frame-up. Stars Alan Ladd and Edward G. Robinson.

HELLDORADO
Cable Films; 1946 • b/w; 55 min; ½" Beta I, ½" Beta II, ½" VHS • Sale: $45 for ½" Beta I, $49.50 for ½" Beta II & VHS

Presents a western set against the background of the Nevada wilderness. Stars Roy Rogers.

HELLFIRE
Niles Cinema; Order No. NM-0019; 1949 • color; 1 hr, 30 min; ½" Beta II, ½" VHS • Sale: $54.95

The Nostalgia Merchant; Order No. 0019; 1949 • color; 1 hr, 30 min; ½" Beta II, ½" VHS • Sale: $54.95

Red Fox, Inc; Order No. 0019; 1949 • color; 1 hr, 30 min; ½" Beta II, ½" VHS • Sale: $54.95

Recounts a western story of a reformed gambler out to capture a notorious woman bandit. Stars William Elliott, Marie Windsor, and Forrest Tucker.

HELLO, DOLLY!
Blackhawk Films, Inc; Order No. 502-49-0006 for ½" Beta II, 515-49-0015 for ½" VHS; 1969 • color; 2 hrs, 28 min; ½" Beta II, ½" VHS • Sale: $74.95

Golden Tapes Video Tape Library; Order No. F-1001; 1969 • color; 2 hrs, 28 min; ½" Beta II, ½" VHS • Sale: $49.95 for ½" Beta II & VHS, $124.95 for ¾"

Magnetic Video Corporation; Order No. CL-1001; 1969 • color; 2 hrs, 28 min; ½" Beta II, ½" VHS • Sale: $64.95

RCA SelectaVision VideoDiscs; Order No. 00113; 1969 • color; 1 hr, 58 min; CED • Sale: $22.98

The Video Library; Order No. MV-1501; 1969 • color; 2 hrs, 28 min; ½" Beta II, ½" VHS • Sale: $74.95

Presents Barbra Streisand as Mrs. Dolly Levi, a well known and effusive young widow who has become a matchmaker. Stars, in addition to Ms. Streisand, Walter Matthau, Michael Crawford, and Louis Armstrong, in this musical directed by Gene Kelly.

HELL'S ANGELS ON WHEELS
Magnetic Video Corporation; Order No. CL-2023; 1967 • b/w; 1 hr, 35 min; ½" Beta II, ½" VHS • Sale: $54.95

Red Fox, Inc; 1967 • color; 1 hr, 35 min; ½" Beta II, ½" VHS • Sale: $54.95

Features Jack Nicholson in an early role as a member of the infamous motorcycle gang, with photography by Laszlo Kovacs. Co-stars Adam Roarke and Sabrina Scharf.

HENRY V
RCA SelectaVision VideoDiscs; Order No. 01003; 1945 • color; 2 hrs, 17 min; CED • Sale: $22.98

Presents an adaptation of Shakespeare's historical drama, with Laurence Olivier producing, directing, and starring in the title role. Opens and closes as if the viewer were seated in the Globe Theatre in early 1600's. Tells of England's most revered King, his battle at Agincourt, France, and the wooing of his future bride. Features Robert Newton, Leslie Banks, Renee Asherson, Esmond Knight, Leo Genn, and Ralph Truman.

HENRY PHIPPS GOES SKIING
Home Vision; Order No. 816-7001 for ½" Beta II, 816-9001 for ½" VHS; Date not listed • color; 52 min; ½" Beta II, ½" VHS • Sale: $49.95

Offers a humorous adult fantasy concerning the misadventures of Henry Phipps, who escapes the routine of the shoe factory for a free weekend at a ski resort.

HERCULES
Magnetic Video Corporation; Order No. CL-4020; 1959 • color; 1 hr, 47 min; ½" Beta II, ½" VHS • Sale: $54.95

Presents the legendary superman as he teams up with Jason and the Argonauts in search of the Golden Fleece and encounters natives, monsters, Amazons, and his princess love. Stars Steve Reeves and Sylva Koscina.

HERCULES UNCHAINED
Magnetic Video Corporation; Order No. CL-4021; 1960 • color; 1 hr, 41 min; ½" Beta II, ½" VHS • Sale: $54.95

Traces the continuation of the Hercules saga as the hero and his new wife are en route to Thebes with their young friend Ulysses and are attacked by the giant Antaeus. Stars Steve Reeves and Sylva Koscina.

HERE COMES MR. JORDAN
Columbia Pictures Home Entertainment; 1941 • b/w; 1 hr, 33 min; ½" Beta II, ½" VHS • Sale: $59.95

Time-Life Video Club Inc; 1941 • b/w; 1 hr, 33 min; ½" Beta II, ½" VHS • Sale: $59.95 to members

Offers a fantasy about a prizefighter who is killed in a plane crash, goes to heaven, and discovers he wasn't supposed to die yet. Features Robert Montgomery, Claude Rains, and Evelyn Keyes, under the direction of Alexander Hall.

HEROES
MCA DiscoVision; Order No. 10-012; 1978 • color; 1 hr, 53 min; LaserVision • Sale: $24.94

Tells of the difficulties a returning Vietnam veteran has in adjusting to his country and the love affair that awaits him. Stars Henry Winkler, in his film debut, and Sally Field.

HESTER STREET
Time-Life Video Club Inc; 1975 • b/w; 1 hr, 32 min; ½" Beta II, ½" VHS • Sale: $44.95 to members

Follows the experiences of a young Jewish immigrant

**Barbra Streisand
in *Hello Dolly!***

wife who joins her husband in the "New World" only to discover he does not consider her American enough. Stars Carol Kane, Steven Keats, Mel Howard, and Doris Roberts.

HEY, THERE'S NAKED BODIES ON MY TV!
Meda/Media Home Entertainment Inc; Order No. M505; Date not listed • color; 1 hr, 25 min; ½" Beta I, ½" Beta II, ½" VHS • Sale: $54.95

Presents a pornographic film.

HI DIDDLE DIDDLE
Video T.E.N.; 1943 • b/w; 1 hr, 12 min; ½" Beta II, ½" VHS • Sale: $49.95 for ½" Beta II, $54.95 for ½" VHS

Traces the misadventures of a young couple on their wedding day, on account of the comic scheming of their parents. Includes Adolphe Menjou, Martha Scott, Pola Negri, Dennis O'Keefe, Billie Burke, June Havoc, and Walter Kingsford.

HIGH NOON
The Nostalgia Merchant; Order No. 0047; 1952 • b/w; 1 hr, 25 min; ½" Beta II, ½" VHS • Sale: $54.95
- -
RCA SelectaVision VideoDiscs; Order No. 00301; 1952 • b/w; 1 hr, 25 min; CED • Sale: $19.98

Offers a western concerning a newly married town marshal who must choose between love and duty. Features Gary Cooper, Grace Kelly, and Thomas Mitchell, under the direction of Fred Zinnemann.

HIGH PLAINS DRIFTER
MCA DiscoVision; Order No. 14-002;.1973 • color; 1 hr, 45 min; LaserVision • Sale: $24.95

Probes the difference between good guys and bad ones as the "man with no name" returns out of the heat waves of the desert to rid a town of three men who have sworn to destroy it. Stars Clint Eastwood, who reprises his mysterious western stranger role and also directs. Features Verna Bloom and Mitchell Ryan.

HIGH RISE
Quality X Video Cassette Company; Date not listed •

color; 1 hr, 7 min; ½" Beta I , ½" Beta II, ½" VHS • Sale: $99.50

Presents a pornographic film.

HIGH VELOCITY
Meda/Media Home Entertainment Inc; 1977 • color; 1 hr, 45 min; ½" Beta II, ½" VHS • Sale: $49.95

Relates how two mercenary Vietnam veterans are engaged as commandos in a hostage rescue attempt. Features Ben Gazzara, Paul Winfield, Britt Eklund, Keenan Wynn, and Alejandro Rey.

HIGHER AND HIGHER
Blackhawk Films, Inc; Order No. 506-88-0741 for ½" Beta II, 525-88-0741 for ½" VHS; 1943 • b/w; 1 hr, 30 min; ½" Beta II, ½" VHS • Sale: $49.95

Presents a musical about a bankrupt aristocrat who schemes with his servants to regain his fortune. Showcases Frank Sinatra in his first leading role, with Leon Errol, Michele Morgan, Jack Haley, Victor Borge, Mel Torme, and Mary McGuire.

HIGHSCHOOL REPORT CARD
Scorpio, Etc; 1979 • color; 30 min; ½" Beta I, ½" Beta II, ½" VHS • Sale: $39.95

Presents a pornographic film.

HILLS OF OLD WYOMING
Videobrary Inc; Order No. 19; 1937 • b/w; 1 hr, 18 min; ½" Beta II, ½" VHS • Sale: $39.95

Offers a Hopalong Cassidy western in which a local Indian tribe is thought to be cattle-rustling. Stars William Boyd and George "Gabby" Hayes.

THE HINDENBURG
MCA DiscoVision; Order No. 11-002; 1975 • color; 2 hrs, 5 min; LaserVision • Sale: $24.95

Dramatizes the maiden flight of the luxury German dirigible which mysteriously crashed after completing its trans-Atlantic voyage. Raises the question of wartime sabotage and uses Academy Award-winning special effects. Stars George C. Scott, Anne Bancroft, William Atherton, and Gig Young.

HIROSHIMA MON AMOUR

Budget Video; 1959 • b/w; 1 hr, 28 min; ½" Beta II, ½" VHS • Sale: $44.95

Explores a 24-hour romantic relationship between a Japanese architect and a French actress, emphasizing the wartime memories of each and their influence on the present. Features Emmanuelle Riva and Eiji Okada under the direction of Alain Resnais; in French with subtitles.

HIS GIRL FRIDAY

Northeast Video and Sound, Inc; 1940 • b/w; 1 hr, 32 min; ¾" U-Matic, ½" EIAJ, ½" Beta II, ½" VHS • Sale: $195; Rental: $75/wk

----

Reel Images Inc; Order No. 128; 1940 • b/w; 1 hr, 32 min; ½" Beta II, ½" VHS • Sale: $49.95 for ½" Beta II, $52.95 for ½" VHS

Presents a comedy remake of "The Front Page." Depicts a scheming newspaper editor who wants his star reporter to cover a hot murder trial and forget about the hayseed she plans to marry. Stars Cary Grant, Rosalind Russell, Ralph Bellamy, Gene Lockhart, Helen Mack, Porter Hall, Roscoe Karns, and Billy Gilbert, under the direction of Howard Hawks.

HISTORY IS MADE AT NIGHT

Time-Life Video Club Inc; 1937 • b/w; 1 hr, 37 min; ½" Beta II, ½" VHS • Sale: $39.95 to members

Presents a comedy-melodrama about a Parisian headwaiter who rescues and falls in love with a married woman who is being tormented by her husband. Stars Charles Boyer, Jean Arthur, and Colin Clive.

HITLER

Blackhawk Films, Inc; Order No. 502-68-0093 for ½" Beta II, 515-68-0093 for ½" VHS; 1962 • b/w; 1 hr, 47 min; ½" Beta II, ½" VHS • Sale: $59.95

Depicts Hitler's career as the leader of the Third Reich, with a Freudian analysis of his inner motivations. Features Richard Basehart as Hitler.

HITLER'S CHILDREN

The Nostalgia Merchant; Order No. 8067; 1943 • b/w; 1 hr, 23 min; ½" Beta II, ½" VHS • Sale: $54.95

Red Fox, Inc; Order No. 8067; 1943 • b/w; 1 hr, 23 min; ½" Beta II, ½" VHS • Sale: $54.95

Recounts the predicament of young people caught in the horror of Nazi Germany. Features Bonita Granville, Tim Holt, and Otto Kruger.

Tim Holt and Bonita Granville in
Hitler's Children.

THE HOLES

Cinema Concepts, Inc.; 1975 • color; 1 hr, 30 min; ¾" U-Matic, ½" Beta II, ½" VHS • Sale: $54.95 for ½" Beta II & VHS, 149.95 for ¾"

Offers a comedy about a busload of tourists in Paris who sink into the ground along with a few buildings, the police, and a number of women. Features Philippe Noiret.

HOLIDAY

National Film and Video Center; 1938 • b/w; 1 hr, 34 min; ¾" U-Matic, ½" Beta II, ½" VHS • Rental: $69/1 showing

Stars Cary Grant as a casual young man engaged to a society girl who falls in love with her younger sister when he becomes disillusioned by the structured life the elder one requires. Co-stars Katharine Hepburn and Lew Ayres, under the direction of George Cukor.

HOLLYWOOD GOES TO WAR

Reel Images Inc; Order No. 801; 1945 • b/w; 41 min; ½" Beta II, ½" VHS • Sale: $39.95 for ½" Beta II, $42.95 for ½" VHS

Presents five short subjects produced by the Office of War Information, the Army Pictorial Service, and the Army-Navy Screen Magazine for the entertainment of the soldiers overseas during World War II. Includes "All Star Bond Rally" with Bob Hope and Bing Crosby, "Hollywood Canteen Overseas Special" with Dinah Shore and Red Skelton, "Mail Call" with Dorothy Lamour, "G.I. Movie Weekly" with a bouncing ball sing-along, and "Invaders In Greasepaint" with Carole Landis and Martha Raye.

HOLLYWOOD HIGH

Niles Cinema; Order No. BT-33 for ½" Beta II, VH-33 for ½" VHS; 1976 • color; 1 hr, 25 min; ½" Beta II, ½" VHS • Sale: $59.95

Depicts the life of teenagers at Hollywood High, where summer vacation lasts all year long. Features March Albrecht, John Young, and Rae Sperling.

HOMBRE

Golden Tapes Video Tape Library; Order No. F-1012; 1967 • color; 1 hr, 51 min; ½" Beta II, ½" VHS • Sale: $49.95 for ½" Beta II & VHS, $124.95 for ¾"

Magnetic Video Corporation; Order No. CL-1012; 1967 • color; 1 hr, 51 min; ½" Beta II, ½" VHS • Sale: $44.95

Tells the story of a man raised by Apaches then forced back into the white man's world. Stars Paul Newman and Richard Boone.

HOME IN OKLAHOMA

Cable Films; 1947 • b/w; 54 min; ½" Beta I, ½" Beta II, ½" VHS • Sale: $45 for ½" Beta I, $49.50 for ½" Beta II & VHS

Presents a western with Carol Hughes as a villainess who is after Gabby Hayes' ranch. Features Roy Rogers and Dale Evans.

THE HOMECOMING

Magnetic Video Corporation; 1973 • color; 1 hr, 56 min; ½" Beta II, ½" VHS • Sale: $80

Offers the American Film Theatre adaptation of Harold Pinter's play about a man who takes his wife home to his family for the first time after being deliberately separated from them. Stars Cyril Cusack, Ian Holm, Michael Jayston, Vivien Merchant, Terence Rigby, and Paul Rogers under Peter Hall's direction.

HOMESTEADERS VALLEY

Cable Films; 1947 • b/w; 54 min; ½" Beta I, ½" Beta II, ½" VHS • Sale: $45 for ½" Beta I, $49.50 for ½" Beta II & VHS

Presents a western in which Red Ryder and Little Beaver lead a wagon train to Paradise Valley, where actor Eugene Roth and his gang make it tough for the eastern greenhorns. Stars Allan Lane and Bobby Blake.

HONEYMOON HAVEN

Quality X Video Cassette Company; Date not listed • color; 1 hr, 20 min; ½" Beta I, ½" Beta II, ½" VHS • Sale: $99.50

Presents a pornographic film.

HONEYPIE

Quality X Video Cassette Company; Date not listed • color; 1 hr, 26 min; ¾" U-Matic, ½" Beta I, ½" Beta II, ½" VHS • Sale: $85 for ½" Beta & VHS, $150 for ¾"

Presents a pornographic film.

HOOK, LINE AND SINKER

Video T.E.N.; 1930 • b/w; 1 hr, 12 min; ½" Beta II, ½" VHS • Sale: $49.95 for ½" Beta II, 54.95 for ½" VHS

Focuses on the popular 30's comedy team of Bert Wheeler and Robert Woolsey, in the story of two insurance salesmen who help a runaway heiress operate her uncle's hotel. Features Dorothy Lee, Natalie Moorhead, and Hugh Herbert.

HOOPER

WCI Home Video Inc; 1978 • color; 1 hr, 30 min; ½" Beta II, ½" VHS • Sale: $55

Follows the attempts of a young man to unseat the champion of all movie stuntmen, and his eventual teaming up with him to perform an "impossible" car stunt. Stars Burt Reynolds, Jan-Michael Vincent, Sally Fields, and Terry Bradshaw, under the direction of a former master movie stuntman, Hal Needham.

HOPALONG CASSIDY (ENTERS); HEART OF THE WEST

Videobrary Inc; Order No. 4-16; 1935 & 1936 • b/w; 2 hrs, 2 min; ½" Beta II, ½" VHS • Sale: $69.95

Presents a Hopalong Cassidy western double feature. Offers the film which introduces Hoppy, explains his name and reveals his first name, and "Heart of the West" in which Hoppy refuses to work for a man he suspects of rustling. Stars William Boyd and "Gabby" Hayes.

HOPALONG CASSIDY (HOPALONG CASSIDY ENTERS)

Videobrary Inc; Order No. 4; 1935 • b/w; 1 hr, 2 min; ½" Beta II, ½" VHS • Sale: $39.95

Presents the western which introduced Hopalong Cassidy. Reveals his first name and how he came to be called Hopalong. Stars William Boyd, George "Gabby" Hayes, and Jimmy Ellison.

HOPALONG CASSIDY RETURNS

Videobrary Inc; Order No. 9; 1936 • b/w; 1 hr, 11 min; ½" Beta II, ½" VHS • Sale: $39.95

Presents a Hopalong Cassidy western. Reveals how Cassidy tries to clean up Mesa Grande even if it means defying beautiful Lilli, who may be at the bottom of the fatal claim-jumping. Stars William Boyd, George "Gabby" Hayes, and Evelyn Brent.

Katharine Hepburn and Cary Grant in *Holiday*.

HOPALONG RIDES AGAIN

Videobrary Inc; Order No. 14; 1937 • b/w; 1 hr, 5 min; ½" Beta II, ½" VHS • Sale: $39.95

Presents a Hopalong Cassidy western. Offers a tale of cattle rustling masterminded by the brother of a young woman Cassidy is very fond of. Stars William Boyd, George "Gabby" Hayes, and Harry Worth.

HOPALONG RIDES AGAIN; TEXAS TRAIL

Videobrary Inc; Order No. 14-21; 1937 • b/w; 2 hrs, 1 min; ½" Beta II, ½" VHS • Sale: $69.95

Presents a Hopalong Cassidy western double feature. Includes "Hopalong Rides Again" in which Cassidy battles rustlers, and "Texas Trail" in which he is accused of horse-stealing. Stars William Boyd and "Gabby" Hayes.

HOPPITY GOES TO TOWN

Tape Club of America; Order No. 2002 B; 1941 • color; 1 hr, 18 min; ½" Beta II, ½" VHS • Sale: $54.95

Presents a full-length cartoon feature which describes the adventures of a small community of humanized insects who live on a tiny patch of land only forty-five inches from Broadway. Tells how their existence is threatened when a new building is constructed right on their homeland. Shows Hoppity, a grasshopper, who goes out in the world to seek a safe new homeland for his people.

HORIZONS OF THE SEA

Video Communications Inc; Date not listed • color; 1 hr, 34 min; ½" Beta II, ½" VHS • Sale: $54.95

Explores the wilderness and the waterways of Australia in a documentary about four young people looking for adventure in the South Seas.

HORRIBLE DOUBLE FEATURE

Blackhawk Films, Inc; Order No. 506-30-0846 for ½" Beta II, 525-30-0846 for ½" VHS: Date not listed •

b/w; 56 min; ¾" U-Matic, ½" Beta I, ½" Beta II, ½" VHS • Sale: $59.95 for ½" Beta I, $39.95 for ½" Beta II & VHS, $69.95 for ¾"

Presents a segment from The History of the Motion Picture Series. Offers condensed versions of "Dr. Jekyll and Mr. Hyde" starring John Barrymore, and "The Hunchback of Notre Dame" starring Lon Chaney. Features a musical score accompaniment.

HORROR EXPRESS
Niles Cinema; Order No. BT-27 for ½" Beta II, VH-27 for ½" VHS; 1973 • color; 1 hr, 35 min; ½" Beta II, ½" VHS • Sale: $59.95
- -
Thunderbird Films; 1973 • color; 1 hr, 35 min; ¾" U-Matic, ½" Beta I, ½" Beta II, ½" VHS • Sale: $69.95 for ½" Beta I, 49.95 for ½" Beta II & VHS, $89.95 for ¾"
- -
VCX; Order No. FC112; 1972 • color; 1 hr, 28 min; ½" Beta II, ½" VHS • Sale: $35.00

Chronicles the mysterious, murderous events on board a train carrying the remains of the "missing link" across Siberia. Features Christopher Lee, Peter Cushing, and Telly Savalas.

HOT LEAD AND COLD FEET
Fotomat Corp; Order No. B1035 for ½" Beta II, V1035 for ½" VHS; 1978 • color; 1 hr, 30 min; ½" Beta II, ½" VHS • Sale: $54.95 ; Rental: $7.95/5 days
- -
Niles Cinema; Order No. WD-19; 1978 • color; 1 hr, 29 min; ½" Beta II, ½" VHS • Sale: $59.95
- -
Walt Disney Home Video; Order No. 19BS for ½" Beta II, 19VS for ½" VHS; 1978 • color; 1 hr, 30 min; ½" Beta II, ½" VHS • Sale: $59.95

Presents a western-spoof from the Walt Disney Studios, with British actor Jim Dale playing two brothers who take part in a wild obstacle race to gain possession of a town and undo the evil mayor. Stars Jim Dale, Darren McGavin, Karen Valentine, Don Knotts, and Jack Elam.

HOT OVEN
VTS; Date not listed • color; 1 hr, 8 min; ½" Beta I, ½" Beta II, ½" VHS • Sale: $99

Presents a pornographic film.

THE HOT ROCK
Blackhawk Films, Inc; Order No. 502-49-0024 for ½" Beta II, 515-49-0020 for ½" VHS; 1972 not listed • color; 1 hr, 37 min; ½" Beta II, ½" VHS • Sale: $54.95
- -
Golden Tapes Video Tape Library; Order No. F-1042; 1972 • color; 1 hr, 37 min; ½" Beta II, ½" VHS • Sale: $49.95 for ½" Beta II & VHS, $124.95 for ¾"
- -
Magnetic Video Corporation; Order No. CL-1042; 1972 • color; 1 hr, 37 min; ½" Beta II, ½" VHS • Sale: $44.95

Presents a misadventure about a quartet of jewel thieves in search of an elusive diamond. Blasts off with the big heist and then on to three more, each one more ingenious than the preceding. Stars Robert Redford, George Segal, and Zero Mostel.

HOUSE CALLS
MCA DiscoVision; Order No. 16-006; 1978 • color; 1 hr, 38 min; LaserVision • Sale: $24.95

Presents a recently widowed surgeon who wants to make up time lost in 31 years of married fidelity, and his romance with a divorcee who demands he be faithful to only her. Stars Walter Matthau and Glenda Jackson, with Art Carney and Richard Benjamin.

HOUSE NEAR PRADO
Monarch Releasing Corporation; Date not listed • color; 1 hr, 15 min; ¾" U-Matic • Sale: $350

Presents a pornographic film.

THE HOUSE OF SEVEN CORPSES
Tape Club of America ; Order No. 2707 B; 1973 • color; 1 hr, 30 min; ½" Beta II, ½" VHS • Sale: $54.95

Tells of a motion picture company that has started filming an occult movie in a Victorian mansion. Relates how the crew members slowly get involved in a grisly death that recently occurred in the mansion. Stars John Ireland, Faith Domergue, and John Carradine.

HOUSE OF THE LIVING DEAD
Video Communications Inc; Order No. 1184; Date not listed • color; 1 hr, 25 min; ½" Beta II, ½" VHS • Sale: $54.95

Reveals an "evil" that kills and feeds in the attic of a South African estate. Features Mark Burns, Shirley Anne Field, and David Oxley.

HOUSE ON HAUNTED HILL
Blackhawk Films, Inc; Order No. 502-86-0092 for ½" Beta II, 515-86-0092 for ½" VHS; 1958 • b/w; 1 hr, 15 min; ½" Beta II, ½" VHS • Sale: $59.95

Recounts the tale of a proprietor of a 100-year-old mansion who offers $10,000 to anyone who can live through a night in "the house." Stars Vincent Price under William Castle's direction.

HOW GREEN WAS MY VALLEY
Magnetic Video Corporation; Order No. CL-1037; Date not listed • b/w; 1 hr, 58 min; ½" Beta II, ½" VHS • Sale: $44.95

Traces the story of the Morgan family over a period of years, revealing their trials, loves, joys, and sorrows. Shows how the family was never conquered, not by armed men, hardship, hunger, or hate. Features Walter Pidgeon, Maureen O'Hara, and Roddy McDowell.

How Green Was My Valley.

HOW THE MYTH WAS MADE

Home Vision; Order No. 811-7001 for ½" Beta II, 811-9001 for ½" VHS; 1978 • color; 59 min; ½" Beta II, ½" VHS • Sale: $49.95

Offers a retrospective view of the making of Robert Flaherty's "Man of Aran," long regarded as a world classic. Includes interviews with participants in the original opus, shot in Ireland's Aran Islands during 1933 and 1934.

HOW TO MARRY A MILLIONAIRE

Golden Tapes Video Tape Library; Order No. F-1023; 1953 • color; 1 hr, 36 min; ½" Beta II, ½" VHS • Sale: $49.95 for ½" Beta II & VHS, $124.95 for ¾"

Magnetic Video Corporation; Order No. CL-1023; 1953 • color; 1 hr, 36 min; ½" Beta II, ½" VHS • Sale: $44.95

Presents the story of three broke beauties who are determined to marry millionaires. Stars Marilyn Monroe.

HOW TO STEAL A MILLION

Golden Tapes Video Tape Library; Order No. F-1035; 1966 • color; 2 hrs, 3 min; ½" Beta II, ½" VHS • Sale: $49.95 for ½" Beta & VHS, $124.95 for ¾"

Magnetic Video Corporation; Order No. CL-1035; 1966 • color; 2 hrs, 3 min; ½" Beta II, ½" VHS • Sale: $44.95

Presents a comedy about the art forging set in the world of fashion. Stars Peter O'Toole and Audrey Hepburn.

HUD

Fotomat Corp; Order No. B0073 for ½" Beta II, V0073 for ½" VHS; 1963 • color; 1 hr, 52 min; ½" Beta II, ½" VHS • Sale: $49.95; Rental: $9.95/up to 5 days, applicable to purchase

RCA SelectaVision VideoDiscs; Order No. 00625; 1963 • b/w; 1 hr, 52 min; CED • Sale: $19.98

Portrays Hud, a man at odds with his father, tradition, and himself, whose only interests are fighting, drinking, hot-rodding his Cadillac, and womanizing. Stars Paul Newman as Hud, Melvyn Douglas as his father, an old-line cattle rancher, Patricia Neal as the understanding housekeeper, and Brandon deWilde, under the direction of Martin Ritt.

HUGO THE HIPPO

Magnetic Video Corporation; Order No. CL-5007; 1976 • color; 1 hr, 31 min; ½" Beta II, ½" VHS • Sale: $54.95

Presents an animated feature recounting a youngster's attempt to save a hippo from extinction in ancient Zanzibar. Includes the voices of Burl Ives, Marie and Donny Osmond, Paul Lynde, and Robert Morley.

THE HUMAN MONSTER

Cable Films; 1939 • b/w; 1 hr, 14 min; ½" Beta I, ½" Beta II, ½" VHS • Sale: $65 for ½" Beta I, $49.50 for ½" Beta II & VHS

Presents a macabre British film based on the Edgar Wallace thriller, "The Dark Eyes of London." Stars Bela Lugosi.

HUNCHBACK OF NOTRE DAME

Blackhawk Films, Inc; Order No. 506-52-0835 for ½" Beta II, 525-52-0835 for ½" VHS; 1923 • b/w; 1 hr, 38 min; ½" Beta II, ½" VHS • Sale: $39.95

Retells the story of the cathedral bell-ringer in medieval Paris who loves a gypsy dancing girl. Stars Lon Chaney in this silent version of Victor Hugo's classic.

THE HUNCHBACK OF NOTRE DAME

Niles Cinema; Order No. NM-8017; 1939 • b/w; 1 hr, 57 min; ½" Beta II, ½" VHS • Sale: $54.95

The Nostalgia Merchant; Order No. 8017; 1939 • b/w; 1 hr, 57 min; ½" Beta II, ½" VHS • Sale: $54.95

RCA SelectaVision VideoDiscs; Order No. 00402; 1939 • b/w; 1 hr, 57 min; CED • Sale: $19.98

Red Fox, Inc; Order No. 8017; 1939 • b/w; 1 hr, 57 min; ½" Beta II, ½" VHS • Sale: $54.95

Vid America; Order No. 938; 1939 • b/w; 1 hr, 56 min; ½" Beta II, ½" VHS • Rental: $10.95/wk

Relates Victor Hugo's story of a gypsy girl in 15th century France and the deformed bell-ringer of the cathedral. Stars Charles Laughton, Maureen O'Hara, Edmond O'Brien, Cedric Hardwicke, Thomas Mitchell, and George Zucco, in this remake of the 1923 film.

Lon Chaney and Nigel De Brulier in _The Hunchback of Notre Dame_ (1923).

100 RIFLES

Magnetic Video Corporation; Order No. CL-1060; 1969 • color; 1 hr, 50 min; ½" Beta II, ½" VHS • Sale: $54.95

Presents a western in which a sheriff chases gunrunners into Mexico and falls in love with an Indian woman. Stars Jim Brown, Burt Reynolds, Raquel Welch, Fernando Lamas, and Dan O'Herlihy.

THE HUNTER

Paramount Home Video; Order No. 1192; 1980 • color; 1 hr, 37 min; ½" Beta II, ½" VHS • Sale: $72.95

Presents Steve McQueen's last film as he portrays Ralph "Papa" Thorson, modern day bounty hunter, who would rather stun than kill his "clients." Adapts a true story of a man who has apprehended over 5,000 fugitives in 30 years. Features Kathryn Harrold, Eli Wallach, LeVar Burton, and Ben Johnson.

HURRICANE
Fotomat Corp; Order No. B0287 for ½″ Beta II, V0287 for ½″ VHS; 1979 • color; 2 hrs, 11 min; ½″ Beta II, ½″ VHS • Sale: $54.95; Rental: $9.95/5 days

Offers a story of forbidden love set in the South Seas. Features ''Disaster-Movie'' type special effects. Stars Jason Robards, Mia Farrow, Max Von Sydow, Trevor Howard, and Dayton Ka'ne.

HURRICANE EXPRESS
Cable Films; 1933 • b/w; 4 hrs; ½″ Beta I, ½″ Beta II, ½″ VHS • Sale: $89.50

Offers a twelve-chapter serial packed with railroad action. Pits John Wayne against the mysterious ''Wrecker'' who is out to sabotage the railroad. Reveals how the mystery man's identity is hidden by a series of ingenious masks by which he is able to look like anyone he chooses. Features Shirley Grey and Conway Tearle.

HURRICANE EXPRESS
Cable Films; 1932 • b/w; 1 hr, 20 min; ½″ Beta I, ½″ Beta II, ½″ VHS • Sale: $65 for ½″ Beta I, $49.50 for ½″ Beta II & VHS

Presents the feature version of the action serial. Stars John Wayne and Shirley Grey.

HUSTLE
Fotomat Corp; Order No. B0265 for ½″ Beta II, V0265 for ½″ VHS; 1975 • color; 2 hrs; ½″ Beta II, ½″ VHS • Sale: $49.95; Rental: $9.95/up to 5 days, applicable to purchase
- -
Paramount Home Video; 1975 • color; 2 hrs; ½″ Beta II, ½″ VHS • Sale: $59.95

Depicts a murder investigation and the love affair between a police detective and a high-priced French hooker. Stars Burt Reynolds, Catherine Deneuve, Ben Johnson, Paul Winfield, Eileen Brennan, Eddie Albert, Ernest Borgnine, and Jack Carter, under the direction of Robert Aldrich.

THE HUSTLE
Blackhawk Films, Inc ; Order No. 502-49-0037 for ½″ Beta II, 515-49-0025 for ½″ VHS; Date not listed • color; 2 hrs, 15 min; ½″ Beta II, ½″ VHS • Sale: $74.95
- -
Golden Tapes Video Tape Library; Order No. F-1006; 1961 • b/w; 2 hrs, 15 min; ½″ Beta II, ½″ VHS • Sale: $49.95 for ½″ Beta II & VHS, $124.95 for ¾″
- -
Magnetic Video Corporation; Order No. CL-1006; 1961 • b/w; 2 hrs, 15 min; ½″ Beta II, ½″ VHS • Sale: $64.95

Presents a drama about a professional pool shark's big gamble. Centers on various attempts of a small-time pool player to beat the reigning champ. Stars Paul Newman, George C. Scott, Jackie Gleason, Piper Laurie, and Myron McCormick, under the direction of Robert Rossen.

I, A WOMAN—II
Vid America; Order No. 972; Date not listed • color; 1 hr, 21 min; ½″ Beta II, ½″ VHS • Rental: $12.95/wk

Presents a pornographic film.

I ACCUSE MY PARENTS
Thunderbird Films; 1943 • b/w; 1 hr, 10 min; ¾″ U-Matic, ½″ Beta I, ½″ Beta II, ½″ VHS • Sale $59.95 for ½″ Beta I, $39.95 for ½″ Beta II & VHS, $79.95 for ¾″

Recounts in flashbacks a young man's decline into crime and why he blames his parents. Stars Robert Lowell and Mary Beth Hughes.

I COVER THE WATERFRONT
Video T.E.N.; 1933 • b/w; 1 hr, 10 min; ½″ Beta II, ½″ VHS • Sale: $49.95 for ½″ Beta II, $54.95 for ½″ VHS

Traces the demise of a fisherman who smuggles illegal Chinese aliens, drowning them when there is trouble, and his innocent daughter's romance with a reporter. Stars Claudette Colbert, Ben Lyon, Ernest Torrance, and Hobart Cavanaugh.

I DRINK YOUR BLOOD
Monarch Releasing Corporation; Date not listed • color; 1 hr, 26 min; ¾″ U-Matic • Sale: $350

Presents a pornographic film.

I GO POGO
Fotomat Corp; Order No. B0455 for ½″ Beta II, V0455 for ½″ VHS; 1979 • color; 1 hr, 30 min; ½″ Beta II, ½″ VHS • Sale: $54.95; Rental: $9.95/5 days

Presents an animated film featuring characters created by cartoonist Walt Kelly. Relates how Pogo Possum ran for the Presidency against his better judgment. Features the voices of Jonathan Winters, Vincent Price, Ruth Buzzi, Arnold Stang, Stan Freberg, and Jimmy Breslin.

I WALKED WITH A ZOMBIE
Niles Cinema; Order No. NM-8018; 1943 • b/w; 1 hr, 9 min; ½″ Beta II, ½″ VHS • Sale: $54.95
- -
The Nostalgia Merchant; Order No. 8018; 1943 • b/w; 1 hr, 9 min; ½″ Beta II, ½″ VHS • Sale: $54.95
- -
Red Fox, Inc; Order No. 8018; 1943 • b/w; 1 hr, 9 min; ½″ Beta II, ½″ VHS • Sale: $54.95

Presents a horror story of voodoo running rampant on a small West Indian island. Features James Ellison, Frances Dee, and Tom Conway.

I WANT YOU
VTS; Date not listed • color; 1 hr, 12 min; ½″ Beta I, ½″ Beta II, ½″ VHS • Sale: $99

Presents a pornographic film.

I WILL, I WILL . . . FOR NOW
Magnetic Video Corporation; Order No. CL-5011; 1976 • color; 1 hr, 48 min; ½" Beta II, ½" VHS • Sale: $54.95

Offers a contemporary satire of sex clinics, marriage counseling, and marital infidelity, in which a husband tries to come to terms with his ex-wife whom he still loves. Stars Elliot Gould, Diane Keaton, Paul Sorvino, Victoria Principal, and Robert Alda, under the direction of Norman Panama.

I WONDER WHO'S KILLING HER NOW
Niles Cinema; Order No. BT-17 for ½" Beta II, VH-17 for ½" VHS; 1976 • color; 1 hr, 27 min; ½" Beta II, ½" VHS • Sale: $59.95

Presents a comedy-mystery about a husband who hires a hit man to kill his wife, then regrets his decision and fights to save her. Features Bob Dishy, Joanna Barnes, and Bill Dana.

ICE CASTLES
Columbia Pictures Home Entertainment; Order No. BE51345 for ½" Beta II, VH10340 for ½" VHS; 1979 • color; 1 hr, 49 min; ½" Beta II, ½" VHS • Sale: $59.95

Follows the attempts of an Olympic-hopeful ice skater to persevere after a freak accident blinds her. Stars Lynn-Holly Johnson, Robby Benson, Colleen Dewhurst, Tom Skerritt, and Jennifer Warren.

THE ICEMAN COMETH
Magnetic Video Corporation; 1973 • color; 3 hrs, 59 min; ½" Beta II, ½" VHS • Sale: $100

Offers the American Film Theatre adaptation of Eugene O'Neill's play about life's meaning as sought for by down and out customers at a seedy bar. Stars Lee Marvin, Robert Ryan, Fredric March, Jeff Bridges, Martyn Green, Moses Gunn, Bradford Dillman, and Edith Evans.

IF I HAD A MILLION
MCA DiscoVision; Order No. 21-003; 1933 • b/w; 1 hr, 28 min; LaserVision • Sale: $15.95

Offers a series of vignettes which tell what individuals do when a wealthy man hands each of them $1,000,000. Stars W.C. Fields, Charlie Ruggles, Charles Laughton, Gary Cooper, Jack Oakie, and George Raft. Features direction by Ernst Lubitsch, James Cruze, Norman Z. McLeod, Stephen S. Roberts, William A. Seiter, Norman Taurog, and H. Bruce Humberstone.

I'M ALL RIGHT, JACK
Fotomat Corp; Order No. B0235 for ½" Beta II, V0235 for ½" VHS; 1959 • b/w; 1 hr, 44 min; ½" Beta II, ½" VHS • Sale: $49.95; Rental: $9.95/up to 5 days, applicable to purchase

- -
Time-Life Video Club Inc; 1960 • b/w; 1 hr, 44 min; ½" Beta II, ½" VHS • Sale: $39.95 to members

Satirizes the British labor-management relationship as an oafish labor leader gets caught between the two sides in a crooked financial scam. Stars Peter Sellers, Ian Carmichael, and Terry-Thomas, under the direction of the Boulting Brothers.

IN CELEBRATION
Magnetic Video Corporation; 1974 • color; 2 hrs, 11 min; ½" Beta II, ½" VHS • Sale: $80

Offers the American Film Theatre's adaptation of David Storey's play about a bitter reunion between an English coal-miner and his grown sons. Stars Alan Bates and features Lindsay Anderson's direction.

IN COLD BLOOD
National Film and Video Center; 1967 • color; 2 hrs, 13 min; ¾" U-Matic, ½" Beta II, ½" VHS • Rental: $89/1 showing

Adapts for the screen Truman Capote's realistic novel which recounts the events leading up to the murder of a prosperous Kansas farmer and his family, the capture of the two murderers, and their trial. Stars John Forsythe, Robert Blake, and Scott Wilson.

IN NAME ONLY
Blackhawk Films, Inc; Order No. 506-07-0736 for ½" Beta II, 525-07-0736 for ½" VHS; 1939 • b/w; 1 hr, 42 min; ½" Beta II, ½" VHS • Sale: $49.95

Recounts the tale of a married man in love with another woman but unable to attain a divorce from his selfish wife until he receives his inheritance. Stars Cary Grant, Carole Lombard, and Kay Francis.

IN OLD CALIFORNIA
The Nostalgia Merchant; Order No. 0242; 1942 • b/w; 1 hr, 28 min; ½" Beta II, ½" VHS • Sale: $54.95

Features John Wayne as a man who settles in a brawling western frontier town and rallies the ranchers to fight the town's criminal element. Co-stars Albert Dekker and Binnie Barnes.

IN OLD MEXICO
Videobrary Inc; Order No. 5; 1938 • b/w; 1 hr, 2 min; ½" Beta II, ½" VHS • Sale: $39.95

Presents a Hopalong Cassidy western. Shows Cassidy being tricked into an unwanted rendezvous with his arch-enemy, The Fox. Stars William Boyd, George "Gabby" Hayes, and Paul Sutton.

IN OLD MEXICO; THE EAGLE'S BROOD
Videobrary Inc; Order No. 5-8; 1938 & 1935 • b/w; 2 hrs, 1 min; ½" Beta II, ½" VHS • Sale: $69.95

Offers a Hopalong Cassidy western double feature. Presents "In Old Mexico" in which Cassidy is tricked into an unwanted rendezvous with his arch-enemy, The Fox, and "The Eagle's Brood" in which Cassidy goes undercover to save the life of a young boy who knows his parents' murderers. Stars William Boyd and George "Gabby" Hayes.

IN OLD NEW MEXICO
Reel Images Inc; Order No. 54; 1945 • b/w; 1 hr, 1 min; ½" Beta II, ½" VHS • Sale: $39.95 for ½" Beta II, $42.95 for ½" VHS

Presents a western adventure in which the Cisco Kid and Pancho set out to prove the innocence of a girl accused of killing an old lady. Stars Duncan Renaldo.

IN OLD SANTA FE
Video Communications Inc; Order No. 1128; 1934 • b/w; 1 hr; ½" Beta II, ½" VHS • Sale: $54.95

Presents an action western featuring Ken Maynard, Gene Autry, and Smiley Burnette. Offers songs by all three, as well as stagecoach robbing and gangsterism on a dude ranch.

IN PRAISE OF OLDER WOMEN
Magnetic Video Corporation; Order No. CL-4057; 1978 • color; 1 hr, 48 min; ½" Beta II, ½" VHS • Sale: $54.95

- -
Vid America; Order No. 328; 1978 • color; 1 hr, 50 min; ½" Beta II, ½" VHS • Rental: $12.95/wk

Depicts the romantic adventures of a young man who prefers the company of mature women to the frustration of adolescent relationships. Stars Tom Berenger, Karen Black, and Susan Strasberg.

IN SEARCH OF ANCIENT ASTRONAUTS
National Film and Video Center; Date not listed • color; 52 min; 3/4" U-Matic, 1/2" Beta II, 1/2" VHS • Rental: $49/1 showing

Explores the evidence that may indicate that our ancestors were visited by extraterrestrial beings, in a short film narrated by Rod Serling, based on the book "Chariots of the Gods."

IN SEARCH OF NOAH'S ARK
Video Communications Inc; Order No. 6003; 1976 • color; 1 hr, 35 min; 1/2" Beta II, 1/2" VHS

Investigates the scientific evidence that exists to verify the universal flood and Noah's Ark as recorded in Genesis. Includes a narration by Brad Crandell.

THE INCREDIBLE SEX-RAY MACHINE
VTS; Date not listed • color; 1 hr, 9 min; 1/2" Beta I, 1/2" Beta II, 1/2" VHS • Sale: $99

Presents a pornographic film.

THE INCREDIBLE SHRINKING MAN
MCA DiscoVision; Order No. 23-004; 1957 • b/w; 1 hr, 21 min; LaserVision • Sale: $15.95

Adapts the novel by Richard Matheson in which a man begins to shrink gradually after exposure to radioactivity. Shows him fighting off a house cat, and now-grown-monstrous spider, as he must struggle to survive with a new perspective of life. Stars Grant Williams, April Kent, and Randy Stuart.

THE INDESTRUCTIBLE MAN
Blackhawk Films, Inc; Order No. 502-86-0073 for 1/2" Beta II, 515-86-0073 for 1/2" VHS; 1956 • b/w; 1 hr, 16 min; 1/2" Beta II, 1/2" VHS • Sale: $59.95

Recounts the story of a man returning from the dead to seek his revenge on three men who double-crossed him. Features Lon Chaney, Jr., Casey Adams, Marian Carr, and Ross Elliot.

INDIAN PAINT
Video Communications Inc; 1963 • color; 1 hr, 31 min; 1/2" Beta II, 1/2" VHS • Sale: $54.95

Shows a 15-year-old Indian boy, son of the tribal chief, raising a colt and encountering many perilous adventures. Stars Johnny Crawford and Jay Silverheels.

THE INFORMER
Niles Cinema; Order No. NM-8036; 1935 • b/w; 1 hr, 31 min; 1/2" Beta II, 1/2" VHS • Sale: $54.95
- -
The Nostalgia Merchant; Order No. 8036; 1935 • b/w; 1 hr, 31 min; 1/2" Beta II, 1/2" VHS • Sale: $54.95
- -
Red Fox, Inc; Order No. 8036; 1935 • b/w; 1 hr, 31 min; 1/2" Beta II, 1/2" VHS • Sale: $54.95
- -
Vid America; 1935 • b/w; 1 hr, 31 min; 1/2" Beta II, 1/2" VHS • Rental: $9.95/wk

Relates the demise of a drunken Irishman who informs on a buddy to collect a reward during the Irish rebellion. Stars Victor McLaglen and Preston Foster, with a score by Max Steiner, under the direction of John Ford.

THE IN-LAWS
Fotomat Corp; Order No. B0291 for 1/2" Beta II, V0291 for 1/2" VHS; 1979 • color; 1 hr, 43 min; 1/2" Beta II, 1/2" VHS • Sale: $54.95

WCI Home Video Inc; 1979 • color; 1 hr, 43 min; 1/2" Beta II, 1/2" VHS • Sale: $60

Follows the antics of a CIA agent who decides to go for the big money and involves his future in-law in his madcap scheme. Stars Alan Arkin, Peter Falk, Richard Libertini, and Penny Peyser.

THE INNOCENT
Time-Life Video Club Inc; Date not listed • color; 1 hr, 40 min; 1/2" Beta II, 1/2" VHS • Sale: $44.95 to members

Relates a story of sensuality and decadence in turn-of-the-century Rome. Depicts a young society bride who takes a lover after learning of her husband's infidelity. Uses locations in the villa and palazzos of Italy. Stars Laura Antonelli, Jennifer O'Neill, and Giancarlo Giannini in Luchino Visconti's last film.

INSIDE DESIREE COUSTEAU
Direct Video; 1980 • color; 1 hr, 20 min; 1/2" Beta II, 1/2" VHS • Sale: $99.50

Presents a pornographic film.

INSIDE MARILYN CHAMBERS
Mitchell Brothers' Film Group; Date not listed • color; 1 hr, 15 min; 1/2" Beta II, 1/2" VHS • Sale: $69 Beta II, $89 for 1/2" VHS

Presents a pornographic film.

THE INSPECTOR GENERAL
Cinema Resources; 1949 • color; 1 hr, 42 min; 1/2" Beta II, 1/2" VHS • Sale: $45

Showcases Danny Kaye as an illiterate who is mistaken for a visiting bureaucrat and friend of Napoleon's in 19th Century Russia. Features Walter Slezak, Elsa Lanchester, and Gene Lockhart in a frantic comedy.

INTERVAL
Magnetic Video Corporation; Order No. CL-4024; 1973 • color; 1 hr, 24 min; 1/2" Beta II, 1/2" VHS • Sale: $54.95

Focuses on a beautiful but lonely woman, recovering from a disappointing romance and a nervous breakdown, who becomes involved with a man as lonely as she is. Stars Merle Oberon and Robert Wolders.

INTIMATE PLAYMATES
Entertainment Video Releasing, Inc; Date not listed • color; 1 hr, 18 min; 1/2" Beta II, 1/2" VHS • Sale: $79.95

Presents a pornographic film.

INTOLERANCE
Ivy Video; 1916? • b/w; 2 hrs, 3 min; 3/4" U-Matic, 1/2" Beta II, 1/2" VHS • Sale: $59.95 for 1/2" Beta II & VHS, trade-in plan available, $295 for 3/4"
- -
Northeast Video and Sound, Inc; Order No. 154S; 1916 • b/w; 2 hrs, 3 min; 3/4" U-Matic, 1/2" EIAJ, 1/2" Beta II, 1/2" VHS • Sale: $295; Rental: $100/wk

Portrays man's inhumanity to his fellow man in a massive epic shuttling back and forth through four historical eras, from ancient Babylon to the present. Showcases an impressive array of early film stars in D.W. Griffith's most ambitious and costly cinematic effort.

INTRODUCTIONS
VTS; Order No. WWV100E7; Date not listed • color; 1 hr, 18 min; 1/2" Beta I, 1/2" Beta II, 1/2" VHS • Sale: $99

Presents a pornographic film.

INVASION FROM INNER EARTH

Video Communications Inc; Order No. 1055; 1974 • color; 1 hr, 32 min; 1/2" Beta II, 1/2" VHS • Sale: $54.95

Relates how five scientists working in the remote reaches of Canada on an advanced ecological research project find people inexplicably dying while at the same time radio communications inform them of growing mass hysteria and death in cities around the world. Stars Nick Holt, Paul Bentzen, and Debbi Pick.

INVASION OF THE BLOOD FARMERS

Thunderbird Films; 1976 • color; 1 hr, 20 min; 3/4" U-Matic, 1/2" Beta I, 1/2" Beta II, 1/2" VHS • Sale: $69.95 for 1/2" Beta I, $49.95 for 1/2" Beta II & VHS, $89.95 for 3/4"

Relates the efforts of a fanatical religious sect to obtain the sacrificial blood necessary to revive their queen. Stars Norman Kelley and Tanna Hunter.

THE INVINCIBLE

Video Gems; 1980 • color; 1 hr, 33 min; 1/2" Beta II, 1/2" VHS • Sale: $59.95

Offers a martial arts film featuring Bruce Li.

THE INVISIBLE GHOST

Video T.E.N.; 1941 • b/w; 1 hr, 10 min; 1/2" Beta II, 1/2" VHS • Sale: $49.95 for 1/2" Beta II, $54.95 for 1/2" VHS

Relates the story of a kindly man who goes berserk when he sees visions of his supposedly dead wife. Features Bela Lugosi, Polly Ann Young, John McGuire, and Clarence Muse.

THE IRON MASK

Cable Films; 1929 • b/w; 1 hr, 39 min; 1/2" Beta I, 1/2" Beta II, 1/2" VHS • Sale: $65 for 1/2" Beta I, $49.50 for 1/2" Beta II & VHS

Offers a silent film adaptation of Alexander Dumas' novel. Includes many swashbuckling scenes as the devious Rochefort attempts to pass off a twin brother as heir to the throne. Stars Douglas Fairbanks and Margaret DeLamotte.

IRON MOUNTAIN TRAIL; SHERIFF OF CIMARRON

The Nostalgia Merchant; Order No. 5003; 1953, 1945 • b/w; 2 hrs; 1/2" Beta II, 1/2" VHS • Sale: $59.95

Offers a western double feature. Opens with "Iron Mountain Trail," a tale of the Pony Express starring Rex Allen. Concludes with "Sheriff of Cimarron" in which an ex-convict tries to clear himself of a crime that sent him to jail; stars Sunset Carson.

THE ISLAND

Budget Video; 1961 • b/w; 1 hr, 36 min; 1/2" Beta II, 1/2" VHS • Sale: $44.95

Documents the day-to-day existence of a farming family on a small Japanese island without dialogue in a film directed by Kaneto Shindo. Features Nobuko Otawa, Taiji Tonoyama, Shinji Tanaka, and Masanori Horimoto.

ISLANDS IN THE STREAM .

Fotomat Corp; Order No. B0079 for 1/2" Beta II, V0079 for 1/2" VHS; 1977 • color; 1 hr, 50 min; 1/2" Beta II, 1/2" VHS • Sale: $49.95; Rental: $9.95/up to 5 days, applicable to purchase

Paramount Home Video; 1977 • color; 1 hr, 50 min; 1/2" Beta II, 1/2" VHS • Sale: $59.95

Presents a screen version of Ernest Hemingway's last novel. Portrays an American expatriate artist on Bimini,

whose talent is not without torment, especially with the arrival of his three sons for the summer. Shows how he tries to lead his sons into manhood, but is haunted by the threat of war and the scars of two unsuccessful marriages. Stars George C. Scott, David Hemmings, Claire Bloom, and Susan Tyrrell.

ISLE OF THE DEAD

Niles Cinema; Order No. NM-8037; 1945 • b/w; 1 hr, 12 min; 1/2" Beta II, 1/2" VHS • Sale: $54.95

The Nostalgia Merchant; Order No. 8037; 1945 • b/w; 1 hr, 12 min; 1/2" Beta II, 1/2" VHS • Sale: $54.95

Red Fox, Inc; Order No. 8037; 1945 • b/w; 1 hr, 12 min; 1/2" Beta II, 1/2" VHS • Sale: $54.95

Tells of a group of travelers stranded on an island during an epidemic who believe they are under a curse. Features Boris Karloff, Ellen Drew, and Marc Cramer.

IT CAME FROM OUTER SPACE

MCA Videocassette, Inc; Order No. 67017; 1953 • b/w; 1 hr, 21 min; 1/2" Beta II, 1/2" VHS • Sale: $65

Niles Cinema; Order No. MC-6017; 1953 • b/w; 1 hr, 21 min; 1/2" Beta II, 1/2" VHS • Sale: $65.00

Offers a science-fiction tale in 3-D of a town attempting to fight off an invasion by an alien. Includes 4 pairs of 3-D glasses. Stars Richard Carlson, Barbara Rush, Charles Drake, and Kathleen Hughes. Adapts a Ray Bradbury story, and shows much of the action through the eyes of the monster.

IT HAPPENED IN NEW ORLEANS

Reel Images Inc; Order No. 29; 1936 • b/w; 1 hr, 33 min; 1/2" Beta II, 1/2" VHS • Sale: $49.95 for 1/2" Beta II, $52.95 for 1/2" VHS

Follows a young boy and an ex-slave as they struggle to survive together in the South just after the Civil War. Features Bobby Breen, May Robson, and Charles Butterworth.

Henry Travers and James Stewart in *It's a Wonderful Life.*

IT'S A JOKE SON
Thunderbird Films; 1947 • b/w; 1 hr; 3/4" U-Matic, 1/2" Beta I, 1/2" Beta II, 1/2" VHS • Sale: $59.95 for 1/2" Beta I, $39.95 for 1/2" Beta II and VHS, $79.95 for 3/4"

Chronicles the unlikely campaign of Senator Claghorn (a Fred Allen radio character) for election on a third party ticket. Features Kenny Delmar, June Lockhart, Una Merkel, and Douglas Drumlittle.

IT'S A WONDERFUL LIFE
Cinema Concepts, Inc.; 1946 • b/w; 2 hrs; 3/4" U-Matic, 1/2" Beta II, 1/2" VHS • Sale: $54.95 for 1/2" Beta II & VHS, $149.95 for 3/4"

- -
Northeast Video and Sound, Inc; Order No. 156S; 1946 • b/w; 2 hrs, 10 min; 3/4" U-Matic, 1/2" EIAJ, 1/2" Beta II, 1/2" VHS • Sale: $250; Rental: $90/wk

- -
Reel Images Inc; Order No. 127; 1946 • b/w; 2 hrs, 10 min; 1/2" Beta II, 1/2" VHS • Sale: $69.95 for 1/2" Beta II, $73.95 for 1/2" VHS

- -
Tape Club of America; Order No. 2411 C; Date not listed • b/w; 2 hrs, 5 min; 1/2" Beta II, 1/2" VHS • Sale: $74.95

Features James Stewart in a film directed by Frank Capra about a man who has worked hard but faces ruin, until help comes to him through his guardian angel. Co-stars Donna Reed and Lionel Barrymore.

IT'S IN THE BAG
The Nostalgia Merchant; Order No. 0210; 1945 • b/w; 1 hr, 27 min; 1/2" Beta II, 1/2" VHS • Sale: $54.95

Offers a comedy about a shiftless flea circus owner who comes into line for a large inheritance. Features Fred Allen, Binnie Barnes, Robert Benchley, Sidney Toler, Jack Benny, and William Bendix.

IT'S LOVE AGAIN
Budget Video; 1936 • b/w; 1 hr, 30 min; 1/2" Beta II, 1/2" VHS • Sale: $44.95

Presents a British musical comedy which highlights the antics of a young woman looking for her "big break" and the society columnist she joins forces with. Features Jessie Matthews, Robert Young, and Sonnie Hale.

IVAN THE TERRIBLE (PART 1)
Reel Images Inc; Order No. 24; 1944 • b/w; 1 hr, 36 min; 1/2" Beta II, 1/2" VHS • Sale: $49.95 for 1/2" Beta II, $52.95 for 1/2" VHS

Presents the first part of Sergei Eisenstein's classic film about Ivan, the first tsar of a united Russia. Dramatizes the story in a manner deliberately larger than life, in a way reminiscent of Greek or Shakespearean tragedy.

IVAN THE TERRIBLE (PART 2)
Reel Images Inc; Order No. 25; 1946 • b/w; 1 hr, 22 min; 1/2" Beta II, 1/2" VHS • Sale: $49.95 for 1/2" Beta II, $52.95 for 1/2" VHS

Presents the second segment of Sergei Eisenstein's classic film version of the life of Ivan, originally banned by the Soviet government until 1958. Features, in the ending, the only color footage Eisenstein ever filmed.

JACK AND THE BEANSTALK
Fotomat Corp; Order No. B0139 for 1/2" Beta II, V0139 for 1/2" VHS; 1952 • color; 1 hr, 18 min; 1/2" Beta II, 1/2" VHS • Sale: $39.95; Rental: $7.95/up to 5 days, applicable to purchase

- -
Video Communications Inc; 1952 • color; 1 hr, 18 min; 1/2" Beta II, 1/2" VHS • Sale: $54.95

Offers Abbott and Costello in their fairytale land debut as they battle the infamous giant. Shows how they rescue the princess and bring back the hen which laid the golden egg.

JACOB: THE MAN WHO FOUGHT WITH GOD
Video Communications Inc; Order No. 1190; Date not listed • color; 1 hr, 58 min; 1/2" Beta II, 1/2" VHS • Sale: $54.95

Recounts the Genesis story of Jacob's struggle to receive his father's blessing and inheritance in spite of Esau's birthright. Follows Jacob's life to his eventual reconciliation with his brother. Features Fosco Giaccheti, Luisa Della Noce, and Jean Mercier.

THE JADE PUSSY CAT
Freeway Video Enterprises; Date not listed • color; 1 hr, 20 min; 1/2" Beta II, 1/2" VHS • Sale: $75 for 1/2" Beta II, $85 for 1/2" VHS

Presents a pornographic film.

JAILHOUSE ROCK
MGM/CBS Home Video; Order No. M50011; 1957 • b/w; 1 hr, 36 min; 1/2" Beta II, 1/2" VHS • Sale: $49.95

- -
Niles Cinema; Order No. GM-728; 1957 • b/w; 1 hr, 36 min; 1/2" Beta II, 1/2" VHS • Sale: $49.95

Presents a pre-Army Elvis Presley film. Follows Elvis as he goes to jail, learns how to play the guitar, and becomes a rock and roll star. Features songs by Leiber-Stoller. Stars Elvis, Judy Tyler, Vaughn Taylor, Dean Jones, and Mickey Shaughnessy.

JAMAICA REEF
FHV Entertainment, Inc; 1974 • color; 1 hr, 24 min; 1/2" Beta II, 1/2" VHS • Sale: $49.95

Relates an unusual adventure which takes place off the coast of Jamaica and concerns the search for sunken treasure. Stars Cheryl Ladd, Stephen Boyd, David Ladd, and Rosie Grier.

JASON AND THE ARGONAUTS
National Film and Video Center; 1963 • color; 1 hr, 44 min; 3/4" U-Matic, 1/2" Beta II, 1/2" VHS • Rental: $49/1 showing

Relates Jason's search for the Golden Fleece in his ship the Argo. Tells of how Medea disobeys her father to guide Jason to the Fleece and of their escape. Stars Todd Armstrong, Nancy Kovack, Gary Raymond, and Laurence Naismith.

Ted Neeley in *Jesus Christ Superstar*.

JAWS

MCA DiscoVision; Order No. 12-001; 1975 • color; 2 hrs, 4 min; LaserVision • Sale: $24.95

MCA Videocassette, Inc; Order No. 66001; 1975 • color; 2 hrs, 4 min;½" Beta II, ½" VHS • Sale: $60

Shows the effect of a 25-foot great white killer shark on a vacation community. Reveals the inability to comprehend such a dangerous situation and then explores the courage needed to combat the problem that will not go away. Uses music, underwater photography, real shark footage, and a mechanical shark to create tension. Stars Roy Scheider, Robert Shaw, Richard Dreyfuss, and Murray Hamilton, under the direction of Steven Spielberg.

JAWS 2

MCA DiscoVision; Order No. 12-010; 1978 • color; 2 hrs; LaserVision • Sale: $24.95

MCA Videocassette, Inc; Order No. 66002; 1978 • color; 2 hrs; ½" Beta II, ½" VHS • Sale: $60

Provides a sequel to the original "Jaws" in which Police Chief Brody must destroy another great white killer shark before it can destroy a group of youngsters out sailing. Stars Roy Scheider, Lorraine Gary, and Murray Hamilton.

JAWS OF DEATH

Video Communications Inc; Order No. 1057; 1975 • color; 1 hr, 31 min; ½" Beta II, ½" VHS • Sale: $54.95

Relates a story of a Marine biologist and his team who, against warnings, attempt inter-species communications with a killer whale.

JAZZ BALL

Golden Tapes Video Tape Library; Order No. CD8; 1956 • b/w; 1 hr; ½" Beta II, ½" VHS • Sale: $47.95 for ½" Beta II & VHS, 79.95 for ¾"

Offers a compilation of acts taken from old short subjects produced by Paramount. Features Cab Calloway, Louis Armstrong, The Mills Brothers, Artie Shaw, Betty Hutton, Jimmy Dorsey, Gene Krupa, and Buddy Rich.

JAZZ 'N' JIVE

Video Action Library ; Order No. BH03; 1930-41 • color; 1 hr; ½" Beta I, ½" Beta II, ½" VHS • Rental: $12.50/1 wk, $6.25 ea add'l wk

Presents four short films that feature music and musicians. Starts with "Cuckoo Murder Case" (1931), a comic horror cartoon. Follows with "Toot That Trumpet" (1941) with Apus and Estrillita. Continues with "Radio Revels" (1935), featuring the Major Bowes Amateur Hour winners. Concludes with "Black and Tan" (1930) starring Duke Ellington.

JERICHO

Budget Video; 1937 • b/w; 1 hr, 15 min; ½" Beta II, ½" VHS • Sale: $44.95

Showcases the talents of Paul Robeson in the ancestor of black superhero films. Follows the adventures of a black soldier accused of an unknown charge who escapes to Africa and lives like a sheik. Includes Henry Wilcoxon and Wallace Ford.

THE JERK

MCA DiscoVision; 1979 • color; 1 hr, 33 min; LaserVision • Sale: $24.95

MCA Videocassette, Inc; Order No. 66005; 1979 • color; 1 hr, 33 min; ½" Beta II, ½" VHS • Sale: $60

Offers Steve Martin in a comedy directed by Carl Reiner. Follows the bungling adventures of a white boy raised by black sharecroppers—who doesn't know that he's adopted. Co-stars Bernadette Peters.

JESSE JAMES AT BAY

Cable Films; 1941 • b/w; 54 min; ½" Beta I, ½" Beta II, ½" VHS • Sale: $45 for ½" Beta I, $49.50 for ½" Beta II & VHS

Presents a saga of Jesse James and his fight against the railroads. Stars Roy Rogers and Gabby Hayes.

JESUS CHRIST SUPERSTAR

MCA DiscoVision; Order No. 17-002; 1973 • color; 1 hr, 43 min; LaserVision • Sale: $24.95

MCA Videocassette, Inc; Order No. 55002; 1973 • color; 1 hr, 43 min; ½" Beta II, ½" VHS • Sale: $50

Depicts the last seven days in the life of Christ, told in rock opera form. Uses the landscape of Israel to enhance the retelling and provide a counterpoint to the unusual imagery. Stars Ted Neeley, Carl Anderson, and Joshua Mostel, under the direction of Norman Jewison.

JESUS OF NAZARETH

Magnetic Video Corporation; Order No. CL-9003; 1976 • color; 6 hrs, 11 min; ½" Beta II, ½" VHS • Sale: $169.95

RCA SelectaVision VideoDiscs; Order No. 00510; 1976 • color; 6 hrs, 29 min; CED • Sale: $99.98

Offers Director Franco Zeffirelli's account of the life of Jesus Christ, written by Anthony Burgess, Suso Cecchi D'amico, and Zeffirelli. Features biblical and historical research by Anglican, Catholic, and Jewish authorities, and location filming in Tunisia and Morocco. Stars Robert Powell, Anne Bancroft, Ernest Borgnine, James Farentino, James Earl Jones, Stacy Keach, Tony Lo Bianco, James Mason, Ian McShane, Laurence Olivier, Donald Pleasance, Christopher Plummer, Anthony Quinn, Rod Steiger, Peter Ustinov, Michael York, and Olivia Hussey. Includes music by Maurice Jarre.

JOE

Time-Life Video Club Inc; 1970 • color; 1 hr, 47 min; ½" Beta II, ½" VHS • Sale: $34.95 to members

Tells of a hippie-hating, bigoted hardhat who conspires with an ad executive to cover up the latter's murder of his daughter's boyfriend. Features Peter Boyle, Dennis Patrick, and Susan Sarandon, under the direction of John Avildsen.

JOE KIDD

MCA DiscoVision; Order No. 14-004; 1972 • color; 1 hr, 28 min; LaserVision • Sale: $24.95

Profiles a gunslinger, hired to hunt down one side, who then decides to choose for himself. Stars Clint Eastwood, Robert Duvall, John Saxon, and Don Stroud, under John Sturges' direction.

JOHN WAYNE DOUBLE FEATURE #1

All Star Video Corp; 1934 • b/w; 2 hrs; ½" Beta II, ½" VHS • Sale: $59.95

Presents two early westerns starring John Wayne. Includes "Blue Steel" and "West of the Divide."

JOHN WAYNE DOUBLE FEATURE #2

All Star Video Corp; 1934; 1933 • b/w; 2 hrs; ½" Beta II, ½" VHS • Sale: $59.95

Presents two early westerns starring John Wayne. Includes "Star Packer" and "Sagebrush Trail."

JOHNNY ANGEL

Blackhawk Films, Inc; Order No. 506-30-0733 for ½" Beta II, 525-30-0733 for ½" VHS ; 1945 • b/w; 1 hr, 19 min; ½" Beta II, ½" VHS • Sale: $49.95

Shows a man solving the murder of his father and breaking up a ring of thugs in a mystery-thriller. Stars George Raft, Claire Trevor, Signe Hasso, Lowell Gilmore, Hoagy Carmichael, and Marvin Miller.

JOHNNY GUITAR

The Nostalgia Merchant; Order No. 0122; 1954 • color; 1 hr, 50 min; ½" Beta II, ½" VHS • Sale: $54.95

Presents an offbeat, multi-leveled western about a female saloon owner, an ex-gunfighter, a gang of misfit outlaws, and a group of mercenary, self-righteous townsfolk, all of whose interests intertwine in a combination of realism, romance, violence, and cynicism.

Scott Brady, Joan Crawford, and Sterling Hayden in *Johnny Guitar.*

Stars Sterling Hayden, Joan Crawford, Mercedes McCambridge, Ward Bond, Scott Brady, and Ernest Borgnine, under the direction of Nicholas Ray.

THE JOLSON STORY

National Film and Video Center; 1946 • color; 2 hrs, 9 min; ¾" U-Matic, ½" Beta II, ½" VHS • Rental: $49/1 showing

Recounts the story of a young vaudevillian who becomes a Broadway star because of his new method of singing. Shows how his love of singing and need for an audience cause his marriage to fail. Stars Larry Parks, Evelyn Keyes, and William Demarest.

JOSEPH AND HIS BRETHREN

Video Communications Inc; Order No. 1058; 1962 • color; 1 hr, 43 min; ½" Beta II, ½" VHS • Sale: $54.95

Dramatizes the Old Testament story of Joseph, beloved son of Jacob, who was sold into slavery by his brothers. Stars Geoffrey Horne and Robert Morley.

JOSEPH ANDREWS

Fotomat Corp; Order No. B0031 for ½" Beta II, V0031 for ½" VHS; 1977 • color; 1 hr, 38 min; ½" Beta II, ½" VHS • Sale: $49.95; Rental: $9.95/up to 5 days, applicable to purchase

Presents a film version of a 1742 Henry Fielding novel which chronicles the rise of Joseph Andrews from servant to personal footman—and fancy of—Lady Booby. Follows him as he battles seductions, robberies, and rogues, trying to remain faithful to his love—an equally innocent servant girl. Stars Ann-Margret, Peter Firth, Jim Dale, Michael Hordern, and Beryl Reid, under the direction of Tony Richardson.

JOY

Quality X Video Cassette Company; Date not listed • color; 1 hr, 15 min; ½" Beta I, ½" Beta II, ½" VHS • Sale: $99.50

Presents a pornographic film.

JUDEX

Budget Video; 1964 • b/w; 1 hr, 43 min; ½" Beta II, ½" VHS • Sale: $44.95

Relates the tale of a cloaked hero-avenger who punishes the wicked and protects the good, in a film by Georges Franju, in French with subtitles. Features Channing Pollock, Francine Berge, Edith Scob, Sylva Koscina, and Michel Vitold.

JUDGE PRIEST

Budget Video; 1934 • b/w; 1 hr, 18 min; 1/2" Beta II, 1/2" VHS • Sale: $44.95

Presents a comedy-drama in which a Kentucky judge saves his nephew from marriage and the town blacksmith from a sentence of jail. Stars Will Rogers, Tom Brown, Anita Louise, and Stepin Fetchit.

JULIA

Magnetic Video Corporation; 1977 • color; 1 hr, 58 min; 1/2" Beta II, 1/2" VHS • Sale: $69.95

Adapts for the screen Lillian Hellman's story in "Pentimento" about how she was drawn into helping anti-Nazi Germans escape Hitler's Germany. Stars Jane Fonda, Vanessa Redgrave, Jason Robards, Maximilian Schell, Hal Holbrook, Rosemary Murphy, Meryl Streep, Lisa Pelikan, and Cathleen Nesbitt.

Jane Fonda and Vanessa Redgrave in *Julia*.

THE JUNGLE BOOK

Cinema Concepts, Inc.; 1942 • color; 1 hr, 40 min; 3/4" U-Matic, 1/2" Beta II, 1/2" VHS • Sale: $54.95 for 1/2" Beta II & VHS, $149.95 for 3/4"

- -

Northeast Video and Sound, Inc; 1942 • color; 1 hr, 49 min; 3/4" U-Matic, 1/2" EIAJ, 1/2" Beta II, 1/2" VHS • Sale: $395; Rental: $75/wk

- -

Reel Images Inc; Order No. 129; 1942 • color; 1 hr, 47 min ; 1/2" Beta JI, 1/2" VHS • Sale: $49.95 for 1/2" Beta II, $52.95 for 1/2" VHS

- -

VCX, Order No. FC109; 1942 • color; 1 hr, 49 min; 1/2" Beta II, 1/2" VHS • Sale: $35.00

- -

Vid America; Order No. 916; 1942 • color; 1 hr, 45 min; 1/2" Beta II, 1/2" VHS • Rental: $9.95/wk

- -

The Video Library; Order No. CC-0126; 1942 • color; 1 hr, 40 min; 1/2" Beta II, 1/2" VHS • Sale: $49.95

Presents Rudyard Kipling's story about the infant son of a prince who wanders off into the jungle and is reared by a pack of wolves. Stars Sabu, Joseph Calleia, and Rosemary DeCamp, under the direction of Zoltan Korda.

JUST CRAZY ABOUT HORSES

Home Vision; Order No. 814-7001 for 1/2" Beta II, 814-9001 for 1/2" VHS; 1978 • color; 1 hr, 45 min; 1/2" Beta II, 1/2" VHS • Sale: $49.95

Documents the varied uses of horses in America today. Includes information about breeding, racing, polo, fox hunts, and auctions.

THE KANSAN

Video T.E.N.; 1943 • b/w; 1 hr, 19 min; 1/2" Beta II, 1/2" VHS • Sale: $49.95 for 1/2" Beta II, $54.95 for 1/2" VHS

Documents how a marshal copes with an old family feud and a murderous tyrant. Includes Richard Dix, Victor Jory, Jane Wyatt, and Albert Dekker.

KARLA

Monarch Releasing Corporation; Date not listed • color; 1 hr, 20 min; 3/4" U-Matic • Sale: $350

Presents a pornographic film.

KEATON SPECIAL AND VALENTINO MYSTIQUE

Blackhawk Films, Inc; Order No. 506-66-0841 for 1/2" Beta II, 525-66-0841 for 1/2" VHS; Date not listed • b/w; 56 min; 3/4" U-Matic, 1/2" Beta I, 1/2" Beta II, 1/2" VHS • Sale: $59.95 for 1/2" Beta I, $39.95 for 1/2" Beta II & VHS, 69.95 for 3/4"

Presents two narrated documentaries from the History of the Motion Picture Series. Shows Buster Keaton in his peak years from the mid-teens to the mid-thirties, combining historical facts with excerpts from "College," "Fatty at Coney Island," and "Steamboat Bill, Jr." Offers Paul Killiam recounting the career of Rudolph Valentino. Uses newsreels, stills, newspaper clippings, home movies, and excerpts from "Son of the Sheik," "Eagle," and "Blood and Sand."

THE KENNEL MURDER CASE

Video T.E.N.; 1933 • b/w; 1 hr, 13 min; 1/2" Beta II, 1/2" VHS • Sale: $49.95 for 1/2" Beta II, $54.95 for 1/2" VHS

Examines a murder committed in a locked room with debonair sleuth Philo Vance, a bumbling police sergeant, and a beautiful woman. Stars William Powell, Mary Astor, Eugene Pallette, and Helen Vinson, under the direction of Michael Curtiz.

KEY TO THE UNIVERSE

Home Vision; Order No. 817-7001 for 1/2" Beta II, 817-9001 for 1/2" VHS; 1977 • color; 2 hrs; 1/2" Beta II, 1/2" VHS • Sale: $49.95

Reports on the latest theories about the links between the macro-world—stars and galaxies—and the micro-world—atoms and their components. Offers an overview of recent scientific breakthroughs toward understanding the laws of creation.

KEYSTONE KRAZIES

Ivy Video; 1929 • b/w; 55 min; 3/4" U-Matic, 1/2" Beta II, 1/2" VHS • Sale: $$59.95 for 1/2" Beta II & VHS trade-in plan available, $150 for 3/4"

- -

Northeast Video and Sound, Inc; Order No. 138S; Date not listed • b/w; 55 min; 3/4" U-Matic, 1/2" EIAJ, 1/2" Beta II, 1/2" VHS • Sale: $149; Rental: $55/wk

Highlights the classic mayhem of Mack Sennett's Keystone Comedies from the era of silent film. Rediscovers the highly creative slapstick of the Keystone Kops, with archetypal chase scenes and pie fights.

THE KID AND THE IDLE CLASS
Magnetic Video Corporation; Order No. CL-3002; 1921 • b/w; 1 hr, 30 min; 1/2" Beta II, 1/2" VHS • Sale: $44.95

Offers Charlie Chaplin silent double feature. Begins with "The Kid," in which Charlie raises an orphan played by Jackie Coogan. Concludes with "The Idle Class," in which Chaplin plays two roles, a poor man and a rich playboy.

THE KID FROM LEFT FIELD
Time-Life Video Club Inc; 1953 • b/w; 1 hr, 30 min; 1/2" Beta II, 1/2" VHS • Sale: $34.95 to members

Follows the adventures of a bat boy whose father used to be on the major league team and now is a vendor. Recounts how the father passes on advice to the team through his son. Stars Dan Dailey, Anne Bancroft, Billy Chapin, Lloyd Bridges, Ray Collins, and Richard Egan.

THE KID FROM LEFT FIELD
Time-Life Video Club Inc; 1979 • color; 1 hr, 40 min; 1/2" Beta II, 1/2" VHS • Sale: $34.95 to members

Presents a made-for-TV movie about baseball and fathers and sons. Concerns a bat boy who shows the San Diego Padres how to get from the cellar to the World Series with a little help from his has-been, and former Padre star, father. Stars Gary Coleman, Robert Guillaume, Tab Hunter, Gary Collins, and Ed McMahon.

KIDNAPPED
Fotomat Corp; 1960 • color; 1 hr, 37 min; 1/2" Beta II, 1/2" VHS • Sale: $49.95; Rental: $9.95/up to 5 days, applicable to purchase
- -
MCA DiscoVision; Order No. D18-506; 1960 • color; 1 hr, 37 min; LaserVision • Sale: $24.95
- -
RCA SelectaVision VideoDiscs; Order No. 00706; 1960 • color; 1 hr, 37 min; CED • Sale: $19.98

Presents an adaptation of Robert Louis Stevenson's novel set in Scotland during the Jacobite rebellion of the early 1700's. Shows a young heir being kidnapped on the orders of his uncle, and follows his adventures with a rebel fighter. Stars Peter Finch, James MacArthur, and Bernard Lee, in a Walt Disney Studios production, filmed in Scotland.

KIDS IS KIDS
Fotomat Corp; Order No. B1042 for 1/2" Beta II, V1042 for 1/2" VHS; Date not listed • color; 47 min; 1/2" Beta II, 1/2" VHS • Sale: $44.95; Rental: $7.95/5 days
- -
MCA DiscoVision ; Order No. D61-504; Date not listed • color; 1 hr; LaserVision • Sale: $9.95
- -
Niles Cinema; Order No. WD-21; Date not listed • color; 46 min; 1/2" Beta II, 1/2" VHS • Sale: $44.95
- -
Walt Disney Home Video; Order No. 21BS for 1/2" Beta II, 21 VS for 1/2" VHS; Date not listed • color; 46 min; 1/2" Beta II, 1/2" VHS • Sale: $44.95

Offers a Walt Disney cartoon collection featuring Prof. Ludwing Von Drake and Donald Duck. Includes "Donald's Happy Birthday," "Good Scouts," "Donald's Fountain of Youth," "Soup's On," and "Lucky Number."

KILLER BATS
Cable Films; 1940 • b/w; 1 hr, 9 min; 1/2" Beta I, 1/2"

Beta II, 1/2" VHS • Sale: $65 for 1/2" Beta I, $49.50 for 1/2" Beta II & VHS

Portrays a quiet unassuming doctor who in reality is training monster bats to kill. Stars Bela Lugosi and Dave O'Brien, under the direction of Jean Yarborough.

KILLER SHARK
Blackhawk Films, Inc; Order No. 502-86-0075 for 1/2" Beta II, 515-86-0075 for 1/2" VHS; 1950 • b/w; 1 hr, 16 min; 1/2" Beta II, 1/2" VHS • Sale: $59.95

Describes what happens when a proper Bostonian gentleman takes a boat out alone for his vacation and gets more than he bargained for. Features Roddy Macdowell and Laurette Luez.

THE KILLING OF SISTER GEORGE
Magnetic Video Corporation; Order No. 8006; 1968 • color; 2 hrs, 18 min; 1/2" Beta II, 1/2" VHS • Sale: $79.95

Adapts Frank Marcus' play about a lesbian love triangle among a soap opera actress, a TV network executive, and an apartment mate. Stars Beryl Reid, Sussanah York, Coral Browne, Ronald Fraser, and Patricia Medina. Uses graphic language.

KIND HEARTS AND CORONETS
Fotomat Corp; Order No. B0237 for 1/2" Beta II, V0237 for 1/2" VHS; 1949 • b/w; 1 hr, 42 min; 1/2" Beta II, 1/2" VHS • Sale: $49.95; Rental: $9.95/up to 5 days, applicable to purchase
- -
Time-Life Video Club Inc; 1949 • b/w; 1 hr, 44 min; 1/2" Beta II, 1/2" VHS • Sale: $49.95 to members

Showcases the versatility of Alec Guinness as he plays eight members of a wealthy family being systematically eliminated by a young man who is ninth in line to the inheritance. Displays a satirical look at "getting away with murder." Stars Guinness, Dennis Price, Valerie Hobson, Joan Greenwood, and Arthur Lowe.

THE KING AND I
Golden Tapes Video Tape Library; Order No. F-1004; 1956 • color; 2 hrs, 13 min; 1/2" Beta II, 1/2" VHS • Sale: $49.95 for 1/2" Beta II & VHS, $124.95 for 3/4"
- -
Magnetic Video Corporation; Order No. CL-1004; 1956 • color; 2 hrs, 13 min; 1/2" Beta II, 1/2" VHS • Sale: $64.95
- -
The Video Library; Order No. MV-1004; 1956 • color; 2 hrs, 13 min; 1/2" Beta II, 1/2" VHS • Sale: $74.95

Stars Yul Brynner as the King of Siam and Deborah Kerr as Anna in this film adaptation of the Rodgers and Hammerstein Broadway musical based on the novel "Anna and the King of Siam." Includes "Getting to Know You," "Hello Young Lovers," and "Whistle A Happy Tune."

THE KING BOXERS
Video Gems; 1980 • color; 1 hr, 30 min; 1/2" Beta II, 1/2" VHS • Sale: $59.95

Offers a martial arts film with Jimmy Manfei, Yasuka Kurata, and Johnny Nainam.

KING CREOLE
Magnetic Video Corporation; Order No. CL-2005; 1958 • b/w; 1 hr, 55 min; 1/2" Beta II, 1/2" VHS • Sale: $44.95
- -
The Video Library; Order No. MV-2005; 1958 • b/w; 1 hr, 55 min; 1/2" Beta II, 1/2" VHS • Sale: $44.95

**Deborah Kerr and Yul Brynner
in *The King and I*.**

Presents a musical drama about a young busboy saved from delinquency when he is coerced into singing at a nightclub and ends up making a big hit. Stars Elvis Presley, Carolyn Jones, and Dean Jagger.

A KING IN NEW YORK
Magnetic Video Corporation; Order No. CL-3011; 1957 • b/w; 1 hr, 45 min; ½" Beta II, ½" VHS • Sale: $44.95

Presents Charlie Chaplin's political satire about a deposed European monarch who visits America during the McCarthy era. Includes a scene in which the King is tricked into appearing on a live TV show. Co-stars Dawn Addams, Michael Chaplin, and Phil Brown, in a film written and directed by Charlie Chaplin.

KING KONG
Niles Cinema; Order No. NM-8001; 1933 • b/w; 1 hr, 45 min; ½" Beta II, ½" VHS • Sale: $54.95
- -
The Nostalgia Merchant; Order No. 8001; 1933 • b/w; 1 hr, 45 min; ½" Beta II, ½" VHS • Sale: $54.95
- -
RCA SelectaVision VideoDiscs; Order No. 00406; 1933 • b/w; 1 hr, 40 min; CED • Sale: $19.98
- -
Red Fox, Inc; Order No. 8001; 1933 • b/w; 1 hr, 45 min; ½" Beta II, ½" VHS • Sale: $54.95
- -
Vid America; Order No. 924; 1933 • b/w; 1 hr, 45 min; ½" Beta II, ½" VHS • Sale: $54.95; Rental: $10.95/wk, applicable to purchase

Presents the original version of the fantasy of a giant ape who terrorizes New York City. Features numerous special effects, considered extremely sophisticated for that era. Stars Fay Wray, Bruce Cabot, and Robert Armstrong, with a score by Max Steiner.

KING KONG
Fotomat Corp; Order No. B0019 for ½" Beta II, V0019 for ½" VHS; 1977 • color; 2 hrs, 15 min; ½" Beta II, ½" VHS • Sale: $69.95; Rental: $9.95/up to 5 days, applicable to purchase
- -
MCA DiscoVision; Order No. P10-522; 1977 • color; 2 hrs, 15 min; LaserVision • Sale: $24.95
- -
Paramount Home Video; 1977 • color; 2 hrs, 15 min; ½" Beta II, ½" VHS • Sale: $79.95

Presents a remake of the film classic. Shows, again, the gargantuan ape as he battles attacking aircraft high above the streets of New York, this time plunging from the top of the World Trade Center. Stars Jeff Bridges, Charles Grodin, and Jessica Lange, in a Dino De Laurentis production.

KING OF KONG ISLAND
Video Communications Inc; Order No. 1187; Date not listed • color; 1 hr, 32 min; ½" Beta II, ½" VHS • Sale: $54.95

Reveals a group of mad scientists causing apes to go berserk. Shows the fate of the world resting in the paws of a mighty descendent of the original Kong. Features Brad Harris and Marc Lawrence.

KING OF THE GYPSIES
Fotomat Corp; Order No. B0227 for ½" Beta II, V0227 for ½" VHS; 1978 • color; 1 hr, 52 min; ½" Beta II, ½" VHS • Sale: $54.95; Rental: $9.95/5 days
- -
Paramount Home Video; Order No. 8868; 1979 • color; 1 hr, 52 min; ½" Beta II, ½" VHS • Sale: $59.95

Adapts for the screen Peter Maas' non-fiction book about a young man who wants to make his way as an American but must take on the responsibility of leading his gypsy clan. Stars Sterling Hayden, Shelley Winters, Susan Sarandon, Judd Hirsch, Eric Roberts, Brooke Shields, and Annette O'Toole.

KING OF THE KONGO
Reel Images Inc; Order No. 703; 1929 • b/w; 3 hrs, 33 min; ½" Beta II, ½" VHS • Sale: $119.95

Offers the first Mascot Studio serial, a silent film featuring Boris Karloff, Jacqueline Logan, and Walter Miller. Tells of a Secret Serviceman who is sent into the Southeast Asian jungles to break up a gang of ivory thieves. Includes prehistoric monsters, musical score, and title cards.

KING OF THE ROCKET MEN
The Nostalgia Merchant; Order No. 0024; 1949 • b/w; 3 hrs; ½" Beta II, ½" VHS • Sale: $109.95

Presents, on two videocassettes, a Republic motion picture serial in 12 episodes. Follows the adventures of Jeff King, "thunderbolt of the air," as he tries to stop Doctor Vulcan and his gang of traitors from stealing scientific secrets. Stars Tris Coffin, Mae Clarke, and I. Stanford Jolley.

KING OF THE TEXAS RANGERS
The Nostalgia Merchant; Date not listed • b/w; 3 hrs; ½" Beta II, ½" VHS • Sale: $109.95

Presents, on two videocassettes, a motion picture serial in 12 episodes. Stars Slingin' Sammy Baugh.

KINGS, QUEENS, JOKERS
Video Action Library; Order No. BH01; 1920-31 • color; 1 hr; ½" Beta I, ½" Beta II, ½" VHS • Rental: $15/1 wk, $7.50 ea add'l wk

Compiles three short films, beginning with "The Stolen Jools" (1931), a humorous mystery starring Buster Keaton, Laurel and Hardy, Loretta Young, Joan Crawford, and many others. Continues with "Dangerous Females" starring Marie Dressler and Polly Moran. Concludes with "Haunted Spooks" (1920) starring Harold Lloyd and Mildred Davis.

KINKY LADIES OF BOURBON STREET
Quality X Video Cassette Company; Date not listed • color; 1 hr, 27 min; ½" Beta I, ½" Beta II, ½" VHS • Sale: $99.50

Presents a pornographic film.

KIPPS

Budget Video; 1941 • b/w; 1 hr, 35 min; 1/2" Beta II, 1/2" VHS • Sale: $44.95

Presents a British satire in which an impoverished draper's apprentice inherits a fortune and is forced to cope with the responsibilities of the wealthy; directed by Sir Carol Reed. Stars Michael Redgrave, Diana Wynyard, and Michael Wilding.

KNIFE IN THE WATER

Reel Images Inc; Order No. 456; 1965 • b/w; 1 hr, 35 min; 1/2" Beta II, 1/2" VHS • Sale: $49.95 for 1/2" Beta II, $52.95 for 1/2" VHS

Relates the story of a conservative couple who pick up a hitchhiker. Shows how their relationship eventually grows into temperamental differences and vicious tensions. Presents the first feature directed by Roman Polanski.

KNIGHTS OF THE RANGE

Video Communications Inc; Order No. 1131; 1940 • b/w; 1 hr, 6 min; 1/2" Beta II, 1/2" VHS • Sale: $54.95

Offers an adaptation of a story by Zane Grey, concerning a reformed outlaw and his efforts to save a cattle ranch from being taken over by criminals. Stars Russell Hayden, Victor Jory, Jean Parker, and Morris Ankrum.

KNOCK ON ANY DOOR

Columbia Pictures Home Entertainment; Order No. BE51355 for 1/2" Beta II, VH10350 for 1/2" VHS; 1949 • b/w; 1 hr, 40 min; 1/2" Beta II, 1/2" VHS • Sale: $59.95

Adapts for the screen Willard Motley's novel about a young man from the slums who is accused of killing a policeman and is defended by a man who escaped the same type of background. Stars Humphrey Bogart, John Derek, and George Macready.

KNOCK THEM OVER

Monarch Releasing Corporation; Date not listed • color; 1 hr, 14 min; 3/4" U-Matic • Sale: $300

Presents a pornographic film.

THE KNOCKOUT AND DOUGH AND DYNAMITE

Reel Images Inc; Order No. 531; 1914 • b/w; 54 min; 1/2" Beta II, 1/2" VHS • Sale: $39.95 for 1/2" Beta II, $42.95 for 1/2" VHS

Pairs two Keystone productions starring Charlie Chaplin. Spotlights "Fatty" Arbuckle, Mabel Norman, and Mack Sennett himself in "The Knockout," a film in which Chaplin has a supporting role as the referee for the big fight. Stars Chaplin by himself as a baker's assistant left alone to mind the shop in "Dough and Dynamite."

KOTCH

Magnetic Video Corporation; Order No. 8008; 1971 • color; 1 hr, 54 min; 1/2" Beta II, 1/2" VHS • Sale: $59.95

Studies a 72-year-old widower who is regarded as a problem by his children but refuses to be cast aside. Shows his involvement with an unmarried, pregnant teenager. Stars Walter Matthau, Deborah Winters, Felicia Farr, and Charles Aidman, under Jack Lemmon's direction.

LA BETE HUMAINE

Budget Video; 1938 • b/w; 1 hr, 30 min; 1/2" Beta II, 1/2" VHS • Sale: $44.95

- -

Cable Films; 1938 • b/w; 1 hr, 44 min; 1/2" Beta I, 1/2" Beta II, 1/2" VHS • Sale: $65 for 1/2" Beta I, $49.50 for 1/2" Beta II & VHS

- -

Reel Images Inc; Order No. 502; 1938 • b/w; 1 hr, 41 min; 1/2" Beta II, 1/2" VHS • Sale: $49.95 for 1/2" Beta II, $52.95 for 1/2" VHS

Examines the psyche of a railroad engineer haunted by memories of alcoholic parents and grandparents, whose fits of madness lead to tragedy. Stars Jean Gabin, Simone Simon, Fernand Ledoux, Carette, and Blanchette Brunoy, under the direction of Jean Renoir; in French with subtitles.

LA CUCCARACHA

Reel Images Inc; Order No. 26; 1934 • color; 21 min; 1/2" Beta II, 1/2" VHS • Sale: $29.95 for 1/2" Beta II, $32.95 for 1/2" VHS

Presents a musical drama filled with Mexican songs and dances in the first 3-strip live-action Technicolor film ever made. Features Steffi Dunna.

LA FAVORITA

Reel Images Inc; Order No. 468; 1952 • b/w; 1 hr, 20 min; 1/2" Beta II, 1/2" VHS • Sale: $49.95 for 1/2" Beta II, $52.95 for 1/2" VHS

Presents a film version of the Italian opera with English narration. Features Sophia Loren in a supporting role.

LA FEMME INFIDELE

Blackhawk Films, Inc; Order No. 502-30-0061 for 1/2" Beta II, 515-30-0061 for 1/2" VHS; 1969 • color; 1 hr, 42 min; 1/2" Beta II, 1/2" VHS • Sale: $59.95

Explores a man's reactions to the first hints and growing certainty that his wife has taken a lover. Presents a blend of comedy and horror. Features Stephane Audran, Michel Bouquet, Maurice Ronet, Michel Duchaussoy, and Stephan Di Napolo, under the direction of Claude Chabrol.

LA GRANDE ILLUSION

Ivy Video; 1938 • b/w; 1 hr, 50 min; 3/4" U-Matic, 1/2" Beta II, 1/2" VHS • Sale: $59.95 for 1/2" Beta II & VHS, trade-in plan available, $225 for 3/4"

- -

Northeast Video and Sound, Inc; 1938 • b/w; 1 hr, 50 min; 3/4" U-Matic, 1/2" EIAJ, 1/2" Beta II, 1/2" VHS • Sale: $225; Rental: $80/wk

Explores the human aspect of war in this Jean Renoir film about the relationships between French prisoners of war and their German commandant, and the conflicts between different classes of society among the prisoners. Stars Jean Gabin, Pierre Fresnay, and Erich Von Stroheim.

LADY CHATTERLY'S LOVER
Budget Video; 1955 • b/w; 1 hr, 42 min; ½" Beta II, ½" VHS • Sale: $44.95

Transcribes for the screen the novel by D.H. Lawrence telling of the affair between a rich married woman and her husband's game-keeper, a celebration of physical love and an indictment of sexual hypocrisy. Stars Danielle Darrieux, Leo Genn, and Erno Crisa under the direction of Marc Allegret; in French with subtitles.

LADY COCOA
Video T.E.N.; 1957 • color; 1 hr, 33 min; ½" Beta II, ½" VHS • Sale: $49.95 for ½" Beta II, $54.95 for ½" VHS

Tells of a racketeer's girlfriend on the run in Las Vegas. Features Lola Falana, Gene Washington, Alex Dreier, "Mean" Joe Green, James A. Watson Jr., and Millie Perkins.

THE LADY FROM SHANGHAI
National Film and Video Center; 1948 • b/w; 1 hr, 27 min; ¾" U-Matic, ½" Beta II, ½" VHS • Rental: $69/1 showing

Deals with an adventurer who accepts $5000 to sign a confession that he killed a man's business partner, when actually that man plans to disappear in a swindle plot. Shows how, when the man is actually murdered, the adventurer must escape from jail to find the real killer. Stars Rita Hayworth and Orson Welles, who also wrote the screenplay and directed.

LADY OF BURLESQUE
Reel Images Inc; Order No. 570; 1943 • b/w; 1 hr, 32 min; ½" Beta II, ½" VHS • Sale: $49.95 for ½" Beta II, $52.95 for ½" VHS
- -
Video Communications Inc; 1943 • b/w; 1 hr, 31 min; ½" Beta II, ½" VHS • Sale: $54.95
- -
Video T.E.N.; 1943 • b/w; 1 hr, 31 min; ½" Beta II, ½" VHS • Sale: $49.95 for ½" Beta II, $54.95 for ½" VHS

Offers a musical/murder mystery based on Gypsy Rose Lee's 'The G-String Murders.' Unfolds a story of strippers found strangled with their own G-strings. Features Barbara Stanwyck, Michael O'Shea, Charles Dingle, Pinky Lee, and Gerald Mohr.

THE LADY REFUSES
Thunderbird Films; 1931 • b/w; 1 hr, 10 min; ¾" U-Matic, ½" Beta I, ½" Beta II, ½" VHS • Sale: $69.95 for ½" Beta I, $49.95 for ½" Beta II & VHS, $89.95 for ¾"

Presents a comedy of manners in which a sophisticated patriarch hires a young woman to lure his son away from a rowdy group of friends. Stars Betty Compson, John Darrow, and Margaret Livingston.

LADY SINGS THE BLUES
Fotomat Corp; Order No. B0085 for ½" Beta II, V0085 for ½" VHS; 1972 • color; 2 hrs, 24 min; ½" Beta II, ½" VHS • Sale: $69.95; Rental: $9.95/up to 5 days, applicable to purchase
- -
Paramount Home Video; 1972 • color; 2 hrs, 24 min; ½" Beta II, ½" VHS • Sale: $79.95
- -
RCA SelectaVision VideoDiscs; Order No. 00616; 1972 • color; 2 hrs, 24 min; CED • Sale: $22.98

Presents a screen version of the life of Billie Holiday, one of America's most loved and memorable blues singers. Stars Diana Ross, Billy Dee Williams, and Richard Pryor.

A LADY TAKES A CHANCE
The Video Library; Order No. CC-1027; 1943 • b/w; 1 hr, 26 min; ½" Beta II, ½" VHS • Sale: $54.95
- -
Video Tape Network; Order No. CD 621 for ½" Beta II, CD 622 for ½" VHS; 1943 • b/w; 1 hr, 26 min; ½" Beta II, ½" VHS • Sale: $59.95

Presents one of John Wayne's most versatile performances as a rope-shy rodeo rider who yearns for the wide-open spaces and no feminine entanglements—only to fall in love with a New York City working girl with matrimonial ideas.

THE LADY VANISHES
Cinema Concepts, Inc.; 1938 • b/w; 1 hr, 20 min; ¾" U-Matic, ½" Beta II, ½" VHS • Sale: $54.95 for ½" Beta II & VHS, $149.95 for ¾"
- -
The Video Library; Order No. AE-6009; 1938 • b/w; 1 hr, 20 min; ½" Beta II, ½" VHS • Sale: $49.95

Combines suspense and humor in this spy story directed by Alfred Hitchcock. Concerns the disappearance of a matronly secret agent aboard a train traveling through Central Europe. Stars Margaret Lockwood, Michael Redgrave, Paul Lukas, Dame May Whitty, and Cecil Parker.

THE LADYKILLERS
Fotomat Corp; Order No. B0243 for ½" Beta II, V0243 for ½" VHS; 1955 • b/w; 1 hr, 27 min ; ½" Beta II, ½" VHS • Sale: $49.95; Rental: $9.95/up to 5 days, applicable to purchase
- -
Time-Life Video Club Inc; 1955 • b/w; 1 hr, 34 min; ½" Beta II, ½" VHS • Sale: $39.95 to members

Depicts the attempt of five crooks to pull the wool over the eyes of a little old landlady, as they pose as musicians to rent rooms in her house so they can pull off a robbery nearby. Showcases the comic talents of Alec Guinness, Cecil Parker, Herbert Lom, Peter Sellers, Danny Green, Katie Johnson, and Frankie Howerd.

LASERBLAST
Meda/Media Home Entertainment Inc; Order No. M135; 1977 • color; 1 hr, 25 min; ½" Beta II, ½" VHS • Sale: $49.95

Offers a sciencefiction film which begins with two aliens killing a third alien in a barren desert area of the United States, only to leave behind a laser gun and "power pendant."

LASSIE'S GREATEST ADVENTURE
The Nostalgia Merchant; Order No. 7006; 1964 • color; 1 hr, 43 min; ½" Beta II, ½" VHS • Sale: $54.95
- -
Red Fox, Inc; Order No. 7006; 1964 • color; 1 hr, 43 min; ½" Beta II, ½" VHS • Sale: $54.95

Relates how a dog saves herself and her young master after they are stranded in the Canadian wilderness. Stars Jon Provost, June Lockhart, and Lassie.

THE LAST BANDIT
The Nostalgia Merchant; Order No. BT0020; 1949 • color; 1 hr, 30 min; ½" Beta II, ½" VHS • Sale: $54.95
- -
Red Fox, Inc; Order No. BT0020; 1949 • color; 1 hr,

30 min; ½″ Beta II, ½″ VHS • Sale: $54.95

Presents a western about a reformed outlaw who is framed for a train robbery. Features William Elliott, Forrest Tucker, and Adrian Booth.

THE LAST CHALLENGE OF THE DRAGON
Video Gems; 1980 • color; 1 hr, 30 min; ½″ Beta II, ½″ VHS • Sale: $59.95

Offers a martial arts film featuring Shih Chien.

THE LAST COMMAND
Niles Cinema; Order No. NM-0123; 1955 • color; 1 hr, 50 min; ½″ Beta II, ½″ VHS • Sale: $54.95
- -
The Nostalgia Merchant; Order No. 0123; 1955 • color; 1 hr, 50 min; ½″ Beta II, ½″ VHS • Sale: $54.95
- -
Red Fox, Inc; Order No. 0123; 1955 • color; 1 hr, 50 min; ½″ Beta II, ½″ VHS • Sale: $54.95

Relates the epic story of Jim Bowie and the defense of the Alamo. Stars Sterling Hayden, Richard Carlson, and Ernest Borgnine.

THE LAST FOUR DAYS
Fotomat Corp; Order No. B0189 for ½″ Beta II, V0189 for ½″ VHS; 1977 • color; 1 hr, 27 min; ½″ Beta II, ½″ VHS • Sale: $39.95; Rental: $7.95/up to 5 days, applicable to purchase

Traces the events in the final days of the life of Benito Mussolini. Features Rod Steiger, Henry Fonda, and Franco Nero.

LAST HOLIDAY
Fotomat Corp; Order No. B0257 for ½″ Beta II, V0257 for ½″ VHS; 1950 • b/w; 1 hr, 26 min; ½″ Beta II, ½″ VHS • Sale: $49.95; Rental: $9.95/up to 5 days, applicable to purchase

Relates the tale of a salesman who decides to take one last fling when he is told he has a limited amount of time to live. Shows him being mistaken for a man of wealth at the fashionable seaside resort he goes to with his life's savings. Stars Alec Guinness, Kay Walsh, Beatrice Campbell, and Wilfred Hyde-White in this comedy-drama.

THE LAST HURRAH
National Film and Video Center; 1958 • b/w; 2 hrs, 1 min; ¾″ U-Matic, ½″ Beta II, ½″ VHS • Rental: $49/1 showing

Depicts the political skirmishes of a mayoral election in a large city through the eyes of a sports writer whose uncle is the incumbent. Stars Spencer Tracy, under John Ford's direction.

THE LAST LAUGH
National Film and Video Center; 1924 • b/w; 1 hr, 13 min; ¾″ U-Matic, ½″ Beta II, ½″ VHS • Rental: $49/1 showing
- -
Northeast Video and Sound, Inc; 1924 • b/w; 1 hr, 11 min; ¾″ U-Matic, ½″ EIAJ, ½″ Beta II, ½″ VHS • Sale: $195; Rental: $75/wk

Contrasts the worlds of rich and poor through the symbolism of a doorman's status and the power that comes from the uniform he wears. Conveys the doorman's sense of shame when he is reduced to being a porter. Stars Emil Jannings and Hermann Vallentin under the direction of F.W. Murnau.

THE LAST MILE
Video T.E.N.; 1932 • b/w; 1 hr, 11 min; ½″ Beta II, ½″ VHS • Sale: $49.95 for ½″ Beta II, $54.95 for ½″ VHS

Probes the realities and myths of prison life in a film which set the pattern for many future cliched movies. Stars Howard Phillips, Preston Foster, George E. Stone, Noel Madison, Alan Roscoe, Paul Fix, and Al Hill.

THE LAST REMAKE OF BEAU GESTE
MCA DiscoVision; Order No. 16-005; 1977 • color; 1 hr, 25 min; LaserVision • Sale: $24.95

Offers a spoof of the Beau Geste films, written and directed by Marty Feldman. Stars Feldman, Ann-Margret, Michael York, Peter Ustinov, James Earl Jones, Trevor Howard, Henry Gibson, and Terry-Thomas.

LAST TANGO IN PARIS
Vid America; Order No. 469; 1972 • color; 2 hrs; ½″ Beta II, ½″ VHS • Rental: $13.95/wk

Showcases Marlon Brando as an expatriate American whose wife has inexplicably committed suicide, who acts out his frustrations in a series of sexual encounters with a young Parisian stranger. Co-stars Maria Schneider and Jean-Pierre Leaud, under the direction of Bernardo Bertolucci.

LAST TRAIN FROM GUN HILL
Magnetic Video Corporation; Order No. CL-2018; 1959 • color; 1 hr, 34 min; ½″ Beta II, ½″ VHS • Sale: $54.95
- -
Red Fox, Inc; Order No. CL-2018; 1959 • color; 1 hr, 34 min; ½″ Beta II, ½″ VHS • Sale: $54.95

Recounts the search of a U.S. Marshal for the man who killed his Indian wife. Stars Kirk Douglas and Anthony Quinn.

L'ATALANTE
Budget Video; 1934 • b/w; 1 hr, 22 min; ½″ Beta II, ½″ VHS • Sale: $44.95
- -
Discount Video Tapes; 1934 • b/w; 1 hr, 22 min; ½″ Beta II, ½″ VHS • Sale: $49.95

Portrays a young pair of newlyweds on a Seine River barge, their disillusionments, near break-up, and eventual reconciliation through the efforts of an elderly barge hand. Features Dita Parlo, Jean Daste, and Michel Simon under the direction of poet Jean Vigo; in French with subtitles.

Dana Andrews, Clifton Webb, and Gene Tierney in _Laura_.

LAUGHFEST
Video Action Library2; Order No. BH04; 1913-23 •
color; 59 min; 1/2″ Beta I, 1/2″ Beta II, 1/2″ VHS • Rental:
$12.50/1 wk, $6.25 ea add'l wk

Comprises five short silent comedies. Begins with
Snub Pollard in "It's a Gift" (1923). Follows with Ben
Turpin in "The Daredevil" (1923), a parody of earlier
films. Continues with "Barney Oldfield's Race for a
Life" (1913) starring Mabel Normand, Ford Sterling,
and Barney Oldfield. Concludes with two Charlie
Chaplin films from 1914, "Kids Auto Race" and "A
Busy Day."

LAURA
Magnetic Video Corporation; Order No. 1094; 1944 •
b/w; 1 hr, 28 min; 1/2″ Beta II, 1/2″ VHS • Sale: $59.95

Niles Cinema; Order No. CL-1094; 1944 • b/w; 1 hr,
28 min; 1/2″ Beta II, 1/2″ VHS • Sale: $59.95
RCA SelectaVision VideoDiscs; Order No. 00106; 1944
• b/w; 1 hr, 28 min; CED • Sale: $14.98

Follows a police detective as he attempts to solve the
murder of a hauntingly beautiful woman, and ends up
in the New York advertising world. Stars Gene Tierney,
Clifton Webb, Dana Andrews, Vincent Price, and Judith Anderson.

LAUREL AND HARDY (VOLUME 1)
The Nostalgia Merchant; Date not listed • b/w; 1 hr,
30 min; 1/2″ Beta II, 1/2″ VHS • Sale: $54.95

Offers a compilation of Laurel and Hardy comedy
shorts. Includes "The Music Box," "County Hospital,"
"The Live Ghost," and "Twice Two."

LAUREL AND HARDY (VOLUME 2)
The Nostalgia Merchant; Date not listed • b/w; 1 hr,
30 min; 1/2″ Beta II, 1/2″ VHS • Sale: $54.95

Presents a compilation of Laurel and Hardy comedy
shorts. Includes "Blotto," "Towed in a Hole," "Brats,"
and "Hog Wild."

LAUREL AND HARDY (VOLUME 3)
The Nostalgia Merchant; Date not listed • b/w; 1 hr,
30 min; 1/2″ Beta II, 1/2″ VHS • Sale: $54.95

Recounts the exploits of Laurel and Hardy in a compi-
lation of comedy shorts. Presents "Oliver the 8th,"
"Busy Bodies," "Their First Mistake," and "Dirty
Work."

LAUREL AND HARDY (VOLUME 4)
The Nostalgia Merchant; Date not listed • b/w; 1 hr,
30 min; 1/2″ Beta II, 1/2″ VHS • Sale: $54.95

Stars Laurel and Hardy in a compilation of comedy
shorts. Offers "Another Fine Mess," "Come Clean,"
"Laughing Gravy," and "Any Old Port."

LAUREL AND HARDY (VOLUME 5)
The Nostalgia Merchant; Order No. 4305; Date not listed • b/w; 1 hr, 29 min; 1/2″ Beta II, 1/2″ VHS • Sale:
$54.95

Offers a compilation of comedy shorts starring Stan
Laurel and Oliver Hardy. Includes "Be Big," "The Perfect Day," "Night Owls," and "Helpmates."

LAUREL AND HARDY (VOLUME 6)
The Nostalgia Merchant; Order No. 4306; Date not listed • b/w; 1 hr, 30 min; 1/2″ Beta II, 1/2″ VHS • Sale:
$54.95

Presents a compilation of comedy shorts starring Stan
Laurel and Oliver Hardy. Includes "Our Wife," "The
Fixer Uppers," "Them Thar Hills," and "Tit for Tat."

**Stanley Holloway and Alec Guinness
in *The Lavender Hill Mob*.**

THE LAVENDER HILL MOB
Fotomat Corp; Order No. B0239 for 1/2″ Beta II, V0239
for 1/2″ VHS; 1951 • b/w; 1 hr, 18 min; 1/2″ Beta II, 1/2″
VHS • Sale: $49.95; Rental: $9.95/up to 5 days, applicable to purchase

Time-Life Video Club Inc; 1950 • b/w; 1 hr, 22 min;
1/2″ Beta II, 1/2″ VHS • Sale: $49.95 to members

Satirizes the British establishment as a timid bank clerk
concocts a scheme for smuggling a fortune in gold
bullion out of the country by melting it down into Eiffel
Tower paperweights. Stars Alec Guinness and Stanley
Holloway.

LAW OF THE LASH; RODEO KING AND THE SENO-
RITA
The Nostalgia Merchant; 1947; 1951 • b/w; 2 hrs; 1/2″
Beta II, 1/2″ VHS • Sale: $59.95

Offers a western double feature. Opens with "Law of
the Lash," in which a cowboy brings rustlers to justice.
Stars Lash LaRue and "Fuzzy" St. John. Follows with
"Rodeo King and the Senorita," in which calamity pre-
vents the star cowboy from joining his rodeo. Features
Rex Allen and Mary Ellen Kay.

LAW OF THE UNDERWORLD
Reel Images Inc; Order No. 422 ; 1938 • b/w; 1 hr, 1
min; 1/2″ Beta II, 1/2″ VHS • Sale: $39.95 for 1/2″ Beta II,
$42.95 for 1/2″ VHS

Depicts an archetypal 1930's gangster story in which
an innocent boy and girl become involved with the
mob and are accused of robbery and murder. Stars
Chester Morris, Anne Shirley, Walter Abel, and Jack
Carson.

LAWRENCE OF ARABIA
National Film and Video Center; 1962 • color; 3 hrs, 5
min; 3/4″ U-Matic, 1/2″ Beta II, 1/2″ VHS • Rental:
$119/1 showing

Lawrence of Arabia.

Dramatizes the revolt of the Arabs against the Turks during World War I in epic style. Features Peter O'Toole as a young British officer caught up in the intrigue of the times, leading raids against Turkish supply and troop trains. Co-stars Omar Sharif, Alec Guinness, and Anthony Quinn, under David Lean's direction.

LE BODY SHOP
Monarch Releasing Corporation; Date not listed • color; 1 hr, 28 min; ¾" U-Matic • Sale: $350

Presents a pornographic film.

LE MAGNIFIQUE
Cinema Concepts, Inc.; 1975 • color; 1 hr, 35 min; ¾" U-Matic, ½" Beta II, ½" VHS • Sale: $54.95 for ½" Beta II & VHS, $149.95 for ¾"

The Video Library; Order No. CC-0129; 1975 • color; 1 hr, 35 min; ½" Beta II, ½" VHS • Sale: $54.95

Features Jean-Paul Belmondo and Jacqueline Bisset in a comedy from director Philippe De Broca.

LE SECRET
Cinema Concepts, Inc.; 1974 • color; 1 hr, 43 min; ¾" U-Matic, ½" Beta II, ½" VHS • Sale: $54.95 for ½" Beta II & VHS, $149.95 for ¾"

The Video Library; Order No. CC-0130; 1974 • color; 1 hr, 33 min; ½" Beta II, ½" VHS • Sale: $54.95

Features Jean-Louis Trintignant and Philippe Noiret in a psychological thriller, under the direction of Robert Enrico.

LEGEND OF AMALUK
Video Communications Inc; Date not listed • color; 1 hr, 43 min; ½" Beta II, ½" VHS • Sale: $54.95

Tells a true life tale, unfolded by Lorne Greene, of a stalwart though unproven Eskimo youth who is rebuffed by the men of his village for participation in their hunts.

THE LEGEND OF COUGAR CANYON
Video Communications Inc; 1974 • color; 1 hr, 38 min; ½" Beta II, ½" VHS • Sale: $54.95

Concerns a 12-year-old boy who lives with his mother and six brothers and sisters in Canyon de Chelly, where preying cougars terrorize their herd of sheep and goats.

LEGEND OF DEATH VALLEY
Video Communications Inc; Order No. 1062; 1977 • color; 1 hr, 35 min; ½" Beta II, ½" VHS • Sale: $54.95

Relates a story of a man who follows his ancestor's footsteps into the remote regions of Death Valley.

THE LEGEND OF JEDEDIAH CARVER
Video Communications Inc; Order No. 3003; 1977 • color; 1 hr, 33 min; ½" Beta II, ½" VHS • Sale: $54.95

Recounts the story of one man's struggle to survive the vast desolation of the wilderness and the vengeance of a renegade. Features DeWitt Lee and Joshua Hoffman.

LEGEND OF LOCH NESS
Video Communications Inc; Date not listed • color; 1 hr, 32 min; ½" Beta II, ½" VHS • Sale: $54.95

Chronicles the search for the world's most famous monster, with the use of advanced technology. Asks if the monster is scientific fact or science-fiction.

THE LEGEND OF THE LONE RANGER
The Nostalgia Merchant; Order No. 7003; 1949 • b/w; 1 hr, 15 min; ½" Beta II, ½" VHS • Sale: $54.95

Offers a three-part serialized Lone Ranger adventure compiled on one videocassette. Tells of the origin of the legendary "Masked Rider of the Plains" and features Clayton Moore, Jay Silverheels, and Glenn Strange.

LEGENDARY PERSONALITIES
Blackhawk Films, Inc; Order No. 506-68-0852 for ½" Beta II, 525-68-0852 for ½" VHS; Date not listed • b/w; 1 hr; ¾" U-Matic, ½" Beta I, ½" Beta II, ½" VHS • Sale: $59.95 for ½" Beta I, $39.95 for ½" Beta II & VHS, $69.95 for ¾"

Presents a compilation of color-toned, Movietone Newsreels from the 1920's and 1930's. Includes clips with Haile Selassie, George Bernard Shaw, and Sir Arthur Conan Doyle. Offers both the serious and the humorous sides of historical figures.

LENNY
Vid America; 1974 • b/w; 1 hr, 52 min; ½" Beta II, ½" VHS • Rental: $13.95/wk

Portrays the controversial 1950's nightclub comic Lenny Bruce. Recreates Bruce's on-going battles with authorities over the sexual and scatological content of his monologues; examines his relationship with stripper Honey Harlowe. Stars Dustin Hoffman, Valerie Perrine, Jan Miner, Stanley Beck, and Gary Morton, under the direction of Bob Fosse.

LEONOR
Magnetic Video Corporation; 1975 • color; 1 hr, 30 min; ½" Beta II, ½" VHS • Sale: $44.95

Depicts a nobleman in the 14th century who, although remarried, still loves his dead first wife and compacts with the devil to bring her back. Stars Liv Ullmann and Michel Piccoli.

THE LEOPARD MAN
Niles Cinema; Order No. NM-8040; 1943 • b/w; 1 hr, 6 min; ½" Beta II, ½" VHS • Sale: $54.95

The Nostalgia Merchant; Order No. 8040; 1943 • b/w; 1 hr, 6 min; ½" Beta II, ½" VHS • Sale: $54.95

Red Fox, Inc; Order No. 8040; 1943 • b/w; 1 hr, 6 min; ½" Beta II, ½" VHS • Sale: $54.95

Relates the story of an escaped leopard who is presumed to be terrorizing a small town, but the killings persist after the cat's death. Stars Dennis O'Keefe and Margo.

A LETTER TO THREE WIVES
Magnetic Video Corporation; Order No. 1093; 1949 • b/w; 1 hr, 43 min; 1/2" Beta II, 1/2" VHS • Sale: $59.95

Niles Cinema; Order No. CL-1093; 1949 • b/w; 1 hr, 43 min; 1/2" Beta II, 1/2" VHS • Sale: $59.95

Studies three marriages in flashback. Shows the reaction of three women who receive a letter saying one of their husbands has run off with another woman. Stars Jeanne Crain, Linda Darnell, Ann Sothern, Kirk Douglas, Paul Douglas, Jeffrey Lynn, Thelma Ritter, and the voice of Celeste Holm.

THE LICKERISH QUARTET
Vid America; Order No. 973; Date not listed • color; 1 hr, 30 min; 1/2" Beta II, 1/2" VHS • Rental: $12.95/wk

Presents a pornographic film.

LIES MY FATHER TOLD ME
National Film and Video Center; 1975 • color; 1 hr, 42 min; 3/4" U-Matic, 1/2" Beta II, 1/2" VHS • Rental: $89/1 showing

Examines a boy's love for his old-fashioned, religious grandfather over his materialistic father. Shows how, when his grandfather leaves and his father bluntly tells him that the old man died, the boy retains his loyalty and waits for the old man to return. Stars Jeffrey Lynas, Yossi Yadin, Marilyn Lightstone, and Len Birman.

THE LIFE AND TIMES OF GRIZZLY ADAMS
Video Communications Inc; 1976 • color; 1 hr, 36 min; 1/2" Beta II, 1/2" VHS • Sale: $54.95

Concerns a fur trapper pursued for a crime he did not commit. Recounts how he finds peace in the mountains where he befriends a massive bear. Stars Dan Haggerty.

THE LIFE AND TIMES OF XAVIERA HOLLANDER
Quality X Video Cassette Company; Date not listed • color; 1 hr, 11 min; 1/2" Beta I, 1/2" Beta II, 1/2" VHS • Sale: $99.50

Presents a pornographic film.

LIFE OF BRIAN
WCI Home Video Inc; 1979 • color; 1/2" Beta II, 1/2" VHS • Sale: $55

Presents Monty Python's irreverent comedy about a reluctant messiah. Satirizes political terrorist groups, the growth of cult religions, and Hollywood epics, among others. Stars Graham Chapman, John Cleese, Eric Idle, Michael Palin, Terry Gilliam, and Terry Jones, under Jones Direction.

LIFE WITH FATHER
Cinema Concepts, Inc.; 1947 • color; 1 hr, 56 min; 3/4" U-Matic, 1/2" Beta II, 1/2" VHS • Sale: $54.95 for 1/2" Beta II & VHS, 149.95 for 3/4"

The Video Library; Order No. AE-6002; 1947 • color; 1 hr, 46 min; 1/2" Beta II, 1/2" VHS • Sale: $49.95

Presents an adaptation of the Broadway play based on the Clarence Day story about growing up in Victorian New York. Depicts a loving but somewhat eccentric patriarch and his dealings with his four sons and very patient wife. Stars William Powell, Irene Dunne, Elizabeth Taylor, and Edmund Gwenn.

LIGHTNING SWORDS OF DEATH
National Film and Video Center; Date not listed •

color; 1 hr, 23 min; 3/4" U-Matic, 1/2" Beta II, 1/2" VHS • Rental: $49/1 showing

Follows the adventures of master swordsman Ogami, who was discredited by a jealous clan and now roams the country with his two-year-old son. Stars Tom Wakayama, Goh Kato, Yuko Hama, and Katsu Wakayama, in a Japanese film directed by Shintaro Katsu.

LI'L ABNER
Video T.E.N.; 1940 • b/w; 1 hr, 18 min; 1/2" Beta II, 1/2" VHS • Sale: $49.95 for 1/2" Beta II, $54.95 for 1/2" VHS

Showcases all of Al Capp's comic strip characters come to life on Sadie Hawkins Day in Dogpatch. Features Cranville Owen, Martha O'Driscoll, and Buster Keaton.

LIMELIGHT
Magnetic Video Corporation; Order No. CL-3010; 1952 • b/w; 2 hrs, 25 min; 1/2" Beta II, 1/2" VHS • Sale: $64.95

Recounts a love story between an over-the-hill British music hall clown and the ballet dancer he nurses back to health after her attempted suicide. Stars Charlie Chaplin, Claire Bloom, Sydney Chaplin, Nigel Bruce, and Buster Keaton, in a film written, produced, and directed by Chaplin.

THE LINCOLN CONSPIRACY
Vid America; Order No. 925; Date not listed • color; 1 hr, 27 min; 1/2" Beta II, 1/2" VHS • Rental: $10.95/wk

Investigates the larger story behind the assassination of Abraham Lincoln. Reconstructs the total conspiracy, of which John Wilkes Booth was only a part, from contemporary diaries and Secret Service documents.

THE LION IN WINTER
Magnetic Video Corporation; Order No. CL-4007; 1968 • color; 2 hrs, 14 min; 1/2" Beta II, 1/2" VHS • Sale: $74.95

Red Fox, Inc; Order No. CL-4007; 1968 • color; 2 hrs, 14 min; 1/2" Beta II, 1/2" VHS • Sale: $74.95

Vid America; 1968 • color; 2 hrs, 15 min; 1/2" Beta II, 1/2" VHS • Rental: $13.95 /wk

Dramatizes the uneasy reunion of the aging King Henry II with his estranged wife Queen Eleanor of Aquitaine and their three surviving sons. Features Peter O'Toole as Henry and Katharine Hepburn as Eleanor in constant conflict over which son will succeed to the throne.

Peter O'Toole and Katharine Hepburn in *The Lion in Winter.*

LIPSTICK

Paramount Home Video; 1976 • color; 1 hr, 28 min; 1/2" Beta II, 1/2" VHS • Sale: $59.95

Presents a tale of the rape of a high-fashion model, the injustice of society, and her ultimate revenge. Features Margaux Hemingway, Anne Bancroft, Chris Sarandon, Perry King, and Mariel Hemingway.

LIQUID LIPS

Freeway Video Enterprises; Date not listed • color; 1 hr, 20 min; 1/2" Beta II, 1/2" VHS • Sale: $75 for 1/2" Beta II, $85 for 1/2" VHS

Presents a pornographic film.

LITTLE ANNIE ROONEY

Blackhawk Films, Inc; Order No. 506-01-0831 for 1/2" Beta II, 525-01-0831 for 1/2" VHS; 1925 • color; 1 hr; 1/2" Beta II, 1/2" VHS • Sale: $39.95

Tells the story of a tomboy and her brother who set out to avenge the murder of their policeman father. Stars Mary Pickford, William Haines, Walter James, Gordon Griffith, and Vola Vale in this silent feature.

LITTLE DARLINGS

Niles Cinema; Order No. PP-1301; 1980 • color; 1 hr, 35 min; 1/2" Beta II, 1/2" VHS • Sale: $64.95

- -
Paramount Home Video; Order No. 1301; 1980 • color; 1 hr, 35 min; 1/2" Beta II, 1/2" VHS • Sale: $79.95

Concerns two adolescent girls at summer camp who try to out-do one another in every way, including who will be first to lose her virginity. Features Tatum O'Neal and Kristy McNichol.

LITTLE LAURA AND BIG JOHN

Video Communications Inc; Order No. 1065; 1973 • color; 1 hr, 22 min; 1/2" Beta II, 1/2" VHS • Sale: $54.95

Chronicles the lives of Laura and John, who start by stealing and go on to form the dread Ashley Gang. Stars Karen Black and Fabian Forte.

LITTLE LORD FAUNTLEROY

Video T.E.N.; 1936 • b/w; 1 hr, 42 min; 1/2" Beta II, 1/2" VHS • Sale: $49.95 for 1/2" Beta II, $54.95 for 1/2" VHS

Depicts a young boy brought up in 1880's Brooklyn who finds his whole life changed when he becomes an English lord. Features Freddie Bartholomew, Mickey Rooney, Dolores Costello, and Guy Kibbee.

LITTLE MEN

Thunderbird Films; 1940 • b/w; 1 hr, 26 min; 3/4" U-Matic, 1/2" Beta I, 1/2" Beta II, 1/2" VHS • Sale: $69.95 for 1/2" Beta I, $49.95 for 1/2" Beta II & VHS, $89.95 for 3/4"

Chronicles the early life of an orphan reared by a con-artist who wishes to give the boy a better life than his own. Features George Bancroft, Kay Francis, and Jack Oakie in this adaptation of Louisa May Alcott's novel.

THE LITTLE MERMAID

Video Gems; 1978 • color; 1 hr, 11 min; 1/2" Beta II, 1/2" VHS • Sale: $53.95

Offers an animated adventure for children. Adapts Hans Christian Anderson's tale of the mermaid princess who rescues a prince.

LITTLE ORPHAN ANNIE

Blackhawk Films, Inc; Order No. 506-01-0729 for 1/2" Beta II, 525-01-0729 for 1/2" VHS; 1932 • b/w; 1 hr; 1/2" Beta II, 1/2" VHS • Sale: $39.95

Chronicles the adventures of the famous comic strip heroine as she is befriended by a bum with a money-making scheme. Features Mitzi Green and Edgar Kennedy.

THE LITTLE PRINCE

Fotomat Corp; Order No. B0221 for 1/2" Beta II, V0221 for 1/2" VHS; 1974 • color; 1 hr, 28 min; 1/2" Beta II, 1/2" VHS • Sale: $49.95; Rental: $9.95/up to 5 days, applicable to purchase

- -
Paramount Home Video; 1974 • color; 1 hr, 28 min; 1/2" Beta II, 1/2" VHS • Sale: $59.95

Adapts the classic children's book by Antoine de Saint-Exupery, about a pilot who makes a forced landing in the Sahara and meets a "little" prince from Asteroid B-612. Follows the prince's lessons in life from a fox, a snake, and the pilot. Features a musical score by Lerner and Loewe. Stars Richard Kiley, Bob Fosse, Steven Warner, Gene Wilder, and Donna McKechnie, under Stanley Donen's direction.

THE LITTLE PRINCESS

Ivy Video; 1939 • color; 1 hr, 30 min; 3/4" U-Matic, 1/2" Beta II, 1/2" VHS • Sale: $59.95 for 1/2" Beta II & VHS, trade-in plan available, $295 for 3/4"

- -
Northeast Video and Sound, Inc; Order No. 144S; 1939 • color; 1 hr, 30 min; 3/4" U-Matic, 1/2" EIAJ, 1/2" Beta II, 1/2" VHS • Sale: $295; Rental: $100/wk

- -
VCX; Order No. FC104; 1939 • color; 1 hr, 31 min; 1/2" Beta II, 1/2" VHS • Sale: $35.00

Showcases Shirley Temple in her first feature film, singing and dancing her way through a Cinderella story with a twist. Centers around a school for girls where poor Shirley is reduced from star boarder to scrub girl before the dénouement restores her to happiness and prosperity.

A LITTLE ROMANCE

WCI Home Video Inc; 1979 • color; 1 hr; 1/2" Beta II, 1/2" VHS • Sale: $55

Tells the romantic tale of an American girl and a French boy who are on the edge of adult awareness. Follows their developing relationship in springtime Paris, showing how they are aided by a dapper pickpocket. Stars Diane Lane, Thelonious Bernard, and Sir Laurence Olivier.

LITTLE ROQUEFORT

Magnetic Video Corporation; Order No. CL-2033; Date not listed • color; 30 min; 1/2" Beta II, 1/2" VHS • Sale: $34.95

Presents a compilation of Terrytoon animated cartoons featuring Little Roquefort.

LITTLE SHOP OF HORRORS

Video T.E.N.; 1960 • b/w; 1 hr, 10 min; 1/2" Beta II, 1/2" VHS • Sale: $49.95 for 1/2" Beta II, 54.95 for 1/2" VHS

Offers a Roger Corman black comedy of a young florist's assistant who raises a giant plant that feeds on blood. Includes Jonathan Haze, Jackie Joseph, Mel Welles, Dick Miller, and Jack Nicholson.

LITTLE SISTERS

VTS; Date not listed • color; 1 hr, 1 min; 1/2" Beta I, 1/2" Beta II, 1/2" VHS • Sale: $99

Presents a pornographic film.

LITTLE TOUGH GUYS
Cable Films; 1938 • b/w; 1 hr, 27 min; 1/2″ Beta I, 1/2″ Beta II, 1/2″ VHS • Sale: $65 for 1/2″ Beta I, $49.50 for 1/2″ Beta II & VHS

Features the group first seen in ''Dead End'' as the Dead End Kids, and also known as the Eastside Kids and Bowery Boys. Stars Billy Halop, Marjorie Main, Helen Parrish, and the Little Tough Guys.

THE LITTLEST OUTLAW
MCA DiscoVision ; Order No. D18-504; 1955 • color; 1 hr, 13 min; LaserVision • Sale: $24.95

Offers a Walt Disney Studios production about a young Mexican stable boy who runs away with a horse to save it from mistreatment. Features authentic tribal dances of the Chichimecas Indians, a bullfight, and rural Mexican locations.

THE LIVES OF A BENGAL LANCER
MCA DiscoVision; Order No. 21-002; 1935 • b/w; 1 hr, 50 min; LaserVision • Sale: $15.95

Follows the adventures of a young man who turns up in his father's battalion which has been ordered to hold off an uprising near the Khyber Pass, India. Stars Gary Cooper, Franchot Tone, Richard Cromwell, C. Aubrey Smith, and Monte Blue, under Henry Hathaway's direction.

THE LODGER
Northeast Video and Sound, Inc; 1926 • b/w; 1 hr, 5 min; 3/4″ U-Matic, 1/2″ EIAJ, 1/2″ Beta II, 1/2″ VHS • Sale: $195; Rental: $75/wk

Presents Alfred Hitchcock's chiller about a family who suspects that their tenant may be Jack the Ripper. Stars Ivor Novello and Malcolm Keen.

THE LONE RANGER
The Nostalgia Merchant; Order No. 7001; 1956 • color; 1 hr, 26 min; 1/2″ Beta II, 1/2″ VHS • Sale: $54.95

Recounts a tale of the masked man and his faithful Indian companion Tonto as they prevent a land-hungry cattle rancher from starting a plains war. Stars Clayton Moore, Jay Silverheels, and Lyle Bettger.

THE LONE RANGER AND THE LOST CITY OF GOLD
The Nostalgia Merchant; Order No. 7002; 1958 • color; 1 hr, 21 min; 1/2″ Beta II, 1/2″ VHS • Sale: $54.95

Chronicles the fight of the Lone Ranger and Tonto against an outlaw gang that is in search of a fabulous treasure belonging to a peaceful Indian tribe. Features Clayton Moore, Jay Silverheels, and Douglas Kennedy.

LONELY ARE THE BRAVE
MCA DiscoVision; Order No. 12-008; 1962 • b/w; 1 hr, 47 min; LaserVision • Sale: $15.95

Follows the attempts of a non-conformist cowboy to remain free in a world in which he is being pursued by walkie-talkies, helicopters, fences, and the modern age. Stars Kirk Douglas as the eacaped prisoner in Dalton Trumbo's adaptation of Edward Abbey's novel. Features Walter Matthau, Carroll O'Connor, Gena Rowlands, and George Kennedy.

LONELY WIVES
Reel Images Inc; Order No. 27; 1931 • b/w; 1 hr, 26 min; 1/2″ Beta II, 1/2″ VHS • Sale: $49.95 for 1/2″ Beta II, $52.95 for 1/2″ VHS

Presents a farce based upon a popular stage play in which a lawyer hires an entertainer to serve as a dou-

ble because of a marital problem. Features Edward Everett Horton in a dual role. Stars Patsy Ruth Miller, Esther Ralston, and Laura Laplante.

THE LONG HOT SUMMER
Golden Tapes Video Tape Library; Order No. F-1045; 1958 • color; 1 hr, 57 min; 1/2″ Beta II & VHS • Sale: $49.95 for 1/2″ Beta II & VHS, $124.95 for 3/4″
- -
Magnetic Video Corporation; Order No. CL-1045; 1958 • color; 1 hr, 57 min; 1/2″ Beta II, 1/2″ VHS • Sale: $44.95

Presents the story of a young man who falls in love with the daughter of a Southern aristocrat. Stars Paul Newman and Joanne Woodward.

THE LONGEST DAY
Blackhawk Films, Inc; Order No. 502-49-0003 for 1/2″ Beta II, 520-49-0012; 1962 • color; 2 hrs, 59 min; 1/2″ Beta II, 1/2″ VHS • Sale: $79.98
- -
Golden Tapes Video Tape Library; Order No. F-1021; 1962 • b/w; 2 hrs, 59 min; 1/2″ Beta II, 1/2″ VHS • Sale: $49.95 for 1/2″ Beta II & VHS, $124.95 for 3/4″
- -
Magnetic Video Corporation; Order No. CL-1021; 1962 • b/w; 2 hrs, 59 min; 1/2″ Beta II, 1/2″ VHS • Sale: $64.95
- -
RCA SelectaVision VideoDiscs; Order No. 00107; 1963 • b/w; 3 hrs; CED • Sale: $22.98
- -
The Video Library; Order No. MV-1021; 1962 • b/w; 2 hrs, 59 min; 1/2″ Beta II, 1/2″ VHS • Sale: $74.95

Details the events leading up to and through the Allied Forces' invasion of Normandy on D-Day, 1944. Stars John Wayne, Robert Mitchum, Henry Fonda and Robert Ryan.

THE LONGEST YARD
Fotomat Corp; Order No. B0037 for 1/2″ Beta II, V0037 for 1/2″ VHS; 1974 • color; 2 hrs; 1/2″ Beta II, 1/2″ VHS • Sale: $49.95; Rental: $9.95/up to 5 days, applicable to purchase
- -
Paramount Home Video; 1974 • color; 2 hrs; 1/2″ Beta II, 1/2″ VHS • Sale: $59.95
- -
RCA SelectaVision VideoDiscs; Order No. 00606; 1974 • color; 2 hrs, 3 min; CED • Sale: $24.98

Steve Forrest and John Wayne in The Longest Day.

Richard Gere and Diane Keaton in *Looking for Mr. Goodbar*.

Portrays a sadistic warden who will make any sacrifice to push his guards' semi-pro football team to a championship. Shows what happens when Paul Crewe, a pro quarterback now behind bars, agrees to organize a prisoners' team, and the warden intercedes to assure that his team meets only passive resistance from Crewe's Mean Machine. Stars Burt Reynolds, Eddie Albert, Dino Washington, Ray Nitschke, and Sonny Sixkiller.

LOOKING FOR MR. GOODBAR

Fotomat Corp; Order No. B0083 for 1/2" Beta II, V0083 for 1/2" VHS; 1977 • color; 2 hrs, 16 min; 1/2" Beta II, 1/2" VHS • Sale: $69.95; Rental: $13.95/up to 5 days, applicable to purchase

- -

MCA DiscoVision; Order No. P10-520; 1977 • color; 2 hrs, 16 min; LaserVision • Sale: $24.95

- -

Paramount Home Video; 1977 • color; 2 hrs, 16 min; 1/2" Beta II, 1/2" VHS • Sale: $79.95

- -

RCA SelectaVision VideoDiscs; Order No. 00617; 1977 • color; 2 hrs, 15 min; CED • Sale: $22.98

Presents a screen version of Judith Rossner's novel. Tells the story of Theresa Dunn, a young woman trying to break away from the claustrophobic atmosphere of her family and search for her own identity. Examines the dual nature of her life: the woman who is a compassionate teacher of deaf children by day, and the woman who seeks uninvolved sexual encounters by night. Stars Diane Keaton, Tuesday Weld, William Atherton, Richard Kiley, and Richard Gere, under the direction of Richard Brooks.

LOONEY TUNES AND MERRIE MELODIES #1

Reel Images Inc; Order No. 604; 1931-34 • b/w; 56 min; 1/2" Beta II, 1/2" VHS • Sale: $39.95 for 1/2" Beta II, $42.95 for 1/2" VHSa

Presents eight cartoons from Warner Brothers and Vitaphone, each based on an extended jazz number. Includes "The Queen Was In The Parlor," "Freddy The

Freshman," "Red Headed Baby," "Battling Bosko," "You're Too Careless With Your Kisses," "It's Got Me Again," "Moonlight For Two," and "You Don't Know What You're Doin!"

LOONEY TUNES AND MERRIE MELODIES #2

Reel Images Inc; Order No. 605; 1931-43 • b/w; 51 min; 1/2" Beta II, 1/2" VHS • Sale: $39.95 for 1/2" Beta II, $42.95 for 1/2" VHS

Presents seven cartoons from Warner Brothers and Vitaphone, each based on an extended jazz number. Includes "Porky Pig's Feat," "Smile Darn Ya Smile," "Get Rich Quick Porky," "One More Time," "Yodeling Yokels," "Scrap Happy Daffy," and "Porky's Preview." Features Porky Pig, Daffy Duck, and Bugs Bunny.

LORD JIM

National Film and Video Center; 1965 • color; 2 hrs, 34 min; 3/4" U-Matic, 1/2" Beta II, 1/2" VHS • Rental: $79/1 showing

Presents the story of a young, idealistic ship's officer who commits an act of cowardice that results in the cancellation of his sailing papers. Recounts his search for a second chance and his success in proving himself a man. Stars Peter O'Toole, James Mason, Curt Jurgens, and Eli Wallach.

THE LORDS OF FLATBUSH

National Film and Video Center; 1974 • color; 1 hr, 22 min; 3/4" U-Matic, 1/2" Beta II, 1/2" VHS • Rental: $89/1 showing

Tells the story of four boys who form a high school gang—their ins and outs with their girlfriends, attempts to steal a car, and the necessary marriage of one couple. Features Henry Winkler.

LOST CITY OF ATLANTIS

Video Communications Inc; Order No. 1066; 1978 • color; 1 hr, 33 min; 1/2" Beta II, 1/2" VHS • Sale: $54.95

Deals with recent excavations on the Greek island of Santorini.

LOST CONTINENT
Video Action Library; 1951 • b/w; 1 hr, 26 min; 1/2"
Beta I, 1/2" Beta II, 1/2" VHS • Sale: $51

Chronicles the adventures of a group of scientists who crash land in the jungle while in search of a missing rocket, and discover a prehistoric world. Stars Cesar Romero and Hillary Brooke.

LOST HORIZON
National Film and Video Center; 1937 • b/w; 1 hr, 50 min; 3/4" U-Matic, 1/2" Beta II, 1/2" VHS • Rental: $69/1 showing

Presents an early screen version of James Hilton's novel. Finds a plane full of people hijacked to a hidden paradise, from which some escape. Ends with the voluntary return of the leader to Shangri-La. Stars Ronald Coleman and Jane Wyatt in a film directed by Frank Capra.

LOST HORIZON
National Film and Video Center; 1973 • color; 2 hrs, 24 min; 3/4" U-Matic, 1/2" Beta II, 1/2" VHS • Rental: $79/1 showing

Dramatizes the story of Shangri-La, based on the novel "Lost Horizon" by James Hilton. Tells of the arrival of a group of people who have been kidnapped and who subsequently choose to escape from paradise. Stars Peter Finch, Liv Ullmann, Sally Kellerman, George Kennedy, Michael York, Olivia Hussey, and John Gielgud.

LOST IN THE STARS
Magnetic Video Corporation; 1974 • color; 1 hr, 54 min; 1/2" Beta II, 1/2" VHS • Sale: $80

Offers the American Film Theatre's adaptation of the Kurt Weill and Maxwell Anderson musical version of Alan Paton's novel "Cry, The Beloved Country." Studies apartheid in South Africa. Stars Brock Peters, Melba Moore, Raymond St. Jacques, Clifton Davis, and Paula Kelly.

THE LOST PATROL
Blackhawk Films, Inc; Order No. 506-75-0728 for 1/2" Beta II, 525-75-0728 for 1/2" VHS; 1934 • b/w; 1 hr, 6 min; 1/2" Beta II, 1/2" VHS • Sale: $49.95

Studies the men who make up a small British military unit lost in the Mesopotamian desert, under attack from Arabs, as their numbers dwindle. Stars Victor McLaglen, Boris Karloff, Wallace Ford, Reginald Denny, and Alan Hale under John Ford's direction.

THE LOST WEEKEND
MCA DiscoVision; Order No. 21-001; 1945 • b/w; 1 hr, 41 min; LaserVision • Sale: $15.95

Offers Billy Wilder's probe into alcoholic addiction, which won four Academy Awards. Follows a disillusioned writer's journey into self-pity which ends in scenes of terrifying hallucinations. Stars Ray Milland, Jane Wyman, Howard da Silva, and Frank Faylen, under Billy Wilder's direction.

THE LOST WORLD
Ivy Video; 1925 • b/w; 45 min; 3/4" U-Matic, 1/2" Beta II, 1/2" VHS • Sale: $59.95 for 1/2" Beta II & VHS, trade-in plan available, $150 for 3/4"
- -
Northeast Video and Sound, Inc; Order No. 158S; 1925 • b/w; 45 min; 3/4" U-Matic, 1/2" EIAJ, 1/2" Beta II, 1/2" VHS • Sale: $149; Rental: $55/wk

Establishes for all time the pattern for future monster movies, and includes many masterful special effects, among them stop-motion animation and elaborate

make-up and costuming. Stars Wallace Beery, Bessie Love, and Lewis Stone in this first of several filmed versions of A. Conan Doyle's adventure novel.

THE LOST YEARS
Video Communications Inc; Order No. 1067; 1977 • color; 1 hr, 33 min; 1/2" Beta II, 1/2" VHS • Sale: $54.95

Deals with the life of Jesus Christ from the age of thirteen to twenty-nine, and suggests that there is evidence of a long pilgrimage which stretched from the city of Rome through Asia Minor to the far reaches of an obscure Tibetan lamasery.

LOT IN SODOM
Northeast Video and Sound, Inc; Order No. 133S; 1933 • b/w; 27 min; 3/4" U-Matic, 1/2" EIAJ, 1/2" Beta II, 1/2" VHS • Sale: $79; Rental: $39/wk

Presents an early experimental film created by J. S. Watson and Melville Webber. Retells the Old Testament story.

LOVE ALL SUMMER
Niles Cinema; Order No. BT-16 for 1/2" Beta II, VH-16 for 1/2" VHS; 1974 • color; 1 hr, 34 min; 1/2" Beta II, 1/2" VHS • Sale: $59.95

Presents the sequel to "The Harrad Experiment," in which Harrad students continue their sex education over the summer vacation, with Richard Doran, Victoria Thompson, Laurie Walters, and Robert Reiser.

LOVE AND KISSES
Monarch Releasing Corporation; Date not listed • color; 1 hr, 15 min; 3/4" U-Matic • Sale: $300

Presents a pornographic film.

THE LOVE BUG
Fotomat Corp; 1969 • color; 1 hr, 47 min; 1/2" Beta II, 1/2" VHS • Sale: $49.95; Rental: $9.95/up to 5 days, applicable to purchase
- -
Niles Cinema; Order No. WD-12; 1969 • color; 1 hr, 48 min; 1/2" Beta II, 1/2" VHS • Sale: $59.95
- -
RCA SelectaVision VideoDiscs; Order No. 00703; 1969 • color; 1 hr, 47 min; CED • Sale: $19.98
- -
Walt Disney Home Video; Order No. 12BS for 1/2" Beta II, 12VS for 1/2" VHS; 1969 • color; 1 hr, 47 min; 1/2" Beta II, 1/2" VHS • Sale: $59.95

Shows a Volkswagen Beatle with a mind of its own, with slapstick humor and many stunts. Presents a Walt Disney Studios production starring Dean Jones, Michele Lee, Buddy Hackett, and Joe Flynn.

LOVE IN STRANGE PLACES
Entertainment Video Releasing, Inc; Order No. 1063; Date not listed • color; 1 hr, 20 min; 1/2" Beta II, 1/2" VHS • Sale: $69.95 for 1/2" Beta II, $74.95 for 1/2" VHS

Presents a pornographic film.

LOVE IS A MANY SPLENDORED THING
Golden Tapes Video Tape Library; Order No. F-1039; 1955 • color; 1 hr, 42 min; 1/2" Beta II, 1/2" VHS • Sale: $49.95 for 1/2" Beta II & VHS, $124.95 for 3/4"
- -
Magnetic Video Corporation; Order No. CL-1039; 1955 • color; 1 hr, 42 min; 1/2" Beta II, 1/2" VHS • Sale: $44.95
- -
The Video Library; Order No. MV-1039; 1955 • color; 1 hr, 42 min; 1/2" Beta II, 1/2" VHS • Sale: $44.95

Presents William Holden and Jennifer Jones in a love

story about a Eurasian doctor and a war correspondent, set in Hong Kong.

THE LOVE SLAVES
VTS; Date not listed • color; 1 hr, 25 min; ½" Beta I, ½" Beta II, ½" VHS • Sale: $99

Presents a pornographic film.

LOVE STORY
Fotomat Corp; Order No. B0059 for ½" Beta II, V0059 for ½" VHS; 1970 • color; 1 hr, 40 min; ½" Beta II, ½" VHS • Sale: $49.95; Rental: $9.95/up to 5 days, applicable to purchase

- -
MCA DiscoVision; Order No. P10-523; 1970 • color; 1 hr, 40 min; LaserVision • Sale: $24.95
- -
Paramount Home Video; 1970 • color; 1 hr, 40 min; ½" Beta II, ½" VHS • Sale: $59.95
- -
RCA SelectaVision VideoDiscs; Order No. 00607; 1970 • color; 1 hr, 39 min; CED • Sale: $24.98

Presents a screen adaptation of Erich Segal's best-selling novel. Portrays a young couple who cross social barriers, marry, and must then cope with the wife's unexpected, impending death. Stars Ryan O'Neal, Ali MacGraw, Ray Milland, and John Marley, under the direction of Arthur Hiller.

Ryan O'Neal and Ali MacGraw in *Love Story*.

LOVE STORY
Scorpio, Etc; 1979 • color; 30 min; ½" Beta I, ½" Beta II, ½" VHS • Sale: $39.95

Presents a pornographic film.

LOVERS AND OTHER STRANGERS
Magnetic Video Corporation; Order No. 8009; 1970 • color; 1 hr, 46 min; ½" Beta II, ½" VHS • Sale: $59.95

Examines the comic effects of a young couple's marriage, especially on the people around them. Stars Gig Young, Bea Arthur, Bonnie Bedelia, Anne Jackson, Harry Guardino, Michael Brandon, Richard Castellano, Bob Dishy, Marian Hailey, Cloris Leachman, and Anne Meara.

THE LOVES AND TIMES OF SCARAMOUCHE
Magnetic Video Corporation; Order No. CL-4008; 1975 • color; 1 hr, 32 min; ½" Beta II, ½" VHS • Sale: $54.95

- -
Red Fox, Inc; Order No. CL-4008; 1975 • color; 1 hr, 32 min; ½" Beta II, ½" VHS • Sale: $54.95

Follows the adventures and womanizing of the elegant rogue Scaramouche in Paris after the French Revolution. Stars Michael Sarrazin and Ursula Andress.

THE LUCIFER COMPLEX
Fotomat Corp; Order No. B0159 for ½" Beta II, V0159 for ½" VHS; 1979 • color; 1 hr, 31 min; ½" Beta II, ½" VHS • Sale: $49.95; Rental: $9.95/up to 5 days, applicable to purchase

- -
Video Communications Inc; Order No. 1068; 1979 • color; 1 hr, 37 min; ½" Beta II, ½" VHS • Sale: $54.95

Presents a science-fiction thriller in which cloning is brought to its ultimate peak of horror as surviving Nazi scientists replace, one by one, all of the world's leaders with cloned look-alikes. Shows that a United Nations agent who uncovers the plot is thought mad but, before he is destroyed, he puts his evidence in a time capsule destined for discovery in the 21st century. Stars Robert Vaughn and Keenan Wynn.

THE LUCK OF GINGER COFFEY
Video Communications Inc; Order No. 4003; 1964 • b/w; 1 hr, 40 min; ½" Beta II, ½" VHS • Sale: $54.95

Relates a story of Ginger Coffey, an Irishman who emigrates to Montreal in an effort to change his luck. Shows that it is not luck which is in question, but rather his own irresponsibility and lack of practicality which tend to defeat him. Stars Robert Shaw, Tom Harvey, and Mary Ure.

LUCKY LUCIANO
Magnetic Video Corporation; Order No. CL-4009; 1974 • color; 1 hr, 48 min; ½" Beta II, ½" VHS • Sale: $54.95

- -
Red Fox, Inc; Order No. CL-4009; 1974 • color; 1 hr, 48 min; ½" Beta II, ½" VHS • Sale: $54.95

Dramatizes the life of Charles "Lucky" Luciano after he was deported to Italy in 1946 and the relentless investigation of narcotics agent Charles Siragusa. Features Gian-Maria Volonte, Rod Steiger, Charles Siragusa, and Edmond O'Brien.

LUCKY TEXAN
Northeast Video and Sound, Inc; Order No. 144S; 1933 • b/w; 60 min; ¾" U-Matic, ½" EIAJ, ½" Beta II, ½" VHS • Sale: $149; Rental: $60/wk

Features John Wayne in one of his first "B" westerns.

THE LUSTY MEN
Fotomat Corp; Order No. B0117 for ½" Beta II, V0117 for ½" VHS; 1952 • color; 1 hr, 53 min; ½" Beta II, ½" VHS • Sale: $39.95; Rental: $7.95/up to 5 days, applicable to purchase

- -
Video Communications Inc; 1952 • color; 1 hr, 53 min; ½" Beta II, ½" VHS • Sale: $54.95

Relates the story of two rival rodeo champions—one on the rise, the other on the wane—both in love with the same high-spirited woman. Stars Susan Hayward, Robert Mitchum, and Arthur Kennedy.

LUTHER
MCA DiscoVision; Order No. 10-016; 1973 • color; 1 hr, 52 min; LaserVision • Sale: $24.95

Presents the American Film Theatre's adaptation of John Osborne's play concerning the life Martin Luther as he moved toward reforming the Christian faith, and his eventual break from the Catholic Church. Stars Stacy Keach, Patrick Magee, and Hugh Griffith.

M
Cinema Concepts, Inc.; 1931 • b/w; 1 hr, 30 min; ¾" U-Matic, ½" Beta II, ½" VHS • Sale: $54.95 for ½" Beta II & VHS, $149.95 for ¾"

- -
Ivy Video; 1931 • b/w; 1 hr, 30 min; ¾" U-Matic, ½" Beta II, ½" VHS • Sale: $59.95 for ½" Beta II & VHS, trade-in plan available, $195 for ¾"

- -
Northeast Video and Sound, Inc; Order No. 126S; 1931 • b/w; 1hr, 30 min; ¾" U-Matic, ½" EIAJ, ½" Beta II, ½" VHS • Sale: $249; Rental: $75/wk

- -
VCX; Order No. FC11; 1931 • b/w; 1 hr, 39 min; ½" Beta II, ½" VHS • Sale: $35.00

- -
The Video Library; 1931 • b/w; 1 hr, 30 min; ½" Beta II, ½" VHS • Sale: $49.95 • Foreign languages: German

Details the crimes and eventual capture of a psychotic child murderer in this film classic directed by Fritz Lang. Features Peter Lorre as the chilling but almost sympathetic killer who becomes the target of a massive manhunt by both the police and the organized crime syndicate of Berlin.

MA AND PA KETTLE
MCA DiscoVision; Order No. 22-002; 1949 • b/w; 1 hr, 15 min; LaserVision • Sale: $15.95

Offers characters first seen in Betty McDonald's novel and film "The Egg and I," the aggressive Ma, and bumbling Pa, and their brood of thirteen children and assortment of barnyard animals. Features Marjorie Main, Percy Kilbridge, Richard Long, and Meg Randall, in the first of many films in this comedy series.

MACAO
Niles Cinema; Order No. NM-8041; 1952 • b/w; 1 hr, 21 min; ½" Beta II, ½" VHS • Sale: $54.95

- -
The Nostalgia Merchant; Order No. 8041; 1952 • b/w; 1 hr, 21 min; ½" Beta II, ½" VHS • Sale: $54.95

- -
Red Fox, Inc; Order No. 8041; 1952 • b/w; 1 hr, 21 min; ½" Beta II, ½" VHS • Sale: $54.95

Tells of a soldier of fortune caught in the intrigue of the Orient's most notorious city. Features Robert Mitchum, Jane Russell, and William Bendix.

MACARTHUR
MCA DiscoVision; Order No. 15-003; 1977 • color; 2 hrs, 10 min; LaserVision • Sale:$24.95

Depicts the life of General Douglas MacArthur, who

prompted conrtoversy throughout his career, including being fired by the President of the U.S. Stars Gregory Peck, Ed Flanders, Dan O'Herlihy, and Marj Dusay.

MACHINE GUN KELLY
Video T.E.N.; 1958 • b/w; 1 hr, 20 min; ½" Beta II, ½" VHS • Sale: $49.95 for ½" Beta II, $54.95 for ½" VHS

Dramatizes the story of a murderous gangster, his girlfriend, and the FBI in this film by Roger Corman. Stars Charles Bronson, Susan Cabot, and Morey Amsterdam.

Charles Bronson and Susan Cabot in *Machine Gun Kelly*.

MACHO CALLAHAN
Magnetic Video Corporation; Order No. CL-4034; 1970 • color; 1 hr, 40 min; ½" Beta II, ½" VHS • Sale: $54.95

Details the revenge of a woman in the Old West who sees her husband killed and decides to kill the slayer herself but finds herself in love with him. Stars David Janssen, Jean Seberg, and Lee J. Cobb.

MACKENNA'S GOLD
National Film and Video Center; 1969 • color; 2 hrs, 8 min; ¾" U-Matic, ½" Beta II, ½" VHS • Rental: $89/1 showing

Tells the story of seventeen men and four women seeking a legendary cache of gold in Apache territory. Stars Gregory Peck, Omar Sharif, Telly Savalas, Julie Newmar, and Camilla Sparv.

THE MAD BOMBER
Niles Cinema; Order No. BT-07 for ½" Beta II, VH-07 for ½" VHS; 1972 • color; 1 hr, 40 min; ½" Beta II, ½" VHS • Sale: $59.95

Details the psychotic progression of a man who believes himself to be meting out justice to society by bombing public buildings. Stars Vince Edwards, Chuck Connors, and Neville Brand.

MAD MONSTER PARTY
Magnetic Video Corporation; Order No. CL-4046; 1967 • color; 1 hr, 34 min; ½" Beta II, ½" VHS • Sale: $54.95

Offers an animated musical feature starring the ingenious Dr. Frankenstein and an international roster of monsters, including Dracula, The Werewolf, The Mummy, and many others. Features the voices of Phyllis Diller, Boris Karloff, Gale Garnett, and Ethel Ennis.

THE MADAM GAMBLES
Northeast Video and Sound, Inc; Date not listed • b/w; 1 hr, 20 min; ¾" U-Matic, ½" EIAJ, ½" Beta II, ½" VHS • Sale: $179; Rental: $70/wk

Presents a British comedy about a dress shop, the owner's effort to save it, and his new invention.

MADAME ROSA
Time-Life Video Club Inc; 1978 • color; 1 hr, 45 min; ½" Beta II, ½" VHS • Sale: $34.95 to members • Foreign languages: French

Offers the story of a woman who once lived as a prostitute, survived Auschwitz, and lives in the slums of Paris earning her living caring for the children of prostitutes. Unveils an old and ill woman who has survived by her wits; follows her search for peace with a young Arab boy. Stars Simone Signoret.

MADE FOR EACH OTHER
Tape Club of America; Order No. 2208 B; 1939 • b/w; 1 hr, 33 min; ½" Beta II, ½" VHS • Sale: $54.95
- -
Thunderbird Films; 1939 • b/w; 1 hr, 40 min; ¾" U-Matic, ½" Beta I, ½" Beta II, ½" VHS • Sale: $69.95 for ½" Beta I, $49.95 for ½" Beta II & VHS, $89.95 for ¾"

Shows John and Jane in a romantic comedy. Tells how they get married after only a few hours' acquaintance and the material problems they encounter afterwards. Stars James Stewart, Carole Lombard, and Charles Coburn.

MADO
Entertainment Video Releasing, Inc; Order No. 1023; 1977 • color; 2 hrs, 10 min; ½" Beta II, ½" VHS • Sale: $49.95 for ½" Beta II, $54.95 for ½" VHS

Relates a story about the complex interrelationship of love and business. Stars Romy Schneider, Ottavia Piccolo, Michel Piccoli, and Jacques Dutronc.

THE MAGIC GARDEN
Reel Images Inc; Order No. 28; 1960 • b/w; 1 hr, 3 min; ½" Beta II, ½" VHS • Sale: $49.95 for ½" Beta II, $52.95 for ½" VHS

Presents a whimsical film in which musical moments enhance a tale of a thief and his efforts to hold on to stolen money. Stars Tommy Machaka, Hariett Qubeka, David Mnkwanazi, and Dolly Rathebe.

MAGICAL MYSTERY TOUR
Cinema Concepts, Inc.; 1967 • color; 55 min; ¾" U-Matic, ½" Beta II, ½" VHS • Sale: $39.95 for ½" Beta II & VHS, $79.95 for ¾"
- -
Golden Tapes Video Tape Library; Order No. CD2; 1967 • color; 1 hr; ½" Beta II, ½" VHS • Sale: $49.95 for ½" Beta II & VHS, $79.95 for ¾"
- -
Ivy Video; 1967 • color; 55 min; ¾" U-Matic, ½" Beta II, ½" VHS • Sale: $59.95 for ½" Beta II & VHS, trade-in plan available, $200 for ¾"
- -
The Video Library; Order No. VN-0121; 1967 • color; 55 min; ½" Beta II, ½" VHS • Sale: $39.95
- -
Video Tape Network; Order No. CT 121 for ½" Beta II, CT 122 for ½" VHS; 1967 • color; 55 min; ½" Beta II, ½" VHS • Sale: $49.95

Follows the Beatles on a traveling bus that takes them

to strange places where they meet unusual people. Includes the songs "Fool on the Hill," "I Am the Walrus," and many others.

THE MAGICIAN
Cinema Resources; 1958 • b/w; 1 hr, 42 min; ½" Beta II, ½" VHS • Sale: $45

Presents a Swedish film directed by Ingmar Bergman with English subtitles. Offers a brooding tale set in 19th century Sweden. Follows a magician and his troupe as they are detained in a small town where their magic becomes involved in murder and the afterlife. Stars Max von Sydow, Ingrid Thulin, Gunnar Bjornstrand, and Bibi Anderson.

THE MAGNIFICENT AMBERSONS
Niles Cinema; Order No. NM-8042; 1942 • b/w; 1 hr, 28 min; ½" Beta II, ½" VHS • Sale: $54.95
- -
The Nostalgia Merchant; Order No. 8042; 1942 • b/w; 1 hr, 28 min; ½" Beta II, ½" VHS • Sale: $54.95
- -
Red Fox, Inc; Order No. 8042; 1942 • b/w; 1 hr, 28 min; ½" Beta II, ½" VHS • Sale: $54.95
- -
Discount Video Tapes; 1942 • b/w; 1 hr, 28 min; ½" Beta II, ½" VHS • Sale: $49.95

Relates the history of a family unwilling to change its way of life with the times, directed by Orson Welles. Stars Joseph Cotten, Anne Baxter, and Tim Holt.

MAHOGANY
Fotomat Corp; Order No. B0087 for ½" Beta II, V0087 for ½" VHS; 1975 • color; 1 hr, 50 min; ½" Beta II, ½" VHS • Sale: $49.95; Rental: $9.95/up to 5 days, applicable to purchase

Follows an ambitious young secretary who becomes a high fashion model and a world famous designer. Portrays the two men in her life: a Chicago politician who fell in love with her before she became a fashion sensation, and a highly successful but malevolent fashion photographer who masterminds, and then tries to sabotage, her career. Stars Diana Ross, Billy Dee Williams, Jean-Pierre Aumont, and Anthony Perkins, under the direction of Barry Gordy.

MAJOR DUNDEE
National Film and Video Center; 1965 • color; 2 hrs, 4 min; ¾" U-Matic, ½" Beta II, ½" VHS • Rental: $49/1 showing

Presents the massacre of "B" Troop of the 3rd U.S. Cavalry at the hands of Sierra Charriba, an Apache Indian chief who escapes into Mexico. Stars Charlton Heston, Richard Harris, Jim Hutton, James Coburn, and Michael Anderson, Jr.

MAKE A WISH
Reel Images Inc; Order No. 32; 1937 • b/w; 1 hr, 17 min; ½" Beta II, ½" VHS • Sale: $49.95 for ½" Beta II, $52.95 for ½" VHS

Presents a family musical in which a noted composer goes stale. Relates a tale of backstage life with scenes also set in a summer camp in the Maine woods. Stars Basil Rathbone, Bobby Breen, Leon Errol, and Ralph Forbes.

THE MAKING OF STAR WARS
Magnetic Video Corporation; Order No. CL-1052; Date not listed • color; 50 min; ½" Beta II, ½" VHS • Sale: $54.95

Goes behind the scenes to chronicle the most popular movie of all time, with secrets never before revealed of

special effects and other pertinent background information.

MALIBU BEACH
Video Communications Inc; 1978 • color; 1 hr, 33
min; ½″ Beta II, ½″ VHS • Sale: $54.95

Offers an ''R'' rated film about life on the beach, with
romance and bikinis. Features Kim Lankford and
James Daughton.

MALIBU HIGH
Video Communications Inc; 1979 • color; 1 hr, 33
min; ½″ Beta II, ½″ VHS • Sale: $54.95

Offers an ''R'' rated film about a prostitute's new profession—''sex and hit.'' Features Jill Lansing and
Stuart Taylor.

MALICIOUS
Fotomat Corp; Order No. B0399 for ½″ Beta II, V0399
for ½″ VHS; 1974 • color; 1 hr, 38 min; ½″ Beta II,
½″ VHS • Sale: $54.95; Rental: $9.95/5 days
- -
Paramount Home Video; 1973 • color; 1 hr, 37 min;
½″ Beta II, ½″ VHS • Sale: $59.95

Offers an Italian comedy for adults. Reveals the yearn-
ings of a 14-year-old boy for his father's intended wife,
the hired housekeeper. Stars Laura Antonelli.

**Humphrey Bogart, Sidney Greenstreet,
Peter Lorre, and Mary Astor
in The Maltese Falcon.**

THE MALTESE FALCON
Vid America; Order No. 424; 1941 • b/w; 1 hr, 40 min;
½″ Beta II, ½″ VHS • Rental: $10.95/wk

Spotlights Humphrey Bogart as private eye Sam Spade
in the story of a group of greedy characters trying to
get hold of a jewel-encrusted statuette. Co-stars Mary
Astor, Sidney Greenstreet, and Peter Lorre, under the
direction of John Huston.

A MAN, A WOMAN, AND A BANK
Magnetic Video Corporation; Order No. 4065; 1979 •
color; 1 hr, 40 min; ½″ Beta II, ½″ VHS • Sale: $59.95

Offers a caper movie about a $4 million bank heist.
Stars Donald Sutherland, Brooke Adams, Paul Mazursky, and Allen Magicovsky.

A MAN ALONE
The Nostalgia Merchant; Order No. 0170; 1955 •
color; 1 hr, 36 min; ½″ Beta II, ½″ VHS • Sale: $54.95

Red Fox, Inc; Order No. 01; 1955 • color; 1 hr, 36
min; ½″ Beta II, ½″ VHS • Sale: $54.95

Tells of an outlaw who is relentlessly pursued for a
crime he did not commit. Features Ray Milland, Mary
Murphy, and Ward Bond.

A MAN CALLED ADAM
Magnetic Video. Corporation; Order No. CL-4040;
1966 • b/w; 1 hr, 42 min; ½″ Beta II, ½″ VHS • Sale:
$54.95

Explores the problems of a potentially great black jazz
trumpeter who alienates his associates, shuns his
friends, and destroys his career. Stars Sammy Davis,
Jr., Louis Armstrong, Cicely Tyson, and Ossie Davis.

A MAN FOR ALL SEASONS
Columbia Pictures Home Entertainment; 1966 • color;
2 hrs, 14 min; ½″ Beta II, ½″ VHS • Sale: $59.95
- -
Time-Life Video Club Inc; 1966 • color; 2 hrs, 14 min;
½″ Beta II, ½″ VHS • Sale: $59.95 to members

Recreates the world of Tudor England in this dramatic
spectacle about the fatal conflict between Sir Thomas
More and King Henry VIII over the establishment of the
Church of England. Stars Paul Scofield, Robert Shaw,
Orson Welles, Wendy Hiller, and Vanessa Redgrave,
under the direction of Fred Zinnemann.

MAN FROM CHEYENNE
Cable Films; 1941 • b/w; 54 min; ½″ Beta I, ½″ Beta
II, ½″ VHS • Sale: $45 for ½″ Beta I, $49.50 for ½″
Beta II & VHS
- -
Thunderbird Films; 1942 • b/w; 1 hr; ¾″ U-Matic, ½″
Beta I, ½″ Beta II, ½″ VHS • Sale: $59.95 for ½″ Beta
I, $39.95 for ½″ Beta II & VHS, $79.95 for ¾″

Presents a western in which Roy Rogers goes to Gabby Hayes' aid when a ruthless gang of cattle rustlers
terrorizes small ranchers. Features songs by Gabby
Hayes; co-stars Gale Storm.

THE MAN FROM CLOVER GROVE
Meda/Media Home Entertainment Inc; Date not listed
• color; 1 hr, 37 min; ½″ Beta II, ½″ VHS • Sale:
$49.95

Offers a comedy about a nutty toy inventor who
creates toys for the orphans of Clover Grove and puts
the sheriff in a spin. Stars Ron Masak, Cheryl Miller,
Jed Allan, and Richard Deacon.

THE MAN FROM LARAMIE
National Film and Video Center; 1955 • color; 1 hr, 44
min; ¾″ U-Matic, ½″ Beta II, ½″ VHS • Rental: $49/1
showing

Stars James Stewart as a man who travels a thousand
miles to find and kill the man who sold Apaches the
repeating rifles they used in a massacre in which his
brother was killed. Co-stars Arthur Kennedy, Donald
Crisp, and Cathy O'Donnell, under the direction of Anthony Mann.

MAN FROM MUSIC MOUNTAIN
Budget Video; 1944 • b/w; 1 hr; ½″ Beta II, ½″ VHS •
Sale: $34.95

Depicts a stock swindle in a western mining town. Stars
Gene Autry and Smiley Burnette.

MAN FROM UTAH
Cable Films; 1934 • b/w; 54 min; ½″ Beta I, ½″ Beta
II, ½″ VHS • Sale: $45 for ½″ Beta I, $49.50 for ½″
Beta II & VHS

Reel Images Inc; Order No. 58; 1934 • b/w; 52 min; 1/2" Beta II, 1/2" VHS • Sale: $39.95 for 1/2" Beta II, $42.95 for 1/2" VHS

Offers a western set against the background of rodeo riders and cowboys. Features stock footage from early 1930's rodeos. Stars John Wayne.

MAN IN THE GLASS BOOTH
Magnetic Video Corporation; 1974 • color; 1 hr, 57 min; 1/2" Beta II, 1/2" VHS • Sale: $80

- -

MCA DiscoVision; Order No. 10-015; 1974 • color; 1 hr, 57 min; LaserVision • Sale: $24.95

Offers the American Film Theatre's adaptation of Robert Shaw's play about a man on trial for atrocities he committed while a Nazi S.S. officer, but who claims he is a Jewish businessman. Stars Maximilian Schell, Lois Nettleton, Luther Adler, Lawrence Pressman, Henry Brown, and Richard Rasof.

THE MAN IN THE WHITE SUIT
Fotomat Corp; Order No. B0241 for 1/2" Beta II, V0241 for 1/2" VHS; 1951 • b/w; 1 hr, 25 min; 1/2" Beta II, 1/2" VHS • Sale: $49.95; Rental: $9.95/up to 5 days, applicable to purchase

- -

Time-Life Video Club Inc; 1952 • b/w; 1 hr, 24 min; 1/2" Beta II, 1/2" VHS • Sale: $49.95, plus $15 annual membership fee

Satirizes modern industry as a timid chemist invents a cloth that won't tear, stain, or wear out. Shows the resulting panic as labor leaders fear loss of jobs and corporate leaders vye for the formula, and the chagrin of the chemist who thought he made a wonderful discovery. Stars Alec Guinness, Cecil Parker, and Joan Greenwood.

THE MAN WHO FELL TO EARTH
Time-Life Video Club Inc; 1976 • color; 2 hrs, 5 min; 1/2" Beta II, 1/2" VHS • Sale: $49.95 to members

Introduces an extra-terrestrial being who comes to Earth to seek water for his dying planet. Shows his ability to outwit earthlings, only to become corrupted by corporate power. Stars David Bowie, Buck Henry, Rip Torn, and Candy Clark, in a film directed by Nicholas Roeg.

THE MAN WHO HAD POWER OVER WOMEN
Magnetic Video Corporation; Order No. CL-4053; 1970 • color; 1 hr, 29 min; 1/2" Beta II, 1/2" VHS • Sale: $54.95

Offers a comedy-drama about a successful public relations executive who has everything—power, money, and women. Stars Rod Taylor, Carol White, James Booth, and Penelope Horner.

THE MAN WHO KNEW TOO MUCH
Northeast Video and Sound, Inc; 1934 • b/w; 1 hr, 24 min; 3/4" U-Matic, 1/2" EIAJ, 1/2" Beta II, 1/2" VHS • Sale: $179; Rental: $70/wk

Presents Alfred Hitchcock's original version of this spy thriller. Concerns a Britisher who inadvertently learns of foreign agents' plans to assassinate a diplomat. Follows his efforts to save his daughter after she is kidnapped by the agents to ensure his silence. Stars Leslie Banks, Edna Best, Peter Lorre, and Frank Vosper.

THE MAN WHO LOVED WOMEN
Columbia Pictures Home Entertainment; Order No. BCF7240 for 1/2" Beta II, VCF3150 for 1/2" VHS; 1977 • color; 1/2" Beta II, 1/2" VHS • Sale: $59.95

Offers French director Francois Truffaut's comedy about a man obsessed with beautiful women. Stars Charles Denner and Brigitte Fossey.

THE MAN WHO SHOT LIBERTY VALANCE
Paramount Home Video ; 1962 • b/w; 2 hrs, 2 min; 1/2" Beta II, 1/2" VHS • Sale: $59.95

Stars John Wayne, James Stewart, Lee Marvin, and Edmond O'Brien in John Ford's modern day western concerning a meek lawyer who becomes famous for shooting a despicable man.

THE MAN WHO TALKS TO WHALES
Video Communications Inc; Order No. 1075; 1977 • color; 1 hr, 31 min; 1/2" Beta II, 1/2" VHS • Sale: $54.95

Follows a man and his young nephew as they search the ocean for Gigi, a rare California Grey Whale. Stars Victor Jory.

MANDINGO
Paramount Home Video; Order No. 8771; Date not listed • color; 2 hrs, 7 min; 1/2" Beta II, 1/2" VHS • Sale: $62.95

Offers a tale of the antebellum South. Centers on the passionate forbidden love between the white owners of the plantation and the black slaves. Includes violence. Features James Mason, Perry King, Susan George, Ken Norton, and Brenda Sykes. Adapts Kyle Onstott's novel.

MANHUNT IN THE AFRICAN JUNGLE
The Nostalgia Merchant; Date not listed • b/w; 3 hrs, 45 min; 1/2" Beta II, 1/2" VHS • Sale: $109.95

Presents, on two videocassettes, a motion picture serial in 15 episodes. Stars Rod Cameron.

THE MANIPULATOR
Video Communications Inc; Order No. 1069; 1971 • color; 1 hr, 32 min; 1/2" Beta II, 1/2" VHS • Sale: $54.95

Portrays Arnold Tiller, head of a huge television and record combine who will stop at nothing to acquire publicity for his budding stars. Shows how he uses any manipulation to promote his fantastic wealth and reputation. Stars Stephen Boyd and Sylva Koscina.

THE MANITOU
Magnetic Video Corporation; Order No. CL-4030; 1978 • color; 1 hr, 43 min; 1/2" Beta II, 1/2" VHS • Sale: $54.95

Recounts a medical story of supernatural terror as a woman suffers from a rapidly growing tumor on her neck which contains a living creature from the dim past. Stars Tony Curtis and Susan Strasberg.

MARASCHINO CHERRY
Quality X Video Cassette Company; Date not listed • color; 1 hr, 23 min ; 1/2" Beta I, 1/2" Beta II, 1/2" VHS • Sale: $99.50

Presents a pornographic film.

MARATHON MAN
Fotomat Corp; Order No. B0095 for 1/2" Beta II, V0095 for 1/2" VHS; 1976 • color; 2 hrs, 5 min; 1/2" Beta II, 1/2" VHS • Sale: $69.95; Rental: $13.95/up to 5 days, applicable to purchase

- -

Paramount Home Video; 1976 • color; 2 hrs, 5 min; 1/2" Beta II, 1/2" VHS • Sale: $79.95

Focuses on a likeable Columbia graduate student and marathon runner unwittingly trapped in a terrifying drama revolving around a murderous Nazi fugitive, Christian Szell. Portrays Szell as a man who administers torture with the instruments of a dental surgeon and the ease of evil personified. Stars Dustin Hoffman, Laurence Olivier, Marthe Keller, and Roy Scheider, under the direction of John Schlesinger.

MARCH OF THE WOODEN SOLDIERS
Thunderbird Films; 1935 • b/w; 1 hr, 13 min; ¾" U-Matic, ½" Beta I, ½" Beta II, ½" VHS • Sale: $69.95 for ½" Beta I, $49.95 for ½" Beta II & VHS, $89.95 for ¾"

Presents a fantasy extravaganza with elaborate sets, songs and dances. Stars Stan Laurel and Oliver Hardy, along with Charlotte Henry and Henry Brandon in this version of Victor Herbert's "Babes in Toyland."

MARIUS
Budget Video; 1931 • b/w; 2 hrs, 5 min; ½" Beta II, ½" VHS • Sale: $64.95
- -
Discount Video Tapes; 1931 • b/w; 2 hrs, 5 min; ½" Beta II, ½" VHS • Sale: $64.95

Offers the first film in Marcel Pagnol's trilogy of life in Marseilles. Recounts how Marius' love for Fanny is surpassed by his love for the sea, and how Fanny unwillingly marries a rich widower to give Marius his freedom. Stars Raimu, Pierre Fresnay, Charpin, and Orane Demazis, under the direction of Alexander Korda; in French with subtitles.

THE MARK OF ZORRO
Blackhawk Films, Inc; Order No. 506-53-0837 for ½" Beta II, 525-53-0837 for ½" VHS; 1920 • b/w; 1 hr, 31 min; ½" Beta II, ½" VHS • Sale: $39.95

Presents the "Robin Hood" of old California, as Don Diego pretends to be a fop, but in reality fights for the rights of the downtrodden. Stars Douglas Fairbanks and Marguerita De La Motte in this silent feature.

MAROONED
National Film and Video Center; 1969 • color; 2 hrs, 6 min; ¾" U-Matic, ½" Beta II, ½" VHS • Rental: $69/1 showing

Offers the story of the Ironman One, a space ship that misfires during return to Earth, stranding its crew in space. Stars Gregory Peck, Richard Crenna, James Franciscus, Gene Hackman, and David Janssen.

THE MARRIAGE OF A YOUNG STOCKBROKER
Golden Tapes Video Tape Library; Order No. F-1027; 1971 • color; 1 hr, 35 min; ½" Beta II, ½" VHS • Sale: $49.95 for ½" Beta II & VHS, $124.95 for ¾"
- -
Magnetic Video Corporation; Order No. CL-1027; 1971 • color; 1 hr, 45 min; ½" Beta II, ½" VHS • Sale: $44.95

Tells the comic tale of a jaded stockbroker with a failing marriage who attempts to spice up his life by going to porno films. Features Richard Benjamin, Joanna Shimkus, and Elizabeth Ashley.

MARRY ME! MARRY ME!
Blackhawk Films, Inc; Order No. 502-30-0062 for ½" Beta II, 515-30-0062 for ½" VHS; 1969 • color; 1 hr, 27 min; ½" Beta II, ½" VHS • Sale: $59.95

Tells the story of a young Frenchman who is ready to marry his fiance, until he meets the other members of her family. Stars Claude Berri and Regine under Berri's direction.

MARTIN LUTHER, HIS LIFE AND TIME
Reel Images Inc; Order No. 533; 1924 • b/w; 1 hr, 41 min; ½" Beta II, ½" VHS • Sale: $49.95 for ½" Beta II, $52.95 for ½" VHS

Traces Martin Luther's youth—his reluctance to obey his father and study law, his study of the Bible, his ordination, and his reconciliation with his father—and the Reformation. Offers a silent film with music score, produced by the Lutheran Film Division, Inc.

MARY OF SCOTLAND
Niles Cinema; Order No. NM-8005; 1936 • b/w; 2 hrs, 3 min; ½" Beta II, ½" VHS • Sale: $54.95
- -
The Nostalgia Merchant; Order No. 8005; 1936 • b/w; 2 hrs, 3 min; ½" Beta II, ½" VHS • Sale: $54.95
- -
Red Fox, Inc; Order No. 8005; 1936 • b/w; 2 hrs, 3 min; ½" Beta II, ½" VHS • Sale: $54.95

Features Katharine Hepburn as Mary, Queen of Scots in this Elizabethan historical drama, also starring Frederic March and John Carradine, under the direction of John Ford.

M*A*S*H
Blackhawk Films, Inc; Order No. 502-49-0011 for ½" Beta II, 515-49-0009 for ½" VHS; 1970 • color; 1 hr, 56 min; ½" Beta II, ½" VHS • Sale: $54.95
- -
Golden Tapes Video Tape Library; Order No. F-1038; 1970 • color; 1 hr, 56 min; ½" Beta II, ½" VHS • Sale: $49.95 for ½" Beta II & VHS, $124.95 for ¾"
- -
Magnetic Video Corporation; Order No. CL-1038; 1970 • color; 1 hr, 56 min; ½" Beta II, ½" VHS • Sale: $44.95
- -
RCA SelectaVision VideoDiscs; Order No. 00108; 1970 • color; 1 hr, 53 min; CED • Sale: $19.98
- -
The Video Library; Order No. MV-1038; 1970 • color; 1 hr, 56 min; ½" Beta II, ½" VHS • Sale: $54.95

Focuses on a corps of army surgeons during the Korean War who develop a lunatic life style in an attempt to cope with the horrors that surround them. Stars Elliott Gould, Donald Sutherland, Sally Kellerman, and Tom Skerritt, under the direction of Robert Altman.

THE MASKED MARVEL
The Nostalgia Merchant; Order No. 0012; 1943 • b/w; 3 hrs; ½" Beta II, ½" VHS • Sale: $109.95

Presents, on two videocassettes, a Republic motion picture serial in 12 episodes. Traces the Masked Marvel's attempts to prevent a reign of sabotage masterminded by the notorious Japanese agent, Sakima, aimed against America's war industries. Stars William Forest, Louise Currie, and Johnny Arthur.

MASTER OF THE HOUSE
Reel Images Inc; Order No. 526; 1925 • b/w; 1 hr, 58 min; ½" Beta II, ½" VHS • Sale: $49.95 for ½" Beta II, $52.95 for ½" VHS

Relates the story of a spoiled husband and an ordinary woman, wife and mother, whose life is confined to the four walls of her home. Offers a silent film from Denmark, with music score and English titles, directed by Carl-Theodore Dreyer.

MASTERPIECE
VTS; Date not listed • color; 1 hr, 10 min; ½" Beta I, ½" Beta II, ½" VHS • Sale: $99

Presents a pornographic film.

MASTER'S DEGREE

Quality X Video Cassette Company; Date not listed • color; 1 hr, 10 min; 1/2" Beta I, 1/2" Beta II, 1/2" VHS • Sale: $99.50

Presents a pornographic film.

MAYERLING

Reel Images Inc; Order No. 34; 1937 • b/w; 1 hr, 35 min; 1/2" Beta II, 1/2" VHS • Sale: $49.95 for 1/2" Beta II, $52.95 for 1/2" VHS

Presents a French film based on the classic love story of the hopeless affair between a crown prince and a baroness. Stars Charles Boyer and Danielle Darrieux under the direction of Anatole Litvak.

MEATBALLS

Time-Life Video Club Inc; 1979 • color; 1 hr, 32 min; 1/2" Beta II, 1/2" VHS • Sale: $449.50 to members

Presents an irreverent comedy inspired by the success of "Animal House." Showcases the talent of Bill Murray as an Activities Director at a summer camp with a coed staff.

MEET DR. CHRISTIAN

Reel Images Inc; Order No. 488; 1939 • b/w; 1 hr, 10 min; 1/2" Beta II, 1/2" VHS • Sale: $49.95 for 1/2" Beta II, 52.95 for 1/2" VHS

Offers the first of a series of "Dr. Christian" films, the character based on a radio series. Presents a doctor who practices medicine in a small American town and also manages to remedy the human ailments of his friends and patients. Stars Jean Hersholt, Dorothy Lovett, and Paul Harvey.

MEET JOHN DOE

Ivy Video; 1941 • b/w; 2 hrs, 3 min; 3/4" U-Matic, 1/2" Beta II, 1/2" VHS • Sale: $59.95 for 1/2" Beta II & VHS, trade-in plan available, $225 for 3/4"

- -

Northeast Video and Sound, Inc; Order No. 138S; 1941 • b/w; 2 hrs, 3 min; 3/4" U-Matic , 1/2" EIAJ, 1/2" Beta II, 1/2" VHS • Sale: $295; Rental: $80/wk

- -

Reel Images Inc; Order No. 35; 1941 • b/w; 2 hrs, 3 min; 1/2" Beta II, 1/2" VHS • Sale: $49.95 for 1/2" Beta II, $52.95 for 1/2" VHS

Presents the story of the disillusionment of a do-gooder whose national campaign of goodwill and friendship nightmarishly backfires upon its creator. Features Gary Cooper and Barbara Stanwyck in Frank Capra's social comedy-melodrama.

MEET ME IN ST. LOUIS

MGM/CBS Home Video; Order No. M60005; 1944 • color; 1 hr, 53 min; 1/2" Beta II, 1/2" VHS • Sale: $59.95

- -

Niles Cinema; Order No. GM-729; 1944 • color; 1 hr, 53 min; 1/2" Beta II, 1/2" VHS • Sale: $59.95

- -

RCA SelectaVision VideoDiscs; Order No. 00205; 1944 • color; 1 hr, 53 min; CED • Sale: $14.98

Offers Vincente Minnelli's musical about life at the 1903 World's Fair. Features "The Boy Next Door," "Trolley Song," "Meet Me In St. Louis," and "Have Yourself A Merry Little Christmas." Stars Judy Garland, Margaret O'Brien, Mary Astor, Marjorie Main, June Lockhart, and Leon Ames.

MEETING AT MIDNIGHT

Northeast Video and Sound, Inc; Order No. 172S; 1944 • b/w;.1 hr, 7 min; 3/4" U-Matic, 1/2" EIAJ, 1/2"

Beta II, 1/2" VHS • Sale: $195; Rental: $65/wk

Presents a Charlie Chan mystery in which the Oriental sleuth solves the murder of a medium and then must face the killer. Stars Sidney Toler, Joseph Crehan, Mantan Moreland, and Frances Chan.

MEMORIES WITHIN MISS AGGIE

Video Home Library; Order No. VX-118; Date not listed • color; 2 hrs; 1/2" Beta II, 1/2" VHS • Sale: $99.95

Presents a pornographic film.

MEN IN WAR

Tape Club of America; Order No. 2301 B; 1957 • b/w; 1 hr, 42 min; 1/2" Beta II, 1/2" VHS • Sale: $54.95

Dramatizes in a realistic manner what happens to an infantry platoon under fire in the Korean war. Stars Robert Ryan, Aldo Ray, Robert Keith, and Vic Morrow.

MEN OF DESTINY (PART 1)—WORLD POLITICAL FIGURES

Magnetic Video Corporation; Order No. CL-7003; Date not listed • b/w; 2 hrs; 1/2" Beta II, 1/2" VHS • Sale: $54.95

Presents a compilation of authentic three-minute newsreels produced by Pathé News, Inc. Focuses on the major world leaders in politics in the first half of the twentieth century. Includes Winston Churchill, Herbert Hoover, Mahatma Ghandi, Charles DeGaulle, Adlai Stevenson, and Queen Elizabeth II.

MEN OF DESTINY (PART 2)—ARTISTS AND INNOVATORS

Magnetic Video Corporation; Order No. CL-7004; Date not listed • b/w; 2 hrs; 1/2" Beta II, 1/2" VHS • Sale: $54.95

Offers a compilation of authentic three-minute newsreels produced by Pathé News, Inc. Focuses on the major artists and innovators of the first half of the twentieth century. Includes Marie Curie, Thomas Edison, Albert Einstein, Jonas Salk, the Wright Brothers, Charles Lindbergh, George M. Cohan, Irving Berlin, and Al Jolson.

MERRIEST PRANKSTERS

Blackhawk Films, Inc; Order No. 506-01-0840 for 1/2" Beta II, 525-01-0840 for 1/2" VHS; Date not listed • b/w; 57 min; 3/4" U-Matic, 1/2" Beta I, 1/2" Beta II, 1/2" VHS • Sale: $59.95 for 1/2" Beta I, $39.95 for 1/2" Beta II & VHS, $69.95 for 3/4"

Margaret O'Brien, Judy Garland, and Hank Daniels in Meet Me in St. Louis.

Mike Kellin and Brad Davis in *Midnight Express*.

Presents a program of comedy highlights. Features Buster Keaton in "The Blacksmith," W. C. Fields in "The Fatal Glass of Beer," and Will Rogers in "Big Moments from Little Pictures." Includes a musical score composed and performed by William Perry.

METROPOLIS

Ivy Video; 1926 • b/w; 1 hr, 24 min; ¾" U-Matic, ½" Beta II, ½" VHS • Sale: $59.95 for ½" Beta II & VHS, trade-in plan available, $195 for ¾"

Northeast Video and Sound, Inc; Order No. 150S; 1926 • b/w; 1 hr, 24 min; ¾" U-Matic, ½" EIAJ, ½" Beta II, ½" VHS • Sale: $250; Rental: $75/wk

---

Reel Images Inc; Order No. 32; 1926 • b/w; 1 hr, 37 min; ½" Beta II, ½" VHS • Sale: $69.98 for ½" Beta II, $73.98 for ½" VHS

Portrays a futuristic society based on underground machinery and robot workers in this Fritz Lang film. Resolves the class conflict between master and slave with the spirit of cooperation and humanity in this allegory, which looks forward to the horrors of fascism based on technology which was soon to polarize Germany and the world.

MICKEY

Reel Images Inc; Order No. 36; 1917 • b/w; 1 hr, 45 min; ½" Beta II, ½" VHS • Sale: $49.95 for ½" Beta II, $52.95 for ½" VHS

Offers a satire on high society which was very popular when released. Presents a silent film starring Mable Normand in a Mack Sennett production.

MIDNIGHT

Reel Images Inc; Order No. 471; 1934 • b/w; 1 hr, 14 min; ½" Beta II, ½" VHS • Sale: $49.95 for ½" Beta II, $52.95 for ½" VHS

Relates the story of the daughter of a jury foreman romantically involved with a gangster who is interested in a particular case before it reaches court. Provides an example of Humphrey Bogart's early screen work in a melodramatic context. Features Bogart, O.P. Hegge, Henry Hull, and Sidney Fox.

*MIDNIGHT BLUE

Ivy Video; 1975-76 • color; 8 30-min tapes; ¾" U-Matic, ½" Beta II, ½" VHS • Sale: $479.60 full series, $59.95 ea tape for ½" Beta II & VHS, trade-in plan available, $1599.60 full series, $199.95 ea tape for ¾" • 8 units: Midnight Blue (Parts 1-8) (These titles are not listed individually in this directory)

Presents a series of pornographic films.

MIDNIGHT BLUE FOLLIES OF 1975

Ivy Video; 1975 • color; 50 min; ¾" U-Matic, ½" Beta II, ½" VHS • Sale: $59.95 for ½" Beta II & VHS, trade-in plan available, $199.95 for ¾"

Presents a pornographic film.

MIDNIGHT BLUE FOLLIES OF 1976

Ivy Video; 1976 • color; 1 hr, 30 min; ¾" U-Matic, ½" Beta II, ½" VHS • Sale: $59.95 for ½" Beta II & VHS, trade-in plan available, $199.95 for ¾"

Presents a pornographic film.

MIDNIGHT EXPRESS

Fotomat Corp; Order No. B0419 for ½" Beta II, V0419 for ½" VHS; 1978 • color; 2 hrs, 1 min; ½" Beta II, ½" VHS • Sale: $54.95; Rental: $9.95/5 days

---

Time-Life Video Club Inc; 1979 • color; 2 hrs, 2 min; ½" Beta II, ½" VHS • Sale: $59.95 to members

Recounts the true story of American student Billy Hayes' imprisonment in Turkey for drug smuggling. Features Brad Davis, Randy Quaid, Irene Miracle, John Hurt, Paul Smith, Bo Hopkins, and Norbert Weisser.

MIDWAY

MCA DiscoVision; Order No. 12-003; 1976 • color; 2 hrs, 12 min; LaserVision • Sale:$24.95

Offers the events leading up to, and including, the Battle of Midway fought in June,1942, six months after the

107

MISTY BEETHOVEN

Quality X Video Cassette Company; 1976 • color; 1 hr, 27 min; ½" Beta I, ½" Beta II, ½" VHS • Sale: $99.50

Presents a pornographic film.

MODERN TIMES

Magnetic Video Corporation; Order No. CL-3007; 1936 • b/w; 1 hr, 29 min; ½" Beta II, ½" VHS • Sale: $44.95

Presents Charlie Chaplin's last silent film, a satire of the machine age. Includes a scene with Charlie as an assembly-line worker who is unable to stop the spastic repetitive movements of his job after leaving the factory. Co-stars Paulette Goddard, Henry Bergman, Chester Conklin, and Stanley Sanford, in a film written, produced, and directed by Chaplin.

MOLLY AND LAWLESS JOHN

FHV Entertainment, Inc; 1972 • color; 1 hr, 36 min; ½" Beta II, ½" VHS • Sale: $49.95

Offers an off-beat, almost-a-love story that pairs Vera Miles and Sam Elliot in a western set against a New Mexico landscape.

MONIQUE

Monarch Releasing Corporation; Date not listed • color; 1 hr, 25 min; ¾" U-Matic • Sale: $350

Presents a pornographic film.

THE MONKEY'S UNCLE

MCA DiscoVision; Order No. D18-512; 1964 • color; 1 hr, 30 min; LaserVision • Sale:$24.95

Follows the adventures of college whiz-kid Merlin Jones as he sets out to prove a monkey has the learning capacity of the average college football hero. Features the Beach Boys title song in this Walt Disney Studio production. Stars Tommy Kirk, Annette Funicello, Leon Ames, Frank Faylen, and Arthur O'Connell.

MONSIEUR VERDOUX

Magnetic Video Corporation; Order No. CL-3009; 1947 • b/w; 2 hrs, 3 min; ½" Beta II, ½" VHS • Sale: $44.95

Presents Charlie Chaplin's black comedy set in the Depression era during the rise of fascism and the beginning of World War II. Centers around the murders of a bluebeard attempting to provide for his wife and child. Co-stars Martha Raye and Isobel Elsom, under Chaplin's direction.

MONSTER FROM GREEN HELL

Reel Images Inc; Order No. 576; 1957 • b/w; 1 hr, 11 min; ½" Beta II, ½" VHS • Sale: $49.95 for ½" Beta II, $52.95 for ½" VHS

Video T.E.N.; 1957 • b/w; 1 hr, 11 min; ½" Beta II, ½" VHS • Sale: $49.95 for ½" Beta II, $54.95 for ½" VHS

Recounts the adventures of scientists on safari in Africa to kill giant wasps which threaten to bring about destruction of the world. Stars Jim Davis and Barbara Turner.

THE MONSTER MAKER

Video T.E.N.; 1944 • b/w; 1 hr, 2 min; ½" Beta II, ½" VHS • Sale: $49.95 for ½" Beta II, $54.95 for ½" VHS

Portrays a mad doctor in love with the daughter of a famed pianist who infects her father with a rare disease. Stars J. Carrol Naish, Ralph Morgan, Wanda McKay, and Tala Birell.

THE MONSTER WALKS

Reel Images Inc; Order No. 407; 1932 • b/w; 1 hr; ½" Beta II, ½" VHS • Sale: $39.95 for ½" Beta II, $42.95 for ½" VHS

Presents a mystery with the complement of stormy nights, suspicious couples, weird servants, and a screaming gorilla in the basement. Stars Rex Harrison, Vera Reynolds, and Mischa Auer.

MONSTERS ON THE MARCH (AND A PAIR OF MARVELS)

Reel Images Inc; Order No. 542; 1932-60 • b/w; 25 min; ½" Beta II, ½" VHS • Sale: $29.95 for ½" Beta II, $32.95 for ½" VHS

Presents preview shorts for fourteen horror/science-fiction movies. Includes "The Return of the Fly," "Isle of the Dead," "It Came from Outer Space," "The Ghost of Frankenstein," "Twenty Million Miles to Earth," "I Walked with a Zombie," "The Wolfman," "House of Dracula," and others.

THE MOON IS BLUE

Magnetic Video Corporation; 1953 • b/w; 1 hr, 35 min; ½" Beta II, ½" VHS • Sale: $59.95

Offers a 1950s comedy considered spicy and daring at the time of its release but quite tame by today's standards. Concerns two young men's determined pursuit of a virgin. Stars William Holden, David Niven, Maggie McNamara, and Tom Tully, under the direction of Otto Preminger.

THE MOON SPINNERS

MCA DiscoVision; Order No. D18-511; 1964 • color; 1 hr, 59 min; LaserVision • Sale:$24.95

Presents a Walt Disney Studio adaptation of Mary Stewart's novel, in the style of Hitchcock. Follows a young girl on vacation on the Isle of Crete who becomes involved with a handsome young man and a jewelry smuggling ring. Stars Hayley Mills, Eli Wallach, Peter McEnery, Joan Greenwood, Irene Papas, and the return to the screen of silent film star Pola Negri.

MORE LITTLE ROQUEFORT

Magnetic Video Corporation; Order No. CL-2033; Date not listed • color; 30 min; ½" Beta II, ½" VHS • Sale: $34.95

Offers a compilation of Terrytoon animated cartoons featuring Little Roquefort.

MORGAN THE PIRATE

Magnetic Video Corporation; Order No. CL-4054; 1961 • color; 1 hr, 36 min; ½" Beta II, ½" VHS • Sale: $54.95

Follows the adventures of Henry Morgan, who, being framed with false evidence, is condemned to death. Shows his career from slave to pirate, to buccaneer, to admiral of the fleet. Offers an Italian-made swashbuckler starring Steve Reeves and Valerie LaGrange.

THE MORNING AFTER

Quality X Video Cassette Company; Date not listed • color; 1 hr, 15 min; ½" Beta I, ½" Beta II, ½" VHS • Sale: $99.50

Presents a pornographic film.

attack on Pearl Harbor. Interweaves personal stories of the men who fought the sea battle that turned the tide for the United States in the Pacific. Stars Charlton Heston, Henry Fonda, James Coburn, Glenn Ford, Hal Holbrook, Toshiro Mifune, Robert Mitchum, and Cliff Robertson.

MIGHTY JOE YOUNG
Niles Cinema; Order No. NM-8006; 1949 • b/w; 1 hr, 34 min; 1/2" Beta II, 1/2" VHS • Sale: $54.95

- -

The Nostalgia Merchant; Order No. 8006; 1949 • b/w; 1 hr, 34 min; 1/2" Beta II, 1/2" VHS • Sale: $54.95

- -

Red Fox, Inc; Order No. 8006; 1949 • b/w; 1 hr, 34 min; 1/2" Beta II, 1/2" VHS • Sale: $54.95

Presents a tale of a large and very human ape who is brought back to civilization. Features Terry Moore, Ben Johnson, and Robert Armstrong.

MIGHTY MOUSE
Magnetic Video Corporation; Order No. CL-2008; Date not listed • color; 30 min; 1/2" Beta II, 1/2" VHS • Sale: $44.95

Presents five Terrytoon cartoons featuring Mighty Mouse.

MILESTONES OF THE CENTURY (PART 1)—THE GREAT WARS
Magnetic Video Corporation; Order No. CL-7001; Date not listed • b/w; 2 hrs; 1/2" Beta II, 1/2" VHS • Sale: $54.95

Offers a compilation of authentic three-minute newsreels produced by Pathé News, Inc. Focuses on the major wars of the first half of the twentieth century. Features "Franklin Delano Roosevelt Leads the Nation," "Europe Ablaze—1914-1917," "Hitler's Germany," "Britain's Finest Hour," and "The Korean Conflict."

MILESTONES OF THE CENTURY (PART 2)—20TH CENTURY TURNING POINTS
Magnetic Video Corporation; Order No. CL-7002; Date not listed • b/w; 2 hrs; 1/2" Beta II, 1/2" VHS • Sale: $54.95

Presents a compilation of authentic three-minute newsreels produced by Pathé News, Inc. Focuses on major events which served as turning points of the first half of the twentieth century. Includes "Invention and Industry," "The Era of Flight," "Suffragettes and Prohibition," "The Russian Revolution," and "The Post-War World."

MILLHOUSE
Video Tape Network; Order No. CD 607 for 1/2" Beta II, CD 608 for 1/2" VHS; Date not listed • b/w; 1 hr, 32 min; 1/2" Beta II, 1/2" VHS • Sale: $59.95

Focuses on Richard M. Nixon, the Checkers Speech and the six crises of his political career before Watergate in this political and social commentary.

MINE OWN EXECUTIONER
Cinema Resources; 1949 • b/w; 1 hr, 43 min; 1/2" Beta II, 1/2" VHS • Sale: $45

Focuses on a psychiatrist who practices without a medical degree and the domestic and professional upheaval that follows him. Presents a British film of suspense which stars Burgess Meredith, Kieron Moore, Dulcie Gray, and Michael Shepley.

THE MIRACLE
The Nostalgia Merchant; Order No. 7007; 1970 •

color; 1 hr, 30 min; 1/2" Beta II, 1/2" VHS • Sale: $54.95

Offers the story of a mute boy who befriends Lassie and her pups and saves them from danger. Stars Lassie, Michael· James Wixted, Jack Bannon, Robert Rockwell, and Skip Homeier.

MIRACLE AT LAKE PLACID
Magnetic Video Corporation; Order No. 8003; 1980 • color; 1 hr, 34 min; 1/2" Beta II, 1/2" VHS • Sale: $49.95

Documents and highlights the 1980 Winter Olympics held at Lake Placid, New York. Features Jim McKay, ABC-TV sportscaster, as host.

MIRACLE OF THE WHITE STALLIONS
MCA DiscoVision; Order No. D18-510; 1963 • color; 1 hr, 55 min; LaserVision • Sale:$24.95

Presents a Walt Disney Studio adaptation of the autobiography of Colonel Podhajsky, director of the Spanish Riding School of Vienna. Shows the attempst to keep the prized Lipizzan stallions safe during World War II from airraid bombings and the clutches of the Nazi army. Offers Austrian locations in a film directed by Arthur Hiller. Stars Robert Taylor, Lilli Palmer, Curt Jurgens,Eddie Albert, and James Franciscus.

MIRACLE ON 34TH STREET
Magnetic Video Corporation; Order No. 1072; 1947 • b/w; 1 hr, 36 min; 1/2" Beta II, 1/2" VHS • Sale: $59.95

- -

Niles Cinema; Order No. Cl-1072; 1947 • b/w; 1 hr, 36 min; 1/2" Beta II, 1/2" VHS • Sale: $59.95

Adapts Valentine Davies' tale of Kris Kringle going to work for Macy's department store as the store "Santa Claus" and then going on trial to prove his identity. Stars Maureen O'Hara, John Payne, Edmund Gwenn, Gene Lockhart, William Frawley, Thelma Ritter, and Natalie Wood as a child.

MIRACLES STILL HAPPEN
Magnetic Video Corporation; Order No. CL-5010; 1977 • color; 1 hr, 27 min; 1/2" Beta II, 1/2" VHS • Sale: $54.95

Offers the true-life story of the lone survivor of a 1971 Christmas Eve plane crash in the Peruvian jungle—a 17-year-old schoolgirl. Features Susan Penhaligon, Graziella Galvani, and Paul Muller.

MISS SADIE THOMPSON
Columbia Pictures Home Entertainment ; Order No. BE51415 for 1/2" Beta II, VH10410 for 1/2" VHS; 1953 • color; 1 hr, 31 min; 1/2" Beta II, 1/2" VHS • Sale: $59.95

Recounts Somerset Maugham's tale of a South Sea woman of easy virtue and her confrontation with a fire-and-brimstone preacher. Stars Rita Hayworth, Jose Ferrer, Aldo Ray, and Charles Bronson.

MISTER KINGSTREET'S WAR
Video Communications Inc; Order No. 1070; 1972 • color; 1 hr, 32 min; 1/2" Beta II, 1/2" VHS • Sale: $54.95

Tells the story of a young married couple who, after the fighting and disillusionment of the Spanish Civil War, seek peace in central Africa, where they devote themselves to setting up a game preserve. Shows how their life is disrupted when a vindictive elder brother suddenly shows up. Stars John Saxon and Rossano Brazzi.

MISTRESS PAMELA
FHV Entertainment, Inc; Date not listed • color; 1 hr, 21 min; 1/2" Beta II, 1/2" VHS • Sale: $49.95

Presents a pornographic film.

MORNING GLORY

Blackhawk Films, Inc; Order No. 506-40-0779 for ½″ Beta II, 525-40-0779 for ½″ VHS; 1933 • b/w; 1 hr, 14 min; ½″ Beta II, ½″ VHS • Sale: $49.95

Traces a young actress' attempts to make it on Broadway and her successful stepping-in at the last minute. Features Katharine Hepburn in her first Oscar-winning role, as well as Douglas Fairbanks Jr. and Adolphe Menjou.

MOSES

Vid America; Order No. 926; Date not listed • color; 1 hr; ½″ Beta II, ½″ VHS • Rental: $9.95/wk

Offers a dramatization from the Sunn Classic series, "Greatest Heroes of the Bible." Recounts the story of Moses from the miracle of the Burning Bush to the parting of the Red Sea. Stars Robert Alda, Julie Adams, Lloyd Bochner, Joseph Campanella, Anne Francis, Frank Gorshin, and John Marley.

THE MOST DANGEROUS GAME

Cinema Concepts, Inc.; 1932 • b/w; 1 hr, 3 min; ¾″ U-Matic, ½″ Beta II, ½″ VHS • Sale: $54.95 for ½″ Beta II & VHS, $149.95 for ¾″

- -

The Video Library; Order No. ME-1037; 1932 • b/w; 1 hr, 3 min; ½″ Beta II, ½″ VHS • Sale: $49.95

Features Joel McCrea and Fay Wray in a horror film about an explorer who lives on a remote island and can only relive the thrill of hunting by using humans as his prey.

MOTHER

Northeast Video and Sound, Inc; Order No. 171S; 1926 • b/w; 1 hr, 13 min; ¾″ U-Matic, ½″ EIAJ, ½″ Beta II, ½″ VHS • Sale: $195; Rental: $75/wk

Offers Pudovkin's classic indictment of Czarist life; discusses the abortive 1905 revolution in terms of a mother and her son. Features Vera Baranovskaia and A. P. Christiakov.

MOTHRA

National Film and Video Center; 1962 • color; 1 hr, 31 min; ¾″ U-Matic, ½″ Beta II, ½″ VHS • Rental: $49/1 showing

Recounts how members of an expedition to Infant Island find that the life on the heavily-radiated island consists of women two feet tall who guard a sacred egg. Stars Franky Sakai and Hiroshi Koizumi.

THE MOUSE THAT ROARED

National Film and Video Center; 1959 • color; 1 hr, 23 min; ¾″ U-Matic, ½″ Beta II, ½″ VHS • Rental: $69/1 showing

Presents Peter Sellers playing all of the leaders of the Duchy of Fenwick, which has declared war on the United States, hoping to be splendidly rehabilitated when they lose. Stars Sellers and Jean Seberg.

MOVIE MOVIE

Magnetic Video Corporation; Order No. 9020; 1978 • b/w & color; 1 hr, 47 min; ½″ Beta II, ½″ VHS • Sale: $59.95

- -

Niles Cinema; Order No. CL-9020; 1978 • b/w & color; 1 hr, 47 min; ½″ Beta II, ½″ VHS • Sale: $59.95

- -

RCA SelectaVision VideoDiscs; Order No. 00506; 1978 • b/w & color; 1 hr, 47 min; CED • Sale: $19.98

Presents a parody of an afternoon at the movies in the 1930s. Offers two separate features and a coming attraction with one cast. Includes a black and white box-

Movie Movie.

ing tale a la John Garfield, and a color Busby Berkeley-ish musical. Stars George C. Scott, Trish Van Devere, Eli Wallach, Red Buttons, Barbara Harris, Barry Bostwock, Harry Hamlin, Art Carney, and Ann Reinking.

MOVIE STRUCK

Cable Films; 1937 • b/w; 1 hr, 9 min; ½″ Beta I, ½″ Beta II, ½″ VHS • Sale: $65 for ½″ Beta I, $49.50 for ½″ Beta II & VHS

Offers a musical comedy of a small town girl who makes it big in Hollywood. Stars Patsy Kelly, Jack Haley, Laurel & Hardy, and Mischa Auer.

THE MOVING PICTURE BOYS IN THE GREAT WAR

Blackhawk Films, Inc; Order No. 506-75-0881 for ½″ Beta II, 525-75-0881 for ½″ VHS ; Date not listed • color; 51 min; ¾″ U-Matic, ½″ Beta I, ½″ Beta II, ½″ VHS • Sale: $59.95 for ½″ Beta I, $39.95 for ½″ Beta II & VHS, $69.95 for ¾″

Presents authentic archive films of World War I taken from three countries. Includes sound effects, music, and narration.

THE MOZART STORY

Reel Images Inc; Order No. 39; 1939 • b/w; 1 hr, 35 min; ½″ Beta II, ½″ VHS • Sale: $49.95 for ½″ Beta II, $52.95 for ½″ VHS

Dramatizes the great composer's life in an Austrian film with English dialogue. Features renditions of Mozart selections by the Vienna Philharmonic.

MR. AND MRS. SMITH

Niles Cinema; Order No. NM-8007; 1941 • b/w; 1 hr, 35 min; ½″ Beta II, ½″ VHS • Sale: $54.95

- -

The Nostalgia Merchant; Order No. 8007; 1941 • b/w; 1 hr, 35 min; ½″ Beta II, ½″ VHS • Sale: $54.95

- -

Red Fox, Inc; Order No. 8007; 1941 • b/w; 1 hr, 35 min; ½″ Beta II, ½″ VHS • Sale: $54.95

Presents a Hitchcock-directed comedy of a married couple who discover their marriage isn't legal. Features Carole Lombard, Robert Montgomery, and Jack Carson.

MR. BLANDINGS BUILDS HIS DREAM HOUSE

Niles Cinema; Order No. NM-8008; 1948 • b/w; 1 hr, 33 min; ½″ Beta II, ½″ VHS • Sale: $54.95

- -

The Nostalgia Merchant; Order No. 8008; 1948 • b/w; 1 hr, 33 min; ½″ Beta II, ½″ VHS • Sale: $54.95

Red Fox, Inc; Order No. 8008; 1948 • b/w; 1 hr, 33 min; 1/2" Beta II, 1/2" VHS • Sale: $54.95

Presents a comedy about a couple's difficulties in trying to build their dream house in the country'. Features Cary Grant, Myrna Loy, and Melvin Douglas.

MR. DEEDS GOES TO TOWN

National Film and Video Center; 1936 • b/w; 1 hr, 58 min; 3/4" U-Matic, 1/2" Beta II, 1/2" VHS • Rental: $69/1 showing

Spins the tale of a small-town boy who arrives in New York to collect a $20 million inheritance and is instantly besieged by relatives, reporters, and con men. Stars Gary Cooper and Jean Arthur in a film directed by Frank Capra.

MR. HULOT'S HOLIDAY

Budget Video; 1953 • b/w; 1 hr, 25 min; 1/2" Beta II, 1/2" VHS • Sale: $44.95

Reel Images Inc; Order No. 437; 1953 • b/w; 1 hr, 54 min; 1/2" Beta II, 1/2" VHS • Sale: $49.95 for 1/2" Beta II, $52.95 for 1/2" VHS

Showcases the comic acting and directing talents of Jacques Tati in a film about people at the seaside working laboriously at trying to have fun. Contains mainly sight gags that need no subtitles to be understood. Includes Nathalie Pascaud, Michelle Rolla, Louis Perrault, and Suzy Willy.

MR. LUCKY

Niles Cinema; Order No. NM-8009; 1943 • b/w; 1 hr, 39 min; 1/2" Beta II, 1/2" VHS • Sale: $54.95

The Nostalgia Merchant; Order No. 8009; 1943 • b/w; 1 hr, 39 min; 1/2" Beta II, 1/2" VHS • Sale: $54.95

Red Fox, Inc; Order No. 8009; 1943 • b/w; 1 hr, 39 min; 1/2" Beta II, 1/2" VHS • Sale: $54.95

Presents a comedy of a professional gambler who falls in love with the wealthy young woman he is trying to fleece. Stars Cary Grant, Laraine Day, and Charles Bickford.

MR. MOTO'S LAST WARNING

Budget Video; 1939 • b/w; 1 hr, 11 min; 1/2" Beta II, 1/2" VHS • Sale: $44.95

Reel Images Inc; Order No. 16; 1939 • b/w; 1 hr, 10

Cary Grant, Myrna Loy, and Melvyn Douglas in *Mr. Blandings Builds a Dream House.*

min; 1/2" Beta II, 1/2" VHS • Sale: $49.95 for 1/2" Beta II, $52.95 for 1/2" VHS

Portrays fanatical saboteurs out to destroy the French fleet at Suez and Mr. Moto's ingenious efforts to stop them. Stars Peter Lorre, Ricardo Cortez, and George Sanders.

MR. ROBERTS

WCI Home Video Inc; 1955 • color; 2 hrs, 3 min; 1/2" Beta II, 1/2" VHS • Sale: $55

Follows the comic/tragic attempts of an officer to lead his men, obey his tyrannical commanding officer, and get himself transferred from a cargo ship to a fighting vessel during World War II. Adapts the Broadway play and stars Henry Fonda in the role he played on the stage, as well as Jack Lemmon, William Powell, James Cagney, Betsy Palmer, and Ward Bond, under the direction of John Ford and Mervyn LeRoy.

MR. ROBINSON CRUSOE

Video T.E.N.; 1932 • b/w; 1 hr, 9 min; 1/2" Beta II, 1/2" VHS • Sale: $49.95 for 1/2" Beta II, $54.95 for 1/2" VHS

Depicts Douglas Fairbanks Sr. in an adventure filmed in Tahiti, about a millionaire who bets he can live alone on a desert island, and wins handily. Features Maria Alba and William Farnum.

MR. SMITH GOES TO WASHINGTON

Columbia Pictures Home Entertainment; 1939 • b/w; 2 hrs, 5 min; 1/2" Beta II, 1/2" VHS • Sale: $59.95

Tells of a naive small-town man who is elected to the U.S. Senate, and is almost destroyed by the big-city power brokers in Washington. Stars James Stewart, Jean Arthur, and Claude Rains, under the direction of Frank Capra.

MR. SUPER ATHLETIC CHARM

Blackhawk Films, Inc; Order No. 506-53-0843 for 1/2" Beta II, 525-53-0843 for 1/2" VHS; Date not listed • b/w; 56 min; 3/4" U-Matic, 1/2" Beta I, 1/2" Beta II, 1/2" VHS • Sale: $59.95 for 1/2" Beta I, $39.95 ofr 1/2" Beta II & VHS, $69.95 for 3/4"

Presents a program from the History of the Motion Picture Series. Offers two swashbucklers starring Douglas Fairbanks, Sr. Includes "Black Pirate" and "Thief of Bagdad."

MRS. BARRINGTON

Monarch Releasing Corporation; Date not listed • color; 1 hr, 20 min; 3/4" U-Matic • Sale: $350

Presents a pornographic film.

THE MUPPET MOVIE

Magnetic Video Corporation; Order No. CL-9001; 1979 • color; 1 hr, 34 min; 1/2" Beta II, 1/2" VHS • Sale: $44.95

RCA SelectaVision VideoDiscs; Order No. 00516; 1979 • color; 1 hr, 34 min; CED • Sale: $19.98

Follows Kermit the frog as he travels across the country to become a Hollywood star. Features Madeline Kahn, Mel Brooks, and Steve Martin, along withMuppet performers Jim Henson, Frank Oz, Jerry Nelson, Richard Hunt, and Dave Goelz.

MURDER

Video T.E.N.; 1930 • b/w; 1 hr, 32 min; 1/2" Beta II, 1/2" VHS • Sale: $49.95 for 1/2" Beta II, $54.95 for 1/2" VHS

Focuses on an innocent woman accused, tried and sentenced for a friend's death, who is helped by a great jurist. Stars Herbert Marshall, Nora Baring, and Phyllis Konstam in this early Hitchcock film.

MURDER BY DEATH
Columbia Pictures Home Entertainment; Order No. BE51418 for ½" Beta II, VH10415 for ½" VHS; 1976 • color; 1 hr, 34 min; ½" Beta II, ½" VHS • Sale: $59.95

Offers Neil Simon's screenplay spoofing famous fiction detectives such as Charlie Chan, Sam Spade, Miss Marple and Nick and Nora Charles. Centers around a dinner to which the world's greatest detectives are invited. Stars Peter Sellers, Peter Falk, David Niven, Maggie Smith, James Coco, Alec Guinness, Elsa Lanchester, Eileen Brennan, Nancy Walker, and Truman Capote.

MURDER BY DECREE
Magnetic Video Corporation; Order No. CL-4059; 1978 • color; 2 hrs; ½" Beta II, ½" VHS • Sale: $54.95

Adapts Nicholas Meyer's novel which depicts Sherlock Holmes and Doctor Watson battling Jack the Ripper. Shows the famous detective stalking the murderer, being thwarted by the Establishment, and threatened by a secret society. Stars Christopher Plummer and James Mason. Uses humor and atmospheric set design to recreate Victorian London.

MURDER BY TELEVISION
Reel Images Inc; Order No. 432; 1935 • b/w; 55 min; ½" Beta II, ½" VHS • Sale: $39.95 for ½" Beta II, $42.95 for ½" VHS

Presents a science-mystery in which a master electronics expert is murdered in view of a room full of people during a TV demonstration. Stars Bela Lugosi.

THE MURDER CLINIC
Video Communications Inc; 1966 • color; 1 hr, 27 min; ½" Beta II, ½" VHS • Sale: $54.95

Tells of a remote asylum, containing an assortment of bizarre characters, and of the monster living in the vicinity. Features William Berger and Francoise Prevost.

MURDER, MY SWEET
Niles Cinema; Order No. NM-8010; 1944 • b/w; 1 hr, 35 min; ½" Beta II, ½" VHS • Sale: $54.95

- -
The Nostalgia Merchant ; Order No. 8010; 1944 • b/w; 1 hr, 35 min; ½" Beta II, ½" VHS • Sale: $54.95

- -
Red Fox, Inc; Order No. 8010; 1944 • b/w; 1 hr, 35 min; ½" Beta II, ½" VHS • Sale: $54.95

Features Dick Powell as Philip Marlowe in this Raymond Chandler story involving homicide and blackmail, also starring Claire Trevor and Mike Mazurki. Creates the dark brooding atmosphere that became the trademark of detective films of that era.

MURDER ON THE ORIENT EXPRESS
Fotomat Corp; Order No. B0097 for ½" Beta II, V0097 for ½" VHS; 1974 • color; 2 hrs, 8 min; ½" Beta II, ½" VHS • Sale: $69.95; Rental: $9.95/up to 5 days, applicable to purchase

- -
Paramount Home Video; 1974 • color; 2 hrs, 8 min; ½" Beta II, ½" VHS • Sale: $79.95

Portrays Agatha Christie's dapper detective Hercule Poirot, for whom murder-solving is a precise, intellectual exercise. Follows as he agrees to interview all aboard the famous train's Calais coach, hoping to find the killer of a millionaire before the local police arrive. Stars Albert Finney, Jacqueline Bissett, Sean Connery,

Michael York, Vanessa Redgrave, Ingrid Bergman, Lauren Bacall, Anthony Perkins, Richard Widmark, John Gielgud, and Martin Balsam, under the direction of Sidney Lumet.

MURDERER'S ROW
Columbia Pictures Home Entertainment; Order No. BE51420 for ½" Beta II, VH10418 for ½" VHS; 1966 • color; 1 hr, 48 min; ½" Beta II, ½" VHS • Sale: $59.95

Presents Dean Martin as secret agent Matt Helm trying to locate the kidnapped father of a beautiful woman and battling an arch-villain. Features Ann-Margret, Karl Malden, and Camilla Sparv.

MUTINY ON THE BOUNTY
MGM/CBS Home Video; Order No. M90031; 1962 • color; 2 hrs, 57 min; ½" Beta II, ½" VHS • Sale: $89.95

Presents, on two videocassettes, the tale of tyranny and defiance on the high seas. Stars Marlon Brando as Mr. Christian, and Trevor Howard as Captain Bligh. Features Richard Harris, Hugh Griffith, Richard Haydn, Tim Seely, Percy Herbert, and Tarita.

MY BRILLIANT CAREER
Time-Life Video Club Inc; 1979 • color; 1 hr, 41 min; ½" Beta II, ½" VHS • Sale: $44.95 to members

Reveals the discoveries of a young woman living in Edwardian Australia and fighting to live an independent and fulfilling life. Follows her from her impoverished beginnings in the outback, through the rejection of her grandmother's society, her life as a governess, and the proposal of a loving suitor. Stars Judy Davis and features location photography.

MY FAVORITE BRUNETTE
Cinema Concepts, Inc.; 1947 • b/w; 1 hr, 30 min; ¾" U-Matic, ½" Beta II, ½" VHS • Sale: $54.95 for ½" Beta II & VHS, $149.95 for ¾"

- -
Golden Tapes Video Tape Library; Order No. CC10; 1947 • b/w; 1 hr, 28 min; ½" Beta II, ½" VHS • Sale: $49.95 for ½" Beta II & VHS, $124.95 for ¾"

- -
Ivy Video; 1947 • b/w; 1 hr, 27 min; ¾" U-Matic, ½" Beta II, ½" VHS • Sale: $59.95 for ½" Beta II & VHS, trade-in plan avalable, $225 for ¾"

- -
Northeast Video and Sound, Inc; Order No. 125S; 1947 • b/w; 1 hr, 27 min; ¾" U-Matic, ½" EIAJ, ½" Beta II, ½" VHS • Sale: $225; Rental: $80/wk

- -
Reel Images Inc; Order No. 428; 1947 • b/w; 1 hr, 25 min; ½" Beta II, ½" VHS • Sale: $49.95 for ½" Beta II, $52.95 for ½" VHS

- -
The Video Library; Order No. AE-6004; 1947 • b/w; 1 hr, 30 min; ½" Beta II, ½" VHS • Sale: $49.95

Features Bob Hope, Dorothy Lamour, Peter Lorre, and Lon Chaney in a comedy about a photographer who assumes the role of a detective and gets mixed up with mobsters.

MY LITTLE CHICKADEE
MCA Videocassette, Inc; Order No. 55005; 1940 • b/w; 1 hr, 23 min; ½" Beta II, ½" VHS • Sale: $50

Offers W.C. Fields and Mae West out in the old West. Co-stars Dick Foran, Margaret Hamilton, and Ruth Donnelly.

MY LOVE FOR YOURS
Cable Films; 1939 • b/w; 1 hr, 39 min; ½" Beta I, ½"

Beta II, ½" VHS • Sale: $65 for ½" Beta I, $49.50 for ½" Beta II & VHS

Offers a romantic comedy with a touch of near tragedy and songs by Allan Jones. Stars Fred MacMurray, Madeleine Carroll, and Allan Jones.

Mae West and W.C. Fields in
My Little Chickadee.

MY MAN GODFREY
Ivy Video; 1936 • b/w; 1 hr, 35 min; ¾" U-Matic, ½" Beta II, ½" VHS • Sale: $59.95 for ½" Beta II & VHS, trade-in plan available, $195 for ¾"

Northeast Video and Sound, Inc; Order No. 162S; 1936 • b/w; 1 hr, 35 min; ¾" U-Matic, ½" EIAJ, ½" Beta II, ½" VHS • Sale: $225; Rental: $75/wk

Reel Images Inc; Order No. 37; 1936 • b/w; 1 hr, 35 min; ½" Beta II, ½" VHS • Sale: $49.95 for ½" Beta II, $52.95 for ½" VHS

Depicts the lunacy and decadence of upper-class American society in this comedy geared to Depression audiences. Features William Powell and Carole Lombard in the story of a down-and-out "forgotten man" who becomes butler to a crazy rich family.

MY PAL TRIGGER
Cinema Resources; 1946 • b/w; ½" Beta II, ½" VHS • Sale: $45

Presents a Roy Rogers western which features Gabby Hayes.

MY SISTER, MY LOVE
Niles Cinema; Order No. BT-32 for ½" Beta II, VH-32 for ½" VHS; 1973 • color; 1 hr, 29 min; ½" Beta II, ½" VHS • Sale: $59.95

Recounts the love-hate relationships between two sisters and their lovers. Stars Susan Strasberg, Nathalie Delon, and Giancarlo Giannini.

MYRA BRECKINRIDGE
Magnetic Video Corporation; 1970 • color; 1 hr, 40 min; ½" Beta II, ½" VHS • Sale: $59.95

Offers Gore Vidal's racy satire about a sex-change operation. Stars Mae West, John Huston, Raquel Welch, Rex Reed, Farrah Fawcett, and Roger C. Carmel in this x-rated production.

THE MYSTERIANS
Video Communications Inc; 1959 • color; 1 hr, 25 min; ½" Beta II, ½" VHS • Sale: $54.95

Chronicles the story of a race of beings from a highly advanced planet who invade Earth. Focuses on the efforts of Earth's scientists to develop new weapons to repel the invaders. Stars Kenji Sahara.

MYSTERIES FROM BEYOND EARTH
Video Communications Inc; Date not listed • color; 1 hr, 35 min; ½" Beta II, ½" VHS • Sale: $54.95

Reveals the bizarre world of psychic phenomena through investigation of UFO's, witchcraft, psychic healing, and the Bermuda Triangle.

MYSTERIES FROM BEYOND THE TRIANGLE
Video Communications Inc; Order No. 1074; 1977 • color; 1 hr, 34 min; ½" Beta II, ½" VHS • Sale: $54.95

Records the sixteen-day expedition of a 75-foot schooner sailing from the island of Tortolla to the Bahamas, through the heart of the Triangle. Offers some possible answers to the puzzle of the Bermuda Triangle.

MYSTERIES OF THE GODS
Tape Club of America; Order No. 2705 B; Date not listed • color; 1 hr, 27 min; ½" Beta II, ½" VHS • Sale: $54.95

Presents a motion picture that blends fantasy with fact. Shows William Shatner, who travels to every corner of the earth to bring "proof" that extra-terrestrial life exists.

MYSTERIOUS ISLAND
Columbia Pictures Home Entertainment; 1961 • color; 1 hr, 41 min; ½" Beta II, ½" VHS • Sale: $59.95

Portrays Jules Verne's tale of a group of escaped Civil War POWs who find huge animals on a lost island. Stars Michael Craig, Joan Greenwood, and Herbert Lom, with special effects by Ray Harryhausen.

THE MYSTERIOUS MONSTERS
Vid America; Order No. 908; Date not listed • color; 1 hr, 30 min; ½" Beta II, ½" VHS • Rental: $10.95/wk

Investigates Big Foot, the Loch Ness monster, the Abominable Snowman, and other creatures attested to be real by witnesses examined with lie detectors and hypnosis. Includes psychic Peter Hurkos, who examines the evidence; features Peter Graves as host.

MYSTERIOUS MR. WONG
Cable Films; 1935 • b/w; 1 hr, 2 min; ½" Beta I, ½" Beta II, ½" VHS • Sale: $65 for ½" Beta I, $49.50 for ½" Beta II & VHS

Depicts the off-beat Chinese villain Mr. Wong, who is out to secure the twelve coins of Confucius, which will give their owner unlimited power. Stars Bela Lugosi, Wallace Ford, and Arlien Judge.

MYSTERY MOUNTAIN
Cable Films; 1934 • b/w; 4 hrs; ½" Beta I, ½" Beta II, ½" VHS • Sale: $89.50

Offers a twelve-chapter serial which was the only one made by the popular Ken Maynard, one of Hollywood's earliest cowboy stars. Features the villainous Rattler, who tries to stop the construction of a railroad over Mystery Mountain. Stars Gene Autry and Smiley Burnette.

THE MYSTERY OF KASPAR HAUSER
Time-Life Video Club Inc; 1975 • color; 1 hr, 50 min; ½" Beta II, ½" VHS • Sale: $39.95 to members

Presents a German Language film, with English subtitles, directed by Werner Herzog. Recounts the true story of a man in 1828 who appeared in a town square barely able to walk and unable to speak, clutching an anonymous note saying he had been abandoned at birth, raised in a cellar prison, frequently beaten, and always alone. Shows the townspeople's attempts to teach him, his own innocent wisdom, and innate goodness. Stars Bruno S., Walter Ladengast, and Brigitte Mira.

THE MYSTERY OF THE MARY CELESTE
Reel Images Inc; Order No. 452; 1937 • b/w; 1 hr, 3 min; 1/2" Beta II, 1/2" VHS • Sale: $49.95 for 1/2" Beta II, $52.95 for 1/2" VHS

Presents a drama based on a true incident that occurred in 1872. Relates the story of the Mary Celeste, a derelict ship whose crew mysteriously disappear. Features Bela Lugosi.

MYSTERY PLANE
Thunderbird Films; 1939 • b/w; 1 hr; 3/4" U-Matic, 1/2" Beta I, 1/2" Beta II, 1/2" VHS • Sale: $59.95 for 1/2" Beta I, $39.95

Features aerial acrobatics in a film about World War II ace pilot "Tailspin Tommy." Recounts the kidnapping of Tommy and his realization that one of the kidnappers is his old idol Captain Brady. Features George Trent, Jason Robards, and Milburn Stone.

MYSTERY SQUADRON
Cable Films; 1933 • b/w; 4 hrs; 1/2" Beta I, 1/2" Beta II, 1/2" VHS • Sale: $89.50

- -
Reel Images Inc; Order No. 704; 1933 • b/w; 3 hrs, 45 min; 1/2" Beta II, 1/2" VHS • Sale: $119.95

Offers a twelve-chapter serial featuring air adventure as the "Black Ace" and his death squadron try to wreck the building of a dam. Shows how two pilots pit their skill against mystery planes, equipped with early-day flame throwers. Stars Bob Steele, Big Boy Williams, and Lucile Browne.

THE NAKED AND THE DEAD
Video Communications Inc; 1958 • color; 2 hrs, 11 min; 1/2" Beta II, 1/2" VHS • Sale: $74.95

Adapts Norman Mailer's novel for the screen. Tells the story of an ill-fated patrol in steamy, enemy-held territory. Explores the peculiar antagonisms among the soldiers. Stars Cliff Robertson, Aldo Ray, and Raymond Massey, under the direction of Raoul Walsh.

NAKED CAME THE STRANGER
Quality X Video Cassette Company; Date not listed • color; 1 hr, 27 min; 1/2" Beta I, 1/2" Beta II, 1/2" VHS • Sale: $99.50

- -
TVX Distributors; Order No. R.T. 82; Date not listed • color; 2 hrs; 1/2" Beta II, 1/2" VHS • Sale: $79.50 for 1/2" Beta II, $89.50 for 1/2" VHS

Presents a pornographic film.

NAKED PARADISE
Video Communications Inc; 1978 • color; 1 hr, 26 min; 1/2" Beta II, 1/2" VHS • Sale: $54.95

Offers an "R" rated film about the sexual problems caused when the daughter from a previous marriage moves in with her stepmother and stepsister. Features Laura Gemser and Annie Bell.

NANOOK OF THE NORTH
National Film and Video Center; 1922 • b/w; 55 min; 3/4" U-Matic, 1/2" Beta II, 1/2" VHS • Rental: $39/1 showing

Documents the life of an Eskimo family in the vast Arctic. Contrasts their struggle for survival with the affection they feel for one another, in a film produced, directed, and photographed by Robert J. Flaherty.

NASHVILLE
Fotomat Corp; Order No. B0205 for 1/2" Beta II, V0205 for 1/2" VHS; 1975 • color; 2 hrs, 39 min; 1/2" Beta II, 1/2" VHS • Sale: $69.95; Rental: $9.95/up to 5 days, applicable to purchase

- -
Paramount Home Video; 1975 • Series: Electrical Maintenance Training Program • color; 2 hrs, 39 min; 1/2" Beta II, 1/2" VHS • Sale: $79.95

Presents, on two cassettes, a collage of incidents involving 24 people in the capital of country music. Explores the larger-scale picture of life in America, success as measured in modern life, and the relationship of politics with fame and violence. Introduces new performers as well as a new style of filmmaking by the director, Robert Altman. Stars Lily Tomlin, in her first film role, Shelley Duvall, Henry Gibson, Ronee Blakely, Karen Black, Geraldine Chaplin, Keenan Wynn, and Keith Carradine, who wrote his own music, including "I'm Easy."

NASTY HABITS
Magnetic Video Corporation; Order No. CL-5003; 1977 • color; 1 hr, 32 min; 1/2" Beta II, 1/2" VHS • Sale: $54.95

Spotlights the Watergate scandal with an international cast in a comic allegory, but the setting isn't Washington—it's a convent! Stars Glenda Jackson, Melina Mercouri, Sandy Dennis, Geraldine Page, Anne Meara, Anne Jackson, and Edith Evans.

NAUGHTY COEDS
Tape Club of America; Order No. 2839 B; Date not listed • color; 1 hr, 20 min; 1/2" Beta II, 1/2" VHS • Sale: $54.95

Presents a pornographic film.

NAUGHTY NOSTALGIA, VOLUME 1
Reel Images Inc ; Order No. 401; 1933 • b/w; 31 min; 1/2" Beta II, 1/2" VHS • Sale: $39.95 for 1/2" Beta II, $42.95 for 1/2" VHS

Presents two pornographic silent films. Features "Mixed Relations" and "Bob's Hot Story."

NAUGHTY NOSTALGIA, VOLUME 2
Reel Images Inc; Order No. 535; 1930-40 • b/w; 42 min; 1/2" Beta II, 1/2" VHS • Sale: $39.95 for 1/2" Beta II, $42.95 for 1/2" VHS

Presents three pornographic films from the late 1930's. Includes "The Baby Sitter," "The Opium Den," and "A Day in the Country."

NEGATIVES
Video Communications Inc; Order No. 4004; 1968 •

color; 1 hr, 30 min; 1/2" Beta II, 1/2" VHS • Sale: $54.95

Presents a tragicomedy which tells the story of Theo and Vivien who, overwhelmed by boredom and isolation, choose to replace reality with extended games. Stars Diane Cilento, Glenda Jackson, and Peter McEnery.

NETWORK
MGM/CBS Home Video; Order No. M60012; 1976 • color; 2 hrs; 1/2" Beta II, 1/2" VHS • Sale: $59.95

- -

Niles Cinema; Order No. GM-730; 1976 • color; 2 hrs; 1/2" Beta II, 1/2" VHS • Sale: $59.95

Presents screenwriter Paddy Chayefsky's black comedy look at TV and how we are all manipulated by it. Focuses on news-caster Howard Beal, who is on the brink of a nervous breakdown, gets fired, announces he is going to commit suicide on TV, and becomes a modern Messiah because he made the ratings. Stars Peter Finch, Faye Dunaway, William Holden, Beatrice Straight, Robert Duvall, and Ned Beatty under Sidney Lumet's direction.

THE NEW ADVENTURES OF TARZAN
Reel Images Inc; Order No. 406; 1935 • b/w; 4 hrs, 27 min; 1/2" Beta II, 1/2" VHS • Sale: $99.95

Presents 12 episodes of Tarzan's adventures. Tells how Tarzan travels to the jungles of Guatemala in search of the "Green Goddess"—a native idol which also contains the formula for a powerful explosive. Stars Herman Brix, Ula Holt, and "Jiggs" as N'Kima the monkey.

THE NEW CENTURIONS
Columbia Pictures Home Entertainment; 1972 • color; 1 hr, 43 min; 1/2" Beta II, 1/2" VHS • Sale: $59.95

- -

Time-Life Video Club Inc; 1972 • color; 1 hr, 43 min; 1/2" Beta II, 1/2" VHS • Sale: $59.95 to members

Depicts life behind-the-scenes on the Los Angeles police force, with George C. Scott as a veteran cop facing retirement, and Stacy Keach as a hot-shot rookie. Co-stars Jane Alexander and Rosalind Cash in this adaptation of Joseph Wambaugh's novel.

THE NEW DEAL—THE THIRTIES
Blackhawk Films, Inc; Order No. 506-66-0680 for 1/2" Beta II, 525-66-0680 for 1/2" VHS; Date not listed • b/w; 5 hrs; 3/4" U-Matic, 1/2" Beta I, 1/2" Beta II, 1/2" VHS • Sale: $249.95 for 1/2" Beta I, $199.95 for 1/2" Beta II & VHS, $349.95 for 3/4"

Presents, on 3 tapes, the major news events of the 1930's. Includes The Great Depression, Mahatma Ghandi, Thomas Edison, George Gershwin, Mt. Rushmore, The Spanish Civil War, Al Capone, The Lindbergh baby kidnapping, FDR, Dillinger, bread lines, the 1936 Olympics, Hindenberg, Howard Hughes, and Lou Gehrig. Uses newsreel format.

A NEW GIRL IN TOWN
Monarch Releasing Corporation; Date not listed • color; 1 hr, 26 min; 3/4" U-Matic • Sale: $300

Presents a pornographic film.

A NICE GIRL LIKE ME
Magnetic Video Corporation; Order No. CL-4029; 1969 • color; 1 hr, 31 min; 1/2" Beta II, 1/2" VHS • Sale: $54.95

Chronicles the comic adventures of a naive and disaster-prone young lady emancipated for the first time with an inheritance, romping through European capitals. Stars Barbara Ferris and Harry Andrews.

NICHOLAS AND ALEXANDRA
National Film and Video Center; 1971 • color; 3 hrs, 3 min; 3/4" U-Matic, 1/2" Beta II, 1/2" VHS • Rental: $89/1 showing

Covers the reign of the last Tsar of Russia in an epic that sweeps from Russia's entry into World War I to the assassination of the entire royal family by the Ural Soviets. Stars Micheal Jayston, Janet Suzman, Harry Andrews, and Irene Worth.

A NIGHT AT THE OPERA
MGM/CBS Home Video; Order No. M50009; 1935 • color; 1 hr, 30 min; 1/2" Beta II, 1/2" VHS • Sale: $49.95

- -

Niles Cinema; Order No. GM-731; 1935 • b/w; 1 hr, 30 min; 1/2" Beta II, 1/2" VHS • Sale: $49.95

- -

RCA SelectaVision VideoDiscs; Order No. 00206; 1935 • b/w; 1 hr, 30 min; CED

Presents the Marx Brothers destroying an opera house. Stars Groucho, Chico, and Harpo Marx, Kitty Carlisle, Allan Jones, Walter King, Margaret Dumont, and Sig Ruman.

NIGHT FLIGHT FROM MOSCOW
Magnetic Video Corporation; Order No. CL-4039; 1973 • color; 1 hr, 53 min; 1/2" Beta II, 1/2" VHS • Sale: $54.95

Offers a complex tale of counter-espionage in Cold War Europe, centering on a KGB officer who is actually a double agent for the West. Stars Yul Brynner, Henry Fonda, Virna Lisi, Dirk Bogarde, and Philippe Noiret, under the direction of Henri Verneuil.

NIGHT GAMES
Magnetic Video Corporation; Order No. 4069; 1979 • color; 1 hr, 40 min; 1/2" Beta II, 1/2" VHS • Sale: $59.95

Explores the world of a privileged young woman who is unable to fulfill herself sexually. Features Cindy Pickett, under Roger Vadim's direction.

NIGHT IN NEVADA
Thunderbird Films; 1939 • b/w; 55 min; 3/4" U-Matic, 1/2" Beta I, 1/2" Beta II, 1/2" VHS • Sale: $59.95 for 1/2" Beta I, $39.95 for 1/2" Beta II & VHS, $79.95 for 3/4"

Presents Roy Rogers in a musical western, with accompaniment by the Sons of the Pioneers.

NIGHT OF THE LIVING DEAD
Niles Cinema; Order No. BT-25 for 1/2" Beta II, VH-25 for 1/2" VHS; 1970 • b/w; 1 hr, 30 min; 1/2" Beta II, 1/2" VHS • Sale: $49.95

- -

Thunderbird Films; 1969 • b/w; 1 hr, 30 min; 3/4" U-Matic, 1/2" Beta I, 1/2" Beta II, 1/2" VHS • Sale: $69.95 for 1/2" Beta I, $49.95 for 1/2" Beta II & VHS, $89.95 for 3/4"

- -

VCX; Order No. FC115; 1968 • b/w; 1 hr, 30 min; 1/2" Beta II, 1/2" VHS • Sale: $35.00

Presents a horror thriller about dead bodies that come back to life and devour the living. Features Judith O'Dea, Duane Jones, and Marilyn Eastman in this film with a large cult following, under the direction of George Ramos.

NIGHT PLEASURES
VTS; Date not listed • color; 1 hr, 16 min; 1/2" Beta I, 1/2" Beta II, 1/2" VHS • Sale: $99

Presents a pornographic film.

NIGHT WATCH

Magnetic Video Corporation; Order No. CL-5005; 1973 • color; 1 hr, 37 min; 1/2" Beta II, 1/2" VHS • Sale: $54.95

Probes a secure, affluent woman whose life is invaded by bizarre dreams and visions of brutal murder. Stars Elizabeth Taylor and Laurence Harvey.

NIGHTMARE CASTLE

Discount Video Tapes; 1966 • b/w; 1 hr, 30 min; 1/2" Beta II, 1/2" VHS • Sale: $49.95

Presents a horror film about a doctor who experiments with electricty to regenerate human blood. Features Barbara Steele and Paul Miller.

NIGHTMARE COUNTY

FHV Entertainment, Inc; 1976 • color; 1 hr, 11 min; 1/2" Beta II, 1/2" VHS • Sale: $49.95

Follows the actions of the leader of a young group of farm workers who manages to outwit and outfight the community's leading citizenry, including the sheriff. Stars Sean MacGregor, Gayle Hemingway, R.N. Bullard, and Woody Lee.

NIGHTMARE IN WAX

Fotomat Corp; Order No. B0161 for 1/2" Beta II, V0161 for 1/2" VHS; 1969 • color; 1 hr, 35 min; 1/2" Beta II, 1/2" VHS • Sale: $39.95; Rental: $7.95/up to 5 days, applicable to purchase

- -
Video Communications Inc; Order No. 1077; 1969 • color; 1 hr, 35 min; 1/2" Beta II, 1/2" VHS • Sale: $54.95

Offers a horror film in which a screen star disfigured by a Hollywood producer turns sculptor and works in a dungeon beneath the Hollywood Wax Museum, exacting his revenge by encasing living bodies in wax. Stars Cameron Mitchell and Anne Helm.

NIJINSKY

Fotomat Corp; Order No. B0453 for 1/2" Beta II, V0453 for 1/2" VHS; 1980 • color; 2 hrs, 5 min; 1/2" Beta II, 1/2" VHS • Sale: $54.95; Rental: $9.95/5 days

Relates the story of the legendary dancer Nijinsky, his wife, and his svengali-like lover, the impresario Diaghilev. Stars Alan Bates, Leslie Browne, and the American Ballet Theatre's dancer, George De La Peña.

NINE AGES OF NAKEDNESS

Meda/Media Home Entertainment Inc; Order No. M508; Date not listed • color; 1 hr, 25 min; 1/2" Beta I, 1/2" Beta II, 1/2" VHS • Sale: $54.95

Presents a pornographic film.

NINE DAYS A QUEEN

Budget Video; 1936 • b/w; 1 hr, 20 min; 1/2" Beta II, 1/2" VHS • Sale: $44.95

Chronicles the court intrigue following the death of King Henry VIII and the tragedy of a young woman who finds herself chosen as the short-lived Queen. Stars Cedric Hardwicke, Nova Pilbearn, and John Mills.

9 TO 5

Magnetic Video Corporation; Order No. 1099; 1980 • color; 1 hr, 50 min; 1/2" Beta II, 1/2" VHS • Sale: $69.95

Offers a comedy-fantasy about the power struggle between women employees and their sadistic bosses. Emphasizes the worst possible situations for comic effect. Stars Jane Fonda, Dolly Parton, Lily Tomlin, and Dabney Coleman.

Dolly Parton, Lilly Tomlin, Jane Fonda, and Dabney Coleman in *Nine to Five.*

1941

MCA Videocassette, Inc; Order No. 66007; 1979 • color; 2 hrs, 1/2" Beta II, 1/2" VHS • Sale: $60

- -
MCA DiscoVision; 1979 • color; 2 hrs; LaserVision • Sale: $24.95

Tells of how California residents, alarmed by Pearl Harbor and Japanese submarines, mobilize themselves against an expected invasion—slapstick-style. Stars John Belushi and Dan Aykroyd, under the direction of Steven Spielberg.

NINOTCHKA

RCA SelectaVision VideoDiscs; Order No. 00212; 1939 • b/w; 1 hr, 50 min; CED • Sale: $14.98

Offers Ernst Lubitsch's comedy about a business-like female Russian agent who falls in love in Paris. Stars Greta Garbo, Melvyn Douglas, Ina Claire, Bela Lugosi, Sig Ruman, Felix Bressart, and Richard Carle.

NO PROBLEM

Cinema Concepts, Inc.; 1976 • color; 1 hr, 34 min; 3/4" U-Matic, 1/2" Beta II, 1/2" VHS • Sale: $54.95 for 1/2" Beta II & VHS, $149.95 for 3/4"

- -
The Video Library; Order No. CC-1036; 1976 • color; 1 hr, 34 min; 1/2" Beta II, 1/2" VHS • Sale: $54.95

Presents a French farce concerning a man being pursued and shot by two killers for reasons unknown. Details the resulting problems of disposing with the dead body. Stars Michel Bouquet.

NONE BUT THE LONELY HEART

Niles Cinema; Order No. NM-8011; 1944 • b/w; 1 hr, 53 min; 1/2" Beta II, 1/2" VHS • Sale: $54.95

- -
The Nostalgia Merchant; Order No. 8011; 1944 • b/w; 1 hr, 53 min; 1/2" Beta II, 1/2" VHS • Sale: $54.95

- -
Red Fox, Inc; Order No. 8011; 1944 • b/w; 1 hr, 53 min; 1/2" Beta II, 1/2" VHS • Sale: $54.95

Presents Cary Grant in a rare dramatic role as a cockney wanderer, with Ethel Barrymore as his mother. Costars Barry Fitzgerald, Jane Wyatt, and Dan Duryea, under the direction of Clifford Odets.

NORMA RAE

Magnetic Video Corporation; Order No. CL-1082; 1979 • color; 1 hr, 54 min; 1/2" Beta II, 1/2" VHS • Sale: $44.95

Offers a romantic drama about a textile worker who

joins forces with a New York labor organizar to unionize a southern mill. Stars Sally Field, Ron Leibman, and Beau Bridges, under the direction of Martin Ritt.

THE NORTH AVENUE IRREGULARS
Fotomat Corp; Order No. B1033 for ½" Beta II, V1033 for ½" VHS; 1979 • color; 1 hr, 39 min; ½" Beta II, ½" VHS • Sale: $54.95; Rental: $7.95/5 days

Niles Cinema; Order No. WD-17; 1979 • color; 1 hr, 39 min; ½" Beta II, ½" VHS • Sale: $59.95

Walt Disney Home Video; Order No. 17BS for ½" Beta II, 17VS for ½" VHS; 1979 • color; 1 hr, 39 min; ½" Beta II, ½" VHS • Sale: $59.95

Offers a Walt Disney Studio comedy about a young priest who tackles organized crime with the help of some of his eccentric parishioners. Stars Edward Herrmann, Barbara Harris, Cloris Leachman, Susan Clark, Karen Valentine, and Michael Constantine.

NORTH BY NORTHWEST
RCA SelectaVision VideoDiscs; Order No. 00207; 1959 • color; 2 hrs, 16 min; CED • Sale: $22.98

Presents Alfred Hitchcock's thriller about a man mistaken for a spy by a group of secret agents and their attempts to kill him. Shows his ingenious means of discovering their secret and what it costs him. Stars Cary Grant, Eva Marie Saint, James Mason, Martin Landau, Leo G. Carroll, and Philip Ober.

NORTH DALLAS FORTY
Fotomat Corp; Order No. B0365 for ½" Beta II, V0365 for ½" VHS; 1979 • color; 1 hr, 57 min; ½" Beta II, ½" VHS • Sale: $54.95; Rental: $9.95/5 days

Paramount Home Video; Order No. 8773; 1979 • color; 1 hr, 59 min; ½" Beta II, ½" VHS • Sale: $66.95

Presents a serious and comic look at the unknown side of pro football in an adaptation of Peter Gent's best seller. Shows an aging wide-receiver who is no longer willing to play the games necessary to keep the owners happy. Stars Nick Nolte, Mac Davis, Charles Durning, G.D. Spradlin, Dayle Haddon, and Steve Forrest. Features many pro players.

NORTH OF THE GREAT DIVIDE; DAYS OF OLD CHEYENNE
The Nostalgia Merchant; 1950; 1943 • b/w; 2 hrs; ½" Beta II, ½" VHS • Sale: $59.95

Presents a western double feature. Opens with Roy Rogers and Trigger bringing cattle rustlers to justice in "North of the Great Divide"; features also Penny Edwards. Concludes with "Days of Old Cheyenne," in which a powerful but dishonest political boss hands down the law in the territory of Wyoming. Stars Don "Red" Barry and Lynn Merrick.

NORTH OF THE RIO GRANDE
Videobrary Inc; Order No. 10; 1937 • b/w; 1 hr, 12 min; ½" Beta II, ½" VHS • Sale: $39.95

Presents a Hopalong Cassidy western. Features Cassidy "undercover" avenging the death of his younger brother. Stars William Boyd, George "Gabby" Hayes, and Lee J. Cobb.

THE NORTH STAR
Video T.E.N.; 1943 • b/w; 1 hr, 42 min; ½" Beta II, ½" VHS • Sale: $49.95 for ½" Beta II, $54.95 for ½" VHS

Focuses on a small village in Russia occupied by the Nazis, and its struggle to resist. Includes Anne Baxter, Dana Andrews, Walter Huston, Eric Von Stroheim, Walter Brennan, Farley Granger, Jane Withers, and Dean Jagger.

NORTHEAST OF SEOUL
Tape Club of America; Order No. 2504 B; 1972 • color; 1 hr, 40 min; ½" Beta II, ½" VHS • Sale: $54.95

Presents three conspirators in their quest for the Kuguru Sword, a jewel-encrusted relic dating back to the days of Genghis Khan. Stars Anita Ekberg, John Ireland, and Victor Buono.

Greta Garbo and Melvyn Douglas in *Ninotchka*.

NOSFERATU

Ivy Video; 1922 • b/w; 1 hr, 10 min; ¾" U-Matic, ½" Beta II, ½" VHS • Sale: $59.95 for ½" Beta II & VHS, trade-in plan available, $195 for ¾"

- -
Northeast Video and Sound, Inc; Order No. 1922; 1922 • b/w; 1 hr, 10 min; ¾" U-Matic, ½" EIAJ, ½" Beta II, ½" VHS • Sale: $225; Rental: $75/wk

Introduces the personage of Dracula to the cinema in F. W. Murnau's expressionistic vampire film. Contains the prototypes for many future horror films, although shot mainly on location unlike many studio productions which are in its debt for characterizations and atmosphere.

Carole Lombard and Fredric March in *Nothing Sacred*.

NOTHING SACRED

Thunderbird Films; 1937 • color; 1 hr, 15 min; ¾" U-Matic, ½" Beta I, ½" VHS • Sale: $69.95 for ½" Beta I, $49.95 for ½" Beta II & VHS, $89.95 for ¾"

- -
VCX; Order No. FC101; 1937 • color; 1 hr, 15 min; ½" Beta II, ½" VHS • Sale: $35.00

Tells of a woman who is informed that she has two weeks to live, and is given a "last fling" by a cynical New York newspaper capitalizing on the "human interest" story. Stars Carole Lombard and Frederic March.

NOTORIOUS

Magnetic Video Corporation; Order No. 8011; 1946 • b/w; 1 hr, 41 min; ½" Beta II, ½" VHS • Sale: $59.95

- -
Niles Cinema; Order No. CL-8011; 1946 • b/w; 1 hr, 41 min; ½" Beta II, ½" VHS • Sale: $59.95

Presents Alfred Hitchcock's thriller about espionage set in World War II South America. Concerns a woman who marries a Nazi in order to get information to pass along to the Allies. Stars Cary Grant, Ingrid Bergman, Claude Rains, Louis Calhern, and Moroni Olsen.

NOW YOU SEE 'EM, NOW YOU DON'T

Fotomat Corp; 1972 • color; 1 hr, 28 min; ½" Beta II, ½" VHS • Sale: $49.95; Rental: $9.95/up to 5 days, applicable to purchase

Shows a student who invents a spray that makes whatever it touches invisible and the crooks who want to steal the formula. Presents a Walt Disney Studios production starring Kurt Russell, Cesar Romero, Joe Flynn, Jim Backus, and William Windom.

NUMBER SEVENTEEN

Discount Video Tape; 1932 • b/w; 1 hr, 4 min; ½" Beta II, ½" VHS • Sale: $49.95

Relates how a detective teams up with a lady jewel thief to prevent an enemy gang from escaping the country. Features Leon M. Lion and Anne Grey, under the direction of Alfred Hitchcock.

NURSE MAIDS

Monarch Releasing Corporation; Date not listed • color; 1 hr; ¾" U-Matic • Sale: $300

Presents a pornographic film.

THE ODD COUPLE

Fotomat Corp; Order No. B0033 for ½" Beta II, V0033 for ½" VHS; 1968 • color; 1 hr, 46 min; ½" Beta II, ½" VHS • Sale: $49.95; Rental: $9.95/up to 5 days, applicable to purchase

- -
Paramount Home Video; 1968 • color; 1 hr, 46 min; ½" Beta II, ½" VHS • Sale: $59.95

Presents a film version of the Neil Simon play. Tells the story of the fastidious Felix and the sloppy Oscar, two divorced men who decide to share an apartment. Stars Jack Lemmon, Walter Matthau, and John Fiedler, under the direction of Gene Saks.

THE ODESSA FILE

National Film and Video Center; 1974 • color; 2 hrs, 8 min; ¾" U-Matic, ½" Beta II, ½" VHS • Rental: $89/1 showing

Pits a journalist against a secret organization formed to protect, finance, and reestablish fugitive S.S. members. Stars Jon Voight as the journalist tracking a death camp's commandant through a clue found in the diary of a camp survivor. Features Mary Tamm and Maximilian Schell.

Jack Lemmon and Walter Matthau in *The Odd Couple*.

**Leslie Howard
and Bette Davis in
Of Human Bondage.**

ODYSSEY
Video Home Library; Order No. VX-108; Date not listed • color; 2 hrs; ½″ Beta II, ½″ VHS • Sale: $99.95

VTS; Order No. WWV10E34; Date not listed • color; 1 hr, 26 min; ½″ Beta I, ½″ Beta II, ½″ VHS • Sale: $99

Presents a pornographic film.

OF HUMAN BONDAGE
Ivy Video; 1934 • b/w; 1 hr, 30 min; ¾″ U-Matic, ½″ Beta II, ½″ VHS • Sale: $59.95 for ½″ Beta II & VHS, trade-in plan available, $195 for ¾″

Northeast Video and Sound, Inc; Order No. 121S; 1934 • b/w; 1 hr, 30 min; ¾″ U-Matic, ½″ EIAJ, ½″ Beta II, ½″ VHS • Sale: $195; Rental: $75/wk

Spares no expense in bringing W. Somerset Maugham's "novel of initiation" to the screen in the first of several versions. Stars Leslie Howard as the young man who is tormented by love for waitress Bette Davis.

OH! CALCUTTA!
Vid America; Order No. 905; 1969 • color; 1 hr, 27 min; ½″ Beta II, ½″ VHS • Rental: $12.95/wk

Presents an expanded production of the erotic Broadway musical comedy with singing and dancing numbers. Features Bill Macy.

OH, GOD!
Fotomat Corp; Order No. B0307 for ½″ Beta II, V0307 for ½″ VHS; 1977 • color; 1 hr, 44 min; ½″ Beta II, ½″ VHS • Sale: $49.95

WCI Home Video Inc; 1977 • color; 1 hr, 44 min; ½″ Beta II, ½″ VHS • Sale: $55

Depicts a young supermarket produce manager who begins receiving messages from God in the form of George Burns. Relates God's wish that mankind acknowledge Him and that He is alive and well. Stars George Burns, John Denver, Teri Garr, Paul Sorvino, George Furth, Ralph Bellamy, and Bernard Hughes, under the direction of Carl Reiner.

OKLAHOMA
MGM/CBS Home Video; Order No. C70020; 1955 • color; 2 hrs, 20 min; ½″ Beta II, ½″ VHS • Sale: $69.95

Adapts for the screen the Rodgers and Hammerstein trend-setting musical about love affairs in small community. Stars Gordon MacRae, Shirley Jones, Charlotte Greenwood, Rod Steiger, Gloria Grahame, Eddie Albert, James Whitmore, and Gene Nelson. Includes "Oh What A Beautiful Morning," "The Surrey With The Fringe On Top," and "People Will Say We're In Love."

OLD BORROWED AND STAG
Quality X Video Cassette Company; Date not listed • b/w; 1 hr, 13 min; ½″ Beta I, ½″ Beta II, ½″ VHS • Sale: $99.50

Presents a pornographic film.

OLD BOYFRIENDS
Magnetic Video Corporation; Order No. CL-4063; 1979 • color; 1 hr, 43 min; ½″ Beta II, ½″ VHS • Sale: $44.95

Offers a drama of a woman searching for herself through the lost loves of her past. Features Talia Shire, Richard Jordan, John Belushi, and Keith Carradine.

THE OLD CURIOSITY SHOP
Magnetic Video Corporation; Order No. CL-4017; 1975 • color; 1 hr, 54 min; ½″ Beta II, ½″ VHS • Sale: $54.95

Offers a lighthearted, yet sometimes sad, musical adaptation of the 19th century Dickens classic, as Quilp, a greedy money-lender, teams up with a corrupt lawyer to take over the Old Curiosity Shop. Stars Anthony Newley and David Hemmings.

OLD YELLER
Fotomat Corp; 1957 • color; 1 hr, 23 min; ½″ Beta II, ½″ VHS • Sale: $49.95; Rental: $9.95/up to 5 days, applicable to purchase

RCA SelectaVision VideoDiscs; Order No. 00708; 1957 • color; 1 hr, 23 min; CED • Sale: $19.98

Presents a film produced by the Walt Disney Studios. Adapts Fred Gipson's novel about a boy who loves his old yellow hunting dog. Takes place on a Texas farm in 1859. Stars Fess Parker, Dorothy McGuire, Tommy Kirk, and Chuck Connors.

Mark Lester and Oliver Reed in *Oliver!*

OLIVER

National Film and Video Center; 1968 • color; 2 hrs, 46 min; ¾" U-Matic, ½" Beta II, ½" VHS • Rental: $89/1 showing

Presents a musical based on Dickens' novel "Oliver Twist," about an orphan raised in the workhouse who is sold as a servant and escapes to London to join a gang of young pickpockets and thieves. Stars Ron Moody, Oliver Reed, Shani Wallis, Mark Lester, and Jack Wild.

OLIVER TWIST

Video T.E.N.; 1933 • b/w; 1 hr, 10 min; ½" Beta II, ½" VHS • Sale: $49.95 for ½" Beta II, $54.95 for ½" VHS

Offers the first sound version of Dickens' story of an orphan boy amid London's underworld. Features Dickie Moore, Irving Pichel, William Boyd, Doris Lloyd, Barbara Kent, and Alec B. Francis.

OLIVER'S STORY

Fotomat Corp; Order No. B0229 for ½" Beta II, V0229 for ½" VHS; 1979 • color; 1 hr, 30 min; ½" Beta II, ½" VHS • Sale: $49.95; Rental: $7.95/5 days

Continues "Love Story" as Oliver Barrett IV faces life after Jennifer's death and approaches a new love. Stars Ryan O'Neal, Candice Bergen, Nicola Pagett, and Ray Milland.

OLLY, OLLY OXEN FREE

Time-Life Video Club Inc; Date not listed • color; 1 hr, 33 min; ½" Beta II, ½" VHS • Sale: $34.95 to members

Offers an adventure story for children about two boys, an old restored balloon, and a lady junkyard owner, including a floating journey from one end of California to the other. Features Katharine Hepburn.

THE OMEN

Magnetic Video Corporation; Order No. CL-1079; 1976 • color; 1 hr, 51 min; ½" Beta II, ½" VHS • Sale: $54.95

Traces the birth of the anti-Christ as the son of an American couple living in England. Unveils the boy's identity through a series of bizarre incidents and omens discovered by a photographer. Follows the anguish of the parents who find out and then must decide what to do with their son. Stars Gregory Peck, Lee Remick, Billie Whitelaw, David Warner, Harvey Stephens, and Patrick Troughton.

ON APPROVAL

Budget Video; 1944 • b/w; 1 hr, 20 min; ½" Beta II, ½" VHS • Sale: $44.95

Presents a British drawing-room comedy in Marx Brothers style, as an impoverished duke sets out to romantically conquer an American heiress. Spotlights Clive Brook, Beatrice Lillie, Googie Withers, and Roland Culver.

ON THE TOWN

RCA SelectaVision VideoDiscs; Order No. 00208; 1949 • color; 1 hr, 38 min; CED • Sale: $14.98

Presents the Comden-Green musical about three sailors on leave in New York City and their new-found girlfriends. Includes "New York, New York." Stars Gene Kelly, Frank Sinatra, Vera-Ellen, Betty Garrett, Ann Miller, Jules Munshin, and Alice Pearce.

ON THE WATERFRONT

National Film and Video Center; 1954 • b/w; 1 hr, 48 min; ¾" U-Matic, ½" Beta II, ½" VHS • Rental: $69/1 showing

Dramatizes the story of a waterfront gang leader's kid brother, who testifies before the Crime Commission after his older brother has been murdered. Stars Marlon Brando as the despised punk who becomes the longshoremen's leader. Features Eva Marie Saint, Rod Steiger, Karl Malden, and Lee J. Cobb, under the direction of Elia Kazan.

ON VACATION WITH MICKEY MOUSE AND FRIENDS

Fotomat Corp; Order No. B1021 for ½" Beta II, V1021 for ½" VHS; Date not listed • color; 47 min; ½" Beta II, ½" VHS • Sale: $44.95; Rental: $7.95/5 days
- -
MCA DiscoVision; Order No. D61-503; Date not listed; LaserVision • color; 1 hr • Sale: $9.95
- -
Niles Cinema; Order No. WD-20; Date not listed • color; 47 min; ½" Beta II, ½" VHS • Sale: $44.95
- -
Vid America ; Order No. 991; 1980 • color; 47 min; ½" Beta II, ½" VHS • Sale: $44.95; Rental: $9.95/wk, applicable to purchase
- -
Walt Disney Home Video; Order No. 20BS for ½" Beta II, 20VS for ½" VHS; Date not listed • color; 47 min; ½" Beta II, ½" VHS • Sale: $44.95

Presents a collection of Walt Disney cartoons featuring

Mickey Mouse, Pluto, and Goofy. Includes "Canine Caddy," "Bumble Bee," "Goofy and Wilbur," "Dude Duck," "Mickey's Trailer," and "Hawaiian Holiday."

ONCE IS NOT ENOUGH
Fotomat Corp; Order No. B0269 for ½" Beta II, V0269 for ½" VHS; 1975 • color; 2 hrs, 1 min; ½" Beta II, ½" VHS • Sale: $49.95; Rental: $9.95/up to 5 days, applicable to purchase

Adapts Jacqueline Susann's final novel about a young woman born into the jet-set world. Tells of her father-fixation and the conflict within her as she tries to reconcile her dreams with the world of the privileged, who become amoral and corrupt. Stars Kirk Douglas, Alexis Smith, David Janssen, George Hamilton, Deborah Raffin, and Brenda Vaccaro.

ONCE UPON A BROTHERS GRIMM
Fotomat Corp; Order No. B0129 for ½" Beta II, V0129 for ½" VHS; Date not listed • color; 1 hr, 42 min; ½" Beta II, ½" VHS • Sale: $49.95; Rental: $9.95/up to 5 days, applicable to purchase
- -
Video Communications Inc; Order No. 1080; 1978 • color; 1 hr, 42 min; ½" Beta II, ½" VHS • Sale: $54.95

Presents a musical fantasy in which the Brothers Grimm meet a succession of their most famous storybook characters. Stars Dean Jones, Paul Sand, Cleavon Little, Arte Johnson, Ruth Buzzi, and Chita Rivera.

ONCE UPON A TIME SHE WAS
Entertainment Video Releasing, Inc; Order No. 1097; Date not listed • color; 1 hr, 20 min; ½" Beta II, ½" VHS • Sale: $69.95 for ½" Beta II, $74.95 for ½" VHS

Presents a pornographic film.

THE ONE AND ONLY
Fotomat Corp; Order No. B0027 for ½" Beta II, V0027 for ½" VHS; 1978 • color; 1 hr, 38 min; ½" Beta II, ½" VHS • Sale: $49.95; Rental: $9.95/up to 5 days, applicable to purchase

Portrays an outrageously self-confident, but out-of-work, actor who dreams of stardom and leaves college to pursue fame and fortune in the most unlikely of arenas—the wrestling ring. Stars Henry Winkler, Kim Darby, and Gene Saks, under the direction of Carl Reiner.

Marie Saint and Marlon Brando in *On The Waterfront*.

THE ONE AND ONLY, GENUINE, ORIGINAL FAMILY BAND
MCA DiscoVision; Order No: D18-513; 1968 • color; 1 hr, 50 min; LaserVision • Sale: $24.95

Offers a Walt Disney Studio production which centers around the adventures of the ten-member Bower family band, which becomes involved in the presidential election between Cleveland and Harrison in the 1880's. Features music and lyrics by Richard M. Sherman and Robert B. Sherman. Stars Walter Brennan, Buddy Ebsen, Lesley Ann Warren, John Davidson, Wally Cox, Richard Deacon, and Kurt Russell.

ONE BODY TOO MANY
Video T.E.N.; 1944 • b/w; 1 hr, 15 min; ½" Beta II, ½" VHS • Sale: $49.95 for ½" Beta II, $54.95 for ½" VHS

Spoofs murder mysteries in this tale of a salesman, a "haunted" house, a group of heirs, a disappearing corpse, and an ominous butler. Stars Jack Haley, Jean Parker, Bela Lugosi, Blanche Yurka, Lyle Talbot, and Douglas Fowley.
The Nostalgia Merchant; Order No. 7004; 1956 • color; 1 hr, 15 min; ½" Beta II, ½" VHS • Sale: $54.95

Offers a three-part serialized Lone Ranger adventure compiled on one video cassette. Relates how the "Masked Rider of the Plains" and Tonto prevent an assassination, stop a series of murders, and capture an outlaw who is pretending to be the Lone Ranger. Features Clayton Moore and Jay Silverheels.

ONE MILLION B.C.
The Nostalgia Merchant; Order No. 4006; 1940 • b/w; 1 hr, 20 min; ½" Beta II, ½" VHS • Sale: $54.95

Relates the saga of primitive cavemen battling dinosaurs and other monsters in the prehistoric world. Stars Victor Mature, Carole Landis, and Lon Chaney, Jr.

ONE RAINY AFTERNOON
Reel Images Inc; Order No. 94; 1936 • b/w; 1 hr, 18 min; ½" Beta II, ½" VHS • Sale: $49.95 for ½" Beta II, $52.95 for ½" VHS
- -
Video T.E.N.; 1936 • b/w; 1 hr, 20 min; ½" Beta II, ½" VHS • Sale: $49.95 for ½" Beta II, $54.95 for ½" VHS

Presents a comedy in which a "kissing bandit" becomes a star. Features Frances Lederer, Ida Lupino, and Hugh Herbert.

1001 DANISH DELIGHTS
Entertainment Video Releasing, Inc; Date not listed • color; 1 hr, 20 min; ½" Beta II, ½" VHS • Sale: $79.95

Presents a pornographic comedy film.

THE ONION FIELD
Magnetic Video Corporation; Order No. 4064; 1979 • color; 2 hrs, 2 min; ½" Beta II, ½" VHS • Sale: $59.95
- -
Vid America; Order No. 465; 1979 • color; 2 hrs, 6 min; ½" Beta II, ½" VHS • Rental: $13.95/wk, applicable to purchase

Adapts for the screen Joseph Wambaugh's book about a true incident involving the kidnapping of two policemen and the murder of one of them. Stars James Woods, John Savage, Franklyn Seales, and Ronny Cox.

THE ONLY GAME IN TOWN
Golden Tapes Video Tape Library; Order No. F-1010; 1970 • color; 1 hr, 53 min; ½" Beta II, ½" VHS • Sale: $49.95 for ½" Beta & II VHS, $124.95 for ¾"

- -
Magnetic Video Corporation; Order No. CL-1010; 1970 • color; 1 hr, 53 min; ½" Beta II, ½" VHS • Sale: $44.95

Presents a drama concerning the romance of a Las Vegas chorus girl and a compulsive gambler. Stars Elizabeth Taylor and Warren Beatty in this adaptation of the play by Frank D. Gilroy.

OPEN CITY
Ivy Video; 1946 • b/w; 1 hr, 45 min; ¾" U-Matic, ½" Beta II, ½" VHS • Sale: $59.95 for ½" Beta II & VHS, trade-in plan available, $225 for ¾"

- -
Northeast Video and Sound, Inc; 1946 • b/w; 1 hr,45 min; ¾" U-Matic, ½" EIAJ, ½" Beta II, ½" VHS • Sale: $225; Rental: $80/wk

Tells a story of underground resistance to the Nazis in Rome during the last days of World War II, through the neo-realistic style of director Roberto Rossellini. Stars Aldo Fabrizi and Anna Magnani as Italian partisans in this first Italian film to surface after the war.

THE OPENING OF MISTY BEETHOVEN
TVX Distributors; Order No. R.T. 86; Date not listed • color; 2 hrs; ½" Beta II, ½" VHS • Sale: $79.50 for ½" Beta II, $89.50 for ½" VHS

Presents a pornographic film.

OPERATION SNATCH
Thunderbird Films; 1962 • b/w; 1 hr, 20 min; ¾" U-Matic, ½" Beta I, ½" Beta II, ½" VHS • Sale: $69.95 for ½" Beta I, $49.95 for ½" Beta II & VHS, $89.95 for ¾"

Recounts a comic tale of attempts to preserve a species of apes on Gibraltar, undertaken in bumbling fashion by the British army. Stars Terry Thomas, Lionel Jeffries, George Sanders, and Jackie Lane.

ORAL CONTRACT
Monarch Releasing Corporation; Date not listed • color; 1 hr, 2 min; ¾" U-Matic • Sale: $350

Presents a pornographic film.

ORCA: THE KILLER WHALE
Fotomat Corp; Order No. B0051 for ½" Beta II, V0051 for ½" VHS; 1977 • color; 1 hr, 32 min; ½" Beta II, ½" VHS • Sale: $49.95; Rental: $9.95/up to 5 days, applicable to purchase

Features special effects on a gigantic scale in this tale of one powerful being against another: a strong, determined fisherman versus a giant whale. Recounts how the whale seeks revenge when his pregnant mate is maimed and killed by the fisherman. Stars Richard Harris, Charlotte Rampling, and Keenan Wynn.

ORPHEUS
Budget Video; 1949 • b/w; 1 hr, 26 min; ½" Beta II, ½" VHS • Sale: $44.95

Reveals the poetic filmmaking gifts of Jean Cocteau in a modern-day version of the Orpheus legend, as a Parisian poet is drawn into a liaison with the shadowy Princess of Death. Stars Jean Marais, Maria Casares, Maria Dea, and Juliette Greco; in French with subtitles.

THE OTHER SIDE OF THE MOUNTAIN
MCA DiscoVision; Order No. 10-003; 1977 • color; 1 hr, 43 min; LaserVision • Sale: $24.95

Portrays the true story of Jill Kinmont, who, while participating at the pre-Olympic ski trials in 1955, suffered a devastating accident which paralyzed her from the neck down. Follows her efforts to achieve a college education and a career and her biggest hurdle, to accept love. Stars Marilyn Hassett, Beau Bridges, Nan Martin, and Belinda J. Montgomery.

OUR DAILY BREAD
Budget Video; 1934 • b/w; 1 hr, 11 min; ½" Beta II, ½" VHS • Sale: $44.95

Focuses upon the hardships of the Depression years as strangers unite to eke out a livelihood from subsistence farming. Stars Karen Morley and Tom Keene under the direction of King Vidor.

OUR RELATIONS
The Nostalgia Merchant; 1936 • b/w; 1 hr, 5 min; ½" Beta II, ½" VHS • Sale: $54.95

Presents a Laurel and Hardy comedy feature involving mistaken identity when the duo are confused with their twin brothers. Stars Stan Laurel, Oliver Hardy, and Alan Hale, under the direction of Harry Lachman. Offers also a Hal Roach comedy short.

OUR TOWN
Northeast Video and Sound, Inc; Order No. 183S; 1940 • b/w; 1 hr, 38 min; ¾" U-Matic, ½" EIAJ, ½" Beta II, ½" VHS • Sale: $195; Rental: $75/wk

Offers an adaptation of Thornton Wilder's play about a small New England town and its inhabitants, who each reveal their private dramas. Stars William Holden, Martha Scott, Thomas Mitchell, and Guy Kibbee.

OUT CALIFORNIA WAY; RED RIVER SHORE
The Nostalgia Merchant; Order No. 5008; 1946, 1953 • b/w & color; 2 hrs; ½" Beta II, ½" VHS • Sale: $59.95

Presents a western double feature. Offers Monte Hale in a behind-the-scenes look at a cowboy trying to break into western movies; filmed in color. Concludes with Rex Allen and Koko trying to stop an oil swindle; filmed in black and white.

OUT OF THE PAST
Niles Cinema; Order No. NM-8012; 1947 • b/w; 1 hr, 37 min ; ½" Beta II, ½" VHS • Sale: $54.95

- -
The Nostalgia Merchant; Order No. 8012; 1947 • b/w; 1 hr, 37 min; ½" Beta II, ½" VHS • Sale: $54.95

- -
Red Fox, Inc; Order No. 8012; 1947 • b/w; 1 hr, 37 min; ½" Beta II, ½" VHS • Sale: $54.95

Tells of a detective's entanglements with double-crosses, deceit and murder in this classic example of "film noir." Features Robert Mitchum, Kirk Douglas, and Jane Greer, with script by Geoffry Holmes, based on his novel "Build My Gallows High."

THE OUTER SPACE CONNECTION
Video Communications Inc; Date not listed • color; 1 hr, 38 min; ½" Beta II, ½" VHS • Sale: $54.95

Proposes the theory that life on earth was carried here by a highly advanced civilization of inter-galactic travelers. Features the narration of Rod Serling.

THE OUTLAW
Astro Video Corporation; Order No. WC-100; 1943 • b/w; 1 hr, 46 min; ½" Beta II, ½" VHS • Sale: $59.95

Cable Films; 1943 • b/w; 1 hr, 43 min; ½" Beta I, ½" Beta II, ½" VHS • Sale: $65 for ½" Beta I, $49.50 for ½" Beta II & VHS

VCX; Order No. FC125; 1943 • b/w; 2 hrs, 3 min; ½" Beta II, ½" VHS • Sale: $35.00

Video T.E.N.; 1943 • b/w; 1 hr, 35 min; ½" Beta II, ½" VHS • Sale: $49.95 for ½" Beta II, $54.95 for ½" VHS

Depicts the legend of Billy the Kid and his relationship with Doc Holliday and Holliday's girl, in a film considered sensational in its time. Stars Jane Russell, Walter Huston, and Thomas Mitchell under the direction of Howard Hughes.

OUTRAGEOUS
Time-Life Video Club Inc; 1977 • color; 1 hr, 40 min; ½" Beta II, ½" VHS • Sale: $39.95 to members

Offers female impersonator Craig Russell doing Channing, Streisand, Merman, Garland, Davis, and Bankhead, while playing a hairdresser involved with a pregnant schizophrenic. Co-stars Hollis McLaren, under the direction of Richard Benner.

OUTSIDE THE LAW
Blackhawk Films, Inc; Order No. 506-52-0844 for ½" Beta II, 525-52-0844 for ½" VHS; 1921 • b/w; 1 hr, 17 min; ¾" U-Matic, ½" Beta I, ½" Beta II, ½" VHS • Sale: $89.95 for ½" Beta I, $39.95 for ½" Beta II & VHS, $99.95 for ¾"

Presents Lon Chaney, Sr. playing two roles in a tale of crime and repentance. Shows him as the underworld hood "Black Mike Sylva" and the Chinese servant "Ah Wing." Includes color-toned black and white film, and a musical score.

OVERBOARD
Time-Life Video Club Inc; Date not listed • color; 1 hr, 38 min; ½" Beta II, ½" VHS • Sale: $39.95 to members

Tells of a couple whose sailing trip to the South Seas becomes a nightmare when the woman falls overboard. Follows the man's desperate search for her and his growing realization of her importance to his life. Stars Cliff Robertson and Angie Dickenson.

OVERLAND STAGE RAIDERS; COLORADO SERENADE
The Nostalgia Merchant; 1938; 1946 • color; 2 hrs; ½" Beta II, ½" VHS • Sale: $59.95

Presents a western double feature. Follows the adventures of a man who learns his partner plans to steal a gold shipment they have been contracted to deliver, starring John Wayne, Ray Corrigan, and Louise Brooks, in "Overland Stage Raiders." Concludes with Eddie Dean in the musical western "Colorado Serenade," in Cinecolor.

OVERLORDS OF THE U.F.O.
Video Communications Inc; Date not listed • color; 1 hr, 42 min; ½" Beta II, ½" VHS • Sale: $54.95

Claims to separate the real from the sham in an examination of photographic evidence of unidentified flying objects. Asks the question who or what is behind their presence on earth.

THE OWL AND THE PUSSYCAT
Columbia Pictures Home Entertainment; Order No. BE51465 for ½" Beta II, VH10460 for ½" VHS; 1970 • color; 1 hr, 35 min; ½" Beta II, ½" VHS • Sale: $59.95

National Film and Video Center; 1970 • color; 1 hr, 35 min; ¾" U-Matic, ½" Beta II, ½" VHS • Rental: $89/1 showing

Adapts for the screen the Broadway comedy about an intellectual writer who falls for a semi-literate prostitute. Stars Barbra Streisand, George Segal, Robert Klein, Allan Garfield, Roz Kelly under Herbert Ross' direction.

PACK UP YOUR TROUBLES
The Nostalgia Merchant; 1932 • b/w; 1 hr, 8 min; ½" Beta II, ½" VHS • Sale: $54.95

Follows Laurel and Hardy's misadventures in the Army when the two serve their country during World War I. Stars Stan Laurel, Oliver Hardy, Mary Carr, and James Finlayson, under the direction of George Marshall and Ray McCarey. Presents also a Hal Roach comedy short.

THE PAINTED STALLION
Reel Images Inc; Order No. 696; 1937 • b/w; 2 hrs, 41 min; ½" Beta II, ½" VHS • Sale: $69.95 for ½" Beta II, $73.95 for ½" VHS

Offers a Republic Studio serial western in six episodes starring Ray Corrigan and Hoot Gibson. Follows a wagon train through dangerous territory as a mysterious girl on a painted stallion warns Jim Bowie and Kit Carson of coming danger.

PAISAN
Video T.E.N.; 1948 • b/w; 1 hr, 30 min; ½" Beta II, ½" VHS • Sale: $49.95 for ½" Beta II, $54.95 for ½" VHS

Discount Video Tape; 1948 • b/w; 1 hr, 30 min; ½" Beta II, ½" VHS • Sale: $49.95

Relates a series of six wartime vignettes by neo-realist Roberto Rossellini. Features Maria Michi, Gar Moore, Dale Edmunds, Dots Johnson, Harriet White, Bill Tubbs, and nonprofessionals.

PAL JOEY
National Film and Video Center; 1957 • color; 1 hr, 49 min; ¾" U-Matic, ½" Beta II, ½" VHS • Rental: $69/1 showing

Tells the story of egotistic, talented Joey Evans, a night club entertainer who convinces a wealthy socialite to finance a night club for him. Stars Rita Hayworth, Frank Sinatra, and Kim Novak.

PALOOKA
Reel Images Inc; Order No. 450; 1934 • b/w; 1 hr, 34 min; ½" Beta II, ½" VHS • Sale: $49.95 for ½" Beta II, $52.95 for ½" VHS

Presents a comedy-drama based on the comic strip of the same name. Features Jimmy Durante as fast-talking manager Knobby Walsh, singing his classic, "Inka-Dinka-Doo." Stars Stuart Erwin and Lupe Velez.

PANCHO VILLA
Niles Cinema; Order No. BT-30 for ½" Beta II, VH-30

for ½" VHS; 1972 • color; 1 hr, 32 min; ½" Beta II, ½" VHS • Sale: $59.95

Presents the story of the illiterate bandit-hero who invaded the United States and outwitted two pursuing armies. Stars Telly Savalas, Clint Walker, Anne Francis, and Chuck Connors.

PANIC IN NEEDLE PARK
Golden Tapes Video Tape Library; Order No. F-1026; 1971 • color; 1 hr, 50 min; ½" Beta II, ½" VHS • Sale: $49.95 for ½" Beta II & VHS, $124.95 for ¾"

Magnetic Video Corporation; Order No. CL-1026; 1971 • color; 1 hr, 50 min; ½" Beta II, ½" VHS • Sale: $44.95

The Video Library; Order No. MV-1026; 1971 • color; 1 hr, 50 min; ½" Beta II, ½" VHS • Sale: $44.95

Dramatizes the lives of two New York youths who become heroin addicts. Chronicles their decline into a low-life world of prostitutes, pimps, and crooks. Stars Al Pacino, Kitty Winn, and Alan Vint.

THE PAPER CHASE
Golden Tapes Video Tape Library; Order No. F-1046; 1973 • color; 1 hr, 51 min; ½" Beta II, ½" VHS • Sale: $49.95 for ½" Beta II & VHS, $124.95 for ¾"

Magnetic Video Corporation; Order No. CL-1046; 1973 • color; 1 hr, 51 min; ½" Beta II, ½" VHS • Sale: $54.95

The Video Library; Order No. MV-1046; 1973 • color; 1 hr, 51 min; ½" Beta II, ½" VHS • Sale: $54.95

Recounts the pressure-filled freshman year of a student at Harvard Law School. Reveals how his romance with the daughter of a tyrannical professor compounds his problems. Stars Timothy Bottoms, John Houseman, and Lindsay Wagner.

PAPER MOON
Paramount Home Video; 1973 • color; 1 hr, 42 min; ½" Beta II, ½" VHS • Sale: $59.95

RCA SelectaVision VideoDiscs; Order No. 00626; 1973 • b/w; 1 hr, 42 min; CED • Sale: $19.98

Follows the antics of a con man in depression-ridden Kansas as he teams up with a cigarette-smoking nine-year-old in order to sell a carload of deluxe bibles to a list of newly-widowed ladies. Stars Ryan O'Neal, his daughter Tatum, Madeline Kahn, and John Hillerman, under the direction of Peter Bogdanovich.

PARADISE, HAWAIIAN STYLE
Magnetic Video Corporation; Order No. CL-2006; 1966 • color; 1 hr, 31 min; ½" Beta II, ½" VHS • Sale: $44.95

The Video Library; Order No. MV-2006; 1968 • color; 1 hr, 31 min; ½" Beta II, ½" VHS • Sale: $44.95

Offers a musical romance concerning an unemployed pilot who starts up a helicopter charter service with his buddy in Hawaii. Shows how the new business flourishes due to old girlfriends sending customers. Stars Elvis Presley, Suzanna Leigh, and James Shigeta.

PARADISE IN HARLEM
Reel Images Inc; Order No. 517; 1940 • b/w; 1 hr, 23 min; ½" Beta II, ½" VHS • Sale: $49.95 for ½" Beta II, $52.95 for ½" VHS

Offers an all-black-cast musical. Tells of the road to skid row as a cabaret performer witnesses a gangland killing and his wife's death. Stars Frank Wilson, Mamie Smith, Edna Mae Harris, Lucky Millender and his Orchestra, and The Juanita Hall Singers.

PARLOR, BEDROOM AND BATH
Video T.E.N.; 1931 • b/w; 1 hr, 15 min; ½" Beta II, ½" VHS • Sale: $49.95 for ½" Beta II, $54.95 for ½" VHS

Highlights Buster Keaton in one of his few sound comedies, the story of a disaster-prone character who is mistaken for a rich playboy. Features Charlotte Greenwood, Reginald Denny, Dorothy Christy, and Cliff Edwards.

**Elvis Presley
in *Paradise,
Hawaiian Style*.**

PARTNERS OF THE PLAINS
Videobrary Inc; Order No. 18; 1938 • b/w; 1 hr, 8 min; 1/2" Beta II, 1/2" VHS • Sale: $39.95

Presents a Hopalong Cassidy western in which an impetuous Englishwoman becomes Cassidy's boss and chief admirer, while at the same time an ex-convict tries to get his revenge on Cassidy. Stars William Boyd and Gwen Goze.

PARTS: THE CLONUS HORROR
Fotomat Corp; Order No. B0191 for 1/2" Beta II, V0191 for 1/2" VHS; 1979 • color; 1 hr, 31 min; 1/2" Beta II, 1/2" VHS • Sale: $49.95; Rental: $9.95/up to 5 days, applicable to purchase

- -
Vid America; Order No. 930; 1979 • color; 1 hr, 30 min; 1/2" Beta II, 1/2" VHS • Rental: $12.95/wk

Tells of a young couple who fall in love at a medical facility, only to discover that they are clones—soon to be frozen and meant to be used as spare parts for their "original" counterparts. Follows their attempts to escape the facility, which is connected to one of the most powerful men on earth, as well as the next President of the United States. Features Timothy Donnelly, Dick Sargent, Keenan Wynn, and Peter Graves.

PASSION
FHV Entertainment, Inc; 1954 • color; 1 hr, 24 min; 1/2" Beta II, 1/2" VHS • Sale: $49.95

Dramatizes the story of one young vaquero who seeks vengeance in California during the Spanish land-grant era of the 1800's. Stars Cornel Wilde and Yvonne De-Carlo.

THE PASSION OF JOAN OF ARC
Reel Images Inc; Order No. 459; 1928 • b/w; 1 hr, 54 min; 1/2" Beta II, 1/2" VHS • Sale: $49.95 for 1/2" Beta II, $52.95 for 1/2" VHS

Presents director Carl Dreyer's view of the trial and execution of the famous Christian martyr. Explores a spartan setting in which the subtle expressions of the characters, as revealed in numerous prolonged close-ups, set the tone. Features Mlle. Falconetti in her most famous role.

THE PASSION POTION
FHV Entertainment, Inc; Date not listed • color; 1 hr, 25 min; 1/2" Beta II, 1/2" VHS • Sale: $49.95

Presents a pornographic film.

PATTON
Blackhawk Films, Inc; Order No. 502-49-0007 for 1/2" Beta II, 515-49-0018 for 1/2" VHS; 1970 • color; 2 hr, 51 min; 1/2" Beta II, 1/2" VHS • Sale: $74.95

- -
Golden Tapes Video Tape Library; Order No. F-1005; 1970 • color; 2 hrs, 51 min; 1/2" Beta II, 1/2" VHS • Sale: $49.95 for 1/2" Beta II & VHS, $124.95 for 3/4"

- -
Magnetic Video Corporation; Order No. CL-1005; 1970 • color; 2 hrs, 51 min; 1/2" Beta II, 1/2" VHS • Sale: $64.95

- -
RCA SelectaVision VideoDiscs; Order No. 00110; 1970 • color; 2 hrs, 49 min; CED • Sale: $22.98

- -
The Video Library; Order No. MV-1005; 1970 • color; 2 hr, 51 min; 1/2" Beta II, 1/2" VHS • Sale: $74.95

Offers a biography of the World War II general who won great acclaim for his achievements despite a fiery personality. Stars George C. Scott, Karl Malden, Stephen Young, and Michael Strong, under the direction of Franklin Schaffner.

PEARL OF THE SOUTH PACIFIC
FHV Entertainment, Inc; 1955 • color; 1 hr, 26 min; 1/2" Beta II, 1/2" VHS • Sale: $49.95

Offers a romantic adventure story set in the tropics in which a woman and two greedy men attempt to steal a wealth in pearls owned by the islanders. Stars Dennis Morgan, Virginia Mayo, and David Farrar.

PECK'S BAD BOY WITH THE CIRCUS
Reel Images Inc; Order No. 457; 1938 • b/w; 1 hr, 11 min; 1/2" Beta II, 1/2" VHS • Sale: $49.95 for 1/2" Beta II, $52.95 for 1/2" VHS

Presents a comedy in which young Peck and his pals almost wreck the circus, then head to a camp where the youngster wins the obstacle race in his own way. Stars Tommy Kelly, Ann Gillis, Spanky Macfarland, Edgar Kennedy, and Billy Gilberto.

PENNIES FROM HEAVEN
National Film and Video Center; 1936 • color; 1 hr, 21 min; 3/4" U-Matic, 1/2" Beta II, 1/2" VHS • Rental: $59/1 showing

Spins a tale of an ex-convict who befriends a poverty-striken family and ends up marrying the social worker who had wanted to send the youngest child to an orphanage. Stars Bing Crosby and Madge Evans.

PENNY SERENADE
Reel Images Inc; Order No. 40; 1941 • b/w; 1 hr, 58 min; 1/2" Beta II, 1/2" VHS • Sale: $49.95 for 1/2" Beta II, $52.95 for 1/2" VHS

- -
Video T.E.N.; 1941 • b/w; 2 hrs, 5 min; 1/2" Beta II, 1/2" VHS • Sale: $59.95 for 1/2" Beta II, $64.95 for 1/2" VHS

Offers a story of a young couple who fall in love, marry, and then adopt a child after their baby dies. Stars Cary Grant and Irene Dunne under George Stevens' direction.

George C. Scott and Karl Malden in _Patton_.

125

THE PEOPLE NEXT DOOR

Magnetic Video Corporation; 1970 • color; 1 hr, 33 min; 1/2" Beta II, 1/2" VHS • Sale: $44.95

Depicts two suburban families struggling with the problem of teenage drug addiction. Stars Eli Wallach, Julie Harris, Hal Holbrook, and Cloris Leachman.

PEOPLE OF THE SEA

Video Communications Inc; Order No. 3011; Date not listed • color; 46 min; 1/2" Beta II, 1/2" VHS • Sale: $44.95

Features Jean-Michel Cousteau and shark photographer Ron Taylor, who explore a plain that was covered by water twenty-five million years ago but is now dry. Follows them as they look for fossils or active remains of life in the sediment and make some interesting discoveries. Relives the shark attack on businessman Rodney Fox and his amazing recovery.

PEPE LE MOKO

Budget Video; 1936 • b/w; 1 hr, 35 min; 1/2" Beta II, 1/2" VHS • Sale: $44.95

Recounts the adventures of a small-time gangster tempted from an Algiers hide-out by his love for a beautiful Parisienne; in French with English subtitles. Stars Jean Gabin and Mireille Balin.

PERFECT FOOLS

Video Action Library; Order No. BH02; 1929-33 • color; 55 min; 1/2" Beta I, 1/2" Beta II, 1/2" VHS • Rental: $15/1 wk, $7.50 ea add'l wk

Offers four short comedies on one tape. Starts with "Faro Nell" (1929) starring Louis Fazanda, a western satire. Continues with W.C. Fields in "The Dentist" (1932). Follows with "In My Merry Oldsmobile" (1932) with Johnny Steele. Concludes with "Techno Cracked" (1933) starring Flip the Frog.

THE PERILS OF PAULINE

All Star Video Corp; 1947 • color; 1 hr, 36 min; 1/2" Beta II, 1/2" VHS • Sale: $49.95
- -
Discount Video Tapes; 1947 • color; 1 hr, 36 min; 1/2" Beta II, 1/2" VHS • Sale: $49.95

Presents a musical-comedy "biography" of silent-screen actress, Pearl White. Features a musical score by Frank Loesser. Stars Betty Hutton, John Lund, Constance Collier, Billy de Wolfe, and William Demarest.

PERMISSION TO KILL

Magnetic Video Corporation; Order No. CL-4010; 1975 • color; 1 hr, 36 min; 1/2" Beta II, 1/2" VHS • Sale: $54.95
- -
Red Fox, Inc; 1975 • color; 1 hr, 36 min; 1/2" Beta II, 1/2" VHS • Sale: $54.95

Recounts the intrigues following Alan Curtis, an agent for Western Intelligence Liaison, whose assignment is to prevent an exiled politician from returning to his dictator-led country. Stars Dirk Bogarde, Ava Gardner, and Bekim Fehmiu.

PERRI

MCA DiscoVision; Order No. D18-505; 1956 • color; 1 hr, 15 min; LaserVision • Sale:$24.95

Offers a Walt Disney Studio adaptation of Felix (Bambi) Saten's novel about two pine squirrels named Perri and Porro. Follows Perri from infancy to her mating with Porro. Features live action nature photography and a cast that includes a flying squirrel, a timid field mouse, a white snowshoe rabbit, and a ferocious marten.

PETER RABBIT AND TALES OF BEATRIX POTTER

Fotomat Corp; Order No. B0259 for 1/2" Beta II, V0259 for 1/2" VHS; 1971 • color; 1 hr, 31 min; 1/2" Beta II, 1/2" VHS • Sale: $39.95; Rental: $7.95/up to 5 days, applicable to purchase
- -
Time-Life Video Club Inc; 1971 • color; 1 hr, 30 min; 1/2" Beta II, 1/2" VHS • Sale: $49.95 to members

Offers five stories by the Victorian children's author, Beatrix Potter, in a ballet choreographed by Sir Frederick Ashton and performed by the Royal Ballet Company. Includes music composed and scored by John Lanchbery. Uses characters from other themes in addition to Peter Rabbit, Jemima Puddleduck, and Mrs. Tiggywinkle, all dressed in life-like animal costumes.

PETE'S DRAGON

Fotomat Corp; Order No. B1037 for 1/2" Beta II, V1037 for 1/2" VHS; 1977 • color; 1 hr, 46 min; 1/2" Beta II, 1/2" VHS • Sale: $54.95; Rental: $9.95/5 days
- -
Niles Cinema; Order No. WD-10; 1977 • color; 1 hr, 45 min; 1/2" Beta II, 1/2" VHS • Sale: $59.95
- -
Walt Disney Home Video; Order No. 10BS for 1/2" Beta II, 10VS for 1/2" VHS; 1977 • color; 1 hr, 45 min; 1/2" Beta II, 1/2" VHS • Sale: $59.95

Combines animation with live action in a musical-fantasy from the Walt Disney Studios. Follows the adventures of an orphan at the turn of the century who has a dragon as a best friend. Stars Helen Reddy, Jim Dale, Mickey Rooney, Red Buttons, Shelley Winters, and Sean Marshall.

PHANTASM

Magnetic Video Corporation; 1977 • color; 1 hr, 30 min; 1/2" Beta II, 1/2" VHS • Sale: $59.95

Lon Chaney in *The Phantom of the Opera*.

Offers a horror tale about two brothers who must fight the living dead and a flying creature that punctures skulls. Features Michael Baldwin, Bill Thornbury, Reggie Bannister, Kathy Lester, and Angus Scrimm.

THE PHANTOM CREEPS
Cable Films; 1939 • b/w; 4 hrs; 1/2" Beta I, 1/2" Beta II, 1/2" VHS • Sale: $89.50

Offers a twelve-chapter serial about a mad scientist who takes on a spy ring and military intelligence. Stars Bela Lugosi, Robert Kent, Dorothy Arnold, and Regis Toomey.

PHANTOM EXPRESS
Thunderbird Films; 1932 • b/w; 1 hr, 10 min; 3/4" U-Matic, 1/2" Beta I, 1/2" Beta II, 1/2" VHS • Sale: $69.95 for 1/2" Beta I, $49.95 for 1/2" Beta II & VHS, $89.95 for 3/4"

Relates the tale of an aging engineer blamed for derailing a train when he is unable to prove the existence of another train that was headed straight at him. Stars William Collier, Jr., Sally Blane, Hobart Bosworth, and J. Farrell McDonald.

PHANTOM FIEND
Northeast Video and Sound, Inc; 1932 • b/w; 1 hr, 19 min; 3/4" U-Matic, 1/2" EIAJ, 1/2" Beta II, 1/2" VHS • Sale: $179; Rental: $70/wk

Presents a remake of Hitchcock's "The Lodger," in which a family suspects that their tenant may be a murderer of young women. Stars Ivor Novello, Elizabeth Allan, and Jack Hawkins.

THE PHANTOM OF THE OPERA
Cinema Concepts, Inc.; 1925 • b/w; 1 hr, 20 min; 3/4" U-Matic, 1/2" Beta II, 1/2" VHS • Sale: $54.95 for 1/2" Beta II & VHS, $149.95 for 3/4"
- -
National Film and Video Center; 1925 • b/w; 1 hr, 20 min; 3/4" U-Matic, 1/2" Beta II, 1/2" VHS • Rental: $49/1 showing
- -
The Video Library; Order No. CC-0137; 1925 • b/w; 1 hr, 20 min; 1/2" Beta II, 1/2" VHS • Sale: $54.95

Presents the classic silent horror film about the embittered, disfigured composer who haunts the sewers beneath the Paris Opera House. Stars Lon Chaney.

PHANTOM OF THE PLAINS; PRAIRIE RUSTLERS
The Nostalgia Merchant; Order No. 5007; 1945 • b/w; 2 hrs; 1/2" Beta II, 1/2" VHS • Sale: $59.95

Offers a western double feature. Opens with Red Ryder trying to save "the Duchess" from a phony suitor; stars Bill Elliott. Concludes with Buster Crabbe attempting to clear his name when his identical twin turns outlaw.

PHANTOM OF THE WEST
Reel Images Inc; Order No. 663; 1931 • b/w; 2 hrs, 46 min; 1/2" Beta II, 1/2" VHS • Sale: $69.95 for 1/2" Beta II, $73.95 for 1/2" VHS

Presents a Mascot Studio serial western in ten episodes starring Tom Tyler. Follows Tom's attempts to discover the identity of the phantom murderer before all of the people who know his name are done away with.

THE PHANTOM RIDER
The Nostalgia Merchant; Date not listed • b/w; 3 hrs; 1/2" Beta II, 1/2" VHS • Sale: $109.95

Presents, on two videocassettes, a motion picture serial in 12 episodes. Stars Robert Kent.

PHANTOM SHIP
Cable Films; 1937 • b/w; 1 hr, 2 min; 1/2" Beta I, 1/2" Beta II, 1/2" VHS • Sale: $65 for 1/2" Beta I, $49.50 for 1/2" Beta II & VHS

Offers a tale of terror based on the bizarre case of the "Marie Celeste," an American ship found adrift and derelict on the Atlantic Ocean on December 5, 1872. Stars Bela Lugosi, Shirley Grey, and Edmund Willard.

Katharine Hepburn and Cary Grant in *The Philadelphia Story*.

THE PHILADELPHIA STORY
RCA SelectaVision VideoDiscs; Order No. 00211; 1940 • color; 1 hr, 52 min; CED • Sale: $19.98

Adapts for the screen Philip Barry's comedy about a wealthy family on Philadelphia's Main Line. Centers on the daughter who is about to remarry, the reporter who falls in love with her, and her ex-husband, who's out to prevent her next marriage. Stars Katharine Hepburn, Cary Grant, James Stewart, Ruth Hussey, and Henry Daniell, under George Cukor's direction.

PICKWICK PAPERS
Video Communications Inc; 1954 • b/w; 1 hr, 49 min; 1/2" Beta II, 1/2" VHS • Sale: $54.95

Adapts the famous Dickens tale for the screen. Relates how Mr. Pickwick and his friends run afoul of the due process of the law. Stars James Hayter, James Donald, and Nigel Patrick.

PICNIC
National Film and Video Center; 1955 • color; 1 hr, 53 min; 3/4" U-Matic, 1/2" Beta II, 1/2" VHS • Rental: $69/1 showing

Follows a young drifter into a town where he thinks he can get a job with an ex-roommate. Shows him romancing his friend's girl at a picnic, which leads to a blow-up that forces him to leave. Ends as the girl decides to go with him. Stars William Holden, Kim Novak, Rosalind Russell, Betty Field, Susan Strasberg, and Cliff Robertson.

PICNIC AT HANGING ROCK
Time-Life Video Club Inc; 1979 • color; 1 hr, 55 min; 1/2" Beta II, 1/2" VHS • Sale: $39.95 to members

Investigates what really occurred during a picnic in Australia on Valentine's Day, 1900, when several schoolgirls disappeared mysteriously. Features Rachel Roberts and the direction of Peter Weir.

PINOCCHIO

Fotomat Corp; Order No. B0131 for ½" Beta II, V0131 for ½" VHS; Date not listed • color; 1 hr, 16 min; ½" Beta II, ½" VHS • Sale: $39.95; Rental: $7.95/up to 5 days, applicable to purchase

----

Video Communications Inc; 1976 • color; 1 hr, 16 min; ½" Beta II, ½" VHS • Sale: $54.95

Retells the children's tale of the lonely woodcarver who makes a puppet that magically comes to life. Stars Danny Kaye, Sandy Duncan, Flip Wilson, Liz Torres, and Clive Revill.

PIPE DREAMS

Magnetic Video Corporation; Order No. CL-4049; 1976 • color; 1 hr, 29 min; ½" Beta II, ½" VHS • Sale: $54.95

Examines an estranged couple caught up in personal and political intrigue during construction of the Alaskan Pipeline. Features music performed by Gladys Knight & The Pips and stars Knight.

PIPPI GOES ON BOARD

Fotomat Corp; Order No. B0143 for ½" Beta II, V0143 for ½" VHS; 1975 • color; 1 hr, 24 min; ½" Beta II, ½" VHS • Sale: $39.95; Rental: $7.95/up to 5 days, applicable to purchase

----

Vid America; Order No. 917; 1975 • color; 1 hr, 23 min; ½" Beta II, ½" VHS • Rental: $10.95/wk

Portrays the impish Pippi Longstocking outwitting both town officials who wish to civilize her, and two thieves who are after a bag of gold coins. Stars Inger Nilsson in this Swedish production directed by Olle Hellblom.

PIPPI LONGSTOCKING IN THE SOUTH SEAS

Fotomat Corp; Order No. B0141 for ½" Beta II, V0141 for ½" VHS; Date not listed • color; 1 hr, 39 min; ½" Beta II, ½" VHS • Sale: $39.95; Rental: $7.95/up to 5 days, applicable to purchase

----

Vid America; Order No. 913; Date not listed • color; 1 hr, 39 min; ½" Beta II, ½" VHS • Rental: $10.95/wk

Follows the adventures of Pippi Longstocking, the young heroine of Astrid Lindgren's well-known Swedish children's books, as she tries to rescue her father, Captain Ephraim Longstocking, from South Sea pirates who want his hidden treasure. Features Inger Nilsson, Maria Persson, Par Sundberg, and Beppe Wolgers.

A PLACE CALLED TRINITY

Tape Club of America; Order No. 2603 B; 1975 • color; 1 hr, 37 min; ½" Beta II, ½" VHS • Sale: 54.95

Tells the story of Jesse Smith, famous in the West for his ability with pistols, fists and women, and his upright brother Lester. Shows how they inherit a piece of land called Trinity for which each one has a different and contradictory plan: Lester wants to build a church, and Jesse wants to build a brothel. Stars Richard Harrison, Anna Zinneman, and Donal O'Brien.

PLAGUE

Vid America; Order No. 946; Date not listed • color; 1 hr, 27 min; ½" Beta II, ½" VHS • Sale: $49.95; Rental: $11.95/wk, applicable to purchase

Offers a science-fiction tale about an accidentally created bacteria that threatens to wipe out mankind.

PLANET OF THE APES

Magnetic Video Corporation; Order No. CL-1054; 1968 • color; 1 hr, 52 min; ½" Beta II, ½" VHS • Sale: $54.95

Roddy McDowall, Kim Hunter, and Charlton Heston in *Planet of the Apes.*

RCA SelectaVision VideoDiscs; Order No. 00109; 1968 • color; 1 hr, 52 min; CED • Sale: $19.98

Presents Pierre Boulle's science-fiction thriller set on a planet on which evolution has been reversed: the great apes are the civilized rulers, men the dumb beasts. Shows how a stranded American astronaut discovers that the planet is a post-atomic Earth. Stars Charlton Heston, Roddy McDowall, and Kim Hunter, under the direction of Franklin J. Schaffner.

PLAY IT AGAIN, SAM

Fotomat Corp; Order No. B0035 for ½" Beta II, V0035 for ½" VHS; 1972 • color; 1 hr, 25 min; ½" Beta II, ½" VHS • Sale: $49.95; Rental: $9.95/up to 5 days, applicable to purchase

----

Paramount Home Video; 1972 • color; 1 hr, 25 min; ½" Beta II, ½" VHS • Sale: $59.95

RCA SelectaVision VideoDiscs; Order No. 00619; 1972 • color; 1 hr, 27 min; CED • Sale: $19.98

Presents the screen version of the Woody Allen play, in which Allen plays a fanatical movie buff with a recurring hallucination: Humphrey Bogart offering tips for success with women. Shows what happens when he discovers that there is one woman he's himself with: Linda, his best friend's wife. Co-stars Diane Keaton, Tony Roberts, and Susan Anspach, under the direction of Herbert Ross.

PLAYERS

Fotomat Corp; Order No. B0367 for ½" Beta II, V0367 for ½" VHS; 1979 • color; 2 hrs; ½" Beta II, ½" VHS • Sale: $54.95; Rental: $9.95/5 days

----

Paramount Home Video; 1979 • color; 2 hrs; ½" Beta II, ½" VHS • Sale: $59.95

Dissects the world of professional tennis, as a young pro falls for a "kept" woman. Features Ali MacGraw, Dean-Paul Martin, Maximilian Schell, and Pancho Gonzalez.

PLAYGIRLS OF MUNICH
Video Home Library; Order No. VX-109; Date not listed
• color; 2 hrs; ½" Beta II, ½" VHS • Sale: $99.95

Presents a pornographic film.

POM-POM GIRLS
Video Communications Inc; 1977 • color; 1 hr, 29
min; ½" Beta II, ½" VHS • Sale: $54.95

Offers an "R" rated film about a last fling at high
school in California. Features Robert Carradine and
Jennifer Ashley.

POPEYE
Ivy Video; 1936 • color; 55 min; ¾" U-Matic, ½" Beta
II, ½" VHS • Sale: $59.95 for ½" Beta II & VHS, trade-
in plan available, $225 for ¾"
- -
Northeast Video and Sound, Inc; Order No. 117S;
1936-39 • color; 55 min; ¾" U-Matic, ½" EIAJ, ½"
Beta II, ½" VHS • Sale: $225; Rental: $80/wk

Presents the three Popeye cartoons made in the late
1930's by Max and Dave Fleischer, in technicolor and
twice the length of regular cartoons. Includes "Popeye
Meets Sinbad", "Popeye Meets Ali Baba", and "Alla-
din."

POPEYE MEETS SINBAD THE SAILOR
National Film and Video Center; Date not listed •
color; 20 min; ¾" U-Matic, ½" Beta II, ½" VHS •
Rental: $19/1 showing

Presents a cartoon in which Popeye, Olive Oyl, and
Wimpy are lost at sea, and land on Sinbad's island.
Follows the action when Sinbad tries to take Olive Oyl
away from Popeye.

POPEYE THE SAILOR
Reel Images Inc; Order No. 651; 1936-39 • color; 54
min; ½" Beta II, ½" VHS • Sale: $39.95 for ½" Beta II,
$42.95 for ½" VHS

Presents three extra-long cartoons from the Max
Fleischer Studio featuring Popeye, Olive Oyl, Wimpy,
and Bluto. Includes "Popeye The Sailor Meets Sinbad
The Sailor" in a fight to the finish, "Popeye The Sailor
Meets Ali Baba's Forty Thieves" who have captured
Olive and Wimpy, and "Aladdin And His Wonderful
Lamp" or Popeye vs. the evil magician.

POPEYE'S FAMOUS FABLES
Video Tape Network; Order No. KI 403 for ½" Beta II,
KI 404 for ½" VHS; Date not listed • color; 55 min; ½"
Beta II, ½" VHS • Sale: $49.95
- -
Presents three classic Popeye cartoons made in the
late 1930's by Max and Dave Fleischer, in technicolor
and twice the length of regular cartoons. Includes "Po-
peye Meets Sinbad," "Popeye Meets Ali Baba," and
"Aladin."

THE POSEIDON ADVENTURE
Magnetic Video Corporation; Order No. CL-1058;
1972 • color; 1 hr, 57 min; ½" Beta II, ½" VHS • Sale:
$54.95

Details the desperate effort of ten survivors to escape
from an ocean liner capsized by a huge wave created
by a submarine earthquake. Combines terror at sea
with the victims' personal stories. Stars Gene Hackman, Ernest Borgnine, Red Buttons, Carol Lynley,
Roddy McDowall, and Stella Stevens.

POSSIBLE POSSUM
Magnetic Video Corporation; Order No. CL-2042; Date
not listed • color; 30 min; ½" Beta II, ½" VHS • Sale:
$34.95

Offers a compilation of Terrytoon animated cartoons
featuring Possible Possum.

POT O'GOLD
Blackhawk Films, Inc; Order No. 506-49-0851 for ½"
Beta II, 525-49-0851 for ½" VHS; 1941 • color; 1 hr,
12 min; ½" Beta II, ½" VHS • Sale: $39.95

Recreates for the screen a famous radio give-away
show, with the big band sound of Horace Heidt. Features James Stewart and Paulette Goddard.

POTEMKIN
Ivy Video; 1925 • b/w; 1 hr, 7 min; ¾" U-Matic, ½"
Beta II, ½" VHS • Sale: $59.95 for ½" Beta II & VHS,
trade-in plan available, $195 for ¾"
- -
Northeast Video and Sound, Inc; Order No. 149S;
1925 • b/w; 1 hr, 7 min; ¾" U-Matic, ½" EIAJ, ½"
Beta II, ½" VHS • Sale: $195; Rental: $75/wk

Dramatizes events during Russia's abortive 1905 revolution in this film by Sergei Eisenstein. Emphasizes the
possibilities of rapid-fire montage in its newsreel style,
culminating in the sequence on the steps of Odessa as
Cossack troops open fire on civilians aiding the muti-
neers on the battleship Potemkin.

PRELUDE TO WAR
Discount Video Tapes; 1942 • b/w; 54 min; ½" Beta
II, ½" VHS • Sale: $39.95

Offers the Oscar winner for Best Documentary of
1942. Presents the years between 1931 and 1939 and
contrasts free societies and totalitarian governments,
under the direction of Frank Capra.

PREMIERE OF "A STAR IS BORN"
Reel Images Inc; Order No. 579; 1954 • b/w; 30 min;
½" Beta II, ½" VHS • Sale: $29.95 for ½" Beta II,
$31.95 for ½" VHS

Shows, from the lobby of the Pantages Theatre in Hollywood, the parade of celebrities who attended the premiere of "A Star Is Born." Includes brief interviews
with, or glimpses of, George Jessel, Dean Martin, Hedda Hopper, Raymond Burr, Edward G. Robinson, Elizabeth Taylor, Dorothy Lamour, Joan Crawford, Doris
Day, Judy Garland, Shelley Winters, Lauren Bacall,
and many others.

PRETTY BABY
Fotomat Corp; Order No. B0015 for ½" Beta II, V0015
for ½" VHS; 1978 • color; 1 hr, 49 min; ½" Beta II,
½" VHS • Sale: $49.95; Rental: $9.95/up to 5 days,
applicable to purchase
- -
Paramount Home Video; 1978 • color; 1 hr, 49 min;
½" Beta II, ½" VHS • Sale: $59.95

Tells the story of E.J. Bellocq, a photographer obsessed with the prostitutes in New Orleans' red-light
district known as Storyville. Shows how twelve-year-old
Violet bewitches Bellocq with her naive coquettish-
ness, and how they marry and remain together until
her mother, a now-reformed prostitute, returns to claim
her. Stars Keith Carradine, Brooke Shields, Susan Sarandon, Frances Faye, and Antonio Fargas, under the
direction of Louis Malle.

PRIDE OF THE BOWERY
Cable Films; 1941 • b/w; 1 hr, 1 min; ½" Beta I, ½"
Beta II, ½" VHS • Sale: $65 for ½" Beta I, $49.50 for
½" Beta II & VHS

Relates a story of a boy of the streets set against the
outdoors of a C.C.C. camp in the late 1930's. Shows
how an aggressive and self-centered young boxer
learns that helping one's fellow man has its own re-
wards. Stars Leo Gorcey and Huntz Hall.

PRIDE OF THE WEST
Videobrary Inc; Order No. 11; 1938 • b/w; 56 min; ½"
Beta II, ½" VHS • Sale: $39.95

Presents a Hopalong Cassidy western. Tells a tale of
an outlaw named Nixon who is involved in a land swindle. Stars William Boyd, George "Gabby" Hayes, and
James Craig.

THE PRINCE AND THE PAUPER
MCA DiscoVision; Order No. D18-508; 1962 • color; 1
hr, 33 min; LaserVision • Sale: $24.95

Offers a Walt Disney Studio adaptation of Mark Twain's
tale of two identical boys who exchange places, one
the son of a drunkard, the other the Prince of Wales
about to be crowned. Stars Guy Williams, Laurence
Naismith, Donald Houston, and Sean Scully.

THE PRIVATE AFTERNOONS OF PAMELA MANN
Quality X Video Cassette Company; 1974 • color; 1 hr
23 min; ½" Beta I, ½" Beta II, ½" VHS • Sale: $99.50

Presents a pornographic film.

PRIVATE BUCKAROO
Video T.E.N.; 1942 • b/w; 1 hr, 5 min; ½" Beta II, ½"
VHS • Sale: $49.95 for ½" Beta II, $54.95 for ½" VHS

Traces the wartime basic training of bandleader Harry
James when he is drafted, along with his orchestra,
Joe E. Lewis, Dick Foran, and the Andrews Sisters.

THE PRIVATE LIFE OF DON JUAN
Video T.E.N.; 1934 • b/w; 1 hr, 37 min; ½" Beta II,
½" VHS • Sale: $49.95 for ½" Beta II, $54.95 for ½"
VHS

Portrays a weary Don Juan forced to maintain his reputation against an imposter, as directed by Alexander
Korda. Stars Douglas Fairbanks Sr. and Merle Oberon.

THE PRIVATE LIFE OF HENRY VIII
Ivy Video; 1933 • b/w; 1 hr, 37 min; ¾" U-Matic, ½"
Beta II, ½" VHS • Sale: $59.95 for ½" Beta II & VHS,
trade-in plan available, $195 for ¾"
- -
Reel Images Inc; Order No. 565; 1933 • b/w; 1 hr, 32
min; ½" Beta II, ½" VHS • Sale: $49.95 for ½" Beta II,
$52.95 for ½" VHS

Features Charles Laughton as King Henry of England
in this humorous historical drama based on the story of
Henry's unsuccessful marital life with·a succession of
six wives. Shows off as well the talents of Robert Donat
and Merle Oberon, and director Alexander Korda.

THE PRODUCERS
Magnetic Video Corporation; Order No. CL-4058;
1968 • color; 1 hr, 28 min; ½" Beta II, ½" VHS • Sale:
$54.95
- -
Vid America; Order No. 466; 1968 • color; 1 hr, 28
min; ½" Beta II, ½" VHS • Rental: $12.95/wk, appli-
cable to purchase

Follows the antics of a Broadway producer who romances old spinsters into investing in a non-existent

musical project. Shows his crisis when he must pick a
flop to produce because he has accepted investments
of several thousand percent—a musical called
"Springtime For Hitler." Presents a film conceived,
written, and directed by Mel Brooks, starring Zero Mostel, Gene Wilder, and Dick Shawn.

THE PROFESSIONALS
National Film and Video Center; 1966 • color; 1 hr, 57
min; ¾" U-Matic, ½" Beta II, ½" VHS • Rental: $89/1
showing

Offers the story of a kidnaped rancher's wife and the
band of men her husband hires to rescue her from the
clutches of one of Pancho Villa's revolutionaries. Reveals that although she is in collaboration with her ab-
ductor, the men take her back to her husband to collect their fee. Stars Burt Lancaster, Lee Marvin,
Claudia Cardinale, Jack Palance, and Robert Ryan.

PROM NIGHT
MCA Videocassette, Inc; Order No. 66021; 1980 •
color; 1 hr, 31 min; ½" Beta II, ½" VHS • Sale: $65

Offers a thriller about a maniac loose at a high school
prom. Features Leslie Nielsen, Jamie Lee Curtis, Casey Stevens, and Antoinette Bower.

PROMISE AT DAWN
Magnetic Video Corporation; Order No. CL-4028;
1970 • color; 1 hr, 41 min; ½" Beta II, ½" VHS • Sale:
$54.95

Depicts a beautiful Russian actress and her young son
who grows up in the 1920's and 30's. Shows how the
mother's overpowering aim is to make him successful,
and his aim in life is to live up to her love and faith in
him. Stars Melina Mercouri and Asaf Dayan, under the
direction of Jules Dassin.

PROMISES! PROMISES!
FHV Entertainment, Inc; 1963 • color; 1 hr, 15 min;
½" Beta II, ½" VHS • Sale: $49.95

Provides a mad marital mix-up of wives, husbands, and
babies. Stars Jayne Mansfield and Tom Noonan.

PROPHECY
Fotomat Corp; Order No. B0369 for ½" Beta II, V0369
for ½" VHS; 1979 • color; 1 hr, 42 min; ½" Beta II,
½" VHS • Sale: $54.95; Rental: $9.95/5 days
- -
Paramount Home Video; 1979 • color; 1 hr, 42 min;
½" Beta II, ½" VHS • Sale: $59.95

Looks at a possible battle between mutant animals and
humans due to industrial dumping in Maine. Includes
an attack by a crazed squirrel. Features Talia Shire,
Robert Foxworth, Armand Assante, and Richard Dysart.

THE PROPHET
Entertainment Video Releasing, Inc; Order No. 1004;
1970 • color; 1 hr, 30 min; ½" Beta II, ½" VHS • Sale:
$49.95 for ½" Beta II, $54.95 for ½" VHS

Traces the story of an amorous disciple's pursuit of her
"guru"—the Prophet—throughout Rome. Stars Ann-
Margret and Vittorio Gassman.

THE PROUD AND THE DAMNED
Video Communications Inc; Order No. 1082; 1970 •
color; 1 hr, 35 min; ½" Beta II, ½" VHS • Sale: $54.95

Focuses on four Civil War veterans who, led by their
former sergeant, roam Latin America hiring out their
guns. Shows how they find themselves involved in the
deadly game of political revolution. Stars Chuck Connors, Jose Greco, and Cesar Romero.

THE PSYCHIC

Fotomat Corp; Order No. B0183 for ½" Beta II, V0183 for ½" VHS; 1978 • color; 1 hr, 28 min; ½" Beta II, ½" VHS • Sale: $49.95; Rental: $9.95/up to 5 days, applicable to purchase

Vid America; Order No. 928; 1978 • color; 1 hr, 29 min; ½" Beta II, ½" VHS • Rental: $11.95/wk

Offers a tale of the supernatural in which a young woman "sees" her life, and death, flash before her eyes while driving through a tunnel. Features Jennifer O'Neill, Marc Porel, Evelyn Stewart, Jenny Tamburi, and Gabriele Ferzetti.

PSYCHO

MCA DiscoVision; Order No. 11-003; 1960 • b/w; 1 hr, 48 min; LaserVision • Sale: $24.95

MCA Videocassette, Inc; Order No. 55001; 1960 • b/w; 1 hr, 48 min; ½" Beta II, ½" VHS • Sale: $50

Offers a tantalizing psychological shocker by Alfred Hitchcock, containing abrupt plot twists and several scenes of grisly violence. Details a series of murders committed by a classic schizophrenic personality. Stars Anthony Perkins, Janet Leigh, and John Gavin, under Hitchcock's direction.

PSYCHOMANIA

Niles Cinema; Order No. BT-29 for ½" Beta II, VH-29 for ½" VHS; 1973 • color; 1 hr, 35 min; ½" Beta II, ½" VHS • Sale: $59.95

Relates the story of an occultist motorcycle gang that learns to cross the barriers of life and death at will. Stars George Sanders, Beryl Reid, and Nicky Henson.

PSYCHOPATH

FHV Entertainment, Inc; 1974 • color; 1 hr, 11 min; ½" Beta II, ½" VHS • Sale: $49.95

Offers a drama of retaliation and murder as one man sets himself up as judge, jury, and executioner, and nobody can escape him. Stars Tom Basham, Gene Carlson, and Barbara Groner.

A PUBLIC AFFAIR

Thunderbird Films; 1962 • b/w; 1 hr, 20 min; ¾" U-Matic, ½" Beta I, ½" Beta II, ½" VHS • Sale: $69.95 for ½" Beta I, $49.95 for ½" Beta II & VHS, $89.95 for ¾"

Chronicles underworld intrigues in California and the birth and passage of a bill to outlaw illegal bill-collecting methods. Stars Edward Binns and Myron McCormick.

PUMPING IRON

Columbia Pictures Home Entertainment; Order No. BDF7280 for ½" Beta II, VCF3175 for ½" VHS; 1977 • color; 1 hr, 25 min; ½" Beta II, ½" VHS • Sale: $59.95

Time-Life Video Club Inc; 1977 • color; 1 hr, 15 min; ½" Beta II, ½" VHS • Sale: $44.95, plus $15 annual membership fee

Documents the world of competitive body-building. Features six-time Mr. Olympic, Arnold Schwarzenegger.

THE PUPPY WHO WANTED A BOY AND THE PUPPY'S GREAT ADVENTURE

Fotomat Corp; Order No. B0179 for ½" Beta II, V0179 for ½" VHS; 1978; 1979 • color; 1 hr; ½" Beta II, ½" VHS • Sale: $39.95; Rental: $7.95/up to 5 days, applicable to purchase

Presents two animated films on one cassette. Offers "The Puppy Who Wanted a Boy," in which Petey, a lonely orphan-puppy, goes to the big city and battles a man who sells puppies for experiments from which they never return, while searching for a boy to love. Follows the further adventures of Petey and his adopted master Tommy, in "The Puppy's Great Adventure," as Petey risks his life to find Tommy when Tommy is adopted from the Public Home for Boys and sent to live many miles away.

THE PURPLE MONSTER STRIKES

The Nostalgia Merchant; Order No. 0037; 1945 • b/w; 3 hrs, 45 min; ½" Beta II, ½" VHS • Sale: $109.95

Presents, on two videocassettes, a Republic motion picture serial in 15 episodes. Traces the attempts of "The Purple Monster," whose mission is to prepare the way for the Martian invasion fleet as it sets out to conquer the Earth. Stars Dennis Moore, Linda Stirling, and Roy Barcroft.

PUTNEY SWOPE

Columbia Pictures Home Entertainment; Order No. BCF7320 for ½" Beta II, VCF3200 for ½" VHS; 1969 • color; 1 hr, 28 min; ½" Beta II, ½" VHS • Sale: $59.95

Satarizes Madison Avenue as it is taken over by streetwise black people who make many irreverent changes. Includes spoofs of TV commercials. Stars Arnold Johnson, Ruth Hermine, Pepi Hermine, and Allen Garfield, under Robert Downey's direction.

PYGMALION

Tape Club of America; Order No. 2407 B; 1938 • b/w; 1 hr, 25 min; ½" Beta II, ½" VHS • Sale: $54.95

Adapts the G.B. Shaw play about Eliza Doolittle, the common cockney flower girl, who is transformed into a beautiful, well-mannered lady by phonetics expert Professor Henry Higgins. Tells a gentle love story, as the professor begins to fall for his creation. Stars Wendy Hiller, Leslie Howard, and Wilfred Lawson.

Arnold Schwarzenegger in *Pumpin Iron.*

QUICK, LET'S GET MARRIED
FHV Entertainment, Inc; 1964 • color; 1 hr, 36 min; 1/2" Beta II, 1/2" VHS • Sale: $49.95

Traces what happens when an ancient map of the legendary treasure of Tolino falls into the hands of a master-thief. Stars Ginger Rogers, Ray Milland, Barbara Eden, and Elliot Gould.

THE QUIET ONE
Budget Video; 1948 • b/w; 1 hr, 7 min; 1/2" Beta II, 1/2" VHS • Sale: $44.95

Tells the story of a black youth in Harlem and his frustrations. Chronicles his descent into juvenile delinquency and his rehabilitation in a reform school, using non-professional actors, documentary style, and a script by James Agee. Features Donald Thompson, Sadie Stockton, Clarence Cooper, and Estelle Evans.

A QUIET PLACE TO KILL
Magnetic Video Corporation; Order No. CL-4022; 1973 • color; 1 hr, 33 min; 1/2" Beta II, 1/2" VHS • Sale: $54.95

Portrays a man and his second wife who invite his ex-wife to stay with them. Offers a complex story of romantic triangles, multiple conspiracies, and murder. Stars Carroll Baker and Jean Sorel.

RABBIT TEST
Magnetic Video Corporation; Order No. CL-4016; 1978 • color; 1 hr, 28 min; 1/2" Beta II, 1/2" VHS • Sale: $54.95

Examines the comic consequences facing the world's first pregnant man. Stars Billy Crystal, Joan Prather, and Alex Rocco, under the direction of Joan Rivers.

RACE FOR YOUR LIFE, CHARLIE BROWN
Fotomat Corp; Order No. B0049 for 1/2" Beta II, V0049 for 1/2" VHS; 1977 • color; 1 hr, 16 min; 1/2" Beta II, 1/2" VHS • Sale: $49.95; Rental: $9.95/up to 5 days, applicable to purchase

- -
Paramount Home Video; 1977 • color; 1 hr, 16 min; 1/2" Beta II, 1/2" VHS • Sale: $59.95

- -
RCA SelectaVision VideoDiscs; Order No. 00630; 1977 • color; 1 hr, 15 min; CED • Sale: $19.98

Presents an animated film based on Charles M. Schulz's comic strip. Shows how bullies threaten Charlie and his friends, making them risk everything in a raft race on a rampaging river.

THE RACKET
Niles Cinema; Order No. NM-8025; 1951 • b/w; 1 hr, 28 min; 1/2" Beta II, 1/2" VHS • Sale: $54.95

- -
The Nostalgia Merchant; Order No. 8025; 1951 • b/w; 1 hr, 28 min; 1/2" Beta II, 1/2" VHS • Sale: $54.95

- -
Red Fox, Inc; Order No. 8025; 1951 • b/w; 1 hr, 28 min; 1/2" Beta II, 1/2" VHS • Sale: $54.95

Recounts the story of a police captain battling corruption in the civic system. Stars Robert Mitchum, Robert Ryan, and Lizabeth Scott.

RACKETEER
Cable Films; 1929 • b/w; 1 hr, 8 min; 1/2" Beta I, 1/2" Beta II, 1/2" VHS • Sale: $65 for 1/2" Beta I, $49.50 for 1/2" Beta II & VHS

Presents an early talking picture. Offers Hollywood's version of the racketeer who falls in love with the pretty girl and wants to "go straight." Stars Carole Lombard, Robert Armstrong, and Hedda Hopper.

RADAR MEN FROM THE MOON
The Nostalgia Merchant; Order No. 0089; 1952 • b/w; 3 hrs; 1/2" Beta II, 1/2" VHS • Sale: $109.95

Presents, on two videocassettes, a Republic motion picture serial in 12 episodes. Follows the adventures of Commander Cody, "Sky Marshall of the Universe," as he battles invaders from the Moon who want to enslave the Earth. Stars George Wallace.

RADIO RANCH
Video T.E.N.; 1935 • b/w; 1 hr, 20 min; 1/2" Beta II, 1/2" VHS • Sale: $49.95 for 1/2" Beta II, $54.95 for 1/2" VHS

Features Gene Autry in his first starring role, from the serial "The Phantom Empire." Tells of evil scientists and a futuristic underground world, with Franie Darro, Betsy King Ross, and Dorothy Christie.

THE RAGE OF PARIS
Video T.E.N.; 1938 • b/w; 1 hr, 18 min; 1/2" Beta II, 1/2" VHS • Sale: $49.95 for 1/2" Beta II, $54.95 for 1/2" VHS

Follows the comic adventures of an unemployed girl trying to snag a rich husband, with the aid of a head waiter and an ex-actress. Stars Danielle Darrieux, Douglas Fairbanks Jr., Mischa Auer, Helen Broderick, and Louis Hayward.

RAIDERS OF RED GAP
Reel Images Inc; Order No. 561; 1943 • b/w; 56 min; 1/2" Beta II, 1/2" VHS • Sale: $39.95 for 1/2" Beta II, $42.95 for 1/2" VHS

Chronicles the confrontation between the Bennett Cattle Company and the homesteaders it is trying to force off the land. Involves a case of mistaken identity when the gunslinger hired by the company changes clothes with the Lone Rider's unsuspecting sidekick. Stars Bob Livingston and Al "Fuzzy" St. John .

RAILROADED
Thunderbird Films; 1947 • b/w; 1 hr, 11 min; 3/4" U-Matic, 1/2" Beta I, 1/2" Beta II, 1/2" VHS • Sale: $69.95 for 1/2" Beta I, $49.95 for 1/2" Beta II & VHS, $89.95 for 3/4"

Presents a mystery film with a detective on the trail of a hired killer responsible for the death of a policeman. Stars John Ireland, Hugh Beaumont, Jane Randolph, and Shiela Ryan.

THE RAILWAY CHILDREN

MCA DiscoVision; Order No. 18-002; 1971 • color; 1 hr, 46 min; LaserVision • Sale: $24.95

Presents the efforts of three children to clear their father's name of espionage charges during the Victorian era in Yorkshire, England. Adapts E. Nesbit's children's book. Features Dinah Sheridan, Jenny Agutter, and Bernard Cribbins, under the direction of Lionel Jeffries.

RAIN

VCX; Order No. FC120; 1932 • b/w; 1 hr, 32 min; 1/2" Beta II, 1/2" VHS • Sale: $35.00

Video T.E.N.; 1932 • b/w; 1 hr, 31 min; 1/2" Beta II, 1/2" VHS • Sale: $49.95 for 1/2" Beta II, $54.95 for 1/2" VHS

Adapts for the screen Somerset Maugham's story of the fire and brimstone preacher and the South Sea island woman of easy virtue. Stars Joan Crawford, Walter Huston, William Gargan, Guy Kibbee, Walter Catlett, and Beulah Bondi.

RAINBOW ON THE RIVER

Reel Images Inc; Order No. 29; 1936 • b/w; 1 hr, 33 min; 1/2" Beta II, 1/2" VHS • Sale: $49.95 for 1/2" Beta II, 52.95 for 1/2" VHS

Presents a musical drama set in the South just after the Civil War. Relates the story of a small boy raised by a former slave. Stars Bobby Breen, May Robson, Charles Butterworth, Louise Beavers, Alan Mowbray, and Benita Hume.

RAISE THE TITANIC

Magnetic Video Corporation; Order No. 9023; 1980 • color; 1 hr, 52 min; 1/2" Beta II, 1/2" VHS • Sale: $59.95

Dramatizes the attempts of world powers to raise the sunken luxury liner because they believe a rare mineral is aboard. Uses lavish special effects. Stars Jason Robards, Alec Guinness, and Richard Jordan.

A RAISIN IN THE SUN

National Film and Video Center; 1961 • color; 2 hrs, 8 min; 3/4" U-Matic, 1/2" Beta II, 1/2" VHS • Rental: $49/1 showing

Adapts the play by Lorraine Hansberry for the screen. Recounts the efforts of a black family to escape life in a crowded Chicago ghetto: the possibility is raised when the widowed mother receives a $10,000 insurance check which makes possible a down payment on a house. Stars Claudia McNeil, Sidney Poitier, and Ruby Dee.

RANCHO NOTORIOUS

Video Communications Inc; 1952 • color; 1 hr, 29 min; 1/2" Beta II, 1/2" VHS • Sale: $54.95

Depicts an outraged rancher setting out to track down the vicious killer of his bride-to-be. Stars Marlene Dietrich, Mel Ferrer, and Arthur Kennedy, under the direction of Fritz Lang.

RANGE LAW; THE DUDE BANDIT

Video Communications Inc; Order No. 1123; 1931, 1933 • b/w; 2 hrs, 7 min; 1/2" Beta II, 1/2" VHS • Sale: $74.95

Offers a western double feature. Stars Ken Maynard in "Range Law," an action western. Presents Hoot Gibson in "The Dude Bandit," in which an unscrupulous moneylender tries to gain control of a ranch.

Walter Huston and Joan Crawford in *Rain*.

RASHOMON

Thunderbird Films; 1951 • b/w; 1 hr, 30 min; 3/4" U-Matic, 1/2" Beta I, 1/2" Beta II, 1/2" VHS • Sale: $69.95 for 1/2" Beta I, $49.95 for 1/2" Beta II & VHS, $89.95 for 3/4"

Presents Toshiro Mifune in a Japanese film by Akira Kurosawa exploring the nature of human honesty and memory. Recounts the story of a rape-murder from the point of view of each protagonist; dubbed in English.

RAWHIDE

Blackhawk Films, Inc; Order No. 506-51-0876 for 1/2" Beta II, 525-51-0876 for 1/2" VHS; 1938 • b/w ; 1 hr; 1/2" Beta II, 1/2" VHS • Sale: $39.95

Video Action Library; Order No. BH07; 1938 • color; 1 hr; 1/2" Beta I, 1/2" Beta II, 1/2" VHS • Rental: $7.50/1 wk, $3.75 ea add'l wk

Relates a western adventure of ranchers versus landowners, filled with brawls, gunplay, and songs. Features Yankee baseball star Lou Gehrig, along with Smith Ballew.

THE RAZOR'S EDGE

Golden Tapes Video Tape Library; Order No. F-1049; 1946 • b/w; 2 hrs, 26 min; 1/2" Beta II, 1/2" VHS • Sale: $49.95 for 1/2" Beta II & VHS, $124.95 for 3/4"

Magnetic Video Corporation; Order No. CL-1049; 1946 • b/w; 2 hrs, 26 min; 1/2" Beta II, 1/2" VHS • Sale: $64.95

Dramatizes the novel by Somerset Maugham, concerning a man's search for goodness and an original way of life in the pre-Depression days of America and Europe. Stars Tyrone Power, Gene Tierney, John Payne, Anne Baxter, Clifton Webb, and Herbert Marshall.

REACHING FOR THE MOON

Cable Films; 1931 • b/w; 1 hr, 8 min; 1/2" Beta I, 1/2" Beta II, 1/2" VHS • Sale: $65 for 1/2" Beta I, $49.50 for 1/2" Beta II & VHS

Presents a Hollywood film concerning the interactions of a financier, his valet, and a girl. Features a brief musical number with young Bing Crosby and Bebe Daniels. Stars Douglas Fairbanks, Sr., Bebe Daniels, Edward Everett Horton, Jack Mulhall, Helen Jerome Eddy, and Bing Crosby.

James Dean,
Sal Mineo,
and Natalie Wood
in *Rebel
Without A Cause.*

THE REAL BRUCE LEE
Video Gems; 1979 • color; 1 hr, 48 min; ½″ Beta II,
½″ VHS • Sale: $59.95

Offers a martial arts film featuring Bruce Lee, Bruce Li,
and Dragon Lee.

REBECCA
Magnetic Video Corporation; Order No. 8012; 1940 •
b/w; 2 hrs, 10 min; ½″ Beta II, ½″ VHS • Sale: $79.95
- -
Niles Cinema; Order No. CL-8012; 1940 • b/w; 2 hrs,
10 min; ½″ Beta II, ½″ VHS • Sale: $79.95

Presents Alfred Hitchcock's adaptation of Daphne du-
Maurier's tale of a girl who marries a man only to find
herself living in the shadow of his former wife. Stars
Laurence Olivier, Joan Fontaine, George Sanders, Judith Anderson, and Nigel Bruce.

REBECCA OF SUNNYBROOK FARM
Magnetic Video Corporation; Order No. CL-1065;
1938 • b/w; 1 hr, 14 min; ½″ Beta II, ½″ VHS • Sale:
$54.95

Showcases Shirley Temple as she becomes a radio
star. Includes a background romance among the
adults. Stars Shirley Temple, Randolph Scott, Jack Haley, Bill ''Bojangles'' Robinson, Gloria Stuart, Phyllis
Brooks, Helen Westley, and Slim Summerville. Uses the
title of a famous children's book, but is not an adaptation.

REBEL ROUSERS
Tape Club of America; Order No. 2501 B; 1967 •
color; 1 hr, 21 min; ½″ Beta II, ½″ VHS • Sale: $54.95

Describes a group of men who hold as their creed: ''If
it feels good, do it.'' Tells how they lay waste to the
flesh and blood of America's daughters. Stars Cameron Mitchell, Jack Nicholson, Diane Ladd, and Bruce
Dern.

REBEL WITHOUT A CAUSE
MCA DiscoVision; Order No. W21-514; 1955 • color;
1 hr, 51 min; LaserVision • Sale:$24.95
- -
WCI Home Video Inc; 1955 • color; 1 hr, 51 min; ½″
Beta II, ½″ VHS • Sale: $55

Offers a study of juvenile delinquency, in which a
young man rebels against his unhappy home, and
makes his reputation with other teenagers by showing
how much courage he has. Stars James Dean, Sal Mineo, Natalie Wood, and Ji m Backus, under the direction of Nicholas Ray.

THE RED BALLOON; OCCURRENCE AT OWL
CREEK BRIDGE
Budget Video; 1956,1962 • b/w & color; 1 hr, 1 min;
½″ Beta II, ½″ VHS • Sale: $34.95

Offers two short subjects. Presents the magical tale of
the friendship between a boy and a balloon with a life
all its own as the two romp through the streets of Paris,
in 'The Red Balloon.' Details the last moments of a
condemned American Civil War prisoner and the images that haunt him before hanging. Contains no dialogue.

THE RED SHOES
RCA SelectaVision VideoDiscs; Order No. 01001; 1948
• color; 2 hrs, 13 min; CED • Sale: $22.98

Offers a romance concerning a young ballerina who
must make the impossible choice between love and
her career. Stars Moira Shearer, Anton Walbrook, Marius Goring, Robert Helpmann, and Albert Basserman.

REDNECK
Niles Cinema; Order No. BT-11 for ½″ Beta II, VH-11
for ½″ VHS; 1973 • color; 1 hr, 32 min; ½″ Beta II,
½″ VHS • Sale: $59.95

Features Telly Savalas in a violent, fast-paced expose
of jewel thieves and kidnappers, with Franco Nero,
Marc Lester, Tom Duggan, and Beatrice Clay.

REEFER MADNESS

Ivy Video; 1937 • b/w; 1 hr, 3 min; 3/4" U-Matic, 1/2" Beta II, 1/2" VHS • Sale: $59.95 for 1/2" Beta II & VHS, trade-in plan available, $195 for 3/4"

- -
Northeast Video and Sound, Inc; Order No. 136S; 1937 • b/w; 1 hr, 3 min; 3/4" U-Matic, 1/2" EIAJ, 1/2" Beta II, 1/2" VHS • Sale: $195; Rental: $75/wk

- -
VCX; Order No. FC128; 1928 • b/w; 1 hr, 11 min; 1/2" Beta II, 1/2" VHS • Sale: $35.00

- -
Video Tape Network; Order No. CD 603 for 1/2" Beta II, CD 604 for 1/2" VHS; 1936 • b/w; 1 hr; 1/2" Beta II, 1/2" VHS • Sale: $49.95

Exaggerates the supposed evils of marijuana "addiction" in this campy anti-drug propaganda film, which has to its credit the creation of an atmosphere of repression and misunderstanding that has only recently been refuted and has not yet entirely been laid to rest.

RELATIVES ARE COMING

Monarch Releasing Corporation; Date not listed • color; 1 hr, 4 min; 3/4" U-Matic • Sale: $300

Presents a pornographic film.

REPULSION

VCX; Order No. FC114; 1965 • b/w; 1 hr, 45 min; 1/2" Beta II, 1/2" VHS • Sale: $35.00

Offers Roman Polanski's horror-study of the mental deterioration of a girl kept from outsiders. Stars Catherine Deneuve, Ian Hendry, John Fraser, and Patrick Wymark.

REQUIEM FOR A HEAVYWEIGHT

National Film and Video Center; 1962 • color; 1 hr, 40 min; 3/4" U-Matic, 1/2" Beta II, 1/2" VHS • Rental: $49/1 showing

Follows the story of Mountain Rivera, a heavyweight boxer who finds himself too old to fight and meets a sympathetic employment counselor who tries to get him a job. Stars Anthony Quinn, Jackie Gleason, Mickey Rooney, and Julie Harris.

RESURRECTION OF EVE

Mitchell Brothers' Film Group; Date not listed • color; 1 hr, 22 min; 1/2" Beta II, 1/2" VHS • Sale: $79

Presents a pornographic film.

THE RESURRECTION OF ZACHARY WHEELER

Fotomat Corp; Order No. B0153 for 1/2" Beta II, V0153 for 1/2" VHS; 1971 • color; 1 hr, 40 min; 1/2" Beta II, 1/2" VHS • Sale: $39.95; Rental: $7.95/up to 5 days, applicable to purchase

- -
Video Communications Inc; 1971 • color; 1 hr, 40 min; 1/2" Beta II, 1/2" VHS • Sale: $54.95

Shows a presidential candidate, having narrowly escaped death after an automobile crash, being escorted in secrecy to a mysterious clinic. Stars Angie Dickinson, Bradford Dillman, and Leslie Neilsen.

RETURN OF CHANDU

Northeast Video and Sound, Inc; 1934 • b/w; 1 hr, 5 min; 3/4" U-Matic, 1/2" EIAJ, 1/2" Beta II, 1/2" VHS • Sale: $179; Rental: $65/wk

Features Bela Lugosi, as Chandu, exercising his powers to conquer the Black Sorcerers who inhabit the island of Lemuria.

THE RETURN OF CHANDU

Reel Images Inc; Order No. 712; 1934 • b/w; 3 hrs, 26 min; 1/2" Beta II, 1/2" VHS • Sale: $119.95

Offers a Principal Studio serial in twelve episodes featuring Bela Lugosi. Shows Chandu the Magician trying to save the Princess of Egypt from her black magic captors who believe they must sacrifice her in order to regain their "powers."

RETURN OF THE BAD MEN

Blackhawk Films, Inc; Order No. 506-57-0717 for 1/2" Beta II, 525-57-0717 for 1/2" VHS; 1948 • b/w; 1 hr, 30 min; 1/2" Beta II, 1/2" VHS • Sale: $49.95

Relates how an angel-faced gun-woman forms a bloodthirsty band of the most notorious outlaws in the west, to plunder the Oklahoma frontier of 1889. Stars Randolph Scott, Robert Ryan, Ann Jeffreys, Gabby Hayes, Jacqueline White, and Jason Robards.

THE RETURN OF THE PINK PANTHER

Vid America; Order No. 453; 1975 • color; 1 hr, 52 min; 1/2" Beta II, 1/2" VHS • Rental: $13.95/wk

Features Peter Sellers as the inept Inspector Clouseau attempting to foil a robbery from a museum (a la "Topkapi"). Co-stars Christopher Plummer, Catherine Schell, and Herbert Lom, under the direction of Blake Edwards.

THE RETURN OF THE TALL BLOND MAN WITH ONE BLACK SHOE

Cinema Concepts, Inc.; 1974 • color; 1 hr, 24 min; 3/4" U-Matic, 1/2" Beta II, 1/2" VHS • Sale: $54.95 for 1/2" Beta II & VHS, $149.95 for 3/4"

- -
The Video Library; Order No. CC-0138; 1974 • color; 1 hr, 24 min; 1/2" Beta II, 1/2" VHS • Sale: $54.95

Presents a slapstick approach to a "James Bond"-type adventure. Follows the misadventures of Francois, a professional violinist mistakenly suspected of being a super-spy, as he narrowly escapes many attempts on his life, without even realizing he is in danger. Stars Pierre Richard.

RETURN TO BOGGY CREEK

Video Communications Inc; Order No. 3004; 1977 • color; 1 hr, 30 min; 1/2" Beta II, 1/2" VHS • Sale: $54.95

Offers a horror movie in which Bigfoot is on the prowl in the swamp region of Louisiana.

THE REVENGE OF FRANKENSTEIN

National Film and Video Center; 1958 • color; 1 hr, 34 min; 3/4" U-Matic, 1/2" Beta II, 1/2" VHS • Rental: $59/1 showing

Recounts how Baron Frankenstein, escaping execution for his crimes of experimentation with the human body, takes up the practice of medicine in a small town and joins forces with another doctor to create a monster out of several bodies. Stars Peter Cushing, Francis Matthews, and Eunice Gayson.

REVENGE OF THE CHEERLEADERS

Monarch Releasing Corporation; Date not listed • color; 1 hr, 30 min; 3/4" U-Matic • Sale: $350

Presents a pornographic film.

RHINOCEROS

Magnetic Video Corporation; 1974 • color; 1 hr, 41 min; 1/2" Beta II, 1/2" VHS • Sale: $80

Offers the American Film Theatre's presentation of

Ionesco's play, directed by Tom O'Horgan. Satirizes man's beastly anger. Stars Gene Wilder and Zero Mostel.

RICHARD PRYOR LIVE IN CONCERT
Time-Life Video Club Inc; 1979 • color; 1 hr, 19 min; 1/2" Beta II, 1/2" VHS • Sale: $44.95 to members

Presents a film of Richard Pryor doing his stand-up routines. Includes profanity.

RIDE IN THE WHIRLWIND
Cinema Resources; 1966 • color; 1 hr, 22 min; 1/2" Beta II, 1/2" VHS • Sale: $45
- -
Video Communications Inc; Order No. 4005; 1967 • color; 1 hr, 22 min; 1/2" Beta II, 1/2" VHS • Sale: $54.95
- -
Video T.E.N.; 1967 • color; 1 hr, 22 min; 1/2" Beta II, 1/2" VHS • Sale: $49.95 for 1/2" Beta II, 54.95 for 1/2" VHS

Presents a western about three cowboys who become mistaken for stagecoach robbers, with a screenplay written by Jack Nicholson. Stars Nicholson, Cameron Mitchell, Millie Perkins, Tom Filer, and Rupert Crosse, under Monte Hellman's direction.

RIDE THE MAN DOWN
The Nostalgia Merchant; Order No. 0172; 1953 • color; 1 hr, 30 min; 1/2" Beta II, 1/2" VHS • Sale: $54.95
- -
Red Fox, Inc; Order No. 0172; 1953 • color; 1 hr, 30 min; 1/2" Beta II, 1/2" VHS • Sale: $54.95

Tells of a ranch foreman who, after the death of his cattle baron-boss, fights off greedy opportunists. Stars Rod Cameron, Ella Raines, and Brian Donlevy.

RIDER ON THE RAIN
Blackhawk Films, Inc; Order No. 502-30-0134 for 1/2" Beta II, 515-30-0134 for 1/2" VHS; 1970 • color; 1 hr, 57 min; 1/2" Beta II, 1/2" VHS • Sale: $54.95
- -
Magnetic Video Corporation; Order No. CL-4011; 1970 • color; 1 hr, 57 min; 1/2" Beta II, 1/2" VHS • Sale: $54.95
- -
Vid America; Order No. 325; 1972 • color; 1 hr, 57 min; 1/2" Beta II, 1/2" VHS • Rental: $12.95/wk

Explores the relationship between a U.S. Army colonel searching for an escaped sex maniac and a young woman who has been victimized by the latter. Stars Charles Bronson and Marlene Jobert, under the direction of Rene Clement.

RIDERS OF THE DESERT
Reel Images Inc; Order No. 52; 1932 • b/w; 57 min; 1/2" Beta II, 1/2" VHS • Sale: $39.95 for 1/2" Beta II, $42.95 for 1/2" VHS

Presents a western adventure with cowboy star Bob Steele. Co-stars Gertrude Messinger and George Hayes.
n
RIDERS OF THE ROCKIES
Fotomat.Corp; Order No. B0107 for 1/2" Beta II, V0107 for 1/2" VHS; 1937 • b/w; 1 hr; 1/2" Beta II, 1/2" VHS • Sale: $39.95; Rental: $7.95/up to 5 days, applicable to purchase

Features Tex Ritter in the tale of a cowboy turned rustler to catch a border gang.

RIDERS OF THE ROCKIES; GUNMAN FROM BODIE
Video Communications Inc; Order No. 1120; 1937, 1941 • b/w; 2 hrs, 2 min; 1/2" Beta II, 1/2" VHS • Sale: $74.95

Offers a western double feature. Features Tex Ritter in "Riders of the Rockies," in which a cowboy turns rustler to catch a border gang. Presents Tim McCoy and Buck Jones in "Gunman from Bodie," an action western.

RIFIFI
Video T.E.N.; 1956 • b/w; 1 hr, 56 min; 1/2" Beta II, 1/2" VHS • Sale: $49.95 for 1/2" Beta II, $54.95 for 1/2" VHS

Details the intricate plotting and execution of a crime and its unexpected aftermath, in a film by Jules Dassin. Features Jean Servais, Carl Mohner, and Marie Sabouret; in French with subtitles.

THE RINK AND THE IMMIGRANT
Reel Images Inc; Order No. 524; 1916-17 • color; 56 min; 1/2" Beta II, 1/2" VHS • Sale: $39.95 for 1/2" Beta II, $42.95 for 1/2" VHS

Pairs two Charlie Chaplin films: "The Rink," in which Chaplin—on roller skates—tries to shield Edna Purviance from the lecherous attentions of Mack Swain; and "The Immigrant," in which Chaplin befriends a widow and her daughter during their adventures upon landing in America.

RIO GRANDE
The Nostalgia Merchant ; 1950 • b/w; 1 hr, 45 min; 1/2" Beta II, 1/2" VHS • Sale: $54.95
- -
Red Fox, Inc; 1950 • b/w; 1 hr, 45 min; 1/2" Beta II, 1/2" VHS • Sale: $54.95

Presents a western directed by John Ford, starring John Wayne, Maureen O'Hara, and Ben Johnson. Examines cavalry life on the frontier, with Wayne as a tough officer whose son is under his command.

RIO LOBO
MGM/CBS Home Video; Order No. C50016; 1970 • color; 1 hr, 54 min; 1/2" Beta II, 1/2" VHS • Sale: $49.95
- -
Niles Cinema; Order No. GM-733; 1970 • color; 1 hr, 54 min; 1/2" Beta II, 1/2" VHS • Sale: $49.95

Follows the adventures of a man on the trail of two traders who killed his best friend. Stars John Wayne, Jorge Rivero, Jennifer O'Neill, Jack Elam, Victor French, Chris Mitchum, Bill Williams, and Jim Davis, under the direction of Howard Hawks.

RIO RATTLER
Thunderbird Films; 1935 • b/w; 55 min; 3/4" U-Matic, 1/2" Beta I, 1/2" Beta II, 1/2" VHS • Sale: $59.95 for 1/2" Beta I, $39.95 for 1/2" Beta II & VHS, $79.95 for 3/4"

Presents a western starring Tom Tyler.

THE ROAD BACK
The Nostalgia Merchant; Order No. 7008; 1970 • color; 1 hr, 36 min; 1/2" Beta II, 1/2" VHS • Sale: $54.95

Spotlights Lassie in San Francisco with a case of canine amnesia in this compilation of TV adventure stories. Features Jed Allen and Lisa Lu.

ROAD TO NASHVILLE
Video Communications Inc; Order No. 1086; 1967 • color; 1 hr, 50 min; 1/2" Beta II, 1/2" VHS • Sale: $54.95

Shows what happens when a Hollywood agent hits the road to Nashville to sign up talent for a new musical. Features Marty Robbins, Doodles Weaver, and Johnny Cash.

ROAD TO SALINA

Magnetic Video Corporation ; Order No. CL-4033; 1971 • color; 1 hr, 36 min; ½" Beta II, ½" VHS • Sale: $54.95

Recounts the story of a drifter who is taken in by a beautiful but deranged woman who believes him to be her long-lost son. Stars Mimsy Farmer, Robert Walker, and Rita Hayworth.

THE ROARING TWENTIES

Blackhawk Films, Inc; Order No. 506-66-0681 for ½" Beta II, 525-66-0681 for ½" VHS; Date not listed • b/w; 5 hrs; ¾" U-Matic, ½" Beta I, ½" Beta II, ½" VHS • Sale: $249.95 for ½" Beta I, $199.95 for ½" Beta II & VHS, $349.95 for ¾"

Presents, on 3 tapes, newsreels of the 1920's which capture the major news events. Includes Ku Klux Klanners, the automobile era, the first solar eclipse in 300 years thoroughly documented, the Charleston, a bathing beauty contest, Babe Ruth, Rudolph Valentino's death, America's Lone Eagle, Charles Lindbergh, and Black Tuesday.

ROBBERY

Magnetic Video Corporation; Order No. CL-4044; 1967 • color; 1 hr, 53 min; ½" Beta II, ½" VHS • Sale: $54.95

Chronicles England's biggest mail-train heist, which, planned like a commando operation and carried out by 25 top professionals, nets $10 million in loot. Features Stanley Baker, Joanna Pettet, and James Booth.

THE ROBE

Blackhawk Films, Inc; Order No. 502-49-0029 for ½" Beta II, 505-49-0027 for ½" VHS; 1953 • color; 2 hrs, 13 min; ½" Beta II, ½" VHS • Sale: $74.95

- -

Golden Tapes Video Tape Library; Order No. F-1022; 1953 • color; 2 hrs, 13 min; ½" Beta II, ½" VHS • Sale: $49.95 for ½" Beta II & VHS, $124.95 for ¾"

- -

Magnetic Video Corporation; Order No. CL-1022; 1953 • color; 2 hrs, 13 min; ½" Beta II, ½" VHS • Sale: $64.95

- -

The Video Library; Order No. MV-1022; 1953 • color; 2 hrs, 13 min; ½" Beta II, ½" VHS • Sale: $74.95

Presents the first Cinemascope feature, an adaptation of Lloyd C. Douglas' novel about the Roman in charge of putting Jesus Christ to death. Stars Richard Burton, Jean Simmons, Victor Mature, Michael Rennie, Richard Boone, and Dean Jagger.

ROBERT YOUNGSON'S BLAZE BUSTERS

Budget Video; Date not listed • b/w; 1 hr; ½" Beta II, ½" VHS • Sale: $34.95

Presents film clips from Warner Brothers compiled by Robert Youngson with an added humorous commentary. Features spectacular firefighting episodes, such as The Hindenburg Disaster.

ROBERT YOUNGSON'S GADGETS GALORE

Budget Video; Date not listed • b/w; 1 hr; ½" Beta II, ½" VHS • Sale: $34.95

Presents film clips from Warner Brothers compiled by Robert Youngson with an added humorous commentary. Features footage of the motorcar.

ROBERT YOUNGSON'S I NEVER FORGET A FACE

Budget Video; Date not listed • b/w; 1 hr; ½" Beta II, ½" VHS • Sale: $34.95

Presents film clips from Warner Brothers compiled by Robert Youngson with an added humorous commentary. Focuses on personalities from the 1920s, including John Barrymore and Johnny Weismuller.

ROBERT YOUNGSON'S SPILLS AND CHILLS

Budget Video; Date not listed • b/w; 1 hr; ½" Beta II, ½" VHS • Sale: $34.95

Presents film clips from Warner Brothers compiled by Robert Youngson with an added humorous commentary. Features the escapades of dare devils.

ROBERT YOUNGSON'S THIS MECHANICAL AGE

Budget Video; Date not listed • b/w; 1 hr; ½" Beta II, ½" VHS • Sale: $34.95

Presents film clips from Warner Brothers compiled by Robert Youngson with an added humorous commentary. Features auto pioneers and auto racing.

ROBERT YOUNGSON'S WORLD OF KIDS

Budget Video; Date not listed • b/w; 1 hr; ½" Beta II, ½" VHS • Sale: $34.95

Presents film clips from Warner Brothers compiled by Robert Youngson with an added humorous commentary. Looks at children.

ROBIN HOOD OF MONTEREY

Fotomat Corp; Order No. B0099 for ½" Beta II, V0099 for ½" VHS; 1947 • b/w; 57 min; ½" Beta II, ½" VHS • Sale: $39.95; Rental: $7.95/up to 5 days, applicable to purchase

Offers a western featuring Gilbert Roland and Chris-Pin Martin.

ROBINSON CRUSOE

Entertainment Video Releasing, Inc; Order No. 1001; Date not listed • color; 1 hr, 30 min; ½" Beta II, ½" VHS • Sale: $49.95 for ½" Beta II, $54.95 for ½" VHS

Recounts Daniel Defoe's tale of a man's struggle to survive on a deserted island for twenty years.

ROCKETSHIP

Cinema Concepts, Inc.; 1935 • b/w; 1 hr, 15 min; ¾" U-Matic, ½" Beta II, ½" VHS • Sale: $54.95 for ½" Beta II & VHS, 149.95 for ¾"

- -

Northeast Video and Sound, Inc; Order No. 115S; 1938 • b/w; 1 hr, 10 min; ¾" U-Matic, ½" EIAJ, ½" Beta II, ½" VHS • Sale: $195; Rental: $65/wk

Features Buster Crabbe in a condensation of the "Flash Gordon" serial.

ROCKETSHIP X-M

Video Action Library; 1951 • b/w; 1 hr, 17 min; ½" Beta I, ½" Beta II, ½" VHS • Sale: $51

Follows the adventures of a group of scientists whose spaceship to the moon veers off course and lands on Mars, where vestiges of civilization are discovered. Stars Lloyd Bridges, Osa Massen, John Emery, Noah Beery Jr., and Hugh O'Brien.

ROCKY

RCA SelectaVision VideoDiscs; Order No. 01401; 1976 • color; 1 hr, 59 min; CED • Sale: $24.98

Depicts a boxer of no particular reputation who gets a chance to fight the heavyweight champion. Stars Sylvester Stallone, Talia Shire, Burt Young, Carl Weathers, Burgess Meredith, and Thayer David.

Olivia Hussey and Leonard Whiting in *Romeo & Juliet*.

ROCKY AND BULLWINKLE CARTOON HOUR
Video Communications Inc; Order No. 1157; Date not listed • color; 1 hr; ½" Beta II, ½" VHS • Sale: $54.95

Offers a collection of cartoons featuring Rocky and His Friends, Bullwinkle, Hoppity Hooper, Dudley Doright, and many more.

ROGUE LION
Video Communications Inc; Order No. 1087; 1978 • color; 1 hr, 35 min; ½" Beta II, ½" VHS • Sale: $54.95

Shows the struggle of two men against local opposition as they attempt to establish a wild animal game reserve in the wilderness of South Africa. Stars Brian O'Shaughnessy and Bruce Millar.

ROLLERBABIES
VTS; Date not listed • color; 1 hr, 24 min; ½" Beta I, ½" Beta II, ½" VHS • Sale: $99

Presents a pornographic film.

ROLLERBALL
Vid America; Order No. 455; 1975 • color; 2 hrs; ½" Beta II, ½" VHS • Rental: $12.95/wk

Portrays a futuristic society in which all forms of violence have been eliminated, except for a fierce gladiatorial-style sport called rollerball. Stars James Caan, John Houseman, Maud Adams, John Beck, Moses Gunn, and Ralph Richardson, under the direction of Norman Jewison.

ROLLERCOASTER
MCA DiscoVision; Order No. 11-009; 1977 • color; 1 hr, 59 min; LaserVision • Sale: $24.95

Follows the efforts of police and a safety inspector to trap a psychopath before he lives up to his promise to sabotage the nation's amusement parks by blowing up their rollercoasters. Stars George Segal, Richard Widmark, Timothy Bottoms, Henry Fonda, and Harry Guardino.

ROMEO AND JULIET
Fotomat Corp; Order No. B0057 for ½" Beta II, V0057 for ½" VHS; 1968 • color; 2 hrs, 18 min; ½" Beta II, ½" VHS • Sale: $69.95; Rental: $9.95/up to 5 days, applicable to purchase

Paramount Home Video; 1968 • color; 2 hrs, 18 min; ½" Beta II, ½" VHS • Sale: $79.95

RCA SelectaVision VideoDiscs; Order No. 00620; 1968 • color; 2 hrs, 18 min; CED • Sale: $22.98

Adapts for the screen Shakespeare's play about the two star-crossed lovers. Offers the much-acclaimed direction of Franco Zeffirelli. Stars Olivia Hussey, Leonard Whiting, Milo O'Shea, Michael York, John McEnery, and Robert Stephens.

ROOM AT THE TOP
Magnetic Video Corporation; Order No. CL-2054; 1959 • b/w; 1 hr, 57 min; ½" Beta II, ½" VHS • Sale: $44.95

Tells of a man's driving ambition to reach the financial apex, which leads him to sacrifice true love and marry the boss' daughter. Stars Laurence Harvey, Simone Signoret, Heather Sears, Hermione Baddeley, and Donald Wolfit, under the direction of Jack Clayton.

ROOM SERVICE
The Nostalgia Merchant; Order No. 8023; 1938 • b/w; 1 hr, 18 min; ½" Beta II, ½" VHS • Sale: $54.95

Vid America; Order No. 936; 1938 • b/w; 1 hr, 18 min; ½" Beta II, ½" VHS • Rental: $10.95/wk

Presents a comedy about a bogus producer who is trying to raise capital for a show and avoid eviction from his hotel at the same time. Stars the Marx Brothers and Lucille Ball.

ROOSTER COGBURN
MCA DiscoVision; Order No. 14-003; 1975 • color; 1 hr, 47 min; LaserVision • Sale: $24.95

Presents John Wayne reprising the role he played in "True Grit" as he attempts to track down the men who killed the father of a missionary, played by Katharine Hepburn. Features Richard Jordan, Anthony Zerbe, John McIntier, and Strother Martin.

ROOTIN' TOOTIN' RHYTHM
Reel Images Inc; Order No. 277; 1937 • b/w; 54 min; ½" Beta II, ½" VHS • Sale: $39.95 for ½" Beta II, $42.95 for ½" VHS

Presents a tale of cattle rustlers after Gene Autry's cattle. Features Autry singing several of his songs. Costars Smiley Burnette, Monte Blue, Armida, Al Clauser and his Oklahoma Outlaws, and Champion.

THE ROSE
Magnetic Video Corporation; 1979 • color; 2 hrs, 14 min; ½" Beta II, ½" VHS • Sale: $79.95

Follows the last days of a Janis Joplin-like rock star succumbing to drugs and alcohol. Stars Bette Midler, Alan Bates, Frederic Forrest, Harry Dean Stanton, and Barry Primus.

ROSEBUD
Monarch Releasing Corporation; Date not listed • color; 1 hr, 22 min; ¾" U-Matic • Sale: $350

Presents a pornographic film.

ROUGH CUT
Paramount Home Video; Order No. 1213; 1980 • color; 1 hr, 52 min; ½" Beta II, ½" VHS • Sale: $72.95

Offers a romantic comedy-adventure. Concerns an ambitious Scotland Yard officer determined to snare an elusive gentleman jewel-thief by using a beautiful lady kleptomaniac as bait. Stars Burt Reynolds, Lesley-Anne Down, and David Niven.

ROUSTABOUT
Magnetic Video Corporation; Order No. CL-2007; 1964 • color; 1 hr, 41 min; 1/2" Beta II, 1/2" VHS • Sale: $44.95

The Video Library; Order No. MV-2007; 1964 • color; 1 hr, 41 min; 1/2" Beta II, 1/2" VHS • Sale: $44.95

Presents a musical romance concerning a free-spirited singer who joins a carnival, woos the owner's daughter, and then leaves when business is in a slump. Recounts his subsequent troubles and eventual return. Stars Elvis Presley, Barbara Stanwyck, Joan Freeman, and Leif Erickson.

THE ROYAL BED
Reel Images Inc; Order No. 43; 1931 • b/w; 1 hr, 13 min; 1/2" Beta II, 1/2" VHS • Sale: $49.95 for 1/2" Beta II, $52.95 for 1/2" VHS

Presents a satirical comedy based on a play by Robert E. Sherwood. Relates the story of a king who would rather play checkers than attend to matters of state. Stars Mary Astor and Lowell Sherman under the direction of the latter.

RUDE BOY
MGM/CBS Home Video; Order No. C60022; 1980 • color; 2 hrs, 3 min; 1/2" Beta II, 1/2" VHS • Sale: $59.95

Niles Cinema; Order No. GM-723; 1980 • color; 1/2" Beta II, 1/2" VHS • Sale: $59.95

Stars The Clash, and Ray Gange in a semi-documentary film about the rise of the British Rock group. Includes the songs ''London's Burning,'' and ''I Fought The Law.''

RUGGLES OF RED GAP
MCA DiscoVision; Order No. 21-018; 1936 • b/w; 1 hr, 30 min; LaserVision • Sale: $15.95

Follows the misadventures of an English manservant who must relocate in the old west when his master loses him in a poker game. Stars Charles Laughton, Mary Boland, Charlie Ruggles, Zasu Pitts, and Roland Young, under the direction of Leo McCarey.

Bette Midler in *The Rose*.

RULES OF THE GAME
Ivy Video; 1939 • b/w; 1 hr, 45 min; 3/4" U-Matic, 1/2" Beta II, 1/2" VHS • Sale: $59.95 for 1/2" Beta II & VHS, trade-in plan available, $225 for 3/4"

Depicts French aristocratic society on the verge of collapse before World War II in this epic by Jean Renoir combining romance, pageantry and farce, and starring some of France's finest actors, including Renoir himself.

RUN, ANGEL, RUN
Video T.E.N.; 1969 • color; 1 hr, 35 min; 1/2" Beta II, 1/2" VHS • Sale: $49.95 for 1/2" Beta II, $54.95 for 1/2" VHS

Explores the world of a motorcycle gang and its revenge on a former member who has revealed its secrets. Features William Smith, Valerie Starrett, Gene Shane, Lee De Broux, Eugene Cornelius, and Ann Fry.

RUN OF THE ARROW
Fotomat Corp; Order No. B0115 for 1/2" Beta II, V0115 for 1/2" VHS; 1956 • color; 1 hr, 25 min; 1/2" Beta II, 1/2" VHS • Sale: $39.95; Rental: $7.95/up to 5 days, applicable to purchase

----
Video Communications Inc; 1957 • color; 1 hr, 25 min; 1/2" Beta II, 1/2" VHS • Sale: $54.95

Deals with a cowpoke who discovers that, despite the gruesome Civil War, he belongs among white men and not warring Indians. Stars Rod Steiger, Brian Keith, Ralph Meeker, and Charles Bronson.

RUSTLER'S VALLEY
Videobrary Inc; Order No. 20; 1937 • b/w; 1 hr; 1/2" Beta II, 1/2" VHS • Sale: $39.95

Offers a Hopalong Cassidy western in which a jealous fiance may not be who he says he is. Stars William Boyd, George ''Gabby'' Hayes, and Lee J. Cobb.

SABOTAGE
Reel Images Inc; Order No. 726; 1936 • b/w; 1 hr, 17 min; 1/2" Beta II, 1/2" VHS • Sale: $49.95 for 1/2" Beta II, $52.95 for 1/2" VHS

Offers an early British thriller by Alfred Hitchcock about a man who runs a movie house and belongs to a group bent on overthrowing the government. Features Oscar Homolka and Sylvia Sidney in an adaptation of Joseph Conrad's ''The Secret Agent.''

SAD CAT
Magnetic Video Corporation; Order No. CL-2038; Date not listed • color; 30 min; 1/2" Beta II , 1/2" VHS • Sale: $34.95

Offers a compilation of Terrytoon animated cartoons featuring Sad Cat.

SAD SACK
Magnetic Video Corporation; Order No. CL-2019; 1957 • b/w; 1 hr, 38 min; 1/2" Beta II, 1/2" VHS • Sale: $54.95

Red Fox, Inc; Order No. CL-2019; 1957 • b/w; 1 hr, 28 min; ½" Beta II, ½" VHS • Sale: $54.95

Showcases the comedy of Jerry Lewis in a story based on the famous comic-strip character who cannot adjust to Army life. Co-stars Phyllis Kirk, David Wayne, and Peter Lorre.

SAGEBRUSH TRAIL

Cable Films; 1934 • b/w; 54 min; ½" Beta I, ½" Beta II, ½" VHS • Sale: $45 for ½" Beta I, $49.50 for ½" Beta II & VHS

Features John Wayne as an escaped convict who falls in with a band of outlaws.

SAHARA

National Film and Video Center; 1943 • b/w; 1 hr, 37 min; ¾" U-Matic, ½" Beta II, ½" VHS • Rental: $69/1 showing

Deals with conflict in the hot desert when a small group of soldiers travels to an isolated fortress to get water, where they are attacked and outnumbered by the Germans until the British arrive. Stars Humphrey Bogart and Dan Duryea.

SAIL TO GLORY

FHV Entertainment, Inc; Date not listed • color; 1 hr; ½" Beta II, ½" VHS • Sale: $49.95

Highlights "America," an exact replica of the original 1851 racing schooner, recreated from 116-year-old plans. Documents the victory over Britain's finest yachts off the Isle of Wight in 1851.

SAILING ALONG

Budget Video; 1938 • b/w; 1 hr, 27 min; ½" Beta II, ½" VHS • Sale: $44.95

Presents a British musical comedy in which the interest of a theatrical backer changes the life of a young girl who lives and works on a barge. Stars Jessie Matthews, Roland Young, and Alistair Sim.

THE SAILOR WHO FELL FROM GRACE WITH THE SEA

Magnetic Video Corporation; Order No. CL-4012; 1976 • color; 1 hr, 48 min; ½" Beta II, ½" VHS • Sale: $54.95

- -

Red Fox, Inc; Order No. CL-4012; 1976, • color; 1 hr, 48 min; ½" Beta II, ½" VHS • Sale: $54.95

- -

Vid America; Order No. 452; 1976 • color; 1 hr, 45. min; ½" Beta II, ½" VHS • Rental: $12.95/wk

Recounts the love story of a British widow and an American merchant seaman. Features Sarah Miles, Kris Kristofferson, and Jonathan Kahn.

THE SAINT IN NEW YORK

Niles Cinema; Order No. NM-8024; 1938 • b/w; 1 hr, 11 min; ½" Beta II, ½" VHS • Sale: $54.95

- -

The Nostalgia Merchant; Order No. 8024; 1938 • b/w; 1 hr, 11 min; ½" Beta II, ½" VHS • Sale: $54.95

- -

Red Fox, Inc; Order No. 8024; 1938 • b/w; 1 hr, 11 min; ½" Beta II, ½" VHS • Sale: $54.95

Portrays the debonaire detective, "The Saint," as he tangles with the underworld to protect an attractive lady. Stars Louis Hayward, Kay Sutton, and Jack Carson.

Hedy Lamarr and Victor Mature in Samson and Delilah.

SALLY OF THE SAWDUST

Blackhawk Films, Inc; Order No. 506-16-0788 for ½" Beta II, 525-16-0788 for ½" VHS; 1925 • b/w; 1 hr, 32 min; ½" Beta II, ½" VHS • Sale: $49.95

Spotlights the only full-fledged comedy directed by D. W. Griffith, the story of a carnival barker who adopts a little girl, and his problems in providing a decent upbringing for her. Stars W.C. Fields, Carol Dempster, and Alfred Lunt in a silent feature.

SALOME

National Film and Video Center; 1953 • color; 1 hr, 43 min; ¾" U-Matic, ½" Beta II, ½" VHS • Rental: $49/1 showing

Stars Rita Hayworth, Stewart Granger, and Charles Laughton in a film which cast Salome as the convert of John the Baptist, who dances for King Herod to save the prophet's life. Ends as her mother wins Herod's consent for John's execution.

SALT IN THE WOUND

Tape Club of America; Order No. 2304 B; 1972 • color; 1 hr, 32 min; ½" Beta II, ½" VHS • Sale: $54.95

Tells the story of two American soldiers—one white, one black—who are court-martialed and sentenced to death. Shows how, just as they face the firing squad, the group is attacked by German parachutists. Stars George Hilton and Klaus Kinski.

SAMAR

Fotomat Corp; Order No. B0123 for ½" Beta II, V0123 for ½" VHS; 1962 • color; 1 hr, 42 min; ½" Beta II, ½" VHS • Sale: $39.95; Rental: $7.95/up to 5 days, applicable to purchase

- -

Video Communications Inc; 1962 • color; 1 hr, 42 min; ½" Beta II, ½" VHS • Sale: $54.95

Shows a prisoner arriving in a penal camp located in Spain and attempting to alleviate the suffering of the inmates. Stars George Montgomery and Gilbert Roland.

SAME TIME, NEXT YEAR
MCA Videocassette, Inc; Order No. 66013; 1978 • color; 1 hr, 59 min; ½" Beta II, ½" VHS • Sale: $60

Adapts the Broadway play about a couple who meet at a motel for an extramarital affair once a year for 26 years. Stars Alan Alda and Ellen Burstyn.

SAMSON AND DELILAH
Vid America; Order No. 907; Date not listed • color; 58 min; ½" Beta II, ½" VHS • Rental: $9.95/wk

Offers an episode from the Sun Classic series "Greatest Heroes of the Bible." Dramatizes the Old Testament story found in Judges 13-16. Features well-known Hollywood actors.

THE SAN ANTONIO KID; KANSAS TERRORS
The Nostalgia Merchant; 1944; 1939 • b/w; 2 hrs; ½" Beta II, ½" VHS • Sale: $59.95

Presents a western double feature. Opens with "Wild Bill" Elliot as Red Ryder in "The San Antonio Kid." Involves a plot to force ranchers to sell their land before oil is found on the property. Follows with "Kansas Terrors" with the Three Mesquiteers selling horses in the Caribbean for the US Army. Stars Bob Livingston, Ray Hatton, and Duncan Renaldo.

SAN FRANCISCO DOCUMENTAL
Astro Video Corporation; Order No. LL101; Date not listed • color; 1 hr; ½" Beta II, ½" VHS • Sale: $39.95

Explores San Francisco using verite techniques and optical effects with music of Bay Area musicians. Includes aerial images and montages of events including a rock concert, the Hookers' Ball, Polk Street on Halloween, cable cars, Golden Gate Park, joggers, street artists, landmarks, and the Grand National Rodeo.

THE SAND PEBBLES
Golden Tapes Video Tape Library; Order No. F-1029; 19666 • color; 2 hrs, 15 min; ½" Beta II, ½" VHS • Sale: $49.95 for ½" Beta II & VHS, $124.95 for ¾"
- -
Magnetic Video Corporation; Order No. CL-1029; 1966 • color; 3 hrs, 15 min; ½" Beta II, ½" VHS • Sale: $64.95
- -
The Video Library; Order No. MV-1029; 1966 • color; 3 hrs, 15 min; ½" Beta II, ½" VHS • Sale: $74.95

Candice Bergen and Steve McQueen in *The San Pebbles*.

Relates the adventure of an American gunboat crew caught between Chinese warlords and foreign powers in post-World War I China. Stars Steve McQueen, Candice Bergen, Richard Attenborough, Richard Crenna, and Simon Oakland, under the direction of Robert Wise.

SANDERS OF THE RIVER
Northeast Video and Sound, Inc; 1935 • b/w; 1 hr, 20 min; ¾" U-Matic, ½" EIAJ, ½" Beta II, ½" VHS • Sale: $195; Rental: $75/wk

Deals with an officer of the river patrol, tracking down those seeking to break the law and stirring up rebellion among the native tribes. Stars Paul Robeson.

SANTA FE MARSHAL
Videobrary Inc; Order No. 25; 1940 • b/w; 1 hr; ½" Beta II, ½" VHS • Sale: $39.95

Presents a Hopalong Cassidy western starring William Boyd and Russell Hayden.

SANTA FE TRAIL
Red Fox, Inc; 1940 • b/w; 1 hr, 20 min; ½" Beta II, ½" VHS • Sale: $49.95
- -
VCX; Order No. FC103; 1940 • b/w; 1 hr, 43 min; ½" Beta II, ½" VHS • Sale: $3 5.00
- -
Video Communications Inc; 1956 • color; 1 hr, 50 min; ½" Beta II, ½" VHS • Sale: $54.95

Presents a pre-Civil War western about a group of soldiers searching for John Brown. Features Errol Flynn, Olivia DeHavilland, Alan Hale, Ronald Reagan, Van Heflin, and Gene Reynolds.

SAPS AT SEA
The Nostalgia Merchant; 1940 • b/w; 57 min; ½" Beta II, ½" VHS • Sale: $54.95
- -
Time-Life Video Club Inc; 1940 • b/w; 57 min; ½" Beta II, ½" VHS • Sale: $44.95 to members

Features Laurel and Hardy on a comic vacation at sea in a boat that is too small for them. Stars Stan Laurel, Oliver Hardy, James Finlayson, Ben Turpin, and Rychard Cramer, under the direction of Gordon Douglas. Provides also a Hal Roach comedy short.

SASQUATCH
Vid America; Order No. 204; Date not listed • color; 1 hr, 36 min; ½" Beta II, ½" VHS • Rental: $9.95/wk

Focuses on the original Bigfoot, the giant believed by many to be a carryover of a sub-human creature. Features people who have encountered the ape-man, and follows an expedition into the Northwest wilds to discover his domain.

SATURDAY NIGHT AND SUNDAY MORNING
Thunderbird Films; 1960 • b/w; 1 hr, 30 min; ¾" U-Matic, ½" Beta I, ½" Beta II, ½" VHS • Sale: $69.95 for ½" Beta I, $49.95 for ½" Beta II & VHS, $89.95 for ¾"

Features Albert Finney as an angry young man in Britain during the 1950's. Recounts his relations with two women played by Shirley Anne Field and Rachel Roberts.

Karen Lynn Gorney and John Travolta in *Saturday Night Fever*.

SATURDAY NIGHT FEVER

Fotomat Corp; Order No. B0003 for ½" Beta II, V0003 for ½" VHS; 1977 • color; 1 hr, 58 min; ½" Beta II, ½" VHS • Sale: $69.95; Rental: $13.95/up to 5 days, applicable to purchase

- -

MCA DiscoVision; Order No. P10-521; 1977 • color; 1 hr, 58 min; LaserVision • Sale: $24.95

Details the life of a local disco kingpin who, after six full days of work at a Brooklyn paint store, ritualistically prepares himself for Saturday night. Shows how he eventually begins to question the narrowness of his perspective. Features disco dance sequences and music by the Bee Gees. Stars John Travolta and Karen Gorney in a Robert Stigwood production directed by John Badham.

SATURDAY NIGHT FEVER (PG)

Paramount Home Video; 1977 • color; 1 hr, 58 min; ½" Beta II, ½" VHS • Sale: $59.95

Presents the film version rated PG.

SATURDAY NIGHT FEVER (R)

Paramount Home Video; 1977 • color; 1 hr, 58 min; ½" Beta II, ½" VHS • Sale: $59.95

- -

RCA SelectaVision VideoDiscs; Order No. 00602; 1977 • color; 1 hr, 59 min; CED • Sale: $24.98

Presents the film version rated R.

SATURN 3

Magnetic Video Corporation; 1980 • color; 1 hr, 28 min; ½" Beta II, ½" VHS • Sale: $59.95

Presents a science-fiction film which features a robot programmed for sex. Stars Kirk Douglas, Farrah Fawcett, Harvey Keitel, and Douglas Lambert.

SAUL AND DAVID

Video Communications Inc; Order No. 1189; Date not listed • color; 2 hrs; ½" Beta II, ½" VHS • Sale: $54.95

Dramatizes the period of David's life while King Saul lived. Includes David's battle with Goliath, Saul's jealousy, and Saul's tragic death. Features Norman Woodland, Giannie Garko, and Lyz Marquez.

SCALPEL

Magnetic Video Corporation; Order No. CL-4056; 1978 • color; 1 hr, 35 min; ½" Beta II, ½" VHS • Sale: $54.95

Presents a bizarre tale of impersonation and double identities, with a Hitchcock-style surprise ending. Features Robert Lansing and Judith Chapman.

SCARED TO DEATH

Reel Images Inc; Order No. 572; 1946 • color; 1 hr, 6 min; ½" Beta II, ½" VHS • Sale: $49.95 for ½" Beta II, $52.95 for ½" VHS

- -

Discount Video Tapes; 1947 • color; 1 hr, 10 min; ½" Beta II, ½" VHS • Sale: $44.95

Presents a story told in flashback by the corpse of a woman who was scared to death by a mask. Features Bela Lugosi, George Zucco, and Joyce Compton.

SCARFACE

MCA Videocassette, Inc; Order No. 55007; 1932 • b/w; 1 hr, 39 min; ½" Beta II, ½" VHS • Sale: $50

Presents a prototypic gangster film set in Chicago. Stars Paul Muni, George Raft, Boris Karloff, and Ann Dvorak, under the direction of Howard Hawks.

THE SCARLET PIMPERNEL

Thunderbird Films; 1934 • b/w; 1 hr, 35 min; ¾" U-Matic, ½" Beta I, ½" Beta II, ½" VHS • Sale: $69.95 for ½" Beta I, $49.95 for ½" Beta II & VHS, $89.95 for ¾"

- -

VCX, Order No. FC107; 1934 • b/w; 1 hr, 35 min; ½" Beta II, ½" VHS • Sale: $35.00

- -

Video T.E.N.; 1935 • b/w; 1 hr, 35 min; ½" Beta II, ½" VHS • Sale: $49.95 for ½" Beta II, $54.95 for ½" VHS

Offers the Alexander Korda classic of an English nobleman attempting to save doomed French aristocrats from the guillotine during the French Revolution. Stars Leslie Howard, Merle Oberon, and Raymond Massey.

SCARLET STREET

Northeast Video and Sound, Inc; 1945 • b/w; 1 hr, 35 min; ¾" U-Matic, ½" EIAJ, ½" Beta II, ½" VHS • Sale: $225; Rental: $80/wk

Presents Fritz Lang's remake of Renoir's "La Chienne." Depicts an unhappily married bank clerk whose talent as an artist has gone undiscovered. Relates how a scheming young woman manages to exploit his infatuation for her. Stars Edward G. Robinson, Joan Bennett, Dan Duryea, and Margaret Lindsey.

SCENES FROM A MARRIAGE

Columbia Pictures Home Entertainment; Order No. BCF7360 for ½" Beta II, VCF32 25 for ½" VHS; 1973 • color; 2 hrs, 48 min; ½" Beta II, ½" VHS • Sale: $59.95

- -

Time-Life Video Club Inc; 1973 • color; 2 hrs, 43 min; ½" Beta II, ½" VHS • Sale: $64.95 to members

Details the disintegration of a marriage and the following relationship. Offers a feature length re-editing of six hours of drama originally produced for Swedish TV, by writer and director Ingmar Bergman. Provides an intimate, painful look at marriage. Stars Liv Ulmann, Erland Josephson, Bibi Anderson, Jan Malmsjo, and Anita Wall.

SCHIZO
Niles Cinema; Order No. BT-15 for 1/2" Beta II, VH-15 for 1/2" VHS; 1976 • color; 1 hr, 49 min; 1/2" Beta II, 1/2" VHS • Sale: $59.95

Traces a young bride's horror-filled search for her mother's murderer through many bloody episodes. Features Lynne Frederick, John Leyton, and Stephanie Beacham.

SCOUMOUNE
Cinema Concepts, Inc.; 1974 • color; 1 hr, 27 min; 3/4" U-Matic, 1/2" Beta II, 1/2" VHS • Sale: $54.95 for 1/2" Beta II & VHS, $149.95 for 3/4"
- -
The Video Library; Order No. CC-0140; 1974 • color; 1 hr, 27 min; 1/2" Beta II, 1/2" VHS • Sale: $54.95

Features Jean-Paul Belmondo and Claudia Cardinale in a comedy-drama that asks the question: "Is there honesty?"

SCROOGE
Reel Images Inc; Order No. 455; 1935 • b/w; 1 hr, 1 min; 1/2" Beta II, 1/2" VHS • Sale: $39.95 for 1/2" Beta II, $42.95 for 1/2" VHS

Relates the story of Charles Dickens' Ebenezer Scrooge, the miser who was transformed by the Ghosts of Christmas. Stars Seymour Hicks.

THE SEA AROUND US
Blackhawk Films, Inc; Order No. 506-66-0716 for 1/2" Beta II, 525-66-0716 for 1/2" VHS; 1953 • color; 1 hr, 1 min; 3/4" U-Matic, 1/2" Beta II, 1/2" VHS • Sale: $89.95 for 1/2" Beta I, $59.95 for 1/2" Beta II & VHS, $99.95 for 3/4"

Presents a science documentary of the fauna, history, and life of the ocean, based on Rachel Carson's study, produced by Irwin Allen, and narrated by Don Forbes.

THE SEA LION
Reel Images Inc; Order No. 532; 1921 • b/w; 1 hr, 7 min; 1/2" Beta II, 1/2" VHS • Sale: $49.95 for 1/2" Beta II, $52.95 for 1/2" VHS

Depicts, in a silent melodrama with music score, the story of a young "wastrel" who ships out to sea to find himself, and instead finds a shipwrecked girl who may be the daughter of "The Sea Lion." Stars Hobart Bosworth and Bessie Love.

SEANCE ON A WET AFTERNOON
Thunderbird Films; 1964 • b/w; 1 hr, 55 min; 3/4" U-Matic, 1/2" Beta I, 1/2" Beta II, 1/2" VHS • Sale: $69.95 for 1/2" Beta I, $49.95 for 1/2" Beta II & VHS, $89.95 for 3/4"

Relates the story of an unrecognized spiritual medium and her husband who stage a kidnapping so that she can "prove" her psychic powers. Features Kim Stanley, Richard Attenborough, and Patrick Magee.

THE SEARCH
The Nostalgia Merchant; Order No. 7005; 1956 • color; 1 hr, 15 min; 1/2" Beta II, 1/2" VHS • Sale: $54.95

Offers a three-part serialized Lone Ranger adventure compiled on one videocassette. Tells of a Christmas-time search for a missing father and a stolen jeweled cross. Features Clayton Moore and Jay Silverheels.

THE SEARCHERS
WCI Home Video Inc; 1956 • color; 1 hr, 59 min; 1/2" Beta II, 1/2" VHS • Sale: $55

Depicts the relentless search spanning many years for a young girl kidnapped by Indians. Stars John Wayne, Jeffrey Hunter, Natalie Wood, Vera Miles, Ward Bond, and Harry Carey Jr., under the direction of John Ford.

SECOND CHANCE
The Nostalgia Merchant; Order No. 8024; 1953 • color; 1 hr, 22 min; 1/2" Beta II, 1/2" VHS • Sale: $54.95
- -
Red Fox, Inc; Order No. 8024; 1953 • color; 1 hr, 22 min; 1/2" Beta II, 1/2" VHS • Sale: $54.95

Presents a thriller of a young girl pursued by a maddened killer across South America. Stars Robert Mitchum, Linda Darnell, and Jack Palance.

SECOND CHORUS
Budget Video; 1940 • b/w; 1 hr, 30 min; 1/2" Beta II, 1/2" VHS • Sale: $44.95
- -
Reel Images Inc; Order No. 494; 1940 • b/w; 1 hr, 24 min; 1/2" Beta II, 1/2" VHS • Sale: $49.95 for 1/2" Beta II, $52.95 for 1/2" VHS

Recounts a musical story of two band leaders trying to keep their band together. Stars Fred Astaire, Paulette Goddard, Burgess Meredith, and Artie Shaw.

SECRET AGENT
Northeast Video and Sound, Inc; 1936 • b/w; 1 hr, 30 min; 3/4" U-Matic, 1/2" EIAJ, 1/2" Beta II, 1/2" VHS • Sale: $195; Rental: $75/wk

Presents an early Alfred Hitchcock spy thriller in which an author and a woman agent must pose as man and wife to seek out and kill a spy. Stars Madeleine Carroll, Peter Lorre, Robert Young, John Gielgud, and Lilli Palmer.

SECRET LIFE OF ADOLPH HITLER
Reel Images Inc; Order No. 33; 1958 • b/w; 53 min; 1/2" Beta II, 1/2" VHS • Sale: $39.95 for 1/2" Beta II, $42.95 for 1/2" VHS

Details the rise of Adolph Hitler and the Third Reich in a documentary narrated by Westbrook van Vooris. Features documentary footage.

THE SECRET WEAPON
National Film and Video Center; 1942 • b/w; 1 hr, 8 min; 3/4" U-Matic, 1/2" Beta II, 1/2" VHS • Rental: $39/1 showing

Pits Sherlock Holmes against the diabolical Professor Moriarty when the professor plans to sell a powerful bomb mechanism to the Nazis. Climaxes in Moriarty's laboratory with Holmes losing his life's blood drop by drop. Stars Basil Rathbone and Nigel Bruce.

SECRETS
Fotomat Corp; Order No. B0361 for 1/2" Beta II, V0361 for 1/2" VHS; 1978 • color; 1 hr, 26 min; 1/2" Beta II, 1/2" VHS • Sale: $59.95; Rental: $9.95/5 days
- -
Vid America; Order No. 921; Date not listed • color; 1 hr, 26 min; 1/2" Beta II, 1/2" VHS • Rental: $12.95/wk
- -
Video Gems; 1971 • color; 1 hr, 26 min; 1/2" Beta II, 1/2" VHS • Sale: $59.95

Examines the relationship of a couple who have grown apart during their nine-year marriage. Follows the extra-marital affairs that lead them to rediscover what they have missed in each other. Stars Jacqueline Bisset, Per Oscarsson, Shirley Knight Hopkins, and Robert Powell.

THE SEDUCTION OF AMY
VTS; Date not listed • color; 1 hr, 14 min; 1/2" Beta I, 1/2" Beta II, 1/2" VHS • Sale: $99

Presents a pornographic film.

THE SEDUCTION OF JOE TYNAN
MCA Videocassette, Inc; Order No. 66008; 1979 • color; 1 hr, 47 min; 1/2" Beta II, 1/2" VHS • Sale: $60

Follows the career of a U.S. senator with presidential aspirations who is seduced by his notoriety, power, and a beautiful co-worker, despite his high ideals and loving family. Stars Alan Alda, who wrote the screenplay as well, Meryl Streep, Melvyn Douglas, and Barbara Harris.

THE SEDUCTION OF LYNN CARTER
Video Home Library; Order No. VX-104; Date not listed • color; 2 hrs; 1/2" Beta II, 1/2" VHS • Sale: $99.95

Presents a pornographic film.

THE SEDUCTION OF MIMI
Magnetic Video Corporation; Order No. CL-2049; 1974 • color; 1 hr, 29 min; 1/2" Beta II, 1/2" VHS • Sale: $44.95

Relates the story of a Sicilian worker's inability to adjust to big-city life in Milan, and his extravagant deeds to reassert his lost honor upon his return home. Stars Giancarlo Giannini and Mariangela Melato, under the direction of Lina Wertmuller.

THE SELFISH GIANT AND THE REMARKABLE ROCKET
Vid America; Order No. 714; Date not listed • color: 60 min; 1/2" Beta II, 1/2" VHS • Rental: $9.95/wk

Features two Oscar Wilde classics animated by The Reader's Digest. Includes the story of the lonely ogre and the comic tale of the feisty firecrackers, narrated by David Niven.

SELLING MOVIES ON TELEVISION
Reel Images Inc; Order No. 583; Date not listed • color; 55 min; 1/2" Beta II, 1/2" VHS • Sale: $39.95 for 1/2" Beta II, $42.95 for 1/2" VHS

Offers a collection of 67 television commercials for movies that include "The Great Dictator," "Divorce American Style," "Casino Royale," "Cool Hand Luke," "Portnoy's Complaint," and many others.

SEMI-TOUGH
Vid America; Order No. 351; 1977 • color; 1 hr, 47 min; 1/2" Beta II, 1/2" VHS • Rental: $13.95/wk

Presents a social satire about two pro football buddies and the team owner's beautiful daughter. Features Burt Reynolds, Kris Kristofferson, Jill Clayburgh, and Robert Preston.

THE SENATOR WAS INDISCREET
Video T.E.N.; 1948 • b/w; 1 hr, 16 min; 1/2" Beta II, 1/2" VHS • Sale: $49.95 for 1/2" Beta II, $54.95 for 1/2" VHS

Offers the only film ever directed by George S. Kaufman, a satire on the world of Washington politics. Features William Powell, Ella Raines, Peter Lind Hayes, Arleen Whelan, and Hans Conreid.

SERPICO
Fotomat Corp; Order No. B0215 for 1/2" Beta II, V0215 for 1/2" VHS; 1974 • color; 2 hrs, 10 min; 1/2" Beta II, 1/2" VHS • Sale: $69.95; Rental: $9.95/up to 5 days, applicable to purchase

Adapts, on two cassettes, Peter Maas' book about a real policeman, Frank Serpico, whose public telling of corruption in the New York City Police Department led to the formation of the much publicized Knapp Commission Hearings, and Serpico's estrangement from the Force. Shows how well-meaning Serpico put his life into jeopardy by trying to get rid of the few bad policemen. Stars Al Pacino, John Randolph, Jack Kehoe, and Cornelia Sharpe, under Sidney Lumet's direction.

THE SERVANT
Fotomat Corp; Order No. B0251 for 1/2" Beta II, V0251 for 1/2" VHS; 1963 • b/w; 1 hr, 52 min; 1/2" Beta II, 1/2" VHS • Sale: $49.95; Rental: $9.95/up to 5 days, applicable to purchase

----

Time-Life Video Club Inc; 1963 • b/w; 1 hr, 56 min; 1/2" Beta II, 1/2" VHS • Sale: $44.95 to members

Explores the relationship between a British manservant and the wealthy, spoiled young man who employs him. Details the moral degradation and class hypocrisy found in this relationship. Stars Dirk Bogarde, James Fox, Sarah Miles, and Wendy Craig, under the direction of Joseph Losey, from a Harold Pinter screenplay.

SEVEN BEAUTIES
Fotomat Corp; Order No. B0437 for 1/2" Beta II, V0437 for 1/2" VHS ; 1976 • color; 1 hr, 56 min; 1/2" Beta II, 1/2" VHS • Sale: $49.95; Rental: $7.95

Time-Life Video Club Inc; 1976 • color; 1 hr, 55 min; 1/2" Beta II, 1/2" VHS • Sale: $44.95 to members

Follows a two-bit Neapolitan hood through his World War II experiences, culminating in his seduction of the gargantuan female commandant of a German concentration camp. Stars Giancarlo Giannini, Fernando Rey, and Shirley Stoler, under the direction of Lina Wertmuller.

SEVEN SAMURAI
Budget Video; 1954 • b/w; 3 hrs, 20 min; 1/2" Beta II, 1/2" VHS • Sale: $74.95

Presents a Japanese film (with English subtitles) directed by Akira Kurosawa. Dramatizes the attempts of a 16th century village to survive repeated raids from bandits by hiring professional warriors. Precedes and serves as the inspiration for the film "The Magnificent Seven." Stars Toshiro Mifune and Takashi Shimura.

THE SEVEN YEAR ITCH
Blackhawk Films, Inc; Order No. 502-49-0025 for 1/2" Beta II, 515-49-0021 for 1/2" VHS; 1955 • color; 1 hr, 45 min; 1/2" Beta II, 1/2" VHS • Sale: $54.95

Golden Tapes Video Tape Library; Order No. F-1043; 1955 • color; 1 hr, 45 min; 1/2" Beta II, 1/2" VHS • Sale: $49.95 for 1/2" Beta II & VHS, $124.95 for 3/4"

Magnetic Video Corporation; Order No. CL-1043; 1955 • color; 1 hr, 45 min; 1/2" Beta II, 1/2" VHS • Sale: $44.95

RCA SelectaVision VideoDiscs; Order No. 00114; 1955 • color; 1 hr, 45 min; CED • Sale: $19.98

The Video Library; Order No. MV-1043; 1955 • color; 1 hr, 45 min; 1/2" Beta II, 1/2" VHS • Sale: $44.95

Tells of a husband of seven years alone in New York while his wife and child are away for the summer, Depicts his almost-affair with the model living in the next apartment until, tortured by guilt, he finally runs off to join his wife. Stars Marilyn Monroe and Tom Ewell, under the direction of Billy Wilder.

THE SEVEN-PER-CENT SOLUTION
MCA DiscoVision; Order No. 11-008; 1976 • color; 1 hr, 53 min; LaserVision • Sale: $24.95

Offers a tale of Sherlock Holmes collaborating with Sigmund Freud in order to track down Professor Moriarty. Stars Nicol Williamson, Robert Duvall, Alan Arkin, Vanessa Redgrave, and Laurence Olivier, under Herbert Ross's direction, in an adaptation of Nicholas Meyer's novel.

1776
National Film and Video Center; 1972 • color; 2 hrs, 28 min; 3/4" U-Matic, 1/2" Beta II, 1/2" VHS • Rental: $79/1 showing

Dramatizes the meetings of the Continental Congress, including the political maneuverings that resulted in Jefferson's authorship of the Declaration of Independence. Culminates in the signing of the Declaration. Stars William Daniels, Howard Da Silva, Ken Howard, Donald Madden, Blythe Danner, and Virginia Vestoff.

THE SEVENTH VOYAGE OF SINBAD
National Film and Video Center; 1958 • color; 1 hr, 29 min; 3/4" U-Matic, 1/2" Beta II, 1/2" VHS • Rental: $69/1 showing

Relates Sinbad's search for a piece of roc's eggshell, which he hopes will restore Princess Parisa to normal size after she has been reduced by the evil spells of magician Sokurah. Stars Kerwin Mathews, Katheryn Grant, Richard Eyer, and Torin Thatcher.

SEX AND THE OFFICE GIRL
Meda/Media Home Entertainment Inc; Order No. M510; 1972 • color; 1 hr, 20 min; 1/2" Beta I, 1/2" Beta II, 1/2" VHS • Sale: $49.95

Presents a pornographic film.

SEX RITUALS OF THE OCCULT
Quality X Video Cassette Company; Date not listed • color; 1 hr, 22 min; 1/2" Beta I, 1/2" Beta II, 1/2" VHS • Sale: $99.50; Preview: $20

Presents a pornographic film.

SEX THROUGH A WINDOW
Niles Cinema; Order No. BT-08 for 1/2" Beta II, VH-08 for 1/2" VHS; Date not listed • color; 1 hr, 35 min; 1/2" Beta II, 1/2" VHS • Sale: $59.95

Tells of a TV newscaster who reports on the ease of invading the privacy of others, and becomes an obsessive spy of people having sex. Stars John Norman, Bara Byrnes, Lynn Kimball, and Glen Jacobsen.

SEX WORLD
TVX Distributors; Order No. R.T. 90; Date not listed • color; 2 hrs; 1/2" Beta II, 1/2" VHS • Sale: $79.50 for 1/2" Beta II, $89.50 for 1/2" VHS

Presents a pornographic film.

SEXTEEN
Quality X Video Cassette Company; Date not listed • color; 1 hr, 16 min; 1/2" Beta I, 1/2" Beta II, 1/2" VHS • Sale: $99.50

Presents a pornographic film.

SEXTON BLAKE AND THE HOODED TERROR
Reel Images Inc; Order No. 425; 1941 • b/w; 1 hr, 10 min; 1/2" Beta II, 1/2" VHS • Sale: $49.95 for 1/2" Beta II, $52.95 for 1/2" VHS

Follows the adventures of a Baker Street sleuth (fashioned after Sherlock Holmes) as he tracks down a master criminal known as "The Snake."

SEXUAL CUSTOMS IN SCANDINAVIA
Quality X Video Cassette Company; Date not listed • color; 1 hr, 15 min; 1/2" Beta I, 1/2" Beta II, 1/2" VHS • Sale: $99.50

Presents a pornographic film.

SEXUAL FREEDOM IN BROOKLYN
Monarch Releasing Corporation; Date not listed • color; 1 hr, 15 min; 3/4" U-Matic • Sale: $300

Presents a pornographic film.

SGT. PEPPER'S LONELY HEARTS CLUB BAND
MCA DiscoVision; Order No. 17-004; 1978 • color; 1 hr, 53 min; LaserVision • Sale: $24.95

Offers a fantasy loosely based on the record album by the Beatles. Presents the attempts of the Lonely Hearts Club Band to overcome a plot to strip Heartland, U.S.A. of its music. Features Peter Frampton, the Bee Gees, Donald Pleasance, and Steve Martin.

SHADOW OF CHINATOWN
Video T.E.N.; 1946 • b/w; 1 hr, 10 min; 1/2" Beta II, 1/2" VHS • Sale: $49.95 for 1/2" Beta II, $54.95 for 1/2" VHS

Tells of a mad scientist, employed by foreign importers to destroy their Chinatown competition, who creates a wave of murder and terror. Stars Bela Lugosi, Herman Brix, and Joan Barclay.

SHADOW OF THE EAGLE
Reel Images Inc; Order No. 789; 1932 • b/w; 3 hrs, 46 min; 1/2" Beta II, 1/2" VHS • Sale: $119.95

Offers a Mascot Studio serial in twelve episodes, starring John Wayne, Pat O'Malley, and Yakima Canutt.

SHADOW OF THE HAWK
National Film and Video Center; 1976 • color; 1 hr, 52 min; 3/4" U-Matic, 1/2" Beta II, 1/2" VHS • Rental: $139/1 showing

Pits a powerful evil force against an old Indian medicine man and his grandson. Features Jan-Michael Vincent, Marilyn Hasset, and Chief Dan George.

THE SHADOW STRIKES
Cable Films; 1937 • b/w; 1 hr, 4 min; 1/2" Beta I, 1/2" Beta II, 1/2" VHS • Sale: $65 for 1/2" Beta I, $49.50 for 1/2" Beta II & VHS

Spotlights Lamont Cranston, alias the Shadow, the cryptic hero of the long-running radio series. Presents a mystery based on the story "The Ghost of the Manor." Stars Rod LaRocque and Lynn Anders.

SHADOWS OF DEATH
Video Communications Inc; Order No. 1125; 1945 • b/w; 1 hr; 1/2" Beta II, 1/2" VHS • Sale: $54.95

Presents a western in which Billy the Kid comes to the rescue. Stars Buster Crabbe and Al "Fuzzy" St. John.

SHALL WE DANCE
Blackhawk Films, Inc; Order No. 506-88-0714 for 1/2"

Harry Carey Jr., Joanne Dru, John Wayne, John Agar, and Ben Johnson in *She Wore a Yellow Ribbon.*

Beta II, 525-88-0714 for ½" VHS; 1937 • b/w; 1 hr, 56 min; ½" Beta II, ½" VHS • Sale: $54.95

Showcases Fred Astaire as a ballet star who falls for snobbish musical comedy primadonna Ginger Rogers, in a musical with a George Gershwin score. Includes the songs "They Can't Take That Away From Me" and "Let's Call The Whole Thing Off," and a dance sequence on roller skates.

SHAMUS

Columbia Pictures Home Entertainment; 1973 • color; 1 hr, 46 min; ½" Beta II, ½" VHS • Sale: $59.95

- -
Fotomat Corp; Order No. B0431 for ½" VHS, V0431 for ½" VHS; 1973 • color; 1 hr, 31 min; ½" Beta II, ½" VHS • Sale: $49.95; Rental: $7.95/5 days

Tells of a private eye and his numerous adventures and amorous exploits as he investigates a government arms deal and a cache of diamonds. Features Burt Reynolds, Dyan Cannon, Giorgio Tozzi, John Ryan, and Joe Santos.

SHANE .

Fotomat Corp; Order No. B0041 for ½" Beta II, V0041 for ½" VHS; 1953 • color; 1 hr, 57 min; ½" Beta II, ½" VHS • Sale: $49.95; Rental: $9.95/up to 5 days, applicable to purchase

- -
Paramount Home Video; 1953 • color; 1 hr, 57 min; ½" Beta II, ½" VHS • Sale: $59.95

- -
RCA SelectaVision VideoDiscs; Order No. 00622; 1953 • color; 1 hr, 58 min; CED • Sale: $19.98

Tells a story of a drifter and retired gunfighter who comes to the assistance of a homestead family terrorized by an aging cattleman and his hired gun. Shows that, in fighting the last, decisive battle, Shane sees the end of his own way of life. Stars Alan Ladd, Jean Arthur, Van Heflin, Brandon de Wilde, and Jack Palance, under the direction of George Stevens.

SHE WORE A YELLOW RIBBON

Niles Cinema; Order No. NM-8026; 1949 • color; 1 hr, 42 min; ½" Beta II, ½" VHS • Sale: $54.95

- -
The Nostalgia Merchant; Order No. 8026; 1949 • color; 1 hr, 43 min; ½" Beta II, ½" VHS • Sale: $54.95

- -
Red Fox, Inc; Order No. 8026; 1949 • color; 1 hr, 43 min; ½" Beta II, ½" VHS • Sale: $54.95

- -
Time-Life Video Club Inc; 1949 • color; 1 hr, 43 min; ½" Beta II, ½" VHS • Sale: $44.95 to members

- -
Vid America; Order No. 933; 1949 • color; 1 hr, 43 min; ½" Beta II, ½" VHS • Rental: $10.95/wk

Presents a John Ford wartime story of duty, country, soldiering, and honor among men. Stars John Wayne, Joanne Dru, and Ben Johnson, under the direction of John Ford.

THE SHE-BEAST

Video Communications Inc; 1966 • color; 1 hr, 14 min; ½" Beta II, ½" VHS • Sale: $54.95

Recounts a tale of the reincarnation of an 18th century Transylvanian witch. Features Barbara Steele, John Karlsen, and Ian Ogilvy.

SHENANDOAH

MCA DiscoVision; Order No. 14-001; 1965 • color; 1 hr, 45 min; LaserVision • Sale: $24.95

Tells of the personal conflict of a Virginia farmer who opposes slavery but cannot sanction war, until his son is taken prisoner during the Civil War and he goes to search for him. Stars James Stewart, Katherine Ross, Doug McClure, and Rosemary Forsyth, under the direction of Andrew V. McLaglen.

SHERLOCK HOLMES AND THE SECRET WEAPON

Video T.E.N.; 1942 • b/w; 1 hr, 8 min; ½" Beta II, ½" VHS • Sale: $49.95 for ½" Beta II, $54.95 for ½" VHS

Shows Sherlock Holmes and Professor Moriarty racing to capture a revolutionary bomb sight which the latter wants to sell to the Nazis. Stars Basil Rathbone, Nigel Bruce, Henry Daniell, Hillary Brooke, and Paul Cavanaugh.

SHERLOCK HOLMES DOUBLE FEATURE #1
All Star Video Corp; 1942; 1946 • b/w; 2 hrs; 1/2" Beta II, 1/2" VHS • Sale: $59.95

Presents two Sherlock Holmes movies starring Basil Rathbone and Nigel Bruce. Offers "Sherlock Holmes and the Secret Weapon," in which Holmes and Dr. Watson vie with their arch enemy Professor Moriarty to capture an invention which could change the course of World War II; and "Terror by Night" in which Watson and Holmes tackle a jewel thief aboard an express train from London to Scotland.

SHERLOCK HOLMES DOUBLE FEATURE #2
All Star Video Corp; 1945; 1946 • b/w; 2 hrs; 1/2" Beta II, 1/2" VHS • Sale: $59.95

Presents two Sherlock Holmes films starring Basil Rathbone and Nigel Bruce. Offers "The Woman in Green," loosely based on Sir A.C. Doyle's "Adventure of the Empty House," in which Holmes suspects Professor Moriarty of the bizarre "finger murders"; and "Dressed to Kill," in which Holmes confronts a beautiful villainess and a secret involving three music boxes constructed by a convict.

SHIP OF FOOLS
National Film and Video Center; 1965 • color; 2 hrs, 30 min; 3/4" U-Matic, 1/2" Beta II, 1/2" VHS • Rental: $49/1 showing

Adapts Katherine Porter's novel to the screen, taking some liberties with the plot. Brings together an oddly assorted group of people as passengers aboard a German freighter in 1933. Stars Vivien Leigh, Jose Ferrer, Oskar Werner, Simone Signoret, Lee Marvin, and George Segal.

SHOCK
Video T.E.N.; 1946 • b/w; 1 hr, 10 min; 1/2" Beta II, 1/2" VHS • Sale: $49.95 for 1/2" Beta II, 54.95 for 1/2" VHS

Portrays a psychiatrist, who has murdered his wife, plotting with his nurse to dispose of a young female witness. Stars Vincent Price, Lynn Bari, Frank Lattimore, Anabel Shaw, and Reed Hadley.

SHOCK CORRIDOR
Video Communications Inc; 1963 • b/w; 1 hr, 38 min; 1/2" Beta II, 1/2" VHS • Sale: $54.95

Portrays a journalist who commits himself to a mental hospital to find a murderer but loses his own mind in the process. Stars Constance Towers and Peter Breck, under the direction of Samuel Fuller.

SHOGUN
Paramount Home Video; 1980 • color; 2 hrs, 4 min; 1/2" Beta II, 1/2" VHS • Sale: $72.95

Condenses the TV mini-series' adaptation of James Clavell's novel into a feature length version. Concerns an English navigator who is shipwrecked in "the Japans" during feudal times. Follows his adventures serving Lord Roranaga who plots to become Shogun, and his ill-fated love affair with Mariko, his interpreter. Stars Richard Chamberlain, Toshiro Mifune, and Yoko Shimada.

SHOOT
Magnetic Video Corporation; Order No. CL-4013; 1976 • color; 1 hr, 34 min; 1/2" Beta II, 1/2" VHS • Sale: $54.95

Red Fox, Inc; Order No. CL-4013; Date not listed • color; 1 hr, 34 min; 1/2" Beta II, 1/2" VHS • Sale: $54.95

Vid America; Order No. 457; 1976 • color; 1 hr, 34 min; 1/2" Beta II, 1/2" VHS • Rental: $12.95/wk

Recounts a bizarre story of six businessmen on a weekend hunting trip who end up choosing fellow hunters as their prey. Stars Cliff Robertson, Ernest Borgnine, and Henry Silva.

THE SHOOTING
Video Communications Inc; Order No. 4006; 1967 • color; 1 hr, 22 min; 1/2" Beta II, 1/2" VHS • Sale: $54.95

Video T.E.N.; 1966 • color; 1 hr, 22 min; 1/2" Beta II, 1/2" VHS • Sale: $49.95 for 1/2" Beta II, 54.95 for 1/2" VHS

Portrays a bounty hunter turned miner who searches for his brother. Stars Jack Nicholson, Will Hutchins, Warren Oates, and Millie Perkins.

THE SHOOTIST
Fotomat Corp; Order No. B0219 for 1/2" Beta II, V0219 for 1/2" VHSi; 1976 • color; 1 hr, 40 min; 1/2" Beta II, 1/2" VHS • Sale: $49.95; Rental: $9.95/up to 5 days, applicable to purchase

Paramount Home Video; 1976 • color; 1 hr, 40 min; 1/2" Beta II, 1/2" VHS • Sale: $59.95

Presents John Wayne's final film. Follows an aged gunslinger as he learns he has terminal cancer, attempts to retire and die in peace, and finds he cannot do as he would like to. Stars Wayne, Lauren Bacall, James Stewart, Ron Howard, Richard Boone, John

Yoko Shimada and Richard Chamberlain in *Shogun*.

Carradine, Scatman Crothers, Harry Morgan, and Hugh O'Brian, under the direction of Don Siegal.

THE SHOUT
Home Vision; Order No. 800-7001 for ½" Beta II, 800-9001 for ½" VHS; 1979 • color; 1 hr, 27 min; ½" Beta II, ½" VHS • Sale: $49.95
- -
Vid America; Order No. 941; 1979 • color; 1 hr, 26 min; ½" Beta II, ½" VHS • Sale: $49.95; Rental: $12.95/wk, applicable to purchase

Offers a story of psychological terror in which a man has learned from Australian aborigines how to kill with a lethal shout. Stars Alan Bates, Susannah York, John Hurt, and Robert Stephens, under the direction of Jerzy Skolimowski.

SHOW BOAT
RCA SelectaVision VideoDiscs; Order No. 00209; 1951 • color; 1 hr, 47 min; CED • Sale: $14.98

Offers a musical version of Edna Ferber's novel about life on the Mississippi River at the turn of the century. Includes "My Bill," "Can't Help Loving That Man," "Old Man River," and "Make Believe." Stars Kathryn Grayson, Ava Gardner, Howard Keel, Joe E. Brown, Marge and Gower Champion, Agnes Moorehead, Robert Sterling, and William Warfield.

A SHRIEK IN THE NIGHT
Video T.E.N.; 1933 • b/w; 1 hr, 14 min; ½" Beta II, ½" VHS • Sale: $49.95 for ½" Beta II, $54.95 for ½" VHS

Relates how an unknown killer terrorizes an apartment building, and how he is tracked down. Stars Ginger Rogers, Lyle Talbot, Arthur Hoyt, and Purnell Pratt.

THE SICILIAN CONNECTION
Entertainment Video Releasing, Inc; Order No. 1015; 1975 • color; 1 hr, 40 min; ½" Beta II, ½" VHS • Sale: $49.95 for ½" Beta II, $54.95 for ½" VHS

Follows one man's fight against drug traffic from the poppy fields of Turkey to the sidewalks of New York. Stars Ben Gazzara.

SIDEWINDER ONE
Magnetic Video Corporation; Order No. CL-4052; 1977 • color; 1 hr, 37 min; ½" Beta II, ½" VHS • Sale: $54.95

Offers an action film centering on the world of motorcycle racing. Features Marjoe Gortner, Michael Parks, Susan Howard, Alex Cord, and Charlotte Rae.

SIDNEY THE ELEPHANT
Magnetic Video Corporation; Order No. CL-2040; Date not listed • color; 30 min; ½" Beta II, ½" VHS • Sale: $34.95

Presents a compilation of Terrytoon animated cartoons featuring Sidney the Elephant.

THE SILENT ENEMY
Reel Images Inc; Order No. 458; 1930 • color; 1 hr, 50 min; ½" Beta II, ½" VHS • Sale: $49.95 for ½" Beta II, $52.95 for ½" VHS

Focuses, in this early documentary, on the Ojibway Indian's way of life before the arrival of the white man, with the "silent enemy" of the title referring to hunger.

SILENT LAUGH MAKERS, VOLUME 1
Reel Images Inc; Order No. 76; 1915-27 • b/w; 1 hr, 16 min; ½" Beta II, ½" VHS • Sale: $49.95 for ½" Beta II, $52.95 for ½" VHS

Offers four silent one-reel comedy shorts. Presents "A One Mama Man" with Charlie Chase; "Lucky Dog" starring Stan Laurel and Oliver Hardy in an excerpt from their first film together (Stan was actually the star); "A Night Out" with Charlie Chaplin and Ben Turpin; and "Hop Along" featuring Arthur Lake.

SILENT LAUGH MAKERS, VOLUME 2
Reel Images Inc; Order No. 77; 1917-27 • b/w; 1 hr, 5 min; ½" Beta II, ½" VHS • Sale: $49.95 for ½" Beta II, $52.95 for ½" VHS

Presents three silent comedy shorts. Features "Fluttering Hearts" with Charlie Chase and Oliver Hardy; "Long Fliv the King," also with Charlie Chase and Oliver Hardy; and "Coney Island" featuring Roscoe "Fatty" Arbuckle, Buster Keaton, and Al St. John.

THE SILENT PARTNER
Time-Life Video Club Inc; 1979 • color; 1 hr, 43 min; ½" Beta II, ½" VHS • Sale: $44.95 to members

Presents a caper in which a bank robber is foiled by a teller, who then keeps some of the money. Follows the cat-and-mouse situation as the robber attempts to regain his lost spoils. Stars Christopher Plummer, Elliot Gould, and Susannah York.

SILVER LODE
FHV Entertainment, Inc; 1954 • color; 1 hr, 20 min; ½" Beta II, ½" VHS • Sale: $49.95

Offers the story of a western town in the 1870's where the whole community is drawn into one man's fight to clear himself of a murder charge. Stars John Payne, Lizabeth Scott, and Dan Duryea.

SILVER ON THE SAGE
Videobrary Inc; Order No. 22; 1939 • b/w; 1 hr, 6 min; ½" Beta II, ½" VHS • Sale: $39.95

Presents a Hopalong Cassidy western in which twin brothers, who are partners in crime, cause double trouble for Cassidy as he attempts to locate his stolen herd. Stars William Boyd, George "Gabby" Hayes, and Stanley Ridges.

SILVER STREAK
Magnetic Video Corporation; Order No. CL-1080; 1976 • color; 1 hr, 53 min; ½" Beta II, ½" VHS • Sale: $54.95

Follows the adventures of a mild-mannered publisher en route from Los Angeles to Chicago aboard a luxury train, as he tries to solve a murder, fights off killers, and jumps the train. Shows the train being hijacked and then becoming a runaway when the engineer is killed. Blends comedy, romance, action, and suspense. Stars Gene Wilder, Richard Pryor, Jill Clayburgh, Patrick McGoohan, Ned Beatty, Ray Walston, and Scatman Crothers.

THE SIN OF HAROLD DIDDLEBOCK
Video T.E.N.; 1946 • b/w; 1 hr, 35 min; ½" Beta II, ½" VHS • Sale: $49.95 for ½" Beta II, $54.95 for ½" VHS

Provides a last look at comedian Harold Lloyd in a film by Preston Sturges about a loser who drinks a magic cocktail. Includes Frances Ramsden, Jimmy Conlin, Edgar Kennedy, Franklin Pangborn, and Lionel Stander.

SINAI COMMANDOS
Discount Video Tapes; 1968 • color; 1 hr, 39 min; ½" Beta II, ½" VHS • Sale: $54.95

Offers an action-war drama set in the desert. Features Robert Fuller and John Hudson.

SINBAD AND THE EYE OF THE TIGER
Columbia Pictures Home Entertainment; 1977 • color; 1 hr, 53 min; 1/2" Beta II, 1/2" VHS • Sale: $59.95

- -
Time-Life Video Club Inc; 1977 • color; 1 hr, 53 min; 1/2" Beta II, 1/2" VHS • Sale: $59.95, plus $15 annual membership fee

Presents a modern adaptation of the Sinbad the Sailor adventures, with special effects by Ray Harryhausen. Features Patrick Wayne and Jane Seymour, under the direction of Sam Wanamaker.

SINBAD THE SAILOR
The Nostalgia Merchant; Order No. 8027; 1947 • color; 1 hr, 57 min; 1/2" Beta II, 1/2" VHS • Sale: $54.95

- -
Vid America; Order No. 218; 1947 • color; 1 hr, 57 min; 1/2" Beta II, 1/2" VHS • Rental: $9.95/wk

Presents a swashbuckler in which the fearless Sinbad pursues a secret amulet and a beautiful princess. Stars Douglas Fairbanks Jr., Maureen O'Hara, and Anthony Quinn.

SING YOUR WORRIES AWAY
Blackhawk Films, Inc; Order No. 506880710 for 1/2" Beta II, 525880710 for 1/2" VHS ; 1942 • b/w; 1 hr, 11 min; 1/2" Beta II, 1/2" VHS • Sale: $49.95

Offers a musical comedy about the theatre and gangsters. Stars June Havoc, Bert Lahr, Buddy Ebsen, Patsy Kelly, Sam Levene, Margaret Dumont, and the King Sisters.

SINGIN' IN THE RAIN
RCA SelectaVision VideoDiscs; Order No. 00210; 1952 • color; 1 hr, 43 min; CED • Sale: $14.98

Spoofs Hollywood's early "talky" days in this classic musical co-directed by Gene Kelly and Stanley Donen. Includes "Make 'Em Laugh," "My Lucky Star," "Broadway Melody," and "Good Morning." Stars Gene Kelly, Debbie Reynolds, Donald O'Connor, Jean Hagen, Cyd Charisse, Madge Blake, and Millard Mitchell.

Donald O'Connor and Gene Kelly in _Singin' In The Rain._

SINGLE ROOM FURNISHED
Video Communications Inc; Order No. 1091; 1968 • color; 1 hr, 42 min; 1/2" Beta II, 1/2" VHS • Sale: $54.95

Presents Jayne Mansfield in her last and most dramatic performance. Follows her as she portrays an innocent, voluptuous teenager, a deserted pregnant wife, a waitress, and a demented streetwalker.

SISTER KENNY
Blackhawk Films, Inc; Order No. 506-30-0709 for 1/2" Beta II, 525-30-0709 for 1/2" VHS; 1946 • b/w; 1 hr, 56 min; 3/4" U-Matic, 1/2" Beta I, 1/2" Beta II, 1/2" VHS • Sale: $89.95 for 1/2" Beta I, $49.95 for 1/2" Beta II & VHS, $99.95 for 3/4"

Offers an adaptation of "And They Shall Walk" by Elizabeth Kenny. Shows Sister Kenny crusading for treatment of the condition known as infantile paralysis. Stars Rosalind Russell, Alexander Knox, Dean Jagger, and Beulah Bondi.

SIX SHOOTIN' SHERIFF
Reel Images Inc; Order No. 472; 1938 • b/w; 59 min; 1/2" Beta II, 1/2" VHS • Sale: $39.95 for 1/2" Beta II, $42.95 for 1/2" VHS

Presents a western adventure with cowboy star Ken Maynard. Tells of a member of a wild gang who is wrongly accused of murder and then mends his ways when released from jail.

SKIN FLICKS
Video Home Library; Order No. VX-115; Date not listed • color; 2 hrs; 1/2" Beta II, 1/2" VHS • Sale: $99.95

Presents a pornographic film.

SKY RIDERS
Magnetic Video Corporation; Order No. CL-1055; 1976 • color; 1 hr, 31 min; 1/2" Beta II, 1/2" VHS • Sale: $54.95

Tells of hooded terrorists who kidnap a millionaire's family, demanding enough weapons for an army as ransom. Features a hang-gliding climax at a medieval monastery. Stars James Coburn, Susannah York, and Robert Culp.

THE SKY'S THE LIMIT
Reel Images Inc; Order No. 534; 1925 • b/w; 50 min; 1/2" Beta II, 1/2" VHS • Sale: $39.95 for 1/2" Beta II, $42.95 for 1/2" VHS

Focuses on the son of the Chief of the U.S. Air Mail Service, who is attracted to a woman who is secretly helping a gang rob the mails by gassing the pilots. Features Jack Geddings, Jane Starr, Alphonse Martell, Mary Jane Irving, Melbourne McDowell, Frank Earle, and Bruce Gordon in a silent film with music score. Includes several early aviation sequences.

SLAP SHOT
MCA DiscoVision; Order No. 16-004; 1977 • color; 2 hrs, 3 min; LaserVision • Sale: $24.95

- -
MCA Videocassette, Inc; Order No. 66012; 1977 • color; 2 hrs, 3 min; 1/2" Beta II, 1/2" VHS • Sale: $60

Follows the efforts of a minor league hockey team coach to catch one last winning season with an assortment of misfits, who finds that he must resort to violence. Uses much profanity to capture the locker room atmosphere. Stars Paul Newman, Michael Ontkean, and Strother Martin, under George Roy Hill's direction.

SLAUGHTER DAY

FHV Entertainment, Inc; 1977 • color; 1 hr, 26 min; ½" Beta II, ½" VHS • Sale: $49.95

Shows how one man's master plan turns into a day of double-cross, terror, and brutal massacre. Stars Rita Tushingham and Gordon Mitchell.

SLAUGHTERHOUSE FIVE

MCA DiscoVision; Order No. 10-007; 1972 • color; 1 hr, 44 min; LaserVision • Sale: $24.95

Presents a film adaptation of the novel by Kurt Vonnegut. Offers a fantasy journey through time by a middle-American, whose mind hovers between memories of his World War II imprisonment and his daydreams of glamor on a distant planet. Features Michael Sacks, Ron Liebman, and Valerie Perrine, under the direction of George Roy Hill.

SLAVES OF LOVE

Meda/Media Home Entertainment Inc; Order No. M511; Date not listed • color; 1 hr, 16 min; ½" Beta I, ½" Beta II, ½" VHS • Sale: $49.95

Presents a pornographic film.

Michael Caine and Laurence Olivier in *Sleuth*.

SLEUTH

Magnetic Video Corporation; Order No. .CL-1085; 1972 • color; 2 hrs, 18 min; ½" Beta II, ½" VHS • Sale: $44.95

Adapts a play by Anthony Shaffer about a mystery writer and the deadly games he plays with his wife's lover. Stars Sir Laurence Olivier and Michael Caine, under the direction of Joseph L. Mankiewicz.

SLIGHTLY SCARLET

FHV Entertainment, Inc; 1956 • color; 1 hr, 39 min; ½" Beta II, ½" VHS • Sale: $49.95

Offers a drama of vice and corruption, of bribes and blackmail, and a big city operator who tries to take over. Stars John Payne, Rhonda Fleming, and Arlene Dahl.

THE SLIPPER AND THE ROSE

MCA DiscoVision; Order No. 18-001; 1976 • color; 2 hrs, 6 min; LaserVision • Sale: $24.95

Presents a musical version of Cinderella with songs by the Sherman Brothers. Stars Richard Chamberlain, Gemma Craven, Annette Crosbie, Dame Edith Evans, Michael Hordern, and Kenneth More, under Bryan Forbes' direction.

SMARTIE PANTS

Tape Club of America; Order No. 2831 B; Date not listed • color; 1 hr, 30 min; ½" Beta II, ½" VHS • Sale: $54.95

Presents a pornographic film.

THE SMASHING OF THE REICH

Reel Images Inc; Order No. 516; 1962 • b/w; 1 hr, 24 min; ½" Beta II, ½" VHS • Sale: $49.95 for ½" Beta II, $52.95 for ½" VHS

Presents a documentary of the fall of the German war machine. Includes footage of the Normandy landings, Bastogne, the Elbe River assault, the liberation of Paris, and concentration camp survivors.

SMASH-UP

Video T.E.N.; 1947 • b/w; 1 hr, 43 min; ½" Beta II, ½" VHS • Sale: $49.95 for ½" Beta II, $54.95 for ½" VHS

Probes the life of a female alcoholic, who loses her husband and child until a near-tragedy to the child causes her to pull together. Stars Susan Hayward, Eddie Albert, Lee Bowman, and Marsha Hunt.

SMOKEY AND THE BANDIT

MCA DiscoVision; Order No. 12-004; 1977 • color; 1 hr, 37 min; LaserVision • Sale: $24.95

- -
MCA Videocassette, Inc; Order No. 66003; 1977 • color; 1 hr, 37 min; ½" Beta II, ½" VHS • Sale: $60

Offers an almost continuous chase film with a Georgia highway patrolman in pursuit of a truck driver who is also a CB radio fanatic. Stars Burt Reynolds, Sally Fields, Jackie Gleason, and Jerry Reed, under the direction of former stunt man Hal Needham.

SMOKEY AND THE BANDIT II

MCA Videocassette, Inc; Order No. 66020; 1980 • color; 1 hr, 41 min; ½" Beta II, ½" VHS • Sale: $65

Follows the hard-driving escapades of a team of "good old boys" hired to deliver a crate containing a pregnant elephant to the Governor of Texas in record time, despite the attempts of sheriff Buford T. Justice to stop them from speeding through his jurisdiction. Stars Burt Reynolds, Sally Field, Jackie Gleason, Jerry Reed, Paul Williams, Pat McCormick, and the Statler Brothers.

SNOWMAN

Video Communications Inc; 1975 • color; 1 hr, 32 min; ½" Beta II, ½" VHS • Sale: $54.95

Recounts the story of a man whose plane crashes in the snow-capped Rockies. Dramatizes the man's rescue with the aid of a giant eagle.

SODOM AND GOMORRAH

Mitchell Brothers' Film Group; Date not listed • color; 1 hr, 36 min; ½" Beta II, ½" VHS • Sale: $69

Presents a pornographic film.

SOLDIER BLUE

Magnetic Video Corporation; Order No. CL-4014; 1970 • color; 1 hr, 45 min; ½" Beta II, ½" VHS • Sale: $54.95

- -
Red Fox, Inc; Order No. CL-4014; 1970 • color; 1 hr, 45 min; ½" Beta II, ½" VHS • Sale: $54.95

Vid America; Order No. 323; 1970 • color; 1 hr, 45 min; ½" Beta II, ½" VHS • Rental: $12.95/wk

Follows the adventures of a U.S. Cavalry unit escorting a large shipment of gold across Cheyenne territory. Stars Candice Bergen and Peter Strauss.

SOME LIKE IT HOT
Vid America; Order No. 458; 1959 • b/w; 2 hrs; ½" Beta II, ½" VHS • Rental: $11.95/wk

Follows the comic adventures of two musicians hiding out from the mob because they witnessed a gangland execution. Shows them in drag joining an all-girl band on a train headed for Miami, being wooed by men and wooing the ladies. Stars Jack Lemmon, Tony Curtis, Marilyn Monroe, Joe E. Brown, George Raft, and Pat O'Brien, under Billy Wilder's direction.

Burt Reynolds in Smokey And The Bandit.

SOMETHING TO SING ABOUT
Tape Club of America; Order No. 2111 B; 1937 • b/w; 1 hr, 24 min; ½" Beta II, ½" VHS • Sale: $54.95
- -
VCX; Order No. FC119; 1937 • b/w; 1 hr, 24 min; ½" Beta II, ½" VHS • Sale: $35.00

Portrays James Cagney as a two-fisted bandleader in a musical melodrama about Hollywood studio life. Stars Cagney, Evelyn Daw, William Frawley, Mona Barrie, Gene Lockhart, James Newill, and Cully Richards.

SOMETIME SWEET SUSAN
Entertainment Video Releasing, Inc; Order No. 1048; Date not listed • color; 1 hr, 16 min; ½" Beta II, ½" VHS • Sale: $69.95 for ½" Beta II, $74.95 for ½" VHS
- -
Vid America; Order No. 975; 1975 • color; 1 hr, 14 min; ½" Beta II, ½" VHS • Sale: $59.95; Rental: $12.95/wk, applicable to purchase

Presents a pornographic film.

SON OF GODZILLA
Cinema Resources; 1969 • color; 1 hr, 26 min; ½" Beta II, ½" VHS • Sale: $45

Offers a humorous Japanese science-fiction story of two monsters, Godzilla and his son, being threatened by giant praying mantises and a huge spider. Features Tadao Takashima.

SON OF KONG
Niles Cinema; Order No. NM-8028; 1933 • b/w; 1 hr, 10 min; ½" Beta II, ½" VHS • Sale: $54.95
- -
The Nostalgia Merchant; Order No. 8028; 1933 • b/w; 1 hr, 10 min; ½" Beta II, ½" VHS • Sale: $54.95
- -
Red Fox, Inc; Order No. 8028; 1933 • b/w; 1 hr, 10 min; ½" Beta II, ½" VHS • Sale: $54.95

Presents a return to Skull Island, the discovery of a young King Kong, and prehistoric creatures galore. Stars Robert Armstrong and Helen Mack.

SON OF MONSTERS ON THE MARCH
Reel Images Inc; Order No. 555; 1955-77 • color; 27 min; ½" Beta II, ½" VHS • Sale: $29.95 for ½" Beta II, $31.95 for ½" VHS

Lines up preview shorts for ten horror/science-fiction films, including "Dark Star," "How to Make a Monster," "I Was a Teenage Frankenstein," "This Island Earth," "The Damned," "Planet of the Apes," "The Vampire Killers," "One Million Years B.C.," "Dracula A.D. 1972," and "The Rocky Horror Picture Show."

SON OF MONTE CRISTO
Video T.E.N.; 1940 • b/w; 1 hr, 42 min; ½" Beta II, ½" VHS • Sale: $49.95 for ½" Beta II, $54.95 for ½" VHS

Follows the adventures of the Count's son as he defeats a would-be dictator and marries a princess. Features Louis Hayward, Joan Bennett, and George Sanders.

SON OF SINBAD
Video Communications Inc; 1955 • color; 1 hr, 22 min; ½" Beta II, ½" VHS • Sale: $54.95

Follows the escapades of Sinbad and how he frees besieged Baghdad from the forces of the mighty Tamarlane. Features Dale Robertson, Vincent Price, and Sally Forrest.

SON OF THE SHEIK
Blackhawk Films, Inc; Order No. 506-55-0842 for ½" Beta II, 525-55-0842 for ½" VHS; 1926 • b/w; 1 hr, 2 min; ½" Beta II, ½" VHS • Sale: $39.95

Shows Ahmed, a desert sheik, who is tricked into believing he has been betrayed by a dancing girl and who, upon learning of her innocence, tracks down the renegades who lied about her. Stars Rudolph Valentino in this silent sequel to "The Sheik."

SON OF ZORRO
The Nostalgia Merchant; Date not listed • b/w; 3 hrs, 15 min; ½" Beta II, ½" VHS • Sale: $109.95

Presents, on two videocassettes, a motion picture serial in 13 episodes. Stars George Turner and Peggy Stewart.

THE SONG OF BERNADETTE
Golden Tapes Video Tape Library; Order No. F-1034; 1943 • b/w; 2 hrs, 36 min; ½" Beta II, ½" VHS • Sale: $49.95 for ½" Beta II & VHS, $124.95 for ¾"
- -
Magnetic Video Corporation; Order No. CL-1034;

1943 • b/w; 2 hrs, 36 min; ½" Beta II, ½" VHS • Sale: $64.95

Tells the story of a peasant French girl in the nineteenth century who has a religious vision and as a result is tormented by the local populace. Stars Jennifer Jones, William Eythe, Charles Bickford, Vincent Price, and Lee J. Cobb.

SONG OF FREEDOM
Northeast Video and Sound, Inc; 1937 • b/w; 1 hr, 8 min; ¾" U-Matic, ½" EIAJ, ½" Beta II, ½" VHS • Sale: $195; Rental: $75/wk

Reel Images Inc; Order No. 559; 1937 • b/w; 1 hr, 11 min; ½" Beta II, ½" VHS • Sale: $49.95 for ½" Beta II, $52.95 for ½" VHS

Features Paul Robeson as a descendant of slaves who longs to return to his homeland in Africa to help his people. Shows how he earns the money he needs by becoming an opera singer. Co-stars Elizabeth Welch.

SONG OF NEVADA
Discount Video Tapes; 1944 • b/w; 1 hr; ½" Beta II, ½" VHS • Sale: $34.95

Offers a western starring Roy Rogers and Dale Evans, in which Dale is nearly deceived into marrying a pompous snob.

SONG OF TEXAS
Reel Images Inc; Order No. 55; 1943 • b/w; 54 min; ½" Beta II, ½" VHS • Sale: $39.95 for ½" Beta II, $42.95 for ½" VHS

Presents the tale of an ex-rodeo champ who wants his daughter to think he's prosperous and owns a ranch. Features several songs by star Roy Rogers. Co-stars Trigger, Sheila Ryan, and the Sons of the Pioneers.

SONS OF THE DESERT
The Nostalgia Merchant; 1933 • b/w; 1 hr, 9 min; ½" Beta II, ½" VHS • Sale: $54.95

Time-Life Video Club Inc; 1933 • b/w; 1 hr, 9 min; ½" Beta II, ½" VHS • Sale: $44.95 to members

Offers a Laurel and Hardy comedy feature in which the duo encounter numerous misadventures at a fraternal convention they are attending—without the knowledge or consent of their wives. Stars Stan Laurel, Oliver Hardy, Charley Chase, and Mae Busch, under the direction of William Seiter. Includes also a Hal Roach comedy short.

SONS OF THE DESERT; TOP FLAT
Vid America; Order No. 947; 1933 • b/w; 1 hr, 26 min; ½" Beta II, ½" VHS • Sale: $49.95; Rental: $10.95/wk; Applicable to purchase

Offers, on one videocassette, a Laurel and Hardy feature plus a Hal Roach comedy short starring Patsy Kelly. Presents Stan Laurel and Oliver Hardy on their way to a convention after lying to their wives. Features Charley Chase and Mae Busch. Includes the misadventures of a beautiful but broke Thelma Todd, impersonating a French maid in a plush apartment.

THE SORROW AND THE PITY
Time-Life Video Club Inc; 1972 • b/w; 4 hrs, 20 min; ½" Beta II, ½" VHS • Sale: $79.95 to members

Presents, on three videocassettes, Marcel Ophuls' documentary about France during the German occupation of World War II. Uses interviews with Frenchmen and Germans present in Clermont, France during the occupation, in footage filmed 20 years later. Asks both sides about their activities during the four years of German rule. Provides a startling contrast and view of what occurred. Includes footage of Anthony Eden and Albert Speer. Discusses the temptations of collaboration and resistance, and the damage done to the human spirit by war.

S.O.S.
Quality X Video Cassette Company; Date not listed • color; 1 hr, 23 min; ½" Beta I, ½" Beta II, ½" VHS • Sale: $99.50

Presents a pornographic film.

S.O.S. COAST GUARD
Cable Films; 1937 • b/w; 4 hrs; ½" Beta I, ½" Beta II, ½" VHS • Sale: $89.50

Offers a twelve-chapter serial featuring action, car chases, fisticuffs, and stuntwork. Stars Bela Lugosi as Dr. Boroff, a mad munitions inventor who locks horns with the hero of the Coast Guard, played by Ralph Byrd.

THE SOUND OF MUSIC
Blackhawk Films, Inc; Order No. 502-88-0019 for ½" Beta II, 515-88-0019 for ½" VHS; 1965 • color; 2 hrs, 54 min; ½" Beta II, ½" VHS • Sale: $74.95

Magnetic Video Corporation; Order No. CL-1051; 1965 • color; 2 hrs, 54 min; ½" Beta II, ½" VHS • Sale: $74.95

Depicts the plight of the singing Von Trapp family during the Nazi annexation of Austria and the woman who left a convent to become the children's governess. Includes Rodgers and Hammerstein songs, "Climb Every Mountain," "My Favorite Things," and "Do Re Mi." Stars Julie Andrews and Christopher Plummer.

SOUTH OF SANTA FE
Cable Films; 1942 • b/w; 55 min; ½" Beta I, ½" Beta II, ½" VHS • Sale: $45 for ½" Beta I, $49.50 for ½" Beta II & VHS

Relates a story in which Roy Rogers and his pals try to help Gabby Hayes save his town, with the help of the girl who owns the nearby gold mine. Features Roy Rogers, Gabby Hayes, and Linda Hayes.

SOUTH OF TEXAS (SOUTH OF THE BORDER); MY PAL TRIGGER
The Nostalgia Merchant; 1939; 1946 • b/w; 2 hrs; ½" Beta II, ½" VHS • Sale: $59.95

Provides a western double feature. Stars Gene Autry in "South of Texas," where he quelches a Mexican uprising; features also Smiley Burnette. Presents also "My Pal Trigger," with Roy Rogers, Gabby Hayes, and their favorite horses.

THE SOUTHERNER
Northeast Video and Sound, Inc; 1945 • b/w; 1 hr, 30 min; ¾" U-Matic, ½" EIAJ, ½" Beta II, ½" VHS • Sale: $250

VCX; Order No. FC123; 1945 • b/w; 1 hr, 31 min; ½" Beta II, ½" VHS • Sale: $35.00

Presents an American film directed by Jean Renoir. Depicts a family's struggle to survive on a farm. Stars Zachary Scott, Betty Field, and Beulah Bondi.

SPARROWS
Blackhawk Films, Inc; Order No. 506-33-0850 for ½" Beta II, 525-33-0850 for ½" VHS; 1926 • color; 1 hr, 15 min; ½" Beta II, ½" VHS • Sale: $39.95

Tells the adventures of a group of orphans kept in vir-

Julie Andrews in
The Sound of Music.

tual slavery at a county baby farm. Stars Mary Pickford in this silent feature.

A SPECIAL DAY
Time-Life Video Club Inc; Date not listed • color; 1 hr, 50 min; ½" Beta II, ½" VHS • Sale: $39.95 to members

Tells of two neighbors in 1938 Rome who share an afternoon's intimacy and gain more positive attitudes about themselves. Stars Sophia Loren and Marcello Mastroianni, under the direction of Ettore Scola.

SPIES
Reel Images Inc; Order No. 44; 1928 • b/w; 2 hrs, 1 min; ½" Beta II, ½" VHS • Sale: $49.95 for ½" Beta II, $52.95 for ½" VHS

Presents an early espionage thriller that helped set the pace for many of the later films of that genre. Features the direction of Fritz Lang in this silent classic.

SPITFIRE
Video T.E.N.; 1943 • b/w; 1 hr, 30 min; ½" Beta II, ½" VHS • Sale: $49.95 for ½" Beta II, $54.95 for ½" VHS

Documents the life of Reginald Mitchell, the man who designed Britain's Spitfire plane in World War II. Stars Leslie Howard, David Niven, Rosamond John, Roland Culver, and Anne Firth.

SPOOKS RUN WILD
Reel Images Inc; Order No. 474; 1941 • b/w; 1 hr, 4 min; ½" Beta II, ½" VHS • Sale: $49.95 for ½" Beta II, $52.95 for ½" VHS

Presents a chiller comedy in which a menace played by Bela Lugosi meets his match. Features the Eastside Kids and Lugosi.

SPRINGTIME IN THE SIERRAS
Cable Films; 1947 • b/w; 54 min; ½" Beta I, ½" Beta II, ½" VHS • Sale: $45 for ½" Beta I, $49.50 for ½" Beta II & VHS

Presents a western in which Roy Rogers and his pals fight a gang of poachers who prey on the wildlife of a game preserve. Stars Roy Rogers and Andy Devine.

THE SPY IN BLACK
Reel Images Inc ; Order No. 46; 1939 • b/w; 1 hr, 17 min; ½" Beta II, ½" VHS • Sale: $49.95 for ½" Beta II, $52.95 for ½" VHS

Presents a British thriller in which a German submarine officer becomes a spy in order to obtain information about the sailing date for a fleet of British cruisers. Stars Conrad Veidt and Valerie Hobson under the direction of Michael Powell.

SPY SMASHER
The Nostalgia Merchant; Date not listed • b/w; 3 hrs; ½" Beta II, ½" VHS • Sale: $109.95

Presents, on two videocassettes, a motion picture serial in 12 episodes. Stars Kane Richmond.

SQUADRON OF DOOM
Video T.E.N.; 1936 • b/w; 1 hr, 10 min; ½" Beta II, ½" VHS • Sale: $49.95 for ½" Beta II, $54.95 for ½" VHS

Details an adventure of Ace Drummond, a government troubleshooter battling a band of jade robbers. Stars John King, Jean Rogers, and Noah Beery Jr.

STAGE DOOR
Blackhawk Films, Inc; Order No. 506-40-0782 for ½" Beta II, 525-40-0782 for ½" VHS; 1937 • b/w; 1 hr, 32 min; ½" Beta II, ½" VHS • Sale: $49.95

Traces the lives of women in a theatrical boarding house and especially that of a wealthy girl trying to make it on her own. Stars Katharine Hepburn, Ginger Rogers, Lucille Ball, Ann Miller, Eve Arden, and Adolphe Menjou.

STAGE DOOR CANTEEN
VCX; Order No. FC126; 1943 • b/w; 2 hrs, 12 min; ½" Beta II, ½" VHS • Sale: $35.00

Offers a World War II romance starring Cheryl Walker and William Terry. Features cameos by Tallulah Bankhead, Katharine Hepburn, Harpo Marx, George Raft, Paul Muni, Merle Oberon, Helen Hayes, and Ed Wynn.

STAGE STRUCK

Video Communications Inc; Order No. 1093; 1957 • color; 1 hr, 35 min; 1/2" Beta II, 1/2" VHS • Sale: $54.95

Recounts the story of an aspiring young actress who bursts on the Broadway scene with excessively high hopes and ambitions. Stars Henry Fonda, Susan Strasberg, and Christopher Plummer.

STAGECOACH

Thunderbird Films ; 1939 • b/w; 1 hr, 40 min; 3/4" U-Matic, 1/2" Beta I, 1/2" Beta II, 1/2" VHS • Sale: $69.95 for 1/2" Beta I, $49.95 for 1/2" Beta II & VHS, $89.95 for 3/4"

- -
Time-Life Video Club Inc; 1939 • b/w; 1 hr, 39 min; 1/2" Beta II, 1/2" VHS • Sale: $39.95 to members

Recounts the adventures of a mismatched troop aboard a stagecoach making its westward journey despite rumors that Geronimo is on the warpath. Features John Wayne, Claire Trevor, Andy Devine, John Carradine, and others in a western directed by John Ford.

STAGECOACH TO DENVER

Cable Films; 1947 • b/w; 56 min; 1/2" Beta I, 1/2" Beta II, 1/2" VHS • Sale: $45 for 1/2" Beta I, $49.50 for 1/2" Beta II & VHS

Presents a western in which Red Ryder is up against the top Republic Studio villain, Roy Bancroft, as Red protects a friend's stagecoach line from evil deeds. Stars Allan Lane.

STAGEDOOR CANTEEN

Thunderbird Films; 1943 • b/w; 2 hrs, 15 min; 3/4" U-Matic, 1/2" Beta I, 1/2" Beta II, 1/2" VHS • Sale: $69.95 for 1/2" Beta I, $49.95 for 1/2" Beta II & VHS, $89.95 for 3/4"

- -
Video T.E.N.; 1943 • b/w; 2 hrs, 6 min; 1/2" Beta II, 1/2" VHS • Sale: $59.95 for 1/2" Beta II, $64.95 for 1/2" VHS

Presents Tallulah Bankhead, Merle Oberon, Katharine Hepburn, Gypsy Rosa Lee, Paul Muni, and many other stars in the story of a soldier who falls for a canteen hostess.

STAIRWAY TO HEAVEN

Video T.E.N.; 1945 • color; 1 hr, 44 min; 1/2" Beta II, 1/2" VHS • Sale: $49.95 for 1/2" Beta II, $54.95 for 1/2" VHS

Offers a fantasy of an RAF flier who escapes death by accident and must prove to a heavenly tribunal that he ought to live. Stars Kim Hunter, David Niven, Roger Livesey, Raymond Massey, and Marius Goring.

STALAG 17

Fotomat Corp; Order No. B0067 for 1/2" Beta II, V0067 for 1/2" VHS; 1953 • color; 2 hrs; 1/2" Beta II, 1/2" VHS • Sale: $69.95; Rental: $9.95/up to 5 days, applicable to purchase

- -
Paramount Home Video; 1953 • b/w ; 2 hrs; 1/2" Beta II, 1/2" VHS • Sale: $59.95

- -
RCA SelectaVision VideoDiscs; Order No. 00627; 1953 • b/w; 2 hrs; CED • Sale: $19.98

Portrays a group of World War II G.I.'s who are thrown together in a German prison camp. Dramatizes what happens when two prisoners are killed in an escape

Persis Khambatta, Leonard Nimoy, Stephen Collins, William Shatner, DeForest Kelley in *Star Trek—The Motion Picture*.

attempt and it becomes obvious that there is a spy among them. Stars William Holden, Don Taylor, Otto Preminger, Neville Brand, Peter Graves, Robert Strauss, and Harvey Lembeck, under the direction of Billy Wilder.

STANLEY

Fotomat Corp; Order No. B0157 for 1/2" Beta II, V0157 for 1/2" VHS; 1972 • color; 1 hr, 48 min; 1/2" Beta II, 1/2" VHS • Sale: $39.95; Rental: $7.95/up to 5 days, applicable to purchase

- -
Video Communications Inc; 1972 • color; 1 hr, 48 min; 1/2" Beta II, 1/2" VHS • Sale: $54.95

Focuses on an embittered Viet Nam veteran who uses a rattlesnake for deadly purposes.

STAR BABE

TVX Distributors; Order No. R.T. 80; Date not listed • color; 2 hrs; 1/2" Beta II, 1/2" VHS • Sale: $79.50 for 1/2" Beta II, 89.50 for 1/2" VHS

Presents a pornographic film.

A STAR IS BORN

Cinema Concepts, Inc.; 1937 • color; 1 hr, 51 min; 3/4" U-Matic, 1/2" Beta II, 1/2" VHS • Sale: $54.95 for 1/2" Beta II & VHS, $149.95 for 3/4"

- -
Golden Tapes Video Tape Library; Order No. CD4; 1937 • color; 1 hr, 51 min; 1/2" Beta II, 1/2" VHS • Sale: $49.95 for 1/2" Beta II & VHS, $124.95 for 3/4"

- -
Ivy Video; 1937 • b/w; 2 hrs, 34 min; 3/4" U-Matic, 1/2" Beta II, 1/2" VHS • Sale: $59.95 for 1/2" Beta II & VHS, trade-in plan available, $350 for 3/4"

- -
Northeast Video and Sound, Inc; Order No. 160S; 1937 • color; 2 hrs, 34 min;3/4" U-Matic, 1/2" EIAJ, 1/2" Beta II, 1/2" VHS • Sale: $395; Rental: $125/wk

- -
VCX; Order No. FC110; 1937 • color; 1 hr, 51 min; 1/2" Beta II, 1/2" VHS • Sale: $35.00

- -
The Video Library; Order No. VW-6003; 1937 • color; 1 hr, 51 min; 1/2" Beta II, 1/2" VHS • Sale: $49.95

Features a David O. Selznick production about an unknown girl who gains stardom when a well-known star falls in love with her, and how his fortunes decline as hers rise. Stars Frederic March, Janet Gaynor, and Adolphe, Menjou, under the direction of William Wellman.

THE STAR PACKER

Cable Films; 1934 • b/w; 54 min; ½" Beta I, ½" Beta II, ½" VHS • Sale: $45 for ½" Beta I, $49.50 for ½" Beta II and VHS

Features John Wayne as an undercover marshal who almost falls victim to another lawman mistaking him for an outlaw. Includes chase sequences and stunt riding.

STAR PILOT

Monarch Releasing Corporation; Date not listed • color; 1 hr, 30 min; ¾" U-Matic • Sale: $350

Presents a pornographic film.

STAR TREK—THE MOTION PICTURE

Niles Cinema; Order No. PP-8858; 1979 • color; 2 hrs, 12 min; ½" Beta II, ½" VHS • Sale: $69.95

- -
Paramount Home Video; Order No. 8858; 1979 • color; 2 hrs, 12 min; ½" Beta II, ½" VHS • Sale: $84.95

- -
RCA SeletaVision VideoDiscs; Order No. 00636; 1979 • color; 2 hrs, 12 min; CED • Sale: $27.98

Presents the first feature length film based on the TV series. Follows the Enterprise's refitting with new technology and it's subsequent attempt to prevent an invasion of Earth in the 23rd century. Features William Shatner, Leonard Nimoy, DeForest Kelley, James Doohan, George Takei, Nichelle Nichols, Walter Koenig, Persis Khambatta, and Stephen Collins.

STARBIRD AND SWEET WILLIAM

Video Communications Inc; 1974 • color; 1 hr, 35 min; ½" Beta II, ½" VHS • Sale: $54.95

Offers the tale of an Indian youth whose solo plane flight crashes in the mountains, forcing him to fight for survival with assistance from a mischievous bear cub. Stars A. Martinez, Skip Homeier, and Dan Haggerty.

STARRING THE RITTS PUPPETS

Home Vision; Order No. 804-7001 for ½" Beta II, 804-9001 for ½" VHS; Date not listed • color; 1 hr, 14 min; ½" Beta II, ½" VHS • Sale: $49.95

Offers two stories for children featuring Sir Geoffrey the Giraffe, Magnolia the Ostrich, and other characters created by Paul Ritts. Includes "The Great Silence" and "For the Love of Fred."

THE STARS LOOK DOWN

Video T.E.N.; 1939 • b/w; 1 hr, 36 min; ½" Beta II, ½" VHS • Sale: $49.95 for ½" Beta II, $54.95 for ½" VHS

Focuses on the plight of Welsh miners a against unsafe conditions, in a drama directed by Carol Reed. Stars Michael ke Redgrave, Margaret Lockwood, and Emlyn Williams.

STARS ON PARADE

Reel Images Inc; Order No. 48; 1946 • b/w; 55 min; ½" Beta II, ½" VHS • Sale: $39.95 for ½" Beta II, $42.95 for ½" VHS

Dramatizes how a small town radio station gets help from some radio personalities in this all-black feature made for black audiences. Stars Milton Wood, Jane Cooley, Francine Everett, Bob Howard, Duke Williams, Clarice Graham, with guest stars Una Mae Carlisle, Eddie South, Phil Moore, and the Phil Moore Four. Includes "Boogie Woogie Dream" with Lena Horne and Ted Wilson.

STARTING OVER

Fotomat Corp; Order No. B0385 for ½" Beta II, V0385 for ½" VHS; 1979 • color; 1 hr, 45 min; ½" Beta II, ½" VHS • Sale: $54.95; Rental: $9.95/5 days

- -
Niles Cinema; Order No. PP-1239; 1979 • color; 1 hr, 46 min; ½" Beta II, ½" VHS • Sale: $64.95

- -
Paramount Home Video; Order No. 1239; 1979 • color; 1 hr, 46 min; ½" Beta II, ½" VHS • Sale: $79.95

- -
RCA SelectaVision VideoDiscs; Order No. 00633; 1979 • color; 1 hr, 46 min; CED • Sale: $24.98

Tells the story of divorce from a male point of view. Depicts a divorced man beginning to date again, finding a new love, but unable to stop loving his ex-wife. Stars Burt Reynolds, Candice Bergen, Jill Clayburgh, Charles Durning, Frances Sternhagen, Austin Pendleton, and Mary Kay Place, under Alan J. Pakula's direction.

Jill Clayburgh and Burt Reynolds in *Starting Over.*

STATE FAIR

Magnetic Video Corporation; Order No. CL-1030; 1962 • color; 1 hr, 58 min; ½" Beta II, ½" VHS • Sale: $44.95

Presents a remake of the 1945 musical concerning a small-town Texas family on a trip to the state fair. Stars Pat Boone, Ann-Margret, Alice Faye, and Tom Ewell.

STATE OF SIEGE

Fotomat Corp; Order No. B0447 for ½" Beta II, V0447 for ½" VHS; 1973 • color; 1 hr, 59 min; ½" Beta II, ½" VHS • Sale: $49.95; Rental: $7.95/5 days

- -
Time-Life Video Club Inc; 1973 • color; 2 hrs; ½" Beta II, ½" VHS • Sale: $39.95 to members

Presents director Costa-Gavras' controversial film based on a true incident, a political kidnapping in Uruguay. Uses fast pacing and suspense. Stars Yves Montand, Renato Salvatori, O.E. Hasse, and Jean-Luc Bideau.

STATE OF THE UNION

MCA Videocassette, Inc; Order No. 55006; 1948 • b/w; 2 hrs, 4 min; 1/2" Beta II, 1/2" VHS • Sale: $50

Adapts the Howard Lindsay-Russell Crouse play about a presidential candidate who must fight everyone to maintain his integrity. Stars Spencer Tracy, Katharine Hepburn, Angela Lansbury, Van Johnson, Adolphe Menjou, and Lewis Stone under the direction of Frank Capra.

STATION WEST

Blackhawk Films, Inc; Order No. 506-57-0782 for 1/2" Beta II, 525-57-0782 for 1/2" VHS; 1948 • b/w; 1 hr, 32 min; 3/4" U-Matic, 1/2" Beta I, 1/2" Beta II, 1/2" VHS • Sale: $89.95 for 1/2" Beta I, $49.95 for 1/2" Beta II & VHS, $99.95 for 3/4"

Adapts a Luke Short story. Presents a U. S. Army undercover agent who investigates a gold robbery and finds himself involved in two murders in a western town. Uses sharp dialogue. Stars Dick Powell, Jane Greer, Agnès Moorehead, Burl Ives, Tom Powers, and Raymond Burr.

STEAMBOAT BILL JR.

Blackhawk Films, Inc; Order No. 506-18-0847 for 1/2" Beta II, 525-18-0847 for 1/2" VHS; 1928 • b/w; 1 hr, 12 min; 3/4" U-Matic, 1/2" Beta I, 1/2" Beta II, 1/2" VHS • Sale: $89.95 for 1/2" Beta I, $39.95 for 1/2" Beta II & VHS, $99.95 for 3/4"

- -

Golden Tapes Video Tape Library; Order No. CC5; 1927 • b/w; 1 hr, 20 min; 1/2" Beta II, 1/2" VHS • Sale: $49.95 for 1/2" Beta II & VHS, $124.95 for 3/4"

Presents a Buster Keaton silent comedy feature. Concerns the efforts of the son of a riverboat captain to prove himself a worthy boatman and win the daughter of a rival steamboat owner. Features numerous acrobatic stunts and precisely executed disasters, under Keaton's own direction.

THE STEEL CLAW

Video Communications Inc; 1961 • color; 1 hr, 35 min; 1/2" Beta II, 1/2" VHS • Sale: $54.95

Portrays a one-handed Marine captain who leads a mission into the interior of the Philippines during early World War II days to rescue an American general. Stars George Montgomery and Charito Luna.

THE STEPFORD WIVES

National Film and Video Center; 1975 • color; 1 hr, 55 min; 3/4" U-Matic, 1/2" Beta II, 1/2" VHS • Rental: $99/1 showing

Produces a chilling effect which grows as a new resident in the town of Stepford notices that all of the women around her are beautifully groomed, model housekeepers who are also strangely lifeless. Stars Katherine Ross, Paula Prentiss, Peter Masterson, Tina Louise, Patrick O'Neal, and Nanette Newman.

THE STEPMOTHER

Video Communications Inc; Order No. 1096; 1972 • color; 1 hr, 34 min; 1/2" Beta II, 1/2" VHS • Sale: $54.95

Presents a sex melodrama which shows that the people involved seem more victims of circumstances than evil, yet the end result is the same. Stars Alejandro Rey and John Anderson.

STILETTO

Magnetic Video Corporation; Order No. CL-4025; 1969 • color; 1 hr, 41 min; 1/2" Beta II, 1/2" VHS • Sale: $54.95

Focuses on a luxury-loving Mafia hit man and the difficulties that face him when he tries to resign from his profession. Stars Alex Cord, Britt Ekland, and Joseph Wiseman.

THE STING

MCA DiscoVision; Order No. 11-001; 1973 • color; 2 hrs, 9 min; LaserVision • Sale: $24.95

- -

MCA Videocassette, Inc; Order No. 66009; 1973 • color; 2 hrs, 9 min; 1/2" Beta II, 1/2" VHS • Sale: $60

Showcases the Redford-Newman duo in 1930's Chicago, as two small-time confidence men pull a "sting" on a big-time gangster from New York. Offers, on the sound track, the ragtime music of Scott Joplin. Stars Paul Newman, Robert Redford, Robert Shaw, Charles Durning, Ray Walston, and Eileen Brennan in George Roy Hill's film, which won seven Oscars.

STINGRAY

Magnetic Video Corporation; Order No. CL-4038; 1978 • color; 1 hr, 40 min; 1/2" Beta II, 1/2" VHS • Sale: $54.95

Relates the story of a red Corvette full of contraband, and how when the unsuspecting owners take it for a drive, the hoodlums who hid the contraband give chase. Stars Christopher Mitchum and Sherry Jackson.

STOLEN KISSES

Fotomat Corp; Order No. B0439 for 1/2" Beta II, V0439 for 1/2" VHS; 1968 • color; 1 hr, 30 min; 1/2" Beta II, 1/2" VHS • Sale: $49.95; Rental: $7.95/5 days

- -

Time-Life Video Club Inc; 1968 • color; 1 hr, 30 min; 1/2" Beta II, 1/2" VHS • Sale: $39.95 to members

Offers director Fancois Truffaut's continuation of the story begun in his "400 Blows." Shares Truffaut's vision of young love as the clumsy hero has various encounters with women. Stars Jean-Pierre Leaud, Delphine Sexrig, Claude DeGivray, and Bernard Revon.

THE STONE KILLER

National Film and Video Center; 1973 • color; 1 hr, 35 min; 3/4" U-Matic, 1/2" Beta II, 1/2" VHS • Rental: $89/1 showing

Lionizes a policeman for being particularly cold-blooded and ruthless as he tracks down lawbreakers. Sets its scenes in New York's Spanish Harlem and Little Italy and in Los Angeles' Skid Row. Stars Charles Bronson in a film directed by Michael Winner.

STONEFACE

Blackhawk Films, Inc; Order No. 506-18-0883 for 1/2" Beta II, 525-18-0883 for 1/2" VHS; Date not listed • b/w; 1 hr; 3/4" U-Matic, 1/2" Beta I, 1/2" Beta II, 1/2" VHS • Sale: $59.95 for 1/2" Beta I, $39.95 for 1/2" Beta II & VHS, $69.95 for 3/4"

Presents a color-toned film with three sketches starring Buster Keaton. Shows him chased by hundreds of cops, atop a balloon thousands of feet in the air, and attempting in vain to assemble a pre-fab, do-it-yourself house. Features a musical score.

STOP! LOOK! LAUGH!

National Film and Video Center; 1960 • color; 1 hr, 18 min; 3/4" U-Matic, 1/2" Beta II, 1/2" VHS • Rental: $49/1 showing

Places the Three Stooges in the midst of a bullfight, a western, the Cinderella story, and the story of Genesis.

STORM IN A TEACUP
Video T.E.N.; 1937 • b/w; 1 hr, 20 min; 1/2" Beta II, 1/2" VHS • Sale: $49.95 for 1/2" Beta II, $54.95 for 1/2" VHS

Studies the events that occur in a small Scottish town when a newspaperman takes on a local magistrate. Stars Rex Harrison, Vivien Leigh, Cecil Parker, Sarah Allgood, Ursula Jeans, and Gus McNaughton.

STORM OVER ASIA
Ivy Video; 1928 • b/w; 1 hr, 13 min; 3/4" U-Matic, 1/2" Beta II, 1/2" VHS • Sale: $59.95 for 1/2" Beta II & VHS, trade-in plan available, $195 for 3/4"
- -
Northeast Video and Sound, Inc; 1928 • b/w; 1 hr, 13 min; 3/4" U-Matic, 1/2" EIAJ, 1/2" Beta II, 1/2" VHS • Sale: $195; Rental: $80/wk

Reveals the mastery of V.I. Pudovkin in his last silent film, concerning the righteous heroism of a young Mongolian hunter seeking redress against oppression and abuse from the foreign masters of his country, and sparking a peasant uprising.

THE STORY OF JOANNA
Video Home Library; Order No. VX-106; Date not listed • color; 2 hrs; 1/2" Beta II, 1/2" VHS • Sale: $99.95

Presents a pornographic film.

THE STORY OF THE SILENT SERIALS AND GIRLS IN DANGER
Blackhawk Films, Inc; Order No. 506-42-0834 for 1/2" Beta II, 525-42-0834 for 1/2" VHS; Date not listed • b/w; 54 min; 3/4" U-Matic, 1/2" Beta I, 1/2" Beta II, 1/2" VHS • Sale: $59.95 for 1/2" Beta I, $39.95 for 1/2" Beta II & VHS, $69.95 for 3/4"

Highlights the best moments of more than 14 silent serials. Features Gloria Swanson tied to the railroad tracks by Wallace Beery, Mae Marsh threatened in caveman times, and other cliffhanger situations. Includes a musical score and narration.

THE STORY OF VERNON AND IRENE CASTLE
Niles Cinema; Order No. NM-8029; 1939 • b/w; 1 hr, 33 min; 1/2" Beta II, 1/2" VHS • Sale: $54.95
- -
The Nostalgia Merchant; Order No. 8029; 1939 • b/w; 1 hr, 33 min; 1/2" Beta II, 1/2" VHS • Sale: $54.95
- -
Red Fox, Inc; Order No. 8029; 1939 • b/w; 1 hr, 33 min; 1/2" Beta II, 1/2" VHS • Sale: $54.95

Features Fred Astaire and Ginger Rogers in their last collaboration at RKO, in a musical biography of a turn-of-the-century dance team.

THE STORY OF WILLIAM S. HART AND THE SAD CLOWNS
Blackhawk Films, Inc; Order No. 506-66-0887 for 1/2" Beta II, 525-66-0887 for 1/2" VHS; Date not listed • b/w; 50 min; 3/4" U-Matic, 1/2" Beta I, 1/2" Beta II, 1/2" VHS • Sale: $59.95 for 1/2" Beta I, $39.95 for 1/2" Beta II & VHS, $69.95 for 3/4"

Offers a color-toned segment from the History of Motion Picture Series. Presents clips from William S. Hart's films, "Hell's Hinges" and "Tumbleweeds," as well as Charlie Chaplin, Buster Keaton, and Harry Langdon performing from their films. Includes narration and a musical score.

THE STRANGER
Ivy Video; 1946 • b/w; 1 hr, 35 min; 3/4" U-Matic, 1/2" Beta II, 1/2" VHS • Sale: $59.95 for 1/2" Beta II & VHS, trade-in plan available, $195 for 3/4"
- -
Northeast Video and Sound, Inc; Order No. 153S; 1946 • b/w; 1 hr, 35 min; 3/4" U-Matic, 1/2" EIAJ, 1/2" Beta II, 1/2" VHS • Sale: $250; Rental: $75/wk
- -
VCX; Order No. FC124; 1946 • b/w; 1 hr, 35 min; 1/2" Beta II, 1/2" VHS • Sale: $35.00

Probes the reactions of a small New England town to the discovery that a trusted, well-liked schoolteacher is in reality a vicious Nazi war criminal. Spotlights Orson Welles as director and star, and showcases Edward G. Robinson as a federal agent and Loretta Young as Welles' fiancée.

THE STRANGER AND THE GUNFIGHTER
National Film and Video Center; 1976 • color; 1 hr, 47 min; 3/4" U-Matic, 1/2" Beta II, 1/2" VHS • Rental: $89/1 showing

Presents the story of a man who accidentally kills a wealthy Chinese lord and is tracked by the victim's family while pursuing a missing fortune. Stars Lee Van Cleef and Lo Lieh.

STRANGER ON THE THIRD FLOOR
Blackhawk Films, Inc; Order No. 506-86-0704 for 1/2" Beta II, 525-86-0704 for 1/2" VHS; 1940 • b/w; 1 hr, 4 min; 1/2" Beta II, 1/2" VHS • Sale: $49.95

Focuses on a man sent to prison for a series of murders he didn't commit and the reporter whose testimony sent him there. Stars Peter Lorre, John McGuire, and Elisha Cook, Jr.

STRANGERS: THE STORY OF A MOTHER AND DAUGHTER
Time-Life Video Club Inc; 1979 • color; 1 hr, 40 min; 1/2" Beta II, 1/2" VHS • Sale: $34.95 to members

Studies the bitter relationship between a lonely woman and her estranged daughter when the daughter visits for the first time in 20 years. Stars Bette Davis, Gena Rowlands, Ford Rainey, Donald Moffat, and Royal Dano.

STRAW DOGS
Magnetic Video Corporation; Order No. 8005; 1972 • color; 1 hr, 53 min; 1/2" Beta II, 1/2" VHS • Sale: $59.95
- -
Niles Cinema; Order No. CL-8005; 1972 • color; 1 hr, 53 min; 1/2" Beta II, 1/2" VHS • Sale: $59.95

Explores the flood of violence aroused when a pacifist American professor and his teasing British wife move into a rural English town, and the local males decide to have their way with the couple. Stars Dustin Hoffman, Susan George, Peter Vauthan, T.P. McKenna, and Peter Arne, under Sam Peckinpah's direction.

THE STREET FIGHTER
MGM/CBS Home Video; Order No. C50018; Date not listed • color; 1 hr, 25 min; 1/2" Beta II, 1/2" VHS • Sale: $49.95
- -
Niles Cinema; Order No. GM-734; Date not listed • color; 1/2" Beta II, 1/2" VHS • Sale: $49.95

Offers a martial arts film featuring Sonny Chiba.

STREET SCENE
Video T.E.N.; 1931 • b/w; 1 hr, 20 min; 1/2" Beta II, 1/2" VHS • Sale: $49.95 for 1/2" Beta II, $54.95 for 1/2" VHS

Portrays the Elmer Rice play of jealousy, murder, manhunt, and a young girl whose life is torn apart by it all, as directed by King Vidor. Stars Sylvia Sidney, William Collier Jr., Max Montor, and Estelle Taylor.

STROKE OF NINE
Monarch Releasing Corporation; Date not listed • color; 1 hr, 4 min; ¾" U-Matic • Sale: $300

Presents a pornographic film.

A STUDY IN SCARLET
Northeast Video and Sound, Inc; 1933 • b/w; 1 hr, 24 min; ¾" U-Matic, ½" EIAJ, ½" Beta II, ½" VHS • Sale: $195; Rental: $75/wk
- -
Reel Images Inc; Order No. 567; 1933 • b/w; 1 hr, 12 min; ½" Beta II, ½" VHS • Sale: $49.95 for ½" Beta II, $52.95 for ½" VHS

Presents a Sherlock Holmes mystery in which the sleuth investigates murders within an organization of seven men who have agreed to divide shares equally whenever a member dies. Stars Reginald Owen and Alan Mowbray.

THE STUNT MAN
Magnetic Video Corporation; 1980 • color; 2 hrs, 10 min; ½" Beta II, ½" VHS • Sale: $69.95

Presents a comedy/adventure/drama about the world of movie-making. Tells of a mysterious fugitive who stumbles onto a movie set and becomes a stunt man. Stars Steve Railsback and Peter O'Toole, under the direction of Richard Rush.

SUBMARINE ALERT
Thunderbird Films; 1943 • b/w; 1 hr, 10 min; ¾" U-Matic, ½" Beta I, ½" Beta II, ½" VHS • Sale: $69.95 for ½" Beta I, $49.95 for ½" Beta II & VHS, $89.95 for ¾"

Presents a wartime thriller involving an American radio technician's struggle against the duplicity of Nazi agents. Stars Richard Arlen, Wendie Barrie, and Dwight Frye.

SUDDENLY, LAST SUMMER
National Film and Video Center; 1959 • b/w; 1 hr, 54 min; ¾" U-Matic, ½" Beta II, ½" VHS • Rental: $89/1 showing

Tells of a young girl committed to a mental institution after witnessing the brutal death of her cousin. Pits a young brain surgeon against the girl's aunt, who wants her to undergo an operation so that she cannot tell the truth about her cousin's death. Stars Montgomery Clift, Elizabeth Taylor, and Katharine Hepburn, in a film based on the play by Tennessee Williams and directed by Joseph L. Mankiewicz.

SUGAR COOKIES
Vid America; Order No. 982; Date not listed • color; 1 hr, 29 min; ½" Beta II, ½" VHS • Sale: $59.95; Rental: $12.95/wk, applicable to purchase

Presents a pornographic film.

SUGARLAND EXPRESS
MCA DiscoVision; Order No. 12-006; 1974 • color; 1 hr, 49 min; LaserVision • Sale: $24.95

Offers director Steven Spielberg's first film, about two parents whose child is being put into a foster home. Shows how they accidently capture a police patrol car, which begins an elaborate chase. Stars Goldie Hawn, Ben Johnson, Michael Sacks, and William Atherton.

SUMMER HEAT
Vid America; Order No. 626; Date not listed • color; 1 hr, 11 min; ½" Beta II, ½" VHS • Sale: $59.95; Rental: $12.95/wk, applicable to purchase

Presents a pornographic film.

SUMMER OF '69
Monarch Releasing Corporation; Date not listed • color; 1 hr, 4 min; ¾" U-Matic • Sale: $350

Presents a pornographic film.

SUMMER WISHES, WINTER DREAMS
National Film and Video Center; 1973 • color; 1 hr, 35 min; ¾" U-Matic, ½" Beta II, ½" VHS • Rental: $89/1 showing

Probes the difficulties a woman faces in reconciling herself to her mother's death and to her son's homosexuality. Stars Joanne Woodward, Martin Balsam, and Sylvia Sidney.

SUMMERDOG
Vid America; Order No. 910; Date not listed • color; 1 hr, 30 min; ½" Beta II, ½" VHS • Rental: $10.95/wk

Offers a tale about an abandoned dog named Hobo who is rescued by a family vacationing in the mountains. Follows Hobo's adventures as he rescues them in return and helps the police to uncover a secret.

SUMMERTIME KILLER
Magnetic Video Corporation; Order No. CL-4015; 1973 • color; 1 hr, 40 min; ½" Beta II, ½" VHS • Sale: $54.95

Dramatizes the revenge of a man who twenty years earlier saw three men beat his father to death, and of the detective who must decide what sort of justice to administer. Features Christopher Mitchum and Karl Malden.

SUNBURN
Fotomat Corp; Order No. B0289 for ½" Beta II, V0289 for ½" VHS; 1979 • color; 1 hr, 50 min; ½" Beta II, ½" VHS • Sale: $59.95; Rental: $9.95/5 days
- -
Paramount Home Video; 1979 • color; 1 hr, 50 min; ½" Beta II, ½" VHS • Sale: $59.95

Presents a mystery/adventure concerning the events following the violent death of an aging millionaire industrialist. Stars Farrah Fawcett-Majors, Charles Grodin, Joan Collins, William Daniels, and Eleanor Parker.

SUNDOWN
Reel Images Inc; Order No. 423; 1941 • b/w; 1 hr, 29 min; ½" Beta II, ½" VHS • Sale: $49.95 for ½" Beta II, $59.95 for ½" VHS

Tells of the British in East Africa during World War II. Shows the problems they encounter with both the natives and the Nazis. Stars Gene Tierney and Bruce Cabot, under the direction of Henry Hathaway.

SUNFLOWER
Magnetic Video Corporation; Order No. CL-4041; 1970 • color; 1 hr, 47 min; ½" Beta II, ½" VHS • Sale: $54.95

Follows a woman as she searches for her lost lover in the Soviet Union during World War II and its aftermath. Stars Marcello Mastroianni and Sophia Loren, under the direction of Vittorio de Sica.

SUNSET BOULEVARD
Fotomat Corp; Order No. B0071 for ½" Beta II, V0071 for ½" VHS; 1950 • b/w; 1 hr, 50 min; ½" Beta II, ½"

VHS • Sale: $49.95; Rental: $9.95/up to 5 days, applicable to purchase

---

Paramount Home Video; 1950 • color; 1 hr, 50 min; ½" Beta II, ½" VHS • Sale: $59.95

RCA SelectaVision VideoDiscs; Order No. 00628; 1950 • b/w; 1 hr, 50 min; CED • Sale: $19.98

Portrays Norma Desmond, an aging silent film queen, and the struggling writer who is held in thrall by her madness. Presents a statement on the dark and desperate side of Hollywood. Stars Gloria Swanson, William Holden, Erich von Stroheim, and Nancy Olson, under the direction of Billy Wilder.

SUNSET TRAIL

Videobrary Inc; Order No. 23; 1939 • b/w; 1 hr; ½" Beta II, ½" VHS • Sale: $39.95

Presents a Hopalong Cassidy western in which Cassidy poses as a tenderfoot at a dude ranch in order to trap a killer. Stars William Boyd, George "Gabby" Hayes, and Charlotte Winters.

THE SUNSHINE BOYS

MGM/CBS Home Video; Order No. M60014; 1975 • color; 1 hr, 51 min; ½" Beta II, ½" VHS • Sale: $59.95

Niles Cinema; Order No. GM-735; 1975 • color; 1 hr, 51 min; ½" Beta II, ½" VHS • Sale: $59.95

Adapts for the screen Neil Simon's play about two ex-vaudeville comedians who broke up because they hated each other but are persuaded to reunite for a TV special. Stars Walter Matthau, George Burns, Richard Benjamin, and Lee Meredith.

SUPERCHICK

Video Communications Inc; Order No. 1097; 1971 • color; 1 hr, 34 min; ½" Beta II, ½" VHS • Sale: $54.95

Tells of an airline hostess and her sexy adventures between flights. Features Joyce Jillson and Louis Quinn.

SUPERMAN

All Star Video Corp; Date not listed • color; 30 min; ½" Beta II, ½" VHS • Sale: $39.95

Video Tape Network; Order No. KI 405 for ½" Beta II, KI 406 for ½" VHS; Date not listed • color; 30 min; ½" Beta II, ½" VHS • Sale: $39.95

Presents beautifully animated cartoons in Technicolor from this rare 1940's Paramount series.

SUPERMAN

Fotomat Corp; Order No. B0295 for ½" Beta II, V0295 for ½" VHS; 1978 • color; 2 hrs, 7 min; ½" Beta II, ½" VHS • Sale: $59.95 Home Theatre Movies; 1941-43 • color; 1 hr; ½" Beta II, ½" VHS • Sale: $49.96

Offers early Superman cartoons made between 1941 and 1943.

SUPERMAN

WCI Home Video Inc; 1978 • color; 2 hrs, 7 min; ½" Beta II, ½" VHS • Sale: $65

Follows the birth of Superman on the disintegrating planet of Krypton, to his growing up in the American Mid-West, to his days as a reporter on the Daily Planet newspaper disguised as Clark Kent. Details his heroic exploits thwarting Lex Luther's plan to cause an earthquake along the San Andreas Fault if he is not paid a huge ransom. Stars Christopher Reeves, Margot Kidder, Marlon Brando, Gene Hackman, and Jackie Cooper.

SUPERMAN COLOR CARTOON FESTIVAL

Discount Video Tapes; 1941-43 • color; 1 hr, 15 min; ½" Beta II, ½" VHS • Sale: $34.95

Offers eight Superman color cartoons of the 40's. Features "Superman," "The Mechanical Monsters," "The Bulleteers," "The Magnetic Telescope," "Terror on the Midway," "The Japoteurs," "The Mummy Strikes," and "Jungle Drums."

THE SUPERWARE PARTY

Scorpio, Etc; 1979 • color; 30 min; ½" Beta I, ½" Beta II, ½" VHS • Sale: $39.95

Presents a pornographic film.

SUSAN SLEPT HERE

Video Communications Inc; 1954 • color; 1 hr, 38 min; ½" Beta II, ½" VHS • Sale: $54.95

Reveals what happens when a man's unexpected Christmas present turns out to be an attractive eighteen-year-old delinquent who has been placed in his custody for the holidays. Features Dick Powell, Debbie Reynolds, and Anne Francis.

SUSPICION

Niles Cinema; Order No. NM-8030; 1941 • b/w; 1 hr, 39 min; ½" Beta II, ½" VHS • Sale: $54.95

The Nostalgia Merchant; Order No. 8030; 1941 • b/w; 1 hr, 39 min; ½" Beta II, ½" VHS • Sale: $54.95

Red Fox, Inc; Order No. 8030; 1941 • b/w; 1 hr, 39 min; ½" Beta II, ½" VHS • Sale: $54.95

Vid America; Order No. 949; 1941 • b/w; 1 hr, 39 min; ½" Beta II, ½" VHS • Rental: $10.95/wk

Relates a Hitchcock-directed tale of a woman who gradually realizes she is married to a murderer. Stars Cary Grant, Joan Fontaine, and Cedric Hardwicke.

Christopher Reeve in *Superman*.

SVENGALI

Golden Tapes Video Tape Library; Order No. CD9; 1931 • b/w; 1 hr, 21 min; 1/2" Beta II, 1/2" VHS • Sale: $49.95 for 1/2" Beta II & VHS, $124.95 for 3/4"

- -

Ivy Video; 1930 • b/w; 1 hr, 16 min; 3/4" U-Matic, 1/2" Beta II, 1/2" VHS • Sale: $59.95 for 1/2" Beta II & VHS, trade-in plan available, $195 for 3/4"

- -

Northeast Video and Sound, Inc; Order No. 147S; 1930 • b/w; 1 hr, 16 min; 3/4" U-Matic, 1/2" EIAJ, 1/2" Beta II, 1/2" VHS • Sale: $195; Rental: $75/wk

- -

Reel Images Inc; Order No. 566; 1931 • b/w; 1 hr, 22 min; 1/2" Beta II, 1/2" VHS • Sale: $49.95 for 1/2" Beta II, $52.95 for 1/2" VHS

Recounts the story of an artist's obsession with a young girl who becomes a singing star under his spell. Stars John Barrymore, Marian Marsh, and Donald Crisp, in a film which features bizarre sets and numerous visual effects.

SWAP MEET

Video Communications Inc; 1979 • color; 1 hr, 26 min; 1/2" Beta II, 1/2" VHS • Sale: $54.95

Offers an "R" rated film about revenge, chase scenes, and wrecked cars. Features Ruth Cox, Jonathan Griss, and Debi Richter.

THE SWASHBUCKLER

Entertainment Video Releasing, Inc; Order No. 1003; 1975 • color; 1 hr, 40 min; 1/2" Beta II, 1/2" VHS • Sale: $49.95 for 1/2" Beta II, $54.95 for 1/2" VHS

Depicts France's salute to American adventure and the swashbuckling films of Errol Flynn. Stars Jean-Paul Belmondo.

SWEET CAKES

Quality X Video Cassette Company; Date not listed • color; 1 hr, 25 min; 1/2" Beta I, 1/2" Beta II, 1/2" VHS • Sale: $99.50

Presents a pornographic film.

SWEET CHARITY

MCA DiscoVision; Order No. 17-003; 1968 • color; 2 hrs, 13 min; LaserVision • Sale: $24.95

Offers a musical based upon a screenplay by Federico Fellini, "Nights of Cabiria." Includes a book by Neil Simon, and music by Dorothy Fields and Cy Coleman. Features the songs "Big Spender," "If They Could See Me Now," and "Rhythm of Life." Follows a prostitute who falls in love with a young man who doesn't know her background. Stars Shirley MacLaine, Ricardo Montalban, Sammy Davis, Jr., and Chita Rivera, in a film which was Bob Fosse's directorial debut.

SWEET HOSTAGE

Magnetic Video Corporation; Order No. CL-5009; 1975 • color; 1 hr, 33 min; 1/2" Beta II, 1/2" VHS • Sale: $54.95

Studies a sensitive, artistically inclined mental-institution inmate who escapes and kidnaps a lonely, confused 16-year-old girl. Stars Linda Blair and Martin Sheen.

SWEET PUN'KIN

Entertainment Video Releasing, Inc; Date not listed • color; 2 hrs; 1/2" Beta II, 1/2" VHS • Sale: $79.95 for 1/2" Beta, $83.95 for 1/2" VHS

Presents a pornographic film.

SWEPT AWAY

Fotomat Corp; Order No. B0441 for 1/2" Beta II, V0441 for 1/2" VHS; 1975 • color; 1 hr, 56 min; 1/2" Beta II, 1/2" VHS • Sale: $49.95; Rental: $7.95/5 days

- -

Time-Life Video Club Inc; 1975 • color; 1 hr, 56 min; 1/2" Beta II, 1/2" VHS • Sale: $44.95 to members

Presents Lina Wertmuller's Italian romantic fantasy about a rich, spoiled woman and her servant-sailor who become stranded together on an island. Explores their ensuing role reversal and eventual love affair. Investigates the role playing and political influences of society. Stars Giancarlo Giannini and Mariangela Melato.

SWING HIGH, SWING LOW

Thunderbird Films; 1937 • b/w; 1 hr, 35 min; 3/4" U-Matic, 1/2" Beta I, 1/2" Beta II, 1/2" VHS • Sale: $69.95 for 1/2" Beta I, $49.95 for 1/2" Beta II & VHS, $89.95 for 3/4"

- -

Video T.E.N.; 1937 • b/w; 1 hr, 35 min; 1/2" Beta II, 1/2" VHS • Sale: $49.95 for 1/2" Beta II, $54.95 for 1/2" VHS

Features Carole Lombard, Fred MacMurray, Charles Butterworth, Jean Dixon, Dorothy Lamour, and Harvey Stephens in the story of a trumpet player's rise and fall in the jazz world.

SWING PARADE OF 1946

Blackhawk Films, Inc; Order No. 502-09-0001 for 1/2" Beta II, 515-09-0001 for 1/2" VHS; 1946 • b/w; 1 hr, 14 min; 1/2" Beta II, 1/2" VHS • Sale: $59.95

Presents a musical review filled with singing, dancing, and slapstick. Features the Three Stooges and Gail Storm.

SWING TIME

Niles Cinema; Order No. NM-8031; 1935 • b/w; 1 hr, 43 min; 1/2" Beta II, 1/2" VHS • Sale: $54.95

- -

The Nostalgia Merchant; Order No. 8031; 1935 • b/w; 1 hr, 43 min; 1/2" Beta II, 1/2" VHS • Sale: $54.95

- -

Red Fox, Inc; Order No. 8031; 1935 • b/w; 1 hr, 43 min; 1/2" Beta II, 1/2" VHS • Sale: $54.95

- -

Time-Life Video Club Inc; 1936 • b/w; 1 hr, 45 min; 1/2" Beta II, 1/2" VHS • Sale: $54.95 to members

Chronicles the story of a dance team whose romance is hampered by a girl back home. Includes the Jerome Kern/Dorothy Fields songs "A Fine Romance," "Pick Yourself Up," and "The Way You Look Tonight." Stars Fred Astaire and Ginger Rogers, under the direction of George Stevens.

SWINGIN' MODELS

Tape Club of America; Order No. 2841 B; Date not listed • color; 1 hr, 18 min; 1/2" Beta II, 1/2" VHS • Sale: $54.95

Presents a pornographic film.

THE SWINGIN' STEWARDESSES

Entertainment Video Releasing, Inc; Date not listed • color; 1 hr, 12 min; 1/2" Beta II, 1/2" VHS • Sale: $79.95

Presents a pornographic film.

A SWINGIN' SUMMER

Video Communications Inc; Order No. 1099; 1962 • color; 1 hr, 21 min; 1/2" Beta II, 1/2" VHS • Sale: $54.95

Presents a beach blanket movie starring Raquel Welch, James Stacy, and Martin West. Features seven song hits by the Righteous Brothers, the Rip Chords, Donnie Brooks, Gary Lewis and the Playboys, and Jody Miller.

SWINGING HIGH
Monarch Releasing Corporation; Date not listed • color; 1 hr, 10 min; 3/4″ U-Matic • Sale: $350

Presents a pornographic film.

SWINGING SKI GIRLS
Meda/Media Home Entertainment Inc; Order No. M512; Date not listed • color; 1 hr, 25 min; 1/2″ Beta I, 1/2″ Beta II, 1/2″ VHS • Sale: $49.95

Presents a pornographic film.

SWINGING SORORITY GIRLS
Meda/Media Home Entertainment Inc; Order No. M513; Date not listed • color; 1 hr, 20 min; 1/2″ Beta I, 1/2″ Beta II, 1/2″ VHS • Sale: $49.95

Presents a pornographic film.

SWISS MISS
The Nostalgia Merchant; 1938 • b/w; 1 hr, 12 min; 1/2″ Beta II, 1/2″ VHS • Sale: $54.95

Offers a Laurel and Hardy comedy feature in which Ollie finds true love. Features romantic tuba playing by Stan. Stars Stan Laurel, Oliver Hardy, Della Lind, Walter Woolf King, and Eric Blore, under the direction of John Blystone. Includes a Hal Roach comedy short.

SYMPATHY FOR THE DEVIL
Magnetic Video Corporation ; Order No. CL-2047; 1970 • color; 1 hr, 50 min; 1/2″ Beta II, 1/2″ VHS • Sale: $54.95

Documents the Rolling Stones rehearsing the title song, alternating with political cartoons and discourses on injustice and imperialism. Stars Mick Jagger and the Stones, in a film in English by Jean-Luc Godard.

TAKE ALL OF ME
Fotomat Corp; Order No. B0187 for 1/2″ Beta II, V0187 for 1/2″ VHS; 1978 • color; 1 hr, 31 min; 1/2″ Beta II, 1/2″ VHS • Sale: $39.95; Rental: $7.95/up to 5 days, applicable to purchase

Offers a tragic love story between a talented, insecure pianist in his 40's and a very young girl who is stricken by leukemia. Features Pamela Vincent, Richard Johnson, Maria Bell, and Leonard John.

TAKE OFF
Quality X Video Cassette Company; Date not listed • color; 1 hr, 43 min; 1/2″ Beta I, 1/2″ Beta II, 1/2″ VHS • Sale: $99.50

Presents a pornographic film.

TAKE THE MONEY AND RUN
Magnetic Video Corporation; Order No. 8007; 1969 • color; 1 hr, 25 min; 1/2″ Beta II, 1/2″ VHS • Sale: $59.95
- -
Niles Cinema; Order No. CL-8007; 1969 • color; 1 hr, 25 min; 1/2″ Beta II, 1/2″ VHS • Sale: $59.95

Presents Woody Allen's first film as writer, director, and star. Follows the episodic misadventures of an incompetent bank robber. Uses psuedo-documentary style with narration by Jackson Beck. Features Janet Margolin, Marcel Hillaire, Jacquelyn Hyde, and Louise Lasser.

TALES OF DEPUTY DAWG
Magnetio Video Corporation; Order No. CL-2035; Date not listed • color; 30 min; 1/2″ Beta II, 1/2″ VHS • Sale: $34.95

Offers a compilation of Terrytoon animated cartoons featuring Deputy Dawg.

THE TALL BLOND MAN WITH ONE BLACK SHOE
Cinema Resources; 1973 • color; 1 hr, 30 min; 1/2″ Beta II, 1/2″ VHS • Sale: $45 Time-Life Video Club Inc; 1972 • color; 1 hr, 30 min; 1/2″ Beta II, 1/2″ VHS • Sale: $39.95 to members

Presents a French farce about two camps of secret agents who mistakenly identify an innocent man as an enemy. Stars Pierre Richard, Bernard Blier, Jean Rochefort, Mireille Darc, and Jean Carmet.

TALL IN THE SADDLE
Niles Cinema; Order No. NM-8033; 1944 • b/w; 1 hr, 19 min; 1/2″ Beta II, 1/2″ VHS • Sale: $54.95
- -
The Nostalgia Merchant; Order No. 8033; 1944 • b/w; 1 hr, 19 min; 1/2″ Beta II, 1/2″ VHS • Sale: $54.95
- -
Red Fox, Inc; Order No. 8033; 1944 • b/w; 1 hr, 19 min; 1/2″ Beta II, 1/2″ VHS • Sale: $54.95

Features John Wayne in the story of a woman-hating cowboy who goes to work for an aging spinster and her young niece, also starring Ella Raines and Gabby Hayes.

TAMING OF THE SHREW
Columbia Pictures Home Entertainment; 1967 • color; 2 hrs, 6 min; 1/2″ Beta II, 1/2″ VHS • Sale: $59.95
- -
Time-Life Video Club Inc; 1966 • color; 2 hrs, 6 min; 1/2″ Beta II, 1/2″ VHS • Sale: $59.95, plus $15 annual membership fee

Offers director Franco Zeffirelli's screen adaptation of Shakespeare's comedy. Tells of a would-be husband who must subdue the fiercely proud, liberated spirit of his bride-to-be. Stars Richard Burton, Elizabeth Taylor, and Cyril Cusack, with music by Nino Rota.

TARGET FOR TONIGHT
Reel Images Inc; Order No. 724; 1941 • b/w; 50 min; 1/2″ Beta II, 1/2″ VHS • Sale: $39.95 for 1/2″ Beta II, $42.95 for 1/2″ VHS

Offers a British documentary feature about a real bombing raid to destroy oil storage tanks in Kiel, Germany during World War II. Features the actual members of the British Royal Air Force who planned and executed the missions, re-enacting their daily lives on the job.

TARZAN AND THE GREEN GODDESS
Video T.E.N.; 1935 • b/w; 1 hr, 12 min; 1/2″ Beta II, 1/2″ VHS • Sale: $49.95 for 1/2″ Beta II, $54.95 for 1/2″ VHS

Spotlights Olympic star Herman Brix as Tarzan in an adventure involving an expedition in search of a statue containing a secret formula. Includes Ula Holt, Frank Baker, Dale Walsh, and Lewis Sargent.

TARZAN AND THE TRAPPERS

Reel Images Inc; Order No. 50; 1958 • b/w; 1 hr, 11 min; 1/2" Beta II, 1/2" VHS • Sale: $49.95 for 1/2" Beta II, $52.95 for 1/2" VHS

Presents an adventure in which the jungle hero fights trappers who are killing animals illegally, and prevents them from taking riches from a lost city. Stars Gordon Scott.

TARZAN OF THE APES

Reel Images Inc; Order No. 529; 1918 • b/w; 1 hr, 1 min; 1/2" Beta II, 1/2" VHS • Sale: $39.95 for 1/2" Beta II, $42.95 for 1/2" VHS

Presents the first Tarzan film ever made, a silent movie with music score, which traces the origin of Tarzan: the baby adopted by a she-ape after the death of his parents grows up to be the "King of the Jungle." Features Elmo Lincoln as Tarzan.

TARZAN THE FEARLESS

Cable Films; 1933 • b/w; 1 hr, 24 min; 1/2" Beta I, 1/2" Beta II, 1/2" VHS • Sale: $65 for 1/2" Beta I, $49.50 for 1/2" Beta II & VHS

- -

Video T.E.N.; 1933 • b/w; 1 hr, 18 min; 1/2" Beta II, 1/2" VHS • Sale: $49.95 for 1/2" Beta II, $54.95 for 1/2" VHS

Relates a story in which Tarzan, helping a young girl find her missing father, must face dangerous evil hunters, treacherous Arabs, people of a lost city, and the perils of the jungle. Stars Buster Crabbe and Jacqueline Wells.

TARZAN'S REVENGE

Video T.E.N.; 1938 • b/w; 1 hr, 10 min; 1/2" Beta II, 1/2" VHS • Sale: $49.95 for 1/2" Beta II, $54.95 for 1/2" VHS

Portrays the original jungle hero in a story of kidnap and rescue. Showcases Olympic champions Glenn Morris and Eleanor Holm, along with George Barbier and C. Henry Gordon.

TEENAGE MILKMAID

Monarch Releasing Corporation; Date not listed • color; 1 hr, 15 min; 3/4" U-Matic • Sale: $350

Presents a pornographic film.

THE TELL TALE HEART

Thunderbird Films; 1964 • b/w; 1 hr, 21 min; 3/4" U-Matic, 1/2" Beta I, 1/2" Beta II, 1/2" VHS • Sale: $69.95 for 1/2" Beta I, $49.95 for 1/2" Beta II & VHS, $89.95 for 3/4"

Presents an expanded version of Edgar Allen Poe's story of psychological terror, murder, and madness. Features Laurence Payne, Adrienne Corri, and Dermont Walsh.

TELL THEM JOHNNY WADD IS HERE

Freeway Video Enterprises; Date not listed • color; 1 hr, 20 min; 1/2" Beta II, 1/2" VHS • Sale: $75 for 1/2" Beta II, $85 for 1/2" VHS

Presents a pornographic film.

10

Fotomat Corp; Order No. BQ371 for 1/2" Beta II, V0371 for 1/2" VHS; 1979 • color; 2 hrs; 1/2" Beta II, 1/2" VHS • Sale: $69.95

Presents a romantic comedy concerning a 42-year-old music composer who has discovered and is obsessed with a woman whose beauty he considers to be perfect. Stars Dudley Moore, Julie Andrews, Bo Derek,

Robert Webber, and Dee Wallace, under the direction of Blake Edwards.

THE TEN COMMANDMENTS

Fotomat Corp; Order No. B0069 for 1/2" Beta II, V0069 for 1/2" VHS; 1956 • color; 3 hrs, 39 min; 1/2" Beta II, 1/2" VHS • Sale: $69.95; Rental: $9.95/up to 5 days, applicable to purchase

- -

MCA DiscoVision; Order No. P21-519; 1956 • color; 3 hrs, 39 min; LaserVision • Sale: $24.95

- -

Paramount Home Video; 1956 • color; 3 hrs, 39 min; 1/2" Beta II, 1/2" VHS • Sale: $79.95

- -

RCA SelectaVision VideoDiscs; Order No. 00623; 1956 • color; 3 hrs, 40 min; CED • Sale: $22.98

Presents an epic screen version, filmed in Egypt and the Sinai with one of the biggest sets ever constructed, of the story of Moses, who turned his back on a privileged life to lead his people to freedom. Stars Charlton Heston, Yul Brynner, Anne Baxter, Edward G. Robinson, Yvonne DeCarlo, Debra Paget, John Derek, Sir Cedric Hardwicke, Nina Foch, Martha Scott, Judith Anderson, and Vincent Price, under the direction of Cecil B. DeMille.

TEN DAYS THAK SHOOK THE WORLD

Reel Images Inc; Order No. 461; 1927 • b/w; 1 hr, 35 min; 1/2" Beta II, 1/2" VHS • Sale: $49.95 for 1/2" Beta II, $52.95 for 1/2" VHS

Presents Sergei Eisenstein's follow-up to "Potemkin." Offers Eisenstein's unique, pioneering editing technique in this classic made to commemorate the tenth anniversary of the Russian Revolution.

TEN LITTLE INDIANS

Magnetic Video Corporation; Order No. CL-4023; 1965 • color; 1 hr, 38 min; 1/2" Beta II, 1/2" VHS • Sale: $54.95

Presents an Agatha Christie mystery which brings together ten total strangers who die one by one. Features Oliver Reed and Elke Sommer.

TENNESSEE'S PARTNER

FHV Entertainment, Inc; 1955 • color; 1 hr, 27 min; 1/2" Beta II, 1/2" VHS • Sale: $49.95

Presents a movie version of Bret Harte's story of the West, set in a California gold-rush town. Depicts gambling, grubstakes, and romance. Stars John Payne, Ronald Reagan, and Rhonda Fleming.

TENSION AT TABLE ROCK

Video Communications Inc; Order No. 1102; 1956 • color; 1 hr, 33 min; 1/2" Beta II, 1/2" VHS • Sale: $54.95

Portrays a rugged cowhand, falsely accused of murder by a woman he spurned, who is forced to leave town and travel under an assumed name to escape his sullied reputation. Stars Richard Egan and Dorothy Malone.

THE TERROR

Cinema Concepts, Inc.; 1963 • color; 1 hr, 21 min; 3/4" U-Matic, 1/2" Beta II, 1/2" VHS • Sale: $54.95 for 1/2" Beta II & VHS, $149.95 for 3/4"

- -

The Video Library; Order No. CC-0143; 1963 • color; 1 hr, 21 min; 1/2" Beta II, 1/2" VHS • Sale: $54.95

Presents a horror story about a lost French officer who is rescued by a girl who disappears as mysteriously as she arrived. Features Boris Karloff, Jack Nicholson, and Sandra Knight.

TERROR BY NIGHT

Northeast Video and Sound, Inc; Order No. 140S; 1946 • b/w; 60 min; 3/4" U-Matic, 1/2" EIAJ, 1/2" Beta II, 1/2" VHS • Sale: $149; Rental: $55/wk

----
Reel Images Inc; Order No. 718; 1946 • b/w; 1 hr; 1/2" Beta II, 1/2" VHS • Sale: $39.95 for 1/2" Beta II, $42.95 for 1/2" VHS

Presents a Sherlock Holmes mystery in which Holmes and Watson foil a jewel thief aboard an express train heading from London to Scotland. Stars Basil Rathbone, Nigel Bruce, and Alan Mowbray.

TERROR FROM UNDER THE HOUSE

Tape Club of America; Order No. 2714 B; 1971 • color; 1 hr, 27 min; 1/2" Beta II, 1/2" VHS • Sale: $54.95

Probes into the terrors that occur when a young couple investigate the rape-murder of their child. Stars Joan Collins and James Booth.

TERRY BEARS

Magnetic Video Corporation; Order No. CL-2041; Date not listed • color; 30 min; 1/2" Beta II, 1/2" VHS • Sale: $34.95

Presents a compilation of Terrytoon animated cartoons featuring the Terry Bears.

TERRYTOONS, VOLUME I, FEATURING MIGHTY MOUSE

RCA SelectaVision VideoDiscs; Order No. 01503; Date not listed • color; 2 hrs; CED • Sale: $14.98

Presents nineteen complete color cartoons featuring Mighty Mouse, Heckle and Jeckle, Deputy Dog, and Little Roquefort.

TEXAS TO BATAAN

Reel Images Inc; Order No. 53; 1942 • b/w; 56 min; 1/2" Beta II, 1/2" VHS • Sale: $39.95 for 1/2" Beta II, $42.95 for 1/2" VHS

Recounts how The Range Busters tangle with enemy spies in this off-beat World War II western. Shows how they take a shipment of badly needed horses to the Philippines. Stars John King, David Sharpe, and Max Terhune.

TEXAS TRAIL

Videobrary Inc ; Order No. 21; 1937 • b/w; 56 min; 1/2" Beta II, 1/2" VHS • Sale: $39.95

Presents a Hopalong Cassidy western in which Cassidy is accused of stealing horses. Stars William Boyd, George "Gabby" Hayes, and Alexander Cross.

THAT UNCERTAIN FEELING

Video T.E.N.; 1941 • b/w; 1 hr, 26 min; 1/2" Beta II, 1/2" VHS • Sale: $49.95 for 1/2" Beta II, $54.95 for 1/2" VHS

Studies the effect of psychoanalysis on a marriage in this comedy directed by Ernst Lubitsch, about a wife who seeks psychiatric relief from her chronic hiccups. Stars Merle Oberon, Melvyn Douglas, Burgess Meredith, Alan Mowbray, and Eve Arden.

THAT'S ENTERTAINMENT

MGM/CBS Home Video; Order No. M60007; 1974 • color; 2 hrs, 12 min; 1/2" Beta II, 1/2" VHS • Sale: $59.95

Niles Cinema; Order No. GM-736; 1974 • b/w & color; 2 hrs, 12 min; 1/2" Beta II, 1/2" VHS • Sale: $59.95

Presents stars hosting scenes from nearly 100 MGM musicals from 1929-58. Includes some little-seen and unexpected moments such as Clark Gable singing and dancing. Stars Fred Astaire, Bing Crosby, Gene Kelly, Peter Lawford, Liza Minelli, Donald O'Connor, Debbie Reynolds, Mickey Rooney, Frank Sinatra, James Stewart, and Elizabeth Taylor. Features direction by Jack Haley, Jr.

THEATRE OF DEATH

Fotomat Corp; Order No. B0155 for 1/2" Beta II, V0155 for 1/2" VHS; 1967 • color; 1 hr, 30 min; 1/2" Beta II, 1/2" VHS • Sale: $39.95; Rental: $7.95/up to 5 days, applicable to purchase

----
Video Communications Inc; 1966 • color; 1 hr, 41 min; 1/2" Beta II, 1/2" VHS • Sale: $54.95

Explores vampire-like murders revolving around Paris' Grand Guignol stage sensation and its beautiful young starlet under a sinister hypnotic trance. Stars Christopher Lee.

THERE'S A GIRL IN MY SOUP

National Film and Video Center; 1970 • color; 1 hr, 35 min; 3/4" U-Matic, 1/2" Beta II, 1/2" VHS • Rental: $69/1 showing

Traces the love affair of a famous chef and a girl who has left her old lover: he falls in love with her, but she returns to the other man. Ends with all three of them living together. Stars Peter Sellers and Goldie Hawn.

THERE'S NO BUSINESS LIKE SHOW BUSINESS

Magnetic Video Corporation; Order No. CL-1086; 1954 • color; 1 hr, 57 min; 1/2" Beta II, 1/2" VHS • Sale: $44.95

Presents an Irving Berlin musical comedy about a vaudeville family. Features Ethel Merman, Donald O'Connor, Marilyn Monroe, Dan Dailey, Johnny Ray, and Mitzi Gaynor.

THESE GIRLS WON'T TALK

Reel Images Inc; Order No. 79; 1918-28 • b/w; 1 hr, 2 min; 1/2" Beta II, 1/2" VHS • Sale: $39.95 for 1/2" Beta II, $42.95 for 1/2" VHS

Presents three silent comedy shorts. Features "Her Bridal Night-mare" with Colleen Moore; "The Campus Carmen" starring Carole Lombard, Daphne Pollard, and Johnny Burke in a Mack Sennett short; and "As Luck Would Have It" with Betty Compson.

THEY CALL ME TRINITY

Magnetic Video Corporation; Order No. CL-4026; 1972 • color; 1 hr, 50 min; 1/2" Beta II, 1/2" VHS • Sale: $54.95

Features two drifters leading underdog Mormon farmers in a fight against outlaws in this comedy-drama set in the Old West. Stars Terence Hill and Farley Granger.

THEY MADE ME A CRIMINAL

Northeast Video and Sound, Inc; 1939 • b/w; 1 hr, 32 min; 3/4" U-Matic, 1/2" EIAJ, 1/2" Beta II, 1/2" VHS • Sale: $195; Rental: $75/wk

----
VCX; Order No. FC121; 1939 • b/w; 1 hr, 32 min; 1/2" Beta II, 1/2" VHS • Sale: $35.00

Features John Garfield as the haunted prizefighter who thinks he has killed his opponent.

THEY SHOOT HORSES, DON'T THEY?

Magnetic Video Corporation; Order No. 8004; 1969 • color; 2 hrs; 1/2" Beta II, 1/2" VHS • Sale: $59.95

Studies the lives of people involved in a dance marathon during the Great Depression of the 1930's. Follows a self-destructive girl who attracts an aimless drifter. Stars Gig Young, Jane Fonda, Michael Sarrazin, Susannah York, Red Buttons, Bonnie Bedelia, and Bruce Dern.

THEY WON'T BELIEVE ME!
The Nostalgia Merchant; Order No. BT8058; 1946 • b/w; 1 hr, 35 min; 1/2" Beta II, 1/2" VHS • Sale: $54.95

Red Fox, Inc; Order No. BT8058; 1946 • b/w; 1 hr, 35 min; 1/2" Beta II, 1/2" VHS • Sale: $54.95

Tells of a young philanderer who gets involved with three women, resulting in tragedy. Features Robert Young, Susan Hayward, and Jane Greer.

THE THIEF OF BAGHDAD
Home Vision; Order No. 805-7001 for 1/2" Beta II, 805-9001 for 1/2" VHS; Date not listed • color; 1 hr, 40 min; 1/2" Beta II, 1/2" VHS • Sale: $49.95

Vid America; Order No. 942; 1978 • color; 1 hr, 43 min; 1/2" Beta II, 1/2" VHS • Sale: $49.95; Rental: $10.95/wk, applicable to purchase

---
Video Gems; 1978 • color; 1 hr, 40 min; 1/2" Beta II, 1/2" VHS • Sale: $59.95

Offers a British and French co-production TV movie adaptation of the "Arabian Nights," with magic carpets and the genie of the lamp. Stars Roddy McDowell, Peter Ustinov, Terence Stamp, and Frank Finlay.

THE THING
Niles Cinema; Order No. NM-8034; 1951 • b/w; 1 hr, 20 min; 1/2" Beta II, 1/2" VHS • Sale: $54.95

The Nostalgia Merchant; Order No. 8034; 1951 • b/w; 1 hr, 20 min; 1/2" Beta II, 1/2" VHS • Sale: $54.95

RCA SelectaVision VideoDiscs; Order No. 00404; 1951 • b/w; 1 hr, 27 min; CED • Sale: $19.98

Red Fox, Inc; Order No. 8034; 1951 • b/w; 1 hr, 20 min; 1/2" Beta II, 1/2" VHS • Sale: $54.95

Vid America; Order No. 944; 1951 • b/w; 1 hr, 26 min; 1/2" Beta II, 1/2" VHS • Sale: $54.95; Rental: $10.95/wk, applicable to purchase

---
Relates the story of an alien who crashes near a polar outpost and goes on a rampage. Stars Kenneth Tobey, Margaret Sheriden, and James Arness.

THINGS TO COME
Cinema Concepts, Inc.; 1936 • b/w; 1 hr, 35 min; 3/4" U-Matic, 1/2" Beta II, 1/2" VHS • Sale: $54.95 for 1/2" Beta II & VHS, $149.95 for 3/4"

Northeast Video and Sound, Inc; 1936 • b/w; 1 hr, 30 min; 3/4" U-Matic, 1/2" EIAJ, 1/2" Beta II, 1/2" VHS • Sale: $195; Rental: $75/wk

---
The Video Library; Order No. ME-1065; 1936 • b/w; 1 hr, 35 min; 1/2" Beta II, 1/2" VHS • Sale: $44.95

Presents an adaptation of H.G. Wells' science-fiction fantasy. Offers a vision of the world of the future with elaborate special effects, including a giant moon cannon. Stars Raymond Massey, Ralph Richardson, and Cedric Hardwicke, under the direction of William Cameron Menzies.

THE THIRD MAN
Fotomat Corp; Order No. B0249 for 1/2" Beta II, V0249 for 1/2" VHS; 1949 • b/w; 1 hr, 39 min; 1/2" Beta II, 1/2" VHS • Sale: $49.95; Rental: $9.95/up to 5 days, applicable to purchase

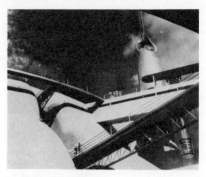

Things to Come.

Thunderbird Films; 1949 • b/w; 1 hr, 45 min; 3/4" U-Matic, 1/2" Beta I, 1/2" Beta II, 1/2" VHS • Sale: $69.95 for 1/2" Beta I, $49.95 for 1/2" Beta II & VHS, $89.95 for 3/4"

VCX; Order No. FC105; 1949 • b/w; 1 hr, 44 min; 1/2" Beta II, 1/2" VHS • Sale: $35.00

Video Communications Inc; Order No. 2024; 1950 • b/w; 1 hr, 40 min; 1/2" Beta II, 1/2" VHS • Sale: $54.95

Presents a classic of intrigue featuring Orson Welles as Harry Lime, an operator in the post-war black market in Vienna. Relates how a writer, arriving on the scene to accept a job from Harry, investigates the facts behind his friend's sudden death and uncovers the truth— Harry is alive and capitalizing on the city's misery. Stars Joseph Cotten, Valli, and Trevor Howard, under the direction of Carol Reed.

THE 39 STEPS
VCX; Order No. FC116; 1935 • b/w; 1 hr, 20 min; 1/2" Beta II, 1/2" VHS • Sale: $35.00 Video T.E.N.; 1935 • b/w; 1 hr, 21 min; 1/2" Beta II, 1/2" VHS • Sale: $49.95 for 1/2" Beta II, $54.95 for 1/2" VHS

Offers Alfred Hitchcock's tale of an innocent man who is believed to be member of a spyring. Stars Robert Donat, Madeleine Carroll, Lucie Mannheim, Godfrey Tearle, and Peggy Ashcroft.

THIS MAN MUST DIE
Blackhawk Films, Inc; Order No. 502-30-0065 for 1/2" Beta II, 515-30-0065 for 1/2" VHS; 1970 • color; 1 hr, 55 min; 1/2" Beta II, 1/2" VHS • Sale: $59.95

Depicts a father's rage at the hit-and-run killing of his son, and his revenge. Features Michael Duchaussoy, Jean Yanne, Caroline Cellier, Lorraine Rainer, Marc Di Napoli, and Guy Marly under Claude Chabrol's direction.

THOROUGHLY MODERN MILLIE
MCA DiscoVision; Order No. 17-001; 1967 • color; 2 hrs, 18 min; LaserVision • Sale: $24.95

Presents a musical set in the Twenties about a secretary who has hopes of marrying her wealthy boss. Stars Julie Andrews, Mary Tyler Moore, Carol Channing, Beatrice Lillie, James Fox, and John Gavin, under the direction of George Roy Hill.

THOSE MAGNIFICENT MEN IN THEIR FLYING MACHINES

Blackhawk Films, Inc ; Order No. 502-49-0026 for ½" Beta II, 515-49-0022 for ½" VHS;.1965 • color; 2 hrs, 18 min; ½" Beta II, ½" VHS • Sale: $74.95

- -

Golden Tapes Video Tape Library; Order No. F-1033; 1965 • color; 2 hrs, 18 min; ½" Beta II, ½" VHS • Sale: $49.95 for ½" Beta II & VHS, $124.95 for ¾"

- -

Magnetic Video Corporation; Order No. CL-1033; 1965 • color; 2 hrs, 18 min; ½" Beta II, ½" VHS • Sale: $64.95

- -

The Video Library; Order No. MV-1033; 1966 • color; 2 hrs, 18 min; ½" Beta II, ½" VHS • Sale: $74.95

Presents a comic valentine to the men who took to the air in the first flying machines. Depicts antique aircraft oddities such as the Bleriot, which was the first plane to fly the English Channel. Stars Terry-Thomas, James Fox, and Stuart Whitman.

THREE BROADWAY GIRLS

Video T.E.N.; 1932 • b/w; 1 hr, 18 min; ½" Beta II, ½" VHS • Sale: $49.95 for ½" Beta II, $54.95 for ½" VHS

Traces the efforts of three gold-digging young ladies to land rich sugar-daddy husbands. Features Madge Evans, Joan Blondell, Ina Claire, David Manners, and Lowell Sherman.

THREE COINS IN THE FOUNTAIN

Magnetic Video Corporation; Order No. CL-1032; 1954 • color; 1 hr, 42 min; ½" Beta II, ½" VHS • Sale: $44.95

Concerns three American secretaries who wish for romance at the Fountain of Trevi in Rome, and eventually find what they seek. Stars Clifton Webb, Dorothy McGuire, Jean Peters, Louis Jourdan, and Rossano Brazzi.

THREE DAYS OF THE CONDOR

Fotomat Corp; Order No. B0093 for ½" Beta II, V0093 for ½" VHS; 1975 • color; 1 hr, 58 min; ½" Beta II, ½" VHS • Sale: $49.95; Rental: $9.95/up to 5 days, applicable to purchase

- -

MCA DiscoVision; Order No. P11-510; 1975 • color; 1 hr, 58 min; LaserVision • Sale: $24.95

- -

Paramount Home Video; 1975 • color; 1 hr, 58 min; ½" Beta II, ½" VHS • Sale: $59.95

Recounts a story of an agent, on the run from a mass slaughter in his CIA research office, who uncovers the possibility of another CIA operating within the organization. Follows him as he suddenly finds himself the target of both his employers and the unknown killers. Stars Robert Redford, Faye Dunaway, Cliff Robertson, and Max Von Sydow, under the direction of Sydney Pollack.

THE THREE MUSKETEERS

Reel Images Inc; Order No. 709; 1933 • b/w; 3 hrs, 36 min; ½" Beta II, ½" VHS • Sale: $119.95

Offers a serial from Mascot Studios in twelve episodes, starring John Wayne. Concerns three legionnaires who battle the evil "Devil of the Desert."

3 NUTS IN SEARCH OF A BOLT

FHV Entertainment, Inc; 1964 • color; 1 hr, 19 min; ½" Beta II, ½" VHS • Sale: $49.95

Offers a comedy of Freudian tomfoolery with three neurotic but resourceful "nuts." Stars Mamie Van Doren and Tom Noonan.

THREE ON THE TRAIL

Videobrary Inc; Order No. 17; 1936 • b/w; 1 hr, 7 min; ½" Beta II, ½" VHS • Sale: $39.95

Presents a Hopalong Cassidy western in which a saloon owner heads a band of outlaws and tries to spoil the morals of a young girl. Stars William Boyd, George "Gabby" Hayes, and Onslow Stevens.

THREE SISTERS

MCA DiscoVision; Order No. 10-014; 1970 • color; 2 hrs, 45 min; LaserVision • Sale: $24.95

Presents Sir Laurence Olivier's film of Anton Chekhov's play, produced for the American Film Theatre. Depicts the three daughters of a deceased Russian colonel living in the provinces at the turn of the century, who yearn for a return to the gentility and culture that they knew in Moscow. Stars Sir Laurence Olivier, Alan Bates, Joan Plowright, Jeanne Watts, Louise Purnell, and Derek Jacoby, under the direction of Olivier.

THE THREE STOOGES, PART 1

Columbia Pictures Home Entertainment; Order No. BE51555 for ½" Beta II, VH10550 for ½" VHS; Date not listed • b/w; 30 min; ½" Beta II, ½" VHS • Sale: $49.95

Presents three slapstick short subjects featuring the original Three Stooges.

THE THREE STOOGES, PART II

Columbia Pictures Home Entertainment; Order No. BE151556 for ½" Beta II, VH10551 for ½" VHS; Date not listed • b/w; 30 min; ½" Beta II, ½" VHS • Sale: $49.95

Presents three slapstick short subjects featuring the original Three Stooges.

THE THREE STOOGES GO AROUND THE WORLD IN A DAZE

National Film and Video Center; 1963 • b/w; 1 hr, 34 min; ¾" U-Matic, ½" Beta II, ½" VHS • Rental: $49/1 showing

Features a spoof of the Jules Verne novel as the Stooges assist Phileas Fogg in duplicating his father's famous trip around the world in 80 days.

THE THREE STOOGES IN ORBIT

National Film and Video Center; 1962 • b/w; 1 hr, 27 min; ¾" U-Matic, ½" Beta II, ½" VHS • Rental: $49/1 showing

Follows the misadventures of the Three Stooges when they discover a Martian plot to steal a Terran scientist's invention.

THE THREE STOOGES MEET HERCULES

National Film and Video Center; 1962 • b/w; 1 hr, 20 min; ¾" U-Matic, ½" Beta II, ½" VHS • Rental: $49/1 showing

Places the Stooges in the tales of Greek mythology, where they try to pass themselves off as Hercules' friends.

THE THREE WORLDS OF GULLIVER

National Film and Video Center; 1960 • color; 1 hr, 40 min; ¾" U-Matic, ½" Beta II, ½" VHS • Rental: $49/1 showing

Adapts the story of Gulliver's adventures in the land of Lilliput, where the people are only six inches high.

Stars Kerwin Mathews, Jo Morrow, and June Thorburn.

TIFFANY JONES
Niles Cinema; Order No. BT-12 for 1/2" Beta II, VH-12 for 1/2" VHS; 1976 • color; 1 hr, 30 min; 1/2" Beta II, 1/2" VHS • Sale: $59.95

Recounts the story of a fashion model who becomes embroiled in the public and private affairs of international intrigue. Stars Anouska Hempel and Ray Brooks.

THE TIGER FROM HONG KONG
Monarch Releasing Corporation; Date not listed • color; 1 hr, 30 min; 3/4" U-Matic • Sale: $350

Presents a pornographic film.

TILL MARRIAGE DO US PART
Time-Life Video Club Inc; 1979 • color; 1 hr, 37 min; 1/2" Beta II, 1/2" VHS • Sale: $44.95 to members

Reveals the problems encountered by a virgin bride in overcoming turn-of-the-century mores and learning the mysteries of the flesh. Stars Laura Antonelli and Michele Placido, under the direction of Luigi Comencini.

TILL THE CLOUDS ROLL BY
Cinema Concepts, Inc.; 1946 • color; 2 hrs; 3/4" U-Matic, 1/2" Beta II, 1/2" VHS • Sale: $54.95 for 1/2" Beta II & VHS, $149.95 for 3/4"

- -
VCX; Order No. FC108; 1946 • color; 2 hrs, 17 min; 1/2" Beta II, 1/2" VHS • Sale: $45.00

- -
The Video Library; Order No. ME-1049; 1946 • color; 2 hrs; 1/2" Beta II, 1/2" VHS • Sale: $69.95

Offers an M-G-M musical depicting the life and music of Jerome Kern. Stars Fred Astaire, Robert Walker, Judy Garland, Lucille Bremer, and Van Heflin.

TILLIE'S PUNCTURED ROMANCE
Golden Tapes Video Tape Library; Order No. CC8; 1914 • b/w; 52 min; 1/2" Beta II, 1/2" VHS • Sale: $49.95 for 1/2" Beta II & VHS, $79.95 for 3/4"

Presents the first full-length comedy feature film, in which a girl from the country is fleeced by a city slicker. Stars Charlie Chaplin, Marie Dressler, and the Keystone Kops, under the direction of Mack Sennett.

TO BE OR NOT TO BE
Time-Life Video Club Inc; 1942 • b/w; 1 hr, 39 min; 1/2" Beta II, 1/2" VHS • Sale: $39.95 to members

Offers a black comedy set in wartime Poland, concerning the efforts of an acting troupe to survive Nazi occupation and the Gestapo. Stars Carole Lombard, Jack Benny, and Robert Stack, under the direction of Ernst Lubitsch.

TO KILL A MOCKINGBIRD
MCA DiscoVision; Order No. 10-009; 1963 • b/w; 2 hrs, 9 min; LaserVision • Sale: $24.95

Adapts the novel by Harper Lee which explores racial prejudice in America's South and the courage needed to fight against it. Follows the trial of a black man accused of raping a white woman. Shows the pressure put on the white lawyer who defends the black man, and its effect upon the children of the widowed lawyer. Stars Gregory Peck in his Oscar-winning role, Brock Peters, Robert Duvall, and Mary Badham.

TO SIR WITH LOVE
National Film and Video Center; 1967 • color; 1 hr, 45 min; 3/4" U-Matic, 1/2" Beta II, 1/2" VHS • Rental: $79/1 showing

Stars Sidney Poitier as an out-of-work engineer turned teacher. Recounts how he earns the respect and affection of his rough and unruly class in London's East End. Features Suzy Kendall and Judy Geeson.

TOKLAT
Video Communications Inc; Date not listed • color; 1 hr, 37 min; 1/2" Beta II, 1/2" VHS • Sale: $54.95

Offers colorful scenes of our American wild as background to the story of a great grizzly bear.

TOM AND JERRY CARTOON FESTIVAL
MGM/CBS Home Video; Order No. M40019; Date not listed • color; 58 min; 1/2" Beta II, 1/2" VHS • Sale: $39.95

Offers a series of cartoons starring Tom and Jerry. Includes "Flying Cats," "Dr. Jeckyl and Mr. Meow," "Cat and Mermouse," and "Cat Concerto."

TOM BROWN'S SCHOOL DAYS
National Film and Video Center; 1951 • b/w; 1 hr, 33 min; 3/4" U-Matic, 1/2" Beta II, 1/2" VHS • Rental: $39/1 showing

- -
Video Communications Inc; 1951 • b/w; 1 hr, 34 min; 1/2" Beta II, 1/2" VHS • Sale: $54.95

Depicts the lifestyle of English schoolboys in 1884. Presents a nostalgic view of the period based on the Thomas Hughes novel. Stars John Howard Davies, Robert Newton, and James Hayter.

Ginger Rogers and Fred Astaire in *Top Hat*.

**Cary Grant,
Roland Young, and
Constance Bennett
in *Topper*.**

TOM, DICK, AND HARRY

Blackhawk Films, Inc; Order No. 506-43-0698 for ½″ Beta II, 525-43-0698 for ½″ VHS; 1941 • b/w; 1 hr, 26 min; ½″ Beta II, ½″ VHS • Sale: $49.95

Spotlights a wide-eyed young girl and her dilemma: which fiance should she marry—the go-getter salesman, the rich playboy, or the non-conformist? Stars Ginger Rogers, George Murphy, Burgess Meredith, Allen Marshall, and Phil Silvers, under Garson Kanin's direction.

TOM SAWYER

MCA DiscoVision; Order No. 19-001; 1973 • color; 1 hr, 16 min; LaserVision • Sale: $15.95

Presents an adaptation of Mark Twain's book about a boy's life in a Mississippi River town in the 1800's. Stars Jane Wyatt as Aunt Polly, and Buddy Ebsen as town ne'er-do-well Muff Potter; features also Vic Morrow and John McGiver, in a made-for-television movie.

TOMBOY

Reel Images Inc; Order No. 479; 1940 • b/w; 1 hr, 10 min; ½″ Beta II, ½″ VHS • Sale: $49.95 for ½″ Beta II, $52.95 for ½″ VHS

Presents a family film in which a bashful country boy and a not-so-shy city girl team up to catch some thieves. Stars Jackie Moran and Marcia Mae Jones.

TONGPAN

Video Action Library; Order No. NV11; Date not listed • b/w; 1 hr; ½″ Beta I, ½″ Beta II, ½″ VHS • Sale: $45; Rental: $12/1 wk, $6 ea add'l wk

Depicts contemporary Thailand and the real dilemmas of development in a feature including many prominent artists and intellectuals, some of them since forced underground.

TOP HAT

The Nostalgia Merchant; Order No. 8035; 1935 • b/w;

1 hr, 37 min; ½″ Beta II, ½″ VHS • Sale: $54.95

Time-Life Video Club Inc; 1935 • b/w; 1 hr, 45 min; ½″ Beta II, ½″ VHS • Sale: $54.95, plus $15 annual membership fee

Presents Fred Astaire, Ginger Rogers, Edward Everett Horton, and Helen Broderick in a musical comedy which revolves around a mistaken identity. Features the Irving Berlin tunes "Cheek to Cheek," "Isn't This a Lovely Day to be Caught in the Rain," and "Top Hat, White Tie and Tails."

TOPPER

The Nostalgia Merchant; Order No. 4005; 1937 • b/w; 1 hr, 37 min; ½″ Beta II, ½″ VHS • Sale: $54.95

Adapts a novel by Thorne Smith about a mild-mannered, henpecked husband who is aided—and manipulated—by a playful ghostly couple and their dog. Stars Cary Grant, Constance Bennett, and Roland Young.

TOPPER RETURNS

Budget Video; 1940 • b/w; 1 hr, 30 min; ½″ Beta II, ½″ VHS • Sale: $44.95

Reel Images Inc; Order No. 47; 1941 • b/w; 1 hr, 28 min; ½″ Beta II, ½″ VHS • Sale: $49.95 for ½″ Beta II, $52.95 for ½″ VHS

Features Topper ably assisted by a beautiful girl ghost as they stalk a killer hiding in a deserted house. Stars Roland Young, Joan Blondell, Carole Landis, and Eddie 'Rochester' Anderson.

TORA! TORA! TORA!

Blackhawk Films, Inc; Order No. 502-49-0014 for ½ ″ Beta II, 515-49-0001 for ½″ VHS; 1965 • color; 2 hrs, 24 min; ½″ Beta II, ½″ VHS • Sale: $74.95

Golden Tapes Video Tape Library; Order No. F-1017; 1970 • color; 2 hrs, 24 min; ½″ Beta II, ½″ VHS •

Sale: $49.95 for ½" Beta II & VHS, $124.95 for ¾"

Magnetic Video Corporation; Order No. CL-1017; 1970 • color; 2 hrs, 24 min; ½" Beta II, ½" VHS • Sale: $64.95

RCA SelectaVision VideoDiscs; Order No. 00111; 1970 • color; 2 hrs, 23 min; CED • Sale: $22.98

The Video Library; Order No. MV-1017; 1970 • color; 2 hrs, 24 min; ½" Beta II, ½" VHS • Sale: $74.95

Chronicles the bombing of Pearl Harbor from both the American and Japanese points of view. Stars Martin Balsam, E. G. Marshall, and James Whitmore.

George Segal and Glenda Jackson in A Touch of Class.

A TOUCH OF CLASS
Magnetic Video Corporation; Order No. CL-5001; 1973 • color; 1 hr, 43 min; ½" Beta II, ½" VHS • Sale: $54.95

Reveals the perils of adultery and its inevitable consequences. Examines two married people having an affair which begins with an illicit Spanish holiday. Stars Glenda Jackson and George Segal.

A TOUCH OF SATAN
Discount Video Tapes; 1974 • color; 1 hr, 27 min; ½" Beta II, ½" VHS • Sale: $54.95

Offers a tale of devil worshippers and Satanic rites. Features Emby Mellay.

TOURIST TRAP
Meda/Media Home Entertainment Inc ; Order No. M134; 1979 • color; 1 hr, 25 min; ½" Beta II, ½" VHS • Sale: $49.95

Presents a horror story in which mannequins come to life to slaughter unsuspecting humans travelling through a desert town. Features Chuck Connors.

THE TOWERING INFERNO
Magnetic Video Corporation; Order No. CL-1071; 1974 • color; 2 hrs, 45 min; ½" Beta II, ½" VHS • Sale: $64.95

Depicts a holocaust engulfing the world's tallest skyscraper on the night of its glamorous and prestigious dedication ceremonies. Combines scenes of blazing terror with the personal stories of the architect and fire chief. Stars Steve McQueen, Paul Newman, William Holden, and Faye Dunaway.

A TOWN CALLED HELL
Tape Club of America; Order No. 2607 B; 1971 • color; 1 hr, 35 min; ½" Beta II, ½" VHS • Sale: $54.95

Describes a dual manhunt set into motion by Porfirio Diaz immediately after the Mexican rebellion. Tells how a whole town is held hostage in this search that involves a revolutionary priest, a mysterious beauty, a fanatical colonel and a brutal bandit-leader. Stars Robert Shaw, Stella Stevens, Martin Landau, and Telly Savalas.

TRAIL DUST
Videobrary Inc; Order No. 12; 1936 • b/w; 1 hr, 17 min; ½" Beta II, ½" VHS • Sale: $39.95

Presents a Hopalong Cassidy western. Offers an adventure in which Cassidy must fight profiteers in order to deliver his herd, to save certain areas from famine. Stars William Boyd, Jimmy Ellison, and George "Gabby" Hayes.

TRAIL OF ROBIN HOOD; ALONG THE NAVAHO TRAIL
The Nostalgia Merchant; 1950; 1945 • b/w; 2 hrs; ½" Beta II, ½" VHS • Sale: $59.95

Offers a Roy Rogers western double feature. Opens with "Trail of Robin Hood," in which Roy is joined by a number of guest cowboy stars in an updated version of the Robin Hood tale. Features Penny Edwards, Gordon Jones, and Riders of the Purple Sage. Concludes with "Along the Navaho Trail," in which Roy hunts the killers of a deputy; features also "Gabby" Hayes.

TRAIL OF THE HAWK
Thunderbird Films; 1935 • b/w; 50 min; ¾" U-Matic, ½" Beta I, ½" Beta II, ½" VHS • Sale: $69.95 for ½" Beta I, $49.95 for ½" Beta II & VHS, $89.95 for ¾"

Recounts the adventures of a young Texan in his attempts to be reunited with his long-lost father. Features Yancey Lane, Betty Jordan, Dickie Jones, and Zandra The Wonder Dog.

TRAIL RIDERS
Reel Images Inc; Order No. 57; 1942 • b/w; 56 min; ½" Beta II, ½" VHS • Sale: $39.95 for ½" Beta II, $42.95 for ½" VHS

Presents a western in which the Range Busters are called into a town to restore law and order and to find the outlaws who murdered the son of the marshal during a bank robbery. Stars John King, David Sharpe, and Max Terhune.

TRAIL STREET
Blackhawk Films, Inc; Order No. 506-57-0692 for ½" Beta II, 525-57-0692 for ½" VHS; 1947 • b/w; 1 hr, 24 min; ½" Beta II, ½" VHS • Sale: $49.95

Tells the story of Bat Masterson saving a town from cattle rustlers and underhanded cattlemen who are trying to take the land away from the farmers. Stars Randolph Scott, Robert Ryan, Anne Jeffreys, Gabby Hayes, Madge Meredith, and Jason Robards. Takes its story from William Corcoran's novel, "Golden Horizon."

TRAILIN TROUBLE
Reel Images Inc; Order No. 56; 1937 • b/w; 1 hr; ½" Beta II, ½" VHS • Sale: $39.95 for ½" Beta II, $42.95 for ½" VHS

Presents a western adventure in which an outlaw steals a roving cowboy's hat, setting off a chain of events involving mistaken identities and a battle between two ranches. Stars Ken Maynard.

TRANSATLANTIC TUNNEL
Video T.E.N.; 1935 • b/w; 1 hr, 10 min; ½″ Beta II, ½″ VHS • Sale: $49.95 for ½″ Beta II, $54.95 for ½″ VHS

Depicts the battle of an American engineer to complete a tunnel under the ocean to England in a science-fiction drama. Stars Richard Dix, Leslie Banks, Madge Evans, C. Aubrey Smith, George Arliss, and Walter Huston.

TREASURE ISLAND
MGM/CBS Home Video; Order No. M50032; 1934 • b/w; 1 hr, 42 min; ½″ Beta II, ½″ VHS • Sale: $49.95

Adapts for the screen Robert Louis Stevenson's 18th century tale of pirates' buried treasure and Long John Silver. Stars Wallace Beery, Jackie Cooper, Lewis Stone, Lionel Barrymore, Otto Kruger, and Nigel Bruce.

THE TREASURE OF JAMAICA REEF
Fotomat Corp; Order No. B0195 for ½″ Beta II, V0195 for ½″ VHS; Date not listed • color; 1 hr, 24 min; ½″ Beta II, ½″ VHS • Sale: $39.95; Rental: $7.95/up to 5 days, applicable to purchase

Presents a chase for a sunken treasure off the Jamaican coast complicated by a race against time to rescue one of the searchers who becomes entombed in the sunken wreck. Features Stephen Boyd, David Ladd, Cheryl Ladd, and Rosey Grier.

TREASURE OF PANCHO VILLA
Video Communications Inc; Order No. 1105; 1955 • color; 1 hr, 36 min; ½″ Beta II, ½″ VHS • Sale: $54.95

Relates how a war-weary colonel in the service of Pancho Villa and a golden-haired spitfire revolutionary rob a Federal gold shipment and head for a rendezvous with Villa. Features Rory Calhoun, Shelley Winters, and Gilbert Roland.

TREASURE OF TAYOPA
Discount Video Tapes; 1974 • color; 1 hr, 25 min; ½″ Beta II, ½″ VHS • Sale: $54.95

Offers a tale of treasure hunting fraught with danger and death. Stars Gilbert Roland, Rena Winters, Bob Corrigan, and Phil Trapani.

TREASURE OF THE SIERRA MADRE
Vid America; Order No. 422; 1948 • b/w; 2 hrs, 6 min; ½″ Beta II, ½″ VHS • Rental: $10.95/wk

Offers a multi-leveled study of the greed for gold and its effect on three prospectors. Stars Humphrey Bogart, Walter Huston, Tim Holt, and Barton MacLane, in a film scripted and directed by John Huston.

THE TRIAL
National Film and Video Center; 1963 • b/w; 1 hr, 58 min; ¾″ U-Matic, ½″ Beta II, ½″ VHS • Rental: $39/1 showing
- -
Video T.E.N.; 1962 • b/w; 1 hr, 58 min; ½″ Beta II, ½″ VHS • Sale: $49.95 for ½″ Beta II, $54.95 for ½″ VHS

Presents Orson Welles' interpretation of the grim novel by Kafka. Stars Anthony Perkins as K, a man arrested for an unknown crime.

TRIANGLE OF PASSION
Monarch Releasing Corporation; Date not listed • color; 1 hr, 28 min; ¾″ U-Matic • Sale: $350

Presents a pornographic film.

TRIGGER JR.; GANGS OF SONORA
The Nostalgia Merchant; Order No. 5006; 1950, 1941 • b/w & color; 2 hrs; ½″ Beta II, ½″ VHS • Sale: $59.95

Offers a western double feature. Presents, in color,

Tim Holt,
Humphrey Bogart,
and Walter Huston
in *The Treasure of
the Sierra Madre.*

"Trigger Jr.," with Roy Rogers trying to stop outlaws from using a wild stallion to threaten ranchers into buying range protection. Concludes with the Three Mesquiteers fighting to save a small frontier newspaper in "Gangs of Sonora."

TRINITY IS STILL MY NAME

Magnetic Video Corporation; Order No. CL-4027; 1972 • color; 1 hr, 57 min; 1/2" Beta II, 1/2" VHS • Sale: $54.95

Follows the exploits of a saddle tramp and his brother who promise their dying father to become successful bandits with a large price on their heads. Stars Terence Hill and Bud Spencer.

THE TRIUMPH OF SHERLOCK HOLMES

Budget Video; 1935 • b/w; 1·hr, 24 min; 3/4" U-Matic, 1/2" Beta I, 1/2" Beta II, 1/2" VHS • Sale: $44.95

Presents Holmes versus arch-villain Professor Moriarty amidst bizarre murders involving a secret society of revenge. Features British actors Arthur Wontner, Ian Fleming, and Lyn Harding.

TRIUMPH OF THE WILL

Reel Images Inc; Order No. 436; 1934 • b/w; 1 hr, 50 min; 1/2" Beta II, 1/2" VHS • Sale: $49.95 for 1/2" Beta II, $52.95 for 1/2" VHS

Presents the classic documentary by Leni Riefenstahl, produced as the official film record of the Sixth Nazi Party Congress held in Nuremberg. Provides an example of a film intended by its producers to function simply as propaganda, but which, through the filmmaker's skills, is now considered as a psychological study of Germany and its leaders. Includes German dialogue with no English subtitles.

TROUBLE IN TEXAS; FARGO EXPRESS

Video Communications Inc; Order No. 1121; 1932, 1937 • b/w; 2 hrs; 1/2" Beta II, 1/2" VHS • Sale: $74.95

Offers a western double feature. Stars Tex Ritter and Rita Hayworth in "Trouble in Texas," in which outlaws go to a rodeo and try to steal the prize money. Presents Ken Maynard in "Fargo Express," a story dealing with a stagecoach hold-up in the Old West.

THE TROUBLE WITH ANGELS

National Film and Video Center; 1966 • color; 1 hr, 52 min; 3/4" U-Matic, 1/2" Beta II, 1/2" VHS • Rental: $49/1 showing

Chronicles the school days of two young girls in a convent. Shows how the two evolve from unscrupulous pranksters into serious young women. Stars Rosalind Russell as Mother Superior, Hayley Mills, Camilla Sparv, Gypsy Rose Lee, and Binnie Barnes.

TRUE GRIT

Fotomat Corp; Order No. B0045 for 1/2" Beta II, V0045 for 1/2" VHS; 1969 • color; 2 hrs, 8 min; 1/2" Beta II, 1/2" VHS • Sale: $69.95; Rental: $9.95/up to 5 days, applicable to purchase
- -
Paramount Home Video; 1969 • color; 2 hrs, 8 min; 1/2" Beta II, 1/2" VHS • Sale: $79.95

Portrays Rooster Cogburn, a drunken, uncouth, one-eyed marshal, who is hired by a girl to kill the man who murdered her father and stole the family nest egg. Shows what happens as she insists on accompanying him. Stars John Wayne, Glen Campbell, Kim Darby, Jeremy Slate, Robert Duvall, and Dennis Hopper, under the direction of Henry Hathaway.

TRUE HEART SUSIE

Reel Images Inc; Order No. 462; 1919 • b/w; 1 hr, 27 min; 1/2" Beta II, 1/2" VHS • Sale: $49.95 for 1/2" Beta II, $52.95 for 1/2" VHS

Recounts a romantic story about a sweet girl in love with a man who marries an unfaithful woman from the city. Stars Lillian Gish and Robert Herron in a silent film directed by D.W. Griffith.

TULSA

Discount Video Tapes; 1949 • color; 1 hr, 36 min; 1/2" Beta II, 1/2" VHS • Sale: $49.95

Offers a story of a woman who wages war against oil drillers when her father is killed. Stars Susan Hayward, Robert Preston, and Pedro Armendarez.

TUMBLEWEEDS

Discount Video Tapes; 1925 • b/w; 1 hr, 20 min; 1/2" Beta II, 1/2" VHS • Sale: $49.95

Presents a silent western concerning the land rush of the Cherokee Strip, noted for its realistic presentation of the Old West. Stars William S. Hart and Barbara Bedford.

TUNNELVISION

Meda/Media Home Entertainment Inc; Order No. M105; 1976 • color; 1 hr, 35 min; 1/2" Beta I, 1/2" Beta II, 1/2" VHS • Sale: $49.95

Presents an absurdist satire on television, under the direction of Brad Swirnoff and Neil Israel. Stars Chevy Chase, Phil Proctor, and Lorraine Newman.

THE TURNING POINT

Magnetic Video Corporation; 1979 • color; 1 hr, 59 min; 1/2" Beta II, 1/2" VHS • Sale: $69.95

Focuses on the mid-life crises of two women friends: one who became a ballet star, and the other who gave up her ballet career to raise a family. Reveals their attempts to come to terms with their own choices and with one another. Stars Anne Bancroft, Shirley MacLaine, Tom Skerritt, and Martha Scott. Features dance sequences with Mikhail Baryshnikov and Leslie Browne.

TUT: THE BOY KING; THE LOUVRE

RCA SelectaVision VideoDiscs; Order No. 01202; Date not listed • color; 1 hr, 41 min; CED • Sale: $19.98

Presents two TV documentaries focusing on art treasures from the past. Includes "Tut: The Boy King" with narrator Orson Welles conducting a tour of the past and the art associated with Tut; plus "The Louvre" with host Charles Boyer guiding the camera through the famous museum's history, its art, and the beauty of the building itself.

TWELVE O'CLOCK HIGH

Magnetic Video Corporation; Order No. CL-1075; 1949 • b/w; 2 hrs, 12 min; 1/2" Beta II, 1/2" VHS • Sale: $64.95

Dramatizes the story of a World War II American Air Force officer stationed in England who must push his men to the point of breaking. Stars Gregory Peck, Hugh Marlowe, Dean Jagger, Gary Merrill, and Millard Mitchell, under the direction of Henry King.

20,000 LEAGUES UNDER THE SEA

Fotomat Corp; Order No. B1041 for 1/2" Beta II, V1041 for 1/2" VHS; 1954 • color; 2 hrs, 7 min; 1/2" Beta II, 1/2" VHS • Sale: $54.95; Rental: $7.95/5 days
- -
Niles Cinema; Order No. WD-15; 1954 • color; 2 hrs,

7 min; ½" Beta II, ½" VHS • Sale: $59.95

RCA SelectaVision VideoDiscs; Order No. 00701; 1954 • color; 2 hrs, 7 min; CED • Sale: $19.98

Vid America; Order No. 990; 1954 • color; 2 hrs, 7 min; ½" Beta II, ½" VHS • Sale: $59.95; Rental: $12.95/wk, applicable to purchase

---

Walt Disney Home Video; Order No. 15BS for ½" Beta II, 15VS for ½" VHS; 1954 • color; 1 hr, 58 min; ½" Beta II, ½" VHS • Sale: $59.95

Presents Walt Disney Studio's adaptation of Jules Verne's fantasy-adventure set at the turn of the century. Tells of the evil Captain Nemo and his futuristic submarine Nautilus. Stars Kirk Douglás, James Mason, Paul Lukas, and Peter Lorre.

TWIST AROUND THE CLOCK
National Film and Video Center; 1961 • color; 1 hr, 22 min; ¾" U-Matic, ½" Beta II, ½" VHS • Rental: $89/1 showing

Relates the story of a band manager and a sax player who discover a new dance craze in a small mountain town, then take the music and the Twist to New York and make it a national craze. Stars Chubby Checker, Dion, Vicki Spencer, The Marcels, Clay Cole, John Cronin, and Mary Mitchell.

TWISTED BRAIN
Video Communications Inc; Order No. 1106; 1974 • color; 1 hr, 25 min; ½" Beta II, ½" VHS • Sale: $54.95

Offers a horror movie in which a gifted student is the subject of a biological experiment that turns him into a creature half man and half beast. Shows how his twisted brain commands him to kill, and kill again. Stars Pat Cardi and John Niland.

TWO FOR THE ROAD
Magnetic Video Corporation; Order No. CL-1084; 1967 • color; 1 hr, 52 min; ½" Beta II, ½" VHS • Sale: $44.95

Shows how an unhappy couple rediscover their lost romance through a series of flashbacks spanning the twelve years of their marriage. Stars Albert Finney and Audrey Hepburn, under the direction of Stanley Donen, with a screenplay by Frederic Raphael.

THE TWO OF US
Time-Life Video Club Inc; 1968 • color; 1 hr, 26 min; ½" Beta II, ½" VHS • Sale: $39.95 to members

Presents the English Language version of Claude Berri's French film. Explores the true story of a young Jewish boy who must conceal his background during World War II. Recounts what happens when his parents send him to the country to live as a Catholic with an elderly couple. Shows his growing relationship with Gramps, a predjudiced old man who especially hates Jews. Stars Michel Simon.

TWO PARE LORENTZ DOCUMENTARIES
Video Action Library; Order No. BH08; 1936-37 • color; 58 min; ½" Beta I, ½" Beta II, ½" VHS • Rental: $10/1 wk, $5 ea add'l wk

Comprises, first, "The River" (1937), a study of the power and destruction, wealth and poverty of the Mississippi, with a score by Virgil Thompson. Concludes with "The Plow That Broke the Plains" (1936), covering the settling of the Great Plains and the subsequent misuses and ravages of the land by man and nature.

TWO RODE TOGETHER
National Film and Video Center; 1961 • color; 1 hr, 49 min; ¾" U-Matic, ½" Beta II, ½" VHS • Rental: $49/1 showing

Spins the tale of a Texas marshal and a U.S. Army lieutenant who lead a wagon train of settlers into Comanche territory to rescue captives held by the Indians. Stars James Stewart, Richard Widmark, and Shirley Jones.

2001—A SPACE ODYSSEY
MGM/CBS Home Video; Order No. M70002; 1968 • color; 2 hrs, 19 min; ½" Beta II, ½" VHS • Sale: $69.95

Niles Cinema; Order No. GM-737; 1968 • color; 2 hrs, 19 min; ½" Beta II, ½" VHS • Sale: $59.95

Presents Stanley Kubrick's science-fiction epic based on a story by Arthur C. Clarke. Offers a view of human evolution as being assisted by unseen aliens whose calling card is a giant monolith. Includes elaborate special effects that set the standard for science-fiction movies to follow. Stars Keir Dullea, Gary Lockwood, and Douglas Rain (as the voice of HAL).

TWO-REELERS—COMEDY CLASSICS (PART 1)
Reel Images Inc; Order No. 580; 1933-44 • b/w; 54 min; ½" Beta II, ½" VHS • Sale: $39.95 for ½" Beta II, $42.95 for ½" VHS

Presents three comedy shorts, starting with "Feather Your Nest," with Edgar Kennedy as a man with an obnoxious brother-in-law. Continues with "How Comedies Are Born," featuring Harry Gibbon and Harry Sweet as would-be comedy writers. Concludes with "Dog Blight," in which Jack Norton buys a dog as a surprise birthday gift for his wife.

TWO-REELERS—COMEDY CLASSICS (PART 2)
Reel Images Inc; Order No. 581; 1938-46 • b/w; 53 min; ½" Beta II, ½" VHS • Sale: $39.95 for ½" Beta II, $42.95 for ½" VHS

Lines up three comedy shorts, beginning with "Twin Husbands," a reworking of the mistaken identity theme that features Leon Errol (as both a henpecked husband and his twin brother), Dorothy Granger, and Jason Robards. Continues with "Chicken Feed," starring Billy Gilbert trying to catch a chicken. Finishes with "False Roomers," starring Edgar Kennedy and Constance Bergen in the story of a man who has let a room to a madman.

TWO-REELERS—COMEDY CLASSICS (PART 3)
Reel Images Inc; Order No. 635; 1933-46 • b/w; 1 hr; ½" Beta II, ½" VHS • Sale: $39.95 for ½" Beta II, $42.95 for ½" VHS

Offers three short subjects. Includes "The Merchant Menace" with Edgar Kennedy, "Coat Tales" with Jed Prouty, and "Social Terrors" with Edgar Kennedy.

TWO-REELERS—COMEDY CLASSICS (PART 4)
Reel Images Inc; Order No. 644; 1934-36 • b/w; 1 hr; ½" Beta II, ½" VHS • Sale: $39.95 for ½" Beta II, $42.95 for ½" VHS

Offers three short subjects. Includes "Bridal Bail" with June Brewster, "No More West" with Bert Lahr, and "Bad Medicine" with Gene Austin.

UB IWERKS CARTOON FEST TWO
Blackhawk Films, Inc; Order No. 506-81-0838 for ½″ Beta II, 525-81-0838 for ½″ VHS; Date not listed • b/w & color; ¾″ U-Matic, ½″ Beta I, ½″ Beta II, ½″ VHS • Sale: $59.95 for ½″ Beta I, $39.95 for ½″ Beta II & VHS, $69.95 for ¾″

Offers six cartoons by one of the pioneers of animation, Ub Iwerks. Presents one black and white Flip the Frog cartoon titled "Spooks," in which Flip takes refuge from a storm in a house haunted by skeletons who play the bass, violin, and piano, and dance. Includes five color cartoons, "Tom Thumb," "Jack Frost," "Aladdin and the Wonderful Lamp," "Ali Baba," and "Sinbad." Uses dialogue.

UB IWERKS CARTOON FESTIVAL
Blackhawk Films, Inc; Order No. 506-81-0888 for ½″ Beta II, 525-81-0888 for ½″ VHS; Date not listed • color; 57 min; ¾″ U-Matic, ½″ Beta I, ½″ Beta II, ½″ VHS • Sale: $59.95 for ½″ Beta I, $39.95 for ½″ Beta II & VHS, $69.95 for ¾″

Presents seven cartoons by one of the pioneers of animation, Ub Iwerks. Offers "The Brave Tin Soldier," in which Laurel and Hardy and the Marx Brothers appear as toys; "Happy Days," which has an "Our Gang" flavor; "Fiddlesticks," which features Flip the Frog; "Jack and the Beanstalk," "The Headless Horseman," and "The Little Red Hen," all animated to catchy tunes; and "Summertime," in which Old Man Winter and the sun illustrate a change of the seasons. Features a musical score.

UFO'S ARE REAL
Fotomat Corp; Order No. B0193 for ½″ Beta II, V0193 for ½″ VHS; 1979 • color; 1 hr, 50 min; ½″ Beta II, ½″ VHS • Sale: $49.95; Rental: $9.95/up to 5 days, applicable to purchase

Investigates the existence of extra-terrestrial beings. Uses photographs, film footage, and secret government and military documents made available through the Freedom of Information Act. Shows that the government of the U.S. has been following this question for more than 30 years.

UGETSU
Budget Video; 1953 • b/w; 1 hr, 36 min; ½″ Beta II, ½″ VHS • Sale: $44.95

Tells of two men, a potter and a farmer, who leave their homes in 16th century Japan to pursue their dreams, the one of wealth, the other of military glory, only to discover that illusory grandeur succumbs to tragic reality. Stars Machiko Kyo and Masayuki Mori under the direction of Kenji Mizoguchi; in Japanese with subtitles.

UNCLE TOM'S CABIN
Northeast Video and Sound, Inc; 1927 • b/w; 1 hr, 2 min; ¾″ U-Matic, ½″ EIAJ, ½″ Beta II, ½″ VHS • Sale: $149

Presents a movie based on the novel of slavery by Har-

riet Beecher Stowe. Stars James R. Lowe, Virginia Grey, and Mona Ray, with narration by Raymond Massey, under the direction of Harry Pollard.

THE UNDEFEATED
Magnetic Video Corporation; Order No. CL-1056; 1969 • color; 1 hr, 59 min; ½″ Beta II, ½″ VHS • Sale: $54.95

Offers a western in which an ex-Union officer is on his way to Mexico to sell horses to the emperor, when he meets up with his enemy, an ex-Confederate officer, and the two of them end up teaming to fight Juarez. Stars John Wayne, Rock Hudson, Ben Johnson, Merlin Olsen, and Roman Gabriel, under the direction of Andrew V. McLaglen.

UNDER CALIFORNIA STARS; ENEMY OF THE LAW
The Nostalgia Merchant; 1948; 1945 • b/w; 2 hrs; ½″ Beta II, ½″ VHS • Sale: $59.95

Offers a western double feature. Follows Roy Rogers as he tames some California horse rustlers in "Under California Stars." Concludes with a Texas Ranger tale, "Enemy of the Law," starring Tex Ritter and Dave O'Brien.

UNDER THE RED ROBE
Discount Video Tapes; 1936 • b/w; 1 hr, 22 min; ½″ Beta II, ½″ VHS • Sale: $49.95

Offers an historical drama of Cardinal Richelieu oppressing the Huguenots. Stars Conrad Veidt, Raymond Massey, and Annabella.

UNDER THE ROOFS OF PARIS
Reel Images Inc; Order No. 441; 1929 • b/w; 1 hr, 35 min; ½″ Beta II, ½″ VHS • Sale: $49.95 for ½″ Beta II, $52.95 for ½″ VHS

Explores the quarters of Paris with a tale of young lovers in a crowded tenement. Features music and innovative sound techniques under the direction of Rene Clair in the first French sound film made. Provides English subtitles for French dialogue.

THE UNDERSEA WORLD OF JACQUES COUSTEAU VOL. I
RCA SelectaVision VideoDiscs; Order No. 02006; Date not listed • color; 1 hr, 41 min; CED • Sale: $19.98

Presents a documentary about the marine environment.

THE UNEXPLAINED
Home Vision; Order No. 813-7001 for ½″ Beta II, 813-9001 for ½″ VHS; 1970 • color; 52 min; ½″ Beta II, ½″ VHS • Sale: $49.95

Offers a documentary film of the future that reveals the investigations of scientists and amateurs into the last unexplained frontiers of knowledge. Pro bes the Continental Drift theory; communication with dolphins in their own "language"; and life in outer space, among other subjects. Includes narration by Rod Serling.

UNIVERSE
National Film and Video Center; Date not listed • color; 27 min; ¾″ U-Matic, ½″ Beta II, ½″ VHS • Rental: $19/1 showing

Explores galaxies, subatomic particles, and cosmic occurrences in a documentary narrated by William Shatner.

UNKNOWN POWERS
Video Gems; 1980 • color; 1 hr, 37 min; ½″ Beta II, ½″ VHS • Sale: $59.95

Investigates in docu-drama style the heightened powers that some people seem to possess, such as spiritual healing.

AN UNMARRIED WOMAN
Magnetic Video Corporation; Order No. 1088; 1978 • color; 2 hrs, 4 min; 1/2" Beta II, 1/2" VHS • Sale: $69.95

Studies what happens to a woman when her husband leaves her after many years of marriage. Stars Jill Clayburgh, Alan Bates, Michael Murphy, Cliff Gorman, Pat Quinn, Kelly Bishop, and Lisa Lucas. Features a script by director Paul Mazursky.

UNWILLING LOVERS
VTS; Date not listed • color; 1 hr, 23 min; 1/2" Beta I, 1/2" Beta II, 1/2" VHS • Sale: $99

Presents a pornographic film.

UP IN SMOKE
Fotomat Corp; Order No. B0457 for 1/2" Beta II, V0457 for 1/2" VHS; 1978 • color; 1 hr, 27 min; 1/2" Beta II, 1/2" VHS • Sale: $54.95; Rental: $9.95/5 days

Niles Cinema; Order No. PP-8966; 1978 • color; 1 hr, 26 min; 1/2" Beta II, 1/2" VHS • Sale: $64.95

Paramount Home Video; Order No. 8966; 1978 • color; 1 hr, 26 min; 1/2" Beta II, 1/2" VHS • Sale: $79.95

Highlights the comedy of Cheech and Chong as two potheads in search of "good grass." Stars Cheech Marin, Tommy Chong, Stacy Keach, Tom Skerritt, Edie Adams, and Strother Martin. Features a screenplay written by Cheech and Chong.

UP POMPEII
Video Communications Inc; Order No. 1108; 1975 • color; 1 hr, 30 min; 1/2" Beta II, 1/2" VHS • Sale: $54.95

Offers a comedy in which a servant in the household of Ludicrus accidentally gains possession of a scroll containing a plot against the Emperor Nero, and must outwit the conspirators who try every means to recover it. Features Frankie Howard and Patrick Cargill.

UP SMOKEY
FHV Entertainment, Inc; Date not listed • color; 1 hr, 20 min; 1/2" Beta II, 1/2" VHS • Sale: $49.95

Presents a pornographic film.

UPA'S CARTOON CLASSICS
Columbia Pictures Home Entertainment; Order No. BE56085 for 1/2" Beta II, VH15080 for 1/2" VHS; Date not listed • color; 30 min; 1/2" Beta II, 1/2" VHS • Sale: $39.95

Offers a collection of cartoons including "The Emperor's New Clothes," "The J-Walker," and "The Man On The Flying Trapeze."

URBAN COWBOY
Paramount Home Video; Order No. 1285; 1980 • color; 2 hrs, 12 min; 1/2" Beta II, 1/2" VHS • Sale: $79.95

Studies a modern cowboy who works at the petrochemical refinery by day and plays at Gilley's, the world's largest country nightclub, by night. Shows the competition in a love triangle between the cowboy, a lady, and a mechanical bull. Stars John Travolta, Debra Winger, and Scott Glenn. Features a country & western soundtrack.

UTOPIA
Golden Tapes Video Tape Library; Order No. CC3;

1950 • b/w; 1 hr, 22 min; 1/2" Beta II, 1/2" VHS • Sale: $49.95 for 1/2" Beta II & VHS, $124.95 for 3/4"

Northeast Video and Sound, Inc; Order No. 166S; 1952 • b/w; 1 hr, 20 min; 3/4" U-Matic, 1/2" EIAJ, 1/2" Beta II, 1/2" VHS • Sale: $195; Rental: $70/wk

Presents Laurel and Hardy's last film, in which the duo inherit an island that is rich in uranium. Stars Stan Laurel, Oliver Hardy, Suzy Delair, and Max Elloy.

VAGABOND LOVER
Video T.E.N.; 1929 • b/w; 1 hr, 15 min; 1/2" Beta II, 1/2" VHS • Sale: $49.95 for 1/2" Beta II, $54.95 for 1/2" VHS

Showcases Rudy Vallee's first screen appearance and one of Hollywood's first musicals, a story of musicians mistaken for burglars. Features Sally Blane, Marie Dressler, Charles Sellon, and Norman Peck.

THE VALACHI PAPERS
National Film and Video Center; 1972 • color; 2 hrs, 5 min; 3/4" U-Matic, 1/2" Beta II, 1/2" VHS • Rental: $89/1 showing

Explores the internal workings of the Cosa Nostra by tracing the career of Joe Valachi, a driver for a powerful syndicate boss who is murdered by rival bosses. Shows how, learning he has been tagged for death, Valachi decides to testify to the Senate Crime Investigation Committee. Stars Lino Ventura, Angelo Infanti, and Gerald S. O'Loughlin.

VALLEY OF TERROR
Blackhawk Films, Inc; Order No. 506-49-0825 for 1/2" Beta II, 525-49-0825 for 1/2" VHS; 1937 • b/w; 59 min; 1/2" Beta II, 1/2" VHS • Sale: $39.95

Relates how a villain wants the mineral deposits under a lady rancher's estate, framing the hero for rustling so he cannot assist her, only to get his comeuppance after the usual western complications. Features Kermit Maynard and Rocky the Horse.

VALLEY OF THE DOLLS
Golden Tapes Video Tape Library; Order No. F-1047; 1967 • color; 2 hrs, 2 min; 1/2" Beta II, 1/2" VHS • Sale: $49.95 for 1/2" Beta II & VHS, $124.95 for 3/4"

Magnetic Video Corporation; Order No. CL-1047; 1967 • color; 2 hrs, 3 min; 1/2" Beta II, 1/2" VHS • Sale: $44.95

The Video Library; Order No. MV-1047; 1967 • color; 2 hrs, 2 min; 1/2" Beta II, 1/2" VHS • Sale: $54.95

Presents the Jacqueline Susann story of show business life and its tensionsStars Barbara Parkins, Sharon Tate, Patty Duke and Paul Burke.

VAMPYR
Thunderbird Films; 1931 • b/w; 1 hr, 6 min; 3/4" U-Matic, 1/2" Beta I, 1/2" Beta II, 1/2" VHS • Sale: $69.95 for 1/2" Beta I, $49.95 for 1/2" Beta II & VHS, $89.95 for 3/4"

Presents an unusual vampire tale with the understated touch of director Carl Dreyer. Approaches the supernatural through inference and suggestion, creating a dreamlike atmosphere punctuated with mysterious music and minimal dialogue. Stars Julian West and Henriette Gerard.

THE VAN
Video Communications Inc; 1977 • color; 1 hr, 30 min; 1/2" Beta II, 1/2" VHS • Sale: $54.95

Offers an "R" rated film. Follows a high school student's plan to get the girl he's after by buying an "R-C." Features Stuart Getz and Deborah White.

VAN NUYS BLVD.
Video Communications Inc; 1979 • color; 1 hr, 33 min; 1/2" Beta II, 1/2" VHS • Sale: $54.95

Offers an "R" rated film about California teenagers who go cruising for "chicks." Features Bill Adler and Cynthia Wood.

VANESSA
FHV Entertainment, Inc; Date not listed • color; 1 hr, 33 min; 1/2" Beta II, 1/2" VHS • Sale $49.95

- -
Vid America; Order No. 976; 1977 • color; 1 hr, 30 min; 1/2" Beta II, 1/2" VHS • Sale: $59.95; Rental: $12.95/wk, applicable to purchase.

Presents a pornographic film.

VANISHING POINT
Magnetic Video Corporation; Order No. CL-1028; 1971 • color; 1 hr, 48 min; 1/2" Beta II, 1/2" VHS • Sale: $54.95

- -
The Video Library; Order No. MV-1028; 1971 • color; 1 hr, 48 min; 1/2" Beta II , 1/2" VHS • Sale: $54.95

Chronicles a car chase from Colorado to California, showing how the driver eludes police with help from a blind disc jockey's radio broadcasts. Stars Barry Newman, Cleavon Little, Dean Jagger, and Victoria Medlin.

VARIETY
Reel Images Inc; Order No. 782; 1925 • b/w; 1 hr, 19 min; 1/2" Beta II, 1/2" VHS • Sale: $49.95 for 1/2" Beta II, $52.95 for 1/2" VHS

Offers a German silent film with musical score, correct projection speed, and title cards in English. Concerns an acrobatic team working in a carnival in pre-war Germany and a love triangle that leads to murder. Features Emil Jannings and Lya de Putti, under the direction of E.A. Dupont.

VERDI'S AIDA
Time-Life Video Club Inc; Date not listed • color; 1 hr, 36 min; 1/2" Beta II, 1/2" VHS • Sale: $49.95 to members

Offers a film version of the opera. Tells of the love an Ethiopian slave has for an Egyptian general and her rivalry for his love with the Pharaoh's daughter, her mistress. Includes English narration and stars Sophia Loren and Renata Tebaldi.

A VERY MERRY CRICKET
Fotomat Corp; Order No. B0711 for 1/2" Beta II, V0711 for 1/2" VHS; 1973 • color; 26 min; 1/2" Beta II, 1/2" VHS • Sale: $39.95; Rental: $5.95/5 days

Provides a lesson for children about brotherhood, nature, geography, and music, in this animated film from Xerox. Takes place during the Christmas holiday in New York's Times Square. Uses characters created by George Selden, including Harry Cat, Tucker Mouse, and Chester C. Cricket.

VICTORY AT SEA
RCA SelectaVision VideoDiscs; Order No. 01201; 1954 • b/w; 1 hr, 48 min; CED • Sale: $14.98

Presents the feature length version of the documentary TV series which highlights the Allied Forces fighting at sea during World War II. Includes narration by Alexander Scourby, outstanding photography, and a score by Richard Rodgers.

THE VILLAIN STILL PURSUES HER
Northeast Video and Sound, Inc; Order No. 165S; 1940 • b/w; 60 min; 3/4" U-Matic, 1/2" EIAJ, 1/2" Beta II, 1/2" VHS • Sale: $195; Rental: $75/wk

Presents a spoof of the old-time melodrama, featuring Buster Keaton., Anit Louise, Richard Cromwell, Hugh Herbert, and Alan Mowbray.

VINCENT, FRANCOIS, PAUL AND THE OTHERS
Entertainment Video Releasing; Order No. 1011; 1974 • color; 1 hr, 53 min; 1/2" Beta II, 1/2" VHS • Sale: $49.95 for 1/2" Beta II, $54.95 for 1/2" VHS

Relates a story of middle-class friendship in an atmosphere of futility and lost love. Stars Yves Montand, Stephane Audran, Michel Piccoli, and Gerard Depardieu, under the direction of Claude Sautet.

THE VIOLATION OF CLAUDIA
Quality X Video Cassette Company; Date not listed • color; 1 hr, 26 min; 1/2" Beta I, 1/2" Beta II, 1/2" VHS • Sale: $99.50

Presents a pornographic film.

VISIONS
Quality X Video Cassette Company; Date not listed • color; 1 hr, 18 min; 1/2" Beta I, 1/2" Beta II, 1/2" VHS • Sale: $99.50

Presents a pornographic film.

VISIONS OF EIGHT
Time-Life Video Club Inc; 1973 • color; 1 hr, 50 min; 1/2" Beta II, 1/2" VHS • Sale: $39.95 to members

Offers eight different views of events at the 1972 Munich Olympics as seen by eight different directors: Juri Ozerov on waiting, Mai Zetterling on weightlifting, Arthur Penn on pole vaulting, Milos Forman on the decathlon, Claude Lelouch on losers, John Schlesinger on the marathon, Ken Ichikawa on the 100-meter sprint, and Michael Phleghar on women contestants.

VISIT TO A SMALL PLANET
Magnetic Video Corporation; Order No. CL-2020; 1960 • b/w; 1 hr, 25 min; 1/2" Beta II, 1/2" VHS • Sale: $54.95

- -
Red Fox, Inc; Order No. CL-2021; 1960 • b/w; 1 hr, 25 min; 1/2" Beta II, 1/2" VHS • Sale: $54.95

Features Jerry Lewis in the story of an extraterrestrial whose hobby is a small planet called Earth. Dramatizes Gore Vidal's satire and co-stars Joan Blackman and Earl Holliman, under the direction of Norman Taurog.

VIVACIOUS LADY
Niles Cinema; Order No. NM-8043; 1938 • b/w; 1 hr, 30 min; 1/2" Beta II, 1/2" VHS • Sale: $54.95

- -
The Nostalgia Merchant; Order No. 8043; 1938 • b/w; 1 hr, 30 min; 1/2" Beta II, 1/2" VHS • Sale: $54.95

- -
Red Fox, Inc; Order No. 8043; 1938 • b/w; 1 hr, 30

min; ½" Beta II, ½" VHS • Sale: $54.95

Presents a romantic comedy about a young college professor who marries a chorus girl. Stars Ginger Rogers and James Stewart.

THE VIXEN
Vid America; Order No. 624; 1968 • color; 1 hr, 10 min; ½" Beta II, ½" VHS • Rental: $12.95/wk

Presents a pornographic film.

VOICES OF DESIRE
Monarch Releasing Corporation; Date not listed • color; 1 hr, 13 min; ¾" U-Matic • Sale: $300

Presents a pornographic film.

VOLUPTUOUS VIXENS '76
Entertainment Video Releasing, Inc; 1976 • color; 1 hr, 12 min; ½" Beta II, ½" VHS • Sale: $79.95

Presents a pornographic film.

VON RYAN'S EXPRESS
Golden Tapes Video Tape Library; Order No. F-1003; 1965 • color; 1 hr, 57 min; ½" Beta II, ½" VHS • Sale: $49.95 for ½" Beta II & VHS, $124.95 for ¾"

- -

Magnetic Video Corporation; Order No. CL-1003; 1965 • color; 1 hr, 57 min; ½" Beta II, ½" VHS • Sale: $44.95

- -

The Video Library; Order No. MV-1003; 1965 • color; 1 hr, 57 min; ½" Beta II, ½" VHS • Sale: $54.95

Presents the adventure story of allied soldiers escaping from a Nazi prison camp. Stars Frank Sinatra and Trevor Howard.

VOYAGE TO THE BOTTOM OF THE SEA
Golden Tapes Video Tape Library; Order No. F-1044; 1961 • color; 1 hr, 45 min; ½" Beta II, ½" VHS • Sale: $49.95 for ½" Beta II & VHS, $124.95 for ¾"

- -

Magnetic Video Corporation; Order No. CL-1044; 1961 • color; 1 hr, 45 min; ½" Beta II, ½" VHS • Sale: $44.95

- -

The Video Library; Order No. MV-1044; 1961 • color; 1 hr, 45 min; ½" Beta II, ½" VHS • Sale: $54.95

Features the story of a giant atomic sub fighting a ring of fire around the world. Stars Walter Pidgeon and Joan Fontaine.

THE WACKIEST SHIP IN THE ARMY
National Film and Video Center; 1960 • color; 1 hr, 39 min; ¾" U-Matic, ½" Beta II, ½" VHS • Rental: $59/1 showing

Stars Jack Lemmon as a Navy lieutenant who is tricked into accepting command of an aged sailing vessel with a crew of "sailors" who have never sailed before. Follows the action, including the Japanese capture of the ship, to the successful completion of the mission. Features Chips Rafferty as the Australian scout who must be put ashore on an enemy-held island.

THE WACKY WORLD OF MOTHER GOOSE
Magnetic Video Corporation; Order No. CL-4035; 1967 • color; 1 hr, 21 min; ½" Beta II, ½" VHS • Sale: $54.95

Presents a song-filled, animated feature starring many characters of the Mother Goose stories. Offers eight new songs and vocal renditions of twelve Mother Goose rhymes.

WAGES OF FEAR
Budget Video; 1953 • b/w; 2 hrs, 18 min; ½" Beta II, ½" VHS • Sale: $64.95

Dramatizes the conflict among four men whose mission it is to drive nitroglycerine-laden trucks through torturous South American terrain; in French with English subtitles. Stars Yves Montand and Peter Van Eyck under the direction of Henri-Georges Clouzot.

WAGONMASTER
Niles Cinema; Order No. NM-8044; 1950 • b/w; 1 hr, 25 min; ½" Beta II, ½" VHS • Sale: $54.95

- -

The Nostalgia Merchant; Order No. 8044; 1950 • b/w; 1 hr, 25 min; ½" Beta II, ½" VHS • Sale: $54.95

- -

Red Fox, Inc; Order No. 8044; 1950 • b/w; 1 hr, 25 min; ½" Beta II, ½" VHS • Sale: $54.95

Relates the John Ford saga of two cowboys who join a Mormon wagon train going west. Stars Ben Johnson, Joanne Dru, and Ward Bond.

A WALK IN THE SUN
Video T.E.N.; 1945 • b/w; 1 hr, 57 min; ½" Beta II, ½" VHS • Sale: $49.95 for ½" Beta II, $54.95 for ½" VHS

Focuses on the Lee Platoon, Texas Division, who hit the beach at Salerno during World War II. Features Dana Andrews, Richard Conte, and Lloyd Bridges.

WANDA
Tape Club of America; Order No. 2814 B; Date not listed • color; 1 hr, 8 min; ½" Beta II, ½" VHS • Sale: $54.95

Presents a pornographic film.

THE WAR BETWEEN THE TATES
Time-Life Video Club Inc; 1977 • color; 1 hr, 37 min; ½" Beta II, ½" VHS • Sale: $36.95 to members

Presents the television adaptation of Alison Lurie's best-seller about Mrs. Tate's war with her college professor-husband over his affair with one of his flower-child students. Follows her retaliations and his attempts to reconcile with comedy and complexity. Stars Elizabeth Ashley, Richard Crenna, and Annette O'Toole.

WAR OF THE WORLDS
Fotomat Corp; Order No. B0053 for ½" Beta II, V0053 for ½" VHS; 1953 • color; 1 hr, 25 min; ½" Beta II, ½" VHS • Sale: $49.95; Rental: $9.95/up to 5 days, applicable to purchase

- -

Paramount Home Video; 1953 • color; 1 hr, 25 min; ½" Beta II, ½" VHS • Sale: $59.95

Presents a screen version of H.G. Wells' chilling novel of the invasion of Earth by Martians. Features special effects for which the movie won an Oscar. Stars Gene Barry, Ann Robinson, and Les Tremayne.

THE WAR YEARS—THE FORTIES
Blackhawk Films, Inc; Order No. 506-66-0679 for ½" Beta II, 525-66-0679 for ½" VHS; Date not listed •

b/w; 5 hrs; 3/4″ U-Matic, 1/2″ Beta I, 1/2″ Beta II, 1/2″ VHS • Sale: $249.95 for 1/2″ Beta I, $199.95 for 1/2″ Beta II & VHS, $349.95 for 3/4″

Presents, on 3 tapes, newsreels which cover the major events of the 1940's. Includes Hitler's invasion and betrayal of Poland, the Battle of Britain, Roosevelt's "I hate war" speech, Stalin, Churchill, MacArthur, Patton, the Battle of the Bulge, Hitler's suicide, Mussolini's execution, Nuremberg, America's focus on Communism, and Harry Truman trouncing Tom Dewey.

WARNER BROS. CARTOONS

Ivy Video; 1940 • color; 50 min; 3/4″ U-Matic, 1/2″ Beta II, 1/2″ VHS • Sale: $59.95 for 1/2″ Beta II & VHS, trade-in plan available, $225 for 3/4″

Presents five of the Looney Tunes and Merrie Melodies from the 30's and 40's. Features Bugs Bunny in "Corny Concerto" and Daffy Duck in "Daffy and the Dinosaur."

WARNER BROTHERS CARTOONS

Reel Images Inc; Order No. 536; 1938-53 • color; 54 min; 1/2″ Beta II; 1/2″ VHS • Sale: $39.95 for 1/2″ Beta II, $42.95 for 1/2″ VHS

Presents seven cartoons featuring Bugs Bunny, Elmer Fudd, and Daffy Duck. Includes "The Wabbit Who Came to Supper," "A Tale of Two Kitties," "Case of the Missing Hare," "Hamateur Night," "Wackiki Wabbit," "Daffy Duck and the Dinosaur," and "Fresh Hare."

THE WARRIORS

Fotomat Corp; Order No. B0283 for 1/2″ Beta II, V0283 for 1/2″ VHS; 1979 • color; 1 hr, 34 min; 1/2″ Beta II, 1/2″ VHS • Sale: $59.95; Rental: $9.95/5 days
- -
Paramount Home Video; 1979 • color; 1 hr, 34 min; 1/2″ Beta II, 1/2″ VHS • Sale: $59.95

Concerns a New York street gang's fight for survival after being framed for murder by a rival gang. Follows The Warriors' struggles through a myriad of streets, parks, and subway stations as they are pursued by the police and other gangs. Stars Michael Beck, James Remer, and Deborah Van Valkenburgh, under the direction of Walter Hill.

WATER RUSTLERS

Thunderbird Films; 1939 • b/w; 50 min; 3/4″ U-Matic, 1/2″ Beta I, 1/2″ Beta II, 1/2″ VHS • Sale: $59.95 for 1/2″ Beta I, $39.95 for 1/2″ Beta II & VHS, $79.95 for 3/4″

Relates the efforts of a rancher's daughter to save her father's land from an unscrupulous neighbor who has built a dam on his part of the watering creek. Stars Dorothy Page and Dave O'Brien.

WATERMELON MAN

National Film and Video Center; 1970 • color; 1 hr, 30 min; 3/4″ U-Matic, 1/2″ Beta II, 1/2″ VHS • Rental: $79/1 showing

Examines the attitudes of a bigoted, wisecracking insurance salesman who wakes up to discover that he has turned into a black man. Stars Godfrey Cambridge and Estelle Parsons.

WATERSHIP DOWN

Fotomat Corp ; Order No. B0311 for 1/2″ Beta II, V0311 for 1/2″ VHS; 1978 • color; 1 hr, 32 min; 1/2″ Beta II, 1/2″ VHS • Sale: $54.95; Rental: $9.95/5 days

Presents the animated adaptation of Richard Adam's book about a family of rabbits who must leave their home to search for a new, safer place. Features the

voices of John Hurt, Richard Briers, Sir Ralph Richardson, Denholm Elliott, Harry Andrews, Joss Ackland, Zero Mostel, and narration by Michael Hordern.

WAY DOWN EAST

Ivy Video; 1925 • b/w; 1 hr, 30 min; 3/4″ U-Matic, 1/2″ Beta II, 1/2″ VHS • Sale: $59.95 for 1/2″ Beta II & VHS, trade-in plan available, $195 for 3/4″
- -
Northeast Video and Sound, Inc; Order No. 163S; 1925 • b/w; 1 hr, 30 min; 3/4″ U-Matic, 1/2″ EIAJ, 1/2″ Beta II, 1/2″ VHS • Sale: $295; Rental: $75/wk

Depicts the tragedies of a New England family, in a romantic style with a climax on flowing river ice. Reveals the talents of director D.W. Griffith and stars Lillian Gish and Richard Barthelmess.

THE WAY OF THE WIND

Video Communications Inc; Order No. 3006; 1977 • color; 1 hr, 44 min; 1/2″ Beta II, 1/2″ VHS • Sale: $54.95

Offers an account of a 30,000 mile odyssey from the Pacific to the Bermuda Triangle to a ghost town of ancient Greece in a film by Charles Tobias.

WAY OUT WEST

The Nostalgia Merchant; 1936 • b/w; 1 hr, 5 min; 1/2″ Beta II, 1/2″ VHS • Sale: $54.95
- -
Time-Life Video Club Inc; 1936 • b/w; 1 hr, 5 min; 1/2″ Beta II, 1/2″ VHS • Sale: $44.95 to members

Follows the comic adventures of Laurel and Hardy when they attempt to hand over a mine deed to the heiress of a late prospector, but are foiled in a case of mistaken identity. Stars Stan Laurel, Oliver Hardy, Sharon Lynn, and James Finlayson, under the direction of James W. Horne. Presents also a Hal Roach comedy short.

W.C. FIELDS FESTIVAL

Ivy Video; 1932 • b/w; 1 hr, 1 min; 3/4″ U-Matic, 1/2″ Beta II, 1/2″ VHS • Sale: $59.95 for 1/2″ Beta II & VHS, trade-in plan available, $195 for 3/4″
- -
Northeast Video and Sound, Inc; Order No. 118S; 1932-33 • b/w; 60 min; 3/4″ U-Matic, 1/2″ EIAJ, 1/2″ Beta II, 1/2″ VHS • Sale: $195; Rental: $75/wk

Provides a look at Fields' routines from his vaudeville career as he developed them in his comic shorts. Includes "The Golf Specialist", "The Fatal Glass of Beer", and "The Dentist".

WE A FAMILY

Monarch Releasing Corporation; Date not listed • color; 1 hr, 10 min; 3/4″ U-Matic • Sale: $300

Presents a pornographic film.

WEDDING IN WHITE

Magnetic Video Corporation; Order No. CL-4037; 1972 • color; 1 hr, 43 min; 1/2″ Beta II, 1/2″ VHS • Sale: $54.95

Depicts family life in a wartime Canadian town, where a sensitive 16-year-old dropout is suppressed by a sterile workingman's world and her dominating father. Stars Donald Pleasance and Carol Kane.

WEEKEND WITH THE BABY SITTER

Discount Video Tape; 1971 • color; 1 hr, 40 min; 1/2″ Beta II, 1/2″ VHS • Sale: $74.95

Spotlights Hollywood as the setting for drug smuggling. Features Susan Romen and George E. Carey.

WELCOME TO ARROW BEACH

Magnetic Video Corporation; Order No. CL-5008; 1974 • color; 1 hr, 39 min; 1/2" Beta II, 1/2" VHS • Sale: $54.95

Details the story of a seemingly harmless beach dweller who likes to invite home drifting young girls who are never seen again. Stars Laurence Harvey, Joanna Pettet, and Stuart Whitman.

WELL OF LOVE

The Nostalgia Merchant; Order No. 7009; 1970 • color; 1 hr, 16 min; 1/2" Beta II, 1/2" VHS • Sale: $54.95

Depicts the rescue of a trapped, near-dead Lassie from an old well. Features Robert Donner and Mary Gregory.

WEST OF THE DIVIDE

Cable Films; 1933 • b/w; 54 min; 1/2" Beta I, 1/2" Beta II, 1/2" VHS • Sale: $45 for 1/2" Beta I, $49.50 for 1/2" Beta II & VHS

Features John Wayne in this early western concerning a man's search for his missing little brother and the man who murdered his father. Includes several hard-hitting scraps and chase sequences.

WESTWARD HO; LAWLESS FRONTIER

The Nostalgia Merchant; 1935 • b/w; 2 hrs; 1/2" Beta II, 1/2" VHS • Sale: $59.95

Presents a John Wayne double feature. Begins with "Westward Ho" in which a vigilante clashes with his outlaw brother; stars also Sheila Manners. Closes with "Lawless Frontier," which tells of the frailty of law and order when the West was young.

A WHALE OF A TALE

Video Communications Inc; 1977 • color; 1 hr, 30 min; 1/2" Beta II, 1/2" VHS • Sale: $54.95

Follows the adventures of a boy who befriends the sea creatures of Marineland. Stars William Shatner and Marty Allen.

WHAT PRICE HOLLYWOOD

Blackhawk Films, Inc; Order No. 506-30-0690 for 1/2" Beta II, 525-30-0690 for 1/2" VHS; 1932 • b/w; 1 hr, 28 min; 1/2" Beta II, 1/2" VHS • Sale: $49.95

Studies an aspiring young starlet whose life, career, and marriage seem headed for the rocks. Stars Constance Bennett, Lowell Sherman, and Neil Hamilton.

WHAT'S UP, DOC?

MCA DiscoVision; Order No. W16-510; 1972 • color; 1 hr, 34 min; LaserVision • Sale: $24.95

Presents an updated screwball comedy in which four suitcases provide confusion, and a young lady provides romance, for a musicologist with a fiancee. Stars Barbra Streisand, Ryan O'Neal, Austin Pendleton, Madeline Kahn, Kenneth Mars, and Michael Murphy, in a film by Peter Bogdanovitch.

WHEN COMEDY WAS KING

Cinema Concepts, Inc.; 1962 • b/w; 1 hr, 24 min; 3/4" U-Matic, 1/2" Beta II, 1/2" VHS • Sale: $54.95 for 1/2" Beta II & VHS, $149.95 for 3/4"
- -
Vid America; Order No. 217; 1962 • b/w; 1 hr, 24 min; 1/2" Beta II, 1/2" VHS • Rental: $9.95/wk
- -
The Video Library; Order No. CC-0146; 1960 • b/w; 1 hr, 24 min; 1/2" Beta II, 1/2" VHS • Sale: $54.95

Presents a documentary offering highlights of comedy in motion pictures. Includes Laurel & Hardy, Charlie Chaplin, Buster Keaton, and Fatty Arbuckle.

WHERE ANGELS GO . . . TROUBLE FOLLOWS

National Film and Video Center ; 1968 • color; 1 hr, 35 min; 3/4" U-Matic, 1/2" Beta II, 1/2" VHS • Rental: $59/1 showing

Relates the adventures of nuns and a group of their students en route to a California youth rally. Stars Rosalind Russell as the mother superior who is at first dismayed when a younger nun instigates peace and civil rights demonstrations at the school, but who is later won over. Features Stella Stevens, Milton Berle, Arthur Godfrey, Van Johnson, and Robert Taylor.

WHERE THE BULLETS FLY

Magnetic Video Corporation; Order No. CL-4045; 1966 • color; 1 hr, 28 min; 1/2" Beta II, 1/2" VHS • Sale: $54.95

Follows a secret agent in his efforts to thwart an evil genius' attempts to steal the essential component of nuclear powered aircraft. Features Tom Adams, Dawn Addams, and Tim Barrett.

WHERE THE LIONS RULE

Video Communications Inc; Order No. 1111; 1976 • color; 1 hr, 32 min; 1/2" Beta II, 1/2" VHS • Sale: $54.95

Relates a story of naturalist Ivan Tors and his family, who are stranded in the great Serengeti Migration where, amidst millions of African animals, they must use all the cunning they can muster to survive.

WHERE THE RED FERN GROWS

Vid America; Order No. 922; 1974 • color; 1 hr, 38 min; 1/2" Beta II, 1/2" VHS • Rental: $11.95/wk

Offers a family entertainment about a young boy, his grandpa, and their hunting dogs, in 1930's Oklahoma. Features James Whitmore, Beverly Garland, Jack Ging, Lonny Chapman, and Stewart Peterson.

WHICH WAY IS UP?

MCA DiscoVision; Order No. 16-009; 1978 • color; 1 hr, 33 min; LaserVision • Sale: $24.95
- -
MCA Videocassette, Inc; Order No. 66014; 1978 • color; 1 hr, 33 min; 1/2" Beta II, 1/2" VHS • Sale: $60

Offers Richard Pryor in a triple role. Tells of love, jealousy, and betrayal, set in central California farm country, in an adaptation of Lina Wertmuller's "Seduction of Mimi." Features Lonette McKee, Margaret Avery, Morgan Woodward, and Marilyn Coleman.

WHIFFS

Magnetic Video Corporation; Order No. CL-5004; 1975 • color; 1 hr, 32 min; 1/2" Beta II, 1/2" VHS • Sale: $54.95

Follows a professional Army "guinea pig" whose system becomes so physically abused that the Army kicks him out, forcing him to turn to a life of petty, and not so petty, crime. Stars Elliot Gould and Jennifer O'Neill.

WHILE THE CAT'S AWAY

Monarch Releasing Corporation; Date not listed • color; 1 hr, 20 min; 3/4" U-Matic • Sale: $350

Presents a pornographic film.

WHILE THE CITY SLEEPS

Video Communications Inc; Order No. 1109; 1956 • b/w; 1 hr, 40 min; 1/2" Beta II, 1/2" VHS • Sale: $54.95

Shows what happens when a murder is committed and a ruthless publisher pits his three rival newschiefs against each other in a contest to crack the case. Features Dana Andrews, Rhonda Fleming, Ida Lupino,

Howard Duff, Sally Forrest, George Sanders, and Vincent Price, under the direction of Fritz Lang.

WHISKEY MOUNTAIN

Video Communications Inc; Order No. 3005; 1978 • color; 1 hr, 35 min; 1/2" Beta II, 1/2" VHS • Sale: $54.95

Relates how the lure of buried treasure attracts two reckless young racers and their wives to legendary Whiskey Mountain. Stars Christopher George, Preston Pierce, and Roberta Collins.

WHITE COMANCHE

Video Communications Inc; Order No. 1112; 1967 • color; 1 hr, 30 min; 1/2" Beta II, 1/2" VHS • Sale: $54.95

Presents a twist to the classic western as twin sons of an Indian mother and a white settler find themselves pitted against each other in the traditional struggle. Shows how a peace officer exceeds his duty in resolving a battle of blood. Stars Joseph Cotten and William Shatner.

WHITE HEAT

Vid America; Order No. 327; 1949 • b/w; 1 hr, 54 min; 1/2" Beta II, 1/2" VHS • Rental: $10.95/wk

Relates the story of Cody Jarrett, a psychopathic murderer with a mother-obsession. Features James Cagney, Virginia Mayo, Edmond O'Brien, Margaret Wycherly, and Steve Cochran, under the direction of Raoul Walsh.

WHITE LINE FEVER

National Film and Video Center; 1975 • color; 1 hr, 30 min; 3/4" U-Matic, 1/2" Beta II, 1/2" VHS • Rental: $119/1 showing

Relates the saga of an independent trucker who is blacklisted by trucking companies because he refuses to carry illegal cargo. Traces his decision to fight back after the companies' violent abuses of his friends and family. Stars Jan-Michael Vincent, Kay Lenz, Slim Pickens, and Don Porter.

THE WHITE SEARCH

FHV Entertainment, Inc; 1971 • color; 1 hr, 25 min; 1/2" Beta II, 1/2" VHS • Sale: $49.95

Stars Jean-Claude Killy, Olympic ski champion, in a ski adventure filmed in the Canadian Rockies, Austria, Switzerland, the wilds of Western America, and the Andes. Features narration by Dick Barrymore.

WHITE ZOMBIE

Northeast Video and Sound, Inc; 1932 • b/w; 1 hr, 10 min; 3/4" U-Matic, 1/2" EIAJ, 1/2" Beta II, 1/2" VHS • Sale: $159; Rental: $65/wk

Recounts the bizarre consequences when a man wishes to possess another man's bride enlists the aid of an evil doctor. Features Bela Lugosi in one of his most archetypal roles, with Madge Bellamy, Robert Frazer, and Brandon Hurst, under the direction of Victor Halperin.

WHO KILLED DOC ROBBIN?

Budget Video; 1948 • color; 50 min; 1/2" Beta II, 1/2" VHS • Sale: $34.95
- -
Discount Video Tape; 1948 • color; 50 min; 1/2" Beta II, 1/2" VHS • Sale: $34.95

Traces the efforts of the Little Rascals as they attempt to clear their friend of the haunted-house murder of a "sinister" doctor. Stars the Our Gang Children, George Zucco, and Virginia Grey.

THE WICKERMAN

Meda/Media Home Entertainment Inc; 1973 • color; 1 hr, 26 min; 1/2" Beta II, 1/2" VHS • Sale: $59.95

Concerns a policeman's experiences with diabolists when he travels to the remote Summerisle in search of a missing young girl. Stars Edward Woodward, Christopher Lee, Diane Cilento, and Britt Ekland.

WIDE OPEN TOWN

Video T.E.N.; 1941 • b/w; 1 hr, 18 min; 1/2" Beta II, 1/2" VHS • Sale: $49.95 for 1/2" Beta II, $54.95 for 1/2" VHS

Explores the world of Hopalong Cassidy in a tale of a town totally without law and a woman outlaw leader. Stars William Boyd, Russell Hayden, Andy Clyde, Evelyn Brent, Victor Jory, and Morris Ankrum.

THE WILD BUNCH

MCA DiscoVision; Order No. W12-513; 1969 • color; 2 hrs, 25 min; LaserVision • Sale:$24.95
- -
WCI Home Video Inc; 1969 • color; 2 hrs, 15 min; 1/2" Beta II, 1/2" VHS • Sale: $60

Offers a western about a gang of gunslingers who opt for one last ride in 1913, for a Mexican renegade general. Explores the theme of men out of synch with the times in which they live, rugged individuals vs. progress and technology. Stars William Holden, Ernest Borgnine, Robert Ryan, Edmund O'Brien, and Warren Oates, under the direction of Sam Peckinpah.

WILD HORSE

Reel Images Inc; Order No. 487; 1931 • b/w; 1 hr, 8 min; 1/2" Beta II, 1/2" VHS • Sale: $49.95 for 1/2" Beta II, $52.95 for 1/2" VHS

Presents an early western which concerns a bank robbery and busting a wild Palomino. Stars Hoot Gibson, Alberta Vaughn, and Stepin Fetchit.

WILD RIDERS

Discount Video Tapes; 1971 • color; 1 hr, 31 min; 1/2" Beta II, 1/2" VHS • Sale: $54.95

Shows two sadistic motorcyclists holding two people prisoner. Features Alex Rocco and Elizabeth Knowles.

WILDERNESS JOURNEY

FHV Entertainment, Inc; 1971 • color; 1 hr, 33 min; 1/2" Beta II, 1/2" VHS • Sale: $49.95

Shows how an accident in Alaska's remote mountains sends a young Tlingit Indian boy on a journey in search of his father. Stars Jimmy Cane.

THE WILL OF A PEOPLE

Reel Images Inc; Order No. 410; 1946 • b/w; 55 min; 1/2" Beta II, 1/2" VHS • Sale: $39.95 for 1/2" Beta II, $42.95 for 1/2" VHS

Details the story of the Spanish Revolution and the rise of Franco told in archive footage from Spain. Presents English narration.

THE WINDOW

The Nostalgia Merchant; Order No. 8045; 1949 • b/w; 1 hr, 13 min; 1/2" Beta II, 1/2" VHS • Sale: $54.95
- -
Red Fox, Inc; Order No. 8045; 1949 • b/w; 1 hr, 13 min; 1/2" Beta II, 1/2" VHS • Sale: $54.95
- -
Discount Video Tapes; 1949 • b/w; 1 hr, 13 min; 1/2" Beta II, 1/2" VHS • Sale: $49.95

Relates the story of a young boy who witnesses a murder, but cannot convince his parents that he's not lying. Stars Barbara Hale, Bobby Driscoll, and Arthur Kennedy.

WINDOWS
Vid America; Order No. 468; 1980 • color; 1 hr, 36 min; ½" Beta II, ½" VHS • Rental: $12.95/wk, applicable to purchase

Offers a love-triangle murder/mystery involving a lesbian, who loves a woman, who loves a cop, who is trying to find a murderer. Features Elizabeth Ashley, TaliqShire, and Joseph Cortese.

WINGS OF AN EAGLE
Astro Video Corporation; Order No. LS-807; 1975 • color; 1 hr, 26 min; ½" Beta II, ½" VHS • Sale: $59.95

Recounts the adventures of an eagle raised by a human in this adaptation of Kent Durden's "Gifts of an Eagle." Shows flight scenes filmed in the Arizona wilderness and stresses the bond between the human protector and the wild eagle. Features Ed Durden, Kent Durden, Christopher Zajie, and Lady the Eagle.

WINNING
MCA DiscoVision; Order No. 12-017; 1969 • color; 2 hrs, 3 min; LaserVision • Sale: $24.95

Probes one man's need to win on the racetrack and how it affects his marriage. Includes footage of the 1968 Indy 500. Stars Paul Newman, Joanne Woodward, Robert Wagner, and Richard Thomas.

WINTER KILLS
Magnetic Video Corporation; 1979 • ; 1 hr, 37 min; ½" Beta II, ½" VHS • Sale: $44.95

Relates a violent story about a complex, all-pervading conspiracy to assassinate a U.S. President. Features Jeff Bridges, Anthony Perkins, Sterling Hayden, Eli Wallach, and John Huston.

WINTERSET
Cable Films; 1937 • b/w; 1 hr, 18 min; ½" Beta I, ½" Beta II, ½" VHS • Sale: $65 for ½" Beta I, $49.50 for ½" Beta II & VHS
- -
Video T.E.N.; 1937 • b/w; 1 hr, 25 min; ½" Beta II, ½" VHS • Sale: $49.95 for ½" Beta II, $54.95 for ½" VHS

Offers a film version of Maxwell Anderson's Broadway play. Tells the story of a young man who sets out to clear the name of his father, who was electrocuted for a crime he did not commit. Stars Burgess Meredith, Eduardo Cianelli, Margo, John Carradine, and Mischa Auer.

THE WITCH WHO CAME FROM THE SEA
Niles Cinema; Order No. BT-09 for ½" Beta II, VH-09 for ½" VHS; 1972 • color; 1 hr, 27 min; ½" Beta II, ½" VHS • Sale: $59.95
- -
Discount Video Tapes; 1972 • color; 1 hr, 27 min; ½" Beta II, ½" VHS • Sale: $54.95

Features Millie Perkins, Rick Jason, Lonny Chapman, and Vanessa Brown in the tale of a woman's obsession with the sea, which causes her to commit several murders.

THE WITCHMAKER
Cinema Concepts, Inc.; 1969 • color; 1 hr, 41 min; ¾" U-Matic, ½" Beta II, ½" VHS • Sale: $54.95 for ½" Beta II & VHS, $149.95 for ¾"
- -
The Video Library; Order No. CC-0147; 1969 • color; 1 hr, 41 min; ½" Beta II, ½" VHS • Sale: $54.95

Offers an occult tale of a warlock who seeks out beautiful young girls to help his harem of witches become youthful again. Stars John Lodge, Alvy Moore, Thordis Brandt, and Anthony Eisley.

WITHOUT RESERVATIONS
Video Communications Inc; 1946 • b/w; 1 hr, 41 min; ½" Beta II, ½" VHS • Sale: $54.95

Chronicles the story of an authoress who scouts for a perfect man to play the hero in the movie version of her new book. Stars Claudette Colbert and John Wayne.

Ray Bolger, Judy Garland, Jack Haley, and Toto in *The Wizard of Oz*.

THE WIZARD OF OZ
MGM/CBS Home Video; Order No. M60001; 1939 • color; 1 hr, 41 min; ½" Beta II, ½" VHS • Sale: $59.95
- -
Niles Cinema; Order No. GM-738; 1939 • b/w & color; 1 hr, 41 min; ½" Beta II, ½" VHS • Sale: $59.95

Presents the musical film adaptation of Frank Baum's tale. Stars Judy Garland, Frank Morgan, Bert Lahr, Jack Haley, Ray Bolger, Billie Burke, Margaret Hamilton, and the Singer Midgets, under the direction of Victor Fleming. Features songs by Harold Arlen and E.Y. Harburg, including "Somewhere Over The Rainbow."

THE WOMAN IN GREEN
Video T.E.N.; 1945 • b/w; 1 hr, 8 min; ½" Beta II, ½" VHS • Sale: $49.95 for ½" Beta II, $54.95 for ½" VHS

Portrays a Sherlock Holmes mystery in which Professor Moriarty is murdering young women and cutting off their right forefingers. Stars Basil Rathbone, Nigel Bruce, Henry Daniell, Hillary Brooke, and Paul Cavanaugh.

WOMAN IN THE DUNES
National Film and Video Center; Date not listed • color; 2 hrs, 3 min; ¾" U-Matic, ½" Beta II, ½" VHS • Rental: $49/1 showing

Uses the metaphor of a man and a woman held captive in the bottom of a sandpit to express the human condition. Stars Eiji Okada and Kyoko Kishida in a Japanese film directed by Hiroshi Teshigahara.

WOMAN IN THE MOON
Video T.E.N.; 1929 • b/w; 1 hr, 55 min; ½" Beta II,

½" VHS • Sale: $49.95 for ½" Beta II, $54.95 for ½" VHS

Presents a silent Fritz Lang science-fiction epic of a trip to the moon in search of gold. Stars Klaus Pohl, Willy Fritsch, Gustav von Wagenheim, Gerda Maurus, and Gustav Stark-Gstettenbauer.

WOMAN IN THE RAIN
FHV Entertainment, Inc; 1976 • color; 1 hr, 30 min; ½" Beta II, ½" VHS • Sale: $49.95

Probes the life of Kelly, played by Barbara Luna, a nightclub singer who had to pay too much for the sins she committed. Co-stars Alex Nichol.

A WOMAN OF PARIS AND SUNNYSIDE
Magnetic Video Corporation; Order No. CL-3003; 1923 • b/w; 1 hr, 55 min; ½" Beta II, ½" VHS • Sale: $44.95

Presents two of Charlie Chaplin's films, "A Woman of Paris," which helped usher in the genre of sophisticated comedy that dominated the American screen in the late 1920's and early 1930's, and "Sunnyside," an experiment in lyric comedy.

A WOMAN REBELS
Blackhawk Films, Inc; Order No. 506-30-0689 for ½" Beta II, 525-30-0689 for ½" VHS; 1936 • b/w; 1 hr, 28 min; ½" Beta II, ½" VHS • Sale: $49.95

Examines the women's rights issue during the time of Victorian England and a young woman's relationship with a divorced man which could lead her to disgrace. Stars Katharine Hepburn, Herbert Marshall, and Elizabeth Allan.

WOMAN TIMES SEVEN
Magnetic Video Corporation; Order No. CL-4047; 1967 • color; 1 hr, 39 min; ½" Beta II, ½" VHS • Sale: $54.95

Offers seven separate stories about seven extraordinary women. Stars Shirley MacLaine, Alan Arkin, Rossano Brazzi, Michael Caine, Vittorio Gassman, Peter Sellers, and Anita Ekberg, under the direction of Vittorio de Sica.

THE WOMEN
Video Communications Inc; Order No. 1115; 1966 • color; 1 hr, 35 min; ½" Beta II, ½" VHS • Sale: $54.95

Presents a comedy in which a prominent author's inability to cope with women is compounded by his relationship with his secretary. Stars Brigitte Bardot and Maurice Ronet.

WOMEN OF THE NIGHT
Mitchell Brothers' Film Group; Date not listed • color; 1 hr, 5 min; ½" Beta II, ½" VHS • Sale: $69

Presents a pornographic film.

WOODSTOCK (PART 1)
WCI Home Video Inc; 1970 • color; 1 hr, 30 min; ½" Beta II, ½" VHS • Sale: $50

Offers a documentary look at the first and most famous of the outdoor rock concerts. Includes performances by Joan Baez, Richie Havens, Crosby, Stills and Nash, Jefferson Airplane, Joe Cocker, Sly and the Family Stone, Ten Years After, Santana, Country Joe and the Fish, John Sebastian, and The Who. Features the direction of Michael Wadleigh.

WOODSTOCK (PART 2)
WCI Home Video Inc; 1970 • color; 1 hr, 30 min; ½" Beta II, ½" VHS • Sale: $50

See Part 1 for description.

THE WORLD GONE MAD
Video T.E.N.; 1931 • b/w; 1 hr, 10 min; ½" Beta II, ½" VHS • Sale: $49.95 for ½" Beta II, $54.95 for ½" VHS

Provides a look at a 'B' film from the earliest sound days, the story of a district attorney, a crooked financier, his daughter, and assorted criminals. Stars Pat O'Brien, Evelyn Brent, Louis Calhern, and J. Carrol Naish.

THE WORLD OF ABBOTT AND COSTELLO
MCA DiscoVision; Order No. 22-006; 1965 • b/w; 1 hr, 19 min; LaserVision • Sale: $15.95

Highlights eighteen of Bud and Lou's features with narration by Jack E. Leonard. Includes "Who's On First" and other routines. Stars Bud Abbott and Lou Costello.

WORLD OF WILDLIFE
RCA SelectaVision VideoDiscs; Order No. 02002; Date not listed • color; 1 hr, 44 min; CED • Sale: $14.98

Offers two nature documentaries originally seen on network TV. Opens with "Snow Geese," providing a look at these rarely photographed birds from the Canadian Arctic to Texas, narrated by Glen Campbell. Includes "Leopard of the Wild," the story of one man's struggle to preserve the wild, narrated by David Niven.

WORLD SAFARI
Video Communications Inc; Order No. 1116; 1971 • color; 1 hr, 33 min; ½" Beta II, ½" VHS • Sale: $54.95

Features safaris seeking animals and adventure in exotic places around the world.

THE WRONG BOX
National Film and Video Center; 1966 • color; 1 hr, 45 min; ¾" U-Matic, ½" Beta II, ½" VHS • Rental: $59/1 showing

Involves the inheritance of a large fortune with many people vying for the role of legatee: one of two brothers will get the money on the death of the other, and the decendants of each brother also begin plotting. Stars John Mills, Ralph Richardson, and Michael Caine.

XANADU
MCA DiscoVision; Order No. 17-006; 1980 • color; 1 hr, 36 min; LaserVision • Sale: $29.95

MCA Videocassette, Inc; Order No. 66019; 1980 • color; 1 hr, 36 min; ½" Beta II, ½" VHS • Sale: $65

Presents, in stereo, a fantasy-musical in which a Muse named Kira helps a few people realize their life's ambitions. Offers a 1940s-type musical updated with 1980s music and technology. Includes "Magic," "I'm Alive," and "Xanadu." Stars Olivia Newton-John, Gene Kelly, and Michael Beck.

THE YANKEE CLIPPER
Blackhawk Films, Inc; Order No. 506-49-0892 for 1/2" Beta II, 525-49-0892 for 1/2" VHS; 1927 • color; 51 min; 1/2" Beta II, 1/2" VHS • Sale: $39.95

Portrays a race from China to New England between the American ship, "The Yankee Clipper," and the English vessel, "Lord of the Isles." Stars William Boyd and Elinor Fair in this silent thriller.

YANKEE DOODLE CRICKET
Fotomat Corp; Order No. B0709 for 1/2" Beta II, V0709 for 1/2" VHS; 1974 • color; 26 min; 1/2" Beta II, 1/2" VHS • Sale: $39.95; Rental: $5.95/5 days

Provides an American history lesson for children in this animated film produced by Xerox films. Features Tucker Mouse, Harry Cat, and Chester Cricket, among other George Selden characters.

YANKEE DOODLE DANDY
Vid America; Order No. 425; 1943 • b/w; 2 hrs, 6 min; 1/2" Beta II, 1/2" VHS • Rental: $10.95/wk

Dramatizes the life of George M. Cohan with song and dance. Recounts his rise to fame, the courtship of his wife Mary, and the triumph of his later years. Stars James Cagney, who won an Oscar for the part.

YELLOW ROSE OF TEXAS
Cable Films; 1944 • b/w; 55 min; 1/2" Beta I, 1/2" Beta II, 1/2" VHS • Sale: $45 for 1/2" Beta I, $49.50 for 1/2" Beta II & VHS

Features Roy Rogers working as an undercover insurance agent on a popular riverboat, as he helps clear the name of an old man falsely accused of a stagecoach robbery. Stars Roy Rogers, Dale Evans, and the Sons of the Pioneers.

Jeanne Cagney, James Cagney, Joan Leslie, Walter Huston, and Rosemary deCamp in *Yankee Doodle Dandy*.

Spring Byington, Ann Miller, James Stewart, and Jean Arthur in *You Can't Take It With You*.

YOJIMBO
Budget Video; 1961 • b/w; 1 hr, 50 min; 1/2" Beta II, 1/2" VHS • Sale: $44.95

Recounts the story of a samurai who comes to a town devastated by civil war between two rival factions, and succeeds in getting the two sides to exterminate each other. Stars Toshiro Mifune under the direction of Akira Kurosawa; in Japanese with subtitles.

YOU CAN'T TAKE IT WITH YOU
National Film and Video Center; 1938 • b/w; 2 hrs, 7 min; 3/4" U-Matic, 1/2" Beta II, 1/2" VHS • Rental: $59/1 showing

Compares the lives of two men, one a corporate magnate who gets pleasure only out of manipulating others, and the other the head of an eccentric family. Brings the two together when the magnate's son becomes engaged to the other's granddaughter. Stars Lionel Barrymore, James Stewart, Jean Arthur, and Edward Arnold, under the direction of Frank Capra.

YOU LIGHT UP MY LIFE
Columbia Pictures Home Entertainment; 1977 • color; 1 hr, 30 min; 1/2" Beta II, 1/2" VHS • Sale: $59.95

- -
Fotomat Corp; Order No. B0435 for 1/2" Beta II, V0435 for 1/2" VHS; 1977 • color; 1 hr, 31 min; 1/2" Beta II, 1/2" VHS • Sale: $54.95; Rental: $9.95/5 days

Profiles a girl trying to make good in the world of show business, and her romantic involvements. Features the title song as interpreted by Didi Conn, who also stars. Includes Joe Silver and Michael Zaslow.

YOUNG AND INNOCENT
Budget Video; 1937 • b/w; 1 hr, 20 min; 1/2" Beta II, 1/2" VHS • Sale: $44.95

- -
Video T.E.N.; 1937 • b/w; 1 hr, 20 min; 1/2" Beta II, 1/2" VHS • Sale: $49.95 for 1/2" Beta II, $54.95 for 1/2" VHS

Presents an Alfred Hitchcock thriller in which a young couple must uncover an unknown killer while themselves the object of a police manhunt. Features English actors Derrick De Marney, Nova Pilbearn, and Percy Marmont.

YOUNG BING CROSBY
Reel Images Inc; Order No. 431; 1932 • b/w; 39 min;

½" Beta II, ½" VHS • Sale: $39.95 for ½" Beta II,
$42.95 for ½" VHS

Presents a series of Mack Sennett comedies starring
the young Bing Crosby prior to his success in feature-
length musical films. Includes the songs "Crooner's
Holiday," "Blue of the Night," and "Bing, Bing, Sing."

YOUNG DILLINGER
Blackhawk Films, Inc; Order No. 502-30-0072 for ½"
Beta II, 515-30-0072 for ½" VHS; 1965 • b/w; 1 hr,
42 min; ½" Beta II, ½" VHS • Sale: $59.95

Depicts the formative years and influences of the soon-
to-be "public enemy number one." Stars Nick Adams,
Mary Ann Mobley, and Victor Buono.

THE YOUNG LIONS
Magnetic Video Corporation; Order No. CL-1057;
1958 • b/w; 2 hrs, 47 min; ½" Beta II, ½" VHS • Sale:
$74.95

Adapts on two video cassettes the Irwin Shaw novel.
Concerns two American soldiers and a Nazi officer in
separate stories which eventually overlap during World
War II. Stars Marlon Brando, Montgomery Clift, Dean
Martin, Hope Lange, Barbara Rush, Maximilian Schell,
and Mai Britt, under the direction of Edward Dmytryk,
with a score by Hugo Friedhofer.

THE YOUNG SEDUCERS
Tape Club of America; Order No. 2834 B; Date not
listed • color; 1 hr, 17 min; ½" Beta II, ½" VHS • Sale:
$54.95

Presents a pornographic film.

YOUNG WINSTON
National Film and Video Center; 1972 • color; 2 hrs,
25 min; ¾" U-Matic, ½" Beta II, ½" VHS • Rental:
$69/1 showing

Depicts the early life of Winston Churchill, focusing on
his career as a war correspondent in India and his service in the British army. Stars Simon Ward, Robert
Shaw, Anne Bancroft, John Mills, Jack Hawkins, and
Pat Heywood.

Z
Fotomat Corp; Order No. B0443 for ½" Beta II, V0443
for ½" VHS; 1969 • color; 2 hrs, 8 min; ½" Beta II, ½"
VHS • Sale: $49.95; Rental: $7.95/5 days

Time-Life Video Club Inc; 1969 • color; 2 hrs, 7 min;
½" Beta II, ½" VHS • Sale: $49.95 to members

Presents Costa-Gavras' oscar-winning political thriller
based on similiar incidents in Greece. Concerns an assassination and its repercussions. Uses fast action and
suspense. Stars Yves Montand, Irene Papas, and
Jean-Louis Trintignant.

ZERO DE CONDUITE
Budget Video; 1933 • b/w; 42 min; ½" Beta II, ½"
VHS • Sale: $34.95

Video T.E.N.; 1933 • b/w; 42 min; ½" Beta II, ½" VHS

• Sale: $39.95 for ½" Beta II, $44.95 for ½" VHS

Tells the story of two young boys who create chaos for
the headmaster of their boarding school; in French
with English subtitles. Stars Jean Daste and Robert Le
Fion under the direction of Jean Vigo.

ZIS BOOM BAH
Video T.E.N.; 1941 • b/w; 1 hr, 2 min; ½" Beta II, ½"
VHS • Sale: $49.95 for ½" Beta II, $54.95 for ½" VHS

Presents a musical starring mother Grace Hayes, her
son Peter Lind Hayes, and his wife Mary Healy, along
with Huntz Hall, Jan Wiley, and Skeets Gallagher. Tells
of a star, her son, and a college going broke.

ZOMBIES OF THE STRATOSPHERE
The Nostalgia Merchant; Date not listed • b/w; 3 hrs;
½" Beta II, ½" VHS • Sale: $109.95

Presents, on two videocassettes, a motion picture serial in 12 episodes. Stars Judd Holdren.

ZORRO'S BLACK WHIP
The Nostalgia Merchant; Order No. 0023; 1944 • b/w;
3 hrs; ½" Beta II, ½" VHS • Sale: $109.95

Presents, on two videocassettes, a Republic motion
picture serial in 12 episodes. Follows the western adventures of a young, beautiful girl who continues the
fight against crime and terror begun by her murdered
brother. Stars Linda Stirling and George Lewis.

ZORRO'S FIGHTING LEGION
Northeast Video and Sound, Inc; Order No. 116S;
1939 • b/w; ¾" U-Matic, ½" EIAJ, ½" Beta II, ½"
VHS • Sale: $495; Rental: $175/wk

Offers a 12-chapter serial starring Reed Hadley as Zorro.

ACTION/ADVENTURE

Adventures of Captain Marvel
Adventures of Frontier Fremont
The Adventures of Tarzan
Africa Texas Style
Algiers
All the Way Boys
Allegheny Uprising
And Then There Were None
Assault on Precinct 13
At Sword's Point
Back from Eternity
Back to Bataan
The Bandits of Orogosolo
Bare Knuckles
The Battle of El Alamein
The Bedford Incident
Behind the Shutters
Berlin Express
The Big Cat
The Black Pirate
The Black Widow
Blood on the Sun
Breakout
The Bridge on the River Kwai
Bruce Lee Superdragon
Bruce Li in New Guinea
Buck Rogers Conquers the Universe
Bulldog Drummond's Peril
Call It Murder
The Call of the Wild
Captain America
Captain Kidd
Castle of Fu Manchu
Chinatown
The Chinese Godfather
Chino
Copkillers
The Count of Monte Cristo
The Crimson Ghost
Daredevils of the Red Circle
Dark Journey
Dark Mountain
The Day of the Dolphin
Death Wish
The Deep
The Deep Six

The Devil at 4 O'Clock
Dick Tracy
Dick Tracy Double Feature
Dick Tracy Meets Gruesome
The Dirty Dozen
Dirty Harry
Dr. Syn
Dressed to Kill
Earthquake
The Eiger Sanction
El Cid
Enter the Dragon
Escape to Burma
Exit the Dragon—Enter the Tiger
The Fallen Sparrow
The Family
Fearless Fighters
55 Days at Peking
Fighter Pilots
Fighting Caravans
The Fighting Devil Dogs
Fire over England
Fist of Fury II
Flying Leathernecks
Flying Tigers
The French Connection
From Here to Eternity
Future Women
Gangbusters
Genghis Khan
Go Tell the Spartans
The Golden Voyage of Sinbad
Good Guys Wear Black
The Great Escape
The Great Locomotive Chase
The Green Archer
The Green Berets
Guerrillas in Pink Lace
Gung Ho!
Gunga Din
The Guns of Navarone
Guns of the Timberland
Hawk of the Wilderness
He Walked by Night
Hell on Frisco Bay
Hells Angels on Wheels
Hercules

Hercules Unchained
Hooper
The Hot Rock
I Wonder Who's Killing Her Now
The Invincible
The Iron Mask
Jamaica Reef
Jason and the Argonauts
Jericho
Johnny Angel
Judex
The Jungle Book
Kidnapped
Killer Shark
The King Boxers
King of the Kongo
King of the Rocket Men
Lady Cocoa
The Last Challenge of the Dragon
Lawrence of Arabia
The Life and Times of Grizzly Adams
Lightning Swords of Death
Little Laura and Big John
The Lives of a Bengal Lancer
The Longest Day
The Lost Patrol
The Loves and Times of Scaramouche
Macao
Machine Gun Kelly
Manhunt in the African Jungle
The Mark of Zorro
The Masked Marvel
Midway
Morgan the Pirate
Mr. Moto's Last Warning
Mr. Robinson Crusoe
Murder by Television
Murder, My Sweet
Murderer's Row
Mysterious Island
Mystery Plane
Mystery Squadron
The New Adventures of Tarzan
Nightmare County
Northeast of Seoul
The Odessa File
Out of the Past
Pancho Villa
Pearl of the South Pacific
Pepe Le Moko
Permission to Kill
The Phantom Creeps
The Proud and the Damned
The Purple Monster Strikes
Quick, Let's Get Married
The Racket
Railroaded
The Real Bruce Lee
Rebel Rousers
Redneck
The Return of Chandu
Rififi
Robinson Crusoe
Run, Angel, Run
Sahara
The Saint in New York
Salt in the Wound
Samar
The Scarlet Pimpernel
Second Chance
The Secret of Big Foot
The Secret Weapon
The Seventh Voyage of Sinbad
Sexton Blake and the Hooded Terror

Shadow of Chinatown
Shadow of the Eagle
Shadow of the Hawk
Shamus
She Wore a Yellow Ribbon
Sherlock Holmes and the Secret Weapon
Sherlock Holmes Double Feature #1
Sherlock Holmes Double Feature #2
Shoot
A Shriek in the Night
Sinbad the Sailor
Sky Riders
The Sky's the Limit
Slaughter Day
Son of Monte Cristo
Son of Sinbad
Son of the Sheik
S.O.S. Coast Guard
The Spy in Black
Spy Smasher
Squadron of Doom
The Steel Claw
The Stone Killer
The Stranger and the Gunfighter
The Street Fighter
Submarine Alert
The Swashbuckler
Tarzan and the Green Goddess
Tarzan and the Trappers
Tarzan of the Apes
Tarzan the Fearless
Tarzan's Revenge
The Thief of Baghdad
The Third Man
The 39 Steps
Three Days of the Condor
The Three Musketeers
The Three Worlds of Gulliver
Tiffany Jones
Tora! Tora! Tora!
Treasure Island
The Treasure of Jamaica Reef
Treasure of Tayopa
The Triumph of Sherlock Holmes
20,000 Leagues Under the Sea
Von Ryan's Express
Wages of Fear
A Walk in the Sun
The White Search
Wild Riders
Wilderness Journey
The Woman in Green
The Yankee Clipper
Young and Innocent
Zorro's Fighting Legion

ADULT
Affair
Alice Goodbody
Alice in Wonderland
The Altar of Lust
Angela—Fireworks Woman
Angelique
Anyone But My Husband
Auditions
Autobiography of a Flea
Bad Penny
Bang Bang You Got It
Barbara Broadcast
Behind the Green Door
Bel Ami
Beneath the Sheets
The Bite
Blue Summer

Breaker Beauties
The Calico Queen
Call Me Angel, Sir
Camille 2000
Campus Girls
Campus Pussycats
Campus Swingers
Candy Stripers
Catherine & Co.
C.B. Mamas
Centerfold
Cheering Section
The Cheerleaders
Cherry, Harry and Raquel
China Cat
Chorus Call
The Clamdigger's Daughter
A Coming of Angels
The Condominium
Congressional Playgirls
Count the Ways
Couples
Cruisers
Cry Uncle!
Curse of the Headless Horseman
Danish Pastries
The Debauchers
Debby Does Dallas
Desires within Young Girls
Dial-a-Girl
Dr. Feelgood
Dracula Sucks
Dutch Treat
Easy Alice
Easy Woman
Eighteen Carat Virgin
Emanuelle in Bangkok
Emilienne
Emmanuelle
Erotic Memoirs of a Male Chauvinist Pig
An Erotic Musical Version of Cinderella
Every Inch a Lady
Expectations
Expose Me, Lovely
Fairytales
Fantasy in Blue
Farmer's Daughters
Felicia
Fiona on Fire
Flesh Factory
Flying Acquaintances
Football Widow
A Formal Faucett
Gabrielle
A Gemini Affair
The Girl from Starship Venus
Hanky Panky
Hard Soap Hard Soap
Hay Country Swingers
Health Spa
Hey, There's Naked Bodies on My TV!
High Rise
Highschool Report Card
Honeymoon Haven
Honeypie
Hot Oven
House near Prado
I, a Woman—II
I Drink Your Blood
I Want You
The Incredible Sex-Ray Machine
Inside Desiree Cousteau
Inside Marilyn Chambers
Intimate Playmates

Introductions
The Jade Pussy Cat
Joy
Karla
Kinky Ladies of Bourbon Street
Knock Them Over
Le Body Shop
The Lickerish Quartet
The Life and Times of Xaviera Hollander
Liquid Lips
Little Sisters
Love and Kisses
Love in Strange Places
The Love Slaves
A Love Story
Malibu Beach
Malibu High
Maraschino Cherry
Masterpiece
Master's Degree
Memories within Miss Aggie
*Midnight Blue
Midnight Blue Follies of 1975
Midnight Blue Follies of 1976
Mistress Pamela
Misty Beethoven
Monique
The Morning After
Mrs. Barrington
Myra Breckinridge
Naked Came the Stranger
Naked Paradise
Naughty Coeds
Naughty Nostalgia, Volume 1
Naughty Nostalgia, Volume 2
A New Girl in Town
Night Pleasures
Nine Ages of Nakedness
Nurse Maids
Odyssey
Old Borrowed and Stag
Once Upon a Time She Was
1001 Danish Delights
The Opening of Misty Beethoven
Oral Contract
The Passion Potion
Playgirls of Munich
Pom-Pom Girls
The Private Afternoons of Pamela Mann
Relatives Are Coming
Resurrection of Eve
Revenge of the Cheerleaders
Rollerbabies
Rosebud
Secrets
The Seduction of Amy
The Seduction of Lynn Carter
Sex and the Office Girl
Sex Rituals of the Occult
Sex World
Sexteen
Sexual Customs in Scandinavia
Sexual Freedom in Brooklyn
Skin Flicks
Slaves of Love
Smartie Pants
Sodom and Gomorrah
Sometime Sweet Susan
S.O.S.
Star Babe
Star Pilot
Sticky Fingers
The Story of Joanna
Stroke of Nine

Sugar Cookies
Summer Heat
Summer of '69
The Superware Party
Swap Meet
Sweet Cakes
Sweet Pun'kin
Swingin' Models
The Swingin' Stewardesses
Swinging High
Swinging Ski Girls
Swinging Sorority Girls
Take Off
Teenage Milkmaid
Tell Them Johnny Wadd Is Here
Things to Come
The Tiger from Hong Kong
Triangle of Passion
Unwilling Lovers
Up Smokey
The Van
Van Nuys Blvd.
Vanessa
The Violation of Claudia
Visions
The Vixen
Voices of Desire
Voluptuous Vixens '76
Wanda
We a Family
While the Cat's Away
Women of the Night
The Young Seducers

ANIMATION/CARTOONS
Abbott and Costello Cartoon Hour
Adventures of Chip 'n' Dale
Adventures of Mighty Mouse (Part 1)
Adventures of Mighty Mouse (Part 2)
Adventures of Mighty Mouse (Part 3)
The Adventures of Pinocchio
Adventures of Superman
Animal Farm
Animation in the 1930's
Astronut
At Home with Donald Duck
The Best of Heckle & Jeckle (Part 1)
The Best of Heckle & Jeckle (Part 2)
The Best of Heckle & Jeckle (Part 3)
The Best of Superman Cartoons
Bon Voyage, Charlie Brown
Bugs and Friends
The Bugs Bunny/Road Runner Movie
Bullwinkle
Camouflage
Cartoon Carnival #1
Cartoon Carnival #2
Cartoon Fest
Cartoon Jamboree
Cartoon Parade No. 1
Cartoon Parade No. 2
Cartoon Parade No. 3
A Charlie Brown Festival
Charlotte's Web
Children's Collection I
Children's Collection II
Chinese Gods
Classic Superman Cartoons
The Color Adventures of Superman
Color Cartoon Parade
Courageous Cat
The Coyote's Lament
The Cricket in Times Square
Deputy Dawg

Dick Deadeye
Dinky Duck
Disney Cartoon Parade, Volume I
Dunder Klumpen
The Fabulous World of Jules Verne
Fantastic Planet
Gandy Goose
Gulliver's Travels
The Happy Prince and The Little Mermaid
Heckle and Jeckle
Hector Heathcote
Hoppity Goes to Town
Hugo the Hippo
I Go Pogo
Kids Is Kids
The Little Mermaid
Little Roquefort
Looney Tunes and Merrie Melodies #1
Looney Tunes and Merrie Melodies #2
Mad Monster Party
Mighty Mouse
More Little Roquefort
On Vacation with Mickey Mouse and Friends
Popeye
Popeye Meets Sinbad the Sailor
Popeye the Sailor
Popeye's Famous Fables
Possible Possum
The Puppy Who Wanted a Boy and The Puppy's
   Great Adventure
Race for Your Life, Charlie Brown
Rocky and Bullwinkle Cartoon Hour
Sad Cat
The Selfish Giant and the Remarkable Rocket
Sidney the Elephant
Superman
Superman
Superman Color Cartoon Festival
Tales of Deputy Dawg
Terry Bears
Terrytoons, Volume I, Featuring Mighty Mouse
Tom and Jerry Cartoon Festival
Ub Iwerks Cartoon Fest Two
Ub Iwerks Cartoon Festival
UPA's Cartoon Classics
A Very Merry Cricket
The Wacky World of Mother Goose
Warner Bros. Cartoons
Warner Brothers Cartoons
Watership Down
Yankee Doodle Cricket

CHILDREN'S
The Absent-Minded Professor
The Adventures of Huckleberry Finn
Almost Angels
The Bad News Bears
The Bad News Bears Go to Japan
The Bad News Bears in Breaking Training
The Bears and I
Bedknobs and Broomsticks
Benji
The Black Stallion
Bless the Beasts and the Children
Candleshoe
Dangerous Holiday
Danny Boy
The Double McGuffin
Dunder Klumpen
Enchanted Forest
Escapade in Japan
Escape to Witch Mountain
The Fabulous World of Jules Verne
The 5,000 Fingers of Dr. T.

The Flight of the Cougar
A Gift for Heidi
The Gold Bug; Rodeo Red and the Runaway
Greyfriars Bobby
The Grizzly and the Treasure
Hansel and Gretel
Heidi (1937)
Heidi (1968)
Hot Lead and Cold Feet
Indian Paint
The Jungle Book
Kidnapped
Lassie's Greatest Adventure
The Legend of Cougar Canyon
The Little Prince
The Littlest Outlaw
The Love Bug
The Miracle
Miracle of the White Stallions
The Muppet Movie
Now You See 'Em, Now You Don't
Old Yeller
Olly, Olly Oxen Free
On Vacation with Mickey Mouse and Friends
Perri
Peter Rabbit and Tales of Beatrix Potter
Pete's Dragon
Pinocchio
Pippi Goes on Board
Pippi Longstocking in the South Seas
The Prince and the Pauper
The Puppy Who Wanted a Boy and The Puppy's
    Great Adventure
Race for Your Life, Charlie Brown
The Railway Children
The Red Balloon; Occurrence at Owl Creek
    Bridge
The Road Back
Sinbad and the Eye of the Tiger
Starbird and Sweet William
Starring the Ritts Puppets
Summerdog
The Thief of Baghdad
Tom Sawyer
Tomboy
Treasure Island
Well of Love
Where the Red Fern Grows
Who Killed Doc Robbin?
The Wizard of Oz

COMEDIES

A Nous la Liberte
Abbott and Costello Meet Captain Kidd
Abbott and Costello Meet Frankenstein
The Absent-Minded Professor
Adam's Rib
The Adventures of Sherlock Holmes' Smarter
    Brother
Affairs of Annabel
Africa Screams
All in a Night's Work
And So They Were Married
Angel on My Shoulder
Animal Crackers
The Apple Dumpling Gang
As You Like It
At War with the Army
The Awful Truth
Bachelor and the Bobby Soxer
The Bad News Bears
Balloonatik
Barefoot in the Park
Beat the Devil

Bell, Book and Candle
Ben Turpin Rides Again (Cross-Eyed!)
Beneath the War of the Worlds
The Big Mouth
Bingo Long Travelling All-Stars and Motor Kings
Blazing Saddles
Blockheads and I'll Take Vanilla
Boccaccio '70
Born Yesterday
Breakfast at Tiffany's
Brothers O'Toole
Buck Privates
Bundle of Joy
Buster Keaton
Cactus Flower
California Split
Car Wash
Carry On Nurse
Casanova '70
Casino Royale
Cat Ballou
Chaplin Mutuals (Volume 1)
Chaplin Mutuals (Volume 2)
Chaplin Mutuals (Volume 3)
Chaplin Mutuals (Volume 4)
The Chaplin Review
Charlie Chaplin Shorts
Check and Double Check
The Circus and A Day's Pleasure
City Lights
Cockeyed Cavaliers
College
*Comedy Cavalcade (5 volumes, 35 parts)
The Days of Thrills and Laughter
Delightfully Dangerous
The Dentist and the Fatal Glass of Beer
Dirty Mary, Crazy Larry
Disorder in the Court
Doctor in Trouble
Dollars
Don't Drink the Water
Don't Give Up the Ship
Don't Raise the Bridge, Lower the River
Dreaming Out Loud
Duck Soup
Dummy Trouble
East Side Kids
The East Side Kids: Let's Get Tough
The East Side Kids: Smart Alecks
Eternally Yours
Every Which Way but Loose
Everything You Always Wanted to Know about
    Sex, but Were Afraid to Ask
The Ex-Mrs. Bradford
The First Traveling Saleslady
A Flask of Fields
Flying Deuces
For Pete's Sake
The Fortune
Foul Play
The Fountain of Love
Francis, the Talking Mule
The Front Page
Fun Factory and Clown Princes of Hollywood
Fun with Dick and Jane
Funny Guys and Gals of the Talkies
Funstuff
Gangway
The General
Gentlemen Prefer Blondes
George
Get Happy
Ghosts on the Loose
The Gold Rush

The Gold Rush and Pay Day
The Golden Age of Comedy
The Golf Specialist and The Pharmacist and The
  Pool Shark
The Gorilla
The Great Dictator
Groove Tube
Gus
Happy Birthday, Wanda June
The Happy Hooker
Harold and Maude
Harold Lloyd Shorts
Harry and Walter Go to New York
Have Rocket, Will Travel
The Headless Horseman and Will Rogers
The Heartbreak Kid
Heaven Can Wait
Heavens Above!
Henry Phipps Goes Skiing
Hi Diddle Diddle
His Girl Friday
History Is Made at Night
The Holes
Holiday
Hook, Line and Sinker
The Hot Rock
How to Marry a Millionaire
How to Steal a Million
I Will, I Will . . . for Now
I'm All Right, Jack
The In-Laws
The Inspector General
It's a Joke Son
It's a Wonderful Life
It's in the Bag
Jack and the Beanstalk
Judge Priest
Keystone Krazies
The Kid and The Idle Class
The Kid from Left Field
Kind Hearts and Coronets
A King in New York
Kings, Queens, Jokers
Kipps
The Knockout and Dough and Dynamite
Kotch
The Lady Refuses
The Ladykillers
Last Holiday
Laughfest ·
Laurel and Hardy (Volume 1)
Laurel and Hardy (Volume 2)
Laurel and Hardy (Volume 3)
Laurel and Hardy (Volume 4)
Laurel and Hardy (Volume 5)
Laurel and Hardy (Volume 6)
The Lavender Hill Mob
Le Magnifique
Li'l Abner
Limelight
Lonely Wives
The Longest Yard
The Love Bug
Lovers and Other Strangers
Ma and Pa Kettle
The Madam Gambles
Made for Each Other
Malicious
The Man from Clover Grove
The Man in the White Suit
The Man Who Loved Women
The Marriage of a Young Stockbroker
Marry Me! Marry Me!
M*A*S*H

Merriest Pranksters
Mickey
Miracle on 34th Street
Modern Times
The Monkey's Uncle
Monsieur Verdoux
The Moon Is Blue
The Mouse That Roared
Mr. and Mrs. Smith
Mr. Blandings Builds His Dream House
Mr. Hulot's Holiday
Mr. Lucky
Murder by Death
My Favorite Brunette
My Little Chickadee
My Man Godfrey
Network
A Nice Girl Like Me
A Night at the Opera
Ninotchka
No Problem
The North Avenue Irregulars
Nothing Sacred
The Odd Couple
On Approval
One Body Too Many
One Rainy Afternoon
Operation Snatch
Our Relations
The Owl and the Pussycat
Pack Up Your Troubles
Palooka
Paper Moon
Parlor, Bedroom and Bath
Peck's Bad Boy with the Circus
Perfect Fools
The Philadelphia Story
Pickwick Papers
Play It Again, Sam
The Private Life of Don Juan
The Producers
Promises! Promises!
The Prophet
Putney Swope
The Rage of Paris
Reaching for the Moon
Reefer Madness
The Return of the Pink Panther
The Return of the Tall Blond Man with One Black
  Shoe
Rhinoceros
The Rink and The Immigrant
Robert Youngson's Blaze Busters
Robert Youngson's Gadgets Galore
Robert Youngson's I Never Forget a Face
Robert Youngson's Spills and Chills
Robert Youngson's This Mechanical Age
Robert Youngson's World of Kids
Room Service
The Royal Bed
Ruggles of Red Gap
Sad Sack
Sally of the Sawdust
Saps at Sea
Scoumoune
The Seduction of Mimi
The Senator Was Indiscreet
Seven Beauties
The Seven Year Itch
Silent Laugh Makers, Volume 1
Silent Laugh Makers, Volume 2
Silver Streak
The Sin of Harold Diddlebock
Some Like It Hot

Sons of the Desert
Sons of the Desert; Top Flat
Spooks Run Wild
Stalag 17
Steamboat Bill Jr.
The Sting
Stolen Kisses
Stoneface
Stop! Look! Laugh!
Storm in a Teacup
Sunburn
The Sunshine Boys
Susan Slept Here
Swiss Miss
Take the Money and Run
The Tall Blond Man with One Black Shoe
The Taming of the Shrew
That Uncertain Feeling
There's a Girl in My Soup
These Girls Won't Talk
Those Magnificent Men in Their Flying Machines
Three Broadway Girls
3 Nuts in Search of a Bolt
The Three Stooges, Part 1
The Three Stooges, Part II
The Three Stooges Go around the World in a
  Daze
The Three Stooges in Orbit
The Three Stooges Meet Hercules
Tillie's Punctured Romance
To Be or Not to Be
Tom, Dick, and Harry
Topper
Topper Returns
The Trouble with Angels
Tunnelvision
Two-Reelers—Comedy Classics (Part 1)
Two-Reelers—Comedy Classics (Part 2)
Two-Reelers—Comedy Classics (Part 3)
Two-Reelers—Comedy Classics (Part 4)
Up in Smoke
Up Pompeii
Utopia
The Villain Still Pursues Her
Visit to a Small Planet
Vivacious Lady
The Wackiest Ship in the Army
Watermelon Man
Way Out West
W.C. Fields Festival
What's Up, Doc?
When Comedy Was King
Where Angels Go . . . Trouble Follows
A Woman of Paris and Sunnyside
The Women
The World of Abbott and Costello
The Wrong Box
You Can't Take It with You
Zero de Conduite

DOCUMENTARIES

The African Adventure
African Safari
Aliens from Spaceship Earth
All Star Jazz Show
The Amazing World of Psychic Phenomena
America at the Movies
America between the Great Wars
The Ark of Noah
Aviation (Volume 1)
The Bengal Tiger
The Bermuda Triangle
Beyond and Back
Beyond Belief

Big Foot—Man or Beast?
The Big Hunt
Birth of a Legend
Born Free
Brother of the Wind
Chariots of the Gods
The Clowns
Coming Attractions (Part 1)—The Super Stars
Coming Next Week—The Great Movie Trailers
Cougar Country
Countdown to World War II
Cry of the Wild
Deadly Fathoms
December 7th
D.W. Griffith: An American Genius
Eisenstein
Encounter with the Unknown
The Fabulous Fifties
The Fantastic Plastic Machine
Fate of the Andrea Doria
Fillmore
Film Firsts
Following the Tundra Wolf
From Broadway to Hollywood
The Genius of Charlie Chaplin
Gimme Shelter
The Grizzly and the Treasure
Guadalcanal Odyssey
Harlan County U.S.A.
Hollywood at War
Hollywood without Makeup
Horizons of the Sea
How the Myth Was Made
Hunters of the Wild
I'm a Stranger Here Myself
In Search of Ancient Astronauts
In Search of Noah's Ark
Instinct for Survival
The Island
Jacques Cousteau's Voyage to the Edge of the
  World
Jungle Cavalcade
Keaton Special and Valentino Mystique
Key to the Universe
Legend of Amaluk
The Legend of Cougar Canyon
Legend of Death Valley
Legend of Loch Ness
Legendary Personalities
The Lincoln Conspiracy
Lost City of Atlantis
The Lost Years
The Making of Star Wars
Martin Luther, His Life and Time
Men of Destiny (Part 1)—World Political Figures
Men of Destiny (Part 2)—Artists and Innovators
Milestones of the Century (Part 1)—The Great
  Wars
Milestones of the Century (Part 2)—20th Century
  Turning Points
Millhouse
Miracle at Lake Placid
Monsters on the March (and a Pair of Marvels)
The Moving Picture Boys in the Great War
The Murder of Fred Hampton
Mysteries from beyond Earth
Mysteries from beyond the Triangle
Mysteries of the Gods
The Mysterious Monsters
Nanook of the North
The New Deal—The Thirties
The Outer Space Connection
Overlords of the U.F.O.
People of the Sea

Prelude to War
Premiere of "A Star Is Born"
Pumping Iron
The Roaring Twenties
Rod Serling's Encounter with the Unknown
San Francisco Documental
Sasquatch
The Sea Around Us
Secret Life of Adolph Hitler
Selling Movies on Television
Sex, Sin and Censorship
The Silent Enemy
The Silent Horror Film
The Smashing of the Reich
Snowman
Somebody Goofed: Movie/TV Bloopers
Son of Monsters on the March
The Sorrow and the Pity
Spirits of the Deep
The Story of the Silent Serials and Girls in Danger
The Story of William S. Hart and the Sad Clowns
Target for Tonight
Ten Days Thak Shook the World
That's Entertainment
Toklat
Triumph of the Will
The True Glory
Tut: The Boy King; The Louvre
Two Pare Lorentz Documentaries
UFO Journals
UFO's Are Real
The Undersea World of Jacques Cousteau Vol. I
The Unexplained
Universe
Unknown Powers
Victory at Sea
Visions of Eight
The War Years—The Forties
The Way of the Wind
Where the Lions Rule
The Will of a People
Wings of an Eagle
Woodstock (Part 1)
Woodstock (Part 2)
World of Wildlife
World Safari

DRAMAS

Abe Lincoln in Illinois
Abraham Lincoln
Accident
Advise and Consent
The African Queen
The Agony and the Ecstasy
Alexander Nevsky
Alice Adams
All about Eve
All Mine to Give
All Screwed Up
All the King's Men
All the President's Men
All Things Bright and Beautiful
Aloha, Bobby and Rose
Alpha Beta
American Graffiti
Anastasia
Anatomy of a Murder
And Then There Were None
The Anderson Tapes
Angel and the Badman
Angel on My Shoulder
Anne of the Thousand Days
Appointment in Honduras
Autumn Leaves

The Baby
Baby Blue Marine
Back Street
Ballad of a Soldier
Barabbas
The Beachcomber
The Bears and I
The Bedford Incident
Ben Hur
Berserk
Beyond a Reasonable Doubt
Beyond Fear
The Bible
Billboard Girl
Bird of Paradise
Birth of a Nation
Bitter Sweet
Bittersweet Love
Black Like Me
Blackmail
Blind Husbands
Blood and Sand (1941)
Blood of a Poet
Blow-Up
The Blue Angel
The Blue Max
Bluebeard
Bob & Carol & Ted & Alice
Bonjour Tristesse
Bonnie and Clyde
Book of Numbers
The Boston Strangler
Boy on a Dolphin
The Boys in the Band
Break of Hearts
Breaking Up
Broken Strings
Brother John
Bullitt
Bus Stop
Butley
Butterflies Are Free
Cactus in the Snow
The Caine Mutiny
The Candidate
The Cardinal
Carnal Knowledge
Casablanca
Catch-22
Catherine the Great
C.C. and Company
Cesar
Chain Gang Women
Charlie Chan in Meeting at Midnight (Black Magic)
Cheers for Miss Bishop
Chinatown
A Christmas Carol
The Christmas Tree
Circus World
Citizen Kane
Clash by Night
Cleopatra
The Collector
Coma
Corridors of Blood
Cousin, Cousine
Crime and Punishment
Cromwell
Curly Top
Cyrano De Bergerac ·
Darling
David Copperfield
The Day of the Dolphin
The Day of the Jackal

Day of Wrath
Deadly Hero
Dear Dead Delilah
The Death Kiss
Death Wish
The Deep Six
A Delicate Balance
Deliverance
The Demi-Paradise
The Desert Fox
The Detective
Diabolique
Diamonds
Diary of a Mad Housewife
The Diary of Anne Frank
Dick Tracy's Dilemma
Dingaka
Dinner at the Ritz
Dirty Gertie from Harlem USA
Dirty Harry
D.O.A.
Doctor Faustus
Doctor Zhivago
Dog Day Afternoon
Doomed to Die
Double Indemnity
Downhill Racer
Dr. Kildare's Strange Case
Dreaming Lips
Dressed to Kill
Dynamite Chicken
The Eagle
East of Eden
Ecstasy
8 1/2
Emperor Jones
Enchanted Island
End of the Road
Executive Action
Eyes Right
Fail Safe
The Fall of the Roman Empire
The Fallen Idol
Family Plot
Fanny
A Farewell to Arms
Fat City
The 5th Day of Peace
Foreign Correspondent
Fortune's Fool
Forty Carats
The Fountainhead
Frantic
Freckles Comes Home
The French Connection
Frenzy
From the Terrace
The Garden of the Finzi-Continis
Generation
Gentleman's Agreement
Georgy Girl
Ginger in the Morning
Glen or Glenda?
Glory
Go Down Death
The Go-Between
The Godfather
The Godfather, Part II
God's Little Acre
Going My Way
Good-bye Nana
The Graduate
The Grand Illusion
The Grapes of Wrath

The Great Gabbo
The Great Gatsby
Great Guy
Great Leaders (Gideon and Samson)
The Great Waldo Pepper
Guess Who's Coming to Dinner
Hamlet
The Harder They Come
The Harder They Fall
The Harlem Globetrotters
The Harrad Experiment
Haunts
Heat
Hedda
Hell on Frisco Bay
Hell's Angels on Wheels
Henry V
Here Comes Mr. Jordan
Hester Street
The Hindenburg
Hiroshima Mon Amour
Hitler
Hitler's Children
Hollywood High
Hombre
The Homecoming
How Green Was My Valley
Hud
The Hunchback of Notre Dame (1923)
The Hunchback of Notre Dame (1939)
Hustle
The Hustler
I Accuse My Parents
I Cover the Waterfront
The Iceman Cometh
If I Had a Million
In Celebration
In Cold Blood
In Name Only
The Informer
Interval
Intolerance
It Happened in New Orleans
It's a Wonderful Life
Ivan the Terrible (Part 1)
Ivan the Terrible (Part 2)
Jacob: The Man Who Fought with God
Jesus of Nazareth
Joe
The Jolson Story
Joseph and his Brethren
The Kennel Murder Case
The Killing of Sister George
Knife in the Water
Knock on Any Door
La Bete Humaine
La Femme Infidele
La Grande Illusion
Lady Chatterly's Lover
The Lady from Shanghai
Lady of Burlesque
Lady Sings the Blues
A Lady Takes a Chance
The Lady Vanishes
The Last Hurrah
The Last Laugh
The Last Mile
Last Tango in Paris
L'Atalante
Laura
Law of the Underworld
Le Secret
Lenny
A Letter to Three Wives

Lies My Father Told Me
Life with Father
The Lion in Winter
Lipstick
Little Annie Rooney
Little Lord Fauntleroy
Little Men
Little Orphan Annie
The Little Princess
Little Tough Guys
The Lodger
The Long Hot Summer
The Longest Day
The Longest Yard
Lord Jim
The Lords of Flatbush
Lost Horizon (1937)
Lost Horizon (1973)
The Lost Weekend
Lot in Sodom
Love All Summer
Love Is a Many Splendored Thing
Love Story
The Luck of Ginger Coffey
Lucky Luciano
Luther
M
The Mad Bomber
Made for Each Other
Mado
The Magic Garden
The Magician
The Magnificent Ambersons
Mahogany
The Maltese Falcon
A Man Called Adam
A Man for All Seasons
Man in the Glass Booth
The Man Who Had Power over Women
The Man Who Knew Too Much
The Manipulator
Marathon Man
The Marcus-Nelson Murders
Marius
The Marriage of a Young Stockbroker
Mary of Scotland
Master of the House
Mayerling
Meet Dr. Christian
Meet John Doe
Meeting at Midnight
Men in War
Midnight
Mine Own Executioner
Miracles Still Happen
Miss Sadie Thompson
Mister Kingstreet's War
The Moon Spinners
Morning Glory
Moses
Mother
Mr. Deeds Goes to Town
Mr. Moto's Last Warning
Mr. Roberts
Mr. Smith Goes to Washington
Murder
Murder on the Orient Express
Mutiny on the Bounty
My Love for Yours
My Sister, My Love
Mysterious Mr. Wong
The Mystery of Kaspar Hauser
The Mystery of the Mary Celeste
Naked and the Dead

Nashville
Negatives
The New Centurions
Nicholas and Alexandra
Night Flight from Moscow
Night Watch
Nine Days a Queen
None But the Lonely Heart
North by Northwest
The North Star
Nothing Sacred
Notorious
Number Seventeen
Of Human Bondage
Old Yeller
Oliver Twist
On the Waterfront
Once Is Not Enough
The Only Game in Town
Open City
Orpheus
Our Daily Bread
Our Town
Outside the Law
Paisan
Panic in Needle Park
The Paper Chase
The Passion of Joan of Arc
Patton
Pennies from Heaven
Penny Serenade
The People Next Door
The Perils of Pauline
Permission to Kill
Phantom Express
Phantom Fiend
Picnic
Pipe Dreams
The Poseidon Adventure
Potemkin
Pride of the Bowery
The Private Life of Henry VIII
Promise at Dawn
Psycho
Psychopath
A Public Affair
Pygmalion
The Quiet One
A Quiet Place to Kill
The Racket
Racketeer
Rain
A Raisin in the Sun
Rashomon
The Razor's Edge
Rebecca
Rebecca of Sunnybrook Farm
Rebel without a Cause
The Red Shoes
Requiem for a Heavyweight
Rider on the Rain
Road to Salina
Robbery
The Robe
Rocky
Romeo and Juliet
Room at the Top
Rules of the Game
Sabotage
Sail to Glory
The Sailor Who Fell from Grace with the Sea
Salome
Samson and Delilah
The Sand Pebbles

Sanders of the River
Saturday Night and Sunday Morning
Saturday Night Fever
Saul and David
Scalpel
Scarface
Scarlet Street
Scenes from A Marriage
Scrooge
The Sea Lion
Seance on a Wet Afternoon
Secret Agent
Secrets
Serpico
The Servant
Seven Beauties
Seven Samurai
The Seven-Per-Cent Solution
1776
Sex through a Window
The Shadow Strikes
Shamus
Shenandoah
Ship of Fools
Shock
Shoot
The Sicilian Connection
Sinai Commandos
Single Room Furnished
Sister Kenny
Sleuth
Slightly Scarlet
Smash-Up
The Song of Bernadette
Song of Freedom
The Southerner
Sparrows
A Special Day
Spies
Spitfire
Stage Door
Stage Door Canteen
Stage Struck
Stairway to Heaven
Stalag 17
A Star Is Born
The Stars Look Down
State of Siege
State of the Union
The Stepmother
Stiletto
Stolen Kisses
Storm over Asia
The Stranger
Stranger on the Third Floor
Strangers: The Story of a Mother and Daughter
Straw Dogs
Street Scene
Study in Scarlet
Suddenly, Last Summer
Sugarland Express
Summer Wishes, Winter Dreams
Summertime Killer
Sundown
Sunflower
Sunset Boulevard
Superchick
Suspicion
Sweet Hostage
Swept Away . . . by an Unusual Destiny in the
    Blue Sea of August
Swing High, Swing Low
The Ten Commandments
Ten Little Indians

Terror by Night
They Made Me a Criminal
They Shoot Horses, Don't They?
They Won't Believe Me!
The Third Man
The 39 Steps
This Man Must Die
Three Coins in the Fountain
Three Days of the Condor
Three Sisters
To Kill a Mockingbird
To Sir with Love
Tom Brown's School Days
Tongpan
A Touch of Class
The Towering Inferno
Treasure of the Sierra Madre
The Trial
True Heart Susie
Tulsa
Twelve O'Clock High
Two for the Road
The Two of Us
Ugetsu
Uncle Tom's Cabin
Under the Red Robe
Under the Roofs of Paris
The Valachi Papers
Valley of the Dolls
Vanishing Point
Variety
Vincent, Francois, Paul and the Others
Way Down East
Wedding in White
Weekend with the Baby Sitter
Welcome to Arrow Beach
What Price Hollywood
Where the Bullets Fly
Whiffs
While the City Sleeps
White Heat
White Line Fever
The Window
Winning
Winterset
The Witch Who Came from the Sea
Without Reservations
Woman in the Dunes
Woman in the Rain
A Woman Rebels
Woman Times Seven
The World Gone Mad
Yojimbo
You Light Up My Life
Young Dillinger
The Young Lions
Young Winston
Z

MUSICALS
Aida
Alice's Adventures in Wonderland
An American in Paris
Battling Hoofer
Bedknobs and Broomsticks
Beggar's Opera
Bing Crosby Festival
Blue Hawaii
Breakfast in Hollywood
Breaking the Ice
Bye, Bye Birdie
Can Can
Carefree
Carmen Jones

Cover Girl
The Dancing Pirate
Disco 9000
Doctor Dolittle
Doll Face
Down to Earth
Easter Parade
Easy Come, Easy Go
Evergreen
The Fabulous Dorseys
Fiddler on the Roof
Flying Down to Rio
Follow the Fleet
Frankie and Johnny
French Line
Fun in Acapulco
Gangway
The Gay Divorcee
Gentlemen Prefer Blondes
George White's Scandals
G.I. Blues
Gigi
Girl Most Likely
Girls, Girls, Girls
Glorifying the American Girl
Grease
Greek Street
Hansel and Gretel
Heart's Desire
Hello, Dolly!
Higher and Higher
Hollywood Goes to War
It's Love Again
Jailhouse Rock
Jazz Ball
Jazz 'n' Jive
Jesus Christ Superstar
The King and I
King Creole
La Cuccaracha
La Favorita
The Little Prince
Lost in the Stars
Magical Mystery Tour
Make a Wish
March of the Wooden Soldiers
Meet Me in St. Louis
Movie Struck
The Mozart Story
Oh! Calcutta!
Oklahoma
The Old Curiosity Shop
Oliver
On the Town
The One and Only, Genuine, Original Family Band
Pal Joey
Paradise, Hawaiian Style
Paradise in Harlem
The Perils of Pauline
Pete's Dragon
Pot O'Gold
Private Buckaroo
Rainbow on the River
Road to Nashville
Roustabout
Sailing Along
Second Chorus
Shall We Dance
Show Boat
Sing Your Worries Away
Singin' in the Rain
The Slipper and the Rose
Something to Sing About
The Sound of Music

Stagedoor Canteen
Stars on Parade
State Fair
The Story of Vernon and Irene Castle
Sweet Charity
Swing Parade of 1946
Swing Time
A Swingin' Summer
Sympathy for the Devil
There's No Business Like Show Business
Thoroughly Modern Millie
Till the Clouds Roll By
Top Hat
Twist around the Clock
Vagabond Lover
Verdi's Aida
The Wizard of Oz
Xanadu
Yankee Doodle Dandy
Young Bing Crosby
Zis Boom Bah

RECENT RELEASES

Airplane!
Airport '77
Alice Sweet Alice
Alien
All That Jazz
American Gigolo
American Hot Wax
Animal House
Annie Hall
Attack of the Killer Tomatoes
Autumn Sonata
The Bad News Bears
The Bad News Bears Go to Japan
The Bad News Bears in Breaking Training
Battlestar Galactica
Being There
Bittersweet Love
Black and White in Color
The Black Hole
The Black Marble
Black Sunday
Bloodline
Blue Collar
The Blues Brothers
Boardwalk
The Boys from Brazil
Bread and Chocolate
Breaking Away
Breaking Glass
Breakout
Brian's Song
Brubaker
The Bugs Bunny/Road Runner Movie
Capricorn One
Carny
The Cassandra Crossing
The Changeling
Chapter Two
Cheech and Chong's Next Movie
The Chicken Chronicles
The China Syndrome
The Choirboys
Circle of Iron
Citizen's Band
Close Encounters of the Third Kind
Close Encounters of the Third Kind, Special Edition
Coal Miner's Daughter
Coast to Coast
Cocaine Cowboys
Coming Home

Conversation Piece
Cruising
Damien, Omen II
Days of Heaven
The Deep
The Deer Hunter
A Different Story
The Double McGuffin
Dracula
A Dream of Passion
Dreamer
The Duellists
The Eagle Has Landed
Eleanor and Franklin
The Electric Horseman
The End
Escape from Alcatraz
The Europeans
Exorcist II: The Heretic
The Eyes of Laura Mars
Fame
Fellini's Casanova
Fingers
First Love
Flash Gordon
FM
The Fog
For the Love of Benji
Foul Play
Fraternity Row
French Postcards
Friday the 13th
Fun with Dick and Jane
The Fury
Ghosts That Still Walk
The Godsend
Goin' Coconuts
Goin' South
Going in Style
Gray Lady Down
Grease
The Greek Tycoon
Hair
Halloween
The Happy Hooker Goes to Washington
Hawmps!
Heaven Can Wait
Heroes
High Velocity
Hot Lead and Cold Feet
House Calls
The Hunter
Hurricane
Ice Castles
In Praise of Older Women
The In-Laws
The Innocent
Islands in the Stream
Jaws 2
The Jerk
Joseph Andrews
Julia
Just Crazy About Horses
The Kid from Left Field
King Kong
King of the Gypsies
Laserblast
The Last Four Days
The Last Remake of Beau Geste
The Legend of Jedediah Carver
Life of Brian
Little Darlings
A Little Romance
Looking for Mr. Goodbar

The Lucifer Complex
MacArthur
Madame Rosa
Malicious
A Man, A Woman, and A Bank
The Man Who Talks to Whales
Mandingo
The Manitou
Meatballs
Midnight Express
Movie Movie
The Muppet Movie
Murder by Decree
My Brilliant Career
Nasty Habits
Night Games
Nijinsky
9 to 5
1941
Norma Rae
North Dallas Forty
Oh, God!
Old Boyfriends
Oliver's Story
Once upon a Brothers Grimm
The One and Only
The Onion Field
Orca: The Killer Whale
The Other Side of the Mountain
Outrageous
Overboard
Parts: The Clonus Horror
Phantasm
Picnic at Hanging Rock
Players
Pretty Baby
Prom Night
Prophecy
The Psychic
Rabbit Test
Raise the Titanic
Return to Boggy Creek
Richard Pryor Live in Concert
Rogue Lion
Rollercoaster
The Rose
Rough Cut
Rude Boy
Same Time, Next Year
Saturday Night Fever
Saturday Night Fever (PG)
Saturday Night Fever (R)
Saturn 3
Secrets
The Seduction of Joe Tynan
Semi-Tough
Sgt. Pepper's Lonely Hearts Club Band
Shogun
The Shout
Sidewinder One
The Silent Partner
Sinbad and the Eye of the Tiger
Slap Shot
Smokey and the Bandit
Smokey and the Bandit II
Star Trek—The Motion Picture
Starting Over
Stingray
The Stunt Man
Sunburn
Superman
Take All of Me
10
Till Marriage.Do Us Part

Tourist Trap
The Turning Point
An Unmarried Woman
Up in Smoke
Urban Cowboy
The War between the Tates
The Warriors
A Whale of a Tale
Which Way Is Up?
Whiskey Mountain
Windows
Winter Kills
Xanadu
You Light Up My Life

SCIENCE FICTION/HORROR

The Andromeda Strain
Andy Warhol's Dracula
Andy Warhol's Frankenstein
Ape Man
The Astro Zombies
Attack of the Crab Monsters
The Avenging Conscience
Barbarella
Bedlam
Beneath the Planet of the Apes
The Bionic Woman
The Birds
Blackenstein
Blood Mania
Blood of Dracula's Castle
Blood of the Vampire
Bluebeard
The Body Snatcher
The Body Snatcher and Cat People
The Boy and His Dog
The Bride of Frankenstein
Bride of the Monster
Buck Rogers Conquers the Universe
Buck Rogers (Planet Outlaws)
Cabinet of Dr. Caligari
Castle of Fu Manchu
Cat People
Chandu on the Magic Island
Chandu the Magician
Children Shouldn't Play with Dead Things
A Clockwork Orange
Corridors of Blood
Crash
Creature from the Black Lagoon
The Creature's Revenge
The Curse of the Cat People
Curse of the Voodoo
Cyborg: The Six Million Dollar Man
Dark Star
The Day of the Triffids
The Day the Earth Stood Still
The Day Time Ended
Dementia 13
Destination Saturn
Devil Doll
The Devil's Daughter
The Devil's Nightmare
The Devil's Rain
Don't Look in the Basement
Don't Look Now
Dracula (1931)
Dracula (1979)
Duel
Earth vs. the Flying Saucers
End of the World
The Evil Mind
The Exorcist
The Eyes of Laura Mars

Fall of the House of Usher
Fantastic Voyage
Fiend without a Face
First Men in the Moon
First Spaceship on Venus
Flash Gordon Conquers the Universe
Flash Gordon: Mars Attacks the World
Flash Gordon:Rocketship
4D Man
Frankenstein
Frankenstein 1970
From the Earth to the Moon
Ghidrah, The Three-Headed Monster
Godzilla vs. Megalon and Godzilla vs. the Cosmic
  Monster
The Haunted Strangler
Horror Express
The House of Seven Corpses
House of the Living Dead
House on Haunted Hill
The Human Monster
I Walked with a Zombie
The Incredible Shrinking Man
The Indestructible Man
Invasion from Inner Earth
Invasion of the Blood Farmers
The Invisible Ghost
Isle of the Dead
It Came from Outer Space
Jaws
Jaws of Death
Killer Bats
King Kong
King of Kong Island
Leonor
The Leopard Man
Little Shop of Horrors
Lost Continent
The Lost World
The Man Who Fell to Earth
Marooned
Metropolis
Mighty Joe Young
Monster from Green Hell
The Monster Maker
The Monster Walks
The Most Dangerous Game
Mothra
The Murder Clinic
The Mysterians
Night of the Living Dead
Nightmare Castle
Nightmare in Wax
Nosferatu
The Omen
One Million B.C.
The Phantom of the Opera
Phantom Ship
Plague
Planet of the Apes
Psycho
Psychomania
Rakar Men from the Moon
Radio Ranch
Reefer Madness
Repulsion
The Resurrection of Zachary Wheeler
Return of Chandu
The Revenge of Frankenstein
Rocketship
Rocketship X-M
Rollerball
Scared to Death
Schizo

The She-Beast
Shock Corridor
Slaughterhouse Five
Son of Godzilla
Son of Kong
Stanley
The Stepford Wives
Svengali
The Tell Tale Heart
The Terror
Terror from under the House
Theatre of Death
The Thing
Things to Come
A Touch of Satan
Transatlantic Tunnel
Twisted Brain
2001—A Space Odyssey
Vampyr
Voyage to the Bottom of the Sea
The War of the Worlds
White Zombie
The Wickerman
The Witch Who Came from the Sea
The Witchmaker
Woman in the Moon
Zombies of the Stratosphere

SILENT

The Adventures of Tarzan
The Americano and Variety
An Andalusian Dog
Avant Garde and Experimental Film Program No.
1
The Avenging Conscience
Balloonatik
Ben Turpin Rides Again (Cross-Eyed!)
The Biograph Shorts: D.W. Griffith
Birth of a Nation
The Black Pirate
Blind Husbands
Blood and Sand (1922)
Burlesque on Carmen
Buster Keaton
Cabinet of Dr. Caligari
Chaplin Mutuals (Volume 1)
Chaplin Mutuals (Volume 2)
Chaplin Mutuals (Volume 3)
Chaplin Mutuals (Volume 4)
The Chaplin Review
Charlie Chaplin Shorts
The Circus and A Day's Pleasure
City Lights
College
D.W. Griffith
The Eagle
Eyes Right
Fortune's Fool
Funstuff
The General
The Gold Rush
The Gold Rush and Pay Day
Hunchback of Notre Dame (1923)
Intolerance
The Iron Mask
Keystone Krazies
The Kid and The Idle Class
King of the Kongo
Kings, Queens, Jokers
The Knockout and Dough and Dynamite
The Last Laugh
Laughfest
Little Annie Rooney

The Lodger
The Lost World
Lot in Sodom
M
The Mark of Zorro
Martin Luther, His Life and Time
Master of the House
Metropolis
Mickey
Modern Times
Mother
Mr. Super Athletic Charm
Naughty Nostalgia, Volume 1
Nosferatu
Outside the Law
The Passion of Joan of Arc
The Phantom of the Opera
Potemkin
The Rink and The Immigrant
Sally of the Sawdust
The Sea Lion
Silent Laugh Makers, Volume 1
Silent Laugh Makers, Volume 2
The Sky's the Limit
Son of the Sheik
Sparrows
Spies
Steamboat Bill Jr.
Stoneface
Storm over Asia
Tarzan of the Apes
Ten Days Thak Shook the World
These Girls Won't Talk
Tillie's Punctured Romance
True Heart Susie
Tumbleweeds
Uncle Tom's Cabin
Variety
Way Down East
Woman in the Moon
A Woman of Paris and Sunnyside
The Yankee Clipper

WESTERNS

Abilene Town
The Adventures of Red Ryder
Against a Crooked Sky
Alvarez Kelly
Angel and the Badman
Arizona Days
The Arizona Ranger; Road Agent
Bad Man's River
Badmen of Nevada
Bandits of Dark Canyon; Hidden Valley Outlaws
Bar 20 Justice
Bar 20 Rides Again
Bar 20 Rides Again; Rustler's Valley
Beauty and the Bandit
Bells of Coronado; King of the Cowboys
Bells of Rosarita
Bells of Rosarita; Under Western Stars
The Big Land
Billy the Kid Returns
Bite the Bullet
Blood on the Moon
Blue Steel
Boots and Saddles
Borderland
Brimstone
Buck and the Preacher
Butch Cassidy and the Sundance Kid
Call of the Prairie
Call of the Prairie; Pride of the West
Calling Wild Bill Elliott; Santa Fe Saddlemates

Captain Apache
Cassidy of Bar 20
Cassidy of Bar 20; Sunset Trail
Cattle Queen of Montana
The Chase
Cheyenne Rides Again
Cheyenne Takes Over; Tulsa Kid
Chino
Cowboy Commandos
Cry Blood Apache
Cry for Me Billy
Dakota
Daniel Boone
The Daring Adventurer
The Daring Rogue; The Devil's Den
The Dark Command
Davy Crockett, King of the Wild Frontier
Dawn on the Great Divide
Death Rides the Plains
Desert Trail
Destry Rides Again
Don't Fence Me In; Sheriff of Wichita
Drum Beat
The Duchess and the Dirtwater Fox
Dynamite Ranch; Local Badman
The Eagle's Brood
El Dorado
Fighting Caravans
The Fighting Kentuckian
Flame of Barbary Coast
Forbidden Trail
Fort Apache
Forty Thieves
Forty Thieves; Santa Fe Marshall
Frontier Justice; Bulldog Courage
The Frontiersman
The Gatling Gun
Gay Ranchero
Ghost Town Law
Ghost Town Renegades
Ghost Town Renegades; Santa Fe Uprising
The Golden Stallion; The Cherokee Flash
The Gun Hawk
Gunfight at the O.K. Corral
The Gunman from Bodie
Guns of the Timberland
Heart of Arizona
Heart of the West
Hearts of the Golden West
Helldorado
Hellfire
High Noon
High Plains Drifter
Hills of Old Wyoming
Home in Oklahoma
Homesteaders Valley
Hopalong Cassidy (Enters); Heart of the West
Hopalong Cassidy (Hopalong Cassidy Enters)
Hopalong Cassidy Returns
Hopalong Rides Again
Hopalong Rides Again; Texas Trail
100 Rifles
Hurricane Express
Hurricane Express
In Old California
In Old Mexico
In Old Mexico; The Eagle's Brood
In Old New Mexico
In Old Santa Fe
Iron Mountain Trail; Sheriff of Cimarron
Jesse James at Bay
Joe Kidd
John Wayne Double Feature #1
John Wayne Double Feature #2

Johnny Guitar
The Kansan
King of the Texas Rangers
Knights of the Range
A Lady Takes a Chance
The Last Bandit
The Last Command
Last Train from Gun Hill
Law of the Lash; Rodeo King and the Senorita
The Legend of the Lone Ranger
The Lone Ranger
The Lone Ranger and the Lost City of Gold
Lonely Are the Brave
Lucky Texan
The Lusty Men
Macho Callahan
Mackenna's Gold
Major Dundee
A Man Alone
Man from Cheyenne
The Man from Laramie
Man from Music Mountain
Man from Utah
The Man Who Shot Liberty Valance
Molly and Lawless John
My Pal Trigger
Mystery Mountain
Night in Nevada
North of the Great Divide; Days of Old Cheyenne
North of the Rio Grande
One Mask Too Many
Out California Way; Red River Shore
The Outlaw
Overland Stage Raiders; Colorado Serenade
The Painted Stallion
Partners of the Plains
Passion
Phantom of the Plains; Prairie Rustlers
Phantom of the West
The Phantom Rider
A Place Called Trinity
Pride of the West
The Professionals
Raiders of Red Gap
Rancho Notorious
Range Law; The Dude Bandit
Rawhide
Return of the Bad Men
Ride in the Whirlwind
Ride the Man Down
Riders of the Desert
Riders of the Rockies
Riders of the Rockies; Gunman from Bodie
Rio Grande
Rio Lobo
Rio Rattler
Robin Hood of Monterey
Rooster Cogburn
Rootin' Tootin' Rhythm
Run of the Arrow
Rustler's Valley
Sagebrush Trail
The San Antonio Kid; Kansas Terrors
Santa Fe Trail
Sante Fe Marshall
The Search
The Searchers
Shadows of Death
Shane
She Wore a Yellow Ribbon
The Shooting

The Shootist
Silver Lode
Silver on the Sage
Six Shootin' Sheriff
Soldier Blue
Son of Zorro
Song of Nevada
Song of Texas
South of Santa Fe
South of Texas (South of the Border);
   My Pal Trigger
Springtime in the Sierras
Stagecoach
Stagecoach to Denver
The Star Packer
Station West
Sunset Trail
Tall in the Saddle
Tennessee's Partner
Tension at Table Rock
Texas to Bataan
Texas Trail
They Call Me Trinity
Three on the Trail
A Town Called Hell
Trail Dust

Trail of Robin Hood; Along the Navaho Trail
Trail of the Hawk
Trail Riders
Trail Street
Trailin Trouble
Treasure of Pancho Villa
Trigger Jr.; Gangs of Sonora
Trinity Is Still My Name
Trouble in Texas; Fargo Express
True Grit
Tumbleweeds
Two Rode Together
The Undefeated
Under California Stars; Enemy of the Law
Valley of Terror
Wagonmaster
Water Rustlers
West of the Divide
Westward Ho; Lawless Frontier
White Comanche
Wide Open Town
The Wild Bunch
Wild Horse
Yellow Rose of Texas
Zorro's Black Whip
Zorro's Fighting Legion

ARROW FILMS & VIDEO
1800 North Highland Avenue, Suite 600
Hollywood, CA 90028
213-461-2868
Michael Balsamo, Sales Director

ASTRO VIDEO CORPORATION
90 Golden Gate Avenue
San Francisco, CA 94102
415-673-4320
Judy Templin, Sales Manager

BLACKHAWK FILMS, INC
The Best Building, 1235 W 5th Street
Davenport, IA 52808
319-323-9735
Carl Lange, Vice President

BUDGET VIDEO
4590 Santa Monica Boulevard
Los Angeles, CA 90029
213-466-2431
Larry Fine, President

CABLE FILMS
Country Club Station, PO Box 7171
Kansas City, MO 64113
913-362-2804
Herbert Miller, Vice President Marketing

CBS VIDEO ENTERPRISES
See MGM/CBS Home Video

CINEMA CONCEPTS, INC.
1805 Berlin Turnpike
Wethersfield, CT 06109
203-529-0575
Joel G. Jacobson, President

CINEMA RESOURCES
Box 41325
Indianapolis, IN 46241
317-291-2407
James Kisner, President

COLUMBIA PICTURES HOME ENTERTAINMENT
711 Fifth Avenue
New York, NY 10022
212-751-4400
Steven Basloe, Marketing Manager

DIRECT VIDEO
1717 N Highland Avenue
Hollywood, CA 90028
800-423-2452
Tommy Sinopoli, Sales Department

DISCOUNT VIDEO TAPES
P.O. Box 7122
Burbank, CA 91510
213-843-3366

ENTERTAINMENT VIDEO RELEASING, INC
1 E 57th Street
New York, NY 10022
212-752-2240
Mark Slade, President

FHV ENTERTAINMENT, INC
8604 White Oak Avenue
Northridge, CA 91325
213-705-1024
Randy C. Luenebrink, President

FOTOMAT CORP
64 Danbury Road
Wilton, CT 06897
800-325-1111

FREEWAY VIDEO ENTERPRISES
6331 Hollywood Boulevard
Hollywood, CA 90028
213-461-8554
Jack Levy, General Sales Manager

GOLDEN TAPES VIDEO TAPE LIBRARY
336 Foothill Road
Beverly Hills, CA 90210
213-550-0659
William K. Beck, President

HOME THEATRE MOVIES
6464 Sunset Boulevard, Suite
Hollywood, CA 90028
213-465-6121
Dran May, National Sales Manager

HOME VISION
Division of Films, Inc
733 Green Bay Road
Wilmette, IL 60091
800-323-1406, 312-256-6600

INOVISION
An EDS Corporation
14580 Midway Road
Dallas, TX 75234
800-527-0263, 800-442-5846 in Texas
Fred Mirick, Vice-President

IVY VIDEO
165 W 46th Street
New York, NY 10036
212-765-3940
Sidney Tager, Vice President, Sales

MAGNETIC VIDEO CORPORATION
23434 Industrial Park Court
Farmington, MI 48024
313-477-6066
Al B. Eicher, Vice President, General Manager

MCA DISCOVISION
100 Universal City Plaza
Universal City, CA91608
213-985-4321

MCA VIDEOCASSETTE, INC
70 Universal City Plaza
Universal City, CA 91608
213-985-4321

MEDA/MEDIA HOME ENTERTAINMENT INC
116 North Robertson Boulevard, Suite 701
Los Angeles, CA 90048
213-652-1542
Jerry Nieves, National and International Coordinator

MGM/CBS HOME VIDEO
CBS Video Enterprises
1700 Broadway
New York, NY 10019
212-975-5277
Herb Mendelsohn, Vice President, Marketing

MITCHELL BROTHERS' FILM GROUP
895 O'Farrell Street
San Francisco, CA 94109
415-441-1930
Jim and Art Mitchell, General Managers

MONARCH RELEASING CORPORATION
8500 Wilshire Boulevard, Suite 506
Beverly Hills, CA 90211
213-652-9900
A. L. Shackleton, President

NATIONAL FILM AND VIDEO CENTER
4321 Sykesville Road
Finksburg,MD 21048
301-795-3000
George Ulysses, President

NILES CINEMA
1141 Mishawaka Avenue
South Bend, IN 46615
219-289-2845, 800-348-2462
Paula Casey, Vice President

NORTHEAST VIDEO AND SOUND, INC
287 Kenyon Street
Stratford, CT 06497
203-377-1444
Paul Seaburg, Vice President

THE NOSTALGIA MERCHANT
6255 Sunset Boulevard, Suite 1019
Hollywood, CA 90028
213-464-1406
Earl Blair, Vice President

PARAMOUNT HOME VIDEO
5451 Marathon Street
Hollywood, CA 90038
213-468-5000
Brenda Mutchnick, Senior Vice President

QUALITY X VIDEO CASSETTE COMPANY
356 W 44th Street
New York, NY 10036
212-541-7860
Robert R. Sumner, President

RCA SELECTAVISION VIDEODISCS
Box 91301
Indianapolis, IN 46291
212-621-6000
Stu Gray, Programming and Marketing Manager

RED FOX, INC
Route 209
East Elizabethville, PA 17023
717-362-3391
Ann Rhodes, Video Department Manager

REEL IMAGES INC
495 Monroe Turnpike
Monroe, CT 06468
203-261-5022
John Sonneborn, President

SCORPIO, ETC
22714 Ventura Boulevard
Woodland Hill, CA 91364
213-884-6692
Sal Esposito, Sales Manager

THUNDERBIRD FILMS
P.O. Box 65157, 3500 Verdugo Road
Los Angeles, CA 90065
213-256-1034
Tom Dunnahoo, Owner

TIME-LIFE VIDEO CLUB INC
Harrisburg, PA 17105
800-523-7601

TVX DISTRIBUTORS
1643 North Cherokee Avenue
Hollywood, CA 90028
213-462-6010, 800-421-4133
David Handley, General Sales Manager

VCX
7313 Varna Avenue
North Hollywood, CA 91605

800-423-2587, 213-764-0319
651-461

VIDAMERICA
Video Corporation of America
P.O. Box 2041
Lathan NY 12111
212-355-1505
Dan Paley, Customer Service

VIDEO ACTION LIBRARY
Division of World Television
1200 South La Cienega Boulevard
Los Angeles, CA 90035
213-657-6978
Al Goodman, President

VIDEO COMMUNICATIONS INC
6555 East Skelly Drive
Tulsa, OK 74145
800-331-4077
Bob Blair, Executive Vice President

VIDEO GEMS
731 North La Brea Avenue
Los Angeles, CA 90038
800-421-3252, 213-938-2385
S. Sommers, Sales Rep.

VIDEO HOME LIBRARY
PO Box G, Madison Square Station
New York, NY 10010
212-929-2340
Andre D'Apice, President

VIDEO IMAGES
See Reel Images Inc.

THE VIDEO LIBRARY
612 Montgomery Ave.
Narberth, PA 19072
215-664-4545
Homer H. Hewitt III, President

VIDEO TAPE NETWORK
115 E. 62nd Street
New York, NY 10021
212-759-8735
John Friede, President

VIDEO T.E.N.
121 La Veta Drive, NE
Albuquerque, NM 87108
505-266-8619, 800-545-6580
John Ralston, President

VIDEO WAREHOUSE, INC
PO Box 275, 500 Highway 36
Atlantic Highlands, NJ 07716
201-291-5300
Caroline Michaels, Customer Service

VIDEOBRARY INC
3518 West Cahuenga, Suite 301
Hollywood, CA 90068
213-851-5811
Tom Corradine, President

VTS
19201-B-Parthenia
North Ridge, CA 91324
213-996-7068, 213-996-7069
Norm Berkoff and Phil Cole, Vice Presidents

WALT DISNEY HOME VIDEO
Walt Disney Telecommunications & Non-Theatrical
  Company
500 South Buena Vista Street
Burbank, CA 91521
800-423-2259 213-841-2000

WCI HOME VIDEO INC
75 Rockefeller Plaza
New York, NY 10019
212-484-8000